# Your future is just four parts away.

Welcome to the Becker CPA Exam Review! Congratulations on taking the first step to becoming a CPA. As the industry's leading partner in CPA Exam preparation, we know you're not just studying for an exam – you are preparing for your future. To help you get there, Becker CPA Exam Review is as close as you can get to the real thing. So let's get started.

## Access Becker's CPA Exam Review course

Log in to your CPA Exam Review course anytime at **cpa.becker.com**. Watch our orientation video and download the mobile app to access your studies on the go. Your progress will automatically sync among all your devices, so you can pick up where you left off. For more on getting started, visit **becker.com/cpa-review/getting-started**.

## Utilize the Becker resources

Make studying more organized with our study planner. With interactive tools to help you determine your ideal study schedule and to recommend your ideal exam-taking time, it's easy to plan your preparation so you're ready when exam day comes. Here are the added benefits of Becker:

- Take advantage of the personalized review sessions at the end of each unit to identify which topics you need to review and strengthen
- Access 1-on-1 academic support from our experienced CPA instructors
- Watch 400+ SkillMaster videos that coach you through task-based simulations
- Improve upon core concepts with the help of more than 1,300 flashcards
- Test your knowledge with our simulated exams – the closest thing you can get to the actual CPA Exam itself

## You're not in it alone!

For tips, stories and advice, visit our blog at **becker.com/blog**. You can also collaborate with other Becker students studying FAR on our Facebook study group at **facebook.com/groups/BeckerFARStudyGroup/**.

---

## Submit your CPA Exam application

It takes time for your CPA Exam application to be approved – so don't wait til the last minute.

Once your CPA Exam application has been processed, your Notice to Schedule will give you a limited window of time to schedule your exam.

Your state board of accountancy sets the amount of time you have, so be sure to check your state's requirements.

Once you schedule your exam, add it to the study planner so we can share tips, strategies and more as your test date approaches.

---

**Becker.**

Join the community!

# Becker.

**ACADEMIC HELP**
Click on Contact Academic Support from within the course software at the top at cpa.becker.com

**CUSTOMER SERVICE AND TECHNICAL SUPPORT**
Call 1-877-CPA-EXAM (outside the U.S. +1-630-472-2213) or contact us at becker.com/cpa-review/cpa-contact

This textbook contains information that was current at the time of printing. Your course software will be updated on a regular basis as the content that is tested on the CPA Exam evolves and as we improve our materials. Note the version reference below and select your replacement textbook under Replacement Products at **becker.com/cpa-replacement-products** to learn if a newer version of this book is available to be ordered.

CPA Exam Review

# Financial

For Exams Scheduled
After December 31, 2020

V 3.7

## COURSE DEVELOPMENT TEAM

| | |
|---|---|
| Timothy F. Gearty, CPA, MBA, JD, CGMA | Editor in Chief, Financial/Regulation (Tax) National Editor |
| Angeline S. Brown, CPA, CGMA | Sr. Director, Product Management |
| Valerie Funk Anderson, CPA | Sr. Manager, Curriculum |
| Stephen Bergens, CPA | Manager, Accounting Curriculum |
| Cheryl Costello, CPA, CGMA | Sr. Specialist, Curriculum |
| Tom Cox, CPA, CMA | Financial (GASB & NFP) National Editor |
| Steven J. Levin, JD | Regulation (Law) National Editor |
| Danita De Jane | Director, Course Development |
| Anson Miyashiro | Manager, Course Development |
| Tim Munson | Project Manager, Course Development |

## CONTRIBUTING EDITORS

| | |
|---|---|
| Teresa C. Anderson, CPA, CMA, MPA | Stephanie Morris, CPA, MAcc |
| Katie Barnette, CPA | Michelle Moshe, CPA, DipIFR |
| Jim DeSimpelare, CPA, MBA | Peter Olinto, JD, CPA |
| Tara Z. Fisher, CPA | Sandra Owen, JD, MBA, CPA |
| Melisa F. Galasso, CPA | Michelle M. Pace, CPA |
| R. Thomas Godwin, CPA, CGMA | Michael Potenza, CPA, JD |
| Holly Hawk, CPA, CGMA | Jennifer J. Rivers, CPA |
| Liliana Hickman-Riggs, CPA, CMA, CIA, CFE, CITP, CFF, CGMA, FCPA, MS | Josh Rosenberg, MBA, CPA, CFA, CFP |
| | Jonathan R. Rubin, CPA, MBA |
| Patrice W. Johnson, CPA | Michael Rybak, CPA, CFA |
| Julie D. McGinty, CPA | Denise M. Stefano, CPA, CGMA, MBA |
| Sandra McGuire, CPA, MBA | Elizabeth Lester Walsh, CPA, CITP |

This textbook is an essential part of Becker's CPA review course and is intended for use in conjunction with the Becker CPA review web and mobile applications ("Becker Apps"). Your use of and access to the Becker Apps is governed by the online end user license agreement (EULA). This textbook is to be used solely by the purchaser of the CPA review course and for personal use only. This textbook as a whole, and any parts therein, may not be shared, copied, reproduced, distributed, licensed, sold, or resold without the prior written consent of Becker Professional Development Corporation. Failure to comply with this notice may expose you to legal action for copyright infringement and/or disciplinary action pursuant to the Student Code of Conduct located at https://www.becker.com/cpa-review/student-code-of-conduct.

Permissions

Material from *Uniform CPA Examination Selected Questions and Unofficial Answers*, 1989–2020, copyright © by American Institute of Certified Public Accountants, Inc., is reprinted and/or adapted with permission.

Any knowing solicitation or disclosure of any questions or answers included on any CPA Examination is prohibited.

Copyright © 2020 by Becker Professional Education Corporation. All rights reserved.

ISBN: 978-1-950713-20-2

Printed in the United States of America.

No part of this work may be reproduced, translated, distributed, published or transmitted without the prior written permission of the copyright owner. Request for permission or further information should be addressed to the Permissions Department, Becker Professional Education Corporation.

# FINANCIAL
*Table of Contents*

Introduction ................................................................................................................. Intro-1

**FINANCIAL 1:** *Conceptual Framework and Financial Reporting*
1. Standards and Conceptual Framework ........................................................... F1-3
2. Income Statement and Balance Sheet ............................................................ F1-13
3. Revenue Recognition: Part 1 ........................................................................... F1-19
4. Revenue Recognition: Part 2 ........................................................................... F1-31
5. Income Statement: Discontinued Operations ............................................... F1-45
6. Accounting Changes and Error Corrections .................................................. F1-51
7. Statement of Comprehensive Income ............................................................ F1-59
8. Adjusting Journal Entries ................................................................................ F1-67

**FINANCIAL 2:** *Financial Reporting and Disclosures*
1. Notes to Financial Statements ........................................................................ F2-3
2. Going Concern .................................................................................................. F2-7
3. Subsequent Events ........................................................................................... F2-11
4. Fair Value Measurements ................................................................................ F2-15
5. Segment Reporting .......................................................................................... F2-21
6. SEC Reporting Requirements ......................................................................... F2-27
7. Special Purpose Frameworks ......................................................................... F2-33
8. Ratio Analysis ................................................................................................... F2-41
9. Partnerships ..................................................................................................... F2-53

**FINANCIAL 3:** *Assets and Related Topics*
1. Cash and Cash Equivalents ............................................................................. F3-3
2. Trade Receivables ............................................................................................ F3-9
3. Inventory ........................................................................................................... F3-21
4. PP&E: Cost Basis .............................................................................................. F3-39
5. PP&E: Depreciation and Disposal .................................................................. F3-49
6. Nonmonetary Transactions ............................................................................. F3-61
7. Intangibles ........................................................................................................ F3-69
8. Impairment ....................................................................................................... F3-79

© Becker Professional Education Corporation. All rights reserved.

**FINANCIAL 4:** *Investments, Business Combinations, and Goodwill*

1. Financial Instruments ........................................................................................................... F4-3
2. Equity Method ..................................................................................................................... F4-19
3. Basic Consolidation Concepts ........................................................................................... F4-31
4. Acquisition Method: Part 1 ................................................................................................ F4-39
5. Acquisition Method: Part 2 ................................................................................................ F4-51
6. Intercompany Transactions ............................................................................................... F4-65
7. Consolidated Financial Statements .................................................................................. F4-73
8. Goodwill, Including Impairment ....................................................................................... F4-85

**FINANCIAL 5:** *Liabilities*

1. Payables and Accrued Liabilities ....................................................................................... F5-3
2. Contingencies and Commitments .................................................................................... F5-17
3. Long-Term Liabilities ......................................................................................................... F5-25
4. Bonds: Part 1 ....................................................................................................................... F5-37
5. Bonds: Part 2 ....................................................................................................................... F5-47
6. Troubled Debt Restructuring and Extinguishment ........................................................ F5-59

**FINANCIAL 6:** *Leases, Derivatives, Foreign Currency Accounting, and Income Taxes*

1. Leases: Part 1 ...................................................................................................................... F6-3
2. Leases: Part 2 ...................................................................................................................... F6-17
3. Derivatives and Hedge Accounting .................................................................................. F6-31
4. Foreign Currency Accounting ........................................................................................... F6-43
5. Income Taxes: Part 1 .......................................................................................................... F6-53
6. Income Taxes: Part 2 .......................................................................................................... F6-65

**FINANCIAL 7:** *Pensions and Equity*

1. Pension Benefits: Part 1 ..................................................................................................... F7-3
2. Pension Benefits: Part 2 ..................................................................................................... F7-15
3. Retirement Benefits Other Than Pensions ...................................................................... F7-27
4. Financial Statements of Employee Benefit Plans ........................................................... F7-33
5. Stockholders' Equity: Part 1 .............................................................................................. F7-39
6. Stockholders' Equity: Part 2 .............................................................................................. F7-51
7. Stock Compensation .......................................................................................................... F7-59

Table of Contents  Financial

**FINANCIAL 8:** *EPS, Cash Flows, and NFP Accounting*
1. Earnings per Share .................................................................................................................. F8-3
2. Statement of Cash Flows ...................................................................................................... F8-15
3. Not-for-Profit Financial Reporting: Part 1 ........................................................................... F8-29
4. Not-for-Profit Financial Reporting: Part 2 ........................................................................... F8-43
5. Not-for-Profit Revenue Recognition .................................................................................... F8-49
6. Not-for-Profit Transfers of Assets and Other Accounting Issues ..................................... F8-61

**FINANCIAL 9:** *State and Local Governments: Part 1*
1. Governmental Accounting Overview .................................................................................. F9-3
2. Fund Structure and Fund Accounting ................................................................................. F9-11
3. Transactions and Events: Part 1 ........................................................................................... F9-17
4. Transactions and Events: Part 2 ........................................................................................... F9-35
5. Governmental Funds Financial Statements: Part 1 ........................................................... F9-49
6. Governmental Funds Financial Statements: Part 2 ........................................................... F9-63

**FINANCIAL 10:** *State and Local Governments: Part 2*
1. Proprietary Funds Financial Statements ............................................................................. F10-3
2. Fiduciary Funds Financial Statements ................................................................................ F10-15
3. Form and Content of the Comprehensive Annual Financial Report .............................. F10-33
4. Government-wide Financial Statements ............................................................................ F10-41
5. Fund Financial Statements ................................................................................................... F10-51
6. Deriving Government-wide Financial Statements and Reconciliation Requirements .... F10-65
7. Notes and Supplementary Information .............................................................................. F10-83

Class Question Explanations .................................................................................................... CQ-1
Blueprint ..................................................................................................................................... BL-1
Glossary ...................................................................................................................................... GL-1
Index ........................................................................................................................................... Index-1

## NOTES

# Introduction
# FAR

1. Financial Accounting and Reporting (FAR) Overview .................................................. 3

2. FAR Exam—Summary Blueprint ......................................................................... 3

3. Becker's CPA Exam Review—Course Introduction ................................................... 3

4. Becker Customer and Academic Support ............................................................... 4

5. The Uniform CPA Exam—Overview ...................................................................... 4

**NOTES**

## Financial Accounting and Reporting (FAR) Overview

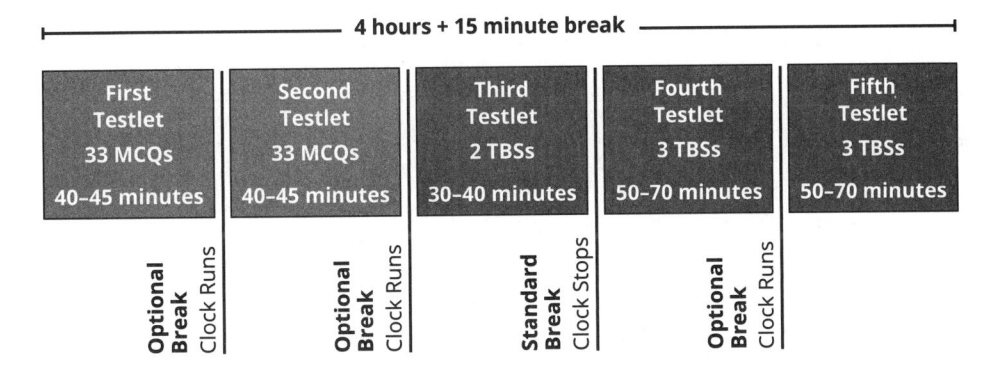

**4 hours + 15 minute break**

| First Testlet | Second Testlet | Third Testlet | Fourth Testlet | Fifth Testlet |
|---|---|---|---|---|
| 33 MCQs | 33 MCQs | 2 TBSs | 3 TBSs | 3 TBSs |
| 40–45 minutes | 40–45 minutes | 30–40 minutes | 50–70 minutes | 50–70 minutes |
| Optional Break — Clock Runs | Optional Break — Clock Runs | Standard Break — Clock Stops | Optional Break — Clock Runs | |

## FAR Exam—Summary Blueprint

| Content Area Allocation | Weight |
|---|---|
| Conceptual Framework, Standard-Setting, and Financial Reporting | 25–35% |
| Select Financial Statement Accounts | 30–40% |
| Select Transactions | 20–30% |
| State and Local Governments | 5–15% |
| **Skill Allocation** | **Weight** |
| Evaluation | — |
| Analysis | 25–35% |
| Application | 50–60% |
| Remembering and Understanding | 10–20% |

The complete FAR exam blueprint appears in the back of the book.

## Becker's CPA Exam Review—Course Introduction

Becker Professional Education's CPA Exam Review products were developed with you, the candidate, in mind. To that end we have developed a series of tools designed to tap all of your learning and retention capabilities. The Becker lectures, comprehensive texts, and course software are designed to be fully integrated to give you the best chance of passing the CPA Exam.

Passing the CPA Exam is difficult, but the professional rewards a CPA enjoys make this a worthwhile challenge. We created our CPA Exam Review after evaluating the needs of CPA candidates and analyzing the CPA Exam over the years. Our course materials comprehensively present topics you must know to pass the examination, teaching you the most effective tactics for learning the material.

## Becker Customer and Academic Support

You can access Becker's Customer and Academic Support from within the course software by clicking Contact Support at the top at:

cpa.becker.com

You can also access customer service and technical support by calling 1-877-CPA-EXAM (outside the U.S. +1-630-472-2213).

## The Uniform CPA Exam—Overview

### Exam Sections

The CPA Examination consists of four sections:

**Financial Accounting and Reporting**

The *Financial* section consists of a four-hour exam covering financial accounting and reporting for commercial entities under U.S. GAAP, governmental accounting, not-for-profit accounting, and the differences between IFRS and U.S. GAAP.

**Auditing and Attestation**

The *Auditing* section consists of a four-hour exam. This section covers all topics related to auditing, including audit reports and procedures, generally accepted auditing standards, attestation and other engagements, and government auditing.

**Regulation**

The *Regulation* section consists of a four-hour exam, combining topics from business law and federal taxation, including the taxation of property transactions, individuals, and entities.

**Business Environment and Concepts**

The *Business* section consists of a four-hour exam covering general business topics, such as corporate governance, economics, financial management, information technology, and operations management, including managerial accounting.

## Question Formats

The chart below illustrates the question format breakdown by exam section.

|  | Multiple-Choice Questions |  | Task-Based Simulations or Written Communication Tasks |  |
| --- | --- | --- | --- | --- |
| Section | Percentage | Number | Percentage | Number |
| Financial | 50% | 66 | 50% | 8 TBSs |
| Auditing | 50% | 72 | 50% | 8 TBSs |
| Regulation | 50% | 76 | 50% | 8 TBSs |
| Business | 50% | 62 | 50% | 4 TBSs/3 WC |

Each exam will contain testlets. A testlet is either a series of multiple-choice questions, a set of task-based simulations, or a set of written communications. For example, the Financial examination will contain five testlets. The first two testlets will be multiple-choice questions and the third, fourth, and fifth testlets will contain task-based simulations. Each testlet must be finished and submitted before continuing to the next testlet. Candidates cannot go back to view a previously completed testlet or go forward to view a subsequent testlet before closing and submitting the earlier testlet. Our mock exams contain these types of restrictions so that you can familiarize yourself with the functionality of the CPA Exam.

## Exam Schedule

Beginning July 1, 2020, in most states and jurisdictions the computer-based CPA Exam moves to continuous testing, which gives candidates the ability to take the exam year-round, without restriction, other than waiting to receive scores from prior attempts of the same section or when there is a major change to the exam. Candidates can schedule an exam date directly with Prometric (www.prometric.com/cpa) after receiving a notice to schedule.

## Eligibility and Application Requirements

Each state sets its own rules of eligibility for the examination. Please visit www.becker.com/state as soon as possible to determine your eligibility to sit for the exam.

## Application Deadlines

With the computer-based exam format, set application deadlines generally do not exist. You should apply as early as possible to ensure that you are able to schedule your desired exam dates. Each state has different application requirements and procedures, so be sure to gain a thorough understanding of the application process for your state.

## Grading System

You must pass all four parts of the examination to earn certification as a CPA. You must score 75 or better on a part to receive a passing grade and you must pass all four exams in 18 months or you will lose credit for the earliest exam that you passed.

# NOTES

# FAR 1

# Conceptual Framework and Financial Reporting

## Module

| | | |
|---|---|---|
| 1 | Standards and Conceptual Framework | 3 |
| 2 | Income Statement and Balance Sheet | 13 |
| 3 | Revenue Recognition: Part 1 | 19 |
| 4 | Revenue Recognition: Part 2 | 31 |
| 5 | Income Statement: Discontinued Operations | 45 |
| 6 | Accounting Changes and Error Corrections | 51 |
| 7 | Statement of Comprehensive Income | 59 |
| 8 | Adjusting Journal Entries | 67 |

# MODULE 1: Standards and Conceptual Framework

# 1 Financial Accounting Standards

## 1.1 Standard-Setting Bodies in the United States

In the United States, the Securities and Exchange Commission (SEC) has the legal authority to establish U.S. generally accepted accounting principles (GAAP). However, in most instances, the SEC has allowed the accounting profession to establish GAAP and self-regulate. The SEC and three different bodies of the accounting profession have determined GAAP since 1934.

### 1.1.1 Securities and Exchange Commission (SEC)

The SEC was established by the Securities Exchange Act of 1934. All companies that issue securities in the United States are subject to SEC rules and regulations. The SEC has issued public company specific accounting rules and regulations in Regulation S-X, Financial Reporting Releases (FRR), Accounting Series Releases (ASR), Interpretative Releases (IR), Staff Accounting Bulletins (SAB), and EITF Topic D and SEC Observer comments.

### 1.1.2 Committee on Accounting Procedure (CAP)

The Committee on Accounting Procedure (CAP) was a part-time committee of the American Institute of Certified Public Accountants (AICPA) that promulgated Accounting Research Bulletins (ARB), which determined GAAP from 1939 until 1959.

### 1.1.3 Accounting Principles Board (APB)

The Accounting Principles Board (APB) was another part-time committee of the AICPA. It issued Accounting Principles Board Opinions (APBO) and APB Interpretations, which determined GAAP from 1959 until 1973.

### 1.1.4 Financial Accounting Standards Board (FASB)

In 1973, an independent full-time organization called the Financial Accounting Standards Board (FASB) was established, and it has determined GAAP since then. Through 2009, the FASB issued Statements of Financial Accounting Standards (SFAS), FASB Interpretations (FIN), FASB Technical Bulletins (FTB), Emerging Issues Task Force Statements (EITF), FASB Staff Positions, FASB Implementation Guides, and Statements of Financial Accounting Concepts (SFAC).

The FASB has seven full-time members, who serve for five-year terms and may be reappointed to one additional five-year term. The Board members must sever connections with firms or institutions before joining the Board.

## 1.2 U.S. GAAP: FASB Accounting Standards Codification®

The vast number of standards issued by the Committee on Accounting Procedures, the Accounting Principles Board, and the Financial Accounting Standards Board, as well as additional guidance provided by the SEC and the AICPA, made it difficult for users to access the full body of U.S. GAAP. Effective July 1, 2009, the FASB *Accounting Standards Codification*® became the single source of authoritative nongovernmental U.S. GAAP. Accounting and financial reporting practices not included in the codification are not GAAP.

## 1.3 Private Company Council (PCC)

The Financial Accounting Foundation (FAF) created the Private Company Council (PCC) to improve standard setting for privately held companies in the U.S. The goal of the PCC is to establish alternatives to U.S. GAAP, where appropriate, to make private company financial statements more relevant, less complex, and cost-beneficial. Accounting alternatives for private companies are incorporated into the relevant sections of the *Accounting Standards Codification* (ASC).

## 1.4 Ongoing Standard-Setting Process

The FASB updates the *Accounting Standards Codification* for new U.S. GAAP issued by the FASB and for amendments to the SEC content with Accounting Standards Updates.

Proposed FASB amendments to the ASC are issued for public comment in the form of exposure drafts. A majority vote of the Board members is required to approve an exposure draft for issuance. At the end of the exposure draft public comment period, the FASB staff analyzes and studies all comment letters and position papers and then the Board re-deliberates the issue. When the Board is satisfied that all reasonable alternatives have been adequately considered, the FASB staff prepares an Accounting Standards Update for Board consideration. A majority vote of the Board members is required to amend the ASC.

Accounting Standards Updates are not authoritative literature, but instead provide background information, update the codification, and describe the basis for conclusions on changes in the codification. All new GAAP and SEC amendments are fully integrated into the existing structure of the codification.

## 1.5 International Financial Reporting Standards (IFRS)

The International Accounting Standards Board (IASB) was established in 2001 as part of the International Financial Reporting Standards (IFRS) Foundation.

When the IASB was created, it adopted the International Accounting Standards (IAS) that had been issued by its predecessor, the Board of the International Accounting Standards Committee. The IASB issues International Financial Reporting Standards (IFRSs) and related documents, including the *Conceptual Framework for Financial Reporting*, exposure drafts, and other discussion documents. The term International Financial Reporting Standards includes IFRSs, IASs, and Interpretations developed by the IFRS Interpretations Committee (IFRIC) and the former Standard Interpretations Committee (SIC).

# 2 Conceptual Framework for Financial Reporting

The FASB has created a conceptual framework (set forth in pronouncements called Statements of Financial Accounting Concepts, or SFAC) that serves as a basis for all FASB pronouncements. The SFAC are not GAAP, but they provide a basis for financial accounting concepts for business and nonbusiness enterprises. As phases of this project are completed, the FASB will issue each component of the conceptual framework as a chapter in Statement of Financial Accounting Concepts No. 8, *Conceptual Framework for Financial Reporting*. The chapters of SFAC No. 8 that have been issued replaced SFAC No. 1, "Objectives of Financial Reporting by Business Enterprises," and SFAC No. 2, "Qualitative Characteristics of Accounting Information."

## 2.1 SFAC No. 8, *Conceptual Framework for Financial Reporting*— Chapter 1: "The Objective of General Purpose Financial Reporting"

The objective of general purpose financial reporting is to provide financial information about the reporting entity that is useful to the primary users of general purpose financial reports in making decisions about providing resources to the reporting entity.

### 2.1.1 Primary Users

The primary users of general purpose financial reports are existing and potential investors, lenders, and other creditors. Other parties, including regulators and members of the public who are not investors, lenders, and other creditors, may also use general purpose financial reports, but are not considered to be primary users.

### 2.1.2 Financial Information Provided in General Purpose Financial Reports

Financial information needed by primary users includes information about the resources of the entity, the claims against the entity, the changes in the resources and claims, and how efficiently and effectively the entity's management and governing board have discharged their responsibilities to use the entity's resources. Financial information should be presented using the accrual basis of accounting.

Existing and potential investors, lenders, and other creditors use financial information to assess the reporting entity's prospects for future net cash inflows to the entity. Such information may be used to estimate the value of the reporting entity.

## 2.2 SFAC No. 8, *Conceptual Framework for Financial Reporting*—Chapter 3: "Qualitative Characteristics of Useful Financial Information"

The qualitative characteristics of useful financial information are the characteristics that are likely to be most useful to existing and potential investors, lenders, and other creditors in making decisions about the reporting entity based on financial information.

### 2.2.1 Fundamental Qualitative Characteristics

The fundamental qualitative characteristics of useful financial information are relevance and faithful representation. Both characteristics must be present for financial information to be useful.

- **Relevance:** Financial information is relevant if it is capable of making a difference in the decisions made by users. To be relevant, financial information must have predictive value and/or confirming value, and must be material.
    - **Predictive Value:** Information has predictive value if it can be used by users to predict future outcomes.
    - **Confirmatory Value:** Information has confirmatory value if it provides feedback about evaluations previously made by users.
    - **Materiality:** Information is material if an omission or misstatement of the information could affect the decisions made by users based on financial information. Materiality is an entity-specific aspect of relevance. The FASB and IASB have not specified a uniform quantitative threshold for materiality and have not specified what would be material in specific situations.
- **Faithful Representation:** To be useful, financial information must faithfully represent the reported economic phenomena. Faithful representation requires the financial information to be complete, neutral, and free from error. Although perfect faithful representation is generally not achievable, these characteristics must be maximized.
    - **Complete:** A complete depiction of financial information includes all information necessary for the user to understand the reported economic event, including descriptions and explanations.
    - **Neutral:** A neutral depiction of financial information is free from bias in selection or presentation.

- **Free From Error:** Free from error means that there are no errors in the selection or application of the process used to produce reported financial information and that there are no errors or omissions in the descriptions of economic events. Free from error does not require perfect accuracy because, for example, it is difficult to determine the accuracy of estimates.

### 2.2.2 Steps to Apply the Fundamental Qualitative Characteristics

The most efficient and effective process for applying the fundamental characteristics of useful financial information is:

1. Identify the economic event or transaction that has the potential to be useful to the users of a reporting entity's financial information.
2. Identify the type of information about the event or transaction that would be most relevant.
3. Determine whether the information is available and can be faithfully represented.

If the information is available and can be faithfully represented, then the fundamental qualitative characteristics have been satisfied. If not, the process is repeated with the next most relevant type of information.

### 2.2.3 Enhancing Qualitative Characteristics

Comparability, verifiability, timeliness, and understandability enhance the usefulness of information that is relevant and faithfully represented. These characteristics can be used to determine how an economic event or transaction should be depicted if two ways are equally relevant and faithfully represented. The enhancing qualitative characteristics should be maximized.

- **Comparability:** Information is more useful if it can be compared with similar information about other entities or from other time periods. Comparability enables users to identify similarities and differences among items. Consistency, which is the use of the same methods for the same items either from period to period within an entity or in a single period across entities, helps to achieve comparability.
- **Verifiability:** Verifiability means that different knowledgeable and independent observers can reach consensus that a particular depiction is faithfully represented. Verifiability does not require complete agreement.
- **Timeliness:** Timeliness means that information is available to users in time to be capable of influencing their decisions.
- **Understandability:** Information is understandable if it is classified, characterized, and presented clearly and concisely. However, even well-informed and diligent users may need the assistance of advisors to understand complex and difficult transactions.

### 2.2.4 The Cost Constraint

The cost constraint is a pervasive constraint on the information provided in financial reporting. The benefits of reporting financial information must be greater than the costs of obtaining and presenting the information. The FASB and IASB consider costs and benefits in relation to financial reporting in general and not at the individual reporting entity level.

## 2.3 SFAC No. 3, *Elements of Financial Statements of a Business*

This statement was replaced by SFAC No. 6.

## 2.4 SFAC No. 4, *Objectives of Financial Reporting by Nonbusiness Organizations*

This statement outlines the characteristics that distinguish nonbusiness organizations from business organizations, describes the users of the financial information provided by nonbusiness organizations, and sets forth the objectives of external financial reporting by nonbusiness organizations.

### 2.4.1 Characteristics of Nonbusiness Organizations

The following characteristics distinguish nonbusiness organizations from business organizations:

- A significant portion of their resources come from contributions and grants.
- Their operating purposes are other than to provide goods or services for profit.
- They lack ownership interests that can be sold, transferred, or redeemed, or that allow a claim on resources upon liquidation.

Nonbusiness organizations include most human service organizations, churches, foundations, and other organizations, such as not-for-profit hospitals and not-for-profit educational institutions that receive a significant portion of their resources from contributions and grants.

### 2.4.2 Users of Financial Information of Nonbusiness Organizations

The following groups are interested in the financial information reported by nonbusiness organizations:

- Resource providers, including lenders, suppliers, employees, members, contributors, and taxpayers.
- Constituents who use and benefit from the services provided by nonbusiness organizations.
- Governing and oversight bodies that are responsible for setting policies and for overseeing and evaluating the managers of nonbusiness organizations.
- Managers who are responsible for carrying out the policy mandates of the governing bodies and managing the day-to-day operations of the nonbusiness organization.

### 2.4.3 Objectives of Financial Reporting of Nonbusiness Organizations

The objectives of the financial reporting of nonbusiness organizations are to provide:

- Information useful in making resource allocation decisions.
- Information useful in assessing services and the ability to provide services.
- Information useful in assessing management stewardship and performance.
- Information about economic resources, obligations, and net resources; organization performance; the nature of and relationship between inflows and outflows; service efforts and accomplishments; and liquidity.

## 2.5 SFAC No. 5, *Recognition and Measurement in the Financial Statements*

This statement sets forth the recognition criteria and guidance on what and when information should be incorporated in the financial statements.

### 2.5.1 Full Set of Financial Statements

- Statement of financial position (the balance sheet)
- Statement of earnings (the income statement)
- Statement of comprehensive income
- Statement of cash flows
- Statement of changes in owners' equity

### 2.5.2 Fundamental Recognition Criteria

Recognition is the process of formally recording or incorporating an item in the financial statements of an entity and classifying it as asset, liability, equity, revenue, or expense.

- **Definitions:** The item meets the definition of an element of financial statements.
- **Measurability:** The item has a relevant attribute measurable with sufficient reliability.
- **Relevance:** The information about it is capable of making a difference to a financial statement user.
- **Reliability:** The information is representationally faithful, verifiable, and neutral.

### 2.5.3 Measurement Attributes for Assets and Liabilities

Items reported in the financial statements are currently measured using different attributes, including those listed below.

- Historical cost
- Current cost
- Net realizable value
- Current market value
- Present value of future cash flows

### 2.5.4 Fundamental Assumptions and Principles

- **Entity Assumption:** Economic activity can be accounted for when considering an identifiable set of activities (e.g., a separate corporation or division).
- **Going Concern Assumption:** For financial accounting, it is presumed (subject to rebuttal by evidence to the contrary) that the entity will continue to operate in the foreseeable future.
- **Monetary Unit Assumption:** It is assumed that money is an appropriate basis by which to measure economic activity. The assumption is that the monetary unit does not change over time; thus, the effects of inflation are not reflected in the financial statements.
- **Periodicity Assumption:** Economic activity can be divided into meaningful time periods.
- **Measurement Principle:** Financial statements use a mixed attribute system that allows assets and liabilities to be measured at various bases, including historical cost, fair value, net realizable value, and present value of future cash flows. As a general rule, however, financial information is accounted for and based on cost, not on current market value.

- **Accrual Accounting:** Revenues are recognized when the performance obligation is satisfied and expenses are recognized in the same period as the related revenue, not necessarily in the period in which the cash is received or expended by the company.
  - **Revenue Recognition Principle:** As a general rule, revenues are recognized when an entity satisfies a performance obligation by transferring either a good or a service to a customer.
  - **Expense Recognition Principle:** Expenses are necessarily incurred to generate revenue. Expenses incurred to generate a specific amount of revenue in a period are matched against that revenue (for example, cost of goods sold). Expenses that do not have a direct link with revenue may be recognized when cash is spent or liabilities are incurred (for example, selling, general and administrative expenses). Other expenses are allocated by systematic and rational procedures to the periods in which the assets provide benefit (for example, depreciation expense). Losses may result when it is evident that future economic benefits of an asset have been reduced or eliminated.
- **Full Disclosure Principle:** It is important that the user be given information that would make a difference in the decision process, but not so much information that the user is impeded in analyzing what is important.

## 2.6 SFAC No. 6, *Elements of Financial Statements*

Elements are the components of the financial statements. They must be measurable and meet the recognition requirements previously discussed.

### 2.6.1 Assets

Assets are probable future economic benefits to be received by the company as a result of past transactions or events. Valuation accounts may be used to show reductions to or increases in an asset that reflect adjustments beyond the historical cost or carrying amount of the asset.

### 2.6.2 Liabilities

Liabilities are probable future sacrifices of economic benefits arising from a present obligation of the company to transfer assets or provide services to other entities in the future as a result of past transactions or events.

### 2.6.3 Equity (or Net Assets)

Equity is the residual interest in the assets of the company that remains after deducting its liabilities.

### 2.6.4 Investments by Owners

Investments by owners are increases in the equity of an entity resulting from transfers of cash, property, or services from owners.

### 2.6.5 Distributions to Owners

Distributions to owners are decreases in the equity of an entity from transfers of cash, property, or services, or the incurrence of a liability to owners.

### 2.6.6 Comprehensive Income

Comprehensive income includes any change in equity other than investments by owners and distributions to owners (i.e., net income plus other comprehensive income).

### 2.6.7 Revenues

Revenues are inflows or enhancements of assets, or settlements of liabilities from delivering goods or services as a part of normal operations. Recognize revenue at the gross amount (less allowances for returns and discounts given).

### 2.6.8 Expenses

Expenses are outflows or uses of assets, or incurrences of liabilities from delivering goods or services as part of normal operations.

### 2.6.9 Gains

Gains are increases in equity from peripheral transactions and other events, except revenues and investments from owners.

### 2.6.10 Losses

Losses are decreases in equity from peripheral transactions and other events, except expenses and distributions to owners.

## 2.7 SFAC No. 7, *Using Cash Flow Information and Present Value in Accounting Measurements*

SFAC No. 7 provides a framework for accountants to employ when using future cash flows as a measurement basis for assets and liabilities, especially when the factors to consider in the measurement are complex. It also provides a set of principles that govern the use of present value, especially when the timing and/or amount of future cash flows are uncertain.

### 2.7.1 Measurements Based on Future Cash Flows Only

SFAC No. 7 applies only to measurement issues for assets and liabilities that are determined using future cash flows only.

### 2.7.2 Five Elements of Present Value Measurement

The FASB identified five elements of present value (or economic value) measurement that were used as the basis for determining the measurement objective of SFAC No. 7.

1. Estimate of future cash flow
2. Expectations about timing variations of future cash flows
3. Time value of money (the risk-free rate of interest)
4. The price for bearing uncertainty
5. Other factors (e.g., liquidity issues and market imperfections)

### 2.7.3 Fair Value Objective

If fair value cannot be determined in the marketplace, the objective must be to obtain an estimate of fair value by using the present value of future cash flows.

### 2.7.4 Present Value Computations

SFAC No. 7 allows the use of two approaches to determine present value (each considering the interest method of allocation), depending on the circumstances.

- **Traditional Approach:** The traditional approach (i.e., one discount rate used to take the present value of a future cash flow stream) to present value computations may be used when assets and liabilities have contractual (i.e., fixed) cash flows that are not expected to vary. In this approach, interest rate selection is paramount.

- **Expected Cash Flow Approach:** In more complex cases, the expected cash flow approach is to be used. Rather than focusing on the interest rate selection, this approach uses only the risk-free rate of return as the discount rate and then turns its attention to the expected future cash flows, considering uncertainties (e.g., default risk) as adjustments to the future cash flows.
    - **Expected Cash Flow:** The expected cash flow approach considers a range of possible cash flows and assigns a (subjective) probability to each cash flow in the range to determine the weighted average, or "expected," future cash flow.
    - **Risk and Uncertainty Adjustments to Cash Flows:** Adjustments to the expected cash flows used in complex present value computations (rather than interest rate adjustments) are required for uncertainties (e.g., default risk).

### 2.7.5 Liability Measurement Considers Additional Factors

The FASB determined that, when using present value, the objective of estimating the fair value of a liability must consider certain other factors, including:

- Costs to settle
- Credit standing of the company

### 2.7.6 Changes in Estimated Cash Flows Using the Catch-up Approach

To use this approach, simply adjust the carrying amount of the asset or liability to the present value determined using the revised estimates and discount using the original effective interest rate.

---

**Question 1**  MCQ-00010

According to the FASB and IASB conceptual frameworks, completeness is an ingredient of:

|    | *Relevance* | *Faithful Representation* |
|----|-------------|---------------------------|
| a. | Yes         | No                        |
| b. | No          | Yes                       |
| c. | Yes         | Yes                       |
| d. | No          | No                        |

## NOTES

# MODULE 2: Income Statement and Balance Sheet

**FAR 1**

## 1 Uses of the Income Statement and Terminology

The purpose of the income statement is to provide information about the uses of funds in the income process (i.e., expenses), the uses of funds that will never be used to earn income (i.e., losses), the sources of funds created by those expenses (i.e., revenues), and the sources of funds not associated with the earnings process (i.e., gains).

### 1.1 Uses of the Income Statement

The income statement is useful in determining profitability, value for investment purposes, and creditworthiness. The income statement is also useful in predicting information about future cash flows (e.g., the amounts, timing, and uncertainty of cash flows) based on past performance.

### 1.2 Terminology

#### 1.2.1 Cost and Unexpired Costs

- **Cost** is an amount (measured in money) expended for items such as capital assets, services (e.g., payroll), and merchandise received. Cost is the amount actually paid for something.
- **Unexpired costs** are costs that will expire in future periods and be charged (allocated in a systematic and rational manner or matched) against revenues from future periods.

| Unexpired Costs (Asset) | Expired Costs (Expense) |
|---|---|
| 1. Inventory | Cost of goods sold |
| 2. Unexpired (prepaid) cost of insurance | Insurance expense |
| 3. Net book value of fixed assets | Depreciation expense |
| 4. Unexpired cost of patents | Patents expense (amortization) |

#### 1.2.2 Gross Concept (Revenues and Expenses)

- **Revenues** are reported in the gross amount of consideration to which the entity expects to be entitled in exchange for the specified goods or services transferred.
- **Expenses** (costs that benefit only the current period or the allocation of unexpired costs to the current period for the benefit received) are reported at their gross amounts.

#### 1.2.3 Net Concept (Gains and Losses)

- **Gains** are reported at their net amounts (i.e., proceeds less net book value). A gain is the recognition of an asset either not in the ordinary course of business (e.g., gains on the sale of a fixed asset) or without the incurrence of an expense (e.g., finding gold on the company's property).
- **Losses** are reported at their net amounts (i.e., proceeds less net book value). A loss is cost expiration either not in the ordinary course of business (e.g., loss on the sale of investment assets) or without the generation of revenue (e.g., abandonment).

Income Statement and Balance Sheet                                                                                    FAR 1

**Note:** The FASB has eliminated the concept of extraordinary items. Items of income or loss that are unusual or infrequent (or both) should be reported separately as part of income from continuing operations. The nature of the item and the financial statement effects should be disclosed on the face of the income statement or in the footnotes. U.S. GAAP and IFRS are now aligned in their treatment of unusual or infrequent items.

# 2   Income From Continuing Operations

## 2.1   Multiple-Step Income Statement

The multiple-step income statement reports operating revenues and expenses separately from nonoperating revenues and expenses and other gains and losses. The benefit of the multiple-step income statement is enhanced user information (because the line items presented often provide the user with readily available data with which to calculate various analytical ratios).

### Example 1    Multiple-Step Income Statement

**Facts:** The following trial balance contains a list of income statement accounts for the year ended December 31, Year 1.

**Trial Balance: Income Statement Accounts *Only***
For the Year Ended December 31, Year 1

| Account | | Debit | Credit |
|---|---|---|---|
| 4000 | Sales revenue | | $380 |
| 4050 | Sales returns | $ 25 | |
| 4060 | Sales discounts | 5 | |
| 4100 | Service revenue | | 200 |
| 4200 | Rental revenue | | 100 |
| 5000 | Cost of goods sold | 200 | |
| 5100 | Cost of services sold | 150 | |
| 5200 | Cost of rental income | 60 | |
| 5250 | Salaries expense* | 70 | |
| 5300 | Freight out | 25 | |
| 5400 | Commissions | 40 | |
| 5500 | Advertising | 15 | |
| 5600 | Insurance expense | 20 | |
| 5800 | Depreciation expense | 80 | |
| 5900 | Income tax expense | 100 | |
| 6000 | Interest revenue | | 170 |
| 6200 | Other revenue | | 130 |
| 6500 | Gain on sale | | 50 |
| 7000 | Interest expense | 50 | |
| 7500 | Loss on sale of assets | 40 | |
| 7550 | Loss on sale of investments | 100 | |

*Salaries expense: $20 relates to salaries for salesmen and $50 relates to salaries for officers of the company.

**Note:** The trial balance does not balance, as the balance sheet accounts are excluded.

(continued)

(continued)

**Required:** Prepare a multiple-step income statement prepared from the trial balance information above.

**Solution:**

Radon Industries Inc.
**Income Statement**
For the Year Ended December 31, Year 1
*(in thousands)*

| | | |
|---|---:|---:|
| Net sales (including goods, services, and rentals), less discounts and returns | | $650 |
| Cost of sales (including goods, services, and rentals): | | (410) |
|     Gross margin | | $240 |
| Selling expenses | $100 | |
| General and administrative expenses | 70 | |
| Depreciation expense | 80 | (250) |
| Income (loss) from operations | | $ (10) |
| Other revenues and gains: | | |
|     Interest revenue | 170 | |
|     Gain on sale of fixed assets | 50 | |
|     Other revenue | 130 | 350 |
| Other expenses and losses: | | |
|     Interest expense | 50 | |
|     Loss on sale of fixed assets | 40 | (90) |
| Income before unusual items and income tax | | $250 |
| Loss on sale of available-for-sale securities | | (100) |
| Income before income tax | | 150 |
| Income tax expense | | (100) |
| **Net income** (or "income from continuing operations")* | | **$ 50** |

*"Income from continuing operations" would be used if the income statement includes "discontinued operations."

1. Inventory cost .......................... Purchase price, freight in
2. Selling expense ........................ Freight out, salaries and commissions, advertising
3. General and administrative ........... Officers' salaries, accounting and legal, insurance
4. Nonoperating .......................... Auxiliary activities, interest expense

## 2.2 Single-Step Income Statement

In the single-step income statement presentation of income from continuing operations, total expenses (including income tax expense) are subtracted from total revenues; thus, the income statement has a single step. The benefits of a single-step income statement are its simple design and the fact that the presentation of types of revenues or expenses do not appear to the user to be classified as more important than others.

### Example 2 — Single-Step Income Statement

**Facts:** Same as Example 1.

**Required:** Using the trial balance from Example 1, prepare a single-step income statement.

**Solution:**

Radon Industries Inc.
**Income Statement**
For the Year Ended December 31, Year 1
*(in thousands)*

| | |
|---|---:|
| **Revenues and other items:** | |
| Sales revenue | $ 350 |
| Service revenue | 200 |
| Interest revenue | 170 |
| Rental revenue | 100 |
| Gain on sale of fixed assets | 50 |
| Other revenue | 130 |
| **Total revenues and other items** | **$1,000** |
| **Expenses and other items:** | |
| Cost of goods sold | $ 200 |
| Cost of services sold | 150 |
| Cost of rental income | 60 |
| Selling expenses | 100 |
| General and administrative expenses | 70 |
| Interest expense | 50 |
| Depreciation expense | 80 |
| Loss on sale of fixed assets | 40 |
| Loss on sale of available-for-sale securities | 100 |
| Income tax expense | 100 |
| **Total expenses and other items** | **$ 950** |
| **Net income** (or income from continuing operations, if necessary) | **$ 50** |

# 3 Balance Sheet

Under U.S. GAAP, entities may present a classified balance sheet that distinguishes current and non-current assets and liabilities. When appropriate, a balance sheet presentation based on liquidity is also permissible. The following is an example of a classified balance sheet.

---

**Company Name**
**Balance Sheet**
As of December 31, Year 1

*Assets*

**Current assets**
    Cash and cash equivalents
    Trading securities, at fair value
    Accounts receivable, net of allowance
    Notes receivable
    Inventory
    Prepaid expenses

**Investments**
    Available-for-sale securities, at fair value
    Held-to-maturity securities
    Investments in affiliates

**Property, plant, and equipment**
    Land
    Building
    Equipment
    Less: accumulated depreciation

**Intangible assets**
    Goodwill
    Patents, net of amortization

**Other assets**
    Pension and other postretirement benefit assets
    Deferred income tax asset

**Total assets**

*Liabilities and Stockholders' Equity*

**Current liabilities**
    Current portion of long-term debt
    Accounts payable
    Notes payable
    Interest payable
    Salaries payable
    Unearned revenue

**Long-term liabilities**
    Bonds payable
    Deferred income tax liability
    Pension and other postretirement benefit liabilities

**Total liabilities**

**Stockholders' equity**
    Capital stock
        Preferred stock, $10 par, 8% cumulative and nonparticipating, 10,000 shares authorized, 5,000 shares issued and outstanding
        Common stock, $0.01 par, 600,000,000 shares authorized, 57,598,000 shares issued and 57,178,485 shares outstanding
    Paid-in capital in excess of par
    Retained earnings
    Accumulated other comprehensive income
    (Treasury stock at cost) (419,515 shares)

**Total stockholders' equity**

**Total liabilities and stockholders' equity**

Income Statement and Balance Sheet

FAR 1

### Question 1 — MCQ-00031

Scott Corporation sold a fixed asset used for operations for greater than its carrying amount. Scott should report the transaction in the income statement using the:

- **a.** Gross concept, showing the proceeds as part of revenues and the carrying amount as part of expenses in the continuing operations section.
- **b.** Net concept, showing the total amount as a component of other comprehensive income, net of income taxes.
- **c.** Net concept, showing the total gain as part of discontinued operations, net of income taxes.
- **d.** Net concept, showing the total gain as part of continuing operations, *not* net of income taxes.

### Question 2 — MCQ-00052

Which of the following should be included in general and administrative expenses?

|  | Interest | Advertising |
|---|---|---|
| **a.** | Yes | Yes |
| **b.** | Yes | No |
| **c.** | No | Yes |
| **d.** | No | No |

# MODULE 3: Revenue Recognition: Part 1

## 1 Overview and Scope

Revenue recognition occurs when an entity satisfies a performance obligation by transferring either a good or a service to a customer. Revenue should be recognized at an amount that reflects the expected consideration the entity is entitled to receive in exchange for the good or service provided.

All entities (public, private, not-for-profit) that either enter into contracts with customers to transfer goods, services, or nonfinancial assets (unless governed by other standards) are subject to the revenue recognition standard. Certain contracts, such as those covering leases, insurance, non-warranty guarantees, and financial instruments, are covered under other standards.

## 2 The Five-Step Approach

In order to properly apply the revenue recognition standard, an entity should implement the five-step approach described below:

- **Step 1:** Identify the contract with the customer
- **Step 2:** Identify the separate performance obligations in the contract
- **Step 3:** Determine the transaction price
- **Step 4:** Allocate the transaction price to the separate performance obligations
- **Step 5:** Recognize revenue when or as the entity satisfies each performance obligation

### 2.1 Step 1: Identify the Contract(s) With the Customer

#### 2.1.1 Definitions

A contract is defined as an agreement between two or more parties that creates enforceable rights and obligations. Depending on an entity's typical business practices, contracts can be verbal, written, or implied.

A customer is a party that has contracted with an entity to exchange consideration in order to obtain goods or services that are an output of the entity's ordinary activities.

#### 2.1.2 Criteria for Revenue Recognition

Revenue is only recognized when a contract meets *all* of the criteria listed below. The criteria assessment is performed at contract inception and if all criteria are met, reassessments should only be needed if significant changes occur. If all of the criteria are not met at inception, regular reassessments should follow.

- All parties have approved the contract and have committed to perform their obligations.
- The rights of each party regarding contracted goods or services are identified.
- Payment terms can be identified.

- The contract has commercial substance, meaning future cash flows (amount, risk, and timing) are expected to change as a result of the contract.
- It is probable (based on the customer's intent and ability to pay when due) that the entity will collect substantially all of the consideration due under the contract.

If the criteria above are not met but consideration has been paid by the customer, an entity can recognize revenue if the consideration is nonrefundable and either there are no remaining obligations to transfer goods/services or the contract has terminated. If not recognized as revenue, the consideration received is booked as a liability.

### Example 1 — Identifying the Contract

**Facts:** On March 1, Year 1, Bulldog Inc. entered into a contract to transfer a product to Kitty Inc. on September 1, Year 1. Kitty will pay the full contract price of $15,000 to Bulldog by August 1, Year 1. Bulldog transferred the product to Kitty on September 1, Year 1. The cost of the product totaled $9,000.

**Required:** Determine the journal entries that Bulldog will book to account for this transaction.

**Solution:**

*March 1, Year 1, journal entry*: No entry is required because neither party has performed according to the contract.

*August 1, Year 1, journal entry*: A contract liability (e.g. unearned sales revenue) is recognized when the cash is received in advance.

| DR | Cash | $15,000 | |
|----|------|---------|---|
| CR | Unearned sales revenue | | $15,000 |

*September 1, Year 1, journal entry*: Revenue is recorded when the product is transferred from the seller to the buyer.

| DR | Unearned sales revenue | $15,000 | |
|----|------|---------|---|
| CR | Sales revenue | | $15,000 |
| DR | Cost of goods sold | 9,000 | |
| CR | Inventory | | 9,000 |

### 2.1.3 Combination of Contracts

When two or more contracts are entered into with the same customer or with related parties of the customer at or near the same time, the contracts should be combined and accounted for as a single contract if either the contracts are negotiated as a package with a single commercial objective, consideration for one contract is tied to the performance or price of another contract, or the goods/services promised represent a single performance obligation.

### 2.1.4 Contract Modification

A contract modification represents a change in the price or scope (or both) of a contract approved by both parties. When a modification occurs, it is either treated as a new contract or as a modification of the existing contract. The modification is treated as a new contract if both the scope increases due to the addition of distinct goods or services and the price increase appropriately reflects the stand-alone selling prices of the additional goods/services. If not accounted for as a new contract, the modification is treated as part of the existing contract (for non-distinct goods and services) with an adjustment to revenue to reflect the change in the transaction price.

## 2.2 Step 2: Identify the Separate Performance Obligations in the Contract

### 2.2.1 Performance Obligation Defined

A performance obligation is a promise to transfer a good or a service to a customer. The transfer can be either an individual good or service (or a bundle of goods or services) that is distinct, or a series of goods or services that are substantially the same and are thereby transferred in the same manner. If the promise to transfer a good or a service is not distinct from other goods or services, they will all be combined into a single performance obligation.

### 2.2.2 A Distinct Good or Service

In order to be distinct, both criteria below must be met:

1. The promise to transfer the good or service is separately identifiable from other goods or services in the contract; and
2. The customer can benefit either from the good or service independently or when combined with the customer's available resources.

### 2.2.3 Separately Identifiable

A transfer of a good or service is separately identifiable if the entity does not integrate the good or service with other goods or services in the contract; the good or service does not customize or modify another good or service in the contract; or the good or service does not depend on or relate to other goods or services promised in the contract.

Factors that indicate two or more promises to transfer a good or a service to a customer are not separately identifiable include (but are not limited to) the following:

- The goods or services are highly interrelated or interdependent.
- The entity provides a significant service of integrating the good or service with other goods or services promised in the contract into a bundle of goods or services that represent the combined output contracted for by the customer.

### Example 2 — Single Performance Obligation

**Facts:** Tanner Co. is building a multi-unit residential complex. The entity enters into a contract with a customer for a specific unit that is under construction. The goods and services to be provided in the contract include procurement, construction, piping, wiring, installation of equipment, and finishing.

**Required:** Identify the performance obligation(s) in this contract.

**Solution:** Although the goods and services provided by the contractor are capable of being distinct, they are not distinct in this contract because the goods and services cannot be separately identified from the promise to construct the unit. The contractor will integrate the goods and services into the unit, so all the goods and services are accounted for as a single performance obligation.

### Example 3 — Separately Identifiable Performance Obligations

**Facts:** A software developer enters into a contract with a customer to transfer a software license, perform installation, and provide software updates and technical support for five years. The developer sells the license, installation, updates, and technical support separately. The entity determines that each good or service is separately identifiable because the installation does not modify the software and the software is functional without the updates and technical support.

**Required:** Identify the performance obligation(s) in this contract.

**Solution:** The software is delivered before the installation, updates, and technical support and is functional without the updates and technical support, so the customer can benefit from each good or service on its own. The developer has also determined that the software license, installation, updates, and technical support are separately identifiable. On this basis, there are four performance obligations in this contract:

1. Software license
2. Installation service
3. Software updates
4. Technical support

## 2.3 Step 3: Determine the Transaction Price

### 2.3.1 Transaction Price Defined

The transaction price represents the amount of consideration that an entity can expect to be entitled to receive in exchange for transferring promised goods or services to a customer. The transaction price should be determined based on considering the effects of: variable consideration (and any constraining estimates), significant financing if applicable, noncash considerations, and any consideration payable to the customer (if applicable).

### 2.3.2 Variable Consideration

The amount of variable consideration should be estimated by taking a range of possible amounts and using either the expected value (which sums probability-weighted amounts) or the most likely amount—whichever is assumed to be the better predictor. Variable consideration should only be included in the price if it is probable that a significant revenue reversal will not be required once any uncertainty tied to the consideration is resolved.

### 2.3.3 Significant Financing

Time value of money should be an adjustment to the transaction price if the timing of the payments per the contract provides either the customer or the entity with a significant benefit in regard to financing the transfer of goods or services. Revenue should be recognized based on the price that would have been paid in cash by the customer at the time of transfer. If the time between the transfer of goods/services and the payment by the customer is anticipated to be less than one year, discounting the transaction price is unnecessary.

### 2.3.4 Noncash Consideration

Noncash consideration should be measured at fair value at contract inception.

### 2.3.5 Consideration Payable to a Customer

Any consideration (cash, credits, vouchers, etc.) that is payable to a customer should be treated as a reduction in the transaction price and revenue recognized by the entity unless the entity is receiving goods or services transferred by the customer.

---

**Example 4     Time Value of Money**

**Facts:** On January 1, Year 5, SDF sold furniture to a customer for $4,000 with three years' interest-free credit. The customer took delivery of the furniture on that day. The $4,000 is payable to SDF on December 31, Year 7. The applicable discount rate based on the customer's credit profile is 8 percent.

**Required:** Determine the transaction price for the sale of furniture.

**Solution:** The transaction price is $3,175 ($4,000 × 1/(1.08)$^3$) because the time value of money must be considered when determining the transaction price.

Note that interest income will also be recognized each year as follows:

Year 5: $3,175 × 8% = $254

Year 6: ($3,175 + $254) × 8% = $274

Year 7: ($3,175 + $254 + $274) × 8% = $296

---

## 2.4 Step 4: Allocate the Transaction Price to the Performance Obligations in the Contract

### 2.4.1 Allocation Defined

If there is more than one performance obligation within a contract, the transaction price should be allocated to each separate performance obligation based on the amount of consideration that would be expected for satisfying each unique obligation. The stand-alone selling price (and any applicable discount or variable consideration) of each distinct good or service underlying each performance obligation should be determined at contract inception.

### 2.4.2 Stand-alone Selling Price

The price an entity would sell the promised good or service to a customer on a stand-alone basis. Once this price is determined for each obligation within the contract, the total transaction price should be allocated in proportion to the stand-alone selling prices.

### 2.4.3 Discounts

A discount exists when the sum of the stand-alone prices for each obligation within a contract exceeds the total consideration for the contract. A discount should be allocated proportionally to all obligations within the contact.

### 2.4.4 Variable Consideration

If applicable, variable consideration may be attributable to the entire contract, individual performance obligations within a contract, or distinct goods or services within a single performance obligation.

### 2.4.5 Transaction Price Changes

If the transaction price changes after contract inception, the change should be allocated to the performance obligations in the contract on the same basis that was used at inception. Changes in stand-alone selling prices after inception should not be reallocated.

---

**Example 5 — Allocating the Transaction Price**

**Facts:** A software company enters into a $250,000 contract with a customer to transfer a software license, perform installation service, and provide technical support for a three-year period. The entity sells the license, installation service, and technical support separately. The installation service and technical support could be performed by other entities and the software remains functional in the absence of these services. The contract price must be paid on installation of the software, which is planned for March 1, Year 1.

**Required:** How should the software company recognize revenue for these transactions?

**Solution:** The entity identifies three performance obligations in the contract for the following goods and services:

1. Software license
2. Installation service
3. Technical support

The stand-alone selling price can be determined for each performance obligation. The license is usually sold for $160,000, the installation service is $20,000, and technical support runs $30,000 per year. The fair value of the contract is determined to be $270,000. Based on the relative fair values, the allocation of revenue is as follows:

| | |
|---|---|
| Software license | [($160,000/$270,000) × $250,000] = $148,148 |
| Installation service | [($20,000/$270,000) × $250,000] = $18,519 |
| Technical support | [($90,000/$270,000) × $250,000] = $83,333 |

(continued)

(continued)

*The journal entry to record the $250,000 payment made on March 1 appears below.*

**March 1, Year 1**

| DR | Cash | $250,000 | |
|---|---|---|---|
| CR | License revenue | | $148,148 |
| CR | Service revenue | | 18,519 |
| CR | Unearned service revenue | | 83,333 |

Revenue is recorded for the sale of the license and the installation at the time of sale. The technical support will be recognized on a monthly basis as the support is provided.

**December 31, Year 1**

| DR | Unearned service revenue | $23,148 | |
|---|---|---|---|
| CR | Service revenue | | $23,148 |

At year-end, an adjusting entry is made to record 10 months of technical support ($83,333/36 = $2,314.80; $2,314.80 × 10 months = $23,148) through the end of Year 1. The remaining technical support will be recorded in Years 2 and 3.

## 2.5 Step 5: Recognize Revenue When (or as) the Entity Satisfies a Performance Obligation

### 2.5.1 Transfer of Control

An entity should recognize revenue when the entity satisfies a performance obligation by transferring the good or service to the customer, who thereby obtains control of the asset. Control implies the ability to obtain the benefits from and direct the usage of the asset while also preventing other entities from obtaining benefits and directing usage. Performance obligations may be satisfied either over time or at a point in time.

### 2.5.2 Satisfied Over Time

Revenue is recognized over time if any one of the criteria below is met:

- The entity's performance creates or enhances an asset that the customer controls.
- The customer receives and consumes the benefits of the entity's performance as the entity performs it (e.g., service contracts, such as a cleaning service or a monthly payroll processing service).
- The entity's performance does not create an asset with alternative use to the entity (assessed at inception) and the entity has an enforceable right to receive payment for performance completed to date.

In order to recognize revenue, the entity must be able to reasonably measure progress toward completion. Progress can be measured using output and input methods.

1. **Output Methods**

   By using output methods, revenue is recognized based on the value to the customer of the goods or services transferred to date relative to the remaining goods or services promised. Examples of output methods include: units produced or delivered, time elapsed, milestones achieved, surveys of performance completed to date, and appraisals of results achieved. These methods should only be used when the output selected represents the entity's performance toward complete satisfaction of the performance obligation. When the outputs used to measure progress are not available or directly observable, an input method may be necessary.

2. **Input Methods**

   By using input methods, revenue is recognized based on the entity's efforts or inputs to the satisfaction of the performance obligation relative to the total expected inputs. Examples of input methods include: costs incurred relative to total expected costs, resources consumed, labor-hours expended, and time elapsed. A disadvantage of input methods is that there may not be a direct relationship between an entity's inputs and the transfer of control of goods and services to a customer. If inputs are used evenly throughout the performance period, revenue can be recognized on a straight-line basis.

> **Illustration 1     Straight-Line Basis**
>
> A health club enters into a contract with a customer for one year of unlimited health club access for $75 per month. The health club determines that the customer simultaneously receives and consumes the benefits of the club's performance, so the contract is a performance obligation satisfied over time. Because the customer benefits from the club's services evenly throughout the year, the best measure of progress toward complete satisfaction of the performance obligation is a time-based measure. Revenue will be recognized on a straight-line basis throughout the year at $75 per month.

In the absence of reliable information used to measure progress, if an entity expects to recover its costs, revenue may be recognized to the extent that costs are recovered until the point at which it can reasonably measure the outcome of the performance obligation.

### 2.5.3 Satisfied at a Point in Time

If the performance obligation is not satisfied over time, then it is satisfied at a point in time. Revenue should be recognized at the point in time when the customer obtains control of the asset.

Control would generally require the following:

- The entity has a right to payment and the customer has an obligation to pay for an asset.
- The customer has legal title to the asset.
- The entity has transferred physical possession of the asset.
- The customer has the significant rewards and risks of ownership.
- The customer has accepted the asset.

## Example 6 — Performance Obligation Satisfied Over Time

**Facts:** Tanner Co. is building a multi-unit residential complex. The entity enters into a contract with a customer for a specific unit that is under construction. The contract has the following terms:

- The customer pays a nonrefundable security deposit upon entering the contract.
- The customer agrees to make progress payments during construction.
- If the customer fails to make the progress payments, the entity has the right to all of the consideration in the contract if it completes the unit.
- The terms of the contract prevent the entity from directing the unit to another customer.

**Required:** Determine whether this performance obligation is satisfied over time or at a point in time.

**Solution:** This performance obligation is satisfied over time because:

- The unit does not have an alternative future use to the entity because it cannot be directed to another customer.
- The entity has a right to payment for performance to date because the entity has a right to all of the consideration in the contract if it completes the unit.

## Example 7 — Performance Obligation Satisfied at a Point in Time

**Facts:** Tanner Co. is building a multi-unit residential complex. The entity enters into a contract with a customer for a specific unit that is under construction. The contract has the following terms:

- The customer pays a deposit upon entering the contract that is refundable if the entity fails to complete the unit in accordance with the contract.
- The remainder of the purchase price is due on completion of the unit.
- If the customer defaults on the contract before completion, the entity only has the right to retain the deposit.

**Required:** Determine whether this performance obligation is satisfied over time or at a point in time.

**Solution:** This is a performance obligation satisfied at a point in time because it is not a service contract, the customer does not control the unit as it is created, and the entity does not have an enforceable right to payment for performance completed to date (i.e., the entity only has a right to the deposit until the unit is completed).

# 3 Presentation

A contract asset or liability should be presented in the statement of financial position when either party has performed in a contract.

A *contract asset* reflects the entity's right to consideration in exchange for goods or services that the entity has transferred to the customer. Essentially, the entity has performed prior to the customer paying or prior to the payment due date. The conditions associated with this right are something other than the passage of time.

**Note:** If the payment due date is conditioned only by the passage of time, the entity should present this separately as a *receivable*.

A *contract liability* must be booked when an entity has an obligation to transfer goods or services to a customer. In this situation, the entity has either already received consideration from the customer or the customer owes consideration and it is unconditional (the customer pays or owes payment before the entity performs).

---

### Example 8 — Contract Liability and Receivable

**Facts:** On January 1, Anderson Co. enters into a noncancelable contract with Tanner Co. for the sale of an excavator for $350,000. The excavator will be delivered to Tanner on April 1. The contract requires Tanner to pay the $350,000 in advance on February 1, and Tanner makes the payment on March 1.

**Required:** Prepare the journal entries that would be used by Anderson to account for this contract.

**Solution:**

*February 1 journal entry*: Anderson recognizes a receivable because it has an unconditional right to the consideration (i.e., the contract is noncancelable).

| | | | |
|---|---|---|---|
| DR | Receivable | $350,000 | |
| CR | Contract liability | | $350,000 |

*March 1 journal entry*: When Tanner makes the payment, Anderson recognizes the cash collection.

| | | | |
|---|---|---|---|
| DR | Cash | $350,000 | |
| CR | Receivable | | $350,000 |

*April 1 journal entry*: Anderson recognizes revenue when the excavator is delivered to Tanner.

| | | | |
|---|---|---|---|
| DR | Contract liability | $350,000 | |
| CR | Revenue | | $350,000 |

## Example 9 — Contract Asset and Receivable

**Facts:** On January 1, Anderson Co. enters into a contract with Tanner Co. for the sale of two excavators for $350,000 each. The contract requires one excavator to be delivered on February 1 and states that the payment for the delivery of the first excavator is conditional on the delivery of the second excavator. The second excavator is delivered on June 1.

**Required:** Prepare the journal entries that would be used by Anderson to account for this contract.

**Solution:**

*February 1 journal entry*: Anderson recognizes a contract asset and revenue when it satisfies the performance obligation to deliver the first excavator.

| | | | |
|---|---|---|---|
| DR | Contract asset | $350,000 | |
| CR | Revenue | | $350,000 |

Note that a receivable is not recognized on February 1, because Anderson does not have an unconditional right to the consideration until the second excavator is delivered.

*June 1 journal entry*: Anderson recognizes a receivable and revenue when it satisfies the performance obligation to deliver the second excavator.

| | | | |
|---|---|---|---|
| DR | Receivable | $700,000 | |
| CR | Contract asset | | $350,000 |
| CR | Revenue | | 350,000 |

---

### Question 1 — MCQ-00549

For $50 a month, Rawl Co. visits its customers' premises and performs insect control services. If customers experience problems between regularly scheduled visits, Rawl makes service calls at no additional charge. Instead of paying monthly, customers may pay an annual fee of $540 in advance. For a customer who pays the annual fee in advance, Rawl should recognize the related revenue under U.S. GAAP:

a. When the cash is collected.
b. At the end of the fiscal year.
c. At the end of the contract year after all of the services have been performed.
d. Evenly over the contract year as the services are performed.

**Question 2**  MCQ-06244

On April 15, Year 3, Landon Co. signed a contract that entailed providing a piece of scientific equipment for $215,000 to Jacobs Inc., with delivery expected to occur on August 31, Year 3. Per the terms of the contract, Jacobs will pay Landon for the full amount on July 31, Year 3. Landon's cost to produce the equipment is $175,000. Assuming delivery occurs as expected, the August 31 journal entry for Landon will involve which of the following debits/credits?

   a. Credit to cash of $215,000.
   b. Debit to inventory of $175,000.
   c. Credit to cost of goods sold of $175,000.
   d. Debit to unearned sales revenue of $215,000.

# MODULE 4: Revenue Recognition: Part 2

FAR 1

# 1 Specific Applications Within Revenue Recognition

## 1.1 Incremental Costs of Obtaining a Contract

The incremental costs of obtaining a contract are costs incurred that would not have been incurred if the contract had not been obtained, and are recognized as an asset (capitalized and amortized) if the entity expects that it will recover these costs. An entity will recognize an expense if the costs would have been incurred regardless of whether the contract was obtained.

### Example 1 — Incremental Costs of Obtaining a Contract

**Facts:** A software developer enters into a contract with a customer to transfer a software license, perform installation, and provide software updates and technical support for three years in exchange for $240,000. In order to win this contract, the developer incurred the following costs:

| | |
|---|---|
| Legal fees for drawing up the contract | $10,000 |
| Travel costs to deliver proposal | 20,000 |
| Commissions to sales employee | 12,000 |
| Total | $42,000 |

**Required:** Determine which costs should be recognized as an asset and which should be expensed.

**Solution:** The travel costs ($20,000) should be expensed because they would have been incurred even if the developer did not get the contract. The legal fees ($10,000) and sales commissions ($12,000) should be recognized as assets because they are costs of obtaining the contract, assuming that the developer expects to recover the costs.

## 1.2 Costs to Fulfill a Contract

The costs that are incurred to fulfill a contract that are not within the scope of another standard will be recognized as an asset if they meet *all* of the following criteria:

- Relate directly to a contract (such as direct labor, materials, allocated costs, and other costs that are explicitly chargeable to the customer per the contract).
- They generate or enhance the resources of the entity.
- They are expected to be recovered.

Costs to be expensed include selling, general and administrative costs, wasted labor and materials costs, and costs tied to satisfied performance obligations.

> **Example 2** **Costs to Fulfill a Contract**
>
> **Facts:** A software developer enters into a contract with a customer to transfer a software license, perform installation, and provide software updates and technical support for three years in exchange for $240,000. In order to fulfill the technical support portion of the project, the developer purchases an additional workstation for the technical support team for $8,000 and assigns one employee to be primarily responsible for providing the technical support for the customer. This employee also provides services for other customers. The employee is paid $30,000 annually and is expected to spend 10 percent of his time supporting the customer.
>
> **Required:** Determine which costs should be recognized as an asset and which should be expensed.
>
> **Solution:** The additional workstation ($8,000) should be recognized as an asset under IAS 16 *Property, Plant, and Equipment*. The cost of the employee assigned to the contract ($30,000) should be recognized as a payroll expense because, although the costs relate to the contract and are expected to be recovered, the employee was already working for the developer and therefore the costs do not generate or enhance the resources of the developer.

## 1.3 Principal vs. Agent

Whenever an entity uses another party to provide goods or services to a customer, the entity needs to determine whether it is acting as a principal or an agent.

- Principal: The entity controls the good or service before it is transferred to the customer. When this is the case, the revenue recognized is equal to the gross consideration an entity expects to receive.

- Agent: The entity arranges for the other party to provide the good or service to the customer. When this is the case, the revenue recognized is equal to the fee or commission for performing the agent function.

Indicators that an entity is an agent and does not control the good or service before it is provided to the customer include:

- another party (the principal) is primarily responsible for fulfilling the contract;

- the entity does not have inventory risk; and

- the entity does not have discretion in establishing prices for the other party's goods or services.

> **Example 3** **Principal vs. Agent**
>
> **Facts:** On January 1, Anderson Co. enters into a contract with Tanner Co. for the sale of an excavator with unique specifications. Anderson and Tanner develop the specifications and Anderson contracts with a construction equipment manufacturer to produce the equipment. The manufacturer will deliver the equipment to Tanner when it is completed.
>
> Anderson agrees to pay the manufacturer $350,000 on delivery of the excavator to Tanner. Anderson and Tanner agree to a selling price of $385,000, which will be paid by Tanner to Anderson. Anderson's profit is $35,000. Anderson's contract with Tanner requires Tanner to seek remedies for defects from the manufacturer, but Anderson is responsible for any corrections due to errors in specifications.
>
> **Required:** Determine whether Anderson is acting as principal or agent in its contract with Tanner.
>
> **Solution:** Anderson is acting as principal in the contract based on the following indicators:
>
> - Anderson is responsible for fulfilling the contract because it is responsible for ensuring that the excavator meets specifications.
> - Anderson has inventory risk because it is responsible for correcting errors in specifications, even though the manufacturer has inventory risk during production.
> - Anderson has discretion in establishing the selling price.

## 1.4 Repurchase Agreements

A repurchase agreement is a contract by which an entity sells an asset and also either promises to or has the option to repurchase the asset. The three main forms of repurchase agreements include: an entity's obligation to repurchase the asset (a forward); an entity's right to repurchase the asset (a call option); and an entity's obligation to repurchase the asset at the customer's request (a put option).

### 1.4.1 Forward or Call Option

The entity's accounting for the contract will be based on whether it must (forward) or can (call) repurchase the asset for either:

- less than the original selling price (it will be a lease); or
- equal to/more than the original price (it will be a financing arrangement).

If the contract is a financing arrangement, the entity will recognize the asset, recognize a financial liability for any consideration received from the customer, and recognize as interest expense the difference between the amount of consideration received from the customer and the amount of consideration to be paid by the customer.

Revenue Recognition: Part 2

| Example 4 | Forward or Call Option |

**Facts:** On January 1, Anderson Co. enters into a contract with Tanner Co. for the sale of an excavator for $350,000. The contract includes a call option that gives Anderson the right to repurchase the excavator for $385,000 on or before December 31. Tanner pays the entity $350,000 on January 1. On December 31, the option lapses unexercised.

**Required:** Explain how Anderson should account for the transaction on January 1, during the year, and on December 31.

**Solution:** Anderson should account for the transaction as a financing arrangement because the repurchase price is greater than the original selling price.

On January 1, Anderson recognizes a financial liability of $350,000:

| DR | Cash | $350,000 | |
|---|---|---|---|
| CR | Financial liability | | $350,000 |

During the year, Anderson recognizes interest expense of $35,000, the difference between the repurchase price of $385,000 and the cash received of $350,000.

| DR | Interest expense | $35,000 | |
|---|---|---|---|
| CR | Financial liability | | $35,000 |

On December 31, when the option lapses, Anderson derecognizes the liability and records a sale:

| DR | Financial liability | $385,000 | |
|---|---|---|---|
| CR | Revenue | | $385,000 |

### 1.4.2 Put Option

If the entity has an obligation to repurchase the asset at the customer's request for less than the original selling price, the entity will account for the contract as either:

- a lease (if the customer has a significant economic incentive to exercise the right); or
- a sale with a right of return (if the customer does not have a significant economic incentive to exercise the right).

If the repurchase price is equal to or greater than the original selling price, the entity accounts for the contract as either:

- a financing arrangement (if the repurchase price is more than the expected market value of the asset); or
- a sale with a right of return (if the repurchase price is less than or equal to the expected market value of the asset and the customer does not have a significant economic incentive to exercise the right).

> ### Example 5 Put Option
>
> **Facts:** On January 1, Anderson Co. enters into a contract with Tanner Co. for the sale of an excavator for $350,000. The contract includes a put option that obliges Anderson to repurchase the excavator at Tanner's request for $315,000 on or before December 31. The market value is expected to be $275,000 on December 31. Tanner pays Anderson $350,000 on January 1.
>
> **Required:** Determine whether Anderson should account for this transaction as a lease, a financing arrangement, or a sale with a right of return.
>
> **Solution:** The transaction should be accounted for as a lease because Anderson has an obligation to repurchase the excavator for less than the original selling price, and Tanner has a significant economic incentive to exercise the option because the repurchase price is greater than the market value expected on December 31.

### 1.5 Bill-and-Hold Arrangements

Bill-and-hold arrangements are contracts in which the entity bills a customer for a product that it has not yet delivered to the customer. Revenue cannot be recognized in a bill-and-hold arrangement until the customer obtains control of the product. Generally, control is transferred to the customer when the product is shipped to or delivered to the customer (depending on the terms of the contract). For a customer to have obtained control of a product in a bill-and-hold arrangement, *all* of the following criteria must be met:

- There must be a substantive reason for the arrangement (e.g., the customer has requested the arrangement because it does not have space for the product).
- The product has been separately identified as belonging to the customer.
- The product is currently ready for transfer to the customer.
- The entity cannot use the product or direct it to another customer.

> ### Example 6 — Bill and Hold
>
> **Facts:** On January 1, Anderson Co. enters into a contract with Tanner Co. for the sale of an excavator and spare parts. The manufacturing lead time is 18 months. On July 1 of the following year, Tanner pays for the machine and spare parts, but only takes possession of the machine. Tanner inspects and accepts the spare parts, but requests that the parts be stored in Anderson's warehouse because Tanner does not have a place to store the parts and its premises are very close to Anderson's warehouse.
>
> Anderson expects to store the spare parts in a separate section of its warehouse for three years. The parts are available for immediate delivery to Tanner. Anderson cannot use the spare parts or transfer them to another customer.
>
> **Required:** Identify the performance obligation(s) in this contract and determine when revenue is recognized on each performance obligation.
>
> **Solution:** There are three performance obligations in this contract:
>
> 1. Promise to provide the excavator
> 2. Promise to provide spare parts
> 3. Custodial services related to the spare parts
>
> Tanner obtains control of the spare parts on July 1 because all of the criteria are met (i.e., there is a substantive reason for Anderson to hold the spare parts, the parts are separately identified and ready to transfer, and Anderson cannot use the parts or transfer them to another customer).
>
> Anderson recognizes revenue for the excavator and spare parts on July 1 when the excavator is transferred to Tanner and Tanner has obtained control of the spare parts.
>
> Anderson recognizes revenue on the custodial services over the three years that the services are provided.

## 1.6 Consignment

Consignment is when the dealer or distributor has not obtained control of the product. Revenue is recognized when the dealer or distributor sells the product to a customer, or when the dealer or distributor obtains control of the product (i.e., after a specified period of time expires).

Indicators of a consignment arrangement include:

- The entity controls the product until a specified event occurs (the sale of the product to the customer or a specific time period expires).

- The dealer does not have an unconditional obligation to pay the entity for the product (although it might be required to pay a deposit).

- The entity can require the return of the product or transfer the product to another party.

| Example 7 | Sale or Consignment |
|---|---|

**Facts:** FMC, a large multinational car manufacturer, delivers cars to a car dealer on the following terms:

- Legal title passes on sale to the public.
- The car dealer must pay for the car when legal title passes. The price to the car dealer is determined on the date FMC delivers the cars to the dealership.
- FMC can require the return of the cars and, if not sold by the car dealer, can transfer the cars to another dealer.

**Required:** Determine whether FMC should account for the delivery of the cars to the car dealer as a sale or a consignment arrangement.

**Solution:** FMC should account for the delivery of cars to the car dealer as a consignment arrangement because the dealer has not obtained control of the cars, as evidenced by the fact that FMC can require the return or transfer of the cars and the dealer does not have an unconditional obligation to pay FMC for the cars. Revenue should not be recognized until the dealer sells a car.

## 1.7 Warranties

The accounting for a warranty will depend on whether a customer has the option to purchase the warranty separately. If it can be purchased separately, the warranty will be considered a distinct service because it is promised to the customer in addition to the product covered by the contract. An entity will therefore account for the warranty as a performance obligation and allocate a portion of the overall transaction price to that obligation. If the warranty cannot be purchased separately, then there is no separate performance obligation.

The following factors should be considered when determining whether the warranty represents a service in addition to the assurance that a product is compliant with agreed-upon specifications:

- If the law requires the warranty, this would indicate that it is not a performance obligation.
- The longer the coverage period, the higher the likelihood that it is a performance obligation.
- If an entity must perform specific tasks to provide assurance regarding product compliance with agreed-upon specifications, these tasks are likely not a performance obligation.

If a warranty provides a service to a customer that is beyond the assurance that the product will comply with agreed-upon specifications, the promised service will represent a performance obligation that will require the transaction price be allocated to both the product itself and the service.

## 1.8 Refund Liabilities and the Right to Return

An entity should recognize a refund liability if it receives or will receive consideration from a customer and anticipates having to refund a portion or all of that consideration. The refund liability represents the amount an entity does not expect to be entitled to receive.

For products with a right of return (which may involve the customer receiving a refund, a credit, or another product in exchange for the original product), an entity should recognize:

- Revenue for transferred products equaling the amount of consideration the entity expects to be entitled to receive (revenue will not be recognized for products that entities anticipate having to return)
- A refund liability
- An asset related to the subsequent recovery of products when the refund liability is settled

### Illustration 1     Sales Returns

Journal entry to record an initial liability on a cash sale of $50,000 where 10 percent of items purchased tend to be returned:

| DR | Cash | $50,000 | |
|---|---|---|---|
| CR | Refund liability | | $ 5,000 |
| CR | Sales revenue | | 45,000 |

Journal entry to record cash paid to customer who returns $3,000 in goods purchased:

| DR | Refund liability | $3,000 | |
|---|---|---|---|
| CR | Cash | | $3,000 |

### Question 1                                                                 MCQ-06248

JoJo Roasters manufactures and sells coffee bean roasters. JoJo entered into an agreement with Smooth and Bold Coffee Company (S&B) to manufacture five roasters for S&B's new production facility. The roasters were manufactured to S&B's specifications and were completed on September 1, Year 2. Due to delays in the construction of S&B's new facility, JoJo agreed to maintain the coffee roasters in a separate section of its warehouse until the S&B facility opened on January 10, Year 3. S&B paid for the roasters on October 1, Year 2. On which date can JoJo recognize the revenue from this bill-and-hold arrangement?

    a. September 1, Year 2
    b. October 1, Year 2
    c. December 31, Year 2
    c. January 10, Year 3

# 2 Long-Term Construction Contracts

## 2.1 Recognizing Revenue Before Delivery

In most instances, companies recognize revenue at the point of sale (delivery). Under certain circumstances companies recognize revenue over time. Long-term construction contracts are an example of this type of revenue recognition.

## 2.2 Percentage-of-Completion Method

### 2.2.1 Requirements

When a long-term construction contract meets the criteria for recognizing revenue over time, it is appropriate to use the percentage-of-completion method if the entity's accounting system can:

1. reasonably estimate profitability; and
2. provide a reliable measure of progress toward completion.

### 2.2.2 Determination of Revenues Recognized

Income recognized is the percentage of estimated total income either:

1. that incurred costs to date bear to total estimated costs based on the most recent cost information, or
2. that may be indicated by such other measure of progress toward completion appropriate to the work performed.

# Revenue Recognition: Part 2

## 2.2.3 Balance Sheet Presentation

Under the percentage-of-completion method, construction costs and estimated gross profit earned are accumulated in the *construction in progress* account (an inventory account) and billings on construction are accumulated in the *progress billings* account (a contra-inventory account). The two accounts are netted against each other for balance sheet reporting.

- **Current Asset Accounts**
  - Due on accounts (receivable)
  - Costs and estimated earnings of uncompleted contracts in excess of progress billings (sometimes called *construction in progress*) *or;*

- **Current Liability Account**

  Progress billings in excess of cost and estimated earnings on uncompleted contracts.

## 2.2.4 Accounting for the Percentage-of-Completion Method

The following are important points to remember in accounting for contracts under the percentage-of-completion method:

- Journal entries and interim balance sheet treatment are the same as the completed contract method (described in the next section), except that the amount of estimated gross profit earned in each period is recorded by charging the construction in progress account and crediting realized gross profit.

- Gross profit or loss is recognized in each period by the following steps:

| | | |
|---|---|---|
| **Step 1** | Compute gross profit of completed contract: | Contract price<br>< Estimated total cost ><br>Gross profit |
| **Step 2** | Compute percentage of completion: | Total cost to date<br>Total estimated cost of contract |
| **Step 3** | Compute gross profit earned (profit to date): | Step 1 × Step 2 = PTD |
| **Step 4** | Compute gross profit earned for current year: | PTD at current FYE<br>< PTD at beginning of period ><br>Current year-to-date GP |

- An estimated loss on the total contract is recognized immediately in the year it is discovered. However, any previous gross profit or loss reported in prior years must be adjusted for when calculating the total estimated loss.

## Example 8: Long-Term Contract Gross Profit Computation

**Facts:**

|  | Year 1 | Year 2 | Year 3 | Year 4 |
|---|---|---|---|---|
| Sales price | $4,000 | $4,000 | $4,000 | $4,000 |
| Total (estimated) cost of contract | 3,000 | 3,200 | 4,200 | 4,300 |
| Costs incurred to date | 1,500 | 2,400 | 3,600 | 4,300 |

**Required:** Compute gross profit in Years 1 through 4 under the percentage-of-completion and completed contract methods.

**Solution:**

### Percentage of Completion

|  | Year 1 | Year 2 | Year 3 | Year 4 |
|---|---|---|---|---|
| **Step 1** Compute GP of completed contract: | | | | |
| Total contract sales price | $ 4,000 | $ 4,000 | $ 4,000 | $ 4,000 |
| Less: Total estimated cost of contract | (3,000) | (3,200) | (4,200) | (4,300) |
| Total gross profit | $ 1,000 | $ 800 | $ (200) | $ (300) |
| **Step 2** Compute percentage of completion: | | | | |
| Costs incurred to date | $ 1,500 | $ 2,400 | $ 3,600 | $ 4,300 |
| Total estimated cost of contract | $ 3,000 | $ 3,200 | $ 4,200 | $ 4,300 |
| Percentage of completion | 50% | 75% | 100% | 100% |
|  |  |  | (Loss Rule) |  |
| **Step 3** Compute GP earned to date: | | | | |
| Total contract GP | $ 1,000 | $ 800 | $ (200) | $ (300) |
| × Percentage of completion | 50% | 75% | 100% | 100% |
| GP earned to date (cumulative) | $ 500 | $ 600 | $ (200) | $ (300) |
| **Step 4** Compute GP earned each year—percentage of completion: | | | | |
| Previously recognized | $ -0- | $ 500 | $ 600 | $ (200) |
| Current year gross profit | $ 500 | $ 100 | $ (800) | $ (100) |

### Completed Contract

Compute GP earned each year—Completed contract method:

| **Computations** | $ -0- | $ -0- | $ (200) | $ (100) |
|---|---|---|---|---|

# Revenue Recognition: Part 2

## 2.3 Completed Contract Method

### 2.3.1 Requirements

When a long-term construction contract does not meet the criteria for recognizing revenue over time, revenue and gross profit are recognized when the contract is completed.

### 2.3.2 Balance Sheet Presentation

Under the completed contract method, construction costs are accumulated in the *construction in progress* account (an inventory account) and billings on construction are accumulated in the *progress billings* account (a contra-inventory account). The two accounts are netted against each other for balance sheet reporting.

- **Current Asset Accounts**
  - Due on accounts (receivable)
  - Cost of uncompleted contracts in excess of progress billings (sometimes called *construction in progress*) or;
- **Current Liability Account**
  - Progress billings on uncompleted contracts in excess of cost

### 2.3.3 Accounting for the Completed Contract Method

The following are important points to remember in accounting for contracts under the completed contract method:

- Under the completed contract method, estimated gross profit is not recognized each period as part of construction in progress. Unless a loss is recognized on the contract, no gross profit is recognized until the contract is completed.
- At completion of the contract, gross profit or loss is recognized as follows:

> **Gross profit or loss = Contract price − Total costs**

- At interim balance sheet dates, the excess of either the construction in progress account or the progress billings account over the other is classified as a current asset or a current liability.
- Losses should be recognized in full in the year they are discovered. An expected loss on the total contract is determined by:
  1. Adding estimated costs to complete the recorded costs to date to arrive at total contract costs.
  2. Adding to advances any additional revenue expected to arrive at total contract revenue.
  3. Subtracting (2) from (1) to arrive at total estimated loss on contract.

### U.S. GAAP VS. IFRS

Under IFRS, the completed contract method is not permitted. The percentage-of-completion method must be used unless the final outcome of the project cannot be reliably estimated, in which case the cost recovery method is required. Under the cost recovery method, revenue can be recognized only to the extent that cash collected exceeds the costs incurred.

# Long-Term Construction Contract Accounting Journal Entries

## Percentage-of-Completion Method | Completed Contract Method

### Journal Entries During Construction Period

**Journal entry to record costs incurred:**
- DR  Construction in progress
- CR  Materials, cash, etc.

**Journal entry to record costs incurred:**
- DR  Construction in progress
- CR  Materials, cash, etc.

**Journal entry to record billings on contract:**
- DR  Accounts receivable
- CR  Progress billings on construction contract

**Journal entry to record billings on contract:**
- DR  Accounts receivable
- CR  Progress billings on construction contract

**Journal entry to record payments received:**
- DR  Cash
- CR  Accounts receivable

**Journal entry to record payments received:**
- DR  Cash
- CR  Accounts receivable

**Journal entry to record estimated gross profit during construction:**
- DR  Cost of long-term construction contracts
- DR  Construction in progress
- CR  Revenue from LT construction contracts*

*Determined based on costs to date relative to total costs. Losses recognized in full in the period incurred.

N/A if project is profitable. Losses are recognized in full in the period incurred.

### Balance Sheet Presentation During Construction Period

CIP > Progress billings = Current asset (costs of uncompleted contracts in excess of progress billings)

Progress billings > CIP = Current liability (progress billings on uncompleted contracts in excess of costs)

CIP includes costs incurred and estimated gross profit earned to date.

---

CIP > Progress billings = Current asset (costs of uncompleted contracts in excess of progress billings)

Progress billings > CIP = Current liability (progress billings on uncompleted contracts in excess of costs)

CIP includes only costs incurred.

### Journal Entries When Construction Completed

**Journal entry to close construction accounts:**
- DR  Progress billings
- CR  Construction in progress

**Journal entry to close billings to revenue:**
- DR  Progress billings
- CR  Revenue

**Journal entry to close construction in progress to expense:**
- DR  Cost of LT construction contract
- CR  Construction in progress

Revenue Recognition: Part 2                                                                                      FAR 1

### Question 2                                                                                        MCQ-00654

Haft Construction Co. has consistently used the percentage-of-completion method. On January 10, Year 1, Haft began work on a $3,000,000 construction contract. At the inception date, the estimated cost of construction was $2,250,000. The following data relate to the progress of the contract:

| | |
|---|---|
| Income recognized at 12/31/Year 1 | $ 300,000 |
| Costs incurred 1/10/ Year 1 through 12/31/Year 2 | 1,800,000 |
| Estimated cost to complete at 12/31/Year 2 | 600,000 |

In its income statement for the year ended December 31, Year 2, what amount of gross profit should Haft report?

  a. $450,000
  b. $300,000
  c. $262,500
  d. $150,000

### Question 3                                                                                        MCQ-00659

During Year 1, Tidal Co. began construction on a project scheduled for completion in Year 3. At December 31, Year 1, an overall loss was anticipated at contract completion. What would be the effect of the project on Year 1 operating income under the U.S. GAAP percentage-of-completion and completed-contract methods?

| | Percentage-of-Completion | Completed-Contract |
|---|---|---|
| a. | No effect | No effect |
| b. | No effect | Decrease |
| c. | Decrease | No effect |
| d. | Decrease | Decrease |

# MODULE 5: Income Statement: Discontinued Operations

FAR 1

## 1 Introduction to Discontinued Operations

Discontinued operations are reported separately from continuing operations in the income statement, net of tax. A discontinued operation may include a component of an entity, a group of components of an entity, or a business or nonprofit activity. Items reported within discontinued operations can consist of an impairment loss, a gain or loss from actual operations, and a gain or loss on disposal. All of these amounts are included in discontinued operations in the period in which they occur.

## 2 Definitions

### 2.1 Component of an Entity

A component of an entity is a part of an entity (the lowest level) for which operations and cash flows can be *clearly distinguished, both operationally and for financial reporting purposes,* from the rest of the entity.

According to U.S. GAAP, a component can refer to:

- an operating segment (as defined in segment reporting);
- a reportable segment (as defined in segment reporting);
- a reporting unit (as defined in goodwill impairment testing);
- a subsidiary; or
- an asset group (a collection of assets to be disposed of together as a group in a single transaction and the liabilities directly associated with those assets that will be transferred in that same transaction).

### 2.2 Business

A business is an integrated set of activities and assets that is capable of being conducted and managed for the purpose of providing a return in the form of dividends, lower costs, or other economic benefits directly to investors or other owners, members, or participants.

### 2.3 Nonprofit Activity

A nonprofit activity is an integrated set of activities and assets that is conducted and managed for the purpose of providing benefits, other than goods or services at a profit, to fulfill an entity's purpose or mission.

Income Statement: Discontinued Operations

## 2.4 Held for Sale

A component of a business is classified as *held for sale* in the period in which *all* of the following criteria are met:

1. Management commits to a plan to sell the component.
2. The component is available for immediate sale in its present condition.
3. An active program to locate a buyer has been initiated.
4. The sale of the component is probable and the sale is expected to be complete within one year. (There are limited exceptions to this one-year rule, when certain events and circumstances occur that are beyond the control of the entity.)
5. The sale of the component is being actively marketed.
6. Actions required to complete the sale make it unlikely that significant changes to the plan will be made or that the plan will be withdrawn.

When a component is classified as held for sale, an impairment analysis of the component must be conducted.

# 3 Accounting Rules

## 3.1 Types of Entities to Be Considered

The results of operations of a component of an entity or a group of components of an entity, or a business or nonprofit activity, will be reported in discontinued operations if it:

- has been disposed of; or
- is classified as held for sale.

## 3.2 Conditions That Must Be Present

All related costs shall be recognized when the obligations to others exist, not necessarily in the period of commitment to a plan. A disposal of a component or group of components is reported in discontinued operations if the disposal represents a strategic shift that has or will have a major effect on an entity's operations and financial results.

Examples of a strategic shift that could have a major effect on operations and financial results may include, among others:

- Disposal of a major geographical area
- Disposal of a major equity method investment
- Disposal of a major line of business

A business or nonprofit activity that, on acquisition, meets the criteria to be classified as held for sale is a discontinued operation.

> **Illustration 1    Discontinued Operation**
>
> Am-Serv Inc. is a food service company that delivers frozen food products to food service providers. Its clients include fast-food restaurants, high-end steak houses, home-delivery diet food companies, and institutions such as schools and hospitals. Historically, the fast-food restaurants have been the largest segment of Am-Serv's business in terms of revenue and operating profit. However, that division is now forecast to begin to decline in revenues because the public is looking for healthier options. Am-Serv has decided to sell its fast-food operation and, instead, focus on selling to locally operated restaurants offering a healthier fare. Such restaurants will generally show lower revenue per unit, but higher operating profit per unit. Because the fast-food division is the largest component in terms of revenue and operating profit, the disposal represents a major strategic shift, and will be reported as a discontinued operation.

## 3.3    Discontinued Operations Calculation

### 3.3.1    Types of Items Included in Results of Discontinued Operations

- Results of operations of the component.
- Gain or loss on disposal of the component.
- Impairment loss (and subsequent increases in fair value) of the component.
  - **Initial and Subsequent Impairment Losses**

    A loss is recognized for recording the impairment of the component (i.e., any initial or subsequent write-down to fair value less costs to sell).
  - **Subsequent Increases in Fair Value**

    A gain is recognized for any subsequent increase in fair value minus the costs to sell (but not in excess of the previously recognized cumulative loss).

### 3.3.2    Report in the Period Disposed of or Held for Sale

The results of discontinued operations of a component are reported in discontinued operations (for the current period and for all prior periods presented) in the period the component is either disposed of or is held for sale. The results of subsequent operations of a component classified as held for sale are reported in discontinued operations in the period in which they occur.

### 3.3.3    Depreciation and Amortization

Once management decides to dispose of the component, assets within the component are no longer depreciated or amortized.

## 3.4    Anticipated Future Gains or Losses

Losses anticipated to occur in future periods are considered when impairment analysis is conducted on the component. Gains anticipated to occur in future periods are not recognized until they occur. A gain or loss not previously recognized that results from the sale of the component is recognized at the date of sale and not before.

Income Statement: Discontinued Operations                                                     FAR 1

## 3.5 Subsequent Adjustments to Amounts Previously Reported

Adjustments to amounts previously reported in discontinued operations that are *directly related* to the disposal of a component of an entity in a prior period are classified in the current period in discontinued operations.

### 3.5.1 Examples

- Resolution of contingencies related to terms of the disposal transaction (e.g., purchase price adjustments and indemnification issues).
- Resolution of contingencies directly related to the operations of the component before it was disposed of (e.g., warranty obligations and environmental responsibilities).
- Settlement of employee benefit plan obligations.

### 3.5.2 Definition of "Directly Related"

In order for a settlement to be considered directly related to a component of an entity, it must:

- have a demonstrated cause-and-effect relationship; and
- occur no later than one year after the date of the disposal transaction (unless circumstances beyond the control of the entity exist).

## 3.6 Measurement and Valuation

A component classified as held for sale is measured at the lower of its carrying amount or fair value less costs to sell. Costs to sell are the incremental direct costs to transact the sale.

## 3.7 Presentation and Disclosure

- **Present as a Separate Component of Income:** The results of discontinued operations, net of tax, are reported as a separate component of income, below income from continuing operations.
- **Disclose in Face or in Notes:** A gain or loss recognized on the disposal shall be disclosed either on the face of the income statement or in the notes to the financial statements.

---

**Example 1 — Discontinued Operations Calculations and Income Statement Presentation**

**Facts:** The trial balance below presents the income statement accounts for Year 1 from All Sports Company's trial balance. The golf division of All Sports has been losing money on a monthly basis. The golf division's income statement accounts are also presented below. The board of directors decides on April 30, Year 1, to dispose of the golf division. The carrying value of the golf division on April 30, Year 1, is $4,000,000, and its fair value less costs to sell is $2,200,000. After months of negotiations, the division's net assets are sold on June 30, Year 2, for $2,000,000. The golf division has continuing losses in Year 2 of $200,000 per month. All Sports' income tax rate is 40 percent for Years 1 and 2. Assume that All Sports' income from continuing operations is $4,875,000 in Year 1 and $5,200,000 in Year 2.

(continued)

(continued)

### All Sports Company Trial Balance
### Year 1

|      |                      | All Components | Golf Division |
|------|----------------------|---------------:|--------------:|
| 4000 | Sales revenue        | $21,000,000    | $2,500,000    |
| 5000 | Cost of goods sold   | $9,500,000     | 1,850,000     |
| 5300 | Freight out          | 155,000        | 135,000       |
| 5400 | Commissions          | 900,000        | 220,000       |
| 5500 | Advertising          | 1,200,000      | 600,000       |
| 5600 | Insurance expense    | 1,400,000      | 750,000       |
| 5700 | Salaries expense     | 2,500,000      | 850,000       |
| 5800 | Depreciation expense | 950,000        | 495,000       |
| 6000 | Interest revenue     | 750,000        |               |
| 6200 | Other revenue        | 300,000        |               |
| 6500 | Gain on sale of assets | 400,000      |               |
| 7000 | Interest expense     | 120,000        |               |
| 7500 | Impairment loss      | 1,800,000      | 1,800,000     |

**Required:** How should the disposal of the golf division be reported on All Sports Company's Year 1 and Year 2 financial statements?

**Solution:**

**Reporting for Year 1:**

The golf division was not disposed of until Year 2 and would be reported as held for sale in the Year 1 financial statements.

The continuing loss from the golf division would be included in discontinued operations in Year 1.

Loss from operations = $2,500,000 − ($1,850,000 + $135,000 + $220,000 + $600,000 + $750,000 + $850,000 + $495,000) = ($2,400,000).

Loss from operations, net of tax = ($2,400,000) × (1 − 40%) = ($1,440,000)

Impairment loss = $2,200,000 − $4,000,000 = ($1,800,000)

Impairment loss, net of tax = ($1,800,000) × (1 − 40%) = ($1,080,000)

*Income Statement Presentation Year 1:*

| | |
|---|---:|
| Income from continuing operations | $4,875,000 |
| Discontinued operations | |
|     Loss from operations of discontinued component, net of tax | (1,440,000) |
|     Loss from impairment of discontinued operations, net of tax | (1,080,000) |
| Net income | $2,355,000 |

(continued)

# Income Statement: Discontinued Operations

*(continued)*

**Reporting for Year 2:**

In Year 2, discontinued operations would include the continuing losses incurred before the sale and the loss on disposal.

    Loss from operations (Jan 1 – June 30) = ($200,000) × 6 = ($1,200,000)

    Loss from operations, net of tax = ($1,200,000) × (1 – 40%) = ($720,000)

    Loss on disposal = $2,000,000 – $2,200,000 = ($200,000)

    Loss on disposal, net of tax = ($200,000) × (1 – 40%) = ($120,000)

*Income Statement Presentation Year 2:*

| | |
|---|---:|
| Income from continuing operations | $5,200,000 |
| Discontinued operations | |
|   Loss from operations of discontinued component, net of tax | (720,000) |
|   Loss from sale (disposal) of discontinued operations, net of tax | (120,000) |
| Net income | $4,360,000 |

---

### Question 1      MCQ-00045

During January Year 3, Doe Corp. agreed to sell the assets and product line of its Hart division. The decision represents a major strategic shift for Doe and will have a significant effect on its operations and financial results. The sale was completed on January 15, Year 4, and resulted in a gain on disposal of $900,000. Hart's operating losses were $600,000 for Year 3 and $50,000 for the period January 1 through January 15, Year 4. Disregarding income taxes, what amount of net gain (loss) should be reported in Doe's comparative Year 4 and Year 3 income statements?

| | Year 3 | Year 4 |
|---|---|---|
| a. | $0 | $250,000 |
| b. | $250,000 | $0 |
| c. | $(600,000) | $850,000 |
| d. | $(650,000) | $900,000 |

# MODULE 6
# Accounting Changes and Error Corrections

**FAR 1**

## 1 Changes in Accounting Estimate (Prospective Application)

A change in accounting estimate occurs when it is determined that the estimate previously used by the company is incorrect.

### 1.1 Events Resulting in Estimate Changes

- Changes in the lives of fixed assets.
- Adjustments of year-end accrual of officers' salaries and/or bonuses.
- Write-downs of obsolete inventory.
- Material, nonrecurring IRS adjustments.
- Settlement of litigation.
- Changes in accounting principle that are inseparable from a change in estimate (e.g., a change from the installment method to immediate recognition method because uncollectible accounts can now be estimated).
- Revisions of estimates regarding discontinued operations.

---

**Example 1**     **Change in Accounting Estimate**

**Facts:** Carlin Company buys a truck for $90,000. The truck is expected to last 10 years. During the third year, Carlin Company realizes that the truck is only going to last a total of five years. The truck is depreciated on the straight-line basis and has no estimated salvage value.

**Required:** Create a depreciation schedule for the life of the truck (five years).

**Solution:**

*Depreciation Schedule*

| Year | Depreciation |
|------|--------------|
| 1 | $ 9,000 [$90,000/10] |
| 2 | $ 9,000 [$90,000/10] |
| 3 | $24,000 [$72,000/3] |
| 4 | $24,000 [$72,000/3] |
| 5 | $24,000 [$72,000/3] |
|   | **$90,000** |

## 1.2 Reporting a Change in Estimate

### 1.2.1 Prospectively

Changes in accounting estimate are accounted for prospectively (i.e., implement in the current period and continue in future periods). They do not affect previous periods (i.e., no effect on previously reported retained earnings).

### 1.2.2 Change in Estimate Affecting Future Periods

If a change in accounting estimate affects several future periods (e.g., a revision of service lives of depreciable assets), the effect on income from continuing operations, net income, and the related per share information for the current year should be disclosed in the notes to the financial statements.

**Note:** Changes in ordinary accounting estimates (e.g., uncollectible accounts and inventory adjustments) usually made each period do not have to be disclosed unless they are material.

# 2 Changes in Accounting Principle (Retrospective Application)

A change in accounting principle is a change in accounting from one accounting principle to another acceptable accounting principle (e.g., GAAP to GAAP).

## 2.1 Rule of Preferability

An accounting principle may be changed only if required by GAAP (a newly issued codification update) or if the alternative principle is preferable and more fairly presents the information.

## 2.2 Effects of a Change

### 2.2.1 Direct Effects

The direct effects of a change in accounting principle are adjustments that would be necessary to restate the financial statements of prior periods.

### 2.2.2 Indirect Effects

The indirect effects of a change in accounting principle are differences in nondiscretionary items based on earnings (e.g., bonuses) that would have occurred if the new principle had been used in prior periods.

## 2.2.3 Cumulative Effect

If noncomparative financial statements are being presented, then the cumulative effect of a change in accounting principle is equal to the difference between the amount of beginning retained earnings in the period of change and what the retained earnings would have been if the accounting change had been retroactively applied to all prior affected periods. It includes direct effects and only those indirect effects that are entered in the accounting records. If comparative financial statements are being presented, then the cumulative effect is equal to the difference between beginning retained earnings in the first period presented and what retained earnings would have been if the new principle had been applied to all prior periods. The cumulative effect of a change in accounting principle is presented net of tax as an adjustment to beginning retained earnings in the statement of stockholders' equity.

---

**Illustration 1  Cumulative Effect of a Change in Accounting Principle**

On January 1, Year 5, Harbor Company decided to switch to the weighted average method of inventory accounting. Prior to Year 5, Harbor used FIFO to account for its inventory. Harbor's effective tax rate is 30 percent.

Pretax income information is as follows:

|  | Pretax Income Under | |
|---|---|---|
|  | **Weighted Average** | **FIFO** |
| Prior to Year 5 | $800,000 | $600,000 |

| | |
|---|---|
| Cumulative effect adjustment as of 1/1/Year 5 | $200,000 |
| Less income tax effect at 30 percent | (60,000) |
| Cumulative effect net of income tax | $140,000 |

The $140,000 cumulative effect net of income tax would adjust the beginning retained earnings balance within the statement of stockholders' equity.

---

## 2.3 Reporting Changes in an Accounting Principle

The general rule is that changes in accounting principle should be recognized by adjusting beginning retained earnings in the earliest period presented for the cumulative effect of the change, and, if prior period (comparative) financial statements are presented, they should be restated (retrospective application).

> **U.S. GAAP VS. IFRS**
>
> Under IFRS, when an entity disclosing comparative information applies an accounting principle retroactively or makes a retrospective restatement of items in the financial statements, the entity must (at a minimum) present three balance sheets (end of current period, end of prior period, and beginning of prior period) and two of each other financial statement (current period and prior period). The cumulative effect adjustment would be shown as an adjustment of the beginning retained earnings on the balance sheet for the beginning of the prior period. U.S. GAAP does not have a three balance sheet requirement.

### 2.3.1 Exceptions to the General Rule

- **Impracticable to Estimate:** To prepare a change in accounting principle handled retrospectively, the amount of the cumulative effect adjustment must be calculated as of the beginning of the first period presented. If it is considered "impractical" to accurately calculate this cumulative effect adjustment, then the change is handled prospectively (like a change in estimate). An example of a change handled in this manner is a change in inventory cost flow assumption to LIFO (under U.S. GAAP). Since a cumulative effect adjustment to LIFO would require the reestablishment and recalculation of old inventory layers, it is considered impractical to try to rebuild those old cost layers. This change is therefore handled prospectively. The beginning inventory of the year of change is the first LIFO layer. Additional LIFO layers are added from that point forward.

- **Change in Depreciation Method:** A change in the method of depreciation, amortization, or depletion is considered to be both a change in accounting principle and a change in estimate. These changes should be accounted for as changes in estimate and are handled prospectively. The new depreciation method should be used as of the beginning of the year of the change in estimate and should start with the current book value of the underlying asset. No retroactive or retrospective calculations should be made, and no adjustment should be made to retained earnings.

### 2.3.2 Applications of the General Rule

- The amount of cumulative effect to be reported on the retained earnings statement is the difference between:
  - retained earnings at the beginning of the earliest period presented; and
  - retained earnings that would have been reported at the beginning of the earliest period presented if the new accounting principle had been applied retrospectively for all prior periods, by recognizing only the direct effects and related income tax effect.
- The new accounting principle is used for all periods presented (prior periods are restated).
- If an accounting change is not considered material in the year of change but is reasonably expected to become material in later periods, it should be fully disclosed in the year of change.

### 2.3.3 Nonrecurring Changes

An accounting change should not be made for a transaction or event in the past that has been terminated or is nonrecurring.

# 3 Changes in Accounting Entity (Retrospective Application)

Under U.S. GAAP, a change in accounting entity occurs when the entity being reported on has changed composition. Examples include consolidated or combined financial statements that are presented in place of statements of the individual companies and changes in the companies included in the consolidated or combined financial statements from year to year.

## 3.1 Restatement to Reflect Information for the New Entity (if Comparative Financial Statements Are Presented)

If a change in accounting entity occurs in the current year, all previous financial statements that are presented in comparative financial statements along with the current year should be restated to reflect the information for the new reporting entity.

## 3.2 Full Disclosure

Full disclosure of the cause and nature of the change should be made, including changes in income from continuing operations, net income, and retained earnings.

> **U.S. GAAP VS. IFRS**
>
> IFRS does not include the concept of a change in accounting entity.

# 4 Error Correction (Prior Period Adjustment)

Error corrections are not accounting changes. Error corrections include:

- Corrections of errors in recognition, measurement, presentation, or disclosure in financial statements resulting from mathematical mistakes, mistakes in the application of U.S. GAAP, or oversight or misuse of facts that existed at the time the financial statements were prepared.

- Changes from a non-GAAP method of accounting to a GAAP method of accounting (e.g., cash basis to accrual basis), which is a specific correction of an error.

## 4.1 Comparative Financial Statements Presented

### 4.1.1 Correct the Information (if the Year Is Presented)

If comparative financial statements are presented and financial statements for the year with the error are presented, merely correct the error in those prior financial statements.

### 4.1.2 Adjust Beginning Retained Earnings of the Earliest Year Presented (if the Year Is Not Presented)

If comparative financial statements are presented and financial statements for the year with the error are not presented (e.g., because it is too far back in years), adjust (net of tax) the opening retained earnings of the earliest year presented.

# Accounting Changes and Error Corrections

## 4.2 Comparative Financial Statements Not Presented

If comparative financial statements are not presented, the error correction should be reported as an adjustment to the opening balance of retained earnings (net of tax).

### U.S. GAAP VS. IFRS

Under IFRS, when it is impracticable to determine either the period-specific effect or the cumulative effect of an error, the entity is required to restate information prospectively from the earliest date that is practicable. U.S. GAAP does not have an impracticality exemption for error corrections.

## 4.3 Effect on the Statement of Retained Earnings

The purpose of the statement of retained earnings is to reconcile the beginning balance of retained earnings with the ending balance. It is usually presented immediately following the income statement or as a component of the statement of stockholders' equity.

### Example 2  Accounting Changes and Error Corrections

**Facts:** In Year 4, Jordan Manufacturing discovered that depreciation expense was incorrectly calculated in Years 1 and 2. In total, $4,500,000 of depreciation expense was not recorded during these two years.

At the beginning of Year 4, Jordan Manufacturing decided to change inventory methods from the last-in first-out (LIFO) cost flow assumption to the first-in first-out (FIFO) cost flow assumption. The following information details the pretax income under LIFO and FIFO for Years 1 through 3.

|  | Pretax Income Under | | |
|---|---|---|---|
|  | LIFO | FIFO | Difference |
| Year 1 | $3,000,000 | $3,750,000 | $ 750,000 |
| Year 2 | 3,400,000 | 5,500,000 | 2,100,000 |
| Year 3 | 4,100,000 | 6,250,000 | 2,150,000 |

Jordan's tax rate is 40 percent.

**Required:**

1. Calculate the required adjustment for the depreciation error and indicate how this correction should be presented in the financial statements.

2. Calculate the cumulative adjustment for the change in principle and indicate how the adjustment should be reported in the financial statements.

3. Prepare the statement of retained earnings for Year 4. Jordan is presenting financial statements for Year 4 only. Assume the balance in retained earnings (as originally reported) at December 31, Year 4, was $28,000,000.

(continued)

(continued)

**Solution:**

1. As Jordan is presenting financial information for the current Year 4 only, the depreciation error should be reported as an adjustment to retained earnings net of tax. The $4,500,000 depreciation not recorded in Years 1–3 results in a $2,700,000 adjustment to beginning retained earnings:

    $4,500,000 × (1 − 40%) = $2,700,000

2. The change in accounting principle (from LIFO to FIFO) should also be reported as an adjustment to retained earnings net of tax. The sum of the increases in pretax income in Years 1–3 as a result of the change is $5,000,000 ($750,000 + $2,100,000 + $2,150,000), and the net of tax adjustment is:

    $5,000,000 × (1 − 40%) = $3,000,000

3. Jordan's statement of retained earnings appears below:

Jordan Manufacturing<br>
Statement of Retained Earnings<br>
For the Year Ended December 31, Year 4

| | | |
|---|---:|---:|
| Beginning balance (as previously reported) | | $28,000,000 |
| Prior period adjustment | $(4,500,000) | |
| Add: income tax benefit | 1,800,000 | (2,700,000) |
| Cumulative effect of accounting change | 5,000,000 | |
| Less: income tax effect | (2,000,000) | 3,000,000 |
| Beginning balance (restated) | | 28,300,000 |
| Add: Net income | | 1,700,000 |
| | | 30,000,000 |
| Less: dividends | | |
|    Cash dividend declared on preferred stock | 500,000 | |
|    Cash dividend declared on common stock | 350,000 | |
|    Property dividend declared on common stock | 100,000 | |
|    Stock dividend declared on common stock | 50,000 | (1,000,000) |
| Ending balance | | $29,000,000 |

## Question 1 — MCQ-00071

Per U.S. GAAP, which of the following statements is correct regarding accounting changes that result in financial statements that are, in effect, the statements of a different reporting entity?

a. Cumulative-effect adjustments should be reported as separate items on the income statement in the year of change.
b. No restatements or adjustments are required if the changes involve consolidated methods of accounting for subsidiaries.
c. No restatements or adjustments are required if the changes involve the cost or equity methods of accounting for investments.
d. The financial statements of all prior periods presented should be restated.

## Question 2 — MCQ-00081

For Year 1, Pac Co. estimated its two-year equipment warranty costs based on $100 per unit sold in Year 1. Experience during Year 2 indicated that the estimate should have been based on $110 per unit. The effect of this $10 difference from the estimate is reported:

a. In Year 2, as income from continuing operations.
b. As an accounting change, net of tax, below Year 2 income from continuing operations.
c. As an accounting change requiring Year 1 financial statements to be restated.
d. As a correction of an error requiring Year 1 financial statements to be restated.

# MODULE 7

# Statement of Comprehensive Income

**FAR 1**

## 1 Definitions

### 1.1 Comprehensive Income

Comprehensive income is the change in equity (net assets) of a business enterprise during a period from transactions and other events and circumstances from nonowner sources. It includes all changes in equity during a period except those resulting from investments by owners and distributions to owners.

$$\begin{array}{r}\text{Net income}\\ +\;\text{Other comprehensive income}\\ \hline \text{Comprehensive income}\end{array}$$

### 1.2 Net Income

Net income includes the following items:

1. Income from continuing operations
2. Discontinued operations

### 1.3 Other Comprehensive Income

Other comprehensive income items are revenues, expenses, gains, and losses that are included in comprehensive income but excluded from net income under U.S. GAAP and/or IFRS.

An entity must classify the specific items by their nature, such as:

- **Pension Adjustments**

    Under U.S. GAAP, changes in the funded status of a pension plan due to gains or losses, prior service costs, and net transition assets or obligations must be recognized in other comprehensive income in the year the changes occur. All gains or losses, prior service costs, and transition assets or obligations are included in other comprehensive income until recognized as a component of net periodic benefit cost.

    Under IFRS, certain actuarial gains and losses may be included in other comprehensive income. These gains and losses are not reclassified to net income in subsequent periods.

- **Unrealized Gains and Losses (Available-for-Sale Debt Securities)**

  The following types of unrealized gains and losses on certain investments in debt securities are reported as components of other comprehensive income until the securities are sold.

  - Unrealized holding gains and losses on "available-for-sale debt securities."
  - Unrealized holding gains and losses that result from a debt security being transferred into the "available-for-sale" category from "held to maturity."
  - Subsequent decreases or increases in the fair value of "available-for-sale" debt securities previously written down as impaired.

- **Foreign Currency Items**

  Foreign currency translation adjustments and gains and losses on foreign currency transactions that are designated as (and are effective as) economic hedges of a net investment in a foreign entity are reported as a component of other comprehensive income. Foreign currency translation adjustments remain in other comprehensive income until the sale or liquidation of the investment in the foreign entity. Also, gains and losses on intra-entity foreign currency transactions that are of a long-term investment nature, when the entities to the transaction are consolidated, are combined or accounted for by the equity method.

- **Instrument-Specific Credit Risk**

  For liabilities for which the fair value option is elected, changes in fair value that are attributable to instrument-specific credit risk are included in comprehensive income.

- **Effective Portion of Cash Flow Hedges**

  The effective portion of a cash flow hedge is reported as a component of other comprehensive income until the cash flows associated with the hedged item are realized.

- **Revaluation Surplus (IFRS Only)**

  Under IFRS, revaluation surpluses (gains) recognized when intangible assets and fixed assets are revalued are also included in other comprehensive income. Revaluation surpluses are not reclassified to net income in subsequent periods, but may be transferred directly to retained earnings when the related asset is used or derecognized.

## 1.4 Reclassification Adjustments

Reclassification adjustments move other comprehensive income items from accumulated other comprehensive income to the income statement.

## 1.5 Accumulated Other Comprehensive Income

Accumulated other comprehensive income is a component of equity that includes the total of other comprehensive income for the current period and all previous periods. Other comprehensive income for the current period is "closed" to this account, which is reconciled each period similar to the manner in which retained earnings are reconciled.

### Pass Key

At the end of each accounting period, all components of comprehensive income are closed to the balance sheet. Net income is closed to retained earnings, and other comprehensive income is closed to accumulated other comprehensive income.

# 2 Financial Statement Reporting

Comprehensive income and its components shall be displayed in a financial statement that is presented with the same prominence as the other financial statements that constitute a full set of financial statements. The requirements to present comprehensive income do not apply to not-for-profit entities or to any company that does not have any item of other comprehensive income. Comprehensive income should not be reported on a per share basis.

Under U.S. GAAP, comprehensive income may be presented in:

- a single statement of comprehensive income (single-statement approach); or
- an income statement followed by a separate statement of comprehensive income that begins with net income (two-statement approach).

> **U.S. GAAP VS. IFRS**
>
> Both U.S. GAAP and IFRS allow the statement of comprehensive income to be presented using the single-statement approach (statement of comprehensive income) or the two-statement approach (statement of income immediately followed by a separate statement of comprehensive income).

## 2.1 Single-Statement Approach

The single-statement approach displays other comprehensive income items individually and in total, below the net income amount, and totals them for comprehensive income.

### Example 1 — Single-Statement Approach

**Facts:** The following other comprehensive income items were noted in the Year 1 trial balance of Sydney Technologies Inc. The tax rate for other comprehensive income items is 30 percent for Year 1.

| | | | |
|---|---|---|---|
| CR | Unrealized holding gains | | $400,000 |
| CR | Foreign currency translation gains | | 50,000 |
| DR | Pension losses | $ 25,000 | |
| DR | Unrealized holding losses | 100,000 | |
| DR | Foreign currency translation losses | 125,000 | |

**Required:** Compute the net of tax amounts to be reported in the statement of comprehensive income and complete the following statement of comprehensive income using the single-statement approach.

(continued)

(continued)

**Solution:**

The net of tax amounts to be reported in the statement of comprehensive income for each other comprehensive income item is as follows:

| | |
|---|---|
| Unrealized holding net gains | $300,000 × (1 − 30%) = 210,000 |
| Foreign currency items | $(75,000) × (1 − 30%) = (52,500) |
| Pension losses | $(25,000) × (1 − 30%) = (17,500) |

**Sydney Technologies Inc.**
**Statement of Comprehensive Income**
For the Year Ended December 31, Year 1

| | |
|---|---:|
| Revenues | $ 20,000,000 |
| Expenses | (18,400,000) |
| Income before income taxes | $ 1,600,000 |
| Income tax (25%) | (400,000) |
| Net income | $ 1,200,000 |
| Other comprehensive income, net of income tax: | |
|    Pension net loss | $ (17,500) |
|    Unrealized holding gains (available-for-sale securities) | 210,000 |
|    Foreign currency items | (52,500) |
|    Other comprehensive income | 140,000 |
|    Comprehensive income | $ 1,340,000 |

## 2.2 Two-Statement Approach

The two-statement approach displays comprehensive income as a separate statement that immediately follows the income statement.

**Sydney Technologies Inc.**
**Statement of Comprehensive Income**
For the Year Ended December 31, Year 1

| | |
|---|---:|
| Net income | $1,200,000 |
| Other comprehensive income, net of income tax: | |
|    Pension net loss | $ (17,500) |
|    Unrealized holding gains (available-for-sale securities) | 210,000 |
|    Foreign currency items | (52,500) |
|    Other comprehensive income | 140,000 |
|    Comprehensive income | $1,340,000 |

# 3 Other Reporting Issues

## 3.1 Other Comprehensive Income

Components of other comprehensive income may be reported either (i) net of tax; or (ii) before related tax effects, with one amount shown for the aggregate income tax expense or benefit related to the total of other comprehensive income items.

## 3.2 Income Tax Expense or Benefit

The amount of income tax expense or benefit allocated to each component of other comprehensive income is disclosed either on the face of the statement in which those components are displayed or in the notes to the financial statements.

## 3.3 Interim Period Reporting

A total for comprehensive income shall be reported in condensed financial statements of interim periods issued to shareholders.

## 3.4 Required Disclosures

All formats must disclose:

- The tax effects of each component included in (current) other comprehensive income, either as part of the statement presentation or in the notes to the financial statements.
- The changes in the accumulated balances of each component of other comprehensive income (e.g., pension adjustments, unrealized holding gains and losses on available-for-sale securities, foreign currency items, the effective portion of cash flow hedges, and IFRS revaluation surplus).
    - The changes in the accumulated balances by component may be shown on the face of the financial statements or in the notes to the financial statements.
- Total accumulated other comprehensive income in the balance sheet as an item of equity.
- The reclassification adjustments, which are made to avoid double counting in other comprehensive income items that are displayed in net income for the current year (e.g., previously reported unrealized gains on available-for-sale securities that were realized during the current year).
    - Disclosure is required for:
        — Changes in AOCI balances by component of other comprehensive income. The entity must separately disclose (i) reclassification adjustments; and (ii) current-period OCI.
        — Significant items reclassified out of AOCI must be disclosed either on the face of the statement where net income is presented, or as a separate disclosure in the notes to the financial statements.
    - Amounts by OCI component may be presented either before-tax or net-of-tax, as long as the tax effect is shown in either the financial statements or the notes.

## Brown and Associates
### Notes to Financial Statements
### Changes in Accumulated Other Comprehensive Income by Component
For the Year Ended December 31, Year 1

| Components | Gains/Losses on Cash Flow Hedges | Foreign Currency Items | Total |
|---|---|---|---|
| Beginning balance | $2,000 | $4,000 | $6,000 |
| Other comprehensive income before reclassifications | 3,000 | 1,500 | 4,500 |
| Amounts reclassified from AOCI | (500) | -0- | (500) |
| Net current-period other comprehensive income | 2,500 | 1,500 | 4,000 |
| **Ending balance** | **$4,500** | **$5,500** | **$10,000** |

**Note:** All amounts are net of tax. Therefore, an additional footnote would disclose the tax effects. Other columns would be added if Brown had other components of OCI in its financial statements.

## Brown and Associates
### Notes to Financial Statements
### Reclassifications out of Accumulated Other Comprehensive Income
For the Year Ended December 31, Year 1

| Details About Accumulated Other Comprehensive Income Components | Amount Reclassified From Accumulated Other Comprehensive Income | Affected Line Item in the Statement Where Net Income Is Presented |
|---|---|---|
| Gains and losses on cash flow hedges: | | |
|   Interest rate contracts | $ 3,000 | Interest income/(expense) |
|   Commodity contracts | (3,750) | Cost of sales |
| | (750) | Total before tax |
| | 250 | Tax (expense) or benefit |
| **Total reclassifications** | **$ (500)** | **Net of tax** |

Alternatively, this information could be presented on the income statement. The amounts would be shown parenthetically on each affected line item.

**Question 1**  MCQ-00102

One of the elements of a financial statement is comprehensive income. Comprehensive income excludes changes in equity resulting from which of the following?

- a. Loss from discontinued operations.
- b. Prior period error correction.
- c. Dividends paid to stockholders.
- d. Unrealized loss on investments in non-current marketable equity securities.

## NOTES

# MODULE 8
# Adjusting Journal Entries

FAR 1

## 1 Matching Revenues and Related Expenses

Accrual basis accounting is in accordance with U.S. GAAP and matches revenues with expenses. In order to properly match revenues with expenses in the periods in which they occur, it is sometimes necessary to *defer* or *accrue* revenues or expenses.

- In the case of unearned (deferred) revenues, cash is received before the revenue is earned (e.g., magazine subscription revenues are collected January 1, Year 1, for the calendar year ending December 31, Year 1).
- In the case of prepaid (deferred) expenses, cash is paid before the expense is incurred (e.g., prepaying rent today for the upcoming year).
- In the case of accrued revenues (receivables), cash is received after the revenue has been earned (e.g., you made a sale on credit and the customer actually pays you 30 days later).
- In the case of accrued expenses (accrued liabilities, accounts payable, or other payables), cash is paid after the expense has been incurred (e.g., you incur utilities expense but don't pay the bill until next month).

## 2 Adjusting Journal Entries

In order for financial statements to be prepared in accordance with the accrual basis of accounting, adjusting entries must be recorded.

### 2.1 Unearned Revenues and Prepaid Expenses

If revenue has been deferred, the company must calculate the amount of revenue that has been earned through year-end and make the appropriate adjusting journal entry.

*Journal entry to record unearned revenue:*

| | | | |
|---|---|---|---|
| DR | Cash | $XXX | |
| CR | Unearned revenue | | $XXX |

*Adjusting journal entry to record unearned revenue that has been earned:*

| | | | |
|---|---|---|---|
| DR | Unearned revenue | $XXX | |
| CR | Revenue | | $XXX |

If expenses have been deferred (prepaid), the company must calculate the amount of expenses that have been incurred through year-end and make the appropriate adjusting journal entry.

*Journal entry to record prepaid expense:*

| | | | |
|---|---|---|---|
| DR | Prepaid expense (asset) | $XXX | |
| CR | Cash | | $XXX |

*Adjusting journal entry to reverse prepaid expense and record incurred expense:*

| | | | |
|---|---|---|---|
| DR | Expense | $XXX | |
| CR | Prepaid expense | | $XXX |

## 2.2 Accrued Revenues and Expense

An entity must assess whether revenues have been earned prior to the cash being received. If so, revenues must be accrued by recording a receivable.

Journal entry to record accrued revenue:

| | | | |
|---|---|---|---|
| DR | Accounts receivable | $XXX | |
| CR | Revenue | | $XXX |

An entity must also assess if expenses have been incurred prior to the cash being paid. If so, expenses must be accrued by recording accrued liabilities, accounts payable, or other payable (e.g., wages payable).

| | | | |
|---|---|---|---|
| DR | Expense | $XXX | |
| CR | Accrued liability | | $XXX |

## 2.3 Error Corrections

In some instances, an entity may record cash receipts (disbursements) to a revenue/expense account when they should have been recorded to an asset/liability account. An adjusting entry may be required in this case to ensure that the financial statements are in accordance with the accrual basis of accounting (e.g., recording the prepayment of insurance directly to insurance expense rather than prepaid insurance).

## 2.4 Rules for Recording Adjusting Journal Entries

- Adjusting journal entries must be recorded by the end of the entity's fiscal year, before the preparation of financial statements.
- Adjusting journal entries *never* involve the cash account.
- All adjusting entries will hit one income statement account and one balance sheet account.

## Example 1 — Adjusting Journal Entries: Unearned Revenue

**Facts:** On December 1, Year 1, Impact Inc. received $250,000 in cash for services to be performed equally during December Year 1, and January Year 2. Impact Inc. recorded the entry as a credit to unearned service revenue.

**Required:** Prepare the journal entry to record the unearned revenue on December 1, Year 1, and the adjusting journal entry required at year-end.

**Solution:**

*December 1, Year 1—journal entry to record deferred revenue:*

| DR | Cash | $250,000 | |
|---|---|---|---|
| CR | Unearned service revenue | | $250,000 |

*December 31, Year 1—adjusting journal entry to record revenue earned during Year 1:*

| DR | Unearned service revenue | $125,000 | |
|---|---|---|---|
| CR | Service revenue | | $125,000 |

## Example 2 — Adjusting Journal Entries: Accrued Interest

**Facts:** On November 1, Year 1, Impact Inc. borrowed $2,000,000 from Federal Bank at a rate of 3 percent with interest due annually on November 1. The principal will be paid back on November 1, Year 11.

**Required:** Prepare the journal entry to record the loan on November 1, Year 1, and the adjusting journal entry for the accrued interest at year-end.

**Solution:**

*November 1, Year 1—journal entry to record loan from Federal Bank:*

| DR | Cash | $2,000,000 | |
|---|---|---|---|
| CR | Note payable | | $2,000,000 |

*December 31, Year 1—adjusting journal entry to record the interest accrued from November–December of Year 1 ($2,000,000 × 3% × 2/12 = $10,000):*

| DR | Interest expense | $10,000 | |
|---|---|---|---|
| CR | Interest payable | | $10,000 |

# Example 3 — Adjusting Journal Entries: Comprehensive Example

**Facts:** Titan Company reported pretax income in Year 2 of $8,000. Upon review of the general ledger, the following information listed in the first column was discovered.

**Required:** If necessary, record an adjustment to pretax income in the table provided so that the income statement and balance sheet will be presented in accordance with the accrual basis of accounting. Prepare the adjusting journal entries required to record these adjustments.

**Solution:**

| | Adjustment to Year 2 Pretax Income | Adjustments to Balance Sheet — Assets | Adjustments to Balance Sheet — Liabilities and Equity |
|---|---|---|---|
| Unadjusted Year 2 pretax income | $8,000 | | |
| 1. The company purchased a $300, three-year insurance policy on 1/1/Year 2 and expensed it all on the payment date. | 200 | $ 200 | |
| 2. $2,000 of credit sales made during Year 2 were not recorded in the ledger because they had not been collected in cash. | 2,000 | 2,000 | |
| 3. Cash totaling $3,000 that was received in advance from customers was recorded to service revenue. Only 30 percent of the services had been performed by year-end. | (2,100) | | $2,100 |
| 4. The accountant discovered that a $450 utility bill covering the month of December had not been entered in the AP system at year-end. | (450) | | 450 |
| 5. $4,000 of rent was prepaid on 1/1/Year 1, covering a four-year rental period. No entry was recorded in Year 2 related to this prepayment. | (1,000) | (1,000) | |
| 6. The direct write-off method (non-GAAP method) was used to write off a $650 bad debt in Year 2, although the company uses the allowance approach to estimate bad debts. | 650 | 650 | |
| 7. The company purchased $1,300 of raw materials at year-end which were shipped FOB shipping point and were in transit at the end of the year. The goods were not included in the actual year-end inventory count (the effect of this correction on the financial statements is the same whether the perpetual or periodic inventory system is used.) | | 1,300 | 1,300 |
| 8. The company purchased available-for-sale securities during Year 2 for $1,500. The fair value at year-end totaled $2,000 but no adjustment to fair value was recorded in the ledger. | | 500 | 500 |
| Total adjustments | $ (700) | $3,650 | $4,350 |
| Adjusted Year 2 pretax income | $7,300 | | |

(continued)

(continued)

1. The $300 paid for insurance during the year should have been debited to *prepaid insurance*. At year-end, two years of insurance coverage are left and one year has expired. The $200 reduction in expense increases pretax income for the year. The $200 debit under balance sheet reflects the correct balance of *prepaid insurance* as of that date. At year-end, two years of insurance coverage remain.

| DR | Prepaid insurance | $200 | |
|---|---|---|---|
| CR | Insurance expense | | $200 |

2. According to the revenue recognition principle and accrual accounting, sales should be recorded when the performance obligation is satisfied. The $2,000 credit to income properly records the sale, and the debit to the balance sheet properly reflects the claim to cash that exists at year-end.

| DR | Accounts receivable | $2,000 | |
|---|---|---|---|
| CR | Sales revenue | | $2,000 |

3. The receipt of cash in advance from a customer should not have been recorded as service revenue because it represents unearned revenue. At year-end, 30 percent of the services had been performed, so $900 is valid service revenue. $2,100 had to be removed from income and recorded as an obligation on the balance sheet at year-end to reflect remaining services to be performed.

| DR | Sales revenue | $2,100 | |
|---|---|---|---|
| CR | Unearned revenue | | $2,100 |

4. Expenses should be recorded in the period incurred. The $450 charge to income records the correct expense incurred. The year-end balance sheet now reflects the $450 as accounts payable (utilities payable).

| DR | Utilities expense | $450 | |
|---|---|---|---|
| CR | A/P (Utilities payable) | | $450 |

5. There was no cash outflow in the current year related to the rent expense, but one year of rent expense must be charged to income. The $1,000 reflects the expense incurred in the current year. The prepaid rent balance from the prior year-end is reduced and the current year-end prepaid balance would total $2,000, as two years of benefit remain.

| DR | Rent expense | $1,000 | |
|---|---|---|---|
| CR | Prepaid rent | | $1,000 |

(continued)

(continued)

6. Because the company uses the allowance approach to record estimated bad debts, we can assume that an estimate of bad debt was recorded when the sale was originally recorded. The direct write-off was recorded to bad debt expense when it should have been recorded to the allowance account. The effect of this correction is to increase income and increase assets (assets increase because we are reducing a contra-asset account).

| | | | |
|---|---|---|---|
| DR | Allowance for doubtful accounts | $650 | |
| CR | Bad debt expense | | $650 |

7. The correct journal to record the inventory in transit at year-end:

| | | | |
|---|---|---|---|
| DR | Inventory (perpetual system, or: Purchases (periodic system) | $1,300 | |
| CR | Accounts payable | | $1,300 |

8. Available-for-sale securities must be reported on the balance sheet at fair value. The valuation account increases the value of the investment on the balance sheet. The unrealized gain affects equity through accumulated other comprehensive income.

| | | | |
|---|---|---|---|
| DR | Valuation account (fair value adjustment) | $500 | |
| CR | Unrealized gain on available-for-sale securities) | | $500 |

### Question 1　　MCQ-08238

On October 31, Year 1, a company with a calendar year-end paid $90,000 for services that will be performed evenly over a six-month period from November 1, Year 1, through April 30, Year 2. The company expensed the $90,000 cash payment in October, Year 1, to its services expense general ledger account. The company did not record any additional journal entries in Year 1 related to the payment. What is the adjusting journal entry that the company should record to properly report the prepayment in its Year 1 financial statements?

a. Debit prepaid services and credit services expense for $30,000.
b. Debit prepaid services and credit services expense for $60,000.
c. Debit services expense and credit prepaid services for $30,000.
d. Debit services expense and credit prepaid services for $60,000.

# FAR 2

# Financial Reporting and Disclosures

## Module

| | | |
|---|---|---|
| 1 | Notes to Financial Statements | 3 |
| 2 | Going Concern | 7 |
| 3 | Subsequent Events | 11 |
| 4 | Fair Value Measurements | 15 |
| 5 | Segment Reporting | 21 |
| 6 | SEC Reporting Requirements | 27 |
| 7 | Special Purpose Frameworks | 33 |
| 8 | Ratio Analysis | 41 |
| 9 | Partnerships | 53 |

# MODULE 1: Notes to Financial Statements

## 1 Summary of Significant Accounting Policies

Both U.S. GAAP and IFRS require that a description of all significant policies be included as an integral part of the financial statements. The preferred presentation is to include the "Summary of Significant Accounting Policies" as the first or second note to the financial statements. Policies presented in other notes should not be duplicated.

> **U.S. GAAP VS. IFRS**
>
> IFRS requires an explicit and unreserved statement of compliance with IFRS in the notes to the financial statements. An entity cannot describe financial statements as complying with IFRSs unless they comply with all IFRS requirements. U.S. GAAP does not have a similar requirement.

### 1.1 Disclosures

The summary of significant accounting policies includes disclosures of:

- Measurement bases used in preparing the financial statements.
- Specific accounting principles and methods used during the period, including:
  - Basis of consolidation
  - Depreciation methods
  - Amortization of intangibles
  - Inventory pricing
  - Use of estimates
  - Fiscal year definition
  - Special revenue recognition issues (e.g., long-term construction contracts, franchising, leasing operations, etc.)

## U.S. GAAP VS. IFRS

IFRS requires disclosure of judgments and estimates that management has made in the process of applying accounting policies and which have a significant effect on the financial statements. Examples of judgments include determining whether financial assets are held-to-maturity securities and determining whether the relationship between an entity and an SPE (special purpose entity) indicates that the entity controls the SPE. This disclosure is generally made in the "Summary of Significant Accounting Policies."

U.S. GAAP requires disclosure of significant estimates, but does not require the disclosure of judgments made in preparing the financial statements

### 1.2 Items Not Included

The summary of significant accounting policies would not include the following items:

- Composition and detailed dollar amounts of account balances
- Details relating to changes in accounting principles
- Dates of maturity and amounts of long-term debt
- Yearly computation of depreciation, depletion, and amortization

## 2 Remaining Notes to the Financial Statements

The remaining notes contain all other information relevant to decision makers (e.g., investors, creditors, etc.) These notes are used to disclose facts not presented in either the body of the financial statements or in the Summary of Significant Accounting Policies. Examples of relevant note information include the following:

- Material information regarding inventory, property, plant, and equipment, and other significant asset/liability balances that require specific disclosures;
- Changes in stockholders' equity, including capital stock, paid-in capital, retained earnings, treasury stock, stock dividends, and other capital changes;
- Required marketable securities disclosure, including carrying value and gross unrealized gains and losses;
- Fair value estimates;
- Contingency losses;
- Contingency gains (if highly probable, but care should be exercised to avoid misleading implications as to the likelihood of realization);
- Contractual obligations (including bonds payable and notes payable), including restrictions on specific assets or liabilities;
- Pension plan description;
- Segment reporting;
- Subsequent events; and
- Changes in accounting principles or implementation of new accounting standards update.

# 3 Disclosure of Risks and Uncertainties (U.S. GAAP)

U.S. GAAP requires the disclosure of risks and uncertainties existing at the date(s) of the financial statements in the following areas:

## 3.1 Nature of Operations

The footnotes should include a description of the entity's major products or services and its principal markets, including the locations of those markets. If the entity operates multiple businesses, the disclosure should describe the relative importance of each business.

## 3.2 Use of Estimates in the Preparation of Financial Statements

The footnotes should include the following statement (or a similar statement):

The preparation of financial statements in conformity with generally accepted accounting principles (GAAP) requires management to make estimates and assumptions that affect the reported amounts of assets and liabilities, the disclosure of contingent assets and liabilities at the date of the financial statements, and the reported amounts of revenues and expenses during the reporting period. Actual results could differ from those estimates.

## 3.3 Certain Significant Estimates

When it is reasonably possible that an estimate will change in the near term and that the effect of the change will be material, an estimate of the effect of the change should be disclosed.

The following are examples of assets and liabilities and related revenues and expenses, including gain and loss contingencies that may be based on estimates that are particularly sensitive to change:

- Inventory or equipment subject to rapid technological obsolescence.
- Deferred tax asset valuation allowances.
- Capitalized computer software costs.
- Loan valuation allowances.
- Litigation-related obligations.
- Amounts reported for long-term obligations, such as pension and postretirement benefits.
- Amounts reported in long-term contracts.

## 3.4 Current Vulnerability Due to Certain Concentrations

### 3.4.1 Definition

Vulnerability due to concentrations arise when an entity is exposed to risk of loss that could be mitigated through diversification.

### 3.4.2 Disclosure Requirements

Concentrations should be disclosed if all of the following criteria are met:

- The concentration exists at the financial statement date.
- The concentration makes the entity vulnerable to the risk of a near-term severe impact (a significant financially disruptive effect on the normal functioning of an entity).
- It is at least reasonably possible that the events that could cause the severe impact will occur in the near term.

### 3.4.3 Examples of Concentrations

The following are common examples of concentrations:

- Concentrations in the volume of business transacted with a particular customer, supplier, lender, grantor, or contributor.
- Concentrations in revenue from particular products, services, or fund-raising events.
- Concentrations in the available supply of resources, such as materials, labor, or services.
- Concentrations in market or geographic area.

> **U.S. GAAP VS. IFRS**
>
> IFRS "risk and uncertainty" disclosure requirements are narrower and focus on sources of estimation uncertainty. IFRS state that an entity should disclose information about the assumptions it makes about the future, and other major sources of estimation uncertainty at the end of the reporting period, that have a significant risk of resulting in a material adjustment to the carrying amount of assets and liabilities within the next financial year. The notes should include details of the nature and carrying amount at the end of the reporting period of these assets and liabilities.

---

**Question 1**  MCQ-00103

Which of the following information should be disclosed in the summary of significant accounting policies?

    **a.** Refinancing of debt subsequent to the balance sheet date.
    **b.** Guarantees of indebtedness of others.
    **c.** Criteria for determining which investments are treated as cash equivalents.
    **d.** Adequacy of pension plan assets relative to vested benefits.

# MODULE 2: Going Concern

FAR 2

## 1 Going Concern Overview

An entity is considered to be a going concern if it is reasonably expected to remain in existence and settle all its obligations for the foreseeable future.

Prior to 2014, U.S. auditing standards addressed the topic of going concern, but there was a lack of guidance in U.S. GAAP specific to going concern. In 2014, the FASB issued a new standard addressing management's responsibilities and disclosures required under U.S. GAAP.

## 2 Going Concern Presumption

Under U.S. GAAP, preparation of financial statements presumes that the reporting entity will continue as a going concern. Under this presumption, financial statements are prepared under the going concern basis of accounting.

If an entity's liquidation is imminent (and the entity is therefore no longer considered to be a going concern), financial statements are prepared under the liquidation basis of accounting.

## 3 Management's Responsibility to Evaluate

Management is required to evaluate whether there is substantial doubt about an entity's ability to continue as a going concern within one year after the date that the financial statements are issued.

- Substantial doubt exists when relevant conditions and events, when considered in the aggregate, indicate it is probable (defined as "likely to occur") that the entity will not be able to meet its obligations as they become due within one year from the financial statement issuance date (in contrast to the balance sheet date).
- Management's evaluation should occur for each annual and interim reporting period.
- Management's evaluation should be based on relevant conditions and events that are known and reasonably knowable at the financial statement issuance date.
- Management's evaluation should consider both quantitative and qualitative factors, such as the following:
  - The entity's current financial condition, including sources of liquidity (e.g., cash and access to credit).
  - The entity's obligations due or anticipated in the next year, even if they are not recognized in the financial statements.
  - Funds necessary to maintain operations based on resources, obligations, and expected cash flows in the next year.
  - Other conditions that could adversely affect the entity's ability to meet its obligations, such as negative financial trends, other indications of financial difficulties, and internal and external matters.

# 4 Mitigating Factors

If conditions or events exist that raise substantial doubt about an entity's ability to continue as a going concern, management should consider whether the entity's plans intended to mitigate those conditions or events will be successful in alleviating the substantial doubt.

The mitigating effect should be evaluated based on:

- whether it is probable that the plans will be effectively implemented; and, if so,
- whether it is probable that the implemented plans will be successful in mitigating the adverse conditions or events.

# 5 Results of Management's Evaluation and Required Disclosures

## 5.1 No Substantial Doubt

No disclosures related to going concern are required if the evaluation does not give rise to substantial doubt.

## 5.2 Substantial Doubt Alleviated

If there is substantial doubt about an entity's ability to continue as a going concern, but the substantial doubt is alleviated as a result of management's plans, the financial statements should be prepared under the going concern basis of accounting and should include the following footnote disclosures:

- The primary conditions or events that initially raised substantial doubt about the entity's ability to continue as a going concern.
- Management's evaluation of the significance of those conditions or events in relation to the entity's ability to meet its obligations.
- Management's plans that alleviated the substantial doubt.

## 5.3 Substantial Doubt Not Alleviated

If there is substantial doubt about an entity's ability to continue as a going concern, and the substantial doubt is not alleviated as a result of management's plans, the financial statements would continue to be prepared under the going concern basis of accounting. The footnotes must state that there is substantial doubt about the entity's ability to continue as a going concern within one year of the financial statement issuance date. In addition, the following footnote disclosures are required:

- The primary conditions or events that raise substantial doubt about the entity's ability to continue as a going concern.
- Management's evaluation of the significance of those conditions or events in relation to the entity's ability to meet its obligations.
- Management's plans that are intended to mitigate the adverse conditions or events.

# 6 U.S. GAAP vs. IFRS

U.S. GAAP and IFRS both emphasize management's responsibility to evaluate the entity's ability to continue as a going concern and provide relevant disclosures when necessary. Differences between U.S. GAAP and IFRS include the following distinctions:

- U.S. GAAP requires the liquidation basis of accounting if liquidation is imminent and the going concern basis requirements are not met, whereas IFRS does not provide guidance on the basis of accounting to use if liquidation is imminent.
- U.S. GAAP requires certain disclosures when there is substantial doubt about an entity's ability to continue as a going concern, even if that doubt is alleviated by management's plans to address it. IFRS requires disclosures when management is aware of material uncertainties that may give rise to substantial doubt about an entity's ability to continue as a going concern.
- U.S. GAAP requires management to assess going concern conditions within one year of the financial statement issuance date, whereas IFRS requires assessment at least one year from the balance sheet date.

---

**Question 1**  MCQ-03689

Management has plans to mitigate conditions causing substantial doubt about the entity's ability to continue as a going concern. Management believes that those plans will be effectively implemented and successful in mitigating the adverse conditions.

Which of the following is true?

   a. The financial statements should be prepared under the going concern basis of accounting with no additional disclosures.

   b. The financial statements should be prepared under the going concern basis of accounting with footnote disclosure explaining the conditions that originally raised doubt about the entity's status as a going concern.

   c. The financial statements should be prepared under the going concern basis of accounting with a supplemental schedule showing anticipated cash receipts and disbursements for the upcoming year, demonstrating that the company expects to remain solvent through the end of the year.

   d. The financial statements should be prepared under the going concern basis of accounting, with supplemental footnote information showing the balance sheet prepared under the liquidation basis of accounting.

# MODULE 3: Subsequent Events

**FAR 2**

## 1 Definition of a Subsequent Event

A subsequent event is an event or transaction that occurs after the balance sheet date but before the financial statements are issued or are available to be issued. Subsequent events can be divided into two categories:

### 1.1 Recognized Subsequent Events

Recognized subsequent events provide additional information about conditions that existed at the balance sheet date. Entities must recognize the effects of all recognized subsequent events in the financial statements. The following subsequent events are considered to be recognized subsequent events:

- **Settlement of Litigation:** If litigation that arose before the balance sheet date is settled after the balance sheet date but before the date that the financial statements are issued or available to be issued, the settlement amount should be considered when determining the liability to be reported on the balance sheet date.

- **Loss on an Uncollectible Receivable:** The effects of a customer's bankruptcy filing after the balance sheet date but before the date that the financial statements are issued or available to be issued should be considered when determining the amount of the uncollectible receivable to be recognized in the financial statements on the balance sheet date.

### 1.2 Nonrecognized Subsequent Events

An entity should not recognize subsequent events that provide information about conditions that did not exist at the balance sheet date.

The following subsequent events occurring after the balance sheet date but before the date the financial statements are issued or are available to be issued are considered to be nonrecognized subsequent events:

- Sale of bond or capital stock
- Business combination
- Settlement of litigation, if the litigation arose after the balance sheet date
- Loss of plant or inventory due to fire or natural disaster
- Changes in the fair value of assets, liabilities, or foreign exchange rates
- Entering into significant commitments or contingent liabilities
- Loss on receivables resulting from conditions occurring after the balance sheet date

A nonrecognized subsequent event should be disclosed if disclosure is necessary to keep the financial statements from being misleading. Disclosure should include the nature of the subsequent event and an estimate of the financial effect of the event or a statement that no estimate can be made. Pro forma financial statements showing the effect of the subsequent event if it had occurred on the balance sheet date may also be presented.

## 2 Subsequent Event Evaluation Period

An entity that files financial statements with the Securities and Exchange Commission (SEC) must evaluate subsequent events through the *date that the financial statements are issued*. All other entities must evaluate subsequent events through the *date that the financial statements are available to be issued*. Financial statements are considered to be issued when they have been widely distributed to financial statement users in a form and format that complies with GAAP. Financial statements are available to be issued when they are in a form and format that complies with GAAP and all approvals for issuance have been obtained.

If an entity is not an SEC filer, then the entity must disclose the date through which subsequent events have been evaluated, including whether that date is the date the financial statements were issued or the date that the financial statements were available to be issued. This disclosure is not required for SEC filers to avoid potential conflicts with current SEC guidance.

## 3 Reissuance of Financial Statements

When an entity reissues its financial statements, the entity should not recognize events that occurred between the date the original financial statements were issued or available to be issued and the date that the financial statements were reissued, unless an adjustment is required by GAAP or other regulatory requirements.

### U.S. GAAP VS. IFRS

Under IFRS, subsequent events are referred to as "events after the reporting period," and the subsequent event evaluation period extends from the reporting period through the date the financial statements are authorized for issuance. Recognized subsequent events are referred to as "adjusting events after the reporting period," and nonrecognized subsequent events are referred to as "non-adjusting events after the reporting period." IFRS specifically addresses going concern issues in the guidance on events after the reporting period, stating that an entity cannot prepare its financial statements on a going concern basis if management determines after year-end that it intends to liquidate the company or cease trading.

## 4 Revised Financial Statements

Revised financial statements are financial statements that have been revised to correct an error or to reflect the retrospective application of U.S. GAAP. Revised financial statements are considered reissued financial statements. If an entity is not an SEC filer, the entity should disclose in its revised financial statements the dates through which subsequent events have been evaluated in both its issued/available-to-be-issued financial statements and its revised financial statements. This disclosure is not required for SEC filers.

## Example 1 — Subsequent Events

**Facts:** Friends of Fido is an SEC filer and has a balance sheet date of December 31, Year 3. The entity will file financial statements by the end of March, Year 4. The following events occurred after the balance sheet date.

1. A lawsuit filed in Year 2 was settled in early February. Friends of Fido must pay $600,000 as a result of the lawsuit. The financial statements currently reflect a contingency amount of $725,000.

2. The entity announced in early March that it will acquire Dawghouse Inc. for $1.5 million. The acquisition, which is planned for September, Year 4, will be made with cash and stock.

3. A customer that had significant aged invoices at year-end announced bankruptcy in January.

4. A second customer that is typically a timely payer had multiple outstanding invoices at year-end. The customer experienced a flood in February and the entire retail location was wiped out. The customer has decided to close its business permanently and is not returning phone calls regarding payment.

**Required:** Determine how these subsequent events should be treated in the financial statements.

**Solution:**

1. This subsequent event relates to a condition that existed at the December 31, Year 3, balance sheet date and should be treated as a recognized subsequent event. The contingency in the financial statements should be adjusted to reflect the settlement amount of $600,000 rather than the current estimate of $725,000.

2. The expected acquisition of Dawghouse Inc. is an example of a nonrecognized subsequent event. The expected acquisition is a material event and should be disclosed in the financial statements but does not required adjustment in the financial statements at December 31, Year 3.

3. The bankruptcy of a customer whose account balances were significantly past due results in a recognized subsequent event. Because the condition (the customer's inability to pay) has occurred over time and existed at the financial statement year-end, the declaration of bankruptcy needs to be accounted for in the analysis of accounts receivable and bad debt expense for December 31, Year 3.

4. Although this customer's receivable balance may be past due, this subsequent event is a nonrecognized subsequent event for two reasons. First, there was no evidence at year-end that this customer, which has always been a timely payer, was not going to pay the past-due invoices. Second, the flood and subsequent decision to close the retail shop did not occur until after year-end. If the outstanding invoices are considered material, this information may require disclosure in the financial statements, but no adjustment is required. If not material, no disclosure would be required.

**Question 1**  MCQ-00733

Ace Co. settled litigation on February 1, Year 2, for an event that occurred during Year 1. An estimated liability was determined as of December 31, Year 1. This estimate was significantly less than the final settlement. The transaction is considered to be material. The financial statements for year-end Year 1 have not been issued. How should the settlement be reported in Ace's year-end Year 1 financial statements?

   a. Disclosure only of the settlement.
   b. Only an accrual of the settlement.
   c. Neither a disclosure nor an accrual.
   d. Both a disclosure and an accrual.

# MODULE 4: Fair Value Measurements

**FAR 2**

## 1 Fair Value Overview

U.S. GAAP and IFRS have standardized the definition of fair value, established a framework for measuring fair value, and outlined required fair value disclosures for all areas that require or permit fair value measurement, *except*:

- share-based compensation;
- measurements based on or using vendor-specific objective evidence of fair value; and
- fair value measurements used for lease classification or measurement.

### 1.1 Fair Value Defined

Fair value is the price that would be received to sell an asset or paid to transfer a liability in an orderly transaction between market participants in the principal (or most advantageous) market at the measurement date under current market conditions.

- Fair value is measured for a specific asset or liability, a group of assets and/or liabilities, or an entity's own equity instrument (e.g., an equity interest issued as consideration in a business combination).
- Fair value is a market-based measure, not an entity-based measure.
- Fair value is measured in the principal market for the asset or liability, or the most advantageous market in the absence of a principal market.
- Fair value is an exit price (the price to sell an asset or transfer a liability), not an entrance price (the price to acquire an asset or assume a liability).
- A fair value measure should reflect all of the assumptions that market participants would use in pricing the asset or liability, including assumptions about risk.
- Fair value does not include transaction costs, but may include transportation costs if location is an attribute of the asset or liability.
- The fair value of a nonfinancial asset assumes the highest and best use of the asset.
- The fair value of a liability should include the liability's nonperformance risk, which is the risk that the obligation will not be fulfilled.
- The fair value of an entity's own equity instrument should be measured from the perspective of a market participant who holds that instrument as an asset.
- Fair value measurement assumes that a liability or an entity's own equity instrument is transferred to a market participant at the measurement date and assumes that the liability or equity interest would remain outstanding and would not be settled, canceled, or extinguished on the measurement date.

# 2 Fair Value Terminology

## 2.1 Orderly Transaction

An orderly transaction is one in which the asset or liability is exposed to the market, for a period before the measurement date, long enough to allow for marketing activities that are usual and customary for transactions involving such assets or liabilities. An orderly transaction cannot be a forced transaction.

## 2.2 Market Participants

Market participants are buyers and sellers who are independent (not related parties), knowledgeable about the asset or liability, able to transact for the asset or liability, and willing to transact for the asset or liability. They are considered to be acting in their economic best interest.

## 2.3 Principal Market

The principal market is the market with the greatest volume or level of activity for the asset or liability. If there is a principal market for an asset or liability, the price in that market will be the fair value measurement, even if there is a more advantageous price in a different market. The reporting entity must have access to the principal market at the measurement date.

## 2.4 Most Advantageous Market

The most advantageous market is the market with the best price for the asset (maximizes selling price of the asset) or liability (minimizes payment to transfer liability), after considering transaction costs. Note that although transactions costs are used to determine the most advantageous market, transaction costs are not included in the final fair value measurement (see the example below). The price in the most advantageous market will be the fair value measurement only if there is no principal market.

---

### Example 1 — Most Advantageous Market

**Facts:**

- Gearty Inc. holds Foxy Co. stock, which trades on two exchanges (Gearty Inc. can access both the New York and London markets).
- The stock price and transaction costs at the measurement date are as follows:

| Exchange | Quoted Stock Price | Transactions Costs | Net |
|---|---|---|---|
| New York | $52 | $6 | $46 |
| London | 50 | 2 | 48 |

**Required:** Determine the fair value of Foxy stock if New York is the principal market, if London is the principal market, and if there is no principal market.

**Solution:**

| | |
|---|---|
| If New York is the principal market | = $52 |
| If London is the principal market | = $50 |
| If no principal market, with London's price (net of transaction costs) having the most advantageous result | = $50 |

## 2.5 Highest and Best Use

### 2.5.1 Nonfinancial Assets

The fair value measurement of a nonfinancial asset takes into account the market participant's ability to generate economic benefits by using the asset in its highest and best use or by selling it to another market participant that would use the asset in its highest and best use.

A reporting entity's current use of a nonfinancial asset is presumed to be its highest and best use, unless market or other factors suggest that a different use by market participants would maximize the value of the asset. The highest and best use of a nonfinancial asset may be to use the asset in combination with other assets, with other assets and liabilities, or on a stand-alone basis.

### 2.5.2 Liabilities and Financial Assets

The highest and best use concept is not relevant when measuring the fair value of financial assets or the fair value of liabilities because such items do not have alternative uses and their fair values do not depend on their use within a group of other assets or liabilities.

---

**Illustration 1    Fair Value Measurement**

As part of a business combination, a reporting entity acquires land that is currently the site of a factory. Similar sites in the area were recently developed for other purposes, including residential and retail space. The highest and best use of the land would be determined by comparing both of the following:

- The value of the land as currently developed for industrial use (value of the land plus the value of the assets/liabilities related to the land, such as the building cost, debt on the land/building, etc.).
- The value of the land as a vacant site for residential or retail use. The cost of tearing down the factory and any related costs must be considered, as well as any uncertainty in converting the land to a vacant site for residential or retail space.

Fair value will be determined based on whichever use results in the highest value.

---

# 3 Fair Value Measurement Framework

U.S. GAAP and IFRS have established a framework for measuring fair value. This framework for measuring fair value (i) outlines the *valuation techniques* that can be used to measure fair value, and (ii) establishes a *hierarchy* of the inputs that can be used in these valuation techniques.

## 3.1 Valuation Techniques

Entities can use the market approach, the income approach, the cost approach, or a combination of these, as appropriate, when measuring the fair value of an asset or a liability. The valuation technique should be appropriate to the circumstances and should maximize the use of observable inputs and minimize the use of unobservable inputs. A change in valuation technique or its application is accounted for as a change in accounting estimate (which is accounted for prospectively).

### 3.1.1 Market Approach

The *market approach* uses prices and other relevant information from market transactions involving identical or comparable assets or liabilities to measure fair value.

### 3.1.2 Income Approach

The *income approach* converts future amounts, including cash flows or earnings, to a single discounted amount to measure fair value. This method can be applied to assets or liabilities.

### 3.1.3 Cost Approach

The *cost approach* uses current replacement cost to measure the fair value of assets.

## 3.2 Hierarchy of Inputs

The fair value hierarchy prioritizes the inputs that can be used in the valuation techniques described above. Level 1 inputs have the highest priority, and Level 3 inputs have the lowest priority. The level in the fair value hierarchy in which a fair value measurement falls is determined by the lowest level input that is significant to the fair value measurement. Valuation techniques should maximize the use of observable inputs (Level 1 and Level 2) and minimize the use of unobservable inputs (Level 3).

### 3.2.1 Level 1 Inputs

*Level 1 inputs* are quoted prices in active markets for identical assets or liabilities that the reporting entity has access to on the measurement date. Quoted prices may be obtained from exchange markets (NYSE), dealer markets, brokered markets and principal-to-principal markets. Level 1 inputs are the most reliable measures of fair value and should be used when available.

### 3.2.2 Level 2 Inputs

*Level 2 inputs* are inputs other than quoted market prices (Level 1) that are directly or indirectly observable for the asset or liability. Level 2 inputs include:

- Quoted prices for similar assets or liabilities in active markets.
- Quoted prices for identical or similar assets in markets that are not active.
- Quoted prices for identical liabilities when traded as assets, if adjustments to the quoted market price of the assets are required.
- Quoted prices for similar liabilities when traded as assets.
- Inputs other than quoted prices that are observable for the asset or liability.
- Inputs that are derived from or corroborated by observable market data.

### 3.2.3 Level 3 Inputs

*Level 3 inputs* are unobservable inputs for the asset or liability. Unobservable inputs reflect the reporting entity's assumptions and should be based on the best available information. Level 3 inputs should be used only when there are no observable (Level 1 or Level 2) inputs or when undue cost and effort is required to obtain observable inputs.

# 4 Fair Value Disclosures

The objective of fair value disclosures is to provide users of financial statements with information about assets and liabilities measured at fair value, including:

1. The valuation techniques and inputs the entity uses to arrive at its measures of fair value, including judgments and assumptions that the entity makes;
2. The uncertainty in the fair value measurements as of the reporting date; and
3. How changes in fair value measurements affect the entity's performance and cash flows.

Specifically, an entity must provide the following disclosures regarding fair value measurements:

- Quantitative information about significant unobservable inputs.
- Discussion of the sensitivity of Level 3 measurements to changes in unobservable inputs disclosed.
- Information about nonfinancial assets and liabilities for which measurements differ from highest and best use.
- Hierarchy for items that are not measured on the balance sheet but are disclosed in the notes to the financial statements.

---

**Example 2**    **Fair Value Measurement**

**Facts:** During the year, Marker Eight Company purchased 3,000 shares of Milledge Inc.'s common stock. At the time of purchase, the stock was trading at a price of $24 per share. The quoted stock price for Milledge Inc. at year-end according to the public exchange was $21.50 per share.

**Required:** Calculate the fair value of the stock at year-end and explain how Marker Eight should record any change in fair value.

**Solution:**

|  | Original Cost | Fair Value at Year-End |
|---|---|---|
| Investment in Milledge Inc. | 3,000 × $24.00/share = $72,000 | 3,000 × $21.50/share = $64,500 |

Marker Eight must record a $7,500 ($72,000 − $64,500) adjusting entry to decrease the value of the investment on the balance sheet to its fair value of $64,500 at year-end. The other side of the entry will affect net income because the stock is an equity security. This is an example of the market approach as the identical asset is used to determine fair value. The market price for the stock is a Level 1 input.

---

# 5 Exceptions to Fair Value Measurement

Exemptions to the requirement to measure fair value exist when:

- it is not practicable to measure fair value;
- fair value cannot be reasonably determined; or
- fair value cannot be measured with sufficient reliability.

## Question 1　　　　　　　　　　　　　　　　　　　　　　　　　　　　MCQ-06057

ABC Company owns stock in XYZ Company. The stock is traded on the New York Stock Exchange and the London Stock Exchange. Stock price information from the two stock exchanges on December 31 is as follows:

| Exchange | Quoted Stock Price | Transactions Costs | Net |
|---|---|---|---|
| New York | $103 | $1 | $102 |
| London | 106 | 5 | 101 |

What is the fair value of the XYZ stock on December 31 if there is no principal market for the stock?

- a. $101
- b. $102
- c. $103
- d. $106

# MODULE 5 Segment Reporting

FAR 2

## 1 Segment Reporting Overview

The objective of segment reporting is to provide information on the business activities and the economic environment of a company to help users of the financial statements:

1. Better understand the entity performance;
2. Better assess its prospects for future net cash flows; and
3. Make more informed judgments about the entity as a whole.

In general, an entity is required to disclose segment profit or loss, segment assets, and certain related items, but it is not required to report segment cash flow.

> **U.S. GAAP VS. IFRS**
>
> IFRS requires the disclosure of segment liabilities if such a measure is regularly provided to the chief operating decision maker. U.S. GAAP does not require the disclosure of segment liabilities.

### 1.1 Required Disclosures for All Public Entities

In order to conform with U.S. GAAP and IFRS, financial statements for public business entities must report information about a company's:

- Operating segments *(annual and interim)*
- Products and services
- Geographic areas
- Major customers

### 1.2 Use Same Accounting Principles as Main Financial Statements

The required financial statement information is essentially a disaggregation of the entity's regular financial statements. The accounting principles used in preparing the financial statements should be used for the segment information. Segment information presented must be reconciled to the related aggregate amounts in the financial statements.

### 1.3 Intercompany Transactions Not Eliminated for Reporting

It is important to remember that transactions between the segments of an entity are not eliminated in a consolidation between the parent company and subsidiaries.

## 1.4 Scope (Public Companies Only)

Segment reporting applies to public companies only. It does not apply to not-for-profit organizations, nonpublic companies, or separate financial statements of members of a consolidated group if both the separate company statements and the consolidated or combined financial statements are included in the same financial report.

# 2 Operating Segments

An operating segment is a component of an entity that has all of the following characteristics:

1. It engages in business activities from which it may earn revenues and incur expenses (including revenues and expenses relating to transactions with other components of the same entity).
2. Its operating results are regularly reviewed by the entity's "chief operating decision maker" to make decisions about resources to be allocated to the segment and assess its performance.
3. Its discrete financial information is available.

The definition of a segment depends on how management uses information, which is called the management approach method. For example, management may report results both by product and service lines and by geographic lines.

## 2.1 Not Every Component Is an Operating Segment

Not every component of an entity is necessarily an operating segment or part of an operating segment.

- **Corporate Headquarters Not an Operating Segment:** A corporate headquarters or certain functional departments may not earn revenues or may earn revenues that are only incidental to the activities of the entity and would not be operating segments.
- **Pension Plan Not an Operating Segment:** An entity's pension and other post-retirement benefit plans are not considered to be operating segments.

## 2.2 Reportable Segments

Reportable segments are operating segments of an entity that meet the criteria for separate reporting.

Those operating segments that exhibit similar long-term financial performance may be aggregated into a single operating segment only if the segments have the same basic characteristics in each of the following areas:

- The nature of the products and services;
- The nature of the production processes;
- The type or class of customer for their products and services;
- The methods used to distribute their products or provide their services; and
- If applicable, the nature of the regulatory environment (e.g., banking, insurance, or public utilities).

## 2.3 Quantitative Thresholds for Reportable Segments

A segment is considered significant and therefore disclosure is required if it meets one or more of the following quantitative thresholds.

### 2.3.1 10 Percent "Size" Test

- **Revenue**

    The segment's revenue, including both sales to external customers and intersegment sales or transfers (but excluding interest income on advances and loans to other segments), is 10 percent or more of the combined revenue, internal and external, of all operating segments.

- **Reported Profit or Loss**

    The absolute amount of the segment's reported profit or loss is 10 percent or more of the greater, in absolute amount, of:

    1. The combined reported profit of all operating segments that did not report a loss.
    2. The combined reported loss of all operating segments that did report a loss.

- **Assets**

    The segment's identifiable assets are 10 percent or more of the combined assets of all operating segments. The assets of a segment are those assets included in the measure of the segment's assets that are reviewed by the chief operating decision maker.

### 2.3.2 75 Percent "Reporting Sufficiency" Test

If the total of external (consolidated) revenue reported by operating segments constitutes less than 75 percent of external (consolidated) revenue, additional operating segments need to be identified as reportable segments, even if they do not meet the above three tests, until at least 75 percent of external (consolidated) revenue is included in reportable segments. The practical limit to the number of segments is 10, which is not a precise limit but is reasonable so as not to overwhelm financial statement users with detailed information.

### 2.3.3 "All Other Segments" Category

Information about other business activities and operating segments that are not reportable based on the above criteria should be combined and disclosed in an "all other segments" category but is reasonable so as not to overwhelm financial statement users with detailed information.

## 2.4 Comparative Reporting

An operating segment that was deemed to be reportable in the immediately preceding period but that does not meet the criteria for reportability in the current period may continue to be reported separately if management judges the segment to have continuing significance.

If an operating segment that was not deemed to be reportable in the prior period meets the criteria for reportability in the current period, segment data for prior periods presented should be restated to reflect the newly reportable segment as a separate segment.

## 2.5 Segment Profit (or Loss) Defined

The segment profit (or loss) is calculated as follows:

> **Revenues**
> Less: directly traceable costs
> Less: reasonably allocated costs
> **Operating profit (or loss)**

### 2.5.1 Income and Expense Allocation

Income and expenses are not allocated to a segment unless they are included in the determination of segment profit or loss reported to the "chief operating decision maker."

### 2.5.2 Items Normally Excluded From Segment Profit (or Loss)

- General corporate revenues
- General corporate expenses
- Interest expense (except for financial institutions)
- Income taxes
- Equity in earnings and losses of an unconsolidated subsidiary (i.e., under the equity method)
- Gains or losses from discontinued operations
- Minority interest

# 3 Reportable Segment Disclosures

## 3.1 Identifying Factors

Factors used to identify the entity's reportable segments, including the basis of organization (e.g., products and services, geographic areas, regulatory environments) should be disclosed. Also disclose whether any operation segments have been aggregated.

## 3.2 Products and Services

The types of products and services from which the reportable segment derives its revenues must be disclosed.

## 3.3 Profit or Loss

The following items must be individually disclosed if the amounts are included in the calculation of segment profit or loss reviewed by the chief operating decision maker:

- Revenues from external customers
- Revenues from transactions with other internal operating segments
- Interest revenue
- Interest expense
- Depreciation, depletion, and amortization
- Unusual items, including unusual events and transactions
- Equity in net income of investees accounted for by the equity method
- Income tax expense or benefit
- Significant noncash items other than depreciation, depletion, and amortization expense

## 3.4 Assets

- The amount of investment in equity method investees.
- Total expenditures for:
  - Additions to long-lived assets other than financial instruments
  - Long-term customer relationships of a financial institution
  - Mortgage and other servicing rights
  - Deferred policy acquisition costs
  - Deferred tax assets

## 3.5 Liabilities (IFRS Only)

Under IFRS, an entity discloses a measure of liabilities for each reportable segment if such an amount is regularly provided to the chief operating decision maker.

## 3.6 Measurement Criteria

The accounting principles used for segment reporting may not be the same as those used to prepare the consolidated statements. Some principles are not expected to apply on a segment basis; therefore, the following information must be disclosed:

- The basis of accounting for any internal transactions.
- The nature of any differences between measurements of the reportable segments' profits or losses and the entity's consolidated income.
- The nature of any differences between measurements of the reportable segments' assets and the entity's consolidated assets, if not apparent from the reconciliation provided.
- The nature of any changes from prior periods in the measurement methods used to determine reported segment profit or loss.
- The nature and effect of any asymmetrical allocations to segments.

## 3.7 Reconciliations

- The total of the reportable segments' revenues to the entity's consolidated revenues.
- The total of the reportable segments' measures of profit or loss to the entity's consolidated income before income taxes, discontinued operations, and the cumulative effects of changes in accounting principles.
- The total of the reportable segments' assets to the entity's consolidated assets.
- The total of the reportable segments' liabilities to the entity's consolidated liabilities (IFRS only).
- The total of the reportable segments' amounts for every other significant item of information disclosed to the corresponding consolidated amount.

# 4 Entity-wide Disclosures

The following disclosures apply to entities regardless of the number of reportable segments. They are required disclosures for all public entities.

## 4.1 Products and Services

Revenues from external customers for each product or service or each group of similar products and services must be disclosed unless it is impracticable to do so, and that fact must be disclosed.

## 4.2 Geographic Areas

### 4.2.1 Revenues

Disclose the revenues from external customers that are:

- Attributable to the entity's domicile country.
- Attributed to all foreign countries if the amount is material.
- Attributed to individual foreign countries if the amount is material.
- The basis for attributing revenues from external customers to individual countries.

### 4.2.2 Long-Lived Assets

Disclose the long-lived assets that are:

- Located in the entity's domicile country.
- Located in all foreign countries in total in which the entity holds assets.
- Located in individual foreign countries if the amount is material.

## 4.3 Major Customers

An entity that generates 10 percent or more of its revenue from sales to a single customer must disclose that fact, the total amount of revenues from each such customer, and the identity of the segment or segments reporting the revenues. The identity of the major customer need not be disclosed.

---

**Question 1**   MCQ-00127

The following information pertains to revenue earned by Timm Co.'s industry segments for the year ended December 31:

| Segment | Sales to Unaffiliated Customers | Intersegment Sales | Total Revenue |
|---|---|---|---|
| Alo | $ 5,000 | $ 3,000 | $ 8,000 |
| Bix | 8,000 | 4,000 | 12,000 |
| Cee | 4,000 | – | 4,000 |
| Dil | 43,000 | 16,000 | 59,000 |
| Combined | 60,000 | 23,000 | 83,000 |
| Elimination | – | (23,000) | (23,000) |
| Consolidated | $60,000 | – | $60,000 |

In conformity with the revenue test, Timm's reportable segments were:

a. Only Dil.
b. Only Bix and Dil.
c. Only Alo, Bix, and Dil.
d. Alo, Bix, Cee, and Dil.

# MODULE 6: SEC Reporting Requirements

FAR 2

## 1 Overview of SEC Reporting Requirements

The SEC requires that more than 50 forms be filed to comply with reporting requirements. These forms are filed electronically through the *electronic data gathering, analysis, and retrieval system* (EDGAR) and are available online to the public. The following is a brief overview of several significant forms that must be filed by companies registered with the SEC.

### 1.1 Securities Offering Registration Statements

When a company issues new securities, it is required to submit a registration statement to the SEC that includes:

- Disclosures about the securities being offered for sale.
- The relationship of the new securities to the company's other securities.
- Information similar to that filed in the annual filing.
- Audited financial statements.
- A description of business risk factors.

### 1.2 Form 10-K

Form 10-K must be filed annually by U.S. registered companies (issuers). The filing deadline for Form 10-K is 60 days after the end of the fiscal year for large accelerated filers, 75 days after the end of the fiscal year for accelerated filers, and 90 days after the end of the fiscal year for all other registrants. These forms contain financial disclosures, including a summary of financial data, management's discussion and analysis (MD&A), and audited financial statements.

> **Pass Key**
>
> A large accelerated filer is defined by the SEC as an issuer with a worldwide market value of outstanding common equity held by nonaffiliates of $700 million or more as of the last business day of the issuer's most recently completed second fiscal quarter. An accelerated filer is defined as an issuer with a worldwide market value of outstanding common equity held by nonaffiliates of $75 million or more, but less than $700 million. Smaller reporting companies, which are entities with annual revenues of less than $100 million, are excluded from the definition of large accelerated filers or accelerated filers.

### 1.3 Form 10-Q

Form 10-Q must be filed quarterly by U.S. registered companies (issuers). The filing deadline for Form 10-Q is 40 days after the end of the fiscal quarter for large accelerated filers and accelerated filers, and 45 days after the end of the fiscal quarter for all other registrants. This form contains unaudited financial statements prepared using U.S. GAAP, interim period MD&A, and certain disclosures.

## 1.4 Form 11-K

This is the annual report of a company's employee benefit plan(s).

## 1.5 Forms 20-F and 40-F

These forms must be filed annually by foreign private issuers. Form 40-F is filed by specific Canadian companies registered with the SEC and Form 20-F is filed by other non-U.S. registrants. These forms are similar to Form 10-K and contain financial disclosures, including a summary of financial data, management's discussion and analysis (MD&A), and audited financial statements. The financial statements may be prepared using U.S. GAAP, IFRS, or a comprehensive body of accounting principles other than U.S. GAAP or IFRS. If a comprehensive body of accounting principles other than U.S. GAAP or IFRS is used, certain reconciliations to U.S. GAAP must be provided.

## 1.6 Form 6-K

This form is filed semiannually by foreign private issuers. This form is similar to the Form 10-Q and contains unaudited financial statements, interim period MD&A, and certain disclosures.

## 1.7 Form 8-K

This form is filed to report major corporate events such as corporate asset acquisitions or disposals, changes in securities and trading markets, changes to accountants or financial statements, and changes in corporate governance or management.

## 1.8 Forms 3, 4, and 5

These forms are required to be filed by directors, officers, or beneficial owners of more than 10 percent of a class of equity securities of a registered company.

# 2 Regulation S-X

In Regulation S-X (17 CFR part 210), the SEC sets forth the form and content of and requirements for interim and annual financial statements to be filed with the SEC. The key provisions of Regulation S-X are outlined below.

## 2.1 Requirements for Interim Financial Statements

### 2.1.1 Review Requirement

Interim financial statements filed with the SEC must be reviewed by an independent public accountant and the review report must be filed with the financial statements.

### 2.1.2 Statements and Periods Presented

The interim financial statements should include the following:

- *Balance sheets* as of the end of the most recent fiscal quarter and as of the end of the preceding fiscal year. A balance sheet for the corresponding fiscal quarter for the preceding fiscal year is not required unless necessary to understand the impact of seasonal fluctuations.

- *Income statements* for the most recent fiscal quarter, for the period between the end of the preceding fiscal year and the end of the most recent fiscal quarter, and for the corresponding periods of the preceding fiscal year. The financial statements may also include income statements for the cumulative 12-month period ended during the most recent fiscal quarter and for the corresponding preceding period.

- *Statements of cash flows* for the period between the end of the preceding fiscal year and the end of the most recent fiscal quarter, and for the corresponding period for the preceding fiscal year. The financial statements may also present statements of cash flows for the cumulative 12-month period ended during the most recent fiscal quarter and for the corresponding preceding period.

### 2.1.3 Adjustments for Fair Presentation

Interim financial statements should reflect adjustments necessary to fairly state the results of the interim period, and a statement to that effect should be included in the notes to the financial statements. Adjustments include estimated provisions for bonus and profit-sharing arrangements that are normally determined or settled at year-end. If all such adjustments are of a normal recurring nature, a statement should be made to that effect. The financial statements should include a detailed description of the nature and amount of adjustments that are not normal recurring adjustments.

### 2.1.4 Condensed Financial Statements

Interim financial statements may be condensed financial statements.

### 2.1.5 Disclosure

Interim financial statement disclosures should be sufficient so that the interim information is not misleading.

- **Omitted Disclosures**

    Because users have access to the most recent annual financial statements, interim reports may omit the summary of significant accounting policies, the details of accounts that have not changed significantly since the end of the most recent fiscal year, and the detailed annual disclosures described below.

- **Required Disclosures**

    Disclosures should include:

    - Material contingencies.
    - Events subsequent to the end of the most recent fiscal year that have a material impact on the entity, including changes in accounting principles and practices (including the date of and reasons for the change), changes in estimates, changes in the status of long-term contracts, significant new borrowings or modifications of financing arrangements, and business combinations or dispositions.

## 2.2 Requirements for Annual Financial Statements

### 2.2.1 Audit Requirement

Annual financial statements filed with the SEC must be audited by an independent public accountant, and the audit report must be filed with the financial statements.

### 2.2.2 Periods Presented

The audited financial statements must include balance sheets for the two most recent fiscal years and statements of income, changes in owners' equity, and cash flows for each of the three fiscal years preceding the date of the most recent audited balance sheet.

> ## U.S. GAAP VS. IFRS
>
> IFRS requires, at a minimum, two balance sheets, two statements of comprehensive income (and net income, if using the two-statement approach), two statements of changes in equity, two statements of cash flows, and related notes.

### 2.2.3 Disclosure Requirements

The following items must be disclosed in the financial statements or notes:

- Dividends per share and in total for each class of shares
- Principles of consolidation or combination
- Assets subject to lien
- Defaults with respect to any issue of securities or credit agreements if the default or breach existed at balance sheet date and has not been subsequently cured
- Preferred shares disclosures
- Restrictions that limit the payment of dividends
- Significant changes in bonds, mortgages, or similar debt
- Summarized financial information of subsidiaries not consolidated and 50 percent or less owned entities
- Income tax expense
- Warrants or rights outstanding
- Related party transactions which affect the financial statements
- Repurchase and reverse repurchase agreements
- Accounting policies for derivative instruments

# 3 SEC XBRL Reporting Requirements

## 3.1 Definition of XBRL

XBRL (eXtensible Business Reporting Language) is a royalty-free, open specification for software that uses XML (eXtensible Markup Language) data tags to describe financial information for business and financial reporting. XBRL is a next-generation language after HTML. HTML tells computers how to display text. XML and XBRL tell computers how to interpret the context of the text.

## 3.2 Key XBRL Terms

### 3.2.1 Tag

A machine-readable code that gives a standard definition for each line item in an income statement, cash flow statement, balance sheet, or other financial or nonfinancial data, including data contained in the notes to the financial statements. Tags include descriptive labels, definitions, references to U.S. GAAP, and other elements that provide contextual information that allow data to be recognized and processed by software.

### 3.2.2 Taxonomy

A taxonomy defines the specific tags used for individual items of business and financial data. XBRL taxonomies include:

- **XBRL U.S. GAAP Financial Reporting Taxonomy:** The XBRL U.S. GAAP taxonomy is maintained and updated by the FASB and the Financial Accounting Foundation to reflect changes in U.S. GAAP and SEC financial statement disclosure requirements, as well as changes in common reporting practices.

- **XBRL IFRS Taxonomy:** The XBRL IFRS taxonomy is maintained by the IFRS Foundation to reflect changes in IFRS disclosure requirements. The development of the IFRS taxonomy is supported by the XBRL Quality Review Team and the XBRL Advisory Council.

- **Global Ledger Taxonomy:** A taxonomy independent of other reporting standards or system types that permits flexible, multinational consolidation.

- **Industry Specific Taxonomies:** Taxonomies have been created to accommodate industry specific financial reporting needs. Industry specific taxonomies exist for the commercial and industrial, banking and savings, real estate, insurance, and broker/dealer industries.

- **Company Specific Tags:** Companies can create their own tags when needed tags are not included in any existing taxonomy.

### 3.2.3 Instance Document

An instance document is an XBRL formatted document that contains tagged data.

## 3.3 SEC Interactive Data Rule

The SEC's Interactive Data Rule requires U.S. public companies and foreign private issuers that use U.S. GAAP, as well as foreign private issuers that use IFRS, to present financial statements and any applicable financial statement schedules in an exhibit prepared using XBRL. This exhibit is required with the filers' SEC registration statements, quarterly and annual reports, and reports 6-K and 8-K containing revised or updated financial statements.

### 3.3.1 Data Tagging Details

Tagged disclosures must include the primary financial statements, notes, and financial statement schedules. A filer's primary financial statements are required to be tagged in detail. Financial statement footnote and financial statement schedule tagging is broken into four different levels. Level 1 tagging is required for a company's first XBRL submission. Level 1 through Level 4 tagging is required starting one year from the filer's initial submission.

- **Level 1:** Each complete footnote and schedule is tagged as a single block of text.
- **Level 2:** Each significant accounting policy within the significant accounting policies footnote is tagged as a single block of text.
- **Level 3:** Each table within each footnote or schedule is tagged as a separate block of text.
- **Level 4:** Within each footnote or schedule, each amount (i.e., monetary value, percentage, and number) is required to be separately tagged.

### 3.3.2 30-Day Grace Period

Each company's initial interactive data exhibit, regardless of filing type, will be required within 30 days after the earlier of the due date or filing date of the related report or registration statement. Filers will also receive a 30-day grace period for the first filing that is required to have footnotes and schedules tagged using all levels of detail.

### 3.3.3 Posting to Corporate Website

Information submitted by a filer to the SEC in interactive data format must also be posted to the filer's corporate website no later than the end of the calendar day on which the filer filed or was required to file the related registration statement or report with the SEC, whichever is earlier.

> **Question 1**     MCQ-06078
>
> Which form is *not* required to include audited financial statements?
> a. Form 10-K
> b. Form 6-K
> c. Form 40-F
> d. Form 20-F

> **Question 2**     MCQ-08590
>
> Each of the following events is required to be reported to the United States Securities and Exchange Commission on Form 8-K, *except*:
> a. The creation of an obligation under an off-balance sheet arrangement of a registrant.
> b. The unregistered sale of equity securities.
> c. A change in a registrant's certifying accountant.
> d. The quarterly results of operations and financial condition of a registrant.

# MODULE 7: Special Purpose Frameworks

**FAR 2**

# 1 Special Purpose Frameworks

Special purpose frameworks, also known as other comprehensive bases of accounting (OCBOA), are non-GAAP presentations that have widespread understanding and support. OCBOA presentations include:

- The cash basis and modified cash basis of accounting.
- The tax basis of accounting.
- A definite set of criteria have substantial support that is applied to all material financial statement elements, such as price-level adjusted financial statements.
- A regulatory basis of accounting.

The cash basis, modified cash basis, and tax basis of accounting are the most commonly used special purpose frameworks.

## 1.1 General Presentation Guidelines

The following guidelines apply to all OCBOA financial statement presentations:

- Financial statement titles should differentiate the OCBOA financial statements from accrual basis financial statements.
- The required financial statements are the equivalents of the accrual basis balance sheet and income statement.
- The financial statements should explain changes in equity accounts.
- A statement of cash flows is not required.
- Disclosures in OCBOA financial statements should be similar to the disclosures in GAAP financial statements and should include:
  - A summary of significant accounting policies.
  - Informative disclosures similar to those required by GAAP for all financial statement items that are the same as or similar to those in GAAP financial statements.
  - Disclosures related to items not shown on the face of the financial statements, such as related party transactions, subsequent events, and uncertainties.

## 1.2 Cash Basis and Modified Cash Basis Financial Statements

Entities that are not required to use the accrual basis of accounting may choose to present cash basis or modified cash basis financial statements because they are simple to prepare and easy to understand. Cash basis financial statements are not well-suited for entities that have complex operations.

### 1.2.1 Cash Basis Financial Statements

Under the cash basis of accounting, revenues are recognized when cash is received and expenses are recognized when cash is paid. Cash basis financial statements are generally used by estates and trusts, civic ventures, and political campaigns and committees.

Cash basis financial statements include a statement of cash and equity and a statement of cash receipts and disbursements.

- **Statement of Cash and Equity**

    In pure cash basis financial statements, cash is the only asset, no liabilities are recorded, and equity is equal to cash.

- **Statement of Cash Receipts and Disbursements**

    The statement of cash receipts and disbursements includes the following:
    - Revenues received
    - Debt and equity proceeds
    - Proceeds from asset sales
    - Expenses paid
    - Debt repayments
    - Dividend payments
    - Payments for purchases of assets

### 1.2.2 Modified Cash Basis Financial Statements

Most for-profit and not-for-profit organizations that produce cash basis financial statements use the modified cash basis of accounting. The modified cash basis is a hybrid method that includes elements of both cash basis and accrual basis accounting. Modifications should not be so extensive that the modified cash basis financial statements become accrual basis financial statements.

- **Common Modifications**

    Modifications made to cash basis financial statements should have substantial support. Substantial support means that the modification is logical and equivalent to the accrual basis of accounting for that item. Common modifications include:
    - Capitalizing and depreciating fixed assets.
    - Accrual of income taxes.
    - Recording liabilities for long-term and short-term borrowings and the related interest expense.
    - Capitalizing inventory.
    - Reporting investments at fair value and recognizing unrealized gains and losses.

- **Presentation**

    Modified cash basis financial statements include the following:
    - A statement of assets and liabilities (modified cash basis) or a statement of assets and liabilities arising from cash transactions.
    - A statement of revenues and expenses and retained earnings (modified cash basis) or a statement of revenues collected and expenses paid.

    The specific elements included in these financial statements depend on the modifications made by the entity.

## 1.3 Income Tax Basis Financial Statements

Entities that are not required to use the accrual basis of accounting may choose to present income tax basis financial statements. In contrast to cash basis financial statements, tax basis financial statements are well-suited for entities that have complex operations.

### 1.3.1 Accounting Issues

Tax basis financial statements are prepared based on the methods and principles used to prepare the entity's tax return. Special accounting treatment must be given to nontaxable revenues and expenses not reported on the tax return.

Nontaxable revenues and expenses must be recognized in tax basis financial statements in the period received or paid for cash-basis taxpayers and in the period accruable for accrual-basis taxpayers. Nontaxable revenues and expenses may be reported as:

- Separate line items in the revenue and expense sections of the statement of revenues and expenses;
- Additions and deductions to net income; or
- A disclosure in a note.

### 1.3.2 Presentation

Tax-basis financial statements include the following:

- A statement of assets and liabilities and equity (income tax basis) or a balance sheet (income tax basis).
- A statement of revenues and expenses and retained earnings (income tax basis) or a statement of income (income tax basis).

The specific elements included in an entity's tax basis financial statements depend on the income and deductions reported on the entity's tax return.

# 2 Converting Cash Basis Financial Statements to the Accrual Basis

Many small businesses use the cash basis or modified cash basis of accounting to account for day-to-day operations. In certain circumstances (e.g., to obtain a loan from a bank, to report to owners, or to go public) such entities may be required to convert cash basis financial statements to accrual basis financial statements.

In order to make this conversion, it is essential to understand the differences between cash basis and accrual basis accounting:

|  | Cash Basis | Accrual Basis |
| --- | --- | --- |
| *Revenue Recognition* | Cash received | Realized or realizable and earned |
| *Expense Recognition* | Cash paid | Incurred/owed/benefit received |

## 2.1 Balance Sheet Conversion

The pure cash basis balance sheet reports only cash and equity. The modified cash basis balance sheet may also include inventory, investments at fair value, fixed assets net of accumulated depreciation, short-term and long-term debt, and/or accrued income taxes. To convert from a cash basis or modified cash basis balance sheet to an accrual basis balance sheet, all assets and liabilities existing at year-end that are not already included on the balance sheet must be added to the balance sheet, with equity equal to the difference between total assets and total liabilities.

Common balance sheet accounts to be recognized (if not already recognized under the modified cash basis) include:

- Accounts receivable
- Inventory
- Prepaid expenses
- Investments at fair value
- Fixed assets, net of accumulated depreciation
- Accounts payable
- Accrued liabilities
- Unearned revenue
- Interest payable
- Income taxes payable
- Short-term and long-term debt

## 2.2 Income Statement Conversion

The primary adjustments required to convert from a cash basis or modified cash basis income statement to an accrual basis income statement include:

- Converting cash basis revenue to accrual basis revenue.
- Converting cash paid for purchases to accrual basis cost of goods sold.
- Converting cash paid for operating expenses to accrual basis operating expenses.

### Pass Key

The process of converting from the cash basis income statement to the accrual basis income statement is the OPPOSITE of the process used to prepare the statement of cash flows from the accrual basis financial statements. If you understand how to prepare the operating section of the statement of cash flows, then you can reverse those calculations to convert cash basis revenues and expenses to accrual basis revenues and expenses.

Additional adjustments may be required to:

- Recognize noncash expenses (i.e., depreciation and amortization).
- Capitalize purchases of fixed assets (fixed asset purchases are cash disbursements under the cash basis).
- Reduce the fixed asset balance for assets sold during the period (fixed asset sales are cash receipts under the cash basis) and recognize gains/losses on the sale.
- Record debt proceeds received during the period as liabilities (debt proceeds are cash receipts under the cash basis).
- Record debt repayments as reductions in liabilities (debt repayments are cash disbursements under the cash basis).

## 2.2.1 Converting Cash Basis Revenue to Accrual Basis Revenue

The following formula can be used to convert from cash basis revenue to accrual basis revenue:

| Formula | Explanation |
|---|---|
| Cash basis revenue | From the cash basis income statement |
| + Ending AR | Revenue earned during the period but not yet collected from customers |
| − Beginning AR | Cash collected during the current period that was earned in prior periods |
| − Ending unearned revenue | Cash collected during the current period that will not be earned until future periods |
| + Beginning unearned revenue | Cash collected in prior periods that was earned in the current period |
| Accrual basis revenue | |

### Pass Key

This conversion process requires knowledge of beginning and ending balance sheet accounts (i.e., accounts receivable and unearned revenue). This is also true when converting cash paid for purchases to cost of goods sold, and when converting from cash paid for operating expenses to accrual basis operating expenses. These balance sheet account balances will be provided to you in any CPA Exam question requiring you to do the cash-to-accrual conversion, just as they are provided to you in questions related to the preparation of the statement of cash flows.

## 2.2.2 Converting Cash Paid for Purchases to Cost of Goods Sold

The following formula can be used to convert from cash paid for purchases to accrual basis cost of goods sold:

| Formula | Explanation |
|---|---|
| Cash paid for purchases | From the cash basis income statement |
| + Ending AP | Expenses incurred during the period but not yet paid |
| − Beginning AP | Expenses incurred during the prior period and paid in the current period |
| − Ending inventory | Purchases made during the current period that have not yet been sold |
| + Beginning inventory | Purchases made in prior periods that were sold during the current period |
| Cost of goods sold | |

# Special Purpose Frameworks

## 2.2.3 Converting Cash Paid for Operating Expenses to Accrual Basis Operating Expenses

The following formula can be used to convert from cash payments for operating expenses to accrual basis operating expenses:

| Formula | Explanation |
|---|---|
| Cash paid for operating expenses | From the cash basis income statement |
| + Ending accrued liabilities | Expenses incurred during the period but not yet paid |
| − Beginning accrued liabilities | Expenses incurred during the prior period and paid in the current period |
| − Ending prepaid expenses | Payments made during the current period that will benefit future periods |
| + Beginning prepaid expenses | Payments made in prior periods that benefited the current period |
| Accrual basis operating expenses | |

### Pass Key

This formula can be used to convert any operating expense, such as wages payable, from the cash basis to the accrual basis and can also be used to determine accrual basis interest payable or income taxes payable.

## 2.2.4 Converting Cash Basis Net Income to Accrual Basis Net Income

The above adjustments and calculations can be combined to calculate accrual basis net income from cash basis net income.

### Example 1 — Converting From Cash Basis to Accrual Basis

**Facts:** ABC Company had cash collections of $50,000, made cash payments of $20,000, and reported cash basis net income of $30,000 for Year 6. The company has determined the following balance sheet amounts for the beginning and ending of Year 6.

| Balance Sheet Account | 12/31/Year 6 | 1/1/Year 6 | Change |
|---|---|---|---|
| Accounts Receivable | $15,000 | $10,000 | $ 5,000 |
| Prepaid Insurance | 4,000 | 2,000 | 2,000 |
| Unearned Service Revenue | 5,000 | 20,000 | (15,000) |
| Salaries Payable | 7,000 | 3,000 | 4,000 |

ABC Company also purchased a piece of equipment on 1/1/ Year 6 for $5,000 in cash. The equipment has no salvage value and will be depreciated on a straight-line basis over five years.

**Required:** Compute ABC Company's Year 6 accrual basis revenue, expenses, and net income.

(continued)

(continued)

**Solution:** Calculate accrual basis revenue for Year 6:

| Formula | | Explanation |
|---|---|---|
| | $50,000 | Cash collections |
| + | 15,000 | Revenue earned during Year 6 but not yet collected from customers |
| − | 10,000 | Cash collected from customers in Year 6 that was earned in prior periods |
| − | 5,000 | Cash collected during Year 6 that will not be earned until future periods |
| + | 20,000 | Cash collected in prior periods that was earned in Year 6 |
| | $70,000 | Accrual basis revenue |

Calculate accrual basis expenses for Year 6:

| Formula | | Explanation |
|---|---|---|
| | $20,000 | Cash payments |
| − | 5,000 | Capitalized fixed asset purchase (not a Year 6 expense) |
| + | 1,000 | Depreciation |
| + | 7,000 | Salaries owed for Year 6 that are not yet paid |
| − | 3,000 | Salaries from Year 5 paid in Year 6 |
| − | 4,000 | Insurance paid in Year 6 that will benefit future periods |
| + | 2,000 | Insurance paid in prior years that benefitted Year 6 |
| | $18,000 | Accrual basis expenses |

Accrual basis net income = $70,000 − $18,000 = $52,000

---

## Question 1 — MCQ-00545

Ward, a consultant, keeps her accounting records on a cash basis. During Year 2, Ward collected $200,000 in fees from clients. At December 31, Year 1, Ward had accounts receivable of $40,000. At December 31, Year 2, Ward had accounts receivable of $60,000, and unearned fees of $5,000. On an accrual basis, what was Ward's service revenue for Year 2?

- a. $175,000
- b. $180,000
- c. $215,000
- d. $225,000

**Question 2**  MCQ-08564

Savor Co. had $100,000 in accrual basis pretax income for the year. At year-end, accounts receivable had increased by $10,000 and accounts payable had decreased by $6,000 from their prior year-end balances. Under the cash basis of accounting, what amount of pretax income should Savor report for the year?

    a. $84,000
    b. $96,000
    c. $104,000
    d. $116,000

# MODULE 8: Ratio Analysis

## 1 Ratio Analysis Overview

Ratios are financial indicators that distill relevant information about a business entity by quantifying the relationship among selected items on the financial statements. An entity's ratios may be compared with ratios of a different period for that entity. An entity's ratios may also be compared with competitor ratios and industry ratios. These comparative analyses identify trends that may be important to investors, lenders, and other interested parties.

Key financial ratios may be classified as liquidity ratios, activity ratios, profitability ratios, and coverage ratios. Gi Company's financial statements provide the financial data for the ratio calculations throughout this module.

> **Pass Key**
>
> Ratio questions on the financial exam may require a simple ratio calculation, an interpretation of what the ratio means, or an analysis of the effects of a change.
>
> When asked to analyze whether a ratio is likely to increase or decrease, you can gain efficiency by knowing the following:
>
> - The numerator has a direct relationship with the ratio. For example, an increase in the numerator results in an increase in the ratio.
>
> $$\frac{\text{Numerator} \uparrow}{\text{Denominator}} = \text{Resulting ratio} \uparrow$$
>
> - The denominator has an inverse relationship with the ratio. For example, an increase in the denominator results in a decrease in the ratio.
>
> $$\frac{\text{Numerator}}{\text{Denominator} \uparrow} = \text{Resulting ratio} \downarrow$$
>
> Sometimes, when both the numerator and denominator are affected by a given change, the final result (increase or decrease) is not easy to determine. The best way to answer questions such as these is to make up numbers and plug them into the ratio formula.

## Gi Company
### Balance Sheet

| Current Assets: | 12/31/Year 2 | 12/31/Year 1 |
|---|---|---|
| Cash and cash equivalents | $ 50,000 | $ 35,000 |
| Trading securities (at fair value) | 75,000 | 65,000 |
| Accounts receivable | 300,000 | 390,000 |
| Inventory (at lower of cost or market) | 290,000 | 275,000 |
| Total current assets | 715,000 | 765,000 |
| Investments available for sale (at fair value) | 350,000 | 300,000 |
| **Fixed Assets:** | | |
| Property, plant, and equipment (at cost) | 1,900,000 | 1,800,000 |
| Less: accumulated depreciation | (180,000) | (150,000) |
| | 1,720,000 | 1,650,000 |
| Goodwill | 30,000 | 35,000 |
| Total assets | $2,815,000 | $2,750,000 |
| **Current Liabilities:** | | |
| Accounts payable | $ 150,000 | $ 125,000 |
| Notes payable | 325,000 | 375,000 |
| Accrued and other liabilities | 220,000 | 200,000 |
| Total current liabilities | 695,000 | 700,000 |
| **Long-Term Debt:** | | |
| Bonds and notes payable | 650,000 | 700,000 |
| Total liabilities | 1,345,000 | 1,400,000 |
| **Stockholders' Equity:** | | |
| Common stock (100,000 shares outstanding) | 500,000 | 500,000 |
| Additional paid-in capital | 670,000 | 670,000 |
| Retained earnings | 300,000 | 180,000 |
| Total equity | 1,470,000 | 1,350,000 |
| Total liabilities and equity | $2,815,000 | $2,750,000 |
| **Income Statement for Year Ended:** | Year 2 | Year 1 |
| Sales | $1,800,000 | $1,700,000 |
| Cost of goods sold | (1,000,000) | (940,000) |
| Gross profit | 800,000 | 760,000 |
| Operating expenses | (486,970) | (476,970) |
| Interest expense | (10,000) | (10,300) |
| Net income before income taxes | 303,030 | 272,730 |
| Income taxes (34 percent) | (103,030) | (92,730) |
| Net income after income taxes | $ 200,000 | $ 180,000 |
| Earnings per share | $ 2 | $ 1.80 |
| **Other Financial Information:** | | |
| Operating cash flows | $ 275,000 | $ 265,000 |
| Dividends per share | 0.80 | -0- |
| Market price per share | 12 | 11 |

## 2　Liquidity Ratios

*Liquidity ratios* are measures of a firm's short-term ability to pay maturing obligations.

### 2.1　Current Ratio

$$\text{Current ratio} = \frac{\text{Current assets}}{\text{Current liabilities}}$$

$$\text{Year 2} = \frac{\$715{,}000}{\$695{,}000} = 1.03$$

$$\text{Year 1} = \frac{\$765{,}000}{\$700{,}000} = 1.09$$

(Industry average = 1.50)

The ratio, and therefore Gi's ability to meet its short-term obligations, is low compared with the industry's average.

### 2.2　Quick Ratio

$$\text{Quick ratio} = \frac{\text{Cash and cash equivalents} + \text{Short-term marketable securities} + \text{Receivable (net)}}{\text{Current liabilities}}$$

$$\text{Year 2} = \frac{\$50{,}000 + \$75{,}000 + \$300{,}000}{\$695{,}000} = 0.61$$

$$\text{Year 1} = \frac{\$35{,}000 + \$65{,}000 + \$390{,}000}{\$700{,}000} = 0.70$$

(Industry average = 0.80)

The industry average of 0.80 is higher than Gi's ratio, which indicates that Gi may have trouble meeting short-term needs.

Ratio Analysis FAR 2

# 3 Activity Ratios

*Activity ratios* are measures of how effectively an enterprise is using its assets.

> **Pass Key**
>
> Turnover ratios generally use average balances [i.e., (beginning balance + ending balance) / 2] for balance sheet components. However, on some recent CPA Exam questions, candidates have been instructed to use year-end balances instead. Please be sure to read the question carefully to determine the appropriate method to use.
>
> The ratios given in this module match the most recent ratios provided by the AICPA as an exhibit on task-based simulations requiring ratio calculations.

## 3.1 Accounts Receivable Turnover

$$\text{Accounts receivable turnover} = \frac{\text{Sales (net)}}{\text{Average accounts receivable (net)}}$$

$$\text{Year 2} = \frac{\$1,800,000}{(\$300,000 + \$390,000) / 2}$$

$$= \frac{\$1,800,000}{\$345,000}$$

$$= 5.22 \text{ times}$$

This ratio indicates the receivables' quality and indicates the success of the firm in collecting outstanding receivables. Faster turnover gives credibility to the current and acid-test ratios.

## 3.2 Days Sales in Accounts Receivable

$$\text{Days sales in accounts receivable} = \frac{\text{Ending accounts receivable (net)}}{\text{Sales (net) / 365}}$$

$$\text{Year 2} = \frac{\$300,000}{\$1,800,000 / 365}$$

$$= 60.83 \text{ days}$$

This ratio indicates the average number of days required to collect accounts receivable.

### 3.3 Inventory Turnover

$$\text{Inventory turnover} = \frac{\text{Cost of goods sold}}{\text{Average inventory}}$$

$$\text{Year 2} = \frac{\$1,000,000}{(\$290,000 + \$275,000)/2}$$

$$= \frac{\$1,000,000}{\$282,500}$$

$$= 3.54 \text{ times}$$

This measure of how quickly inventory is sold is an indicator of enterprise performance. The higher the turnover, in general, the better the performance.

### 3.4 Days in Inventory

$$\text{Days in inventory} = \frac{\text{Ending inventory}}{\text{Cost of goods sold}/365}$$

$$\text{Year 2} = \frac{\$290,000}{\$1,000,000/365}$$

$$= 105.85 \text{ days}$$

This ratio indicates the average number of days required to sell inventory.

### 3.5 Accounts Payable Turnover

$$\text{Accounts payable turnover} = \frac{\text{Cost of goods sold}}{\text{Average accounts payable}}$$

$$\text{Year 2} = \frac{\$1,000,000}{(\$150,000 + \$125,00)/2}$$

$$= 7.27 \text{ times}$$

This ratio indicates the number of times trade payables turn over during the year. A low turnover may indicate a delay in payment, such as from a shortage of cash.

# Ratio Analysis

## 3.6 Days of Payables Outstanding

$$\text{Days of payables outstanding} = \frac{\text{Ending accounts payable}}{\text{Cost of goods sold} / 365}$$

$$\text{Year 2} = \frac{\$150,000}{\$1,000,000 / 365}$$

$$= 54.75$$

This ratio indicates the average length of time trade payables are outstanding before they are paid.

## 3.7 Cash Conversion Cycle

$$\text{Cash conversion cycle} = \text{Days sales in accounts receivable} + \text{Days in inventory} - \text{Days of payables outstanding}$$

$$\text{Year 2} = 60.83 \text{ days} + 105.85 \text{ days} - 54.75 \text{ days}$$

$$= 111.93 \text{ days}$$

This ratio indicates the average length of time it takes from when the company pays cash for an inventory purchase to when the company receives cash from a sale.

## 3.8 Asset Turnover

$$\text{Asset turnover} = \frac{\text{Sales (net)}}{\text{Average total assets}}$$

$$\text{Year 2} = \frac{\$1,800,000}{(\$2,815,000 + \$2,750,000) / 2}$$

$$= \frac{\$1,800,000}{\$2,782,500}$$

$$= 0.65 \text{ times}$$

This ratio is an indicator of how Gi makes effective use of its assets. A high ratio indicates effective asset use to generate sales.

# 4 Profitability Ratios

*Profitability ratios* are measures of the success or failure of an enterprise for a given time period.

## 4.1 Profit Margin

$$\text{Profit margin} = \frac{\text{Net income}}{\text{Sales (net)}}$$

$$\text{Year 2} = \frac{\$200{,}000}{\$1{,}800{,}000}$$

$$= 11.11\%$$

## 4.2 Return on Assets (ROA)

$$\text{Return on assets} = \frac{\text{Net income}}{\text{Average total assets}}$$

$$\text{Year 2} = \frac{\$200{,}000}{\$2{,}782{,}500}$$

$$= 7.2\%$$

## 4.3 DuPont Return on Assets

$$\text{DuPont return on assets} = \text{Profit margin} \times \text{Asset turnover}$$

$$\text{Year 2} = \frac{\text{Net income}}{\text{Sales (net)}} \times \frac{\text{Sales (net)}}{\text{Average total assets}}$$

$$= 11.11\% \times 0.65 \text{ times} = 7.22\%$$

Note that this ratio uses both profit margin and the asset turnover. This ratio allows for increased analysis of the changes in the percentages. The profit margin indicates the percentage return on each sale, and the asset turnover indicates the effective use of assets in generating that sale.

## 4.4 Return on Equity

$$\text{Return on equity} = \frac{\text{Net income}}{\text{Average total equity}}$$

$$\text{Year 2} = \frac{\$200{,}000}{(\$1{,}470{,}000 + \$1{,}350{,}000)/2}$$

$$= 14.18\%$$

## 4.5 Return on Sales

$$\text{Return on sales} = \frac{\text{Income before interest income, interest expense, and taxes}}{\text{Sales (net)}}$$

$$\text{Year 2} = \frac{\$303{,}030 + \$10{,}000}{\$1{,}800{,}000}$$

$$= 17.39\%$$

## 4.6 Gross (Profit) Margin

$$\text{Gross (profit) margin} = \frac{\text{Sales (net)} - \text{Cost of goods sold}}{\text{Sales (net)}}$$

$$\text{Year 2} = \frac{\$800{,}000}{\$1{,}800{,}000}$$

$$= 44.44\%$$

## 4.7 Operating Cash Flow Ratio

$$\text{Operating cash flow ratio} = \frac{\text{Cash flow from operations}}{\text{Current liabilities}}$$

$$\text{Year 2} = \frac{\$275{,}000}{\$695{,}000}$$

$$= 0.396$$

# 5 Coverage Ratios

*Coverage ratios* are measures of security or protection for long-term creditors/investors.

## 5.1 Debt-to-Equity

$$\text{Debt-to-equity ratio} = \frac{\text{Total liabilities}}{\text{Total equity}}$$

$$\text{Year 2} = \frac{\$1,345,000}{\$1,470,000} = 0.91$$

$$\text{Year 1} = \frac{\$1,400,000}{\$1,350,000} = 1.04$$

This ratio indicates the degree of protection to creditors in case of insolvency. The lower this ratio the better the company's position.

## 5.2 Total Debt Ratio

$$\text{Total debt ratio} = \frac{\text{Total liabilities}}{\text{Total assets}}$$

$$\text{Year 2} = \frac{\$1,345,000}{\$2,815,000} = 47.78\%$$

$$\text{Year 1} = \frac{\$1,400,000}{\$2,750,000} = 50.91\%$$

This debt ratio indicates that approximately half of the assets are financed by creditors.

## 5.3 Equity Multiplier

$$\text{Equity multiplier} = \frac{\text{Total assets}}{\text{Total equity}}$$

$$\text{Year 2} = \frac{\$2,815,000}{\$1,470,000} = 1.91$$

$$\text{Year 1} = \frac{\$2,750,000}{\$1,350,000} = 2.01$$

Ratio Analysis

FAR 2

## 5.4 Times Interest Earned

$$\text{Times interest earned} = \frac{\text{Income before interest expense and taxes}}{\text{Interest expense}}$$

Or:

$$= \frac{\text{Earnings before interest and taxes}}{\text{Interest expense}}$$

$$\text{Year 2} = \frac{\$303,030 + \$10,000}{\$10,000}$$

$$= 31.30 \text{ times}$$

This ratio reflects the ability of a company to cover interest charges. It uses income before interest and taxes to reflect the amount of income available to cover interest expense.

# 6 Investor Ratios

## 6.1 Earnings per Share

$$\text{Earnings per share} = \frac{\text{Income available to common shareholders}}{\text{Weighted average common shares outstanding}}$$

$$\text{Year 2} = \frac{\$200,000}{100,000 \text{ shares}}$$

$$= \$2/\text{share}$$

## 6.2 Price Earnings Ratio

$$\text{Price earnings ratio} = \frac{\text{Price per share}}{\text{Basic earnings per share}}$$

$$\text{Year 2} = \frac{\$12}{\$2}$$

$$= 6$$

This statistic indicates the investment potential of an enterprise; a rise in this ratio indicates that investors are pleased with the firm's opportunity for growth.

## 6.3 Dividend Payout

$$\text{Dividend payout} = \frac{\text{Cash dividends}}{\text{Net income}}$$

$$\text{Year 2} = \frac{\$0.80 \text{ dividend per share} \times 100{,}000 \text{ shares outstanding}}{\$200{,}000}$$

$$= 40\%$$

This ratio indicates the portion of current earnings being paid out in dividends. (Alternatively, calculate dividend payout as Dividends per share / Earnings per share = $0.80 / $2 = 40%.)

# 7 Limitations of Ratios

Although ratios are easy to compute, they depend entirely on the reliability of the data on which they are based (e.g., estimates, historical costs, fair value, etc.). Additional information is also valuable when analyzing a company. Horizontal analysis measures the dollar and percentage change over a period of time, which is useful in evaluating trends and noting material changes from period to period. Vertical analysis is helpful in reducing statement items to a common size, as all elements are expressed as a percentage of a common number (e.g., income statement elements are expressed as a percentage of sales revenue). Vertical analysis assists in period-to-period comparison, but also allows for comparability among other entities as the statement is in a common size format.

---

**Question 1**  MCQ-05956

The following information was taken from Baxter Department Store's financial statements:

| | |
|---|---|
| Inventory at January 1 | $ 100,000 |
| Inventory at December 31 | 300,000 |
| Net sales | 2,000,000 |
| Net purchases | 700,000 |

What was Baxter's inventory turnover for the year ending December 31?

a. 2.5
b. 3.5
c. 5
d. 10

**Question 2**  MCQ-05432

Stent Co. had total assets of $760,000, capital stock of $150,000, and retained earnings of $215,000. What was Stent's debt-to-equity ratio?

- a. 2.63
- b. 1.08
- c. 0.52
- d. 0.48

# MODULE 9
# Partnerships

FAR 2

## 1 Admission of a Partner

A new partner may be admitted by the purchase of an existing partnership interest or by investing additional capital into the partnership.

### 1.1 By Purchase or Sale of Existing Partnership Interest

A partner, with the consent of all partners, may sell his partnership interest to a new partner. Payment for the partnership interest by the new partner would go directly to the selling partner. The retiring partner could sell his interest in the same manner to the remaining partners.

- **No Journal Entry**

    No entries are made on the partnership books, except for the change of name on the capital account. Transactions of this type do not affect the assets, liabilities, or total capital of the partnership.

### 1.2 Formation of a Partnership

Contributions to a partnership are recorded as follows:

1. Assets are valued at fair value.
2. Liabilities assumed are recorded at their present value.
3. Partner's capital account therefore equals the difference between the fair value of the contributed assets less the present value of liabilities assumed.

> **Pass Key**
>
> It is important to distinguish the tax and GAAP rules relating to the formation of a partnership:
> - GAAP Rule = Use FV of asset contributed
> - Tax Rule = Use NBV of assets contributed

### 1.3 Creation of a New Partnership Interest With Investment of Additional Capital

When a new partnership interest is created by the investment of additional capital into the partnership, the total capital of the partnership does change, and the purchase price can be equal to, more than, or less than book value.

# Partnerships

## 1.3.1 Exact Method—Equal to Book Value

When the purchase price is equal to the book value of the capital account purchased, no goodwill or bonuses are recorded.

- **Rules—Problem-Solving Steps**

  1. Determine the exact amount a new partner will have to pay to get his capital account in the exact proportional interest to the new net assets of the partnership.
  2. There is no goodwill or bonus.
  3. Old partners' capital account "dollars" stay the same.
  4. Old partners' "% ownership" changes, but that change is generally not a requirement on the CPA Exam.

### Pass Key

Problems that deal with the exact method will always ask, "How much should the new partner contribute in order to have an x% interest in the new partnership?" and will not include references to goodwill or bonuses in the transaction.

### Example 1  New Partner Pays Book Value

**Facts:** A, B, and C are partners in a three-person partnership. They have capital accounts of $20,000, $30,000, and $50,000, respectively. A, B, and C decide to admit D as a new partner with a 25 percent interest in the new partnership.

**Required:** If D pays book value, how much should D contribute in order to have a 25 percent interest in the partnership?

**Solution:**

Equity of new partnership = $20,000 + $30,000 + $50,000 + D's contribution

Since D will contribute an amount equal to 25 percent of the total book value of the new partnership, D's contribution can be shown as 25 percent of total new equity.

Total new equity = $100,000 + 0.25 Total new equity

$100,000 = 0.75 Total new equity;  $\dfrac{\$100{,}000}{0.75}$ = Total new equity

Total new equity = $133,333

0.25 total new equity = $33,333

Thus, D should pay $33,333 for a 25 percent interest.

## 1.3.2 Bonus Method—Recognize Intercapital Transfer

When the purchase price is more or less than the book value of the capital account purchased, bonuses are adjusted between the old and new partners' capital accounts and do not affect partnership assets.

- **Rules—Problem-Solving Steps**
    1. Determine total capital and the interest to the new partner.
    2. If interest less than amount contributed, bonus to old partner(s).
    3. If interest greater than amount contributed, bonus to new partner.

---

### Pass Key

**B** = **B**onus = **B**alance in total capital accounts controls the capital account allocation.

---

### Pass Key

Under the bonus method, the bonus will be credited to the following partner:

- Existing partners—when new partner pays more than NBV
- New partner—when new partner pays less than NBV

---

### Illustration 1    Bonus to Existing Partners

A and B share profits and losses 60:40, and have capital accounts of $30,000 and $10,000, respectively. C has agreed to invest $35,000 for a one-third interest in the new ABC partnership. Since the partnership has decided not to recognize goodwill, the total capital of the resulting partnership is $75,000 ($30,000 + $10,000 + $35,000). C has purchased a one-third interest, so the balance in C's capital account should equal one-third of $75,000 or $25,000. The extra $10,000 paid by C is recorded as a bonus to the old partners and is shared according to their profit and loss ratio.

*Journal entry to record the admission of C into the partnership and recognize the bonus to existing partners:*

| DR/CR | Account | Debit | Credit |
|---|---|---|---|
| DR | Cash | $35,000 | |
| CR | A, Capital ($10,000 × 60%) | | $ 6,000 |
| CR | B, Capital ($10,000 × 40%) | | 4,000 |
| CR | C, Capital (30,000 + 10,000 + 35,000 = 75,000 × 1/3) | | 25,000 |

# Illustration 2 — Bonus to New Partners

It is possible for the existing partners to credit a bonus to a new partner. In the example above, if C had invested $14,000 for a one-third interest in the resulting partnership, C would have received a bonus from A and B, because the one-third interest in the partnership is $18,000 [1/3 ($30,000 + $10,000 + $14,000)] and exceeds C's contribution of $14,000. The $4,000 ($18,000 − $14,000) is a bonus credited to C by A and B, and is charged to A's and B's capital accounts according to their profit and loss ratio (60:40).

*Journal entry to record the partnership and recognize the bonus to new partners:*

| | | | |
|---|---|---|---|
| DR | Cash | $14,000 | |
| DR | A, Capital ($4,000 × 60%) | 2,400 | |
| DR | B, Capital ($4,000 × 40%) | 1,600 | |
| CR | C, Capital (30,000 + 10,000 + 14,000 = 54,000 × 1/3) | | $18,000 |

### 1.3.3 Goodwill Method—Recognized Intangible Asset

Goodwill is recognized based upon the total value of the partnership implied by the new partner's contribution.

- **Rules—Problem-Solving Steps**

    1. Compute new "net assets before GW" (before goodwill) after admitting new (or paying old) partner.

    2. Memo: Compute new "capitalized" net assets (= total net worth) and compare "Capitalized Net Assets" with "Net Assets before Goodwill;" and

    3. The "Difference" is "Goodwill" to be allocated to the old partners according to their old partnership profit ratios.

## Pass Key

**G** = **G**oodwill = **G**oing in investment (dollars) controls capital account allocation and goodwill calculation.

## Illustration 3  Goodwill Credited to Capital Accounts of Existing Partners

A and B share profits and losses 60:40, and have capital accounts of $30,000 and $10,000, respectively. On the basis of A and B's present total capital, C has agreed to invest $35,000 for a one-third interest in the new ABC partnership. The partnership decides to recognize goodwill.

C pays $35,000 for a one-third interest in the partnership; goodwill is recognized as the difference between the implied value of the business and the total of the tangible net assets represented by the partners' capital account.

| | |
|---|---:|
| Implied value ($35,000 × 3 = $105,000) | $105,000 |
| Total partner's capital accounts ($35,000 + $10,000 + $30,000 = $75,000) | (75,000) |
| Goodwill | $ 30,000 |

*Journal entry to record the admission of C into the partnership and recognize goodwill:*

| | | | |
|---|---|---:|---:|
| DR | Cash | $35,000 | |
| DR | Goodwill | 30,000 | |
| CR | A, Capital (60% × $30,000) | | $18,000 |
| CR | B, Capital (40% × $30,000) | | 12,000 |
| CR | C, Capital (equals amount contributed by C) | | 35,000 |

### Pass Key

The following summary will help you remember the differences among the above approaches:

**Exact Method**
- The incoming partner's capital account is their actual contribution. (You must calculate.)
- No adjustment to the existing partner's capital accounts is required.

**Bonus Method**
- Balance in total capital accounts controls the computation.
- The incoming partner's capital account is their percentage of the partnership total NBV (after their contribution).
- Adjust the existing partner's capital accounts to balance.

**Goodwill Method**
- Going in investment (dollars) controls the computation.
- The incoming partner's capital account is their actual contribution.
- Goodwill (implied) is determined based upon the incoming partner's contribution, and shared by the existing partners.

Partnerships    FAR 2

---

**Question 1**    MCQ-04646

Eagle and Falk are partners with capital balances of $45,000 and $25,000, respectively. They agree to admit Robb as a partner. After the assets of the partnership are revalued, Robb will have a 25 percent interest in capital and profits, for an investment of $30,000.

What amount should be recorded as a *bonus* to the original partners?

- a. $0
- b. $5,000
- c. $7,500
- d. $20,000

---

**Question 2**    MCQ-00721

Eagle and Falk are partners with capital balances of $45,000 and $25,000, respectively. They agree to admit Robb as a partner. After the assets of the partnership are revalued, Robb will have a 25 percent interest in capital and profits, for an investment of $30,000.

What amount should be recorded as *goodwill* to the original partners?

- a. $0
- b. $5,000
- c. $7,500
- d. $20,000

---

# 2 Profit and Loss Distribution

Income or loss is distributed among the partners in accordance with their agreement, and in the absence of an agreement all partners share equally irrespective of what their capital accounts reflect or the amount of time each partner spends on partnership affairs.

Unless the partnership agreement provides otherwise, all payments for interest on capital, salaries, and bonuses are deducted prior to any distribution in the profit and loss ratio. Such payments are provided for in full, even in a loss situation.

---

### Pass Key

Partnership accounts may be different from their respective profit and loss ratios. The reason for this is that distributions/withdrawals will be at different times and for different reasons.

## Example 2 — Profit and Loss Distribution

**Facts:** A, B, and C, copartners, had capital balances at the end of the year (but before profit distribution) of $30,000, $60,000, and $90,000, respectively. The partnership's profit for the year, excluding any payments to partners, was $200,000. The partnership agreement provided for interest of 8 percent on ending capital balances, a salary to A of $10,000, and a bonus to C of 15 percent of partnership profits before any distribution to partners. The profit and loss ratios were 20 percent to A, 30 percent to B, and 50 percent to C.

**Required:** On the basis of this data, what was the total distribution to each partner?

**Solution:**

|  | Total | A | B | C |
|---|---|---|---|---|
| Total profit | $200,000 |  |  |  |
| 15% guaranteed bonus to C | (30,000) |  |  | $ 30,000 |
| Interest on ending capital balances (8% × capital balance) | (14,400) | $ 2,400 | $ 4,800 | 7,200 |
| Salary to A | (10,000) | 10,000 |  |  |
| Balances | 145,600 | 12,400 | 4,800 | 37,200 |
| Distribution of balance in P&L ratio 20%; 30%; 50% | (145,600) | 29,120 | 43,680 | 72,800 |
| Total distribution of P&L | $ 0 | $41,520 | $48,480 | $110,000 |

**Note:** All interest, salaries, and bonuses are deducted from total profit to arrive at the amount of profit and loss distributed in the profit and loss ratio. If these items exceed the amount of profit, then the resulting loss is distributed in the profit and loss ratio.

---

### Question 3 — MCQ-00722

During the current year, Young and Zinc maintained average capital balances in their partnership of $160,000 and $100,000, respectively. The partners receive 10 percent interest on average capital balances, and residual profit or loss is divided equally. Partnership profit before interest was $4,000. By what amount should Zinc's capital account change for the year?

- a. $1,000 decrease.
- b. $2,000 increase.
- c. $11,000 decrease.
- d. $12,000 increase.

# 3 Withdrawal of a Partner

## 3.1 Bonus Method

The difference between the balance of the withdrawing partner's capital account and the amount that person is paid is the amount of the "bonus." The "bonus" is allocated among the remaining partners' capital accounts in accordance with their remaining profit and loss ratios. Although the partnership's identifiable assets may be revalued to their fair value at the date of withdrawal, any goodwill implied by the excess payment to the retiring partner is *not* recorded.

*Step 1: Journal entry to revalue the assets to reflect fair value:*

| | | | |
|---|---|---|---|
| DR | Asset adjustment | $XXX | |
| CR | A, Capital (%) | | $XXX |
| CR | B, Capital (%) | | XXX |
| CR | X, Capital (%) | | XXX |

*Step 2: Journal entry to pay off withdrawing partner:*

| | | | |
|---|---|---|---|
| DR | A, Capital (%) | $XXX | |
| DR | B, Capital (%) | XXX | |
| DR | X, Capital (100%) | XXX | |
| CR | Cash | | $XXX |

## 3.2 Goodwill Method

The partners may elect to record the implied goodwill in the partnership based on the payment to the withdrawing partner. The amount of the implied goodwill is allocated to *all* of the partners in accordance with their profit and loss ratios. After the allocation of the implied goodwill of the partnership, the balance in the withdrawing partner's capital account should equal the amount that person is to receive in the final settlement of his or her interest.

*Step 1: Journal entry to revalue the assets to reflect fair value:*

| | | | |
|---|---|---|---|
| DR | Asset adjustment | $XXX | |
| CR | A, Capital (%) | | $XXX |
| CR | B, Capital (%) | | XXX |
| CR | X, Capital (%) | | XXX |

*Step 2: Journal entry to record goodwill to make withdrawing partner's capital account equal payoff:*

| | | | |
|---|---|---|---|
| DR | Goodwill | $XXX | |
| CR | A, Capital (%) | | $XXX |
| CR | B, Capital (%) | | XXX |
| CR | X, Capital (%) | | XXX |

*Step 3: Journal entry to pay off withdrawing partner:*

| | | | |
|---|---|---|---|
| DR | X, Capital (100%) | $XXX | |
| CR | Cash | | $XXX |

# 4 Liquidation of a Partnership

The process of winding up the affairs of a partnership after dissolution is generally referred to as liquidation. Liquidation involves the realization of cash from the disposal of partnership assets. Creditors or partners may agree to accept specific partnership assets in full or partial satisfaction of their claims against the partnership.

## 4.1 Order of Preference Regarding Distribution of Assets

Where a solvent partnership is dissolved and its assets are reduced to cash, the cash must be used to pay the partnership's liabilities in the following order:

### 4.1.1 Creditors

Creditors, including partners who are creditors, must be paid before the noncreditor partners receive any payments.

### 4.1.2 Partners' Capital

Right of offset between a partner's loans to and from the partnership and that person's capital balances generally exists in liquidation.

## 4.2 Losses Considered in Liquidation

1. All possible losses must be provided for in a liquidation before any distribution is made to the partners. The rule to follow is not to distribute any cash until maximum potential losses have been taken into consideration.

2. Losses in liquidating a partnership are charged to the partners in accordance with the partnership agreement; in the absence of such an agreement, the losses are shared equally.

## 4.3 Convert Noncash Assets

The general procedure in a liquidation is that all noncash assets are converted into cash, all liabilities are paid, and the remainder, if any, is distributed to the partners.

## 4.4 Gain or Loss on Realization

The liquidation of partnership assets may result in:

1. A gain on realization;
2. A loss on realization; or
3. A loss on realization resulting in a capital deficiency.

## 4.5 Capital Deficiency

A capital deficiency is a debit balance in a partner's capital account and indicates that the partnership has a claim against the partner for the amount of the deficiency.

### 4.5.1 Right of Offset

If a partner with a capital deficiency has a loan account (the partnership has payable to the partner), the partnership has a legal right to offset and may use the loan account to satisfy the capital deficiency.

# Partnerships

## 4.5.2 Remaining Partners Charged

If a deficiency still exists, the remaining partners must absorb the deficiency according to their respective (remaining) profit and loss ratios.

## 4.6 Partnership Liquidation Schedule

The objective of the schedule is to distribute cash, as it becomes available, to the partners.

It is important that no partner is either overpaid or underpaid as the result of any cash distributed by the liquidator because that person could be personally liable for overpayments made to a partner that were not repaid.

### Pass Key

Generally, the "poor" partners do not have any money to repay their shortage; so (generally), the "richest" partners are paid first.

Many multiple-choice exam questions ask for ending partners' balances after liquidation of a partner or the partnership; some questions merely ask for amount of "cash" to be paid upon liquidation. If all "other" assets and all liabilities are liquidated, the answer will be the same: Cash = Partners' balances.

### Illustration 4  Partnership Liquidation Schedule

After discontinuing the regular business operations and closing the books, A, B, and C decide to liquidate their partnership. The partnership agreement provides for income or loss to be divided 50 percent to A, 30 percent to B, and 20 percent to C. The following is an adjusted trial balance before commencing liquidation:

| | | |
|---|---|---|
| Cash | $20,000 | |
| Noncash assets | 75,000 | |
| Liabilities, creditors | | $25,000 |
| Partner advance, A | | 15,000 |
| Partner advance, C | | 5,000 |
| Partner's capital, A | | 10,000 |
| Partner's capital, B | | 20,000 |
| Partner's capital, C | | 20,000 |
| | $95,000 | $95,000 |

## Illustration 5: A, B, C Partnership—Statement of Liquidation and Realization Date

| | Cash | Noncash Assets | Liabilities Outside Creditors | Liabilities Partner's Advance A | Liabilities Partner's Advance C | Partner's Capital A 50%* | Partner's Capital B 30%* | Partner's Capital C 20%* |
|---|---|---|---|---|---|---|---|---|
| **Assumption 1: Gain on realization (noncash assets sold for $125,000)** | | | | | | | | |
| Balances—before realization | 20,000 | 75,000 | 25,000 | 15,000 | 5,000 | 10,000 | 20,000 | 20,000 |
| Sale of *noncash* assets & division of gain | 125,000 | (75,000) | | | | 25,000 | 15,000 | 10,000 |
| Balances after realization | 145,000 | 0 | 25,000 | 15,000 | 5,000 | 35,000 | 35,000 | 30,000 |
| Payment of liabilities | (25,000) | | (25,000) | | | | | |
| Balances | 120,000 | | 0 | 15,000 | 5,000 | 35,000 | 35,000 | 30,000 |
| Payment of partners' advances | (20,000) | | | (15,000) | (5,000) | | | |
| Balances | 100,000 | | | 0 | 0 | 35,000 | 35,000 | 30,000 |
| Distribution of cash | (100,000) | | | | | (35,000) | (35,000) | (30,000) |
| **Assumption 2: Loss on realization (noncash assets sold for $65,000)** | | | | | | | | |
| Balances—before realization | 20,000 | 75,000 | 25,000 | 15,000 | 5,000 | 10,000 | 20,000 | 20,000 |
| Sale of noncash assets & division of loss | 65,000 | (75,000) | | | | (5,000) | (3,000) | (2,000) |
| Balances—after realization | 85,000 | 0 | 25,000 | 15,000 | 5,000 | 5,000 | 17,000 | 18,000 |
| Payment of liabilities | (25,000) | | (25,000) | | | | | |
| Balances | 60,000 | | 0 | 15,000 | 5,000 | 5,000 | 17,000 | 18,000 |
| Payment of partners' advances | (20,000) | | | (15,000) | (5,000) | | | |
| Balances | 40,000 | | | 0 | 0 | 5,000 | 17,000 | 18,000 |
| Distribution of cash | (40,000) | | | | | (5,000) | (17,000) | (18,000) |
| **Assumption 3: (see the notes that follow) Loss on realization—capital deficiency (noncash assets sold for $15,000)** | | | | | | | | |
| Balances—before realization | 20,000 | 75,000 | 25,000 | 15,000 | 5,000 | 10,000 | 20,000 | 20,000 |
| Sale of noncash assets & division of loss | 15,000 | (75,000) | | | | (30,000) | (18,000) | (12,000) |
| Balances—after realization | 35,000 | 0 | 25,000 | 15,000 | 5,000 | (20,000) | 2,000 | 8,000 |
| Payment of liabilities | (25,000) | | (25,000) | | | | | |
| Balances | 10,000 | | 0 | 15,000 | 5,000 | (20,000) | 2,000 | 8,000 |
| Transfer of A—advance account | | | | (15,000) | | 15,000 | | |
| Balances | 10,000 | | | 0 | 5,000 | (5,000) | 2,000 | 8,000 |
| Division of "A's" deficiency | | | | | | 5,000 | (3,000) | (2,000) |
| Balances | 10,000 | | | | 5,000 | 0 | (1,000) | 6,000 |
| Division of "B's" deficiency | | | | | | | 1,000 | (1,000) |
| Balances | 10,000 | | | | 5,000 | | 0 | 5,000 |
| Distribution of cash | (10,000) | | | | (5,000) | | | (5,000) |

*Profit and loss ratio

**Notes to Assumption 3:**

1. It is important to remember that a partnership has a claim against any partner with a capital deficiency. In this example the $15,000 credit balance in A's advance account constitutes a preferred claim once A's capital balance is in a deficiency position. A's advance account is transferred to A's capital account to offset part of the $20,000 capital deficiency balance.

2. All possible losses must be charged to the partners' capital accounts in their income and loss ratios before any distribution is made. A still has a $5,000 capital deficiency that B and C must absorb in their respective income and loss ratios before any cash distribution is made. B and C will have a claim of $3,000 and $2,000, respectively, against A for absorbing the $5,000 capital deficiency that is calculated as follows:

    (B) 3/5 x $5,000 = $3,000
    (C) 2/5 x $5,000 = $2,000

3. Any partner may pay a capital deficiency in cash directly to the partnership.

4. A partnership is not completely liquidated and their affairs wound up until all claims, including those of partners, are settled.

## NOTES

# FAR 3

# Assets and Related Topics

## Module

| | | |
|---|---|---|
| 1 | Cash and Cash Equivalents | 3 |
| 2 | Trade Receivables | 9 |
| 3 | Inventory | 21 |
| 4 | PP&E: Cost Basis | 39 |
| 5 | PP&E: Depreciation and Disposal | 49 |
| 6 | Nonmonetary Transactions | 61 |
| 7 | Intangibles | 69 |
| 8 | Impairment | 79 |

# MODULE 1
# Cash and Cash Equivalents

FAR 3

## 1 Definition and Classifications

Cash includes both currency and demand deposits with banks and/or other financial institutions. It also includes deposits that are similar to demand deposits (can be added to or withdrawn at any time without penalty).

The term cash equivalents broadens the definition of cash to include short-term, highly liquid investments that are both readily convertible to cash and so near their maturity when acquired by the entity (90 days or less from date of purchase) that they present insignificant risk of changes in value.

### 1.1 Examples of Cash and Cash Equivalents

- Coin and currency on hand (including petty cash)
- Checking accounts
- Savings accounts
- Money market funds
- Deposits held as compensating balances against borrowing arrangements with a lending institution that are *not* legally restricted
- Negotiable paper
  - Bank checks, money orders, traveler's checks, bank drafts, and cashier's checks
  - Commercial paper and Treasury bills
  - Certificates of deposit (having original maturities of 90 days or less)

### 1.2 Items Not Cash or Cash Equivalents

- Time certificates of deposit (if original maturity over 90 days)
- Legally restricted deposits held as compensating balances against borrowing arrangements with a lending institution

### 1.3 Restricted or Unrestricted

Cash is classified as *unrestricted* or *restricted*. Restricted cash is cash that has been set aside for a specific use or purpose (e.g., the purchase of property, plant, and equipment). Unrestricted cash is used for all current operations. The nature, amount, and timing of restrictions should be disclosed in the footnotes.

- If the restriction is associated with a current asset or current liability, classify as a current asset but separate from unrestricted cash.
- If the restriction is associated with a non-current asset or non-current liability, classify as a non-current asset but separate from either the Investments or Other Assets section.

# Cash and Cash Equivalents

- **Examples of Restrictions**
  - If any portion of cash and cash equivalents is contractually restricted because of financing arrangements with a credit institution (called a compensating balance), that portion should be separately reported as "restricted cash" in the balance sheet.
  - If any portion of cash and cash equivalents is restricted by management, it should be reported as restricted cash and as a current or long-term asset (depending on the anticipated date of disbursement).
  - Some industries (such as public utilities) report the amount of cash and cash equivalents as the last asset on the balance sheet because they report assets in inverse order of liquidity.

---

### Example 1     Items Included in Cash Balance

**Facts:** Smith Corporation's cash ledger balance on December 31, Year 7, was $160,000. On the same date Smith held the following items in its safe:

- A $5,000 check payable to Smith, dated January 2, Year 8, that was not included in the December 31 checkbook balance.
- A $3,500 check payable to Smith, deposited December 22 and included in the December 31 checkbook balance, which was returned non-sufficient funds (NSF). The check was redeposited January 2, Year 8, and cleared January 7.
- A $25,000 check, payable to a supplier and drawn on Smith's account, that was dated and recorded December 31, but was not mailed until January 15, Year 8.

**Required:** Determine the amount of cash that Smith should report in its December 31, Year 7, balance sheet.

**Solution:** Smith's cash balance is calculated as follows:

| | |
|---|---:|
| Unadjusted balance of Smith's cash ledger account, December 31, Year 7 | $160,000 |
| Add: check payable to supplier dated and recorded on December 31, Year 7, but not mailed until January 15, Year 8 | 25,000 |
| Less: NSF check returned by bank on December 30, Year 7 | (3,500) |
| Adjusted balance, December 31, Year 7 | $181,500 |

---

# 2 Bank Reconciliations

There are two general forms of bank reconciliations. One form is called a simple reconciliation. The other widely used form is entitled reconciliation of cash receipts and disbursements.

## 2.1 Components of a Simple Reconciliation

Differences between the cash balance reported by the bank and the cash balance per the depositor's records are explained through the preparation of the bank reconciliation. Several factors bring about this differential.

- **Deposits in Transit**

    Funds sent by the depositor to the bank that have not been recorded by the bank and deposits made after the bank's cutoff date will not be included in the bank statement. In both cases, the balance per the depositor's records will be higher than those of the bank.

- **Outstanding Checks**

    Checks written for payment by the depositor that have not been presented to the bank will result in a higher balance per bank records than per depositor records.

- **Service Charges**

    Service charges are deducted by the bank. The depositor will not deduct this amount from its records until it is made aware of the charge, usually in the following month. Balance per books is overstated until this amount is subtracted.

- **Bank Collections**

    The bank may make collections on the depositor's behalf, increasing the depositor's bank balance. If the depositor is not aware the collection was credited to its balance, the balance per depositor's records will be understated.

- **Errors**

    Errors made by either the bank or the depositors are another cause for difference.

- **Non-sufficient Funds (NSF)**

    The bank may have charged the depositor's account for a dishonored check and the check may not have been redeposited until the following month. This would overstate the depositor's book balance as of the balance sheet date.

- **Interest Income**

    Usually the depositor does not keep track of average daily cash balances, and so will add this amount to its records once made aware of this revenue. Balance per books is understated until this amount is added.

## 2.2 Steps in a Simple Bank Reconciliation

Although other methods can be used, the most common procedure is to reconcile both book and bank balances to a common "true" balance. That balance should then appear on the balance sheet under the caption "cash and cash equivalents."

Procedures:

1. Book balance is adjusted to reflect any corrections reported by the bank (e.g., NSF checks, notes collected by the bank and credited to the account, monthly service charges, and other bank charges, such as check printing charges).

2. After the above adjustments are made:

    > **Adjusted book balance = True balance**

3. The bank balance per the bank statement is reconciled to the "true balance," determined above.

# Example 2 — Simple Bank Reconciliation

**Facts:** Burbank Company's records reflect a $12,650 cash balance on November 30, Year 3. Burbank's November bank statement reports the following amounts:

| | |
|---|---:|
| Cash balance | $10,050 |
| Bank service charge | 10 |
| NSF check | 90 |

Deposits in transit equal $3,000 and outstanding checks are $500.

**Required:** Determine Burbank's November 30, Year 3, adjusted cash balance.

**Solution:** Bank reconciliation for November Year 3.

| | | |
|---|---:|---:|
| Balance per books | | $12,650 |
| Less: bank service charge | $10 | |
| NSF check | 90 | (100) |
| Adjusted cash balance | | $12,550 |
| | | |
| Balance per bank | | $10,050 |
| Add: deposits in transit | | 3,000 |
| | | $13,050 |
| Less: outstanding checks | | (500) |
| Adjusted cash balance | | $12,550 |

## 2.3 Reconciliation of Cash Receipts and Disbursements

The reconciliation of cash receipts and disbursements, commonly referred to as the four-column reconciliation, or proof of cash, serves as a proof of the proper recording of cash transactions.

Additional information is required in preparing the four-column reconciliation. The bank reconciliation information for the present month and that of the prior month must be obtained.

The object of the four-column approach is to reconcile any differences between the amount the depositor has recorded as cash receipts and the amount the bank has recorded as deposits. Likewise, this approach determines any differences between amounts the depositor has recorded as cash disbursements and amounts the bank has recorded as checks paid.

## Illustration 1    Four-Column Reconciliation

Based on the information in the previous example and additional information for the month of December, Burbank's reconciliation of cash receipts and disbursements follows:

**Burbank Company**
**Reconciliation of Cash Receipts and Cash Disbursements**
For the Month of December, Year 3

|  | Balance 11/30/Year 3 | December Receipts | December Payments | Balance 12/31/Year 3 |
|---|---|---|---|---|
| **Balance per depositor's books** | $12,550 | $12,950 | $4,948 | $20,552 |
| Note collected by bank |  | 3,050 |  | 3,050 |
| Bank service charge |  |  | 15 | (15) |
| NSF check received from customer |  | (285) |  | (285) |
| Error in recording check No. 350 |  |  | 54 | (54) |
| Adjusted balances | $12,550 | $15,715 | $5,017 | $23,248 |
|  |  |  |  |  |
| **Balance per bank records** | $10,050 | $15,000 | $2,400 | $22,650 |
| Deposit in transit: |  |  |  |  |
|   November 30 | 3,000 | (3,000) |  |  |
|   December 31 |  | 4,000 |  | 4,000 |
| Outstanding checks: |  |  |  |  |
|   November 30 | (500) |  | (500) |  |
|   December 31 |  |  | 3,402 | (3,402) |
| NSF check |  | (285) | (285) |  |
| Adjusted balances | $12,550 | $15,715 | $5,017 | $23,248 |

Cash and Cash Equivalents

**Question 1**  MCQ-00061

Cook Co. had the following balances at December 31, Year 2:

| | |
|---|---|
| Cash in checking account | $350,000 |
| Cash in money market account | 250,000 |
| U.S. Treasury bill, purchased 12/1/Year 2, maturing 2/28/Year 3 | 800,000 |
| U.S. Treasury bond, purchased 3/1/Year 2, maturing 2/28/Year 3 | 500,000 |

Cook's policy is to treat as cash equivalents all highly liquid investments with a maturity of three months or less when purchased. What amount should Cook report as cash and cash equivalents in its December 31, Year 2, balance sheet?

    a. $600,000
    b. $1,150,000
    c. $1,400,000
    d. $1,900,000

# MODULE 2 Trade Receivables

FAR 3

## 1 Accounts Receivable

Accounts receivable are oral promises to pay debts and are generally classified as current assets. They are classified either as trade receivables (accounts receivable from purchasers of the company's goods and services) or nontrade receivables (accounts receivable from persons other than customers, such as advances to employees, tax refunds, etc.).

The net realizable value of accounts receivable is the balance of the accounts receivable account adjusted for allowances for receivables that may be uncollectible, sales discounts, and sales returns and allowances.

### 1.1 Account Analysis Format

The preparation of an account analysis may increase your ability to "squeeze" or otherwise derive various answers to CPA Exam questions regarding accounts receivable, allowance for doubtful accounts, and many other accounts.

**Blank Analysis Format**

| | |
|---|---|
| ○ Beginning balance | $ _____ |
| ○ Add: _____ | _____ |
| _____ | _____ |
| Subtotal | _____ |
| ○ Subtract: _____ | _____ |
| _____ | _____ |
| ○ Ending balance | $ _____ |

### Pass Key

The blank analysis format is a tool that is merely an "add-subtract" form of a t-account that can be used to obtain the correct result to many examination questions. You will find that this format will assist you in "squeezing" answers to many questions related to balance sheet accounts on the CPA Exam.

Trade Receivables FAR 3

### Illustration 1    Accounts Receivable Account Analysis Format

| | | | |
|---|---|---:|---:|
| Beginning balance | | | $ 90,000 |
| Add: | Credit sales | | 800,000 |
| | Subtotal | | 890,000 |
| Subtract: | Cash collected on account | $810,000 | |
| | Accounts receivable converted to notes receivable | 7,000 | |
| | Accounts receivable written off as bad debts | 23,000 | (840,000) |
| Ending balance | | | $ 50,000 |

## 1.2 Valuation of Accounts Receivable With Discounts

In general, accounts receivable should be initially valued at the original transaction amount (i.e., historical cost); however, that amount may be adjusted for sales or cash discounts.

The offer of a cash discount on payments made within a specified period is widely used by many companies. This practice encourages prompt payment and assumes that customers will take advantage of the discount.

### 1.2.1 Sales or Cash Discounts

The discount is generally based on a percentage of the sales price. For example, a discount of 2/10, n/30 offers the purchaser a discount of 2 percent of the sales price if the payment is made within 10 days. If the discount is not taken, the entire (gross) amount is due in 30 days. The calculation of cash discounts typically follows one of two forms; the determination of which method to use is generally based on the company's experience with its customers taking discounts.

1. **Gross Method**

    The gross method records a sale without regard to the available discount. If payment is received within the discount period, a sales discount (contra-revenue) account is debited to reflect the sales discount.

2. **Net Method**

    The net method records sales and accounts receivable net of the available discount. An adjustment is not needed if payment is received within the discount period. However, if payment is received after the discount period, a sales discount not taken account (revenue) must be credited.

## Example 1 — Sales Discounts, Gross and Net Methods

**Facts:** Gearty Company sells $100,000 worth of goods to Smith Company. The terms of the sale are 2/10, n/30.

**Required:** Prepare the journal entries for the accounts receivable Gearty Company would record using both the gross method and the net method.

**Solution:**

*The journal entries at the date of sale:*

|     |                      | Gross     |           | Net      |          |
| --- | -------------------- | --------- | --------- | -------- | -------- |
| DR  | Accounts receivable  | $100,000  |           | $98,000  |          |
| CR  | Sales                |           | $100,000  |          | $98,000  |

*The journal entries if payment is <u>received within</u> the discount period:*

|     |                       | Gross     |           | Net      |          |
| --- | --------------------- | --------- | --------- | -------- | -------- |
| DR  | Cash                  | $98,000   |           | $98,000  |          |
| DR  | Sales discounts taken | 2,000     |           |          |          |
| CR  | Accounts receivable   |           | $100,000  |          | $98,000  |

*The journal entries if payment is <u>not received within</u> the discount period.*

|     |                           | Gross     |           | Net       |          |
| --- | ------------------------- | --------- | --------- | --------- | -------- |
| DR  | Cash                      | $100,000  |           | $100,000  |          |
| CR  | Accounts receivable       |           | $100,000  |           | $98,000  |
| CR  | Sales discounts not taken |           |           |           | 2,000    |

### 1.2.2 Trade Discounts

Trade discounts (quantity discounts) are quoted in percentages. Sales revenues and accounts receivable are recorded net of trade discounts. Trade discounts are applied sequentially.

## Example 2 — Application of Trade Discounts

**Facts:** Caitlyn & Brown sells coats with a list price of $1,000. They are sold to stores for list price minus trade discounts of 40 percent and 10 percent.

**Required:** Calculate the Caitlyn & Brown accounts receivable balance if 100 coats are sold on credit.

**Solution:**

| | |
|---|---:|
| List price | $100,000 |
| Less: 40% discount | (40,000) |
| List price after 40% discount | 60,000 |
| Less: 10% discount | (6,000) |
| Accounts receivable balance | $ 54,000 |

## 1.3 Estimating Uncollectible Accounts Receivable

Accounts receivable should be presented on the balance sheet at their net realizable value. Thus, the amount recorded at initial transaction should be reduced by the amount of any uncollectible receivables. Two methods of recognizing uncollectible accounts receivable exist, the direct write-off method and the allowance method. However, only the allowance method is consistent with accrual accounting (and thus acceptable for GAAP).

### 1.3.1 Direct Write-off Method (Not GAAP)

Under the direct write-off method, the account is written off and the bad debt is recognized when the account becomes uncollectible. The direct write-off method is not GAAP because it does not properly match the bad debt expense with the revenue (note, however, that the direct write-off method is the method used for federal income tax purposes). An additional weakness of this method is that accounts receivable are always overstated because no attempt is made to account for the unknown bad debts included in the balance on the financial statements.

---

**Example 3  Direct Write-off Method**

**Facts:** On December 15, Year 1, Roe Company recorded a credit sale of $10,000. On July 1, Year 2, the company determined that the account receivable was uncollectible.

**Required:** Prepare the journal entry.

**Solution:**

*Journal entry to record the account balance of $10,000 as uncollectible:*

| DR | Bad debt expense | $10,000 | |
|---|---|---|---|
| CR | Accounts receivable | | $10,000 |

The revenue recorded in Year 1 is not properly matched to the bad debt expense recorded in Year 2.

---

### 1.3.2 Allowance Method (GAAP)

Under the current expected credit losses (CECL) model, the balance in the allowance for uncollectibles should be based on current conditions, past experience, and future expectations. The allowance should take into account the possibility of credit losses over the entire life of each receivable.

A percentage of each period's ending accounts receivable is estimated to be uncollectible. The amount determined is charged to bad debts of the period and the credit is made to a valuation account such as "allowance for uncollectible accounts." When specific known amounts are written off, they are debited to the allowance account. There are two generally accepted methods of estimating uncollectible or doubtful accounts under the allowance method.

- **Percentage of Accounts Receivable at Year-end Method (Balance Sheet Approach)**

    Uncollectible accounts may also be estimated as a certain percentage of accounts receivable at year-end. Note that under this method, the amount calculated is the ending balance that should be in the allowance for doubtful accounts on the balance sheet. Therefore, the difference between the unadjusted balance and the desired ending balance is debited (or credited) to the bad debt expense account. This percentage is also based on the company's experience.

## Example 4 — Percentage of Accounts Receivable Method

**Facts:** DEF Co. uses a percentage for uncollectibles based on the year-end balance in accounts receivable. DEF Co. estimates that the balance in the allowance account must be 2 percent of year-end accounts receivable of $80,000. The balance in the allowance account is $1,000 credit before adjustment.

**Required:** Prepare the journal entry to record the adjustment to the allowance account at year-end.

**Solution:**

| | |
|---|---:|
| Required ending balance ($80,000 × 0.02) | $1,600 |
| Minus existing balance before adjustment | (1,000) |
| Increase (credit) to allowance account needed | $ 600 |

*Journal entry to record increase in allowance account:*

| | | | |
|---|---|---:|---:|
| DR | Bad debt expense | $600 | |
| CR | Allowance for uncollectible accounts | | $600 |

**Note:** If the $1,000 balance in the allowance account had been a debit, we would have added it to the required ending balance. The entry would have then been for $2,600.

- **Aging of Receivables Method (Balance Sheet Approach)**

    Another method that can be used in estimating uncollectible accounts is aging of accounts receivable. A schedule is prepared categorizing accounts by the number of days or months outstanding. Each category's total dollar amount is then multiplied by a percentage representing uncollectibility based on past experience. The sum of the product for each aging category will be the desired ending balance in the allowance account.

## Illustration 2 — Aging of Receivables Method

The balance in the allowance account before adjustment is $1,000 credit. The analysis of the aging of receivables requires the allowance account to have a net balance of $1,600.

| Classification by Due Date | Balances in Each Category | Estimated % Uncollectible | Estimated Uncollectible Account |
|---|---:|---:|---:|
| Current | $10,000 | 0.01 | $ 100 |
| 31–61 days | 6,667 | 0.03 | 200 |
| 61–90 days | 5,000 | 0.10 | 500 |
| Over 90 days | 4,000 | 0.20 | 800 |
| | $25,667 | | $1,600 |

Summarized from an analysis of individual invoices. The journal entry would be the same as that shown in the previous example.

## 1.4 Bad Debt Expense

The amount charged to earnings for the bad debt expense of the period includes the following:

1. The provision made each period throughout the year; and
2. An adjustment made at year-end to increase/decrease the balance in the allowance for uncollectible accounts, if needed.

## 1.5 Write-off of a Specific Account Receivable

When a receivable is formally determined to be uncollectible, the following entry is made:

| | | | |
|---|---|---|---|
| DR | Allowance for doubtful accounts | $XXX | |
| CR | Accounts receivable | | $XXX |

## 1.6 Subsequent Collection of Accounts Receivable Written Off

If a collection is made on a receivable that was previously written off, the accounting procedure depends on the method of accounting used.

### 1.6.1 Direct Write-off Method

*The "uncollectible accounts recovered" account is a revenue account.*

| | | | |
|---|---|---|---|
| DR | Cash | $XXX | |
| CR | Uncollectible accounts recovered | | $XXX |

### 1.6.2 Allowance Method

*To restore the account previously written off:*

| | | | |
|---|---|---|---|
| DR | Accounts receivable | $XXX | |
| CR | Allowance for uncollectible accounts | | $XXX |

*To record the cash collection on the account:*

| | | | |
|---|---|---|---|
| DR | Cash | $XXX | |
| CR | Accounts receivable | | $XXX |

## Example 5 — Calculation of Bad Debt Expense

**Facts:** Bost Company, at December 31, Year 5, changed to the aging of accounts receivable approach for measuring its allowance for uncollectible accounts. Bost previously used the percent of sales approach.

The following data are available:

| | |
|---|---:|
| Allowance for uncollectible accounts, 1/1/Year 5 | $20,000 |
| Provision for uncollectible accounts during Year 5 (2% of credit sales of $700,000) | 14,000 |
| Bad debts written off, 11/30/Year 5 | 12,500 |
| Estimated total of uncollectible accounts, per aging at 12/31/Year 5 | 20,500 |

**Required:** Calculate the bad debt expense for Year 5 using the new approach. Prepare the journal entry to record the write-off of bad debts at November 30, Year 5. Prepare the journal entry to record any necessary adjustment to the allowance for uncollectible accounts at year-end Year 5.

**Solution:**

*Allowance*

| | |
|---|---:|
| Balance, 1/1/Year 5 | $20,000 |
| Plus: Year 5 provision | 14,000 |
| Less: Year 5 write-offs | (12,500) |
| Preliminary balance | 21,500 |
| Desired balance | (20,500) |
| Decrease needed | $ 1,000 |

*Provision*

| | |
|---|---:|
| Original provision | $14,000 |
| Less: necessary adjustment | (1,000) |
| Year 5 bad debt expense | $13,000 |

*Journal entry to record the write-off of bad debts at November 30, Year 5:*

| | | | |
|---|---|---:|---:|
| DR | Allowance for uncollectible accounts | $12,500 | |
| CR | Accounts receivable | | $12,500 |

*Journal entry to record the adjustment at December 31, Year 5:*

| | | | |
|---|---|---:|---:|
| DR | Allowance for uncollectible accounts | $1,000 | |
| CR | Bad debt expense | | $1,000 |

## 1.7 Pledging (Assignment)

Pledging is the process whereby the company uses existing accounts receivable as collateral for a loan. The company retains title to the receivables but "pledges" that it will use the proceeds to pay the loan. Pledging requires only note disclosure. The accounts receivable account is not adjusted.

## 1.8 Factoring of Accounts Receivable

Factoring is a process by which a company can convert its receivables into cash by assigning them to a "factor" either without or with recourse. Under factoring arrangements, the customer may or may not be notified.

### 1.8.1 Without Recourse

If a sale is nonrecourse, it means that the sale is final and that the assignee (the factor) assumes the risk of any losses on collections. If the buyer is unable to collect all of the accounts receivable, it has no recourse against the seller.

*Journal entry to factor accounts receivable without recourse:*

| | | | |
|---|---|---|---|
| DR | Cash | $XXX | |
| DR | Due from factor (factor's margin) | XXX | |
| DR | Loss on sale of receivable | XXX | |
| CR | Accounts receivable | | $XXX |

The entry to the asset account "Due from Factor" reflects the proceeds retained by the factor. This amount protects the factor against sales returns, sales discounts, allowances, and customer disputes. If the returns, discounts, and allowances are less than the retained amount, the balance will be returned to the seller.

### 1.8.2 With Recourse

If a sale is on a recourse basis, it means that the factor has an option to re-sell any uncollectible receivables back to the seller.

If accounts receivable are transferred to a factor *with recourse*, two treatments are possible. The transfer may be considered either a sale or a borrowing (with the receivables as mere collateral).

- In order to be considered a sale, the transfer must meet the following conditions:
  - The transferor's (seller's) obligation for uncollectible accounts can reasonably be estimated.
  - The transferor surrenders control of the future economic benefits of the receivables to the buyer.
  - The transferor cannot be required to repurchase the receivables, but may be required to replace the receivables with other similar receivables.
- If any of the above conditions are not met, the transfer is treated as a loan.

## 1.9 Securitization

In a securitization, accounts receivable are transferred to a different entity, such as a trust or subsidiary. The entity then sells securities that are collateralized by the accounts receivable. Investors receive cash as the accounts receivable are paid.

# 2 Notes Receivable

Notes receivable are written promises to pay a debt, and the writing is called a promissory note. Notes receivable are classified the same as accounts receivable. They are either a current asset or a long-term asset, depending on when collection will occur.

## 2.1 Valuation and Presentation

For financial statement purposes, unearned interest and finance charges are deducted from the face amount of the related promissory note. This is necessary in order to state the receivable at its present value.

Also, if the promissory note is noninterest bearing or the interest rate is below market, the value of the note should be determined by imputing the market rate of interest and determining the value of the promissory note by using the effective interest method. Interest-bearing promissory notes issued in an arm's-length transaction are presumed to be issued at the market rate of interest.

## 2.2 Discounting Notes Receivable

Discounted notes receivable arise when the holder endorses the note (with or without recourse) to a third party and receives a sum of cash. The amount received by the holder is determined by applying a *discount rate* to the maturity value of the note. The difference between the amount of cash received by the holder and the maturity value of the note is the *discount*.

### 2.2.1 With Recourse

If the note is discounted with recourse, the holder remains contingently liable for the ultimate payment of the note when it becomes due. Notes receivable that have been discounted with recourse are reported on the balance sheet with a corresponding contra-account (Notes Receivable Discounted) indicating that they have been discounted to a third party. Alternatively, the notes receivable may be removed from the balance sheet and the contingent liability disclosed in the notes to the financial statements.

### 2.2.2 Without Recourse

If the note is discounted without recourse, the holder assumes no further liability. Notes receivable that have been discounted without recourse have essentially been sold outright and should, therefore, be removed from the balance sheet.

---

**Example 6  Discounting a Note at a Bank**

**Facts:** Jordan Corporation has a $40,000, 90-day note from a customer dated September 30, Year 3, due December 30, Year 3, and bearing interest at 12 percent. On October 30, Year 3 (30 days after issue), Jordan Corporation takes the note to its bank, which is willing to discount it at a 15 percent rate. The note was paid by Jordan's customer at maturity on December 30, Year 3 (60 days later).

**Required:** Compute the amount to be paid by the bank for the note. Determine the amount that Jordan Corporation should report as net interest income from the note.

(continued)

Trade Receivables

# (continued)

**Solution:**

1. Calculate the *maturity value* of the note by *adding the interest to the face* amount of the note, as follows:

   | | |
   |---|---|
   | Face value of the note | $40,000 |
   | Interest on note to maturity | 1,200  ($40,000 × 12% × 90/360) |
   | Payoff value of note at maturity | $41,200 |

2. Calculate the *bank discount on the payoff value at maturity*, as follows:

   15% discount × 60/360 days × $41,200 = $1,030

3. Compute the amount *paid by the bank* for the note.

   | | |
   |---|---|
   | Payoff value at maturity | $41,200 |
   | Less: bank's discount | (1,030) |
   | Amount paid by bank for note | $40,170 |

4. Determine the *interest income* (or expense) by subtracting the face value of the note from the amount paid by the bank for the note, as follows:

   | | |
   |---|---|
   | Amount paid by bank for the note | $40,170 |
   | Less: face value of the note | (40,000) |
   | Interest income to Jordan Corporation | $   170 |

## 2.2.3 Dishonored Discounted Notes Receivable

When a discounted note receivable is dishonored, the contingent liability should be removed by a debit to Notes Receivable Discounted and a credit to Notes Receivable. Notes Receivable Dishonored should be recorded to the estimated recoverable amount of the note. A loss is recognized if the estimated recoverable amount is less than the amount required to settle the note and any applicable penalties.

---

**Question 1**  MCQ-00034

Gar Co. factored its receivables without recourse with Ross Bank. Gar received cash as a result of this transaction, which is best described as a:

   **a.** Loan from Ross collateralized by Gar's accounts receivable.
   **b.** Loan from Ross to be repaid by the proceeds from Gar's accounts receivable.
   **c.** Sale of Gar's accounts receivable to Ross, with the risk of uncollectible accounts retained by Gar.
   **d.** Sale of Gar's accounts receivable to Ross, with the risk of uncollectible accounts transferred to Ross.

| **Question 2** | MCQ-00059 |
|---|---|

Roth Inc. received from a customer a one-year, $500,000 note bearing annual interest of 8 percent. After holding the note for six months, Roth discounted the note at Regional Bank at an effective interest rate of 10 percent. What amount of cash did Roth receive from the bank?

- a. $540,000
- b. $523,810
- c. $513,000
- d. $495,238

**NOTES**

# MODULE 3 Inventory

FAR 3

## 1 Types of Inventories

Inventories of goods must be periodically counted, valued, and recorded in the books of account of a business. In general, there are four types of inventories, which are assets that are held for resale.

- **Retail Inventory:** Retail inventory is inventory that is resold in substantially the same form in which it was purchased.
- **Raw Materials Inventory:** Raw materials inventory is inventory that is being held for use in the production process.
- **Work-in-Process Inventory (WIP):** WIP is inventory that is in production but incomplete.
- **Finished Goods Inventory:** Finished goods inventory is production inventory that is complete and ready for sale.

## 2 Goods and Materials to Be Included in Inventory

The general rule is that any goods and materials in which the company has legal title should be included in inventory, and legal title typically follows possession of the goods. Of course, there are many exceptions and special applications of this general rule.

### 2.1 Goods in Transit

Title passes from the seller to the buyer in the manner and under the conditions explicitly agreed on by the parties. If no conditions are explicitly agreed on ahead of time, title passes from the seller to the buyer at the time and place where the seller's performance regarding delivery of goods is complete.

FOB means "free on board" and requires the seller to deliver the goods to the location indicated as FOB at the seller's expense. The following terminology is most commonly used in passing title from the seller to the buyer:

- **FOB Shipping Point:** With FOB shipping point, title passes to the buyer when the seller delivers the goods to a common carrier. Goods shipped in this manner should be included in the buyer's inventory upon shipment.
- **FOB Destination:** With FOB destination, title passes to the buyer when the buyer receives the goods from the common carrier.

### 2.2 Shipment of Nonconforming Goods

If the seller ships the wrong goods, the title reverts to the seller upon rejection by the buyer. Thus, the goods should not be included in the buyer's inventory, even if the buyer possesses the goods prior to their return to the seller.

## 2.3 Consigned Goods

In a consignment arrangement, the seller (the "consignor") delivers goods to an agent (the "consignee") to hold and sell on the consignor's behalf. The consignor should include the consigned goods in its inventory because title and risk of loss is retained by the consignor even though the consignee possesses the goods.

If all of the conditions in 2.3 (above) are not met, there is no revenue recognition from a sale. Revenue will be recognized when the goods are sold to a third party. Until the sale, the goods remain in the consignor's inventory. Title passes directly to the third-party buyer (not to the consignee and then to the third-party buyer) at the point of sale.

## 2.4 Public Warehouses

Goods stored in a public warehouse and evidenced by a warehouse receipt should be included in the inventory of the company holding the warehouse receipt. The reason is that the warehouse receipt evidences title even though the owner does not have possession.

## 2.5 Sales With a Mandatory Buyback

Occasionally, as part of a financing arrangement, a seller has a requirement to repurchase goods from the buyer. If so, the seller should include the goods in inventory even though title has passed to the buyer.

## 2.6 Installment Sales

If the seller sells goods on an installment basis but retains legal title as security for the loan, the goods should be included in the seller's inventory if the percentage of uncollectible debts cannot be estimated. However, if the percentage of uncollectible debts can be estimated, the transaction would be accounted for as a sale, and an allowance for uncollectible debts would be recorded.

# 3 Valuation of Inventory

U.S. GAAP requires that inventory be stated at its *cost*. Where evidence indicates that cost will be recovered with an approximately normal profit on a sale in the ordinary course of business, no loss should be recognized even though replacement or reproduction costs are lower.

## 3.1 Cost

Inventories are generally accounted for at cost, which is defined as the price paid or consideration given to acquire an asset. Methods used to determine the cost of inventory include first-in, first-out (FIFO); last-in, first-out (LIFO); average cost; and the retail inventory method. IFRS does not permit the use of LIFO.

## 3.2 Departures From the Cost Basis

### 3.2.1 Precious Metals and Farm Products

Gold, silver, and other precious metals, and meat and some agricultural products are valued at *net realizable value*, which is net selling price less costs of disposal. When inventory is stated at a value in excess of cost, this fact should be fully disclosed in the financial statements. Inventories reported at net realizable value include:

- Inventories of gold and silver, when there is effective government-controlled market at a fixed monetary value.
- Inventories of agricultural, mineral, or other products meeting all of the following criteria:
  - Immediate marketability at quoted prices;
  - Unit interchangeability; and
  - Inability to determine appropriate costs.

### 3.2.2 Lower of Cost or Market, and Lower of Cost and Net Realizable Value

In the ordinary course of business, when the utility of goods is no longer as great as their cost, a departure from the cost basis principle of measuring inventory is required. This is usually accomplished by stating such goods at market value or net realizable value, as appropriate. The purpose of reducing inventory to an amount below cost is to show the probable loss sustained (conservatism) in the period in which the loss occurred (matching principle).

### 3.2.3 Recognize Loss in Current Period

Under U.S. GAAP, the write-down of inventory is usually reflected in cost of goods sold, unless the amount is material, in which case the loss should be identified separately in the income statement. IFRSs do not specify where an inventory write-down should be reported on the income statement.

### 3.2.4 Reversal of Inventory Write-downs

Under U.S. GAAP, reversals of inventory write-downs are prohibited. IFRSs allow the reversal of inventory write-downs for subsequent recoveries of inventory value. The reversal is limited to the amount of the original write-down and is recorded as a reduction of total inventory costs on the income statement (COGS) in the period of reversal.

### 3.2.5 Exceptions

The lower of cost or market and lower of cost and net realizable value rules will not apply when:

- the subsequent sales price of an end product is not affected by its market value; or
- the company has a firm sales price contract.

## 3.3 Lower of Cost and Net Realizable Value (IFRS and U.S. GAAP)

Under U.S. GAAP, the lower of cost and net realizable value method is used for all inventory that is *not* costed using LIFO or the retail inventory method. This method is required to value all inventory under IFRS. The lower of cost and net realizable value principle may be applied to a single item, a category, or total inventory, provided that the method most clearly reflects periodic income.

### 3.3.1 Net Realizable Value

Net realizable value is an item's net selling price less the costs to complete and dispose of the inventory. Net realizable value is the same as the "market ceiling" in the lower of cost or market method.

## 3.4 Lower of Cost or Market (U.S. GAAP Only)

Under U.S. GAAP, the lower of cost or market method is used when inventory is costed using LIFO or the retail inventory method. The lower of cost or market principle may be applied to a single item, a category, or total inventory, provided that the method most clearly reflects periodic income.

### 3.4.1 Market Value

Under U.S. GAAP, the term *market* in the phrase *lower of cost or market* generally means current replacement cost (whether by purchase or reproduction), provided the current replacement cost does not exceed net realizable value (the *market ceiling*) or fall below net realizable value reduced by normal profit margin (the *market floor*).

### 3.4.2 Definitions

- **Market Value**

    Under U.S. GAAP, market value is the median (middle value) of an inventory item's replacement cost, its market ceiling, and its market floor.

- **Replacement Cost**

    Replacement cost is the cost to purchase the item of inventory as of the valuation date.

- **Market Ceiling**

    Market ceiling is an item's net selling price less the costs to complete and dispose (called the net realizable value).

- **Market Floor**

    Market floor is the market ceiling less a normal profit margin.

## Example 1: Lower of Cost or Market

**Facts:** The following information pertains to a company's inventory at the end of the current year. The company uses LIFO and values its ending inventory using the lower of cost or market method.

| Item | Cost | Replacement Cost | Selling Price | Costs of Completion | Normal Profit |
|---|---|---|---|---|---|
| 1 | $20.50 | $19.00 | $25.00 | $1.00 | $6.00 |
| 2 | 26.00 | 20.00 | 30.00 | 2.00 | 7.00 |
| 3 | 10.00 | 12.00 | 15.00 | 1.00 | 3.00 |
| 4 | 40.00 | 55.00 | 60.00 | 6.00 | 4.00 |

**Required:** Calculate the lower of cost or market for the above four items.

**Solution:**

**Item 1:** Determine the maximum ("ceiling") and minimum ("floor") limits for the replacement cost.

    Ceiling = $24.00 ($25 − $1)

    Floor = $18.00 ($25 − $1) − $6

Since replacement cost ($19) falls between the maximum and minimum, market price is $19.00. Market ($19.00) is lower than cost ($20.50); therefore inventory would be valued at market ($19.00).

**Item 2:** Determine the maximum and minimum limits for the replacement cost.

    Ceiling = $28.00 ($30 − $2)

    Floor = $21.00 ($30 − $2) − $7

Since replacement cost ($20) is less than the minimum, market value is the minimum, or $21.00. Market ($21.00) is lower than cost ($26.00), therefore inventory would be valued at market ($21.00).

**Item 3:** Determine the maximum and minimum limits for the replacement cost.

    Ceiling = $14.00 ($15 − $1)

    Floor = $11.00 ($15 − $1) − $3

Replacement cost ($12) falls within these limits. Since cost ($10.00) is less than replacement cost ($12.00), the cost of $10.00 is used.

**Item 4:** Determine the maximum and minimum limits for the replacement cost.

    Ceiling = $54.00 ($60 − $6)

    Floor = $50.00 ($60 − $6) − $4

Since the replacement cost ($55) exceeds the maximum limit, the maximum ($54.00) is compared with cost ($40.00). Inventory is valued at cost ($40.00).

When market is lower than cost, the maximum prevents a loss in future periods by valuing the inventory at its estimated selling price less costs of completion and disposal. The minimum prevents any future periods from realizing any more than a normal profit.

*Journal entry to record the write-down to a separate account:*

| | | | |
|---|---|---|---|
| DR | Inventory loss due to decline in market value | $XXX | |
| CR | Inventory | | $XXX |

## Example 2 — Lower of Cost and Net Realizable Value

**Facts:** The following information pertains to a company's year-end inventory. The company uses FIFO and values its ending inventory using the lower of cost and net realizable value method.

| Item | Cost | Selling Price | Costs of Completion |
|---|---|---|---|
| 1 | $28.50 | $30.00 | $3.00 |
| 2 | 21.00 | 26.00 | 4.00 |

**Required:** Calculate the lower of cost and market for the above two items.

**Solution:** Determine the lower of cost or net realizable value for the above two items.

**Item 1:** Determine the net realizable value (NRV):

NRV = $27.00 ($30 − $3)

Net realizable value ($27.00) is lower than cost ($28.50); therefore, inventory would be valued at net realizable value ($27.00).

**Item 2:** Determine the net realizable value:

NRV = $22.00 ($26 − $4)

Net realizable value ($22.00) is greater than cost ($21.00); therefore, inventory would be valued at cost ($21.00).

## 3.5 Disclosure

Substantial and unusual losses from the subsequent measurement of inventory should be disclosed in the financial statements. Small losses from a decline in value are included in the cost of goods sold.

The basic principle of consistency must be applied in the valuation of inventory and the method should be disclosed in the financial statements. In the event that a significant change takes place in the measurement of inventory, adequate disclosure of the nature of the change and, if material (materiality principle), the effect on income should be disclosed in the financial statements.

# 4 Periodic Inventory System vs. Perpetual Inventory System

Two types of inventory systems are used to count inventory.

## 4.1 Periodic Inventory System

With a periodic inventory system, the quantity of inventory is determined only by physical count, usually at least annually. Therefore, units of inventory and the associated costs are counted and valued at the end of the accounting period. The actual cost of goods sold for the period is determined after each physical inventory by "squeezing" the difference between beginning inventory plus purchases less ending inventory, based on the physical count.

The periodic method does not keep a running total of the inventory balances. Ending inventory is physically counted and priced. Cost of goods sold is calculated as shown below:

|   | | |
|---|---|---|
| | Beginning inventory | $ 70,000 |
| + | Purchases | 300,000 |
| | Cost of goods available for sale | 370,000 |
| − | Ending inventory (physical count) | (270,000) |
| | Cost of goods sold | $ 100,000 |

## 4.2 Perpetual Inventory System

With a perpetual inventory system, the inventory record for each item of inventory is updated for each purchase and each sale as they occur. The actual cost of goods sold is determined and recorded with each sale. Therefore, the perpetual inventory system keeps a running total of inventory balances.

## 4.3 Hybrid Inventory Systems

### 4.3.1 Units of Inventory on Hand: Quantities Only

Some companies maintain a perpetual record of quantities only. A record of units on hand is maintained on the perpetual basis, and this is often referred to as the *modified perpetual system*. Changes in quantities are recorded after each sale and purchase.

### 4.3.2 Perpetual With Periodic at Year-end

Most companies that maintain a perpetual inventory system still perform either complete periodic physical inventories or test count inventories on a random (or cyclical) basis.

Inventory                                                                                                          FAR 3

> ### Example 3 — Comparison of Periodic and Perpetual Inventory Methods (Sales)
>
> **Facts:** ABC Company sold 20,000 units of inventory for $7 per unit. The inventory had originally cost $5 per unit.
>
> **Required:** Prepare the journal entries to record the sale using the periodic and perpetual methods.
>
> **Solution:** *Journal entry to record sale under periodic method (cost of goods sold will be recorded after the periodic inventory count):*
>
> | | | | |
> |---|---|---|---|
> | DR | Cash | $140,000 | |
> | CR | Sales | | $140,000 |
>
> *Journal entry to record sale under perpetual method:*
>
> | | | | |
> |---|---|---|---|
> | DR | Cash | $140,000 | |
> | CR | Sales | | $140,000 |
> | DR | Cost of goods sold | 100,000 | |
> | CR | Inventory | | 100,000 |

> ### Example 4 — Comparison of Periodic and Perpetual Inventory Methods (Purchases)
>
> **Facts:** ABC Company purchased 50,000 units of merchandise for $6 a unit to be held as inventory.
>
> **Required:** Prepare the journal entries to record the purchase of inventory under the periodic and the perpetual methods.
>
> **Solution:** The periodic method debits purchases; the perpetual method debits inventory.
>
> *Journal entry to record purchase under periodic method:*
>
> | | | | |
> |---|---|---|---|
> | DR | Purchases | $300,000 | |
> | CR | Cash | | $300,000 |
>
> *Journal entry to record purchase under perpetual method:*
>
> | | | | |
> |---|---|---|---|
> | DR | Inventory | $300,000 | |
> | CR | Cash | | $300,000 |

# 5 Primary Inventory Cost Flow Assumptions

Inventory valuation is dependent on the cost flow assumption underlying the computation. Under U.S. GAAP, the cost flow assumption used by a company is not required to have a rational relationship with the physical inventory flows; however, the primary objective is the selection of the method that will most clearly reflect periodic income.

When similar goods are purchased at different times, it may not be possible to identify and match the specific costs of the item sold. Frequently, the identity of goods and their specific related costs are lost between the time of acquisition and the time of sale. This has resulted in the development and general acceptance of several assumptions with respect to the flow of cost factors (FIFO, LIFO, and average cost) to provide practical bases for the measurement of periodic income.

> **U.S. GAAP VS. IFRS**
>
> Under IFRS, the accounting method used to account for inventory should be based on the order in which the products are sold relative to when they were put in inventory. Specific identification should be used whenever possible. The LIFO method is prohibited under IFRS because it rarely reflects actual physical inventory flows. IFRS requires the use of the same cost flow assumption for all inventories having a similar nature and use to the entity. U.S. GAAP does not have this restriction.

## 5.1 Specific Identification Method

Under the specific identification method, the cost of each item in inventory is uniquely identified to that item. The cost follows the physical flow of the item in and out of inventory to cost of goods sold. Specific identification is usually used for physically large or high-value items and allows for greater opportunity for manipulation of income.

## 5.2 First In, First Out (FIFO) Method

Under FIFO, the first costs inventoried are the first costs transferred to cost of goods sold. Ending inventory includes the most recently incurred costs; thus, the ending balance approximates replacement cost. Ending inventory and cost of goods sold are the same whether a periodic or perpetual inventory system is used.

> **Pass Key**
>
> In periods of rising prices, the FIFO method results in the highest ending inventory, the lowest costs of goods sold, and the highest net income (i.e., current costs are not matched with current revenues).

# Inventory

## Example 5 — FIFO Method

**Facts:** During its first year of operations, Helix Corporation has purchased all of its inventory in three batches. Batch 1 was for 4,000 units at $4.25 per unit. Batch 2 was for 2,000 units at $4.50 per unit. Batch 3 was for 3,000 units at $4.75 per unit. In total, 4,000 units were sold, 3,000 units after the first purchase and 1,000 units after the second purchase.

**Required:** Determine the amounts of ending inventory and cost of goods sold using the FIFO method and the periodic and perpetual systems.

**Solution:**

**FIFO: Periodic Inventory System**

| Units Bought | Cost/Unit | Ending Inventory | Goods Available for Sale |
|---|---|---|---|
| 4,000 | $4.25 |  | $17,000 |
| 2,000 | 4.50 | $ 9,000 | 9,000 |
| 3,000 | 4.75 | 14,250 | 14,250 |
|  |  | $23,250 | 40,250 |

Ending inventory **23,250**
Cost of goods sold **$17,000**

**FIFO: Perpetual Inventory System**

| Units Bought | Units Sold | Cost/Unit | Change in Inventory | Inventory Balance | COGS |
|---|---|---|---|---|---|
| 4,000 |  | $4.25 | $17,000 |  |  |
|  | 3,000 | 4.25 | (12,750) | 4,250 | $12,750 |
| 2,000 |  | 4.50 | 9,000 | 13,250 |  |
|  | 1,000 | 4.25 | (4,250) | 9,000 | 4,250 |
| 3,000 |  | 4.75 | 14,250 | 23,250 |  |

Ending inventory **$23,250**
Cost of goods sold **$17,000**

Note that the ending inventory under both methods is $23,250 and the amount of cost of goods sold under both methods is $17,000.

## 5.3 Weighted Average Method

Under the weighted average method, at the end of the period, the average cost of each item in inventory would be the weighted average of the costs of all items in inventory. The weighted average is determined by dividing the total costs of inventory available by the total number of units of inventory available, remembering that the beginning inventory is included in both totals. This method is particularly suitable for homogeneous products and a periodic inventory system.

# Example 6 — Weighted Average Method

**Facts:** Assume the same information for Helix Corporation as in the previous example for FIFO.

**Requirement:** Determine the amounts of ending inventory and cost of goods sold under the weighted average method.

**Solution:**

| Unit Cost | Units Purchased | Total |
|---|---|---|
| $4.25 | 4,000 | $17,000 |
| 4.50 | 2,000 | 9,000 |
| 4.75 | 3,000 | 14,250 |
| Total | 9,000 | $40,250 |

Weighted average cost per unit = $4.4722 ($40,250/9,000)

**Cost of goods sold = $17,889** (4,000 units × $4.4722)

**Ending inventory = $22,361** (5,000 units × $4.4722)

## 5.4 Moving Average Method

The moving average method computes the weighted average cost after each purchase by dividing the total cost of inventory available after each purchase (inventory plus current purchase) by the total units available after each purchase. The moving average is more current than the weighted average. A *perpetual inventory* system is necessary to use the moving average method.

# Example 7 — Moving Average Method

**Facts:** Assume the same information for Helix Corporation as in the previous example for FIFO.

**Required:** Determine the amounts of ending inventory and cost of goods sold under the moving average method.

**Solution:**

| Purchases/(Sales) ||| Inventory Balances (Rounded) |||
|---|---|---|---|---|---|
| Quantity | Cost | Total | Quantity | Average Cost | Total |
| 4,000 | $4.25 | $17,000 | 4,000 | $4.25 | $17,000 |
| (3,000) | 4.25 | (12,750) | 1,000 | 4.25 | 4,250 |
| 2,000 | 4.50 | 9,000 | 3,000 | 4.4167* | 13,250 |
| (1,000) | 4.4167 | (4,417) | 2,000 | 4.4167 | 8,833 |
| 3,000 | 4.75 | 14,250 | 5,000 | 4.6166** | 23,083 |

*Weighted average cost per unit = ($4,250 + $9,000) / 3,000 = $4.4167

**Weighted average cost per unit = ($8,833 + $14,250) / 5,000 = $4.6166

**Cost of goods sold is $17,167** ($12,750 + $4,417)

**Ending inventory is $23,083**

# 5.5 Last In, First Out (LIFO) Method (Not Permitted Under IFRS)

Under LIFO, the last costs inventoried are the first costs transferred to cost of goods sold. Ending inventory, therefore, includes the oldest costs. The ending balance of inventory will typically not approximate replacement cost.

- LIFO does not generally relate to actual flow of goods in a company because most companies sell or use their oldest goods first to prevent holding old or obsolete items.
- If LIFO is used for tax purposes, it must also be used in the GAAP financial statements.

### 5.5.1 LIFO Financial Statement Effects

The use of the LIFO method generally better matches expense against revenues because it matches current costs with current revenues; thus, LIFO eliminates holding gains and reduces net income during times of inflation.

- If sales exceed production (or purchases) for a given period, LIFO will result in a distortion of net income because old inventory costs (called "LIFO layers") will be matched with current revenue.
- LIFO is susceptible to income manipulation by intentionally reducing purchases in order to use old layers at lower costs.

> **Pass Key**
>
> In periods of rising prices, the LIFO method generally results in the lowest ending inventory, the highest costs of goods sold, and the lowest net income.
>
> **Remember: LIFO = Lowest**

### 5.5.2 LIFO Layers

The last in, first out method of determining inventory requires that records be maintained as to the base year inventory amount and additional layers that may be added yearly.

- After an original LIFO amount is created (base year), it may decrease, or additional layers may be created in each year according to the amount of ending inventory. An additional LIFO layer is created in any year in which the ending inventory is greater than the beginning inventory.
- An additional LIFO layer is priced at the earliest costs of the year in which it was created, because the LIFO method matches the most current costs incurred with current revenues, leaving the first cost incurred to be included in any inventory increase.

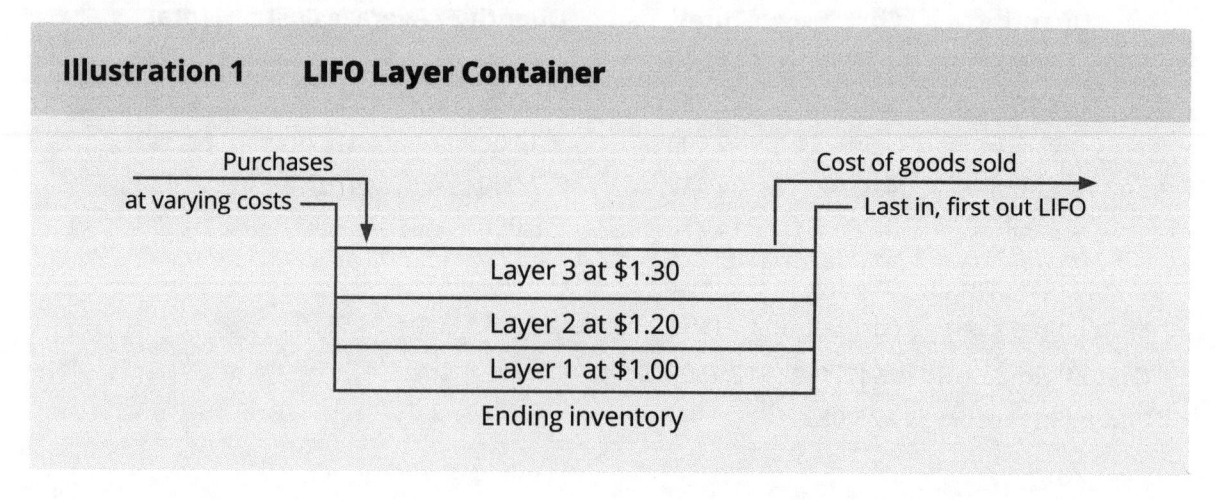

**Illustration 1    LIFO Layer Container**

Purchases at varying costs → [Layer 3 at $1.30 / Layer 2 at $1.20 / Layer 1 at $1.00] → Cost of goods sold — Last in, first out LIFO

Ending inventory

# Example 8 — LIFO Method

**Facts:** Assume the same facts for Helix Corporation as in previous examples.

**Required:** Determine the amounts of ending inventory and cost of goods sold using the LIFO method and periodic and the perpetual systems.

**Solution:**

**LIFO: Periodic Inventory System**

| Units Bought | Cost/Unit | Ending Inventory | Goods Available for Sale |
|---|---|---|---|
| 4,000 | $4.25 | $17,000 | $17,000 |
| 2,000 | 4.50 | 4,500 | 9,000 |
| 3,000 | 4.75 |  | 14,250 |
|  |  |  | 40,250 |
| Ending inventory |  | **$21,500** | (21,500) |
| Cost of goods sold |  |  | **$18,750** |

**LIFO: Perpetual Inventory System**

| Units Bought | Units Sold | Cost/Unit | Inventory Balance | COGS |
|---|---|---|---|---|
| 4,000 |  | $4.25 | $17,000 |  |
|  | 3,000 | 4.25 | (12,750) | $12,750 |
| 2,000 |  | 4.50 | 9,000 |  |
|  | 1,000 | 4.50 | (4,500) | 4,500 |
| 3,000 |  | 4.75 | 14,250 |  |
|  |  |  | **$23,000** | **$17,250** |

Under the *periodic inventory system*, ending inventory is $21,500 and cost of goods sold is $18,750.
Under the *perpetual inventory system*, ending inventory is $23,000 and cost of goods sold is $17,250.

## Pass Key

Comparison of FIFO, LIFO, and the average methods:

| Periodic Inventory System | Ending Inventory | Cost of Goods Sold |
|---|---|---|
| FIFO | $23,250 | $17,000 |
| Weighted Average | 22,361 | 17,889 |
| LIFO | 21,500 | 18,750 |

| Perpetual Inventory System | Ending Inventory | Cost of Goods Sold |
|---|---|---|
| FIFO | $23,250 | $17,000 |
| Moving Average | 23,083 | 17,167 |
| LIFO | 23,000 | 17,250 |

These examples illustrate that in a period of rising prices, FIFO results in the highest ending inventory and the lowest cost of goods sold, LIFO results in the lowest ending inventory and the highest cost of goods sold, and the average method balances fall between the LIFO and FIFO balances. Note that the moving average method results in higher ending inventory and lower cost of goods sold than with the weighted average method.

# Inventory

## 5.6 Dollar-Value LIFO

Under the regular LIFO method, inventory is measured in units and is priced at unit prices. Under the dollar-value LIFO method, inventory is measured in dollars and is adjusted for changing price levels. When converting from LIFO inventory to dollar-value LIFO, a price index will be used to adjust the inventory value. In some problems the price index will be internally computed. In other problems, the price index will be supplied.

### 5.6.1 Internally Computed Price Index

When the price index is computed internally by the company, the price index will be ending inventory at current year cost divided by ending inventory at base year cost:

$$\text{Price index} = \frac{\text{Ending inventory at current year cost}}{\text{Ending inventory at base year cost}}$$

To compute the LIFO layer added in the current year at dollar-value LIFO, the LIFO layer at base year cost is multiplied by the internally generated price index.

---

**Example 9 — Dollar-Value LIFO—Internally Computed Price Index**

**Facts:** Brock Co. adopted the dollar-value LIFO inventory method as of January 1, Year 1. A single inventory pool and an internally computed price index are used to compute Brock's LIFO inventory layers. Information about Brock's dollar-value inventory follows:

| Date | At Base Year Cost | At Current Year Cost | At Dollar-Value LIFO |
|---|---|---|---|
| 1/1/Year 1 | $40,000 | $40,000 | $40,000 |
| Year 1 layer | 5,000 | 14,000 | 6,000* |
| 12/31/Year 1 | $45,000 | $54,000 | 46,000** |
| Year 2 layer | 15,000 | 26,000 | 20,000*** |
| 12/31/Year 2 | $60,000 | $80,000 | $66,000**** |

**Required:** Compute the LIFO layers added and ending inventory for Years 1 and 2 at dollar-value LIFO.

**Solution:**

$$\text{Year 1 price index} = \frac{\$54,000}{\$45,000} = \frac{6}{5}$$

*Year 1 LIFO layer added = 6/5 × $5,000 = $6,000

**Year 1 ending inventory = $40,000 + $6,000 = $46,000

$$\text{Year 2 price index} = \frac{\$80000}{\$60,000} = \frac{4}{3}$$

***Year 2 LIFO layer added = 4/3 × $15,000 = $20,000

****Year 2 ending inventory = $46,000 + $20,000 = $66,000

## 5.6.2 Price Index Supplied

Where the price index is given in the problem, the year-end price index is multiplied by the LIFO layer at the base year cost to calculate the LIFO layer added at dollar-value LIFO.

> **Example 10**    **Dollar-Value LIFO—Price Index Supplied**
>
> **Facts:** Walt Company adopted the dollar-value LIFO inventory method as of January 1, Year 1, when its inventory was valued at $500,000. Walt's entire inventory constitutes a single pool. Using a relevant price index of 1.10, Walt determined that its December 31, Year 1, inventory was $577,500 at current year cost, and $525,000 at base year cost.
>
> **Required:** Calculate Walt's dollar-value LIFO inventory at December 31, Year 1.
>
> **Solution:**
>
> | Date | At Base Year Cost | At Current Year Cost | At Dollar-Value LIFO |
> |---|---|---|---|
> | 1/1/Year 1 | $500,000 | $500,000 | $500,000 |
> | Year 1 layer | | | |
> | 12/31/Year 1 | 525,000 | 577,500 | |
>
> The Year 1 layer at base year cost is $525,000 − $500,000 = $25,000
>
> The Year 1 layer at current year cost is $577,500 − $500,000 = $77,500
>
> The Year 1 layer at dollar-value LIFO is $25,000 (base year layer) × 1.10 = $27,500
>
> The dollar-value LIFO ending inventory is $500,000 + $27,500 = $527,500

# 6 Gross Profit Method

The gross profit method is used for interim financial statements as part of a periodic inventory system. Inventory is valued at retail, and the average gross profit percentage is used to determine the inventory cost for the interim financial statements. The gross profit percentage is known and is used to calculate cost of sales.

> **Example 11    Gross Profit Method**
>
> **Facts:** Dahl Co. sells soap at a gross profit percentage of 20 percent. The following figures apply to the eight months ended August 31, Year 1:
>
> | | |
> |---|---:|
> | Sales | $200,000 |
> | Beginning inventory | 100,000 |
> | Purchases | 100,000 |
>
> On September 1, Year 1, a flood destroys all of Dahl's soap inventory.
>
> **Required:** Estimate the cost of the destroyed inventory.
>
> **Solution:**
>
> | | |
> |---|---:|
> | Sales | $200,000 |
> | COGS % (1.00 − 0.20) | × 80% |
> | Cost of goods sold | $160,000 |
>
> Cost of goods sold is deducted from the total goods available to determine ending inventory, as follows:
>
> | | |
> |---|---:|
> | Beginning inventory | $100,000 |
> | Add: purchases | + 100,000 |
> | Cost of goods available | $200,000 |
> | Less: cost of goods sold | (160,000) |
> | Estimated cost of inventory destroyed | $ 40,000 |

# 7 Firm Purchase Commitments

A firm purchase commitment is a legally enforceable agreement to purchase a specified amount of goods at some time in the future. All material firm purchase commitments must be disclosed in either the financial statements or the notes thereto.

If the contracted price exceeds the market price and if it is expected that losses will occur when the purchase is actually made, the loss should be recognized at the time of the decline in price. A description of losses recognized on these commitments must be disclosed in the current period's income statement.

> ### Example 12 — Loss on Purchase Commitments
>
> **Facts:** J and S Incorporated signed timber-cutting contracts in Year 1 to be executed at $5,000,000 in Year 2. The market price of the rights at December 31, Year 1, is $4,000,000 and it is expected that the loss will occur when the contract is effected in Year 2.
>
> **Required:** Determine the amount that should be reported as a loss on purchase commitments at December 31, Year 1.
>
> **Solution:**
>
> | | |
> |---|---:|
> | Price of purchase commitment | $5,000,000 |
> | Market price at 12/31/Year 1 | (4,000,000) |
> | Loss on purchase commitments | $1,000,000 |
>
> Journal entry to record the loss:
>
> | | | | |
> |---|---|---:|---:|
> | DR | Estimated loss on purchase commitment | $1,000,000 | |
> | CR | Estimated liability on purchase commitment | | $1,000,000 |
>
> Note that the loss is recognized in the period in which the price declined. The estimated loss on purchase commitment is reported in the income statement under other expenses and losses.

---

### Question 1                                                                 MCQ-00114

Bren Co.'s beginning inventory at January 1, Year 3, was understated by $26,000, and its ending inventory was overstated by $52,000. As a result, Bren's cost of goods sold for Year 3 was:

a. Understated by $26,000.
b. Overstated by $26,000.
c. Understated by $78,000.
d. Overstated by $78,000.

---

### Question 2                                                                 MCQ-00084

Nest Co. recorded the following inventory information during the month of January:

| | Units | Unit Cost | Total Cost | Units on Hand |
|---|---|---|---|---|
| Balance on 1/1 | 2,000 | $1 | $2,000 | 2,000 |
| Purchased on 1/8 | 1,200 | 3 | 3,600 | 3,200 |
| Sold on 1/23 | 1,800 | | | 1,400 |
| Purchased on 1/28 | 800 | 5 | 4,000 | 2,200 |

Nest uses the U.S. GAAP LIFO method to cost inventory. What amount should Nest report as inventory on January 31 under each of the following methods of recording inventory?

| | Perpetual | Periodic |
|---|---|---|
| a. | $2,600 | $5,400 |
| b. | $5,400 | $2,600 |
| c. | $2,600 | $2,600 |
| d. | $5,400 | $5,400 |

## NOTES

# MODULE 4
# PP&E: Cost Basis

**FAR 3**

## 1 Property, Plant, and Equipment

- Property, plant, and equipment (PP&E), or fixed assets, are assets that are acquired for use in operations and not for resale.
- They possess physical substance, are long-term in nature, and are subject to depreciation.

The following fixed assets must be shown separately on the balance sheet (or footnotes) at original cost (historical cost):

- **Land (Property)**
- **Buildings (Plant)**
- **Equipment:** May show machinery, tools, furniture, and fixtures separately, if these categories are significant.
- **Accumulated Depreciation Account (Contra-Asset):** May be combined for two or more asset categories.

## 2 Valuation of Fixed Assets Under U.S. GAAP

### 2.1 Historical Cost

Historical cost is the basis for valuation of purchased fixed assets. Historical cost is measured by the cash or cash equivalent price of obtaining the asset and bringing it to the location and condition necessary for its intended use.

### 2.2 Donated Fixed Assets

Donated fixed assets are recorded at fair market value along with incidental costs incurred. Donated fixed assets result in the recognition of a gain on the income statement.

| | | | |
|---|---|---|---|
| DR | Fixed asset (FMV) | $XXX | |
| CR | Gain on nonreciprocal transfer | | $XXX |

# 3 Valuation of Fixed Assets Under IFRS

Under IFRS, fixed assets are initially recognized at the cost to acquire the asset. Subsequent to acquisition, fixed assets can be valued using the cost model or the revaluation model.

## 3.1 Cost Model

Under the cost model, fixed assets are reported at historical cost adjusted for accumulated depreciation and impairment.

$$\text{Cost model carrying value} = \text{Historical cost} - \text{Accumulated depreciation} - \text{Impairment}$$

## 3.2 Revaluation Model

Under the revaluation model, a class of fixed assets is revalued to fair value and then reported at fair value less subsequent accumulated depreciation and impairment. Revaluations must be made frequently enough to ensure that carrying amount does not differ materially from fair value at the end of the reporting period. When fair value differs materially from carrying value, a further revaluation is required.

$$\text{Revaluation model carrying value} = \text{Fair value at revaluation date} - \text{Subsequent accumulated depreciation} - \text{Subsequent impairment}$$

Revaluation must be applied to all items in a class of fixed assets, not to individual fixed assets. Land and buildings, machinery, furniture and fixtures, and office equipment are examples of fixed asset classes. When fixed assets are reported at fair value, the historical cost equivalent (cost − accumulated depreciation − impairment) must be disclosed.

### 3.2.1 Revaluation Losses

When fixed assets are revalued, revaluation losses (fair value < carrying value before revaluation) are reported on the income statement, unless the revaluation loss reverses a previously recognized revaluation gain. A revaluation loss that reverses a previously recognized revaluation gain is recognized in other comprehensive income and reduces the revaluation surplus in accumulated other comprehensive income.

### 3.2.2 Revaluation Gains

Revaluation gains (fair value > carrying value before revaluation) are reported in other comprehensive income and accumulated in equity as revaluation surplus, unless the revaluation gain reverses a previously recognized revaluation loss. Revaluation gains are reported on the income statement to the extent that they reverse a previously recognized revaluation loss.

### 3.2.3 Impairment

If revalued fixed assets subsequently become impaired, the impairment is recorded by first reducing any revaluation surplus to zero with further impairment losses reported on the income statement.

## Example 1 — Revaluation Model (IFRS)

**Facts:** On December 31, Year 1, an entity chose to revalue all of its fixed assets under IFRS. On that date, the fixed assets had the following carrying values and fair values:

|  | Carrying Value | Fair Value |
|---|---|---|
| Land | $10,500,000 | $11,100,000 |
| Buildings | 6,400,000 | 6,000,000 |
| Equipment | 3,300,000 | 3,600,000 |

**Required:** Calculate the revaluation gain and loss to be reported on the December 31, Year 1, financial statements.

**Solution:**

**Revaluation Loss:** The entity will report a loss on the revaluation of the buildings because fair value is less than carrying value:

Loss on revaluation of buildings = $6,000,000 − $6,400,000
= ($400,000)

The loss, which is essentially an impairment loss, will be reported on the income statement.

**Revaluation Gain:** The entity will report a gain on the revaluation of the land and equipment because the fair values of these assets exceed their respective carrying values:

Gain on revaluation of land = $11,100,000 − $10,500,000
= $600,000

Gain on revaluation of equipment = $3,600,000 − $3,300,000
= $300,000

The total revaluation gain of $900,000 would be reported as revaluation surplus in other comprehensive income.

# 4 Property

## 4.1 Cost of Land

When land has been purchased for the purpose of constructing a building, all costs incurred up to excavation for the new building are considered land costs. All the following expenditures are included.

- Purchase price
- Brokers' commissions
- Title and recording fees
- Legal fees
- Draining of swamps
- Clearing of brush and trees

# PP&E: Cost Basis

- Site development (e.g., grading of mountain tops to make a "pad")
- Existing obligations assumed by buyer, including mortgages and back taxes
- Costs of razing (tearing down) an old building (demolition)
- Less proceeds from sale of existing buildings, standing timber, etc.

## 4.2 Land Improvements

Land Improvements are depreciable, and include the following:

- Fences
- Water systems
- Sidewalks
- Paving
- Landscaping
- Lighting

## 4.3 Interest Costs

Interest costs during the construction period should be added to the cost of land improvements based on the weighted average of accumulated expenditures.

# 5 Plant

## 5.1 Cost of Plant

Cost of plant or buildings includes:

- Purchase price, etc.
- All repair charges neglected by the previous owner ("deferred maintenance")
- Alterations and improvements
- Architect's fees
- Possible addition of construction-period interest

> **Pass Key**
>
> When preparing the land for the construction of a building:
> - Land cost: filling in a hole or leveling
> - Building cost: digging a hole for the foundation

## 5.2 "Basket Purchase" of Land and Building

Allocate the purchase price based on the ratio of appraised values of individual items.

# 6 Equipment

Equipment includes office equipment, machinery, furniture, fixtures, and factory equipment.

## 6.1 Cost of Equipment

Cost includes all expenditures related directly to the acquisition or construction of the equipment:

- Invoice price
- Less cash discounts and other discounts (if any)
- Add freight-in (and insurance while in transit and while in construction)
- Add installation charges (including testing and preparation for use)
- Add sales and federal excise taxes
- Possible addition of construction period interest

## 6.2 Capitalize vs. Expense

Proper accounting is determined based on the purpose of the expenditure.

### 6.2.1 Additions

*Additions increase the quantity of fixed assets and are capitalized:*

| | | | |
|---|---|---|---|
| DR | Asset (machinery, etc.) | $XXX | |
| CR | Cash/accounts payable | | $XXX |

### 6.2.2 Improvements and Replacements

Improvements (betterments) improve the quality of fixed assets and are capitalized to the fixed asset account (e.g., a tile or steel roof is substituted for an old asphalt roof). In a replacement, a new, similar asset is substituted for the old asset (e.g., an asphalt shingle roof is replaced with a roof of similar material).

- If the carrying value of the old asset is *known*, remove it and recognize any gain or loss. Capitalize the cost of the improvement/replacement to the asset account.
- If the carrying value of the old asset is *unknown*, and:
  - *The asset's life is extended, debit accumulated depreciation for the cost of the improvement/replacement:*

    | | | | |
    |---|---|---|---|
    | DR | Accumulated depreciation | $XXX | |
    | CR | Cash/accounts payable | | $XXX |

- The usefulness (utility) of the asset is increased, capitalize the cost of the improvement/replacement to the asset account.

### 6.2.3 Repairs

- Ordinary repairs should be expensed as repair and maintenance.
- Extraordinary repairs should be capitalized. Treat the repair as an addition, improvement, or replacement, as appropriate.

| Summary Chart | | Expense | Capitalize | Reduce Accumulated Depreciation |
|---|---|---|---|---|
| Additions: Increase quantity | | | ✓ | |
| *Improvement/replacement:* | Increase life | | | ✓ |
| | Increase usefulness | | ✓ | |
| Ordinary repair | | ✓ | | |
| *Extraordinary repair:* | Increase life | | | ✓ |
| | Increase usefulness | | ✓ | |

# 7 Fixed Assets Constructed by a Company

## 7.1 Costs to Capitalize

When a fixed asset is constructed by a company, the cost of the fixed asset includes:

- Direct materials and direct labor.
- Repairs and maintenance expenses that add value to the fixed asset.
- Overhead, including direct items of overhead (any "idle plant capacity" expense).
- Construction period interest.

## 7.2 Capitalization of Interest Costs

Construction period interest should be capitalized based on weighted average of accumulated expenditures as part of the cost of producing fixed assets, such as:

- Buildings, machinery, or land improvements, constructed or produced for others or to be used internally.
- Fixed assets intended for sale or lease and constructed as discrete projects, such as real estate projects.
- Land improvements. If a structure is placed on the land, charge the interest cost to the structure, not the land.

### 7.2.1 Computing Capitalized Cost

- **Weighted Average Amount of Accumulated Expenditures:** Capitalized interest costs for a particular period are determined by applying an interest rate to the average amount of accumulated expenditures for the qualifying asset during the period (this is known as the avoidable interest).

- **Interest Rate on Borrowings:** The interest rate paid on borrowings (specifically for asset construction) during a particular period should be used to determine the amount of interest cost to be capitalized for the period. Where a qualifying asset is related to a specific new borrowing, the allocated interest cost is equal to the amount of interest incurred on the new borrowing.

- **Interest Rate on Excess Expenditures (Weighted Average):** If the average accumulated expenditures outstanding exceed the amount of the related specific new borrowing, interest cost should be computed on the excess. The interest rate that should be used on the excess is the weighted average interest rate for other borrowings of the company.
- **Not to Exceed Actual Interest Costs:** Total capitalized interest costs for any particular period may not exceed the total interest costs actually incurred by an entity during that period. In consolidated financial statements, this limitation should be applied on a consolidated basis.
- **Do Not Reduce Capitalizable Interest:** Do not reduce capitalizable interest by income received on the unexpended portion of the loan.

### Pass Key

For the CPA Exam, it is important to remember two rules concerning capitalized interest:

**Rule 1:** Only capitalize interest on money actually spent, not on the total amount borrowed.

**Rule 2:** The amount of capitalized interest is the lower of:
- actual interest cost incurred, or
- computed capitalized interest (avoidable interest).

### Example 2 Capitalized Interest

**Facts:** On January 1, Year 1, Conviser Soup Kitchen Inc. signed a fixed-price contract to have a new kitchen built for $1,000,000. On the same day, Conviser borrowed $500,000 to finance the construction. The loan is payable in five $100,000 annual payments plus interest at 11 percent. Conviser planned to finance the balance of the construction costs using the company's existing debt, which had a weighted average interest rate of 9 percent. During Year 1, Conviser had average accumulated expenditures of $600,000 and incurred actual interest costs on all borrowings of $150,000.

**Required:** Calculate Conviser's capitalized interest cost?

**Solution:**

| Weighted Average of Accumulated Expenditures | × | Applicable Interest Rate | = | Amount of Interest to Be Capitalized |
|---|---|---|---|---|
| $500,000 | × | 11% | = | $55,000 |
| 100,000 | × | 9% | = | 9,000 |
|  |  | Total capitalizable interest |  | $64,000 |

Note that because the capitalizable interest of $64,000 is less than the actual interest of $150,000, the full $64,000 is capitalized. The remainder of the actual interest is expensed.

### 7.2.2 Capitalization of Interest Period

- Begins when three conditions are present:
  - Expenditures for the asset have been made.
  - Activities that are necessary to get the asset ready for its intended use are in progress.
  - Interest cost is being incurred.

# PP&E: Cost Basis

- Continues as long as the three conditions are present.
- Stops during intentional delays in construction, but continues during ordinary construction delays.
- Ends when the asset is (or independent parts of the asset are) substantially complete and ready for the intended use (regardless of whether it is actually used).

### 7.2.3 Disclose in Financial Statements

- Total interest cost incurred during the period.
- Capitalized interest cost for the period, if any.

## Illustration 1 Construction Period

| Date | | Interest Capitalized | Expense |
|---|---|---|---|
| 1/2/Year 1 | Purchased $1,000,000 parcel of land for speculation; paid $600,000 down, borrowed $400,000 at 12% per year | | |
| 3/1 | Paid interest cost of $8,000 (2 months) | | $8,000 |
| 3/2 | Decision made to build condo project on the land, and attorneys apply for zoning permits* | | |
| 5/1 | Paid interest cost of $8,000 (2 months) (charge to building) | $ 8,000 | |
| 5/2 | Permits received—*architects begin plans* | | |
| 9/1 | Begin grading and developing land and foundation; paid four months' interest (charge building) | 16,000 | |
| 9/2 | Incurred expenses to date for attorney, architect, and land development = $300,000, all paid with additional borrowed money | | |
| 12/31/Year 1 | Paid four months interest** | 28,000 | |
| | **Total interest** | **$52,000** | **$8,000** |
| 12/31/Year 1 | Required disclosure of interest: **Total interest cost incurred during year = $60,000** **Interest cost capitalized = $52,000*** | | |
| 1/2/Year 2 | Wildcat strike stops construction (unintentional delay) | $$$ | |
| 2/1 | Wildcat strike over—*construction continues* | $$$ | |
| 4/1 | Glut on condo market; construction delayed intentionally | | $$$ |
| 8/1 | Construction continued | $$$ | |
| 10/1 | Floors 1–3 of the 10-story condo building are completed and ready for sale (except for light fixtures and wall coverings) | Floors 4–10 | Floors 1–3 |
| 12/15/Year 2 | Building and project completed | | $$$ |

*Construction period begins at point the decision is made to build on land, and ends when asset is substantially complete and ready for intended use.

**$400,000 + 300,000 = $700,000 × 12% × 4/12 = $28,000

***Capitalizable interest is based on weighted average of accumulated expenditures to date.

## Question 1 — MCQ-00139

On December 1, Year 1, Boyd Co. purchased a $400,000 tract of land for a factory site. Boyd razed an old building on the property and sold the materials it salvaged from the demolition. Boyd incurred additional costs and realized salvage proceeds during December Year 1 as follows:

| | |
|---|---:|
| Demolition of old building | $50,000 |
| Legal fees for purchase contract and recording ownership | 10,000 |
| Title guarantee insurance | 12,000 |
| Proceeds from sale of salvaged materials | 8,000 |

In its December 31, Year 1, balance sheet, Boyd should report a balance in the land account of:

- a. $464,000
- b. $460,000
- c. $442,000
- d. $422,000

## Question 2 — MCQ-08592

Sea Manufacturing Corp. is constructing a new factory building. During the current calendar year, Sea made the following payments to the construction company:

| | |
|---|---|
| January 2 | $1,000,000 |
| December 31 | $1,000,000 |

Sea has an 8 percent, three-year construction loan of $3,000,000. What is the amount of interest costs that Sea may capitalize during the current year?

- a. $0
- b. $80,000
- c. $160,000
- d. $240,000

## NOTES

# MODULE 5: PP&E: Depreciation and Disposal

FAR 3

## 1 Overview

The basic principle of matching revenue and expenses is applied to long-lived assets that are not held for sale in the ordinary course of business. The systematic and rational allocation used to achieve "matching" is usually accomplished by depreciation, amortization, or depletion, according to the type of long-lived asset involved.

### 1.1 Types of Depreciation

- **Physical Depreciation:** This type of depreciation is related to an asset's deterioration and wear over a period of time.
- **Functional Depreciation:** Functional depreciation arises from obsolescence or inadequacy of the asset to perform efficiently. Obsolescence may result from diminished demand for the product that the depreciable asset produces or from the availability of a new depreciable asset that can perform the same function for substantially less cost.

### 1.2 Definitions

- **Salvage Value:** Salvage or residual value is an estimate of the amount that will be realized at the end of the useful life of a depreciable asset. Frequently, depreciable assets have little or no salvage value at the end of their estimated useful life and, if immaterial, the amount(s) may be ignored in calculating depreciation.
- **Estimated Useful Life:** Estimated useful life is the period of time over which an asset's cost will be depreciated. It may be revised at any time, but any revision must be accounted for prospectively, in current and future periods only (change in estimate).

> **Pass Key**
>
> The CPA Exam frequently will have an asset placed in service *during* the year. Therefore, it requires computing depreciation for a part of the year rather than the full year. Candidates must always check the date the asset was placed in service.

> **U.S. GAAP VS. IFRS**
>
> Under IFRS, the depreciation method used should reflect the expected pattern of fixed asset consumption. This is not required under U.S. GAAP.

# 2 Composite Depreciation and Component Depreciation

## 2.1 Component Depreciation

Component depreciation is the separate depreciation of each part of an item of property, plant, and equipment that is significant to the total cost of the fixed asset. Component depreciation is permitted but rarely used under U.S. GAAP.

> **U.S. GAAP VS. IFRS**
>
> IFRSs require component depreciation. Separate significant components of a fixed asset with different lives should be recorded and depreciated separately. The carrying amount of parts or components that are replaced should be derecognized.

> **Example 1    Component Depreciation**
>
> **Facts:** On January 1, Year 1, an entity that uses IFRS acquired a machine with a cost of $250,000 and an estimated life of 20 years. The cost of the machine included the cost of a cylinder that must be replaced every five years for $20,000 and an inspection cost of $5,000. The machine must be reinspected every 10 years at an additional cost of $5,000 pe inspection.
>
> **Required:** Compute Year 1 depreciation using component depreciation.
>
> **Solution:** Under the component approach, the machine, the cylinder, and the inspection cost are recognized and depreciated separately:
>
> |  | Cost | Useful Life | Depreciation |
> |---|---|---|---|
> | Machine | $225,000 | 20 | $11,250 |
> | Cylinder | 20,000 | 5 | 4,000 |
> | Inspection cost | 5,000 | 10 | 500 |
> | Total | $250,000 |  | $15,750 |

## 2.2 Composite or Group Depreciation

Composite depreciation is the process of averaging the economic lives of a number of property units and depreciating the entire class of assets over a single life (e.g., all at five years), thus simplifying record keeping of assets and depreciation calculations.

### 2.2.1 Asset Retirement

When a group or composite asset is sold or retired, the accumulated depreciation is treated differently from the accumulated depreciation of a single asset. If the average service life of the group of assets has not been reached when an asset is retired, the gain or loss that results is absorbed in the accumulated depreciation account. The accumulated depreciation account is debited (credited) for the difference between the original cost and the cash received.

## 2.2.2 Depreciation Methods

Composite and component depreciation can be done using any acceptable depreciation method, including the straight-line, sum-of-the-years'-digits, and declining balance methods.

### Example 2 — Composite (Group) Depreciation

**Facts:** A schedule of machinery owned by Lester Manufacturing Company is presented below:

| | Total Cost | Estimated Salvage Value | Estimated Life in Years |
|---|---|---|---|
| Machine A | $550,000 | $50,000 | 20 |
| Machine B | 200,000 | 20,000 | 15 |
| Machine C | 40,000 | – | 5 |

Lester computes depreciation on the straight-line method.

**Required:** Depreciate the machinery using composite depreciation.

**Solution:** Based on the information presented, the composite life of these assets (in years) should be 16 years, computed as follows:

| Machine | Total Cost | Estimated Salvage Value | Depreciable Cost | Estimated Life in Years | Annual Depreciation |
|---|---|---|---|---|---|
| A | $550,000 | $50,000 | $500,000 | 20 | $25,000 |
| B | 200,000 | 20,000 | 180,000 | 15 | 12,000 |
| C | 40,000 | – | 40,000 | 5 | 8,000 |
| Totals | $790,000 | $70,000 | $720,000 | | $45,000 |

Average composite life = $720,000 divided by $45,000 = 16 years

### Illustration 1 — Disposal of Group or Composite Asset

Assume that the Lester Company sells Machine A in 10 years for $260,000. Because the loss on disposal is not recognized, accumulated depreciation must be reduced or debited.

*The journal entry is as follows:*

| | | | |
|---|---|---|---|
| DR | Cash | $260,000 | |
| DR | Accumulated depreciation | 290,000 | |
| CR | Asset A | | $550,000 |

# 3 Basic Depreciation Methods

The goal of a depreciation method should be to provide for a reasonable, consistent matching of revenue and expense by systematically allocating the cost of the depreciable asset over its estimated useful life.

The actual accumulation of depreciation in the books is accomplished by using a contra-account, such as accumulated depreciation or allowance for depreciation.

## 3.1 Straight-Line Depreciation

Straight-line depreciation is determined by the formula:

$$\frac{\text{Cost} - \text{Salvage value}}{\text{Estimated useful life}} = \text{Depreciation}$$

Estimated useful life is usually stated in periods of time, such as years or months.

---

### Illustration 2    Straight-Line Depreciation

Assume that an asset cost $11,000, has a salvage value of $1,000, and has an estimated useful life of five years.

$$\frac{\$11{,}000 - \$1{,}000}{5 \text{ years}} = \$2{,}000 \text{ depreciation per year}$$

If the asset was acquired within the year instead of at the beginning of the year, a partial depreciation expense is taken in the first year.

---

## 3.2 Sum-of-the-Years'-Digits Depreciation

The sum-of-the-years'-digits method is one of the accelerated methods of depreciation that provides higher depreciation expense in the early years and lower charges in the later years.

### 3.2.1 Calculation

To find the sum-of-the-years'-digits, each year is progressively numbered and then added. For example, the sum-of-the-years'-digits for a five-year life would be: 1 + 2 + 3 + 4 + 5 = 15

For four years: 1 + 2 + 3 + 4 = 10

For three years: 1 + 2 + 3 = 6

### 3.2.2 Formula

The sum-of-the-years'-digits becomes the denominator. The numerator is the remaining life of the asset at the beginning of the current year. For example, the first year's depreciation for a five-year life would be 5/15 of the depreciable base of the asset.

$$\text{Depreciation expense} = (\text{Cost} - \text{Salvage value}) \times \frac{\text{Remaining life of asset}}{\text{Sum-of-the-years' digits}}$$

### 3.2.3 Calculating the Sum-of-the-Years' Digits

When dealing with an asset with a long life, use the general formula for finding the sum-of-the-years'-digits:

$$S = \frac{N \times (N + 1)}{2}$$

Where:

$N$ = Estimated useful life

**Note:** The CPA Exam rarely tests sum-of-the-years'-digits depreciation for asset lives longer than five years.

---

**Example 3    Sum-of-the-Years'-Digits Method**

**Facts:** Assume that an asset cost $11,000, has a salvage value of $1,000, and has an estimated useful life of four years.

**Required:** Calculate the amount of depreciation expense for each of the four years of the asset's useful life.

**Solution:** The first step is to determine the depreciable base:

| | |
|---|---|
| Cost of asset | $11,000 |
| Less: salvage value | (1,000) |
| Depreciable base | $10,000 |

The sum-of-the-years'-digits for four years is:

1 + 2 + 3 + 4 = 10

The first year's depreciation is 4/10, the second year's is 3/10, the third year's is 2/10, and the fourth year's is 1/10, as follows:

| | | | |
|---|---|---|---|
| 1st Year: | 4/10 × $10,000 | = | $4,000 |
| 2nd Year: | 3/10 × $10,000 | = | 3,000 |
| 3rd Year: | 2/10 × $10,000 | = | 2,000 |
| 4th Year: | 1/10 × $10,000 | = | 1,000 |
| Total depreciation | | = | $10,000 |

## 3.3 Units-of-Production (Productive Output) Depreciation

The units-of-production method relates depreciation to the estimated production capability of an asset and is expressed in a rate per unit or hour.

**The formula is:**

$$\frac{\text{Cost} - \text{Salvage value}}{\text{Estimated units or hours}} = \text{Rate per unit or hour}$$

$$\text{Rate per unit (or hour)} \times \text{Number of units produced (or hours worked)} = \text{Depreciation expense}$$

## 3.4 Declining Balance Depreciation

The most common of these accelerated methods is the double-declining-balance method, although other alternative (less than double) methods are acceptable.

### 3.4.1 Calculation

Under double-declining balance, each year's depreciation rate is double the straight-line rate. In the final year, the asset is depreciated to its salvage value, if any.

Double-declining-balance depreciation is calculated using the following formula:

$$\text{Depreciation expense} = 2 \times \frac{1}{N} \times (\text{Cost} - \text{Accumulated depreciation})$$

### 3.4.2 Salvage Value

No allowance is made for salvage value because the method always leaves a remaining balance, which is treated as salvage value. However, the asset should not be depreciated below the estimated salvage value.

> **Pass Key**
>
> The only methods that ignore salvage value in the annual calculation of depreciation are the declining balance methods. Salvage value is only used as the limitation on total depreciation.

> ### Example 4  Double-Declining-Balance Method
>
> **Facts:** An asset costing $10,000 with a salvage value of $2,000 has an estimated useful life of 10 years.
>
> **Required:** Using the double-declining-balance method, calculate the depreciation expense for each year of the useful life of the asset.
>
> **Solution:** First, the regular straight-line method percentage is determined, which in this case is 10 percent (10-year life). The amount is doubled to 20 percent and applied each year to the remaining book value, as follows:
>
> | Year | Double Percentage | Net Book Value Remaining | Amount of Depreciation Expense |
> |---|---|---|---|
> | 1 | 20 | $10,000 | $2,000 |
> | 2 | 20 | 8,000 | 1,600 |
> | 3 | 20 | 6,400 | 1,280 |
> | 4 | 20 | 5,120 | 1,024 |
> | 5 | 20 | 4,096 | 819 |
> | 6 | 20 | 3,277 | 655 |
> | 7 | 20 | 2,622 | 524 |
> | 8 | 20 | 2,098 | 98 |
> | Salvage value | | 2,000 | 0 |
>
> **Note:** Had the preceding illustration been 1½ times declining balance (150 percent), the rate would have been 15 percent of the remaining book value.
>
> If the asset had been placed in service halfway through the year, the first year's depreciation would have been $1,000 (one-half of $2,000), and the second year's depreciation would have been 20 percent of $9,000 (remaining value after the first year), or $1,800.
>
> In Year 8, only $98 depreciation expense is taken because book value cannot drop below salvage value. In addition, no depreciation expense is recorded in Years 9 and 10.

## 3.5 Partial-Year Depreciation

When an asset is placed in service during the year, the depreciation expense is typically taken only for the portion of the year that the asset is used. For example, if an asset (of a company on a calendar year basis) is placed in service on July 1, only six months' depreciation is taken.

Some companies may choose to use other specific variations for assets placed in service during the year. The half-year convention means one-half year's depreciation is taken in both the year of acquisition and the year of disposal. Other variations include taking no depreciation in the year of acquisition and a full year's depreciation in the year of disposal, or taking a full year's depreciation in the year of acquisition and no depreciation in the year of disposal.

# 4 Disposals

## 4.1 Sale of an Asset During Its Useful Life

| | | | |
|---|---|---|---|
| DR | Cash received from sale | $XXX | |
| DR | Accumulated depreciation of sold asset | XXX | |
| CR | Sold asset at cost | | $XXX |
| CR/DR | The difference is gain/loss | | XXX |

## 4.2 Write-off Fully Depreciated Asset

| | | | |
|---|---|---|---|
| DR | Accumulated depreciation (100 percent) | $XXX | |
| CR | Old asset at full cost (100 percent) | | $XXX |

## 4.3 Total and Permanent Impairment

| | | | |
|---|---|---|---|
| DR | Accumulated depreciation per records | $XXX | |
| DR | Loss due to impairment (the difference) | XXX | |
| CR | Asset at full cost | | $XXX |

# 5 Disclosure

Allowances for depreciation and depletion should be deducted from the assets to which they relate.

The following disclosures of depreciable assets and depreciation should be made in the financial statements or notes thereto:

- Depreciation expense for the period.
- Balance of major classes of depreciable assets by nature or function.
- Accumulated depreciation allowances by classes or in total.
- The methods used, by major classes, in computing depreciation.

# 6 Depletion

Depletion is the allocation of the cost of wasting natural resources such as oil, gas, timber, and minerals to the production process.

## 6.1 Definitions

- **Purchase Cost:** Purchase cost includes any expenditures necessary to purchase and then prepare the land for the removal of resources, such as drilling costs or the costs for tunnels or shafts for the oil industry (intangible development costs) or to prepare the asset for harvest, such as in the lumber industry.
- **Residual Value:** The residual value is similar to salvage value. It is the monetary worth of a depleted asset after the resources have been removed.

- **Depletion Base (Cost − Residual Value):** The depletion base is the cost to purchase the property minus the estimated net residual value remaining after all resources have been removed from the property.

## 6.2 Methods

### 6.2.1 Cost Depletion (GAAP)

Cost depletion is computed by dividing the current estimated recoverable units into unrecovered cost (less salvage) to arrive at a cost depletion rate, which is multiplied by units produced to allocate the costs to production.

### 6.2.2 Percentage Depletion (Not GAAP/Tax Only)

- Percentage depletion is based on a percentage of sales. It is allowed by Congress as a tax deduction to encourage exploration in very risky businesses.
- Percentage depletion can (and usually does) exceed cost depletion.
- It is limited to 50 percent of net income from the depletion property computed before the percentage depletion allowance.

## 6.3 Calculation of Depletion

Depletion for a period is calculated as follows:

$$\text{Total depletion} = \text{Unit depletion rate} \times \text{Number of units extracted}$$

### 6.3.1 Unit Depletion Rate (Depletion per Unit)

Unit depletion is the amount of depletion recognized per unit (e.g., ton, barrel, etc.) extracted.

$$\text{Unit depletion rate} = \frac{\text{Depletion base}}{\text{Estimated recoverable units}}$$

### 6.3.2 Depletion Base

The depletion base may be calculated as:

Cost to purchase property
Plus: development costs to prepare the land for extraction
Plus: any estimated restoration costs
Less: residual value of land after the resources (e.g., mineral ore, oil, etc.) are extracted

### 6.3.3 Recognition of Depletion

If all units extracted are not sold, then depletion must be allocated between cost of goods sold and inventory. The amount of depletion to be included in cost of goods sold is calculated by multiplying the unit depletion rate by the number of units sold. Depletion applicable to units extracted but not sold is allocated to inventory as direct materials.

### Example 5 — Total Depletion and Cost of Goods Sold Depletion

**Facts:** In Year 1, Happy Mine Corporation purchased a mineral mine for $3,400,000 with removable ore estimated by geological surveys at 4,000,000 tons. The property has an estimated value of $200,000 after the ore has been extracted. The company incurred $800,000 of development costs preparing the mine for production. During Year 1, 400,000 tons were removed and 375,000 tons were sold.

**Required:**

1. Calculate the depletion base for the mineral mine.
2. Calculate the amount of depletion the mine should record for Year 1.
3. Determine the amount of depletion the mine should include in cost of goods sold for Year 1.

**Solution:**

1. **Depletion base:**

    Cost of land + Development costs + Restoration − Residual value

    $4,000,000 = $3,400,000 + $800,000 + 0 − $200,000

    Then, calculate unit depletion rate:

    $$\text{Unit depletion} = \frac{\text{Depletion base}}{\text{Estimated recoverable units}} = \frac{\$4,000,000}{4,000,000 \text{ tons}} = \$1 \text{ per ton}$$

2. **Depletion for Year 1:**

    = Unit depletion × Units extracted
    = $1 per unit × 400,000 units
    = $400,000

3. **Depletion to be included in cost of goods sold:**

    = Unit depletion × Units sold
    = $1 per unit × 375,000 units
    = $375,000

    Note that the remaining $25,000 would be included in inventory as direct materials ($400,000 − $375,000 = $25,000).

## Pass Key

When computing depletion on land, remember it is **REAL** property:

**Residual** value (subtract)

**Extraction**/development cost

**Anticipated** restoration cost

**Land** purchase price

---

### Question 1                                             MCQ-05651

Carr Inc. purchased equipment for $100,000 on January 1, Year 1. The equipment had an estimated 10-year useful life and a $15,000 salvage value. Carr uses the 200 percent declining balance depreciation method. In its Year 2 income statement, what amount should Carr report as depreciation expense for the equipment?

- a. $13,600
- b. $16,000
- c. $17,000
- d. $20,000

### Question 2                                             MCQ-00143

In January, Vorst Co. purchased a mineral mine for $2,640,000 with removable ore estimated at 1,200,000 tons. After it has extracted all the ore, Vorst will be required by law to restore the land to its original condition at an estimated cost of $180,000. Vorst believes that it would be able to sell the property afterward for $300,000. During the year, Vorst incurred $360,000 of development costs preparing the mine for production and removed and sold 60,000 tons of ore. In its year-end income statement, what amount should Vorst report as depletion?

- a. $135,000
- b. $144,000
- c. $150,000
- d. $159,000

## NOTES

# MODULE 6 Nonmonetary Transactions

FAR 3

## 1 Exchanges Having Commercial Substance

U.S. GAAP requires that exchanges of nonmonetary assets be categorized as either having "commercial substance" or lacking "commercial substance."

An exchange has commercial substance if the future cash flows change as a result of the transaction. The change can be in the areas of risk, timing, or amount of cash flows. In other words, if the economic position of the two parties changes because of the exchange, then the exchange has "commercial substance." A fair value approach is used.

> **Pass Key**
>
> The fair value of assets given up is assumed to be equal to the fair value of assets received, including any cash given or received in the transaction.

### 1.1 Recognizing Gains and Losses

Gains and losses are always recognized in exchanges having commercial substance and are computed as the difference between fair value and book value of the asset given up.

---

**Example 1**    **Exchange With Commercial Substance**

**Facts:** Foxy Company exchanged used cars for a building that could possibly become Foxy Company's storage space. Future cash flows will significantly change. The book value of the cars totals $40,000 (cost of $102,000 − accumulated depreciation of $62,000). The cars' fair value is $45,000. In addition, Foxy must pay $20,000 cash as part of the exchange.

**Required:** Calculate the gain to be recognized on the exchange.

**Solution:**

| | | |
|---|---:|---:|
| Fair value of cars | | $45,000 |
| Book value of cars: | | |
|   Cost of cars | $102,000 | |
|   Accumulated depreciation | (62,000) | |
|     Book value | | (40,000) |
| Gain on disposal of cars | | $ 5,000 |

The cash given up does not enter into the calculation of gain on exchange, which is fair value less book value.

## 1.2 Calculation of Basis of Acquired Asset

The cash given up in the exchange is used to calculate the building's basis on Foxy's books.

### Example 2 Journal Entry for Exchange

**Part 1**

**Facts:** Assume the same facts as in the previous example.

**Required:** Calculate the basis of the new building and prepare the journal entry to record the exchange.

**Solution:**

| | |
|---|---|
| Fair value of cars given up | $45,000 |
| Plus: cash paid | 20,000 |
| Building cost (basis) | $65,000 |

*Journal entry to record the exchange and the gain on the exchange:*

| | | | |
|---|---|---|---|
| DR | Building | $65,000 | |
| DR | Accumulated depreciation—cars | 62,000 | |
| CR | Cars | | $102,000 |
| CR | Gain on disposal of cars | | 5,000 |
| CR | Cash | | 20,000 |

**Note:** If the FV of the cars in the previous example was $38,000 instead of $45,000, a loss of $2,000 (FV $38,000 − BV $40,000) would be recognized and the basis of the building would be $58,000 ($38,000 FV + $20,000 cash).

*Journal entry to record the exchange and the loss on the exchange:*

| | | | |
|---|---|---|---|
| DR | Building | $58,000 | |
| DR | Accumulated depreciation—cars | 62,000 | |
| DR | Loss | 2,000 | |
| CR | Cars | | $102,000 |
| CR | Cash | | 20,000 |

> **U.S. GAAP VS. IFRS**
>
> Under IFRS, nonmonetary exchanges are characterized as exchanges of similar assets and exchanges of dissimilar assets. Exchanges of dissimilar assets are regarded as exchanges that generate revenue, and are accounted for in the same manner as exchanges having commercial substance under U.S. GAAP. Exchanges of similar assets are not regarded as exchanges that generate revenue, and no gains are recognized.

## 2 Exchanges Lacking Commercial Substance

If projected cash flows after the exchange are not expected to change significantly, then the exchange lacks commercial substance. The following accounting treatment is used (note that this method also must be used in any exchange in which fair values are not determinable, or if the exchange is made to facilitate sales to customers).

### 2.1 Gains

#### 2.1.1 No Boot Is Received = No Gain

If the exchange lacks commercial substance and no boot is received, no gain is recognized.

#### 2.1.2 Boot Is Paid = No Gain (< 25 Percent Rule)

If the exchange lacks commercial substance and boot paid is less than 25 percent of the total consideration, no gain is recognized.

#### 2.1.3 Boot Is Received = Recognize Proportional Gain (< 25 Percent Rule)

If the exchange lacks commercial substance and the boot received is less than 25 percent of the total consideration received, a proportional amount of the gain is recognized. A ratio (the total boot received/the total consideration received) is calculated, and that proportion of the total gain realized is recognized.

#### 2.1.4 Boot Is 25 Percent or More of Total Consideration

When the boot received equals or exceeds 25 percent of the total consideration, both parties account for the transaction as a monetary exchange, and gains and losses are recognized in their entirety by both parties to the exchange.

### 2.2 Losses

If the transaction lacks commercial substance and a loss is indicated, the loss should be recognized.

# Nonmonetary Transactions

## Example 3 — No Boot = No Gain Recognized

**Facts:**

- Machine A is exchanged for Machine B
- Machine A, carrying value (BV) = $10,000
- Machine A, fair value (FV) = $12,000
- Machine B, fair value (FV) = $12,000 (FV given = FV received)

**Required:** Calculate the total gain on the transaction. Indicate whether the gain is recognized and calculate the basis of the acquired asset.

**Solution:**

FV of asset given − BV of asset given

$12,000 − $10,000 = $2,000 gain

The gain is not recognized because the exchange lacks commercial substance and boot is not included in the transaction. As a result, the basis of the acquired asset is equal to the basis of the old asset, which is also equal to the asset's fair value less the deferred gain.

*Journal entry to record the above transaction:*

| DR | Machine B | $10,000 | |
|---|---|---|---|
| CR | Machine A | | $10,000 |

## Example 4 — Boot Is Paid (< 25 Percent Rule) = No Gain Recognized

**Facts:**

- Machine A and $2,500 is exchanged for Machine B
- Machine A, carrying value (BV) = $10,000
- Machine A, fair value (FV) = $12,000
- Machine B, fair value (FV) = $14,500 (FV given = FV received)

**Required:** Calculate the total gain on the exchange. Indicate whether the gain is recognized, and calculate the basis of the new asset.

*(continued)*

(continued)

**Solution:**

FV of asset given* − BV of asset given*

$14,500 − $12,500 = $2,000 gain

*Note that the assets given include Machine A plus $2,500.

The gain is not recognized because the exchange lacks commercial substance and boot is paid. As a result, the basis of the acquired asset is equal to the basis of the old asset plus the cash paid.

*Journal entry to record the above transaction:*

| DR | Machine B | $12,500 | |
|----|-----------|---------|---|
| CR | Machine A | | $10,000 |
| CR | Cash | | 2,500 |

### Example 5 — Boot Is Received (< 25 Percent Rule) = Proportional Gain Recognized

**Facts:**
- Machine A is exchanged for Machine B and $2,500
- Machine A, carrying value (BV) = $10,000
- Machine A, fair value (FV) = $12,000
- Machine B, fair value (FV) = $9,500 (FV given = FV received)

**Required:** Calculate the total gain recognized on the exchange. Prepare the journal entry to record the transaction.

**Solution:**

FV of asset given − BV of asset given

$12,000 − $10,000 = $2,000 total gain

The $2,500 cash is 21% of the consideration received ($2,500 / $12,000 = 21%), so a proportional amount of the gain is recognized:

Recognized gain = Realized gain × (Boot received / FV received)

= $2,000 × ($2,500 / $12,000)

= $417

*Journal entry to record the above transaction:*

| DR | Machine B (plug) | $7,917 | |
|----|------------------|--------|---|
| DR | Cash | 2,500 | |
| CR | Machine A | | $10,000 |
| CR | Gain on exchange | | 417 |

## Example 6 — Boot Received (≥ 25 Percent Rule) = All Gain Recognized

**Facts:**

- Machine A is exchanged for Machine B and $6,000
- Machine A, carrying value (BV) = $10,000
- Machine A, fair value (FV) = $12,000
- Machine B, fair value (FV) = $6,000 (FV given = FV received)

**Required:** Calculate the total gain on the exchange, and determine how much is recognized. Prepare the journal entry to record the transaction.

**Solution:**

FV of asset given − BV of asset given

$12,000 − $10,000 = $2,000 total gain

The $6,000 cash is 50% of the consideration received ($6,000 / $12,000 = 50%), so the entire gain is recognized and the machine acquired is recognized at fair value.

*Journal entry to record the above transaction:*

| | | | |
|---|---|---|---|
| DR | Machine B (plug) | $6,000 | |
| DR | Cash | 6,000 | |
| CR | Machine A | | $10,000 |
| CR | Gain on exchange | | 2,000 |

## Example 7 — Losses Recognized in Full

**Facts:**

- Machine A is exchanged for Machine B
- Machine A, carrying value (BV) = $10,000
- Machine A, fair value (FV) = $8,000
- Machine B, fair value (FV) = $8,000 (FV given = FV received)

**Required:** Calculate the loss on the exchange, show the amount recognized, and prepare the journal entry to record the exchange transaction.

(continued)

*(continued)*

**Solution:**

FV of asset given − BV of asset given

$8,000 − $10,000 = $(2,000)

Losses are recognized in full in all exchanges lacking commercial substance.

*Journal entry to record the above transaction:*

| | | | |
|---|---|---|---|
| DR | Machine B | $8,000 | |
| DR | Loss on exchange | 2,000 | |
| CR | Machine A | | $10,000 |

# 3  Involuntary Conversions

## 3.1  Overview

Whenever a nonmonetary asset is involuntarily converted (e.g., fire loss, theft, or condemnation) to cash, the entire gain or loss is recognized for financial accounting purposes.

### Example 8 — Gain on Condemnation

**Facts:** On 12/1/Yr 1, Sykes Company received a condemnation award of $100,000 for the forced sale of Sykes Company's factory building. At that time, Sykes Company's building had a book value of $75,000.

**Required:** Compute the gain or loss on the condemnation and prepare the journal entry to record the event.

**Solution:**

| | |
|---|---:|
| Proceeds from condemnation | $100,000 |
| Less: book value of nonmonetary asset (factory building) | (75,000) |
| Gain on condemnation | $ 25,000 |

*Journal entry to record the above transaction:*

| | | | |
|---|---|---|---|
| DR | Cash | $100,000 | |
| CR | Building | | $75,000 |
| CR | Gain on involuntary conversion | | 25,000 |

## 3.2  Tax Treatment

The rules for involuntary conversions are different for tax purposes. If a gain is recognized for financial purposes in one period and for tax purposes in another period, a temporary difference will result. Interperiod tax allocation will be necessary.

Nonmonetary Transactions

### Question 1 — MCQ-00720

On July 1, Year 1, Balt Co. exchanged a truck for 25 shares of Ace Corp.'s common stock. On that date, the truck's carrying amount was $2,500, and its fair value was $3,000. Also, the book value of Ace's stock was $60 per share. On December 31, Year 1, Ace had 250 shares of common stock outstanding and its book value per share was $50. What amount should Balt report in its December 31, Year 1, balance sheet as investment in Ace, assuming the transaction had commercial substance?

- a. $3,000
- b. $2,500
- c. $1,500
- d. $1,250

### Question 2 — MCQ-08514

A transaction was reported as a nonmonetary exchange of assets. Under which of the following circumstances should the exchange be measured based on the reported amount of the nonmonetary asset surrendered?

- a. When the entity's future cash flows are expected to change as a result of the exchange.
- b. When the timing of future cash flows of the asset received differs significantly from the configuration of the future cash flows of the asset transferred.
- c. When the transaction lacks commercial substance.
- d. When the transaction has commercial substance.

# MODULE 7: Intangibles

FAR 3

## 1 Intangible Assets

Intangible assets are long-lived legal rights and competitive advantages developed or acquired by a business enterprise. They are typically acquired to be used in operations of a business and provide benefits over several accounting periods.

Intangible assets differ considerably in their characteristics, useful lives, and relationship to operations of an enterprise, and are classified accordingly.

### 1.1 Classification of Intangible Assets

- Patents, copyrights, franchises, trademarks, and goodwill are the common intangible assets tested on the CPA Examination.
- Intangible assets may be either specifically identifiable (e.g., patents, copyrights, franchise, etc.) or not specifically identifiable (e.g., goodwill).

#### 1.1.1 Manner of Acquisition

- **Purchased Intangible Assets**

  Intangible assets acquired from other enterprises or individuals should be recorded as an asset at cost. Legal and registration fees incurred to obtain an intangible asset should also be capitalized.

- **Internally Developed Intangible Assets**
  - Under U.S. GAAP, the cost of intangible assets not acquired from others (i.e., developed internally) should be expensed when incurred because U.S. GAAP prohibits the capitalization of research and development costs.
  - Examples (must be expensed):
    — Trademarks (except for the capitalizable costs identified below)
    — Goodwill from advertising
    — The cost of developing, maintaining, or restoring goodwill
  - The exception is that certain costs associated with internally developed intangibles that are specifically identifiable can be capitalized, such as:
    — Legal fees and other costs related to a successful defense of the asset
    — Registration or consulting fees
    — Design costs (e.g., of a trademark)
    — Other direct costs to secure the asset

#### 1.1.2 Expected Period of Benefit

Classification of the intangible asset depends on whether the economic life can be determined or is indeterminable.

### 1.1.3 Separability

The classification of the intangible asset depends on whether the asset can be separated from the entity (e.g., a patent) or is substantially inseparable from it (e.g., a trade name or goodwill).

> **U.S. GAAP VS. IFRS**
>
> Under IFRS, research costs related to an internally developed intangible asset must be expensed, but an intangible asset arising from development is recognized if the entity can demonstrate all of the following:
>
> - Technological feasibility has been established.
> - The entity intends to complete the intangible asset.
> - The entity has the ability to use or sell the intangible asset.
> - The intangible asset will generate future economic benefits.
> - Adequate resources are available to complete the development and sell or use the asset.
>
> The entity can reliably measure the expenditure attributable to the development of the intangible asset.

## 1.2 Capitalization of Costs

A company should record the cost of intangible assets acquired from other enterprises or individuals in an "arm's-length" transaction as assets.

- Cost is measured by:
  - the amount of cash disbursed or the fair value of other assets distributed;
  - the present value of amounts to be paid for liabilities incurred; and
  - the fair value of consideration received for stock issued.
- Cost may be determined either by the fair value of the consideration given or by the fair value of the property acquired, whichever is more clearly evident.
- The cost of unidentifiable intangible assets is measured as the difference between the cost of the group of assets or enterprise acquired and the sum of the costs assigned to identifiable assets acquired, less liabilities assumed.
- The cost of identifiable assets should not include goodwill.

## 1.3 Amortization

The value of intangible assets eventually disappears; therefore, the cost of each type of intangible asset (except for goodwill and assets with indefinite lives) should be amortized by systematic charges to income over the period estimated to be benefited.

> **Pass Key**
>
> A patent is amortized over the shorter of its estimated life or remaining legal life.

### 1.3.1 Method

The straight-line method of amortization should be applied, unless a company demonstrates that another systematic method is more appropriate. The method and estimated useful lives of intangible assets should be adequately disclosed in the notes to the financial statements. Expenses that increase the useful life of the intangible asset require an adjustment to the calculation of the annual amortization.

### 1.3.2 Change in Useful Life

If the life of an existing intangible asset is reduced or extended, the remaining net book value is amortized over the new remaining life.

## 1.4 Sale of Intangible Assets

If an intangible asset is sold, simply compare its carrying value at the date of sale with the selling price to determine the gain or loss.

## 1.5 Valuation

### 1.5.1 U.S. GAAP

Under *U.S. GAAP*, finite life intangible assets are reported at cost less amortization and impairment. Indefinite life intangible assets are reported at cost less impairment.

### 1.5.2 IFRS

Under *IFRS*, intangible assets can be reported under either the cost model or the revaluation model.

- **Cost Model:** Under the *cost model*, intangible assets are reported at cost adjusted for amortization (finite life intangible assets only) and impairment.

- **Revaluation Model:** Under the *revaluation model*, intangible assets are initially recognized at cost and then revalued to fair value at a subsequent revaluation date. Revalued intangible assets are reported at fair value on the revaluation date adjusted for subsequent amortization (finite life intangible assets only) and subsequent impairment.

$$\text{Revaluation model carrying value} = \text{Fair value on revaluation date} - \text{Subsequent amortization} - \text{Subsequent impairment}$$

Revaluations must be performed regularly so that at the end of each reporting period the carrying value of the intangible asset does not differ materially from fair value. If an intangible asset is accounted for using the revaluation model, all other assets in its class must also be revalued unless there is no active market for the intangible assets.

- **Revaluation Losses:** *Revaluation losses* (fair value on revaluation date < carrying value before revaluation) are reported on the income statement, unless the revaluation loss reverses a previously recognized revaluation gain. A revaluation loss that reverses a previously recognized revaluation gain is recognized in other comprehensive income and reduces the revaluation surplus in accumulated other comprehensive income.

- **Revaluation Gains:** *Revaluation gains* (fair value on revaluation date > carrying value before revaluation) are reported in other comprehensive income and accumulated in equity as revaluation surplus, unless the revaluation gain reverses a previously recognized revaluation loss. Revaluation gains are reported on the income statement to the extent that they reverse a previously recognized revaluation loss.

- **Impairment:** If revalued intangible assets subsequently become impaired, the *impairment* is recorded by first reducing any revaluation surplus in equity to zero with further impairment losses reported on the income statement.

### Example 1   IFRS Intangible Asset Revaluation

**Facts:** On December 31, Year 2, an entity that had adopted the IFRS revaluation model in Year 1 adjusted its patents to fair value. On that date, the patents had the following carrying value and fair value:

|  | Carrying Value | Fair Value |
|---|---|---|
| Patents | $8,200,000 | $9,100,000 |

The entity had recorded a revaluation loss of $500,000 in Year 1.

**Required:** Compute the revaluation gains to be reported in Year 2 net income and other comprehensive income.

**Solution:** Total revaluation gain = $9,100,000 − $8,200,000 = $900,000

Of this gain, $500,000 will be reported on the income statement as a reversal of the $500,000 revaluation loss reported in Year 1. The remaining $400,000 ($900,000 − $500,000) gain will be reported in other comprehensive income as revaluation surplus.

# 2 Franchisee Accounting

## 2.1 Initial Franchise Fees

The present value of the amount paid (or to be paid) by a franchisee is recorded as an intangible asset on the balance sheet and amortized over the expected period of benefit of the franchise (i.e., the expected life of the franchise).

## 2.2 Continuing Franchise Fees

These fees are received for ongoing services provided by the franchisor to the franchisee (often referred to as franchise royalties). Usually, such fees are calculated based on a percentage of franchise revenues. Such services might include management training, promotion, and legal assistance. Fees should be reported by the franchisee as an expense and as revenue by the franchisor, in the period incurred.

> **Example 2** **Franchisee's Intangible Assets**
>
> **Facts:** Peter signed an agreement on July 1, Year 1, with Disco Records to operate as a franchisee in New York City. The initial franchise fee was $75,000 and was paid by a $25,000 down payment with the balance payable in five equal annual payments of $10,000 beginning July 1, Year 2. The expected life of the franchise is 10 years. The present value of the five annual payments is $37,908. The amount to be capitalized as an intangible franchise asset on July 1, Year 1, is $62,908 ($25,000 + $37,908).
>
> **Required:** Prepare the journal entry to record the franchise on Peter's books at the acquisition date. Explain the accounting treatment required over the life of the franchise for the discount account. Calculate the amortization of the franchises account for Year 1.
>
> **Solution:**
>
> *Franchisee's journal entry to record the franchise at July 1, Year 1:*
>
> | | | | |
> |---|---|---|---|
> | DR | Franchises | $62,908 | |
> | DR | Discount on notes payable (contra-liability) | 12,092 | |
> | CR | Notes payable | | $50,000 |
> | CR | Cash | | 25,000 |
>
> The discount will be recognized as interest expense by the franchisee over the payment period on an effective interest basis. The franchise account would appear in the franchisee's intangible assets section of the balance sheet and would be amortized over the expected life of the franchise:
>
> Year 1 amortization = (Franchise balance / Expected life) × Months
> = ($62,908 / 10) × 6/12 (July through December, Year 1)
> = $3,145

# 3 Start-up Costs

Expenses incurred in the formation of a corporation (e.g., legal fees) are considered organizational costs and are an example of start-up costs.

Start-up costs, including organizational costs, should be expensed when incurred.

- Start-up costs include costs of the one-time activities associated with:
  - Organizing a new entity (e.g., legal fees for preparing a charter, partnership agreement, bylaws, original stock certifications, filing fees, etc.)
  - Opening a new facility
  - Introducing a new product or service
  - Conducting business in a new territory or with a new class of customer
  - Initiating a new process in an existing facility

# Intangibles

- Start-up costs do not include costs associated with:
  - Routine, ongoing efforts to refine, enrich, or improve the quality of existing products, services, processes, or facilities
  - Business mergers or acquisitions
  - Ongoing customer acquisition

> **Pass Key**
>
> Remember that organizational expenses are *not* capitalized as an intangible asset. Rather, they are expensed immediately.

## 4 Research and Development Costs

Research is the planned efforts of a company to discover new information that will help either create a new product, service, process, or technique or significantly improve the one in current use. Development takes the findings generated by research and formulates a plan to create the desired item or to improve significantly the existing one.

### 4.1 Accounting for Research and Development Costs (U.S. GAAP)

Under U.S. GAAP, the only acceptable method of accounting for research and development costs is a direct charge to expense, with two exceptions:

1. Materials, equipment, or facilities (i.e., tangible assets) that have alternative future uses. Capitalize and depreciate the assets over their useful lives (not the life of the research and development project).
2. Research and development costs of any nature undertaken on behalf of others under a contractual arrangement.
   - The purchaser (buying the R&D) will expense as research and development the amount paid; and the provider (performing the R&D for the purchaser) will expense the costs incurred as cost of sales.
   - The conclusion for charging most research and development costs to expense under U.S. GAAP is the high degree of uncertainty of any future benefits.
   - Disclosure is required in the financial statements or notes of the amount of research and development charged to expense for the period.

### 4.2 Items Not Considered Research and Development

- Routine periodic design changes to old products or troubleshooting in the production stage (these are manufacturing costs, not research and development expenses).
- Marketing research.
- Quality control testing.
- Reformulation of a chemical compound.

## U.S. GAAP VS. IFRS

Under IFRS, research costs must be expensed but development costs may be capitalized if certain criteria are met, as stated in the discussion of intangible assets.

### Example 3 — Research and Development

**Facts:** Julile Co. incurred research and development costs in the current year as follows:

| | |
|---|---|
| Materials used in research and development projects | $ 400,000 |
| Equipment acquired that will have alternative future uses in future research and development projects | 2,000,000 |
| Depreciation on above equipment | 500,000 |
| Personnel costs of persons involved in research and development projects | 1,000,000 |
| Consulting fees paid to outsiders for research and development projects | 100,000 |
| Indirect costs reasonably allocable to research and development projects | 200,000 |

**Required:** Calculate the amount of research and development costs that should be expensed for the current year.

**Solution:** The following items would qualify as research and development costs and should be expensed in the current year:

| | |
|---|---|
| Materials used in research and development projects | $ 400,000 |
| Depreciation on equipment used in research and development | 500,000 |
| Personnel costs of people involved in research and development projects | 1,000,000 |
| Consulting fees paid to outsiders for research and development projects | 100,000 |
| Indirect costs reasonably allocable to research and development projects | 200,000 |
| Total | $2,200,000 |

The equipment is not charged to research and development costs because it has alternative future uses. It should be capitalized as a tangible asset and depreciated over the useful life of the equipment. The depreciation expense should be charged to research and development.

*Intangibles*     FAR 3

# 5 Computer Software Development Costs

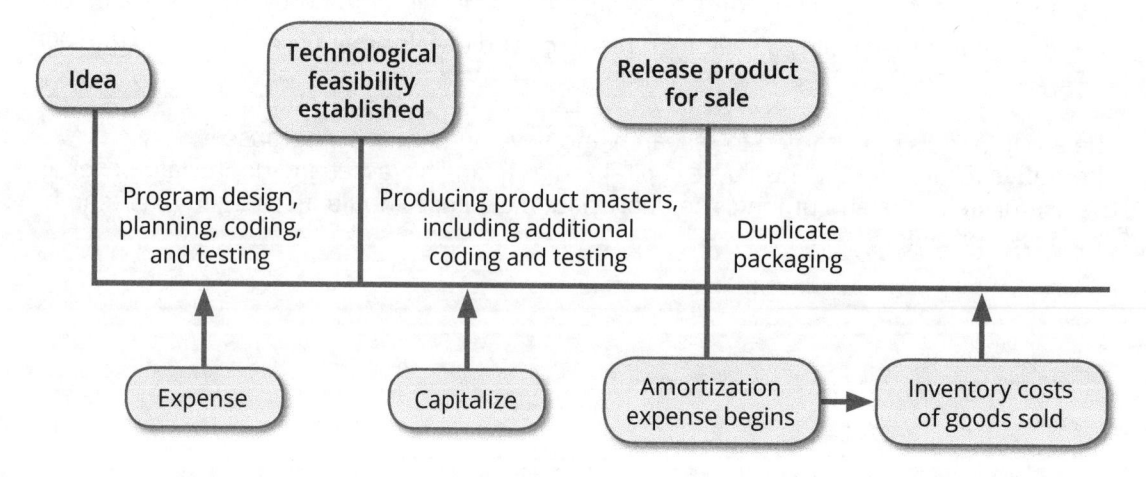

## 5.1 Computer Software Developed to Be Sold, Leased, or Licensed

### 5.1.1 Accounting for Costs

- Expense costs (planning, design, coding, and testing) incurred until technological feasibility has been established for the product.
- Capitalize costs (coding, testing, and producing product masters) incurred after technological feasibility has been established up to the point that the product is released for sale.
- Technological feasibility is established upon completion of a detailed program design or working model.

### 5.1.2 Amortization of Capitalized Software Costs

Annual amortization (on a product by product basis) is the *greater* of:

$$\text{Percentage of revenue} = \text{Total capitalized amount} \times \frac{\text{Current gross revenue for period}}{\text{Total projected gross revenue for product}}$$

$$\text{Straight line} = \text{Total capitalized amount} \times \frac{1}{\text{Estimate of economic life}}$$

### 5.1.3 Inventory

Costs incurred to actually produce the product are product costs charged to inventory. Capitalized software costs are reported at the *lower of cost or market*, where market is equal to net realizable value.

**Accounting for Costs**

```
   Idea          Technological           Release product
                 feasibility              for sale
                 established

   Program design,    Producing product masters,
   planning, coding,  including additional        Duplicate
   and testing        coding and testing          packaging
        ↑                    ↑                        ↑
     Expense            Capitalize         Amortization  →  Inventory costs
                                           expense begins    of goods sold
```

## 5.2 Computer Software Developed Internally or Obtained Only for Internal Use

### 5.2.1 Accounting for Costs

- Expense costs incurred for the preliminary project state and costs incurred for training and maintenance.
- Capitalize costs incurred after the preliminary project state and for upgrades and enhancements, including:
  - Direct costs of materials and services;
  - Costs of employees directly associated with project; and
  - Interest costs incurred for the project.

### 5.2.2 Amortization

Capitalized costs should be amortized on a straight-line basis.

### 5.2.3 Revenue Recognition

If software previously developed for internal use is subsequently sold to outsiders, proceeds received (e.g., from the license of computer software, net of incremental costs) should be applied first to the carrying amount of the software, then recognized as revenue (after the carrying amount of the software has reached zero).

---

**U.S. GAAP VS. IFRS**

IFRS does not provide separate guidance regarding computer software development costs. Under IFRS, computer software development costs are internally generated intangibles. Research costs must be expensed and development costs may be capitalized if certain criteria are met (see the discussion of intangible assets).

---

**Question 1**  MCQ-00542

Gray Co. was granted a patent on January 2, Year 1, and appropriately capitalized $45,000 of related costs. Gray was amortizing the patent over its estimated useful life of 15 years. During Year 4, Gray paid $15,000 in legal costs in successfully defending an attempted infringement of the patent. After the legal action was completed, Gray sold the patent to the plaintiff for $75,000. Gray's policy is to take no amortization in the year of disposal. In its Year 4 income statement, what amount should Gray report as a gain from the sale of the patent?

- a. $15,000
- b. $24,000
- c. $27,000
- d. $39,000

Intangibles FAR 3

### Question 2 — MCQ-00554

On January 2 of the current year, Rafa Co. purchased a franchise with a useful life of 10 years for $50,000. An additional franchise fee of 3 percent of franchise operation revenues must be paid each year to the franchisor. Revenues from franchise operations amounted to $400,000 during the year. In its December 31 balance sheet, what amount should Rafa report as an intangible asset franchise?

- a. $33,000
- b. $43,800
- c. $45,000
- d. $50,000

### Question 3 — MCQ-05947

Stam Co. incurred the following research and development project costs during the current year:

| | |
|---|---:|
| Equipment purchased for current and future projects | $100,000 |
| Equipment purchased for current projects only | 200,000 |
| Research and development salaries for current projects | 400,000 |
| Legal fees to obtain patent | 50,000 |
| Material and labor costs for prototype product | 600,000 |

The equipment has a five-year useful life and is depreciated using the straight-line method. What amount should Stam recognize as research and development expense at year-end under U.S. GAAP?

- a. $450,000
- b. $1,000,000
- c. $1,220,000
- d. $1,350,000

# MODULE 8: Impairment

## 1 Impairment of Intangible Assets Other Than Goodwill

Intangible assets with indefinite useful life (including goodwill) are tested for impairment at least annually, and intangible assets with finite useful life are tested whenever events or changes in circumstances indicate that the carrying amount may not be recoverable.

Under U.S. GAAP, the impairment test applied to an intangible asset other than goodwill is determined by the asset's life. An intangible asset has a finite life when it is possible to estimate the useful life of the asset. If it is not possible to determine the useful life of an intangible asset, then the asset has an indefinite (not infinite) life. If an intangible asset has a finite life, it is amortized over that life. If it has an indefinite life, it is not amortized.

### 1.1 Intangible Assets With Finite Lives (Two-Step Impairment Test)

An intangible asset with a finite life is tested for impairment using a two-step impairment test.

**Step 1:** The carrying amount of the asset is compared with the sum of the undiscounted cash flows expected to result from the use of the asset and its eventual disposition.

**Step 2:** If the carrying amount exceeds the total undiscounted future cash flows, then the asset is impaired and an impairment loss equal to the difference between the carrying amount of the asset and its fair value is recorded.

> **Pass Key**
>
> It is important to note the following when testing property, plant, and equipment, or an intangible asset with a finite life, for impairment:
>
> - **Determining the Impairment:** Use undiscounted future net cash flows.
> - **Amount of Impairment:** Use fair value (FV).

### 1.2 Intangible Assets With Indefinite Lives (One-Step Impairment Test)

When testing an intangible asset with an indefinite life (including goodwill) for impairment, it is generally not possible to estimate total future cash flows expected to result from the use of the assets and its disposition. As a result, an intangible asset with an indefinite life is tested for impairment by comparing the fair value of the intangible asset to its carrying amount. If the asset's fair value is less than its carrying amount, an impairment loss is recognized in an amount equal to the difference.

This quantitative impairment test is not necessary if, after assessing relevant qualitative factors, an entity determines that it is not more likely than not that the fair value of the indefinite-life intangible asset is less than its carrying amount (see expanded discussion of the qualitative evaluation of impairment in F4).

## 1.3 Reporting an Impairment Loss

An impairment loss is reported as a component of income from continuing operations before income taxes, unless the impairment loss is related to discontinued operations. The carrying amount of the asset is reduced by the amount of the impairment loss. Restoration of previously recognized impairment losses is prohibited, unless the asset is held for disposal.

### U.S. GAAP VS. IFRS

Under IFRS, an impairment loss for an intangible asset other than goodwill is calculated using a one-step model in which the carrying value of the intangible asset is compared with the intangible asset's recoverable amount. IFRS defines the recoverable amount as the greater of the asset's fair value less costs to sell and the asset's value in use. Value in use is the present value of the future cash flows expected from the intangible asset. IFRS allows the reversal of impairment losses.

### Pass Key

|  | U.S. GAAP | |
|---|---|---|
|  | *Finite Life* | *Indefinite Life* |
| *Characteristics* | Useful life is limited | Life extends beyond the foreseeable future or cannot be determined |
| *Amortization* | Over useful economic life | None |
| *Impairment test* | Two-step test:<br>• Undiscounted net cash flows<br>• Fair value | One-step test:<br>• Fair value |

## 1.4 Calculation of the Impairment Loss

The impairment loss is calculated as the amount by which the carrying amount exceeds the fair value of the asset.

## Impairment Test

**Qualitative test for impairment (indefinite life intangibles only)**

↓

**Undiscounted future net cash flows***
< Net carrying value >

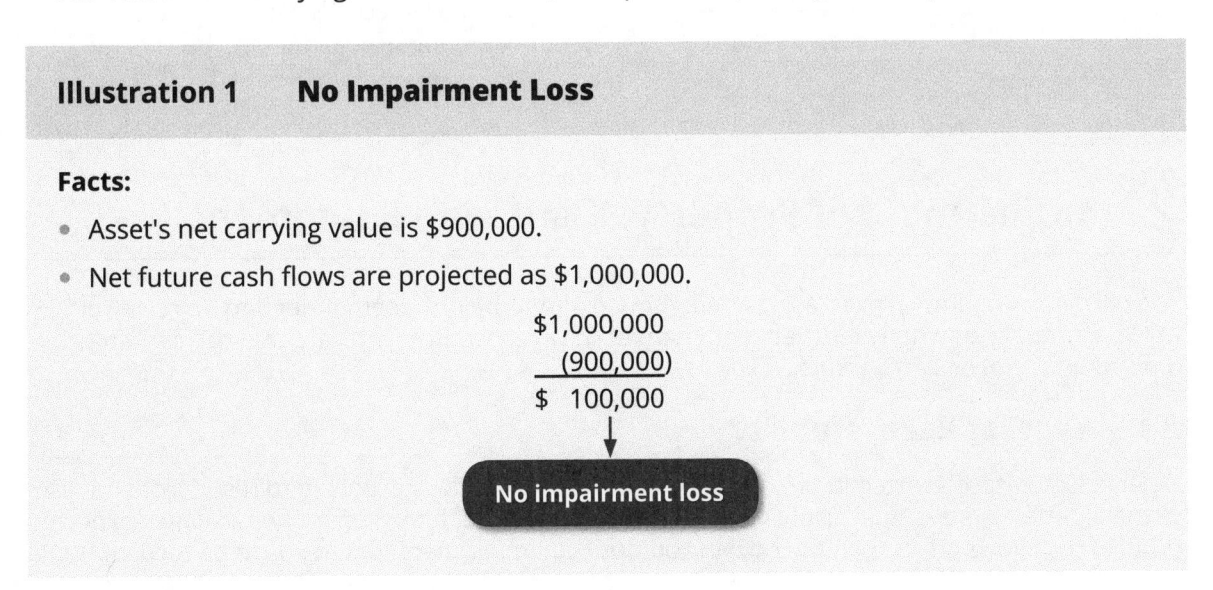

- Positive → No impairment loss
- Negative → Impairment
  - Assets held for use:
    
    Fair value
    < Net carrying value >
    Impairment loss
    
    1. Write asset down
    2. Depreciate new cost
    3. Restoration not permitted
  
  - Assets held for disposal:
    
    Fair value
    < Net carrying value >
    Impairment loss
    + Cost of disposal
    Total impairment loss
    
    1. Write asset down
    2. No depreciation taken
    3. Restoration permitted

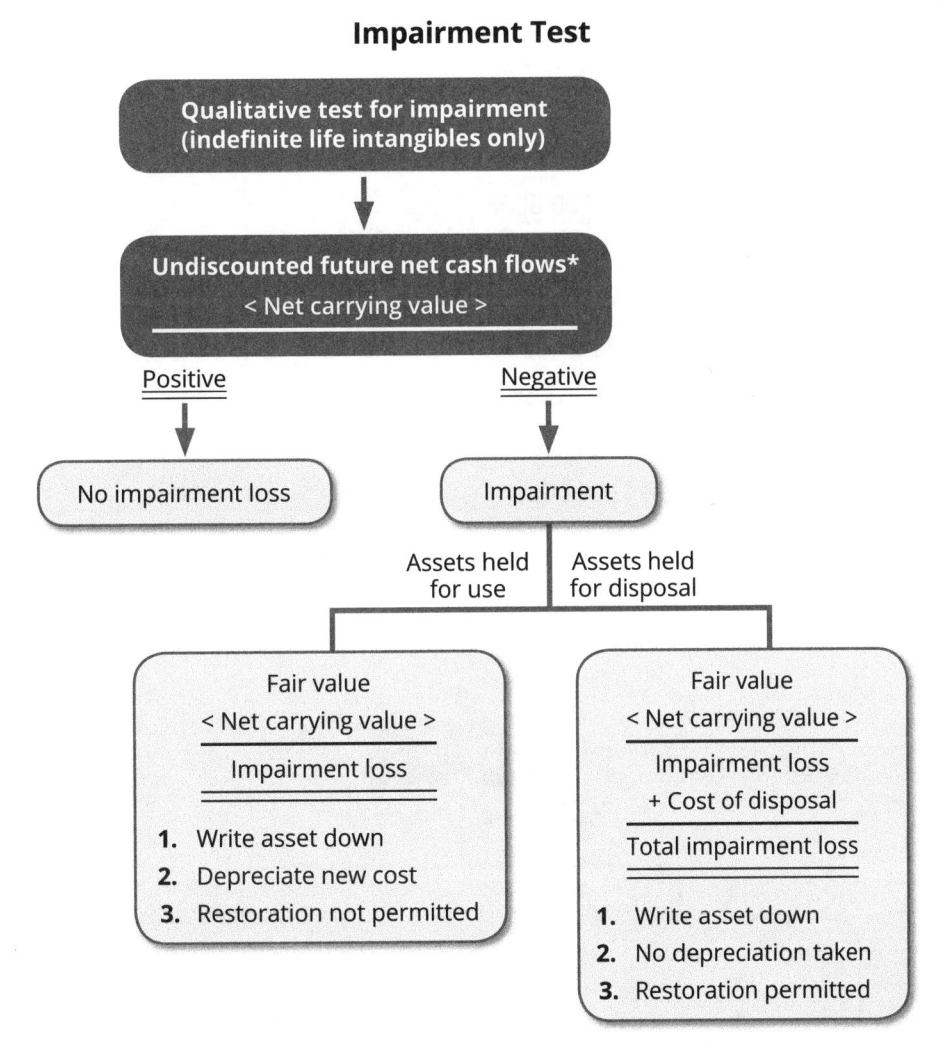

*When testing indefinite-life intangible assets for impairment, fair value must be used instead of undiscounted future net cash flows:

Fair value − Net carrying value = Positive (no impairment) or negative (impairment)

### Illustration 1     No Impairment Loss

**Facts:**

- Asset's net carrying value is $900,000.
- Net future cash flows are projected as $1,000,000.

$1,000,000
(900,000)
$ 100,000

↓

**No impairment loss**

# Impairment

FAR 3

### Illustration 2    Impairment Loss

**Facts:**

- Asset's net carrying value is $1,200,000.
- Net future cash flows are projected as $1,000,000.
- Assumption 1: Asset held for use, and
  - FV/PV net cash flows are $700,000.
- Assumption 2: Asset is held for disposal, and
  - FV/PV net cash flows are $700,000.
  - Cost of disposal will be $100,000.

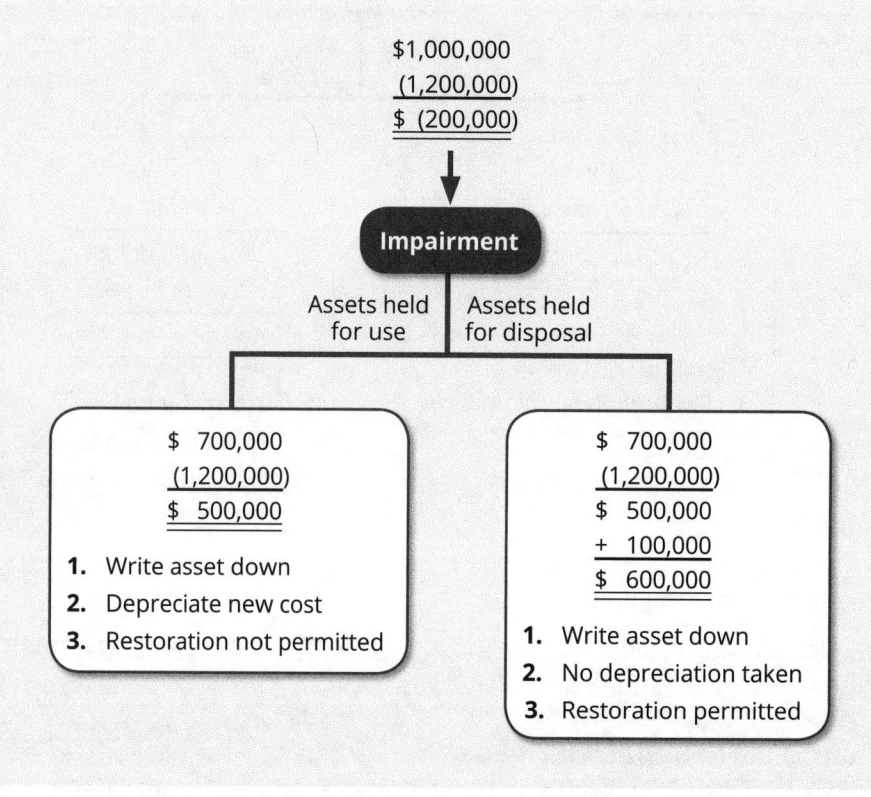

```
        $1,000,000
       (1,200,000)
      $ (200,000)
           ↓
      Impairment
```

**Assets held for use**

```
$   700,000
 (1,200,000)
$   500,000
```

1. Write asset down
2. Depreciate new cost
3. Restoration not permitted

**Assets held for disposal**

```
$   700,000
 (1,200,000)
$   500,000
+   100,000
$   600,000
```

1. Write asset down
2. No depreciation taken
3. Restoration permitted

## 2  Impairment of Property, Plant, and Equipment

The carrying amounts of fixed assets held for use and to be disposed of need to be reviewed at least annually or whenever events or changes in circumstances indicate that the carrying amount may not be recoverable.

### 2.1  Test for Recoverability

When a fixed asset is tested for impairment, the future cash flows expected to result from the use of the asset and its eventual disposition need to be estimated. If the sum of *undiscounted* expected (future) cash flows is less than the carrying amount, an impairment loss needs to be recognized.

## 2.2 Calculation of the Impairment Loss

The impairment loss is calculated as the amount by which the carrying amount exceeds the fair value of the asset.

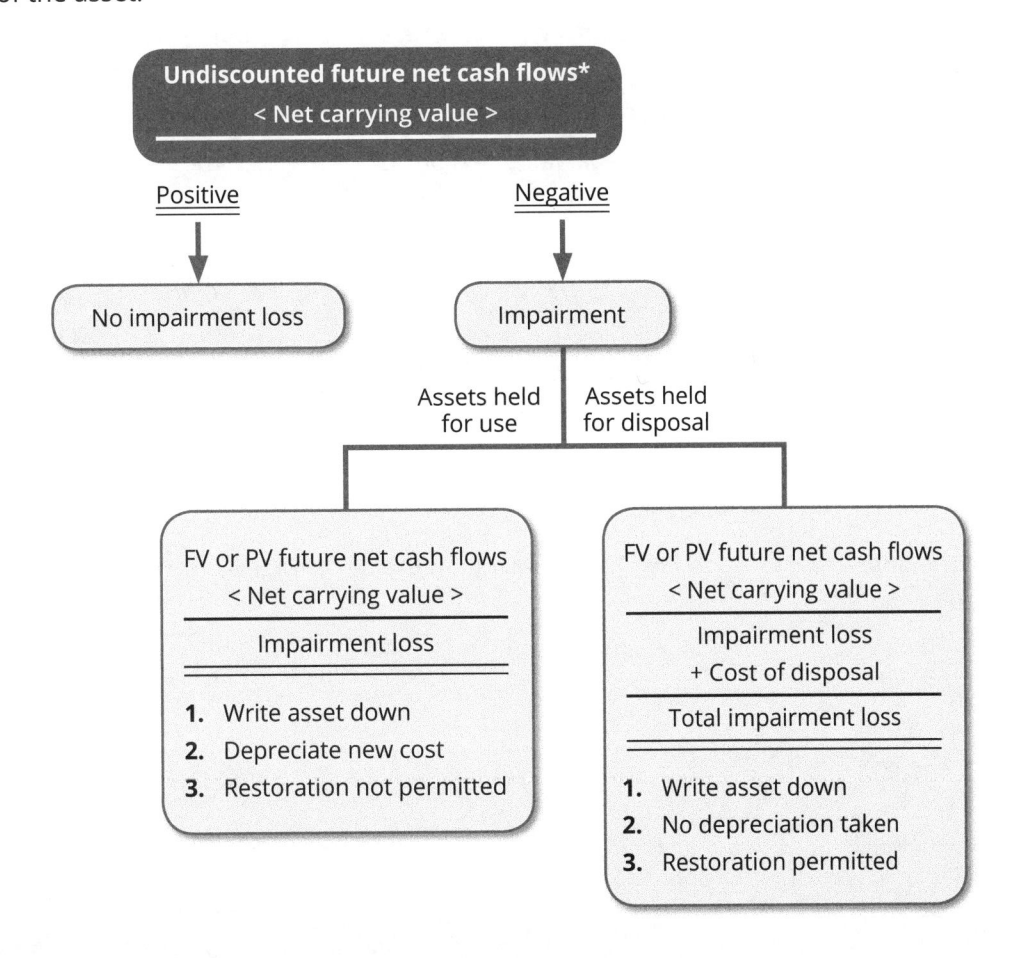

```
              Undiscounted future net cash flows*
                    < Net carrying value >
                    _____

           Positive                    Negative
              ↓                           ↓
      No impairment loss              Impairment
                                 Assets held │ Assets held
                                 for use     │ for disposal
```

**Assets held for use:**
FV or PV future net cash flows
< Net carrying value >
_____
Impairment loss
===================
1. Write asset down
2. Depreciate new cost
3. Restoration not permitted

**Assets held for disposal:**
FV or PV future net cash flows
< Net carrying value >
_____
Impairment loss
+ Cost of disposal
_____
Total impairment loss
===================
1. Write asset down
2. No depreciation taken
3. Restoration permitted

## 2.3 Reporting the Impairment Loss: General

The impairment loss is reported as a component of income from continuing operations before income taxes or in a statement of activities (related to not-for-profit entities). The impairment loss is recognized by reducing the carrying value of the asset to its lower fair value. Restoration of previously recognized impairment losses is prohibited under U.S. GAAP unless the asset is held for disposal.

### U.S. GAAP VS. IFRS

A fixed asset impairment loss under IFRS is calculated using a one-step model in which the carrying value of the fixed asset is compared with the fixed asset's recoverable amount. IFRSs define the recoverable amount as the greater of the asset's fair value less costs to sell and the asset's value in use. Value in use is the present value of the future cash flows expected from the fixed asset. IFRSs allow the reversal of impairment losses.

# Pass Key

It is important to remember the following rules when performing your calculations under U.S. GAAP:

- **Determining the Impairment:** Use undiscounted future net cash flows.
- **Amount of the Impairment:** Use fair value (FV) or discounted (PV) future net cash flows.

---

### Question 1 — MCQ-06390

On December 31, an entity analyzed a patent with a net carrying value of $500,000 for impairment. The entity determined the following:

| | |
|---|---|
| Fair value | $ 495,000 |
| Undiscounted future cash flows | 515,000 |

What is the impairment loss that will be reported on the December 31 income statement under U.S. GAAP?

- a. $0
- b. $5,000
- c. $15,000
- d. $20,000

---

### Question 2 — MCQ-06570

Last year, Katt Co. reduced the carrying amount of its long-lived assets used in operations from $120,000 to $100,000, in connection with its annual impairment review. During the current year, Katt determined that the fair value of the same assets had increased to $130,000. What amount should Katt record as restoration of previously recognized impairment loss in the current year's financial statements under U.S. GAAP?

- a. $0
- b. $10,000
- c. $20,000
- d. $30,000

# FAR 4

# Investments, Business Combinations, and Goodwill

## Module

| | | |
|---|---|---|
| 1 | Financial Instruments | 3 |
| 2 | Equity Method | 19 |
| 3 | Basic Consolidation Concepts | 31 |
| 4 | Acquisition Method: Part 1 | 39 |
| 5 | Acquisition Method: Part 2 | 51 |
| 6 | Intercompany Transactions | 65 |
| 7 | Consolidated Financial Statements | 73 |
| 8 | Goodwill, Including Impairment | 85 |

# NOTES

# MODULE 1

# Financial Instruments

FAR 4

## 1 Financial Instruments Overview

### 1.1 Financial Assets and Financial Liabilities

Financial instruments include financial assets and financial liabilities.

#### 1.1.1 Financial Assets

The following are financial assets:

- Cash (e.g., demand deposits and foreign currencies)
- Evidence of an ownership interest in an entity (e.g., stock certificates, partnership interests, and LLC interests)
- A contract that conveys to one entity a right to:
  - receive cash or another financial instrument from a second entity (e.g., bond investments, notes receivable); or
  - exchange other financial instruments on potentially favorable terms with the second entity (e.g., stock options, futures/forward contracts, and other derivatives).

#### 1.1.2 Financial Liabilities

A financial liability is a contract that imposes on one entity an obligation to:

- deliver cash or another financial instrument to a second entity (e.g., bond obligations, notes payable); or
- exchange other financial instruments on potentially unfavorable terms with the second entity (e.g., stock options, futures/forward contracts, and other derivatives).

### 1.2 Fair Value Option

On specified election dates, entities may choose to measure at fair value eligible financial instruments that are not typically measured at fair value. Under the fair value option, unrealized gains and losses are reported in earnings. The fair value option is irrevocable and is applied to individual financial instruments.

#### 1.2.1 Eligible Financial Instruments

Entities may elect the fair value option for recognized financial assets and financial liabilities. For example, an entity can choose to measure at fair value a debt investment that would otherwise be classified as available-for-sale, with unrealized gains and losses recorded in earnings rather than in OCI. Or an entity can choose to measure at fair value an equity investment that would otherwise be accounted for using the equity method.

Financial instruments not eligible for the fair value option include investments in subsidiaries or VIEs that an entity is required to consolidate, pension benefit assets or liabilities, financial assets or liabilities recognized under leases, deposit liabilities of financial institutions, and financial instruments classified as equity.

### 1.2.2 Fair Value Changes Attributable to Instrument-Specific Credit Risk

For financial liabilities other than derivative liabilities that are designated under the fair value option, the portion of the change in fair value that relates to a change in instrument-specific credit risk is recognized in other comprehensive income. Derivative liabilities recognize these changes in net income. Once the financial liability is derecognized, any accumulated gains or losses in other comprehensive income are recognized in earnings.

### 1.2.3 Election Dates

The fair value option may only be applied on certain dates, including the date that an entity first recognizes an eligible financial instrument, the date that an investment becomes subject to equity method accounting, or the date that an entity ceases to consolidate an investment in a subsidiary or VIE.

## 2 Investments in Debt Securities

### 2.1 Debt Securities

A debt security is any security representing a creditor relationship with an entity.

- Debt securities include:
  - Corporate bonds
  - Redeemable preferred stock
  - Government securities
  - Convertible debt
  - Commercial paper
- Debt securities do not include:
  - Option, futures, or forward contracts
  - Lease contracts
  - Accounts and notes receivable

### 2.2 Classification

Debt securities should be classified into one of three categories, based on the intent of the company.

#### 2.2.1 Trading Securities

Trading securities are debt securities that are bought and held principally for the purpose of selling them in the near term. Trading securities generally reflect active and frequent buying and selling with the objective of generating profits on short-term differences in price. Debt securities classified as trading securities are generally reported as current assets, although they can be reported as non-current, if appropriate.

#### 2.2.2 Available-for-Sale Debt Securities

Available-for-sale debt securities are those not meeting the definitions of the other two classifications (trading or held-to-maturity). Debt securities classified as available-for-sale securities are reported as either current assets or non-current assets, depending on the intent of the corporation.

### 2.2.3 Held-to-Maturity Debt Securities

Investments in debt securities are classified as held-to-maturity only if the corporation has the positive intent and ability to hold these securities to maturity. If the intent is to hold the security for an indefinite period of time, but not necessarily to maturity, then the security is classified as available-for-sale. If a security can be paid or otherwise settled in a manner that the holder may not recover substantially all of its investment, the held-to-maturity classification may not be used. Securities classified as held-to-maturity are reported as current or non-current assets, based on their time to maturity.

## 2.3 Valuation

### 2.3.1 Debt Securities Reported at Fair Value

Debt securities classified as trading and available-for-sale must be reported at fair value. Fair value is the market price of the security or what a willing buyer and seller would pay and accept to exchange the security. Changes in the fair value of trading and available-for-sale debt securities result in unrealized holdings gains or losses. The reporting of these gains or losses in the financial statements depends on the classification of the securities. Although two general ledger accounts are normally maintained (i.e., one for the original cost of the security and the other for the valuation account), the presentation on the balance sheet is one *net* amount.

- **Unrealized Gains and Losses (Trading Securities):** Unrealized holding gains and losses on debt securities classified as trading securities are included in earnings. Therefore, the unrealized gain or loss on trading securities is recognized in net income.

    *Journal entry to record loss in net income:*

    | | | | |
    |---|---|---|---|
    | DR | Unrealized loss on trading securities | $XXX | |
    | CR | Valuation account (fair value adjustment) | | $XXX |

- **Unrealized Gains and Losses (Available-for-Sale Debt Securities):** Unrealized holding gains and losses on available-for-sale securities are recognized in other comprehensive income.

    *Journal entry to record unrealized loss in other comprehensive income:*

    | | | | |
    |---|---|---|---|
    | DR | Unrealized loss on available-for-sale securities | $XXX | |
    | CR | Valuation account (fair value adjustment) | | $XXX |

- **Realized Gains and Losses:** Realized gains or losses are recognized when a debt security is sold and when an available-for-sale debt security is deemed to be impaired. All realized gains or losses are recognized in net income.

### 2.3.2 Financial Assets Reported at Amortized Cost

Held-to-maturity debt securities are reported at amortized cost. Amortized cost accounting is described in detail in the bonds section of F5. Unrealized gains and losses on held-to-maturity securities are not recognized in the financial statements, as held-to-maturity securities are not marked-to-market at period end.

| Classification | Balance Sheet | Reported | Unrealized Gain/Loss | Cash Flow |
|---|---|---|---|---|
| Trading | Current or non-current | Fair value | Net income | Operating or investing* |
| Available-for-sale | Current or non-current | Fair value | Other comprehensive income (PUFIER) | Investing |
| Held-to-maturity | Current or non-current | Amortized cost | None | Investing |

*Under U.S. GAAP, trading debt security transactions are classified in operating cash flows or investing cash flows based on the nature and purpose for which the securities were acquired. If trading debt securities are classified as non-current on the balance sheet, then trading debt security transactions will be reported as investing cash flows. If trading debt securities are classified as current on the balance sheet, then trading debt security transactions will be reported as operating cash flows.

## 2.4 Reclassification

Transfers between categories should occur only when justified. Transfers from the held-to-maturity category should be rare and should only be made when there is a change in the entity's intent to hold a specific security to maturity that does not call into question the entity's intent to hold other debt securities to maturity. Transfers to and from the trading category should also be rare.

Any transfer of a particular security from one group (trading, available-for-sale, or held-to-maturity) to another group (trading, available-for-sale, or held-to-maturity) is accounted for at fair value. Any unrealized holding gain or loss on that security is accounted for as follows:

- **From Trading Category:** The unrealized holding gain or loss at the date of transfer is already recognized in earnings and shall not be reversed.

- **To Trading Category:** The unrealized holding gain or loss at the date of transfer shall be recognized in earnings immediately.

- **Held-to-Maturity Transferred to Available-for-Sale:** The unrealized holding gain or loss at the date of transfer shall be reported in other comprehensive income. Remember that this debt security was valued at amortized cost as a held-to-maturity security and is being transferred to a category valued at fair value.

- **Available-for-Sale Transferred to Held-to-Maturity:** The unrealized holding gain or loss at the date of transfer is already reported in other comprehensive income. The unrealized holding gain or loss shall be amortized over the remaining life of the security as an adjustment of yield in a manner consistent with the amortization of any premium or discount.

| Summary of Transfers Between Categories ||||
|---|---|---|---|
| *From* | *To* | *Transfer Acct. For* | *Unrealized Holding Gain/Loss* |
| Trading | Any other | FV | It has already been recognized in income so no adjustment is necessary |
| Any other | Trading | FV | Recognized in current earnings |
| Held-to-maturity | Available-for-sale | FV | Record in other comprehensive income |
| Available-for-sale | Held-to-maturity | FV | Amortize gain or loss from other comprehensive income with any bond premium/discount amortization |

## 2.5 Income From Investments in Debt Securities

Interest income from an investment in debt securities classified as trading or available-for-sale is recorded on the income statement.

*Journal entry to record interest income:*

| DR | Cash | $XXX | |
|---|---|---|---|
| CR | Interest income | | $XXX |

### Pass Key

Interest income from investments reported at amortized cost (held-to-maturity securities) is discussed in the Bonds module of F5.

## 2.6 Impairment of Debt Securities

Under the current expected credit losses (CECL) model, available-for-sale debt securities and held-to-maturity debt securities should be reported at the net amount expected to be collected using an allowance for expected credit losses. Expected credit losses are determined based on current conditions, past experience, and future expectations. A credit loss is recognized as a current period expense on the income statement and as an offsetting allowance on the balance sheet. Increases and decreases in expected credit losses are reflected on the income statement in the period incurred when the estimate of expected credit losses changes.

### 2.6.1 Impairment of Held-to-Maturity Securities

If it is determined that all amounts due (principal and interest) will not be collected on a debt investment reported at amortized cost, the investment should be reported at the present value of the principal and interest that is expected to be collected. The credit loss is the difference between the present value and the amortized cost.

---

**Example 1 — Held-to-Maturity Security Impairment**

**Facts:** On January 2, Year 3, TGPO Co. purchased a $500,000, four-year bond at par with annual interest at 4.25 percent paid on December 31 each year. TGPO classified the investment as held-to-maturity. At the end of Year 3, TGPO received the full interest payment of $21,250, but determined that it would only collect $11,500 each year in interest for the remaining three years (along with the face value of $500,000 at maturity).

Present value of $1 at 4.25 percent for three periods = 0.88262

Present value of an ordinary annuity of 1 at 4.25 percent for three periods = 2.76198

**Required:** Prepare the entry that TGPO will record at the end of Year 3 to recognize the impairment.

(continued)

(continued)

**Solution:**

The first step is to calculate the present value as of December 31, Year 3.

Present value:

    Interest payments: $11,500 × 2.76198 = $31,763

    Principal payment: $500,000 × 0.88262 = $441,310

        Total present value = $473,073

The credit loss is calculated as: Present value − Amortized cost = $473,073 − $500,000 = ($26,927)

*The journal entry will be as follows:*

| | | | |
|---|---|---|---|
| DR | Credit loss | $26,927 | |
| CR |    Allowance for credit losses | | $26,927 |

### 2.6.2 Impairment of Available-for-Sale Debt Securities

Impairment on available-for-sale securities is accounted for differently from impairment on held-to-maturity securities, because the investor has the option to sell an available-for-sale security if the loss on the sale will be less than the expected credit loss. As a result, the credit loss reported in net income on an available-for-sale security is limited to the amount by which fair value is below amortized cost. Any additional loss is reported as an unrealized loss in other comprehensive income.

---

**Example 2     Available-for-Sale Security Impairment**

**Facts:** The same facts as in Example 1, except the investment is an available-for-sale debt security.

**Required:** Determine the expected credit loss and/or unrealized holding gain/loss to be recognized on December 31, Year 3, for each of the following fair-value scenarios, and prepare the journal entry for each scenario.

Scenario 1: $510,000 fair value

Scenario 2: $480,000 fair value

Scenario 3: $450,000 fair value

(continued)

(continued)

**Solution:**

|  | Scenario 1 | Scenario 2 | Scenario 3 |
|---|---|---|---|
| Amortized cost, 1/2/Year 3 | $500,000 | $500,000 | $500,000 |
| Fair value, 12/31/Year 3 | $510,000 | $480,000 | $450,000 |
| Expected credit loss* | $26,927 | $26,927 | $26,927 |
| Expected credit loss (net income) | 0 | $20,000 | $26,927 |
| Unrealized gain (OCI) | $10,000 | 0 | 0 |
| Unrealized loss (OCI) | 0 | 0 | $23,073 |

* The expected credit loss is the difference between present value and amortized cost, calculated as shown in Example 1 for the held-to-maturity debt security.

*For Scenario 1, the journal entry would be:*

| DR | Valuation account (fair value adjustment) | $10,000 |  |
|---|---|---|---|
| CR | Unrealized gain on available-for-sale security |  | $10,000 |

*For Scenario 2, the journal entry would be:*

| DR | Credit loss | $20,000 |  |
|---|---|---|---|
| CR | Allowance for credit losses |  | $20,000 |

*For Scenario 3, the journal entry would be:*

| DR | Credit loss | $26,927 |  |
|---|---|---|---|
| DR | Unrealized loss on available-for-sale security | 23,073 |  |
| CR | Allowance for credit losses |  | $26,927 |
| CR | Valuation account (fair value adjustment) |  | 23,073 |

## 2.7 Sale of Debt Securities

A sale of a debt security from any category results in a realized gain or loss and is recognized in net income for the period. The valuation account, if used, also would have to be removed on the sale of a security.

- **Trading Securities:** The realized gain or loss reported when a trading debt security is sold is the difference between the adjusted cost (original cost plus or minus unrealized gains and losses previously recognized in net income) and the selling price.

*Trading securities:*

| DR | Cash | $XXX |  |
|---|---|---|---|
| CR | Trading security |  | $XXX |
| CR | Realized gain on trading security (IDA) |  | XXX |

# Financial Instruments

■ **Available-for-Sale Securities:** The realized gain or loss reported when an available-for-sale debt security is sold is the difference between the selling price and the original cost of the security. Any unrealized gains or losses in accumulated other comprehensive income must be reversed at the time the security is sold.

*Available-for-sale securities:*

| | | | |
|---|---|---|---|
| DR | Cash | $XXX | |
| DR | Unrealized gain on available-for-sale security (PUFIER) | XXX | |
| CR | Available-for-sale security | | $XXX |
| CR | Realized gain on available-for-sale security (IDA) | | XXX |

# 3  Investments in Equity Securities

## 3.1  Equity Securities

An equity security is a security that represents an ownership interest in an enterprise or the right to acquire or dispose of an ownership interest in an enterprise at fixed or determinable prices.

■ Equity securities include:
- ownership shares (common, preferred, and other forms of capital stock);
- rights to acquire ownership shares (stock warrants, rights, and call options); and
- rights to dispose of ownership shares (put options).

■ Equity securities do *not* include:
- preferred stock redeemable at the option of the investor or stock that must be redeemed by the issuer;
- treasury stock (the company's own stock repurchased and held); and
- convertible bonds.

## 3.2  Classification

### 3.2.1  Fair Value Through Net Income (FVTNI)

Equity securities are generally carried at fair value through net income (FVTNI). This requirement does not apply to investments accounted for under the equity method, consolidated investees, or when the practicability exception is applied.

### 3.2.2  Practicability Exception

The practicability exception allows an entity to measure an equity investment at cost less impairment, plus/minus observable price changes (in orderly transactions) of identical or similar investments from the same issuer. This exception is applicable for equity investments that do not have a readily determinable fair value. Reporting entities that are broker-dealers in securities, investment companies, or postretirement benefit plans cannot use this exception.

## 3.3 Valuation

Equity securities are generally reported at fair value through net income (FVTNI). Unrealized holding gains and losses on equity securities are included in earnings as they occur.

*Journal entry to record loss in net income:*

| | | | |
|---|---|---|---|
| DR | Unrealized loss on equity security | $XXX | |
| CR | Valuation account (fair value adjustment) | | $XXX |

## 3.4 Income From Investments in Equity Securities

Dividend income from an equity security investment is recognized in net income, unless the dividend is a liquidating dividend.

- **Normal (Nonliquidating) Dividend**

  *Journal entry to record normal dividend income:*

  | | | | |
  |---|---|---|---|
  | DR | Cash | $XXX | |
  | CR | Dividend income | | $XXX |

- **Liquidating Dividend:** A liquidating dividend is a distribution that exceeds the investor's share of the investee's retained earnings. A liquidating dividend is a return of capital that decreases the investor's basis in the investment.

  *Journal entry to record liquidating dividend:*

  | | | | |
  |---|---|---|---|
  | DR | Cash | $XXX | |
  | CR | Investment in investee | | $XXX |

---

### Example 3 — Liquidating Dividend

**Facts:** ABC Corporation owns a 10 percent interest in XYZ Corporation. During the current year, XYZ Corp. paid a dividend of $10,000,000. XYZ had retained earnings of $8,000,000 when the dividend was declared. ABC will receive a dividend of $1,000,000 ($10,000,000 × 10%) from XYZ and will record dividend income of $800,000 for its share of XYZ's retained earnings ($8,000,000 × 10%). The $200,000 difference reduces ABC's investment in XYZ.

**Required:** Prepare the journal entry that ABC will record for this liquidating dividend.

**Solution:**

*Journal entry to record $1,000,000 ($10,000,000 × 10%) dividend received from XYZ Corporation:*

| | | | |
|---|---|---|---|
| DR | Cash | $1,000,000 | |
| CR | Dividend income ($8,000,000 × 10%) | | $800,000 |
| CR | Investment in XYZ Corporation | | 200,000 |

## 3.5 Impairment

Equity investments that do not have readily determinable fair values are measured at cost minus impairment (the practicability exception). An entity should consider the following qualitative indicators in order to determine whether an equity investment with no readily determinable fair value is impaired:

- Heightened concerns regarding the ability of an investee to continue as a going concern due to factors such as noncompliance with capital or debt requirements, deficiencies in working capital, or negative operating cash flows.
- Significant and adverse changes in the industry, geographic area, technology, or regulatory or economic environment of the investee.
- A significant decline in earnings, business prospects, asset quality, or credit rating of the investee.
- Offers to buy from the investee (and willingness to sell on the part of the investee) the same or a similar investment for less than the investor's carrying value.

When a qualitative assessment indicates that impairment exists, the cost basis of the security is written down to fair value and the amount of the write-down is accounted for as a realized loss and included in earnings.

## 3.6 Sale of Security

The sale of an equity security does not give rise to a gain or loss if all changes in the equity's fair value have been reported in earnings as unrealized gains or losses as they occurred.

*Journal entry for sale with no gain or loss:*

| DR | Cash | $XXX | |
|---|---|---|---|
| CR | Equity security* | | $XXX |

If an entity has not recorded an equity security's change in fair value up to the point of sale, a gain or loss is recorded at the time of the sale equal to the difference between adjusted cost (original cost plus or minus unrealized gains and losses previously recognized in earnings) and the selling price.

*The journal entry for sale of equity security with a gain:*

| DR | Cash | $XXX | |
|---|---|---|---|
| CR | Equity security* | | $XXX |
| CR | Gain on equity security | | XXX |

\* Note that any valuation account would also have to be removed when the security is sold.

# 4 Required Disclosures

## 4.1 Disclosures for Investments in Debt Securities

The following information concerning securities classified as available-for-sale and separately for held-to-maturity securities must be disclosed in the financial statements or appropriate notes thereto:

- Aggregate fair value;
- Gross unrealized holding gains and losses;
- Amortized cost basis by major security type; and
- Information about the contractual maturities of debt securities.

## 4.2 Disclosures for Investments in Equity Securities

Entities should disclose the portion of unrealized gains and losses for the period that relates to equity securities still held at the end of the reporting period. This amount is calculated as follows:

|   |
|---|
| Net gains and losses recognized during the period on equity securities |
| − Net gains and losses recognized during the period on equity securities sold during the period |
| Unrealized gains and losses recognized during the reporting period on equity securities still held at the reporting date |

## 4.3 Fair Value

All public and private entities must disclose on the balance sheet or in the notes to the financial statements all financial assets and liabilities, grouped by measurement category (fair value through net income, other comprehensive income, or amortized cost), and, if a financial asset, the form of that asset.

Public business entities (PBEs) must provide fair value information regarding the classification level in the measurement hierarchy (Levels 1, 2, or 3). For assets and liabilities measured at amortized cost, fair value should be disclosed in accordance with the exit price. Exceptions are for payables and receivables due within one year, deposit liabilities with no defined maturities, and equity investments reported under the practicability exception.

For entities that have elected the practicability exception, the following must be disclosed:

- The carrying amount of all investments without readily determinable fair values.
- Any impairment charges incurred during the reporting period.
- The amount of the upward or downward adjustment made to the carrying amount due to any observable price changes, with the intent of the adjustments designed to reflect the fair value of the security.

Financial Instruments

## 4.4 Concentrations of Credit Risk

Entities must disclose all significant concentrations of credit risk arising from all financial instruments, whether from a single party or a group of parties engaged in similar activities and that have similar economic characteristics.

Credit risk is the possibility of loss from the failure of another party to perform according to the terms of a contract. A concentration of credit risk occurs when an entity has contracts of material value with one or more parties in the same industry or region or having similar economic characteristics (e.g., a group of highly leveraged entities).

Under U.S. GAAP, these disclosures apply to all entities (except nonpublic entities that have total assets less than $100 million and have no instruments that are accounted for as derivatives).

## 4.5 Market Risk

Market risk is the possibility of loss from changes in market value (not necessarily due to the failure of another party, but due to changes in economic circumstances).

Under U.S. GAAP, all entities are encouraged, but not required, to disclose quantitative information about the market risk of financial instruments that is consistent with the way it manages or adjusts those risks.

---

**Example 4**     **Investments in Debt and Equity Securities**

**Facts:** The following information pertains to Fox Inc.'s portfolio of marketable investments for the year ended December 31, Year 2:

|  | Cost | Fair value at 12/31/Year 1 | Year 2 activity Purchases | Sales | Fair value at 12/31/Year 2 |
|---|---|---|---|---|---|
| **Held-to-maturity debt securities** | | | | | |
| Security ABC | | | $100,000 | | $ 95,000 |
| **Available-for-sale debt securities** | | | | | |
| Security GHI | | 190,000 | 165,000 | $175,000 | |
| Security JKL | | 170,000 | 175,000 | | 160,000 |
| **Equity Securities** | | | | | |
| Security DEF | $150,000 | $160,000 | | | 155,000 |

Security ABC was purchased at par. There are no expected credit losses on Fox's portfolio of debt investments.

**Required:**

1. Calculate the carrying amount of each security on the balance sheet at December 31, Year 2.
2. Calculate any realized gain or loss recognized in Year 2 net income.
3. Calculate any unrealized gain or loss recognized in Year 2 net income.
4. Calculate any unrealized gain or loss to be recognized in Year 2 other comprehensive income.

(continued)

(continued)

**Solution:**

1. **Carrying amount of each security at December 31, Year 2**

    Security ABC          $100,000

    At year-end, the held-to-maturity debt investment is reported at amortized cost, because there is no expected credit loss. The amortized cost of security ABC is the purchase price of $100,000.

    Security DEF          $155,000

    The year-end carrying amount of the equity investment is the fair value at year-end. Fair value of security DEF is $155,000.

    Security GHI was sold

    Security JKL          $160,000

    The year-end carrying amount of available-for-sale debt investments is the fair value at year-end because there are no expected credit losses. Fair value of security JKL is $160,000.

2. **Realized gain or loss in net income**

    Security GHI          ($15,000)

    The $175,000 sales proceeds less the $190,000 cost yields a realized loss of $15,000. The sale of security GHI will be recorded with the following journal entry:

    | | | | |
    |---|---|---|---|
    | DR | Cash | $175,000 | |
    | DR | Realized loss | 15,000 | |
    | CR | Security GHI | | $165,000 |
    | CR | Unrealized loss (OCI) | | 25,000 |

3. **Unrealized gain or loss in net income**

    Security DEF          ($5,000)

    The unrealized loss on the equity investment is reported in net income. The $160,000 carrying value of security DEF must be reduced to the $155,000 fair value and an unrealized loss of $5,000 is recognized in net income.

4. **Unrealized gain or loss (current year change):** Other comprehensive income

    Security GHI & JKL (net)    $10,000

    | | 12/31/Year 1 Accumulated OCI Gain <Loss> | Year 2 OCI Gain <Loss> | 12/31/Year 2 Accumulated OCI Gain <Loss> |
    |---|---|---|---|
    | Security GHI | <$25,000>[1] | $25,000 | –0– |
    | Security JKL | 5,000[2] | <15,000> | <10,000> |
    | | <$20,000> | $10,000 | <$10,000> |

    [1] Security GHI – Loss in 12/31/Y1 AOCI = $165,000 fair value – $190,000 cost = <$25,000>

    [2] Security JKL – Gain in 12/31/Y1 AOCI = $175,000 fair value – $170,000 cost = $5,000

… Financial Instruments

# 5 Accounting for Financial Instruments Under IFRS 9

## 5.1 Classification and Measurement of Financial Assets

Under IFRS 9, financial assets are initially recognized at fair value and then subsequently measured at either amortized cost or fair value.

### 5.1.1 Single Model for Classification and Measurement

IFRS 9 requires a single model for classification and measurement that applies to all types of financial assets, including those that contain embedded derivatives. The model consists of two parts: a business model for managing the financial assets and a contractual cash flow model.

1. **Business Model for Managing Financial Assets:** The business model for managing the financial assets is the entity's purpose for holding the assets (e.g., for collecting contractual payments or for holding assets in order to realize returns upon the sale of the assets).

2. **Contractual Cash Flow Model:** The contractual cash flow model refers to how cash is received, either solely payments of principal and interest (SPPI) or the collection of proceeds upon the sale of the asset.

### 5.1.2 Debt Instruments

Financial assets that are debt instruments are reported at amortized cost, fair value through other comprehensive income (FVOCI), or fair value through profit or loss (FVPL).

- **Amortized Cost Measurement:** A financial asset that is a debt instrument is measured at amortized cost if both of the following conditions are met:

    1. **Business Model Test:** The asset is held in a business model in which the objective is to hold assets in order to collect contractual cash flows.

    2. **Cash Flow Characteristics Test:** The contractual terms of the financial asset give rise on specified dates to cash flows that are solely payments of principal and interest.

- **Fair Value Measurement:** If the conditions for amortized cost measurement are not met, the debt instrument is measured at fair value:

    1. Financial assets that are held in a portfolio where an entity holds to collect cash flows (SPPI) from portfolio assets and also sells portfolio assets may be classified as FVOCI.

    2. Financial assets that do not contain cash flows that are SPPI must be measured at FVPL (e.g., derivatives).

### 5.1.3 Equity Instruments

A financial asset that is an equity instrument is reported at fair value with gains and losses recognized in earnings (FVPL), unless the entity makes an irrevocable election on initial recognition to present gains and losses in other comprehensive income (FVOCI).

Gains and losses recognized in other comprehensive income are never recognized in earnings, but may be reclassified within equity.

### 5.1.4 Reclassifications

Reclassification of financial assets between amortized cost and fair value are required only when the entity changes the business model under which it manages financial instruments. Such changes should be infrequent and are accounted for prospectively. The asset should be remeasured at fair value on the date of the reclassification, with any gain or loss recognized in earnings.

## 5.2 Classification and Measurement of Financial Liabilities

Under IFRS 9, financial liabilities are initially recognized at fair value and then subsequently measured at either amortized cost or fair value.

- **Amortized Cost Measurement**

  In general, financial liabilities are subsequently measured at amortized cost using the effective interest method.

- **Fair Value Measurement**

  Financial liabilities may be subsequently measured at fair value in certain circumstances, such as when an entity at initial recognition irrevocably designates a financial liability as measured at fair value through profit or loss. Gains and losses on financial liabilities measured at fair value are recognized in earnings, unless the entity is required to present the effects of changes in the liability's credit risk in other comprehensive income.

- **Reclassification**

  Financial liabilities may not be reclassified between amortized cost and fair value.

## 5.3 Impairment

IFRS 9 requires a forward-looking impairment model referred to as the *expected credit loss model*.

### 5.3.1 Applicability

This model does not apply to financial assets measured at fair value through profit or loss.

It does apply to financial assets that are measured at amortized cost or at fair value through other comprehensive income. The model also applies to trade receivables, lease receivables, commitments to lend money, and financial guarantee contracts.

### 5.3.2 12-Month and Lifetime Expected Credit Losses

The entity must recognize expected credit losses at all times (including at purchase) and must update the amount of *expected* credit losses recognized at each reporting date to reflect changes in the credit risk of financial instruments.

- As soon as a financial instrument is originated or purchased, 12-month expected credit losses are recognized in profit or loss.

- If the credit risk increases significantly and the resulting credit quality is not considered to be low credit risk, full lifetime expected credit losses are recognized. Lifetime expected credit losses are only recognized if the credit risk increases significantly from when the entity originates or purchases the financial instrument.

### 5.3.3 Loss Allowance

Impairment losses and, when necessary, the reversal of previously recognized impairment losses are recognized through the use of a loss allowance account, rather than a direct write-down of the assets.

- **Financial Assets Measured at Amortized Cost:** For financial assets that are measured at amortized cost, impairment losses and the reversal of previously recognized impairment losses are recognized in earnings.

- **Financial Assets Measured at FVOCI:** For financial assets that are measured at fair value through other comprehensive income, the impairment losses or the reversal of previously recognized impairment losses should be recognized in other comprehensive income.

Financial Instruments

## Question 1 — MCQ-00265

Entities should report marketable debt securities classified as trading at:

- a. Lower of cost or market, with holding gains and losses included in earnings.
- b. Lower of cost or market, with holding gains included in earnings only to the extent of previously recognized holding losses.
- c. Fair value, with holding gains included in earnings only to the extent of previously recognized holding losses.
- d. Fair value, with holding gains and losses included in earnings.

## Question 2 — MCQ-00273

Information regarding Stone Co.'s available-for-sale portfolio of marketable debt securities is as follows:

| | |
|---|---|
| Aggregate cost as of 12/31/Y2 | $170,000 |
| Market value as of 12/31/Y2 | 148,000 |

At December 31, Year 1, Stone reported an unrealized loss of $1,500 to reduce investments to market value. This was the first such adjustment made by Stone on these types of securities. There is no expected credit loss on this investment. In its Year 2 statement of comprehensive income, what amount of unrealized loss should Stone report?

- a. $30,000
- b. $20,500
- c. $22,000
- d. $0

## Question 3 — MCQ-00287

An investor uses fair value through net income to account for an investment in common stock. Dividends received this year exceeded the investor's share of investee's undistributed earnings since the date of investment. The amount of dividend revenue that should be reported in the investor's income statement for this year would be:

- a. The portion of the dividends received this year that were in excess of the investor's share of investee's undistributed earnings since the date of investment.
- b. The portion of the dividends received this year that were not in excess of the investor's share of investee's undistributed earnings since the date of investment.
- c. The total amount of dividends received this year.
- d. Zero.

# MODULE 2 Equity Method

FAR 4

## 1 When to Use the Equity Method

The equity method is used to account for investments if significant influence can be exercised by the investor over the investee. Consolidated statements should be presented when ownership is greater than 50 percent and there is control over the investee.

A parent company that does not consolidate a subsidiary that is more than 50 percent owned must use the equity method when presenting the investment in that subsidiary in consolidated financial statements. Such a situation could result, for example, when there is lack of control because a company is controlled by a bankruptcy trustee or a subsidiary is likely to be a temporary investment.

### 1.1 Significant Influence

A company that owns 20 percent to 50 percent of voting stock of another "investee" company is presumed to be able to exercise significant influence over the operating and financial policies of that investee and, therefore, must use the equity method when presenting the investment in that investee in:

- consolidated financial statements that include other consolidated entities, but not that investee; or
- unconsolidated parent company financial statements.

> **Pass Key**
>
> The CPA Examination frequently presents questions in which the ownership percentage is below 20 percent, but the "ability to exercise significant influence" exists. The *equity method* is the correct method of accounting for these investments.

### 1.2 Equity Method Not Appropriate

In the following situations, the equity method is not appropriate, even if an investor owns 20 percent to 50 percent of subsidiary:

- Bankruptcy of subsidiary.
- Investment in subsidiary is temporary.
- A lawsuit or complaint is filed.
- A "standstill agreement" is signed (under which the investor surrenders significant rights as a shareholder).
- Another small group has majority ownership and operates the company without regard to the investor.

Equity Method                                                                                      FAR 4

- The investor cannot obtain the financial information necessary to apply the equity method.
- The investor cannot obtain representation on the board of directors in order to exercise significant influence.

# 2  Equity Method Accounting

Under the equity method the investment is originally recorded at the price paid to acquire the investment. The investment account is subsequently adjusted as the net assets of the investee change through the earning of income and payment of dividends. The investment account increases by the investor's share of the investee's net income with a corresponding credit to the investor's income statement account, Equity in Subsidiary/Investee Income. The distribution of dividends by the investee reduces the investment balance. Continuing losses by an investee may result in a decrease of the investment account to a zero balance.

## 2.1  Journal Entries

Three main journal entries are used to account for an equity method investment:

*Journal entry to record investment at cost (FV of consideration plus legal fees):*

| DR | Investment in investee | $XXX |      |
|----|------------------------|------|------|
| CR | Cash                   |      | $XXX |

*Journal entry to record increase in the investment by the investor's share of the earnings of the investee:*

| DR | Investment in investee          | $XXX |      |
|----|---------------------------------|------|------|
| CR | Equity in earnings/investee income* |  | $XXX |

\* Equity in earnings is reported as income on the income statement.

*Journal entry to record decrease in the investment by the investor's share of the cash dividends from the investee:*

| DR | Cash                   | $XXX |      |
|----|------------------------|------|------|
| CR | Investment in investee |      | $XXX |

### Pass Key

An easy way to remember the GAAP accounting rules for the equity method is to think of it as a **bank account** and use your **BASE** account analysis:

- **Beginning** balance
- **Add:** Investor's share of investee's earning (like bank interest; it is income when earned, not when taken out).
- **Subtract:** Investor's share of investee's dividends (like bank withdrawals; and it is not income)
- **Ending** balance

## Example 1 — Equity Method

**Facts:** On January 1, Year 1, Big Corporation acquired a 40 percent interest in Small Company for $300,000. At the date of acquisition, Small Co.'s equity (net assets) had a book value of $750,000. Therefore, there was no difference between the purchase price and the book value of the net assets acquired ($300,000 = 40% × $750,000). During Year 1, Small Co. had net income of $90,000 and paid a $40,000 dividend.

**Required:**

1. Prepare the journal entries required in Year 1 to account for the investment in Small Co.
2. Determine the investment-related amounts to be reported at year-end on Big's balance sheet and income statement.

**Solution:**

1. *Journal entry to record the initial investment of 40 percent:*

   | | | | |
   |---|---|---|---|
   | DR | Investment in Small Co. | $300,000 | |
   | CR | Cash | | $300,000 |

   *Journal entry to recognize the investee's net income (40% × $90,000):*

   | | | | |
   |---|---|---|---|
   | DR | Investment in Small Co. | $36,000 | |
   | CR | Equity in investee income | | $36,000 |

   *Journal entry to recognize the dividend paid by the investee (40% × $40,000):*

   | | | | |
   |---|---|---|---|
   | DR | Cash | $16,000 | |
   | CR | Investment in Small Co. | | $16,000 |

2. On December 31, Year 1, the investment account on the balance sheet would show $320,000 ($300,000 + $36,000 − $16,000), and the income statement would show $36,000 as Big's equity in subsidiary income.

## 2.2 Investments in Investee Common Stock and Preferred Stock

If an investor company owns both common and preferred stock of an investee company:

- The "significant influence" test is generally met by the amount of common stock owned (which is usually the only voting stock).
- The calculation of the income from subsidiary (or investee) to be reported on the income statement includes:
  - Preferred stock dividends
  - Share of earnings available to common shareholders (net income reduced by preferred dividends)

Equity Method

## Question 1 — MCQ-00320

On January 2, Year 3, Well Co. purchased 10 percent of Rea, Inc.'s outstanding common shares for $400,000. Well is the largest single shareholder in Rea, and Well's officers are a majority on Rea's board of directors. Rea reported net income of $500,000 for Year 3 and paid dividends of $150,000. In its December 31, Year 3, balance sheet, what amount should Well report as investment in Rea?

- a. $450,000
- b. $435,000
- c. $400,000
- d. $385,000

## Question 2 — MCQ-00318

Moss Corp. owns 20 percent of Dubro Corp.'s preferred stock and 40 percent of its common stock. Dubro's stock outstanding at December 31, Year 1, is as follows:

| | |
|---|---|
| 10% cumulative preferred stock | $100,000 |
| Common stock | 700,000 |

Dubro reported net income of $60,000 and paid dividends of $10,000 to its preferred shareholders for the year ended December 31, Year 1. How much total revenue should Moss record due to its investment in Dubro?

- a. $22,000
- b. $20,000
- c. $70,000
- d. $50,000

## 2.3 Differences Between the Purchase Price and Book Value (NBV) of the Investee's Net Assets

Additional adjustments to the investment account under the equity method result from differences between the price paid for the investment and the book value of the investee's net assets. This difference is attributable to:

1. **Asset Fair Value Differences:** Differences between the book value and fair value of the net assets acquired.
2. **Goodwill:** Any remaining difference is goodwill.

> **Pass Key**
>
> An easy way to analyze an equity method investment is to set up a building block box and plug in the respective dollar amounts, and then compare to the purchase price:
>
> | | | |
> |---|---|---|
> | Goodwill | Excess = $ | |
> | FV | × % = $ | Purchase Price |
> | NBV | × % = $ | |

The following diagram illustrates the relationships between the purchase price of the equity method investment and the fair value and book value of the equity interest acquired:

**Equity Method**

- Purchase price of investment ↔ Fair value of equity acquired → Difference is goodwill
- Fair value of equity acquired ↔ Book value of equity acquired → Difference is asset fair value difference (premium)

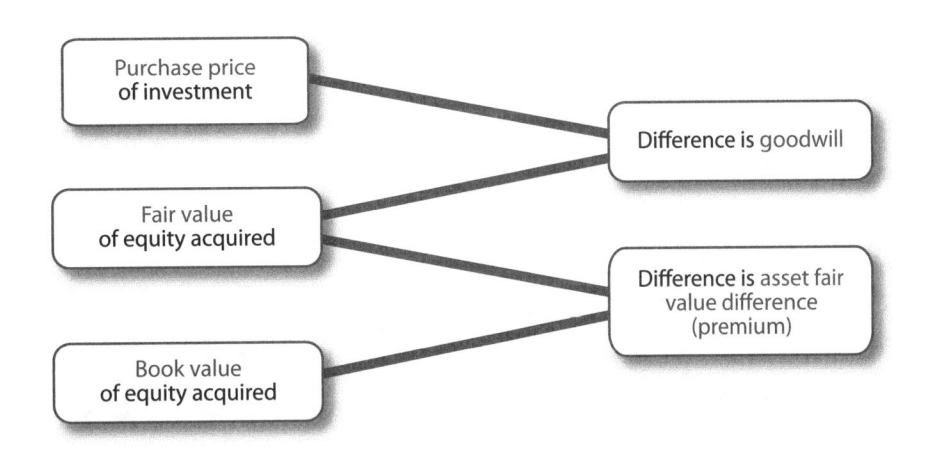

### 2.3.1 Accounting for Asset Fair Value Differences

The excess of an asset's fair value over its book value is amortized over the life of the asset (excess caused by land is not amortized). This additional amortization causes the investor's share of the investee's net income to decrease.

| DR | Equity in investee income | $XXX | |
|---|---|---|---|
| CR | Investment in investee | | $XXX |

> **Pass Key**
>
> To better understand the journal entry and its impact, think of the amortization of excess purchase price (premium) as a bank service charge. The *equity method*, which we treat like a bank account, will have the account balance (balance sheet asset) reduced by this *bank service charge* and also will have the net earnings from the account reduced by this (service) charge.

## 2.3.2 Accounting for Equity Method Goodwill

The fair value excess attributable to goodwill is not amortized and is not subject to a separate impairment test. However, the total equity method investment (including goodwill) must be analyzed at least annually for impairment.

> **Example 2** **Equity Method With Fair Value Difference and Goodwill**
>
> **Facts:** On January 1, Year 1, Big Corporation acquired a 40 percent interest in Small Company for $300,000. At the date of acquisition, Small Co.'s equity (net assets) had a book value of $550,000 and a fair value of $600,000. The difference between the book value and fair value relates to equipment being depreciated over a remaining useful life of 10 years. During Year 1, Small Co. had net income of $90,000 and paid a $40,000 dividend.
>
> **Required:**
>
> 1. Prepare the journal entries required in Year 1 to account for the investment in Small Co.
> 2. Compute the asset fair value difference and goodwill.
> 3. Record the journal entry to depreciate the fair value difference.
> 4. Determine the investment-related amounts to be reported at year-end on Big's balance sheet and income statement.
>
> **Solution:**
>
> **1. Investment and subsidiary activity**
>
> *Journal entry to record the initial investment of 40 percent:*
>
> | | | | |
> |---|---|---|---|
> | DR | Investment in Small Co. | $300,000 | |
> | CR | Cash | | $300,000 |
>
> *Journal entry to recognize the investee's net income (40% × $90,000):*
>
> | | | | |
> |---|---|---|---|
> | DR | Investment in Small Co. | $36,000 | |
> | CR | Equity in investee income | | $36,000 |
>
> *Journal entry to recognize the dividend paid by the investee (40% × $40,000):*
>
> | | | | |
> |---|---|---|---|
> | DR | Cash | $16,000 | |
> | CR | Investment in Small Co. | | $16,000 |
>
> *(continued)*

(continued)

2. **Asset adjustment and depreciation**

| Goodwill | Excess = $60,000 | |
|---|---|---|
| FV | $600,000 × 40% = $240,000 | $300,000 Purchase Price |
| NBV | $550,000 × 40% = $220,000 | |

**Asset Adjustment:** The difference between the book value and fair value of net assets acquired:

| | |
|---|---|
| FV of net assets acquired | $240,000 |
| Less BV of net assets acquired | (220,000) |
| Asset adjustment | $ 20,000 |

**Goodwill:** The excess of the purchase price over the fair value of net assets:

| | |
|---|---|
| Purchase price of the investment in Small Co. | $300,000 |
| Less: Fair value of Big Corp.'s equity in net assets of Small Co. (40% × 600,000) | (240,000) |
| Goodwill | $ 60,000 |

3. *Journal entry to record depreciation on undervalued equipment ($20,000 ÷ 10 years):*

| DR | Equity in investee income | $2,000 | |
|---|---|---|---|
| CR | Investment in Small Co. | | $2,000 |

4. On December 31, Year 1, Big Corp.'s investment in Small Co.'s account would show a balance of $318,000 ($300,000 + $36,000 − $16,000 − $2,000), and the income statement would show $34,000 ($36,000 − $2,000) equity in investee income.

## 2.4 Equity Method Impairment

An impairment loss on an equity method investment is recognized when the following two conditions occur:

1. The fair value of the investment falls below the carrying value of the investment.
2. The entity believes the decline in value is other than temporary.

If both conditions are met, the entity reports the impairment loss on the income statement and the carrying value of the investment is reduced to the lower fair value on the balance sheet.

Under U.S. GAAP, the impairment loss is not permitted to be reversed if the fair value of the investment increases in subsequent periods.

Equity Method FAR 4

> ### Example 3 Impairment
>
> **Facts:** Precious Metals Co. owns a 25 percent investment in Gems Inc. Precious Metals accounts for the investment using the equity method. On the December 31, Year 1, balance sheet, the investment was reported at a carrying value of $5,000,000.
>
> During Year 2, Gems reported a net loss of $80,000 and paid no dividends. At the end of Year 2, Precious Metals' management estimated the fair value of its Gems Inc. investment at $4,000,000 due to the permanent closure of two factories and corresponding loss of sales. This decrease in fair value is considered to be other than temporary.
>
> **Required:** Calculate the impairment loss to be reported on the Year 2 income statement of Precious Metals.
>
> **Solution:** Before considering the effects of impairment, the investment in Gems would have a carrying value of $4,980,000 on the balance sheet of Precious Metals:
>
> | | | |
> |---|---|---|
> | Year 2, beginning balance | $5,000,000 | |
> | + (Share of Year 2 earnings) | (20,000) | [($80,000) × 25%] |
> | − Share of Year 2 dividends | 0 | |
> | Year 2, ending balance | $4,980,000 | |
> | − Fair value at end of Year 2 | (4,000,000) | |
> | Impairment loss | $ 980,000 | |
>
> Precious Metals would recognize an impairment loss of $980,000 on its Year 2 income statement.

---

### Question 3 MCQ-00348

Park Co. uses the equity method to account for its January 1, Year 1, purchase of Tun, Inc.'s common stock. On January 1, Year 1, the fair values of Tun's FIFO inventory and land exceeded their carrying amounts. How do these excesses of fair values over carrying amounts affect Park's reported equity in Tun's Year 1 earnings?

| | *Inventory Excess* | *Land Excess* |
|---|---|---|
| a. | Decrease | Decrease |
| b. | Decrease | No effect |
| c. | Increase | Increase |
| d. | Increase | No effect |

## Question 4 — MCQ-00289

Birk Co. purchased 30 percent of Sled Co.'s outstanding common stock on December 31 for $200,000. On that date, Sled's stockholders' equity was $500,000, and the fair value of its identifiable net assets was $600,000. On December 31, what amount of goodwill should Birk attribute to this acquisition?

- a. $0
- b. $20,000
- c. $30,000
- d. $50,000

## Question 5 — MCQ-00288

Puff Co. acquired 40 percent of Straw, Inc.'s voting common stock on January 2, Year 1 for $400,000. The carrying amount of Straw's net assets at the purchase date totaled $900,000. Fair values equaled carrying amounts for all items except equipment, for which fair values exceeded carrying amounts by $100,000. The equipment has a five-year life. During Year 1, Straw reported net income of $150,000. What amount of income from this investment should Puff report in its Year 1 income statement?

- a. $40,000
- b. $52,000
- c. $56,000
- d. $60,000

# 3 Comparison of Fair Value and Equity Methods

## Do Not Consolidate

### Fair Value
No significant influence
< 20%

**Purchase Price**

| DR | Investment |
|---|---|
| CR | Cash |

**Financial Asset at Fair Value Accounting**

Report investment at fair value with gains and losses reported in net income (trading securities).

**Liquidating Dividends**

| DR | Cash |
|---|---|
| CR | Investment |
| CR | Dividend income |

**Nonliquidating Dividends**

| DR | Cash |
|---|---|
| CR | Dividend income |

### Balance Sheet
"Investment Account"

### Income Statement
"Reportable Income"

### Equity
Significant influence
20%–50%

**Purchase Price**

| DR | Investment in investee |
|---|---|
| CR | Cash |

**+ Investee Income**

| DR | Investment in investee |
|---|---|
| CR | Equity in earnings |

**− Amortized FV > NBV**

| DR | Equity in earnings |
|---|---|
| CR | Investment in investee |

**− Investee Dividends**

| DR | Cash |
|---|---|
| CR | Investment in investee |

**Investee Income**

| DR | Investment in investee |
|---|---|
| CR | Equity in earnings |

**− Amortized FV > NBV**

| DR | Equity in earnings |
|---|---|
| CR | Investment in investee |

**Goodwill**
(*equity method only*)
- Not amortized
- Not impaired

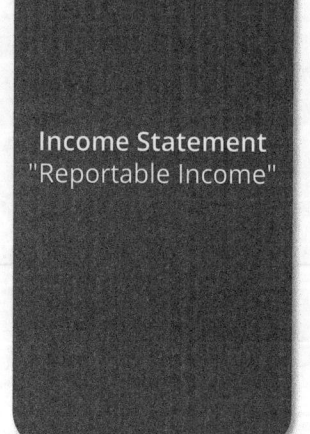

# 4 Transition to the Equity Method

When significant influence is acquired, it is necessary to record a change from the fair value method to the equity method by doing the following on the date the investment qualifies for the equity method:

1. Add the cost of acquiring the additional interest in the investee to the carrying value of the previously held investment.
2. Adopt the equity method as of that date and going forward. Retroactive adjustments are not required.

### Example 4  Transition to Equity Method

**Facts:** On January 1, Year 1, Big Co. paid $15,000 for a 15 percent interest in Small Co. Big did not have significant influence over Small. On January 1, Year 2, Big Co. increased its ownership in Small Co. to 45 percent, paying $60,000.

**Required:** Prepare the journal entry to be recorded on January 1, Year 2, to account for the transition to the use of the equity method for the investment in Small Co.

**Solution:**

*Journal entry to record the acquisition of the additional interest in Small Co. on January 1, Year 2:*

| | | | |
|---|---|---|---|
| DR | Investment in Small Co. | $60,000 | |
| CR | Cash | | $60,000 |

For equity securities without readily determinable fair values, if transitioning to the equity method due to an observable transaction, the investment must be remeasured immediately *before* the transition. If transitioning from the equity method, the investment must be remeasured immediately *after* the transition.

## NOTES

# MODULE 3
# Basic Consolidation Concepts

FAR 4

## 1 Voting Interest Model

### 1.1 Control (Over 50 Percent Ownership)

Under the voting interest model, consolidated financial statements are prepared when a parent-subsidiary relationship has been formed. An investor is considered to have parent status when control over an investee is established or more than 50 percent of the voting stock of the investee has been acquired.

Under U.S. GAAP, all majority-owned subsidiaries (domestic and foreign) must be consolidated except when significant doubt exists regarding the parent's ability to control the subsidiary, such as when:

1. the subsidiary is in legal reorganization; or
2. bankruptcy and/or the subsidiary operates under severe foreign restrictions.

> **U.S. GAAP VS. IFRS**
>
> Under IFRS, a parent company must consolidate its investments in subsidiaries unless all of the following conditions are met:
>
> 1. The parent company is itself a wholly owned subsidiary, or is a partially owned subsidiary of another entity and the other owners do not object to the parent not presenting consolidated financial statements.
>
> 2. The parent company is not publicly traded and is not in the process of issuing securities in a public market.
>
> 3. The ultimate or any intermediate parent of the parent company produces consolidated financial statements in compliance with IFRS.

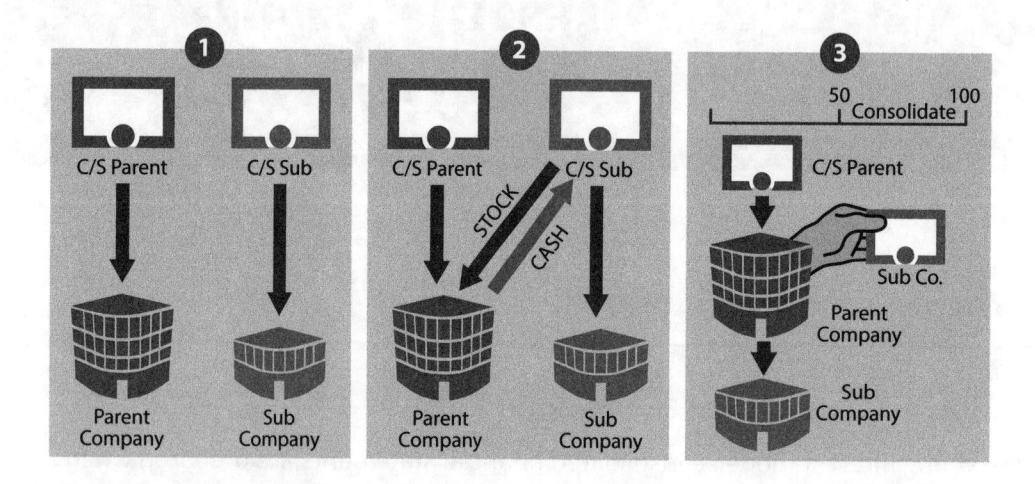

## 1.2 Controlling Interest and Noncontrolling Interest (NCI)

Business combinations that do not establish 100 percent ownership of a subsidiary by a parent company result in a portion of the subsidiary's equity (net assets) being attributable to noncontrolling shareholders.

### 1.2.1 Controlling Interest

An investor owning more than 50 percent of a subsidiary has a controlling interest in that subsidiary.

### 1.2.2 Noncontrolling Interest

Noncontrolling interest is the portion of the equity (net assets) of a subsidiary that is not attributable to the parent. Noncontrolling interest is reported at fair value in the equity section of the consolidated balance sheet, separately from the parent's equity.

---

**Question 1**     MCQ-04697

Sun Co. is a wholly owned subsidiary of Star Co. Both companies have separate general ledgers, and prepare separate financial statements. Sun requires stand-alone financial statements. Which of the following statements is correct?

- a. Consolidated financial statements should be prepared for both Star and Sun.
- b. Consolidated financial statements should only be prepared by Star and *not* by Sun.
- c. After consolidation, the accounts of both Star and Sun should be changed to reflect the consolidated totals for future ease in reporting.
- d. After consolidation, the accounts of both Star and Sun should be combined together into one general-ledger accounting system for future ease in reporting.

# 2 Variable Interest Entity (VIE) Model

## 2.1 Definitions

### 2.1.1 Variable Interest Entities (VIEs)

A corporation, partnership, trust, LLC, or other legal structure used for business purposes that either does not have equity investors with voting rights or lacks the sufficient financial resources to support its activities.

### 2.1.2 Primary Beneficiary

The entity that is required to consolidate the VIE. The primary beneficiary is the entity that has the power to direct the activities of a variable interest entity that most significantly impact the entity's economic performance and:

1. absorbs the expected VIE losses; or
2. receives the expected VIE residual returns.

> **Pass Key**
>
> The primary beneficiary of a variable interest entity must consolidate the variable interest entity. Under U.S. GAAP, all consolidation decisions are evaluated first under the VIE model. If consolidation is not required under the VIE model, then the investor (parent) company determines whether consolidation is necessary under the voting interest model (consolidate when ownership is more than 50 percent of the investee's voting stock).

## 2.2 Identifying a Variable Interest in a Business Entity

A company has a variable interest in a business entity when all of the following conditions are met:

1. The company and business entity have an arrangement
2. The business entity is a legal entity
3. The business fails to qualify for an exclusion
4. The interest is more than insignificant
5. The company has an explicit or implicit variable interest in the entity

### 2.2.1 Company and Business Entity Have an Arrangement

A VIE may exist when a company has any one of four arrangements with a business entity, including:

1. The company or a related party significantly participated in the business entity's design.
2. Substantially all of the business entity's activities, by its design, involve or are conducted on behalf of the company.
3. More than half of the total of the equity, subordinated debt, and other forms of financial support is provided by the company.
4. Securitizations or other forms of asset-backed financing agreements or single-lessee leasing arrangements are the primary activities of the entity.

### 2.2.2 Business Entity Is a Legal Entity

Legal entities include corporations, partnerships, LLCs, trusts, and majority-owned subsidiaries.

### 2.2.3 Business Entity Fails to Qualify for Exclusion

The following types of entities are ordinarily not subject to consolidation as VIEs:

- Nonprofit organizations
- Employee benefit plans
- Registered investment companies
- Separate accounts of life insurance companies
- Governmental organizations and financing entities established by governments

### 2.2.4 Interest Is More Than Insignificant

An entity with an insignificant variable interest is unlikely to be considered the primary beneficiary. The term "insignificant" should be considered in the context of whether the variable interest is large enough for the company to even remotely be considered the primary beneficiary that would consolidate the VIE.

### 2.2.5 Company Has an Explicit or Implicit Variable Interest in the Entity

A variable interest exists when the company must:

- absorb a portion of the business entity's losses; or
- receive a portion of the business entity's expected residual returns.

> **Pass Key**
>
> Examples of variable interests include:
> - Explicit investments at risk
> - Explicit guarantees of debt, the values of assets, or residual values of leased assets
> - Implicit guarantees with related party involvement
> - Most liabilities, excluding short-term trade payables
> - Most forward contracts to sell assets owned by the entity
> - Options to acquire leased assets at the end of the lease terms at specified prices
>
> *Explicit* means in writing and legally enforceable.

## 2.3 Business Entity Is a Variable Interest Entity

Once a company has established that it has a variable interest in a business entity, the company must determine whether the business entity is a variable interest entity (VIE). The business entity is a VIE if it has any of the following characteristics:

### 2.3.1 Insufficient Level of Equity Investment at Risk

A business entity has an insufficient level of equity investment at risk, and is a VIE, if it cannot operate on its own without additional subordinated financial support in the form of variable interests.

An entity has sufficient equity investment at risk, and is not a VIE, when:

- The entity can finance its own activities.
- The entity's equity investment at risk is at least as much as the equity investment of other non-VIE entities that hold similar assets of similar quality.
- Other facts and circumstances indicate that the equity investment at risk is sufficient.
- The fair value of the equity investment at risk is greater than expected losses.

> **Illustration 1  Insufficient Equity at Risk**
>
> In order to receive a bank loan, Little Corporation must obtain a loan guarantee from one of its shareholders. Little Corporation's total equity at risk is insufficient because it must obtain additional financial support in the form of the guarantee in order to obtain outside bank financing. A guarantee is a variable interest and Little Corporation is a VIE.

### 2.3.2 Inability to Make Decisions or Direct Activities

An entity is a VIE if the holders of the total equity investment at risk, as a group, do not have the power to direct the activities of the entity that most significantly impact the entity's economic performance.

### 2.3.3 No Obligation to Absorb Entity's Expected Losses

An entity is a VIE if the holders of the total equity investment at risk have no obligation to absorb the entity's expected losses.

### 2.3.4 No Right to Receive Expected Residual Returns

An entity is a VIE if the holders of the total equity investment at risk have no right to receive the entity's expected residual returns.

### 2.3.5 Disproportionately Few Voting Rights

An entity is a VIE if some of the equity investors have disproportionately few voting rights in comparison to their economic interests. An entity is automatically deemed to be a variable interest entity when all three of the following conditions are present:

1. Substantially all of the activities of the entity are conducted on behalf of an equity investor or substantially all of the activities are involving an equity investor.
2. The voting rights of that equity investor are small in comparison with the focus of the entity on that investor.
3. The voting rights of one or more of the equity investors, including that equity investor, are out of line with the investor's obligation to absorb expected losses, the investor's right to receive expected residual returns, or both.

# Basic Consolidation Concepts

> **Illustration 2 Disproportionately Few Voting Rights**
>
> Gearty Inc. and Small Inc. start a joint venture, Team LLC, to produce and sell gadgets. Their Team LLC investment and voting rights are:
>
> |  | Investment | Voting Rights |
> | --- | --- | --- |
> | Gearty Inc. | $100,000 | 10% |
> | Small Inc. | 25,000 | 90% |
>
> All gadgets produced by Team LLC are sold to Gearty Inc.
>
> Team LLC is a VIE because:
>
> - All activities are on behalf of Gearty Inc.
> - Gearty Inc.'s voting rights are small in comparison with the focus of Team LLC on Gearty Inc.
> - Gearty Inc.'s voting rights are out of line with the variable interest Gearty Inc. has in Team LLC ($100,000 ÷ $125,000 = 80% investment versus 10% voting rights).
>
> If all the gadgets produced by Team LLC were manufactured for an unrelated third party, then Team LLC would not be a VIE because the activities of the entity are not conducted on behalf of the equity investor.

## 2.4 Primary Beneficiary Consolidates

Once a company has established that it has a variable interest in a business entity that is a variable interest entity (VIE), the primary beneficiary must be determined. The primary beneficiary must consolidate the VIE.

The company is the primary beneficiary if it has the power to direct the activities of a variable interest entity that most significantly impact the entity's economic performance and the company:

- absorbs the expected VIE losses; or
- receives the expected VIE residual returns.

If one party receives the expected residual returns and another party absorbs the expected losses, the party that absorbs the expected losses consolidates. It is possible for an entity to be a VIE, but have no primary beneficiary and, therefore, nobody consolidates.

> **U.S. GAAP VS. IFRS**
>
> IFRS focuses on the accounting for special purpose entities. A special purpose entity is a specific type of VIE created by a sponsoring company to hold assets or liabilities, often for structured financing purposes (e.g., sales of receivables, synthetic leases, securitization of loans). Under IFRS, a sponsoring company controls and must consolidate an SPE when the company:
>
> - Is benefited by the SPE's activities.
> - Has decision-making powers that allow it to benefit from the SPE.
> - Absorbs the risks and rewards of the SPE.
> - Has a residual interest in the SPE.

## Private Company Accounting Alternative

Under U.S. GAAP, a private company (an entity that is not a public entity or a not-for-profit entity) may elect to not consolidate a lessor entity that would otherwise be consolidated under existing VIE guidance if the following four criteria are met:

1. The lessee (the reporting entity) and the lessor are under common control.

2. The lessee has a leasing arrangement with the lessor.

3. Substantially all activities between the lessee and lessor are related to leasing activities.

4. If the lessee explicitly guarantees or collateralizes any obligation of the lessor, then the principal amount of the obligation does not exceed the value of the asset leased by the private company from the lessor.

This is an accounting policy elected by the lessee and applies to all current and future leasing arrangements. It is applied using a full retrospective approach to all periods presented.

# MODULE 4: Acquisition Method: Part 1

**FAR 4**

## 1 Calculating the Acquisition Price

In a business combination accounted for as an acquisition, the subsidiary may be acquired for cash, stock, debt securities, etc.

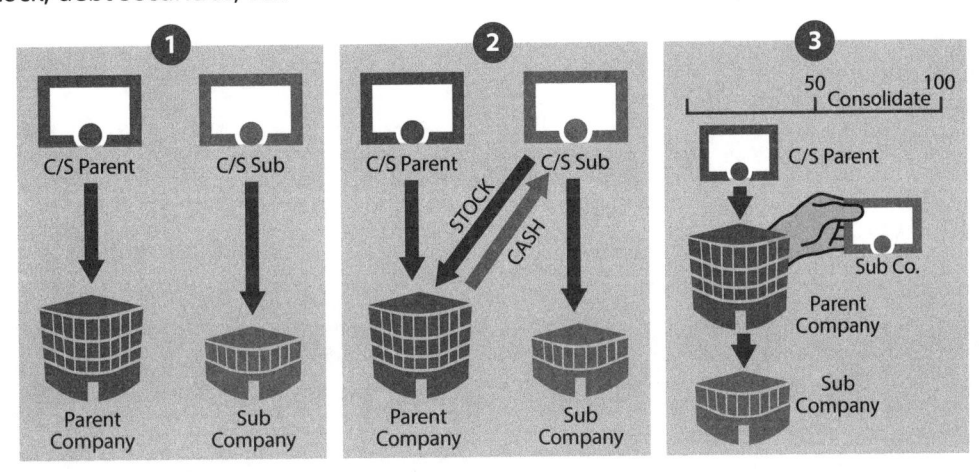

The investment is valued at the fair value of the consideration given or the fair value of the consideration received, whichever is the more clearly evident. The accounting for an acquisition begins at the date of acquisition.

*Journal entry to record the acquisition for cash:*

| | | | |
|---|---|---|---|
| DR | Investment in subsidiary | $XXX | |
| CR | Cash | | $XXX |

*Journal entry to record the acquisition for parent common stock (use FV at date transaction closes):*

| | | | |
|---|---|---|---|
| DR | Investment in subsidiary | $XXX | |
| CR | Common stock (parent at par) | | $XXX |
| CR | APIC (parent/FV—par) | | XXX |

## Example 1 — Date of Purchase: Stock Price Goes Up

**Facts:**

- TAG Inc. announces that it has agreed to buy a Sub Co. on April 1, Year 1, for 1 million shares of its own common stock.
- Transaction closes on September 30, Year 1.

| Market Price of Stock | Stock Price Goes Up |
|---|---|
| 4/1/Y1 (announced) | $10 |
| 9/30/Y1 (closed) | $14 |

**Required:** Compute the acquisition price.

**Solution:**

| Acquisition Price |
|---|
| 1,000,000 × $14 = $14,000,000 |

## Example 2 — Date of Purchase: Stock Price Goes Down

**Facts:**

- TAG Inc. announces that it has agreed to buy a Sub Co. on April 1, Year 1, for 1 million shares of its own common stock.
- Transaction closes on September 30, Year 1.

| Market Price of Stock | Stock Price Goes Down |
|---|---|
| 4/1/Y1 (announced) | $10 |
| 9/30/Y1 (closed) | $7 |

**Required:** Compute the acquisition price.

**Solution:**

| Acquisition Price |
|---|
| 1,000,000 × $7 = $7,000,000 |

# 2 Application of the Acquisition Method

The acquisition method has two distinct accounting characteristics: (1) 100 percent of the net assets acquired (regardless of percentage acquired) are recorded at fair value with any unallocated balance remaining creating goodwill; and (2) when the companies are consolidated, the subsidiary's entire equity (including its common stock, APIC, and retained earnings) is eliminated (not reported).

> **Pass Key**
>
> The parent's basis is the acquisition price. The easy-to-remember formula is:
>
> Acquisition price = Investment in subsidiary

## 2.1 Consolidation Adjustments

An acquiring corporation should adjust the following items during consolidation:

1. **Common Stock, APIC, and Retained Earnings of Subsidiary Are Eliminated**

    The pre-acquisition equity (common stock, APIC, and retained earnings) of the subsidiary is not carried forward in an acquisition. Consolidated equity will be equal to the parent's equity balance (plus any noncontrolling interest). The subsidiary's equity is eliminated by debiting each of the subsidiary's equity accounts in the eliminating journal entry (EJE) on the consolidating workpapers.

2. **Investment in Subsidiary Is Eliminated**

    The parent company will eliminate the "investment in subsidiary" account on its balance sheet as part of the eliminating journal entry (EJE). This credit will be posted on the consolidating workpapers.

3. **Noncontrolling Interest (NCI) Is Created**

    As part of the eliminating journal entry (EJE) on the consolidating workpapers, the fair value of any portion of the subsidiary that is not acquired by the parent must be reported as noncontrolling interest in the equity section of the consolidated financial statements, separately from the parent's equity.

4. **Balance Sheet of Subsidiary Is Adjusted to Fair Value**

    All of the subsidiary's balance sheet accounts are to be adjusted to fair value on the acquisition date. This is accomplished as part of the eliminating journal entry (EJE) on the consolidating workpapers. This adjustment is done, regardless of the amount paid to acquire the subsidiary. The adjustment is for the full (100 percent) fair value of the subsidiary's assets and liabilities, even if the parent acquires less than 100 percent of the subsidiary.

5. **Identifiable Intangible Assets of the Subsidiary Are Recorded at Their Fair Value**

    As part of the eliminating journal entry (EJE) on the consolidating workpapers, it is required that the parent record the fair value of all identifiable intangible assets of the subsidiary. This is done even if no amount was incurred to acquire these items in the acquisition.

6. **Goodwill (or Gain) Is Required**

    If there is an excess of the fair value of the subsidiary (acquisition cost plus any noncontrolling interest) over the fair value of the subsidiary's net assets, then the remaining/excess is debited to create goodwill. If there is a deficiency in the acquisition cost compared with the subsidiary's fair value, then the shortage/negative amount is recorded as a gain.

Acquisition Method: Part 1 FAR 4

# 3 Consolidated Workpaper Eliminating Journal Entry

The year-end consolidating journal entry known as the consolidating workpaper eliminating journal entry (JE) is:

| | | | |
|---|---|---|---|
| DR | Common stock—subsidiary | $XXX | |
| DR | APIC—subsidiary | XXX | |
| DR | Retained earning—subsidiary | XXX | |
| CR | Investment in subsidiary | | $XXX |
| CR | Noncontrolling interest | | XXX |
| DR | Balance sheet adjustments to FV | XXX | |
| DR | Identifiable Intangible assets to FV | XXX | |
| DR | Goodwill | XXX | |

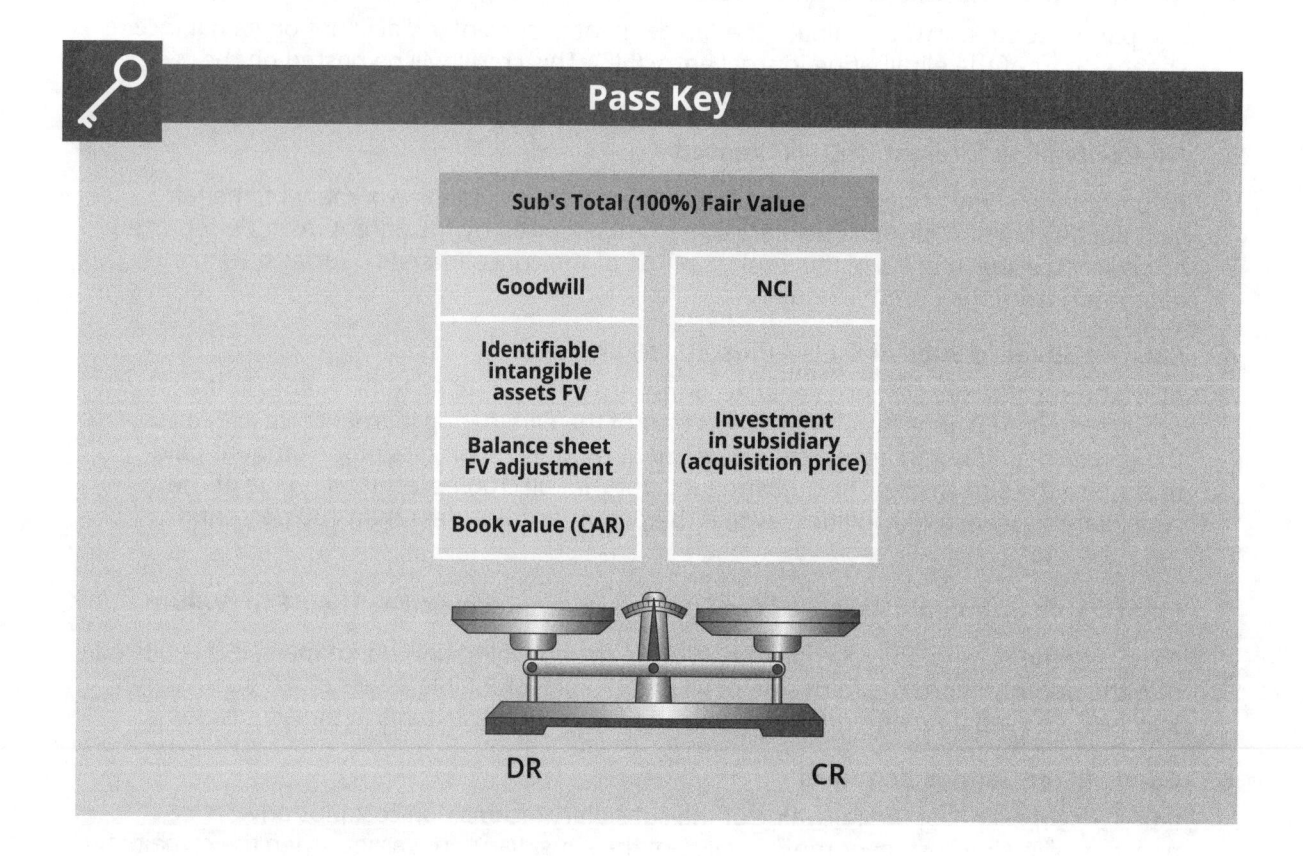

### Pass Key

**Sub's Total (100%) Fair Value**

DR side:
- Goodwill
- Identifiable intangible assets FV
- Balance sheet FV adjustment
- Book value (CAR)

CR side:
- NCI
- Investment in subsidiary (acquisition price)

## Journal Entry Flow Chart—Acquisition Date Calculation

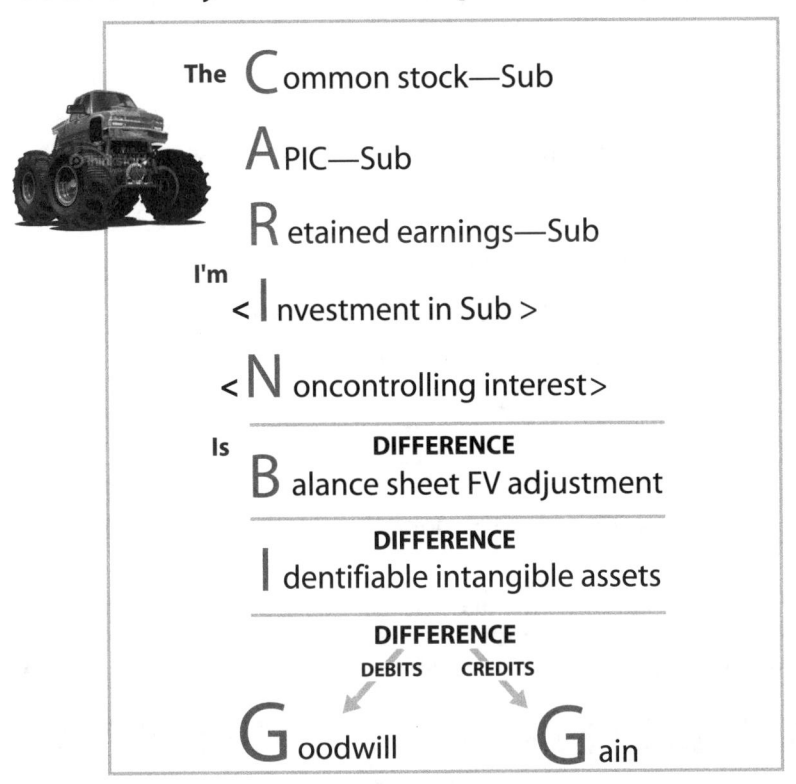

The **C**ommon stock—Sub

**A**PIC—Sub

**R**etained earnings—Sub

I'm <**I**nvestment in Sub>

<**N**oncontrolling interest>

Is  **DIFFERENCE**
**B**alance sheet FV adjustment

**DIFFERENCE**
**I**dentifiable intangible assets

**DIFFERENCE**
DEBITS ↙   ↘ CREDITS
**G**oodwill    **G**ain

The following diagram illustrates the relationships between the fair value of the subsidiary, the fair value of the subsidiary's net assets, and the book value of the subsidiary's net assets.

### Acquisition Method

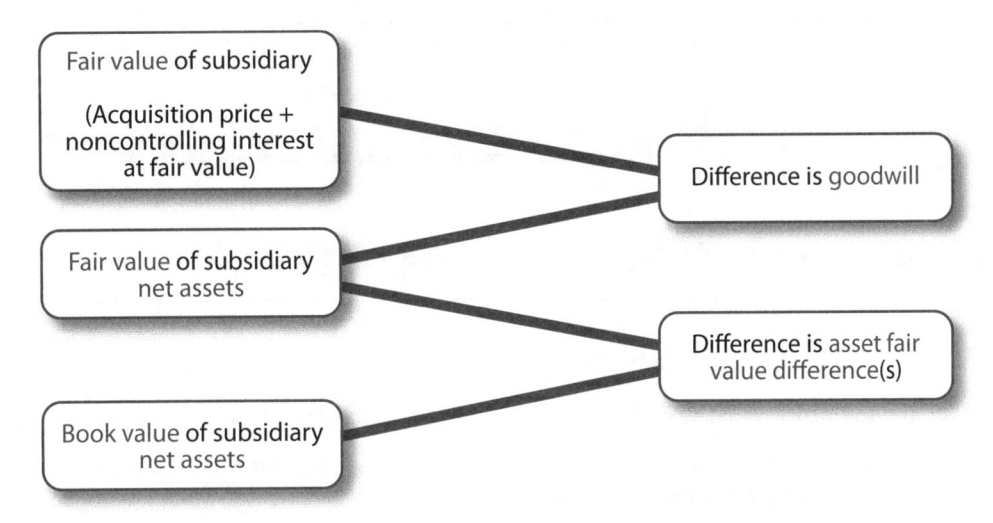

- Fair value of subsidiary (Acquisition price + noncontrolling interest at fair value)
- Fair value of subsidiary net assets
- Book value of subsidiary net assets

- Difference is goodwill
- Difference is asset fair value difference(s)

Acquisition Method: Part 1

# 4 "CAR": Subsidiary Equity Acquired  CAR IN BIG

## 4.1 CAR Formula

The following formula is used to determine the book value of the assets acquired from the subsidiary:

> Assets − Liabilities = Equity
> Assets − Liabilities = Net book value
> Assets − Liabilities = CAR

## 4.2 Acquisition Date Calculation (of CAR)

The determination of the difference between book value and fair value is computed as of the acquisition date.

When the subsidiary's financial statements are provided for a subsequent period, it is necessary to reverse the activity (income and dividends) in the subsidiary's retained earnings in order to squeeze back into the book value (Assets − Liabilities = CAR) at the acquisition date.

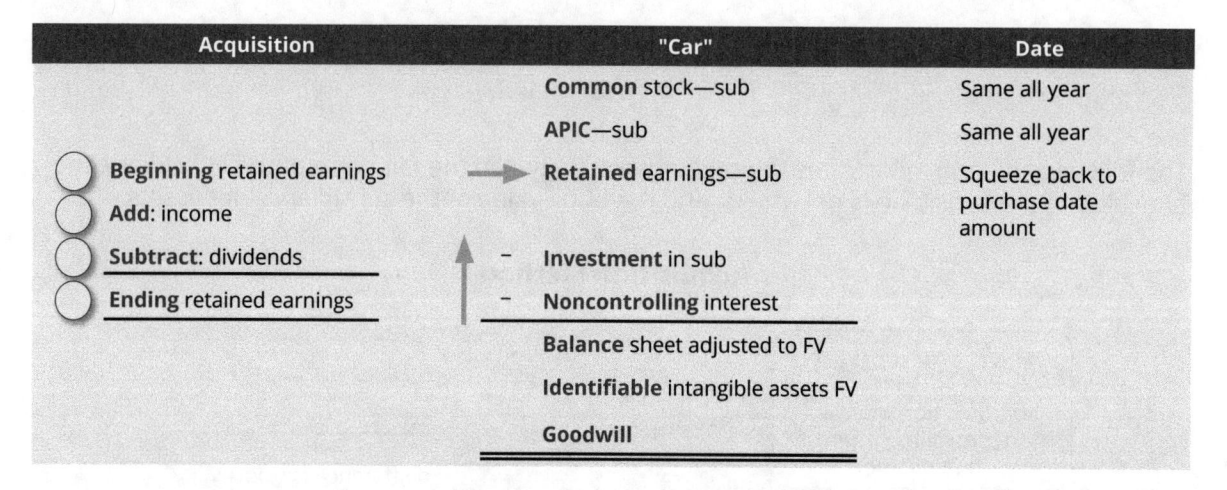

| Acquisition | "Car" | Date |
|---|---|---|
|  | Common stock—sub | Same all year |
|  | APIC—sub | Same all year |
| Beginning retained earnings → | Retained earnings—sub | Squeeze back to purchase date amount |
| Add: income |  |  |
| Subtract: dividends | − Investment in sub |  |
| Ending retained earnings | − Noncontrolling interest |  |
|  | Balance sheet adjusted to FV |  |
|  | Identifiable intangible assets FV |  |
|  | Goodwill |  |

# 5 Investment in Subsidiary  CAR IN BIG

## 5.1 Original Carrying Amount

The original carrying amount of the investment in subsidiary account on the parent's books is:

- Original cost: measured by the fair value (on the date the acquisition is completed) of the consideration given (debit: investment in sub).
- Business combination costs/expenses in an acquisition are treated as follows:
    - Direct out-of-pocket costs and indirect costs are expensed (debit: expense).
    - Stock registration and issuance costs such as SEC filing fees are a direct reduction of the value of the stock issued (debit: additional paid-in capital account).

## Example 3 — Business Combination Accounted for as an Acquisition

**Facts:** On January 1, Year 1, Big Company exchanged 10,000 shares of $10 par value common stock with a fair value of $415,000 for 100 percent of the outstanding stock of Sub Company in a business combination properly accounted for as an acquisition. In addition, Big Co. paid $35,000 in legal fees. At the date of acquisition, the fair and book value of Sub Co.'s net assets totaled $300,000. Registration fees were $20,000:

**Required:**
1. Prepare the journal entry to record the acquisition.
2. Prepare the acquisition date consolidating workpaper eliminating journal entry.

**Solution:**

*Journal entry to record the acquisition price and legal fees:*

| | | | |
|---|---|---|---|
| DR | Investment in subsidiary | $415,000 | |
| DR | Legal expense | 35,000 | |
| CR | Common stock—$10 par value | | $100,000 |
| CR | Additional paid-in capital—Big Co. ($315,000 − $20,000) | | 295,000* |
| CR | Cash ($35,000 + $20,000) | | 55,000 |

*APIC—Big Co. = $415,000 − $100,000 = $315,000 − $20,000 = $295,000

**Sub's Total (100%) Fair Value**

| | | | |
|---|---|---|---|
| Goodwill | $115,000 | -0- | NCI |
| Identifiable intangible assets FV | -0- | | |
| Balance sheet FV adjustment | -0- | $415,000 | Investment in subsidiary |
| Book value (CAR) | $300,000 | | |

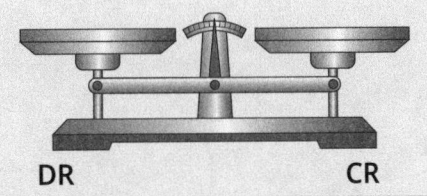

DR                CR

| | | | | |
|---|---|---|---|---|
| ○ | DR | Common stock—subsidiary | | |
| ○ | DR | APIC—subsidiary | $300,000 | |
| ○ | DR | Retained earnings—subsidiary | | |
| ○ | CR | Investment in subsidiary | | $415,000 |
| ○ | CR | Noncontrolling interest | | -0- |
| ○ | DR | Balance sheet adjustments to FV | -0- | |
| ○ | DR | Identifiable Intangible assets to FV | -0- | |
| ○ | DR | Goodwill | 115,000 | |

## 5.2 Contingent Consideration

Contingent consideration is an obligation of the parent company to transfer additional assets or equity interests to the former shareholders of the subsidiary if specified conditions are met.

### 5.2.1 Recording Contingent Consideration

Contingent consideration is recorded by the parent on the acquisition date by:

- adding an estimate of the probable settlement cost to the investment in subsidiary; and
- crediting the liability expected value of contingent consideration.

---

**Example 4    Recording Contingent Consideration**

**Facts:** On January 1, Year 1, Big Company exchanged 10,000 shares of $10 par value common stock with a fair value of $415,000 for 100 percent of the outstanding common stock of Sub Company. In addition to the stock issue, Big Co. agreed to pay an additional $85,000 on January 1, Year 5, if Sub's average income during Years 1–4 exceeds $50,000 annually. On the acquisition date, Big believes that there is a 50 percent probability that Sub will achieve the earnings target over the four-year period. On the date of acquisition, the fair value and book value of Sub Co.'s net assets totaled $300,000.

**Required:**

1. Calculate the expected value of the contingent consideration and prepare the journal entry to record the acquisition.
2. Prepare the acquisition date consolidating workpaper eliminating journal entry.

**Solution:** Expected value of contingent consideration = $85,000 × 50% = $42,500

| | | | |
|---|---|---|---|
| DR | Investment in subsidiary | $457,500 | |
| CR | Estimated liability for contingent consideration | | $ 42,500 |
| CR | Common stock ($10 par value × 10,000 shares) | | 100,000 |
| CR | APIC – Big Co. ($415,000 – $100,000) | | 315,000 |

| | | | |
|---|---|---|---|
| DR | Common stock—subsidiary | | |
| DR | APIC—subsidiary | $300,000 | |
| DR | Retained earnings—subsidiary | | |
| CR | Investment in subsidiary | | $457,500 |
| CR | Noncontrolling interest | | -0- |
| DR | Balance sheet adjustment—PP&E | -0- | |
| DR | Identifiable intangible assets—in-process R&D | -0- | |
| DR | Goodwill | 157,500 | |

### 5.2.2 Changes in Contingent Consideration

The contingent consideration estimate may be adjusted after the acquisition date based on improved information. The adjustment is included in earnings in the period of the adjustment.

> **Illustration 1  Change in Contingent Consideration**
>
> Sub Company's income exceeded $50,000 in Years 1 and 2. On January 1, Year 3, Big Company determined that there is an 80 percent probability that Sub will achieve the four-year average earnings target. In Year 3, the expected value of the contingent consideration is $68,000 ($85,000 × 80%) and an adjustment of $25,500 ($68,000−$42,500) is recognized:
>
> | | | | |
> |---|---|---|---|
> | DR | Expense—increase in estimated contingent consideration | $25,500 | |
> | CR | Estimated liability for contingent consideration | | $25,500 |

## 5.3 Parent Company Accounting for the Investment in Subsidiary

After the acquisition date, the parent uses either the cost method or the equity method to account for the investment in subsidiary in its accounting records.

> **Pass Key**
>
> The equity method and cost method are used by the parent company for internal accounting purposes only. When the consolidated financial statements are prepared, the investment in subsidiary account is eliminated.

### 5.3.1 Cost Method

Under the cost method, the investment in subsidiary account does not change after the acquisition date. No adjustments are made to account for the parent's share of subsidiary income. Dividends received from the subsidiary are recorded by the parent as dividend income.

### 5.3.2 Equity Method

The equity method that is used by the parent company to account for the investment in subsidiary is the same method used by an investor that exercises significant influence over an investee.

Under the equity method, the investment in subsidiary increases by the parent company's share of the subsidiary's net income with a corresponding credit to the income statement account, equity in subsidiary/subsidiary income.

Dividends received from the subsidiary decrease the investment in subsidiary.

## Pass Key

The advantage of the equity method is that changes in the subsidiary's equity are reflected in the parent's investment in subsidiary account, which simplifies the elimination of the investment in subsidiary when the consolidated financial statements are prepared.

### Example 5 — Equity Method

**Facts:** On January 1, Year 1, Gearty Corporation acquired 100 percent of Olinto Corporation. Gearty Corp. issued 100,000 shares of its $10 par common stock, with a market price of $15 on the date the acquisition was announced and $25 on the date the acquisition was completed, for all of Olinto Corp.'s common stock. For the year ended December 31, Year 1, Olinto reported net income of $350,000 and paid cash dividends of $150,000. Gearty accounts for its investment in Olinto using the equity method.

**Required:** Determine the balance in the Gearty's investment in subsidiary account on January 1, Year 1, and December 31, Year 1.

**Solution:**

January 1, Year 1: Investment in subsidiary = 100,000 shares × $25/share = $2,500,000

December 31, Year 1: Investment in subsidiary = $2,700,000, calculated as follows:

| | |
|---|---|
| 1/1/Y1 Investment in subsidiary | $2,500,000 |
| + Share of subsidiary income | 350,000 |
| − Share of subsidiary dividends | (150,000) |
| 12/31/Y1 Investment in subsidiary | $2,700,000 |

---

### Question 1 — MCQ-00430

Company J acquired all of the outstanding common stock of Company K in exchange for cash. The acquisition price exceeds the fair value of net assets acquired. How should Company J determine the amounts to be reported for the plant and equipment and long-term debt acquired from Company K?

| | Plant and Equipment | Long-Term Debt |
|---|---|---|
| a. | K's carrying amount | K's carrying amount |
| b. | K's carrying amount | Fair value |
| c. | Fair value | K's carrying amount |
| d. | Fair value | Fair value |

## Question 2 — MCQ-00389

A business combination is accounted for as an acquisition. Which of the following expenses related to the business combination should be included, in total, in the determination of net income of the combined corporation for the period in which the expenses are incurred?

|    | Fees of Finders and Consultants | Registration Fees for Equity Securities Issued |
|----|---------------------------------|------------------------------------------------|
| a. | Yes | Yes |
| b. | Yes | No |
| c. | No  | Yes |
| d. | No  | No |

## NOTES

# MODULE 5: Acquisition Method: Part 2

FAR 4

## 1 Noncontrolling Interest (NCI)   CAR IN BIG

Business combinations that do not establish 100 percent ownership of a subsidiary by a parent will result in a portion of the subsidiary's equity (net assets) being attributed to noncontrolling shareholders. Noncontrolling interest must be reported at fair value in the equity section of the consolidated balance sheet, separately from the parent's equity. This includes the noncontrolling interest's share of any goodwill.

### 1.1 Balance Sheet

The consolidated balance sheet will include 100 percent of the subsidiary's assets and liabilities (not the sub's equity/CAR). The noncontrolling interest's share of the subsidiary's net assets should be presented on the balance sheet as part of stockholders' equity, separately from the equity of the parent company.

#### 1.1.1 Acquisition Date Computation

The noncontrolling interest is calculated by multiplying the total subsidiary fair value times the noncontrolling interest percentage:

> Fair value of subsidiary
> × Noncontrolling interest %
> ─────────────────────────
> Noncontrolling interest

#### 1.1.2 Noncontrolling Interest After the Acquisition Date

After the acquisition date, the noncontrolling interest reported on the consolidated balance sheet is accounted for using the equity method:

> Beginning noncontrolling interest
> + NCI share of subsidiary net income
> − NCI share of subsidiary dividends
> ────────────────────────────────────
> Ending noncontrolling interest

## 1.2 Income Statement

The consolidated income statement will include 100 percent of the subsidiary's revenues and expenses (after the date of acquisition). The consolidated income statement should show net income attributable to the noncontrolling interest separately from the net income attributable to the parent.

### 1.2.1 Computation of Net Income Attributable to the Noncontrolling Interest

Compute by multiplying the subsidiary's net income times the noncontrolling interest percentage.

> Subsidiary's income
> − Subsidiary's expenses
> ―――――――――――――――
> Subsidiary's net income
> × Noncontrolling interest %
> ―――――――――――――――
> Net income attributable
>   to the noncontrolling interest

---

### U.S. GAAP VS. IFRS

Under IFRS, noncontrolling interest (and goodwill, as discussed below) can be calculated using either the "partial goodwill" method or the "full goodwill" method. The partial goodwill method is the preferred method under IFRS, but entities can elect to use the full goodwill method on a transaction-by-transaction basis.

**Full goodwill method**

The full goodwill method is the method used under U.S. GAAP, in which noncontrolling interest on the balance sheet is calculated as follows:

> NCI = Fair value of subsidiary × Noncontrolling interest %

**Partial goodwill method**

Under the partial goodwill method, noncontrolling interest is calculated as follows:

> NCI = Fair value of subsidiary's net identifiable assets
>       × Noncontrolling interest %

An example of the partial goodwill method is shown following the discussion of goodwill.

## Example 1 — Noncontrolling Interest: U.S. GAAP

**Facts:**

- Gearty Co. acquires 60 percent of Foxy Inc. for $69,000,000
- The fair value of Foxy Inc. is $115,000,000 ($115,000,000 × 60% = $69,000,000)
- Noncontrolling interest is $46,000,000 ($115,000,000 × 40% = $46,000,000)
- Fair value of Foxy Inc. (includes goodwill)           $115,000,000   ⎫
- Fair value of Foxy Inc. identifiable net assets      $100,000,000   ⎬ $15,000,000
- Book value of Foxy Inc. net assets                   $80,000,000    ⎭ $20,000,000

**Required:** Prepare the acquisition date consolidated workpaper eliminating journal entry.

**Solution:**

Sub's Total (100%) Fair Value = $115,000,000

| | | | |
|---|---|---|---|
| Goodwill | $15,000,000 | $46,000,000 | NCI |
| Identifiable intangible assets FV | -0- | $69,000,000 | Investment in subsidiary |
| Balance sheet FV adjustment | $20,000,000 | | |
| Book value (CAR) | $80,000,000 | | |

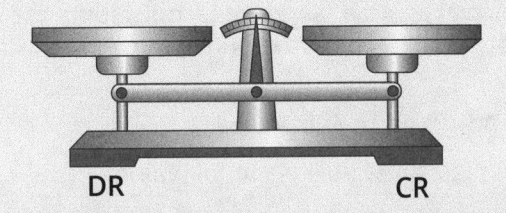

| | | Account | DR | CR |
|---|---|---|---|---|
| ○ | DR | Common stock—subsidiary | | |
| ○ | DR | APIC—subsidiary | $ 80,000,000 | |
| ○ | DR | Retained earnings—subsidiary | | |
| ○ | CR | Investment in subsidiary | | $ 69,000,000 |
| ○ | CR | Noncontrolling interest | | 46,000,000 |
| ○ | DR | Balance sheet adjustments to FV | 20,000,000 | |
| ○ | DR | Identifiable Intangible assets to FV | -0- | |
| ○ | DR | Goodwill | 15,000,000 | |
| | | | $115,000,000 | $115,000,000 |

# 2 Balance Sheet Adjustment to Fair Value, Identifiable Intangible Asset Adjustment to Fair Value, and Goodwill (Gain)   `CAR IN BIG`

## 2.1 Fair Value of Subsidiary

Under the acquisition method, the fair value of the subsidiary is equal to the acquisition cost plus any noncontrolling interest at fair value.

> FV subsidiary = Acquisition cost + NCI at FV

On the acquisition date, the fair value of the subsidiary must be compared with the respective assets and liabilities of the subsidiary. Any difference between the fair value of the subsidiary and the book value acquired will require an adjustment to the following three areas:

1. **Balance Sheet:** Adjustment of the subsidiary's assets and liabilities from book value to fair value.
2. **Identifiable Intangible Assets:** Related to the acquisition of the subsidiary are recorded at fair value.
3. **Goodwill:** Is recognized for any excess of the fair value of the subsidiary over the fair value of the subsidiary's net assets. If the fair value of the subsidiary is less than the fair value of the subsidiary's net assets, a gain is recognized.

## 2.2 Acquisition With Goodwill

**Rule:** When acquiring a subsidiary with a fair value (acquisition price + fair value of NCI) that is greater than the fair value of 100 percent of the underlying assets acquired, the following steps are required:

- **Step 1: Balance Sheet Adjusted to Fair Value**

    Adjust the subsidiary's assets and liabilities to fair value.

- **Step 2: Identifiable Intangible Assets to Fair Value**

    Allocate the remaining acquisition cost to the fair value of any identifiable intangible assets acquired.

| Illustrative List of Identifiable Intangible Assets ||
|---|---|
| • Agreements and contracts | • Computer software and licenses |
| • Rights | • Technical drawings and manuals |
| • Permits | • Customer lists |
| • Patents | • Unpatented technology |
| • Copyrights | • In-process research and development |
| • Trademarks and trade names | • Noncompetes |
| • Franchises | |

> **Pass Key**
>
> **In-Process Research and Development**
>
> Recognize as an intangible asset separately from goodwill at the acquisition date (need valuation).
>
> - Do not immediately write off.
> - In-process research and development meets the definition of an *asset*—it has probable future economic benefit.

These identifiable intangible assets are separated into two categories:

1. **Finite Life:** Amortize over the remaining life. Subject to the two-step impairment test.
2. **Indefinite Life:** Do not amortize. Subject to the one-step impairment test.

> **Pass Key**
>
> |  | Indefinite Life | Finite Life |
> | --- | --- | --- |
> | Characteristics | Life extends beyond the foreseeable future | Useful life is limited |
> | Amortization | None | Over useful economic life |
> | Impairment test | One-step test | Two-step test |

### Step 3: Goodwill

Allocate any remaining acquisition cost to goodwill.

$$\text{Goodwill} = \text{FV subsidiary} - \text{FV subsidiary net assets}$$

This goodwill is generally not amortized. Acquisition goodwill is subject to impairment testing. In the period it is determined to be impaired, it is written down and charged as an expense against income on the income statement.

# Private Company Accounting Alternative

Under U.S. GAAP, a private company (an entity that is not a public entity or not-for-profit entity) may elect an accounting policy under which it would not separately recognize the following intangible assets when accounting for a business combination:

1. Intangible assets that would otherwise arise from noncompete agreements; or

2. Customer-related intangible assets that cannot be separately sold or licensed, such as customer lists, order backlogs, and customer contracts.

Instead, the value of these assets would be included in goodwill. This accounting alternative also applies where a private company is required to recognize the fair value of intangible assets as a result of:

1. Applying the equity method to joint ventures.

2. Adopting fresh-start reporting in a reorganization.

A private company may elect this alternative only if it also elects the private company goodwill accounting alternative. However, a private company can elect the goodwill accounting alternative without electing this alternative for a business combination. Once elected, a private company should apply this accounting alternative prospectively to all business combinations.

## Question 1 — MCQ-00391

On September 29, Year 1, Wall Co. paid $860,000 for all the issued and outstanding common stock of Hart Corp. On that date, the carrying amounts of Hart's recorded assets and liabilities were $800,000 and $180,000, respectively. Hart's recorded assets and liabilities had fair values of $840,000 and $140,000, respectively. In Wall's September 30, Year 1, balance sheet, what amount should be reported as goodwill?

a. $20,000
b. $160,000
c. $180,000
d. $240,000

## Question 2 — MCQ-06457

Penn Corp. paid $300,000 for 75 percent of the outstanding common stock of Star Co. At that time, Star had the following condensed balance sheet:

|  | Carrying Amounts |
|---|---|
| Current assets | $ 40,000 |
| Plant and equipment, net | 380,000 |
| Liabilities | 200,000 |
| Stockholders' equity | 220,000 |

The fair value of the plant and equipment was $60,000 more than its recorded carrying amount. The fair value and carrying amounts were equal for all other assets and liabilities.

What amount of goodwill related to Star's acquisition should Penn report on its consolidated balance sheet under U.S. GAAP?

- a. $20,000
- b. $40,000
- c. $90,000
- d. $120,000

## U.S. GAAP VS. IFRS

Under IFRS, goodwill (and noncontrolling interest as discussed above) can be calculated using either the "partial goodwill" method or the "full goodwill" method.

### Full goodwill method

The full goodwill method is the method used under U.S. GAAP, in which goodwill is calculated as follows:

> Goodwill = Fair value of subsidiary − Fair value of subsidiary's net assets

### Partial goodwill method

Under the partial goodwill method, goodwill is calculated as follows:

> Goodwill = Acquisition cost − Fair value of subsidiary's net assets acquired

**Note:** Partial goodwill and full goodwill methods differ only when the parent owns less than 100 percent of the subsidiary.

## Example 2 — U.S. GAAP and IFRS: Full Goodwill

**Facts:** TAG Inc. purchases 60 percent of Gearty Co.'s equity for $75,000,000 in cash. The fair value of Gearty is $125,000,000 ($125,000,000 × 60% = $75,000,000). TAG uses the full goodwill method under IFRS. The fair value of Gearty Co.'s net identifiable assets is $60,000,000 and carrying amount of Gearty's net assets is $50,000,000. Under the full goodwill method:

$$\text{Noncontrolling interest} = \$125{,}000{,}000 \times 40\% = \$50{,}000{,}000$$
$$\text{Goodwill} = \$125{,}000{,}000 - \$60{,}000{,}000 = \$65{,}000{,}000$$

**Required:** Prepare the acquisition date consolidated workpaper eliminating journal entry.

**Solution:**

Sub's Total (100%) Fair Value = $125,000,000

| | | | |
|---|---|---|---|
| Goodwill | $65,000,000 | $50,000,000 | NCI |
| Identifiable intangible assets FV | -0- | | |
| Balance sheet FV adjustment | $10,000,000 | $75,000,000 | Investment in subsidiary |
| Book value (CAR) | $50,000,000 | | |

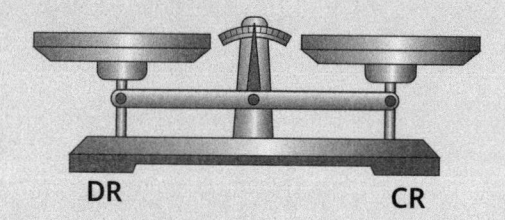

| | | DR | CR |
|---|---|---|---|
| DR | Common stock—subsidiary | | |
| DR | APIC—subsidiary | $ 50,000,000 | |
| DR | Retained earnings—subsidiary | | |
| CR | Investment in subsidiary | | $ 75,000,000 |
| CR | Noncontrolling interest | | 50,000,000 |
| DR | Balance sheet adjustments to FV | 10,000,000 | |
| DR | Identifiable Intangible assets to FV | -0- | |
| DR | Goodwill | 65,000,000 | |
| | | $125,000,000 | $125,000,000 |

## Example 3 — IFRS: Partial Goodwill

**Facts:** TAG Inc. purchases 60 percent of Gearty Co.'s equity for $75,000,000 in cash. TAG uses the partial goodwill method under IFRS. The fair value of Gearty Co.'s net identifiable assets is $60,000,000 and carrying amount of Gearty's net assets is $50,000,000. Under the partial goodwill method:

$$\text{Noncontrolling interest} = \$60,000,000 \times 40\% = \$24,000,000$$

$$\text{Goodwill} = \$75,000,000 - (\$60,000,000 \times 60\%) = \$75,000,000 - \$36,000,000 = \$39,000,000$$

**Required:** Prepare the acquisition date consolidated workpaper eliminating journal entry.

**Solution:**

Sub's Total (100%) Fair Value = $99,000,000

| | | | |
|---|---|---|---|
| Goodwill | $39,000,000 | $24,000,000 | NCI |
| Identifiable intangible assets FV | -0- | | |
| Balance sheet FV adjustment | $10,000,000 | $75,000,000 | Investment in subsidiary |
| Book value (CAR) | $50,000,000 | | |

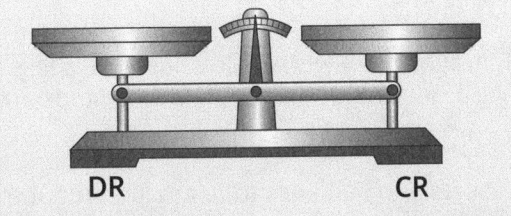

| | | | DR | CR |
|---|---|---|---|---|
| ○ | DR | Common stock—subsidiary | | |
| ○ | DR | APIC—subsidiary | $50,000,000 | |
| ○ | DR | Retained earnings—subsidiary | | |
| ○ | CR | Investment in subsidiary | | $75,000,000 |
| ○ | CR | Noncontrolling interest | | 24,000,000 |
| ○ | DR | Balance sheet adjustments to FV | 10,000,000 | |
| ○ | DR | Identifiable Intangible assets to FV | -0- | |
| ○ | DR | Goodwill | 39,000,000 | |
| | | | $99,000,000 | $99,000,000 |

# Acquisition Method: Part 2

## Question 3 — MCQ-06458

Penn Corp. paid $300,000 for 75 percent of the outstanding common stock of Star Co. At that time, Star had the following condensed balance sheet:

|  | Carrying Amounts |
|---|---|
| Current assets | $ 40,000 |
| Plant and equipment, net | 380,000 |
| Liabilities | 200,000 |
| Stockholders' equity | 220,000 |

The fair value of the plant and equipment was $60,000 more than its recorded carrying amount. The fair value and carrying amounts were equal for all other assets and liabilities.

What amount of goodwill related to Star's acquisition should Penn report on its consolidated balance sheet under the IFRS partial goodwill method?

- a. $20,000
- b. $40,000
- c. $90,000
- d. $120,000

## 2.3 Acquisition With Gain

When acquiring a corporation/subsidiary with a fair value that is less than the fair value of 100 percent of the underlying assets acquired, the following steps are required:

- **Step 1: Balance Sheet Adjusted to Fair Value**

  Adjust the subsidiary's assets and liabilities to fair value accounts (even if the acquisition cost is less than the fair value to be assigned). This will create a negative balance in the acquisition cost account.

- **Step 2: Identifiable Intangible Assets to Fair Value**

  Allocate any remaining acquisition cost (if any) to the fair value of any identifiable intangible assets acquired (even if the remaining acquisition cost is less than the fair value to be assigned). This will create or increase the negative balance in the acquisition cost account.

- **Step 3: Gain**

  The negative balance in the acquisition cost account is recorded as a gain.

## Example 4 — Gain Allocation

**Facts:**

- Gearty Co. purchases 100 percent of Sub Co. for $1,000,000.
- Total net book value of Sub Co. is $800,000.
- Fair value of 100 percent of Sub Co.'s identifiable net assets is $1,200,000.

**Required:** Prepare the acquisition date consolidated workpaper eliminating journal entry.

**Solution:**

Subsidiary's Total (100%) Fair Value = $1,200,000

| | | | |
|---|---|---|---|
| Goodwill | -0- | $200,000 | Gain |
| | | -0- | NCI |
| Identifiable intangible assets FV | -0- | | |
| Balance sheet FV adjustment | $400,000 | $1,000,000 | Investment in subsidiary |
| Book value (CAR) | $800,000 | | |

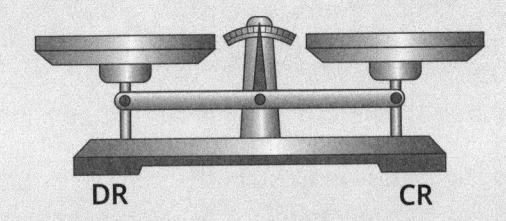

DR / CR

| | | Account | DR | CR |
|---|---|---|---|---|
| | DR | Common stock—subsidiary | | |
| | DR | APIC— subsidiary | $ 800,000 | |
| | DR | Retained earnings—subsidiary | | |
| | CR | Investment in subsidiary | | $1,000,000 |
| | CR | Noncontrolling interest | | -0- |
| | DR | Balance sheet adjustments to FV | 400,000 | |
| | DR | Identifiable Intangible assets to FV | -0- | |
| | CR | Gain | | 200,000 |
| | | | $1,200,000 | $1,200,000 |

# 3 Measurement Period Adjustments

The values assigned to the assets and liabilities of a subsidiary are not always known with certainty on the acquisition date. When this is the case, the values recorded on the acquisition dated are provisional and may be adjusted during the measurement period. Provisional fair values are used in the consolidated financial statements that are prepared before the end of the measurement period.

## 3.1 Measurement Period

The measurement period:

- Cannot exceed one year from the date of acquisition.
- Ends when improved information is available or it becomes obvious that no better information will become available.

## 3.2 Adjustments

During the measurement period, the following adjustments can be made:

- The subsidiary's assets and liabilities may be adjusted to better reflect their values on the acquisition date.
- New subsidiary assets and liabilities that existed on the acquisition date may be recognized.

Measurement period adjustments are offset against goodwill (or gain). Adjustments to depreciation and amortization are reported in the period the adjustments are determined (no restatement required).

Changes in value caused by events after the acquisition date are not included in the measurement period adjustments.

### Example 5 — Measurement Period Adjustments

**Facts:** Pathways Corp. acquired 100 percent of Sidewalk Inc. on July 1, Year 1, for $500,000. Provisional fair values were determined for Sidewalk's assets and liabilities on the acquisition date. Final acquisition date fair values were established on December 31, Year 1.

|  | Book Value | Provisional Fair Value | Final Fair Value |
|---|---|---|---|
| Current assets | $100,000 | $100,000 | $100,000 |
| Long-term investments | 25,000 | 25,000 | 25,000 |
| Property, plant, and equipment | 200,000 | 250,000 | 260,000 |
| In-process R&D |  | 100,000 | 75,000 |
| Liabilities | 50,000 | 50,000 | 50,000 |
| Common stock | 100,000 |  |  |
| Additional paid-in capital | 100,000 |  |  |
| Retained earnings | 75,000 |  |  |

*(continued)*

(continued)

**Required:**

1. Calculate the goodwill recognized on July 1, Year 1, based on the provisional fair values.
2. Calculate the adjustment to goodwill necessary to reflect the final fair values.
3. Prepare the consolidating workpaper eliminating journal entry based on the provisional fair values and the adjusting entry needed to reflect the final fair values.

**Solution:**

1. On July 1, Year 1, goodwill of $75,000 would be recognized:

    Goodwill = Fair value of subsidiary − FV subsidiary net assets (provisional)
    = $500,000 − $425,000
    = $75,000

2. Based on the final fair values, goodwill should be $90,000:

    Goodwill = Fair value of subsidiary − FV subsidiary net assets (provisional)
    = $500,000 − $410,000
    = $90,000

    Therefore, goodwill should be increased by $15,000.

3. Consolidating workpaper eliminating journal entry based on provisional fair values:

| | | | |
|---|---|---|---|
| DR | Common stock—subsidiary | $100,000 | |
| DR | APIC—subsidiary | 100,000 | |
| DR | Retained earnings—subsidiary | 75,000 | |
| CR | Investment in subsidiary | | $500,000 |
| CR | Noncontrolling interest | | -0- |
| DR | Balance sheet adjustment—PP&E | 50,000 | |
| DR | Identifiable intangible assets—in-process R&D | 100,000 | |
| DR | Goodwill | 75,000 | |

Adjusting entry to reflect the final fair values:

| | | | |
|---|---|---|---|
| DR | Property, plant, and equipment | $10,000 | |
| DR | Goodwill | 15,000 | |
| CR | In-process R&D | | $25,000 |

**Note:** In the consolidated financial statements as of December 31, Year 1, depreciation on the building should include depreciation of the $60,000 ($260,000 − $200,000) final fair value adjustment, and amortization of the in-process R&D should be based on the final fair value of $75,000.

## NOTES

# MODULE 6: Intercompany Transactions

**FAR 4**

## 1 Eliminating Intercompany Transactions

When consolidating, 100 percent of intercompany transactions must be eliminated, even when the parent owns less than 100 percent of the subsidiary. Intercompany transactions must be eliminated because they lack the criteria of being "arm's length."

### 1.1 Simple Balance Sheet Eliminations

Eliminate 100 percent of all intercompany payables and receivables.

| | | | |
|---|---|---|---|
| DR | Accounts payable | $XXX | |
| CR | Accounts receivable | | $XXX |

| | | | |
|---|---|---|---|
| DR | Bonds payable (intercompany portion only) | $XXX | |
| CR | Bonds investment (in affiliate) | | $XXX |

| | | | |
|---|---|---|---|
| DR | Accrued bond interest payable | $XXX | |
| CR | Accrued bond interest receivable | | $XXX |

| | | | |
|---|---|---|---|
| DR | Dividends payable (affiliate portion only) | $XXX | |
| CR | Dividends receivable (from affiliate) | | $XXX |

### 1.2 Simple Income Statement Eliminations

- Interest expense / Interest income (bonds)
- Gain on sale / Depreciation expense (intercompany fixed asset sales)
- Sales / Cost of goods sold (intercompany inventory transactions)

# 2 Commonly Tested Intercompany Transactions

## 2.1 Intercompany Inventory/Merchandise Transactions

It is common for affiliated companies to sell inventory/merchandise to one another. Often this inventory/merchandise is sold at a profit. The total amount of this intercompany sale and cost of goods sold should be eliminated prior to preparing consolidated financial statements. In addition, the intercompany profit must be eliminated from the ending inventory and the cost of goods sold of the purchasing affiliate. 100 percent of the profit should be eliminated even if the parent's ownership interest is less than 100 percent. The intercompany profit in beginning inventory that was recognized by the selling affiliate in the previous year must be eliminated by an adjustment (debit) to retained earnings.

### Workpaper Elimination: Intercompany Merchandise Transactions

| | | | |
|---|---|---|---|
| DR | Intercompany sales | $XXX | |
| DR | Retained earnings (profit in beginning inventory) | XXX | |
| CR | Intercompany cost of goods sold | | $XXX |
| CR | Cost of goods sold (intercompany profit included in COGS of the purchasing affiliate) | | XXX |
| CR | Ending inventory (intercompany profit in the inventory remaining) | | XXX |

### Pass Key

When inventory has been sold intercompany and the CPA Examination requires you to correct the accounts, remember to reverse the original intercompany transaction (sale and cost of goods sold, internally) and:

Inventory sold to outsiders ⟶ Correct cost of goods sold

Inventory still on hand ⟶ Correct ending inventory

## Example 1  Intercompany Profit in Inventories

**Facts:** Gearty Corporation owns 100 percent of the common stock of Olinto Corporation. Gearty sold inventory with a cost of $1,000,000 to Olinto for $1,100,000 during Year 1. The Year 1 ending inventory of Olinto included goods purchased from Gearty for $660,000. Olinto had a remaining account payable balance to Gearty of $200,000 on December 31, Year 1. The following journal entries were prepared by Gearty and Olinto to record this intercompany inventory transaction:

*Journal entry to record the sale by Gearty:*

| DR | Accounts receivable | $1,100,000 | |
|---|---|---|---|
| CR | Intercompany sales | | $1,100,000 |
| DR | Intercompany cost of goods sold | 1,000,000 | |
| CR | Inventory | | 1,000,000 |

*Journal entry to record the purchase by Olinto:*

| DR | Inventory | $1,100,000 | |
|---|---|---|---|
| CR | Accounts payable | | $1,100,000 |

**Required:** Prepare the entry to eliminate the intercompany inventory transaction.

**Solution:** The intercompany sales and intercompany cost of goods sold must be eliminated from Gearty's books and the intercompany profit on the sale of inventory must be eliminated from Olinto's books. The intercompany accounts payable and accounts receivable must also be eliminated.

**Step 1:** Calculate intercompany profit on sale of inventory:

Intercompany profit on sale of inventory = $1,100,000 sales price − $1,000,000 cost = $100,000

**Step 2:** Allocate intercompany profit between purchaser's ending inventory and cost of goods sold:

| | | |
|---|---:|---|
| Beginning inventory | $ 0 | |
| Purchases | 1,100,000 | |
| Cost of goods available | 1,100,000 | |
| Ending inventory | 660,000 | 60% |
| Cost of goods sold | 440,000 | 40% |
| Intercompany profit in Olinto's cost of goods sold ($100,000 × 40%) | $ 40,000 | [1] |
| Intercompany profit in Olinto's ending inventory ($100,000 × 60%) | $ 60,000 | [2] |

| DR | Intercompany sales—Gearty | $1,100,000 | |
|---|---|---|---|
| CR | Intercompany cost of goods sold—Gearty | | $1,000,000 |
| CR | Cost of goods sold—Olinto | | 40,000 [1] |
| CR | Inventory—Olinto | | 60,000 [2] |
| DR | Accounts payable | 200,000 | |
| CR | Accounts receivable | | 200,000 |

Intercompany Transactions

## 2.2 Intercompany Bond Transactions

If one member of the consolidated group acquires an affiliate's debt from an outsider, the debt is considered to be retired and a gain/loss is recognized on the consolidated income statement. This gain/loss on extinguishment of debt is calculated as the difference between the price paid to acquire the debt and the book value of the debt. This gain/loss is not reported on either company's books, but is recorded through an elimination entry. All intercompany account balances are also eliminated.

### Example 2 — Intercompany Bond Transactions

**Facts:** On December 31, Year 1, Gearty Corporation issued bonds with a carrying value of $300,000 and a face value of $250,000. The premium on bonds payable was recorded as $50,000. Gearty recorded the following journal entry when the bonds were issued:

*Journal entry to record the sale of the bonds on Gearty's books:*

| | | | |
|---|---|---|---|
| DR | Cash | $300,000 | |
| CR | Bonds payable | | $250,000 |
| CR | Premium on bonds payable | | 50,000 |

On December 31, Year 1, before any portion of the premium was amortized, Olinto Corporation acquired all the outstanding bonds from the original purchasers at a price of $275,000 and recorded the following journal entry:

*Journal entry to record the purchase of the bonds on Olinto's books:*

| | | | |
|---|---|---|---|
| DR | Investment in Gearty bonds | $275,000 | |
| CR | Cash | | $275,000 |

**Required:** Prepare the entry to eliminate the intercompany bond transaction.

**Solution:** *Workpaper elimination entry*—Eliminate the intercompany balances and recognize the gain on extinguishment of debt.

| | | | |
|---|---|---|---|
| DR | Bonds payable | $250,000 | |
| DR | Premium | 50,000 | |
| CR | Investment in Gearty bonds | | $275,000 |
| CR | Gain on extinguishment of bonds | | 25,000 |

- **Intercompany Interest:** Eliminate intercompany accounts such as interest expense, interest income, interest payable, and interest receivable.

- **Amortization of Discount or Premium:** Eliminate amortization of the discount or premium, which serves as an increase or decrease in the amount of interest expense/revenue that is recorded. The unamortized discount or premium on the intercompany bond is eliminated.

- **Subsequent Years:** The elimination for realized but unrecorded gain/loss on extinguishment of bonds in subsequent years would be adjusted to retained earnings. Noncontrolling interest would be adjusted if the bonds were originally issued by the subsidiary.

## 2.3 Intercompany Sale of Land

The intercompany gain/loss on the sale of land remains unrealized until the land is sold to an outsider. A workpaper elimination entry in the period of sale eliminates the intercompany gain/loss and adjusts the land to its original cost.

---

### Example 3 — Intercompany Sale of Land

**Facts:** On July 1, Year 1, Gearty Corporation sold land to Olinto Corporation for $200,000. The initial cost of the land to Gearty was $175,000. Gearty and Olinto recorded the following journal entries on the transaction date:

*Journal entry to record the sale on Gearty's books:*

| | | | |
|---|---|---|---|
| DR | Cash | $200,000 | |
| CR | Land | | $175,000 |
| CR | Intercompany gain on sale of land | | 25,000 |

*Journal entry to record the purchase on Olinto's books:*

| | | | |
|---|---|---|---|
| DR | Land | $200,000 | |
| CR | Cash | | $200,000 |

**Required:** Prepare the entry required to eliminate the intercompany sale of land.

**Solution:** *Workpaper elimination entry*—Elimination of the intercompany gain and adjustment of land to its original cost:

| | | | |
|---|---|---|---|
| DR | Intercompany gain on sale of land | $25,000 | |
| CR | Land ($200,000 − $175,000) | | $25,000 |

---

In the subsequent year and every year thereafter until the land is sold to a third party, retained earnings (Gearty) would be debited and land would be credited to eliminate the intercompany profit. Retained earnings are debited in subsequent years because the gain would have been closed to this account. Because Gearty (parent) was the seller of the land and Olinto (subsidiary) was the purchaser, there is no need to divide the intercompany gain between retained earnings and noncontrolling interest.

## 2.4 Intercompany Profit on Sale of Depreciable Fixed Assets

The gain or loss on the intercompany sale of a depreciable asset is unrealized from a consolidated financial statement perspective until the asset is sold to an outsider. A working paper elimination entry in the period of sale eliminates the intercompany gain/loss and adjusts the asset and accumulated depreciation to their original balance on the date of sale.

# Example 4 — Intercompany Sale of Fixed Assets

**Facts:** Olinto Corporation (subsidiary) sold equipment on January 1, Year 1, to Gearty Corporation (parent) for $100,000. The equipment had a net book value of $70,000 (cost of $90,000 and accumulated depreciation of $20,000), and a remaining life of 10 years. Gearty and Olinto prepared the following journal entries on the date of the transaction:

*January 1, Year 1, journal entry to record the sale on Olinto's books:*

| | | | |
|---|---|---|---|
| DR | Cash | $100,000 | |
| DR | Accumulated depreciation | 20,000 | |
| CR | Machinery (original cost) | | $90,000 |
| CR | Intercompany gain on sale of machinery | | 30,000 |

*January 1, Year 1, journal entry to record the purchase on Gearty's books:*

| | | | |
|---|---|---|---|
| DR | Machinery | $100,000 | |
| CR | Cash | | $100,000 |

At year-end, Gearty recorded the following journal entry: *December 31, Year 1, journal entry to record the depreciation on Gearty's books:*

| | | | |
|---|---|---|---|
| DR | Depreciation expense ($100,000 ÷ 10) | $10,000 | |
| CR | Accumulated depreciation | | $10,000 |

**Required:** Prepare the journal entries to eliminate the intercompany equipment sale and the excess depreciation.

**Solution:** December 31, Year 1, *workpaper elimination entry*—Elimination of intercompany gain and adjustment of the machine and accumulated depreciation accounts to their original balance:

| | | | |
|---|---|---|---|
| DR | Intercompany gain on sale of machinery | $30,000 | |
| CR | Machinery ($100,000 − $90,000) | | $10,000 |
| CR | Accumulated depreciation | | 20,000 |

The depreciation expense recorded by Gearty is overstated by the intercompany profit included in the cost of the machinery.

| | GAAP Original | Non-GAAP Intercompany | Difference |
|---|---|---|---|
| NBV | $70,000 | $100,000 | $30,000 |
| Depreciation years | ÷ 10 Yrs | ÷ 10 Yrs | ÷ 10 Yrs |
| Depreciation | $ 7,000 | $ 10,000 | $ 3,000 |

*Workpaper elimination entry*—Elimination of excess depreciation:

| | | | |
|---|---|---|---|
| DR | Accumulated depreciation | $3,000 | |
| CR | Depreciation expense | | $3,000 |

## Illustration 1  Subsequent Year Workpaper Elimination Journal Entry

In the subsequent years, the intercompany gain/loss on the sale of the asset and the excess depreciation has been closed to retained earnings. The elimination entries in subsequent years therefore adjust retained earnings and, if appropriate, noncontrolling interest for the original gain or loss less the excess depreciation previously recorded (unrealized gain/loss at the beginning of the year). Continuing with the previous example, in Year 2 the workpaper elimination entries would be:

*Journal entry to adjust fixed assets:*

| DR | Retained earnings | $27,000* | |
|---|---|---|---|
| CR | Machinery | | $10,000 |
| CR | Accumulated depreciation | | 17,000** |

*Journal entry to adjust depreciation:*

| DR | Accumulated depreciation | $3,000 | |
|---|---|---|---|
| CR | Depreciation expense | | $3,000 |

\* Original gain: Excess depreciation previously recorded = Unrealized gain at the beginning of the year. $30,000 − $3,000 = $27,000.

\*\* Original accumulated depreciation difference of $20,000 less excess depreciation of $3,000 previously recorded.

---

### Question 1                                                                 MCQ-00455

Wright Corp. has several subsidiaries that are included in its consolidated financial statements. In its December 31, Year 2, trial balance, Wright had the following intercompany balances before eliminations:

| DR | Current receivable due from Main Co. | $32,000 | |
|---|---|---|---|
| DR | Non-current receivable from Main | 114,000 | |
| DR | Cash advance to Corn Corp. | 6,000 | |
| CR | Cash advance from King Co. | | $15,000 |
| CR | Intercompany payable to King | | 101,000 |

In its December 31, Year 2, consolidated balance sheet, what amount should Wright report as intercompany receivables?

    a. $152,000
    b. $146,000
    c. $36,000
    d. $0

# Intercompany Transactions

### Question 2
**MCQ-00448**

Perez, Inc. owns 80 percent of Senior, Inc. During Year 1, Perez sold goods with a 40 percent gross profit to Senior. Senior sold all of these goods in Year 1. For Year 1 consolidated financial statements, how should the summation of Perez and Senior's income statement items be adjusted?

a. Sales and cost of goods sold should be reduced by the intercompany sales.
b. Sales and cost of goods sold should be reduced by 80 percent of the intercompany sales.
c. Net income should be reduced by 80 percent of the gross profit on intercompany sales.
d. No adjustment is necessary.

### Question 3
**MCQ-00484**

On January 1, Year 10, Poe Corp. sold a machine for $900,000 to Saxe Corp., its wholly owned subsidiary. Poe paid $1,100,000 for this machine, which had accumulated depreciation of $250,000. Poe estimated a $100,000 salvage value and depreciated the machine on the straight-line method over 20 years, a policy that Saxe continued. In Poe's December 31, Year 10, consolidated balance sheet, this machine should be included in cost and accumulated depreciation as:

|    | Cost | Accumulated Depreciation |
|----|------|--------------------------|
| a. | $1,100,000 | $300,000 |
| b. | $1,100,000 | $290,000 |
| c. | $900,000 | $40,000 |
| d. | $850,000 | $42,500 |

# MODULE 7
# Consolidated Financial Statements

FAR 4

## 1 Illustrative Consolidated Financial Statements

The following are samples of a comparative consolidated balance sheet, a consolidated income statement, a statement of consolidated comprehensive income, and a consolidated statement of changes in equity.

### 1.1 Sample: Consolidated Balance Sheet

The consolidated balance sheet includes 100 percent of the parent's and subsidiary's assets and liabilities (after eliminating intercompany transactions), but does not include the subsidiary's equity. Noncontrolling interest is presented as part of equity, separately from the equity of the parent company.

**Consolidated Businesses Inc. (CBI)**
**Consolidated Balance Sheet as of December 31**

| | Year 4 | Year 3 |
|---|---|---|
| **Assets** | | |
| Cash | $ 250,000 | $ 195,000 |
| Accounts receivable | 125,000 | 140,000 |
| Available-for-sale debt securities | 320,000 | 315,000 |
| Plant and equipment | 675,000 | 590,000 |
| Total assets | $1,370,000 | $1,240,000 |
| **Liabilities** | | |
| Accounts payable | $ 207,000 | $ 135,000 |
| Accrued expenses | 75,000 | 80,000 |
| Long-term notes payable | 400,000 | 400,000 |
| Total liabilities | $ 682,000 | $ 615,000 |
| **Equity** | | |
| CBI shareholders' equity: | | |
|   Common stock, $1 par | $ 275,000 | $ 275,000 |
|   Additional paid-in capital | 130,000 | 130,000 |
|   Retained earnings | 220,000 | 165,000 |
|   Accumulated other comprehensive income | 23,000 | 19,000 |
| Total CBI shareholders' equity | $ 648,000 | $ 589,000 |
| Noncontrolling interest | 40,000 | 36,000 |
| Total equity | 688,000 | 625,000 |
| Total liabilities and equity | $1,370,000 | $1,240,000 |

## 1.2 Sample: Consolidated Statement of Income

The consolidated income statement includes 100 percent of the parent's revenues and expenses and all of the subsidiary's revenues and expenses after the date of acquisition. The subsidiary's pre-acquisition revenues and expenses are not included in the consolidated income statement.

The consolidated income statement should show, separately, consolidated net income, net income attributable to noncontrolling interests, and net income attributable to the parent company.

**Consolidated Businesses Inc. (CBI)**
**Consolidated Statement of Income for the year ended December 31**

|  | Year 4 | Year 3 | Year 2 |
|---|---|---|---|
| Sales | $620,000 | $570,000 | $595,000 |
| Cost of goods sold | (280,000) | (255,000) | (265,000) |
| Gross profit | 340,000 | 315,000 | 330,000 |
| Selling, general, and administrative expenses | (224,000) | (190,000) | (226,000) |
| Operating income | 116,000 | 125,000 | 104,000 |
| Net interest expense | (12,000) | (8,000) | (6,000) |
| Income before tax | 104,000 | 117,000 | 98,000 |
| Income tax expense | (36,000) | (40,000) | (44,000) |
| Net income | 68,000 | 77,000 | 54,000 |
| Less: Noncontrolling interest in net income | (3,000) | (7,000) | (2,000) |
| Net income attributable to CBI | $ 65,000 | $ 70,000 | $ 52,000 |

## 1.3 Sample: Statement of Consolidated Comprehensive Income

The statement of comprehensive income should show, separately, consolidated comprehensive income, comprehensive income attributable to the noncontrolling interest, and comprehensive income attributable to the parent company.

**Consolidated Businesses Inc. (CBI)**
**Statement of Consolidated Comprehensive Income for the year ended December 31**

|  | Year 4 | Year 3 | Year 2 |
|---|---|---|---|
| Net income | $68,000 | $77,000 | $54,000 |
| Other comprehensive income, net of tax: | | | |
| Unrealized holding gain on available-for-sale debt securities, net of tax | 5,000 | 6,000 | 4,500 |
| Total other comprehensive income, net of tax | 5,000 | 6,000 | 44,500 |
| Comprehensive income | 73,000 | 83,000 | 58,500 |
| Comprehensive income attributable to noncontrolling interest | (4,000) | (8,500) | (3,000) |
| Comprehensive income attributable to CBI | $69,000 | $74,500 | $55,500 |

## 1.4 Sample: Consolidated Statement of Changes in Equity

Because noncontrolling interest is part of the equity of the consolidated group, it is presented in the statement of changes in equity. The consolidated statement of changes in equity should present a reconciliation of the beginning-of-period and end-of-period carrying amount of total equity, equity attributable to the parent, and equity attributable to the noncontrolling interest.

**Consolidated Businesses Inc. (CBI)**
**Consolidated Statement of Changes in Equity for the year ended December 31, Year 1**

*CBI Shareholders*

| | Total | Comprehensive Income | Retained Earnings | AOCI | Common Stock | APIC | NCI |
|---|---|---|---|---|---|---|---|
| Beginning balance | $625,000 | | $165,000 | $19,000 | $275,000 | $130,000 | $36,000 |
| Comprehensive income: | | | | | | | |
| Net income | 68,000 | $68,000 | 65,000 | | | | 3,000 |
| OCI, net of tax: | | | | | | | |
| Unrealized gain on securities | 5,000 | 5,000 | | 4,000 | | | 1,000 |
| Comprehensive income | 73,000 | | | | | | |
| Dividends on common stock | (10,000) | | (10,000) | — | — | — | — |
| Ending balance | $688,000 | $73,000 | $220,000 | $23,000 | $275,000 | $130,000 | $40,000 |

# 2 Consolidated Statement of Cash Flows

## 2.1 Period of Acquisition

The preparation of the consolidated statement of cash flows in the period of acquisition is complicated by the fact that the prior year financial statements reflect parent-only balances while the year-end financial statements reflect consolidated balances. The following steps are necessary in order to prepare a consolidated statement of cash flows in the period of acquisition:

1. The net cash spent or received in the acquisition must be reported in the investing section of the statement of cash flows.

> **Illustration 1     Cash Outflow for Acquisition**
>
> If the parent company spent $2,500,000 to acquire a subsidiary that had $800,000 cash, the net decrease in cash of $1,700,000 would be shown as an investing outflow on the statement of cash flows as follows:
>
> Payment for acquisition of subsidiary, net of cash acquired = $1,700,000

2. The assets and liabilities of the subsidiary on the acquisition date must be added to the parent's assets and liabilities at the beginning of the year in order to determine the change in cash due to operating, investing, and financing activities during the period.

---

**Example 1 — Consolidated Cash Flow From Notes Payable**

**Facts:** A parent company that reported notes payable of $600,000 on January 1 acquired a subsidiary on May 1 that reported notes payable of $250,000 on the acquisition date. The December 31 consolidated balance sheet reported notes payable of $750,000.

**Required:** Determine the cash inflow or outflow from long-term debt.

**Solution:**

| | |
|---|---:|
| Beginning parent notes payable | $600,000 |
| + Acquisition date subsidiary notes payable | 250,000 |
| − Ending consolidated notes payable | 750,000 |
| Cash outflow | $100,000 |

---

## 2.2 Subsequent Periods

In subsequent periods, the preparation of the consolidated statement of cash flows is simplified by the fact that consolidated financial statements are available for the beginning and end of the period. The consolidated statement of cash flows should present the cash inflows and outflows of the consolidated entity, excluding cash flows between the parent and subsidiary.

The preparation of the consolidated statement of cash flows should be similar to the preparation of a statement of cash flows for a nonconsolidated entity, except for the following considerations:

1. When reconciling net income to net cash provided by operating activities, total consolidated net income (including net income attributable to both the parent and the noncontrolling interest) should be used.

2. The financing section should report dividends paid by the subsidiary to noncontrolling shareholders. Dividends paid by the subsidiary to the parent company should not be reported.

3. The investing section may report the acquisition of additional subsidiary shares by the parent if the acquisition was an open-market purchase.

# 3 Preparing Consolidated Financial Statements

## Example 2 — Exercise: Consolidation Eliminating Journal Entries

**Facts:**

On January 1, Year 1, Gearty Corporation (parent) acquired 100 percent of Olinto Corporation. Gearty Corp. issued 100,000 shares of its $10 par common stock, with a market price of $15 on the date the acquisition was announced and $25 on the date the acquisition was completed, for all of Olinto Corp.'s common stock.

On that date the fair value of Olinto Corp.'s assets and liabilities equaled their respective carrying amounts with the exception of land, which had a fair value that exceeded its book value by $200,000.

The fair value of Olinto Corp.'s identifiable intangibles (in process R&D) is $100,000. The in-process R&D will be amortized over a useful life of eight years.

For the year ending December 31, Year 1, Olinto reported net income of $350,000 and paid cash dividends of $150,000.

The stockholders' equity section of each company's balance sheet as of December 31, Year 1, was:

|  | Gearty | Olinto |
|---|---|---|
| Common stock | $5,000,000 | $1,000,000 |
| Additional paid-in capital | 1,000,000 | 400,000 |
| Retained earnings | 3,000,000 | 500,000 |
|  | $9,000,000 | $1,900,000 |

**Required:** Prepare the acquisition date and year-end consolidation workpaper eliminating journal entries.

**Solution:** Acquisition date calculation:

| | |
|---|---|
| Common stock—subsidiary | $1,000,000 |
| APIC—subsidiary | 400,000 |
| Retained earnings—subsidiary (at purchase date) | 300,000 |

| | |
|---|---|
| Beginning | $300,000 |
| Add: income | 350,000 |
| Subtract: dividends | <150,000> |
| Ending | $500,000 |

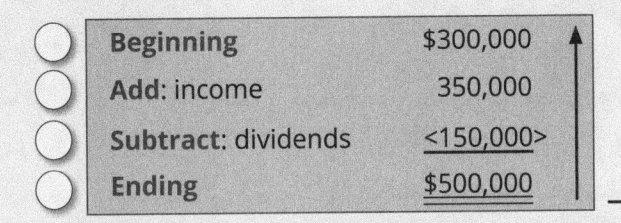

(continued)

# Consolidated Financial Statements

*(continued)*

| | |
|---|---:|
| Net book value | 1,700,000 |
| Investment (100,000 shares × $25 FV) | 2,500,000 |
|   Difference | 800,000 |
| Noncontrolling interest | -0- |
|   Difference | 800,000 |
| Balance sheet adjustment to asset land | 200,000 |
|   Difference | 600,000 |
| Identifiable intangible assets | 100,000 |
| Goodwill | $ 500,000 |

### Acquisition Date: Subsidiary's Total (100%) Fair Value $2,500,000

| | | | |
|---|---|---|---|
| Goodwill | $500,000 | -0- | NCI |
| Identifiable intangible assets FV | $100,000 | | |
| Balance sheet FV adjustment | $200,000 | $2,500,000 | Investment in subsidiary |
| Book value (CAR) | $1,700,000 | | |

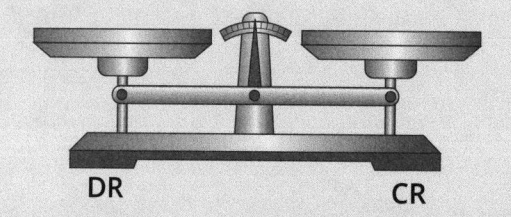

**DR**           **CR**

### Acquisition Date Eliminating Journal Entry

| | | | |
|---|---|---:|---:|
| DR | Common stock—subsidiary | $1,000,000 | |
| DR | APIC—subsidiary | 400,000 | |
| DR | Retained earnings—subsidiary | 300,000 | |
| CR |     Investment in subsidiary | | $2,500,000 |
| CR |     Noncontrolling interest | | -0- |
| DR | Balance sheet adjustment fair value | 200,000 | |
| DR | Identifiable intangible assets fair value | 100,000 | |
| DR | Goodwill | 500,000 | |

*(continued)*

(continued)

Assuming that Gearty accounts for its investment in Olinto using the equity method for internal accounting purposes, Gearty would report an investment in subsidiary of $2,700,000:

| | |
|---|---|
| Beginning investment in sub | $2,500,000 |
| + Share of subsidiary income | 350,000 |
| − Share of subsidiary dividends | (150,000) |
| Ending investment in sub | $2,700,000 |

| | Year-End Eliminating Journal Entry | | |
|---|---|---|---|
| DR | Common stock—subsidiary | $1,000,000 | |
| DR | APIC—subsidiary | 400,000 | |
| DR | Retained earnings—subsidiary | 500,000 | |
| CR | Investment in subsidiary | | $2,700,000 |
| CR | Noncontrolling interest | | -0- |
| DR | Balance sheet adjustment fair value | 200,000 | |
| DR | Identifiable intangible assets fair value | 100,000 | |
| DR | Goodwill | 500,000 | |

# Consolidated Financial Statements

## Example 3 — Preparing Consolidated Financial Statements

**Required:** Prepare the December 31, Year 1, consolidated financial statements of Gearty Corporation and Olinto Corporation using the Consolidation Eliminating Journal Entries example on the previous pages and the intercompany transaction examples from Module 7 (the footnotes refer to the list of explanations of consolidated adjustments, which follows).

**Solution:**

|  | Gearty Dr(Cr) | Olinto Dr(Cr) | Elimination Debits | Elimination Credits | Adjusted Balance |
|---|---|---|---|---|---|
| **Income Statement** | | | | | |
| Sales | $(18,400,000) | $(6,000,000) | $1,100,000[1] | | $(23,300,000) |
| Cost of goods sold | 11,480,000 | 4,210,000 | | 1,000,000[1] 40,000[1] | 14,650,000 |
| Operating expenses | 5,505,000 | 1,330,000 | 12,500[2] | 3,000[3] | 6,844,500 |
| Equity in earnings | (350,000) | 0 | 350,000[4] | | 0 |
| Investment income | (100,000) | 0 | | | (100,000) |
| Interest expense | 80,000 | 140,000 | | | 220,000 |
| Gain on fixed asset sales | (25,000) | (30,000) | 25,000[5] 30,000[6] | | 0 |
| Gain on debt | 0 | 0 | | 25,000[7] | (25,000) |
| Net income | $(1,810,000) | $(350,000) | $1,517,500 | $1,068,000 | $1,710,500 |
| **Statement of Retained Earnings** | | | | | |
| RE, 1/1/Year 1 | $(1,190,000) | $(300,000) | $300,000[4] | | $(1,190,000) |
| Net income | (1,810,000) | (350,000) | 1,517,500 | $1,068,000 | (1,710,500) |
| Dividends | 0 | 150,000 | | 150,000[4] | 0 |
| RE, 12/31/Year 1 | $(3,000,000) | $(500,000) | $1,817,500 | $1,218,000 | $(2,900,500) |
| **Balance Sheet** | | | | | |
| Cash | $1,120,000 | $ 520,000 | | | $1,640,000 |
| AR | 2,075,000 | 1,605,000 | | $200,000[8] | 3,480,000 |
| Inventory | 2,000,000 | 1,000,000 | | 60,000[1] | 2,940,000 |
| Marketable securities | 1,225,000 | 275,000 | | 275,000[7] | 1,225,000 |
| Fixed Assets (net) | 3,470,000 | 1,500,000 | 200,000[4] 3,000[3] | 25,000[5] 10,000[6] 20,000[6] | 5,118,000 |
| In-process R&D | 0 | 0 | 100,000[4] | 12,500[2] | 87,500 |
| Goodwill | 0 | 0 | 500,000[4] | | 500,000 |
| Investment in Sub | 2,700,000 | 0 | | 2,700,000[4] | 0 |
| Total Assets | $12,590,000 | $4,900,000 | $803,000 | $3,302,500 | $14,990,500 |
| AP | $(2,290,000) | $(1,250,000) | $200,000[8] | | $(3,340,000) |
| Bonds payable (net) | (1,300,000) | (1,750,000) | 250,000[7] 50,000[7] | | (2,750,000) |
| Common stock | (5,000,000) | (1,000,000) | 1,000,000[4] | | (5,000,000) |
| APIC | (1,000,000) | (400,000) | 400,000[4] | | (1,000,000) |
| RE | (3,000,000) | (500,000) | 1,817,500 | $1,218,000 | (2,900,500) |
| Liabilities and Equity | $(12,590,000) | $(4,900,000) | $3,717,500 | $1,218,000 | $(14,990,500) |

(continued)

*Explanation of consolidation adjustments:*

1. Elimination of the intercompany sale of inventory:

   | | | | |
   |---|---|---|---|
   | DR | Intercompany sales—Gearty | $1,100,000 | |
   | CR | Intercompany cost of goods sold—Gearty | | $1,000,000 |
   | CR | Cost of goods sold—Olinto | | 40,000 |
   | CR | Inventory—Olinto | | 60,000 |

2. Amortization of in-process R&D over 8 years ($100,000/8 = $12,500):

   | | | | |
   |---|---|---|---|
   | DR | Amortization expense | $12,500 | |
   | CR | In-process R&D | | $12,500 |

3. Elimination of excess depreciation resulting from the intercompany sale of machinery:

   | | | | |
   |---|---|---|---|
   | DR | Amortization depreciation | $3,000 | |
   | CR | Depreciation expense | | $3,000 |

4. Elimination of Olinto's equity and Gearty's investment in Olinto and the recognition of the land fair-value adjustment, in-process R&D, and goodwill on December 31, Year 1:

   | | | | |
   |---|---|---|---|
   | DR | Common stock—subsidiary | $1,000,000 | |
   | DR | APIC—subsidiary | 400,000 | |
   | DR | Retained earnings—subsidiary | 500,000 | |
   | CR | Investment in subsidiary | | $2,700,000 |
   | CR | Noncontrolling interest | | -0- |
   | DR | Balance sheet adjustment FV | $200,000 | |
   | DR | Identifiable intangible assets FV | 100,000 | |
   | DR | Goodwill | 500,000 | |

5. Elimination of intercompany land transaction:

   | | | | |
   |---|---|---|---|
   | DR | Intercompany gain on sale of land | $25,000 | |
   | CR | Land | | $25,000 |

6. Elimination of intercompany sales of equipment:

   | | | | |
   |---|---|---|---|
   | DR | Intercompany gain on sale of machinery | $30,000 | |
   | CR | Machinery ($100,000 − $90,000) | | $10,000 |
   | CR | Accumulated depreciation | | 20,000 |

(continued)

(continued)

7. Record the retirement of intercompany bonds:

| | | | |
|---|---|---|---|
| DR | Bonds payable | $250,000 | |
| DR | Premium (Gearty's records) | 50,000 | |
| CR | Investment in Gearty bonds (Olinto's records) | | $275,000 |
| CR | Gain on extinguishment of bonds | | 25,000 |

8. Elimination of intercompany AR and AP resulting from intercompany sale of inventory:

| | | | |
|---|---|---|---|
| DR | Accounts payable | $200,000 | |
| CR | Accounts receivable | | $200,000 |

## Question 1     MCQ-00427

On January 1, Year 1, Dallas, Inc. acquired 80 percent of Style, Inc.'s outstanding common stock for $120,000. On that date, the carrying amounts of Style's assets and liabilities approximated their fair values. During Year 1, Style paid $5,000 cash dividends to its stockholders. Summarized balance sheet information for the two companies follows:

| | Dallas | Style | Style |
|---|---|---|---|
| | 12/31/Year 1 | 12/31/Year 1 | 1/1/Year 1 |
| Investment in Style (equity method) | $132,000 | | |
| Other assets | 138,000 | $115,000 | $100,000 |
| | $270,000 | $115,000 | $100,000 |
| Common stock | $ 50,000 | $ 20,000 | $ 20,000 |
| Additional paid-in capital | 80,250 | 44,000 | 44,000 |
| Retained earnings | 139,750 | 51,000 | 36,000 |
| | $270,000 | $115,000 | $100,000 |

What amount of total stockholders' equity should be reported in Dallas' December 31, Year 1, consolidated balance sheet?

a. $270,000
b. $286,000
c. $303,000
d. $385,000

## Question 2 — MCQ-00421

On September 1, Year 1, Phillips, Inc. issued common stock in exchange for 20 percent of Sago, Inc.'s outstanding common stock. On July 1, Year 3, Phillips issued common stock for an additional 75 percent of Sago's outstanding common stock. Sago continues in existence as Phillips' subsidiary. How much of Sago's Year 3 net income should be reported as accruing to Phillips?

- a. 20 percent of Sago's net income to June 30 and all of Sago's net income from July 1 to December 31.
- b. 20 percent of Sago's net income to June 30 and 95 percent of Sago's net income from July 1 to December 31.
- c. 95 percent of Sago's net income.
- d. All of Sago's net income.

## Question 3 — MCQ-05920

On January 2 of the current year, Peace Co. paid $310,000 to purchase 75 percent of the voting shares of Surge Co. Peace reported retained earnings of $80,000, and Surge reported contributed capital of $300,000 and retained earnings of $100,000. The purchase differential was attributed to depreciable assets with a remaining useful life of 10 years. Surge reported net income of $20,000 and paid dividends of $8,000 during the current year. Peace reported income, exclusive of its income from Surge, of $30,000 and paid dividends of $15,000 during the current year. What amount will Peace report as dividends declared and paid in its current year's consolidated statement of retained earnings?

- a. $8,000
- b. $15,000
- c. $21,000
- d. $23,000

## NOTES

# MODULE 8
# Goodwill, Including Impairment

FAR 4

## 1 Goodwill

Goodwill represents the intangible resources and elements connected with an entity that cannot be separately identified and reported on the balance sheet (e.g., management or marketing expertise, or technical skill and knowledge that cannot be identified or valued separately). Goodwill is capitalized excess earnings power.

### 1.1 Goodwill Arising From Business Combinations

#### 1.1.1 Acquisition Method

Under the acquisition method, goodwill is the excess of an acquired entity's fair value over the fair value of the entity's net assets, including identifiable intangible assets.

#### 1.1.2 Equity Method

The equity method involves the purchase of a company's capital stock. Goodwill is the excess of the stock purchase price over the fair value of the net assets acquired.

### 1.2 Maintaining Goodwill

Costs associated with maintaining, developing, or restoring goodwill are not capitalized as goodwill (they are expensed). In addition, goodwill generated internally or not purchased in an arm's-length transaction is not capitalized as goodwill.

## 2 Goodwill Impairment

Under U.S. GAAP, goodwill impairment is calculated at the reporting unit level. Impairment exists when the carrying amount of the reporting unit including goodwill exceeds its fair value including goodwill.

### 2.1 Definition of Reporting Unit

A reporting unit is an operating segment, or one level below an operating segment. The goodwill of one reporting unit may be impaired, while the goodwill for other reporting units may or may not be impaired.

## 2.2 Qualitative Evaluation of Goodwill Impairment

- Under U.S. GAAP, the goodwill impairment test has been simplified by allowing companies to test qualitative factors to determine whether it is necessary to perform the quantitative goodwill impairment test. Examples of qualitative factors include:
  - Macroeconomic conditions
  - Overall financial performance
  - Entity-specific events such as bankruptcy, litigation, or changes in management, strategy, or customers
  - Industry and market conditions
  - Sustained decrease in share-price
  - Cost factors that could have a negative effect on earnings and cash flows

- The quantitative impairment test is not necessary if, after assessing the relevant qualitative factors, an entity determines that *it is not more likely than not* that the fair value of the reporting unit is less than its carrying amount.

- If the qualitative assessment indicates that there is a greater than 50 percent chance that the fair value of the reporting unit is less than its carrying amount, then the entity must perform the quantitative impairment test.

## 2.3 Quantitative Evaluation of Goodwill Impairment

The evaluation of goodwill impairment involves comparing the carrying value of the reporting unit including goodwill to the fair value of the reporting unit including goodwill. If the fair value exceeds the carrying value, there is no impairment. If the fair value is less than the carrying value, there will be an impairment charge equal to the difference between the fair value and carrying value. The impairment charge cannot exceed the value of the goodwill that is allocated to that reporting unit.

### Private Company Accounting Alternative

Under U.S. GAAP, a private company (an entity that is not a public entity or a not-for-profit entity) may elect to apply the following alternative method of goodwill accounting:

1. Amortize goodwill on a straight-line basis over 10 years, or less than 10 years if it can demonstrate that another useful life is more appropriate.

2. Make an accounting policy election, disclosed in the summary of significant accounting policies (SSAP) in the footnotes, to test goodwill for impairment at either the entity level or the reporting unit level when a triggering event occurs that indicates that the fair value of an entity (or reporting unit) may be below its carrying amount.

Because goodwill is being amortized, impairment is less likely to occur. This alternative method must be applied to all existing goodwill and any goodwill generated in future business combinations.

## Example 1  Goodwill Impairment (U.S. GAAP)

**Facts:** Omega Inc. has two reporting units, Alpha and Beta, which have book values including goodwill of $500,000 and $675,000, respectively. Alpha reports goodwill of $50,000 and Beta reports goodwill of $75,000. As part of the company's annual review for goodwill impairment, Omega determined that the fair values including goodwill of Alpha and Beta were $480,000 and $700,000, respectively, at December 31, Year 1.

**Required:** Determine whether the reporting units' goodwill is potentially impaired.

**Solution:**

Alpha: Reporting Unit FV − Reporting Unit BV = $480,000 − 500,000 = ($20,000)

Beta: Reporting Unit FV − Reporting Unit BV = $700,000 − 675,000 = $25,000

Because Alpha's fair value is less than its book value, there is goodwill impairment. Beta's goodwill is not impaired.

The impairment charge for Alpha will be equal to the difference between the book value of $500,000 and the fair value of $480,000. Because this difference of $20,000 is less than Alpha's reported goodwill of $50,000, the full $20,000 will be recognized as an impairment loss. If goodwill had been reported as $15,000 instead of $50,000, the impairment charge would have been capped at $15,000.

*Journal entry to record goodwill impairment at December 31, Year 1:*

| DR | Loss due to impairment | $20,000 | |
|---|---|---|---|
| CR | Goodwill | | $20,000 |

## U.S. GAAP VS. IFRS

Under IFRS, goodwill impairment testing is done at the cash-generating unit (CGU) level. A cash-generating unit is defined as the smallest identifiable group of assets that generates cash inflows that are largely independent of the cash inflows from other assets or groups of assets. The goodwill impairment test is a one-step test in which the carrying value of the CGU is compared with the CGU's recoverable amount, which is the greater of the CGU's fair value less costs to sell and its value in use. Value in use is the present value of the future cash flows expected from the CGU. An impairment loss is recognized to the extent that the carrying value exceeds the recoverable amount. The impairment loss is first allocated to goodwill and then allocated on a pro rata basis to the other assets of the CGU.

## Question 1    MCQ-06393

On December 31, an entity had a reporting unit that had a book value of $3,450,000, including goodwill of $225,000. As part of its annual review of goodwill impairment, the entity determined that the fair value of the reporting unit including goodwill was $3,310,000. What is the goodwill impairment loss to be reported on December 31 under U.S. GAAP?

- a. $0
- b. $85,000
- c. $140,000
- d. $225,000

## Question 2    MCQ-06379

On December 31, an entity tested its goodwill for impairment and determined the following for one of its cash-generating units:

| Carrying value | $2,425,000 |
|---|---|
| Fair value | 2,600,000 |

The entity estimated that if it were to sell the cash-generating unit, it would incur costs of $250,000. The entity also determined that the present value of the future cash flows expected from the cash-generating unit is $2,400,000. The cash-generating unit reports goodwill of $65,000. What is the goodwill impairment loss that will be reported on the December 31 income statement under IFRS?

- a. $0
- b. $25,000
- c. $65,000
- d. $75,000

# Liabilities

## Module

| | | |
|---|---|---|
| 1 | Payables and Accrued Liabilities | 3 |
| 2 | Contingencies and Commitments | 17 |
| 3 | Long-Term Liabilities | 25 |
| 4 | Bonds: Part 1 | 37 |
| 5 | Bonds: Part 2 | 47 |
| 6 | Troubled Debt Restructuring and Extinguishment | 59 |

FAR
5

## NOTES

# MODULE 1
# Payables and Accrued Liabilities

**FAR 5**

## 1 Overview

Liabilities are probable future sacrifices of economic benefits arising from present obligations of an entity to transfer assets or provide services to other entities in the future as a result of past transactions or events.

Liabilities must be identified as current or non-current for financial reporting purposes. Current liabilities are obligations whose liquidation is reasonably expected to require the use of current assets, the creation of other current liabilities, or the provision of services within the next year or operating cycle, whichever is longer.

Regular business operations can result in current liabilities as can bank borrowings to meet the cash needs of the entity. Current liabilities are valued on the balance sheet at their settlement value. Current liabilities are an important indication of financial strength and solvency. The ability to pay current debts as they mature is analyzed by interested parties both within and outside the company.

### 1.1 Trade Accounts Payable

Trade accounts payable are amounts owed for goods, raw materials, and supplies that are not evidenced by a promissory note. Purchases of goods and services on credit are usually determinable as to amounts due and the due date. Cash discounts associated with accounts payable can be anticipated and journalized. The purchase may be recorded gross or net.

- **Gross Method**

  The gross method records the purchase without regard to the discount. If invoices are paid within the discount period, a purchase discount is credited.

- **Net Method**

  Under the net method, purchases and accounts payable are recorded net of the discount. If payment is made within the discount period, no adjustment is necessary. If payment is made after the discount period, a purchase discount lost account is debited.

## Example 1 — Trade Accounts Payable

**Facts:** An entity purchases $5,000 of inventory with terms 2/10, net 45 days near the end of Year 1. The entity accounts for discounts using the gross method. Assume that the entity pays for the invoice after year-end, but prior to expiration of the discount period.

**Required:** Prepare the journal entries when the trade payable is initially recorded in Year 1 and when the account is paid in Year 2.

**Solution:** *The following entry will be recorded when the trade payable is initially recorded in Year 1:*

| | | | |
|---|---|---|---|
| DR | Inventory/purchases | $5,000 | |
| CR | Accounts payable | | $5,000 |

The accounts payable balance is current as it will be paid within 45 days. *The following entry would be recorded when the account is paid:*

| | | | |
|---|---|---|---|
| DR | Accounts payable | $5,000 | |
| CR | Cash | | $4,900 |
| CR | Purchase discounts* | | 100 |

*The Inventory account would be credited if the entity uses a perpetual inventory system.

## 1.2 Trade Notes Payable

Trade notes payable are formal, written promises to pay on a certain date that arise from the purchase of goods, supplies, or services. Trade notes payable may include a stated interest rate.

## Example 2 — Trade Notes Payable

**Facts:** To purchase supplies, Dogs and Cats LLC borrows $50,000 from Credit Hall Bank on March 1, signing a 12-month, 5 percent note. Interest payments are due quarterly.

**Required:** Prepare the journal entries that Dogs and Cats records when the note is issued, when interest is paid on June 1, September 1, December 1, and at year-end.

**Solution:** *The following entry records the issuance of the note:*

| | | | |
|---|---|---|---|
| DR | Cash | $50,000 | |
| CR | Notes payable | | $50,000 |

On June 1, September 1, and December 1, the following entries related to interest expense will be recorded:

| | | | |
|---|---|---|---|
| DR | Interest expense (50,000 × 5% × 3/12) | $625 | |
| CR | Cash | | $625 |

(continued)

(continued)

*At the end of December, one month of interest must be accrued as the interest expense has been incurred but not yet paid in cash (cash payment will not be made until March 1).*

| DR | Interest expense (50,000 × 5% × 1/12) | $208 | |
|---|---|---|---|
| CR | Interest payable | | $208 |

## 1.3 Interest Payable

Short-term and long-term debt instruments with a stated interest rate whose payment date does not coincide with the fiscal year-end will result in an interest payable balance at year-end. The amount accrued should represent the interest expense incurred that has not been paid in cash as of the balance sheet date. The previous example includes an accrual for interest expense.

## 1.4 Current Portions of Long-Term Debt

Debt instruments may be set up such that periodic principal payments are made during the life of the borrowing. In this case the principal due within the next year (or operating cycle) will be classified as a current liability.

### 1.4.1 Current Obligations Expected to Be Refinanced

Under U.S. GAAP, a short-term obligation may be excluded from current liabilities and included in non-current debt if the company intends to refinance it on a long-term basis and the intent is supported by the ability to do so as evidenced either by:

- the actual refinancing prior to the issuance of the financial statements; or
- the existence of a noncancelable financing agreement from a lender having the financial resources to accomplish the refinancing.

The amount excluded from current liabilities and a full description of the financing agreement shall be fully disclosed in the financial statements or notes thereto.

*The following journal entry would be used to record the reclassification:*

| DR | Short-term liability | $XXX | |
|---|---|---|---|
| CR | Long-term liability | | $XXX |

## 1.5 Accrued Liabilities/Expenses

Accrued salaries and wages payable is the unpaid portion of salaries and wages as of the balance sheet date. Unpaid salaries and wages generally result from pay periods that overlap the balance sheet date. Accruals are calculated as the ratio of days occurring prior to the balance sheet date divided by the total days in the pay period times the amount of the affected payroll.

Other accrued liabilities relate to expenses incurred that have not been paid in cash at the financial statement date (such as utilities, rent, etc.).

## Example 3 — Accrued Liabilities/Expenses

**Facts:** An employee works five days during the last week of the year and earns $1,250 a week. Three of the days fall in fiscal Year 1 and two of the days fall in fiscal Year 2.

**Required:** Prepare the journal entry to record the accrued liability at the end of fiscal Year 1 and when the employee is paid in fiscal Year 2.

**Solution:** *The following journal entry is recorded at the end of Year 1:*

| | | | |
|---|---|---|---|
| DR | Salaries and wages expense | $750 | |
| CR | Salaries and wages payable ($1,250 × 3/5) | | $750 |

*When the employee is paid the next year, the following journal entry is recorded:*

| | | | |
|---|---|---|---|
| DR | Salaries and wages payable | $750 | |
| DR | Salaries and wages expense | 500 | |
| CR | Cash | | $1,250 |

## 1.6 Taxes Payable

Several types of taxes payable may exist on an entity's balance sheet.

### 1.6.1 Property Taxes Payable

Property taxes are often invoiced in arrears. There are two methods of accrual:

1. Property taxes payable may be accrued prior to the receipt of the tax invoice and matched in the year for which the invoice pertains.

2. Property taxes also may be recorded as a payable upon the receipt of the tax invoice and expensed in the year of receipt (which is often different from the year to which the invoice pertains).

Either method is acceptable, provided the method used is consistently applied.

### 1.6.2 Sales Taxes Payable

Sales taxes payable are sales taxes collected from customers on behalf of the taxing authority and held in trust until remission to the taxing authority. Sales taxes payable should be credited to a payable account after collection and until remitted. Sales taxes are not an expense of the company collecting the sales taxes from customers.

## Example 4 — Sales Taxes Payable

**Facts:** Jewelry Unlimited sells a $10,000 bracelet and collects 7 percent sales tax.

**Required:** Prepare the journal entry for the sale.

**Solution:** *The following entry will be recorded:*

| | | | |
|---|---|---|---|
| DR | Cash | $10,700 | |
| CR | Sales revenue | | $10,000 |
| CR | Sales tax payable | | 700 |

## 1.7 Employee-Related Liabilities

### 1.7.1 Unemployment Taxes and Employer's Share of Payroll Taxes

Unemployment taxes and the employer's share of payroll taxes (e.g., Social Security and Medicare) should be accrued by the employer as an expense. The liability will not be liquidated until the amounts are remitted to the appropriate taxing authority.

### 1.7.2 Payroll Deductions

Payroll deductions for Social Security, Medicare, and income taxes are withheld from employees out of the gross pay of their paychecks. These deductions are the responsibility of the employee and are therefore not recorded as an expense, but credited to a payable account until remitted.

---

**Example 5 — Payroll Deductions**

**Facts:** Hodge Corporation's weekly payroll totals $25,000. The entire balance is subject to FICA and Medicare (7.65 percent) and unemployment taxes (2 percent). The company withholds $3,000 for income taxes.

**Required:** Prepare the journal entries to record the weekly payroll and the employer's weekly tax expense.

**Solution:** *The following entry will be recorded for the weekly payroll:*

| | | | |
|---|---|---|---|
| DR | Salaries and wages expense | $25,000 | |
| CR | FICA taxes payable | | $ 1,913 |
| CR | Withholding taxes payable | | 3,000 |
| CR | Cash | | 20,087 |

*An additional entry related to the employer's tax expense must also be recorded:*

| | | | |
|---|---|---|---|
| DR | Payroll tax expense | $2,413 | |
| CR | FICA taxes payable | | $1,913 |
| CR | Unemployment taxes payable | | 500 |

---

## 1.8 Bonuses

Companies may pay employees bonuses in addition to their regular salaries or wages. These amounts should be recorded to salaries and wages expense. The amount of the bonus is normally based on company profits. Computation problems result because although the bonuses are based on net income, they are a business expense that also reduces net income. The example that follows illustrates the difficulties.

> ### Example 6  Bonuses
>
> **Facts:** X Corp. offers its sales vice president a bonus equal to 10 percent of net income after deducting taxes but before deducting the bonus. Income without taxes or the bonus is $100,000, and the tax rate is 40 percent.
>
> **Required:** Calculate the bonus.
>
> **Solution:** Although the bonus is based on after-tax income, the bonus is deductible from pretax income.
>
> 1. Bonus = 10% ($100,000 − Taxes)
> 2. Taxes = 40% ($100,000 − Bonus)
>
> Substitute equation 2 for "Taxes" in equation 1.
>
> $$\begin{aligned} \text{Bonus} &= 10\%\,[\$100{,}000 - 40\%\,(\$100{,}000 - \text{Bonus})] \\ B &= 10\%\,[\$100{,}000 - 40\%\,(\$100{,}000 - B)] \\ B &= 10\%\,[\$100{,}000 - \$40{,}000 + 40\%\,B] \\ B &= \$6{,}000 + 4\%\,B \\ 96\%\,B &= \$6{,}000 \\ B &= \underline{\$6{,}250} \end{aligned}$$

## 1.9 Compensated Absences

### 1.9.1 Liability Recognition

Compensated absences are paid absences from employment that can relate to vacation, holidays, or sick pay. Liabilities related to these future absences are accrued in the year earned if *all* of the following conditions are met:

1. The employer's obligation to compensate employees for future absences is attributable to services already rendered by employees.
2. The obligation relates to rights that vest (are not contingent on an employee's future service) or *accumulate* (may be carried forward to one or more accounting periods subsequent to that in which earned).
3. Payment of the compensation is probable.
4. The amount can be reasonably estimated.

If only the first three conditions are met, disclosure in a note to the financial statements is adequate.

### 1.9.2 Sick Pay Benefits

Some companies only pay sick pay if an illness occurs. Other companies may allow employees to take time off related to accumulated sick pay, even if an employee is not ill. An employer is not required to accrue a liability for nonvesting accumulating rights to receive sick pay benefits. Estimates of future sick pay are not reliable, and the cost of making and evaluating those estimates do not justify making an accrual. However, the employer should accrue sick pay benefits if the four criteria are met and the estimate is reliable.

# Example 7: Compensation for Future Absences

**Facts:** Taney Company's employees earn two weeks of paid vacation for each year of employment. Unused vacation time is carried forward and paid at the current salary in effect at the balance sheet date. As of December 31, Year 1, James had earned a total of eight weeks and had taken four weeks of vacation. His salary as of December Year 1 was $300 per week. In Year 2 his salary increased to $400 per week.

**Required:** Calculate the amount Taney Company should carry as a liability for James' accumulated vacation time and prepare the journal entries recorded at the end of Year 1 and when James takes four weeks of vacation in Year 2.

**Solution:**

Accrued vacation at 12/31/Year 1 = Current salary rate × Number of weeks of accumulated vacation
= $300 × 4
= $1,200

*Taney Company would record the following journal entry at the end of Year 1:*

| | | | |
|---|---|---|---|
| DR | Salaries and wages expense | $1,200 | |
| CR | Salaries and wages payable | | $1,200 |

Even if James' salary is raised in Year 2, Taney Company would still record the liability at the end of Year 1 based on the $300-per-week salary, as the vacation was earned during that period.

*When the four weeks of vacation are taken in the following year, the additional expense for increased wages would be recorded to salaries and wage expense.*

| | | | |
|---|---|---|---|
| DR | Salaries and wages payable | $1,200 | |
| DR | Salaries and wages expense | 400 | |
| CR | Cash | | $1,600 |

## U.S. GAAP VS. IFRS

IFRS requires the accrual of sick pay benefits as services are rendered by employees.

# 2 Exit or Disposal Activities

A liability must be recognized for the costs associated with an exit or disposal activity.

## 2.1 Exit and Disposal Costs

Costs associated with exit and disposal activities include:

- Involuntary employee termination benefits.
- Costs to terminate a contract that is not a capital lease.
- Other costs associated with exit or disposal activities, including costs to consolidate facilities or relocate employees.

## 2.2 Criteria for Liability Recognition

An entity's commitment to an exit or disposal plan, by itself, is not enough to result in liability recognition. A liability associated with an exit or disposal activity should be recognized only when all of the following criteria are met:

1. An obligating event has occurred;
2. The event results in a present obligation to transfer assets or to provide services in the future; and
3. The entity has little or no discretion to avoid the future transfer of assets or providing of services.

Future operating losses expected to be incurred as part of an exit or disposal activity are recognized in the period(s) incurred.

## 2.3 Liability Measurement

The liability should be measured at fair value. The liability may be adjusted in future periods as a result of revisions to the timing of or estimated cash flows from the exit or disposal activity. Revisions are accounted for prospectively (change in estimate).

## 2.4 Income Statement Presentation

Costs associated with an exit or disposal activity related to a discontinued operation will be reported in discontinued operations. Costs associated with an exit or disposal activity not related to a discontinued operation will be reported in income from continuing operations.

## 2.5 Disclosure

All of the following must be disclosed in the notes to the financial statements in the period the exit or disposal activity is initiated and all subsequent periods until the activity is completed:

- A description of the exit or disposal activity, including the facts and circumstances leading to the expected activity and the expected completion date.
- For each major cost associated with an activity:
  - The total amount expected to be incurred in connection with the activity, the amount incurred in the period, and the cumulative amount incurred to date.
  - A reconciliation of the beginning and ending liability balances showing the changes during the period for costs incurred, costs paid or otherwise settled, and any other adjustments with an explanation of the reasons.

- The line item(s) in the income statement in which the costs are aggregated.
- For each reportable segment, the total amount of costs expected to be incurred, the amount incurred in the period and incurred to date, net of any adjustments with an explanation of the reasons.
- If a liability for a cost associated with the activity is not recognized because fair value cannot be reasonably estimated, that fact and the reasons for that should be disclosed.

> **Illustration 1  Exit and Disposal Activities**
>
> An entity plans to close its facility in a particular location and determines that it no longer needs the 100 employees who work at the facility. The entity notifies the employees that they will be terminated in six months. A termination benefit will be provided to each employee totaling $5,000 on the date the employee stops working. On the communication date (the obligating event), a liability of $500,000 will be recognized.

## 3  Asset Retirement Obligations (AROs)

An asset retirement obligation is a legal obligation associated with the retirement of a tangible long-lived asset that results from the acquisition, construction or development, and/or normal operation of a long-lived asset, except for certain lease obligations (minimum lease payment and contingent rentals).

Asset retirement obligations were initially required for nuclear decommissioning and were then expanded to other similar closure or removal-type costs in other industries, such as oil and gas and mining industries.

A balance sheet approach is required to recognize AROs.

### 3.1  ARO Recognition

An ARO qualifies for recognition when it meets the definition of a liability:

- Duty or responsibility
- Little or no discretion to avoid
- Obligating event

Uncertainty about whether performance will be required does not defer the recognition of a retirement obligation; rather, that uncertainty is factored into the measurement of the fair value of the liability through assignment of probabilities to cash flows.

### 3.2  Initial Measurement (Balance Sheet Approach)

When an asset retirement obligation exists and qualifies for recognition, an entity records an asset and a liability on the balance sheet equal to the fair value of the asset retirement obligation, if a reasonable estimate of fair value can be made. Fair value is generally equal to the present value of the future obligation. If a reasonable estimate of fair value cannot be made, the liability and related asset are recognized when a reasonable estimate of fair value can be made.

- **Asset Retirement Obligations (ARO)**

    The ARO is the obligation (liability) associated with the retirement of a tangible long-lived asset.

- **Asset Retirement Cost (ARC)**

    The ARC is the amount capitalized (asset) that increases the carrying amount of the long-lived asset when a liability for an ARO is recognized.

    | DR | Asset retirement cost (asset) | $XXX | |
    |---|---|---|---|
    | CR | Asset retirement obligation (liability) | | $XXX |

> ### U.S. GAAP VS. IFRS
>
> Under IFRS, an asset retirement obligation is called a decommissioning liability. A decommissioning liability is initially measured at the best estimate of the expenditure required to settle the obligation. U.S. GAAP requires initial measurement at fair value.

## 3.3 Subsequent Measurement

### 3.3.1 Accretion and Depreciation

In periods after the initial measurement, the ARO liability is adjusted for accretion expense due to the passage of time, and the ARC asset is depreciated.

- **Accretion Expense**

    Accretion expense is the increase in the ARO liability due to the passage of time calculated using the appropriate accretion rate. The accretion expense is added to the ARO liability each period. At the end of the accretion period, the ARO liability reported on the balance sheet should be (approximately) equal to the asset retirement obligation to be paid.

    *Journal entry to record accretion expense associated with the ARO (liability):*

    | DR | Accretion expense | $XXX | |
    |---|---|---|---|
    | CR | Asset retirement obligation (liability) | | $XXX |

> ### Pass Key
>
> The asset retirement obligation is recorded at a discounted amount. Accretion expense is the growth of the liability over time so that at the time the liability is satisfied, it is reported at its total non-discounted value.

- **Depreciation Expense**

    Depreciation expense decreases the ARC asset reported on balance sheet. At the end of the accretion period, the asset retirement cost (asset) should be fully depreciated.

    *Journal entry to record depreciation expense associated with the ARC (asset):*

    | DR | Depreciation expense | $XXX | |
    |---|---|---|---|
    | CR | Accumulated depreciation (asset retirement cost) | | $XXX |

> ## Pass Key
>
> The cumulative accretion expense plus depreciation expense recognized on the income statements over the accretion period should be equal to the total asset retirement obligation:
>
> Cumulative accretion expense + Cumulative depreciation expense = Asset retirement obligation (ARO)

### 3.3.2 Revisions to Cash Flow Estimates

Estimated cash flows are used to calculate the discounted ARO liability reported on the balance sheet. Under U.S. GAAP, these cash flow estimates may be revised over time.

- Upward revisions to undiscounted cash flows are "new" liabilities—use current discount rate.
- Downward revisions require removal of "old" liabilities—use historical (or weighted average) discount rate.

> ## U.S. GAAP VS. IFRS
>
> Under IFRS, a decommissioning obligation is remeasured each period for changes in the amount or timing of cash flows and changes in the discount rate. Under U.S. GAAP, the obligation is only adjusted for changes in the amount or timing of cash flows.

## Illustration 2 Asset Retirement Obligation

On January 1, Year 1, Brown Mining Enterprises purchased an existing coal mine. Brown expects to operate the mine for four years, after which it is legally required to dismantle the mine. Brown estimates that it will pay $500,000 in Year 5 to dismantle the mine. Brown uses straight-line depreciation and an accretion rate of 10 percent. The present value of $1, four periods, and 10 percent is 0.68301.

*Journal entry to record the asset retirement obligation of $341,505 ($500,000 × 0.68301) on January 1, Year 1:*

| DR | Asset retirement cost | $341,505 | |
|---|---|---|---|
| CR | Asset retirement obligation | | $341,505 |

On December 31, Year 1, Brown Mining Enterprises will record accretion expense and depreciation expense as follows:

$$\begin{aligned}
\text{Accretion expense} &= \text{Beginning asset retirement obligation} \times \text{Accretion rate} \\
&= \$341{,}505 \times 10\% \\
&= \$34{,}150.50 \\
\text{Depreciation expense} &= \text{Asset retirement cost}/\text{Useful life} \\
&= \$341{,}505/4 \text{ years} \\
&= \$85{,}376.25
\end{aligned}$$

*Prepare the journal entries to record the accretion expense and depreciation expense related to the ARO on December 31, Year 1:*

| DR | Accretion expense | $34,150.50 | |
|---|---|---|---|
| CR | Asset retirement obligation | | $34,150.50 |
| DR | Depreciation expense | 85,376.25 | |
| CR | Accumulated depreciation | | 85,376.25 |

On December 31, Year 1, Brown Mining Enterprises will report the following on its balance sheet:

Asset retirement cost (asset) = $256,128.75 ($341,505 − $85,376.25)

Asset retirement obligation (liability) = $375,655.50 ($341,505 + $34,150.50)

*(continued)*

(continued)

The following table shows the calculation of the accretion expense on the ARO over the four-year accretion period:

| Date | Accretion Expense (10% × ARO) | Carrying Amount of ARO |
|---|---|---|
| 01/01/Yr 1 | | $341,505.00 |
| 12/31/Yr 1 | $ 34,150.50 | 375,655.50 |
| 12/31/Yr 2 | 37,565.55 | 413,221.05 |
| 12/31/Yr 3 | 41,322.11 | 454,543.16 |
| 12/31/Yr 4 | 45,456.84 | 500,000.00 (rounded) |
| | $158,495.00 | |

Over the four-year period ending December 31, Year 4, the total expense (accretion and depreciation) related to the ARO is:

Total expense = $341,505 depreciation + $158,495 accretion
= $500,000 ARO

During Year 5, Brown Mining Enterprises paid $510,000 to dismantle the mine. Prepare the journal entry to record the cost of dismantling in Year 5:

| | | | |
|---|---|---|---|
| DR | Asset retirement obligation | $500,000 | |
| DR | Mine dismantling expense | 10,000 | |
| CR | Cash/Accounts payable | | $510,000 |

## Question 1  MCQ-03931

Paisley Incorporated borrowed $2,000,000 from State Bank on March 1, Year 1, at a rate of 6 percent. According to the loan agreement, Paisley must make principal payments of $200,000 plus appropriate interest payments every March 1 until the loan balance is paid off. Paisley has made timely principal and interest payments since the loan began. The interest payable balance to report on the December 31, Year 3, balance sheet should total:

a. $100,000
b. $98,000
c. $96,000
d. $80,000

## NOTES

# MODULE 2: Contingencies and Commitments

FAR 5

## 1 Definition of Contingencies

A contingency is an existing condition, situation, or set of circumstances involving uncertainty as to possible gain (gain contingency) or loss (loss contingency) that will ultimately be determined when a future event occurs or fails to occur. The resolution may result in the acquisition of an asset, the reduction of a liability, the loss or impairment of an asset, or the incurrence of a liability.

### 1.1 Loss Contingencies

A loss contingency involves a possible future loss whose existence is proven by subsequent events. Examples of loss contingencies include:

- Collectibility of receivables
- Obligations regarding product warranties and defects and unredeemed coupons
- Risk of loss of property by fire, explosion, or other hazards
- Threat of expropriation of assets
- Pending or threatened litigation
- Actual or possible claims and assessments
- Risk of loss from catastrophes assumed by property and casualty insurance companies
- Guarantees of indebtedness of others
- Obligations of commercial banks under standby letters of credit
- Agreements to repurchase receivables (or related property) that have been sold
- Environmental damages

### 1.2 Gain Contingencies

Examples of gain contingencies include:

- Expected favorable settlement from a pending court case
- Possible refunds regarding tax disputes

## 2 Recognition and Measurement of Gain Contingencies

Gain contingencies are claims or rights to receive assets whose existence is uncertain but may become valid upon the occurrence of future events. Gain contingencies are not recognized in the financial statements because to do so may cause recognition of revenue prior to its realization. An entity should disclose a contingency that might result in a gain in the notes to the financial statements, but should be careful to avoid misleading implications about the likelihood of realization.

# 3 Recognition and Measurement of Loss Contingencies

The recognition of contingent losses in the financial statements depends on the likelihood that future events will confirm the contingent loss. GAAP classifies the likelihood of contingent losses as follows:

- **Probable:** Likely to occur.
- **Reasonably possible:** More than remote, but less than likely.
- **Remote:** Slight chance of occurring.

### U.S. GAAP VS. IFRS

Under IFRS, probable is defined as more likely than not to occur and possible is defined as may but probably will not occur.

## 3.1 Loss Is Probable and Can Be Reasonably Estimated

Provision for a loss contingency should be accrued by a charge to income, providing that both of the following conditions exist:

1. *It is probable that as of the date of the financial statements an asset has been impaired or a liability incurred*, based on information available prior to the issuance of the financial statements.

2. *The amount of loss can be reasonably estimated*. In the event that a range of probable losses is given (e.g., $100,000 to $250,000), GAAP requires that the best estimate of the loss be accrued. If no amount in the range is a better estimate than any other amount within the range, the minimum amount in the range should be accrued (in this case $100,000), and a note disclosing the possibility of an additional $150,000 loss should be presented.

### U.S. GAAP VS. IFRS

Under IFRS, a contingent liability is defined as a possible obligation that arises from past events and whose existence will be confirmed only by the occurrence or nonoccurrence of one or more uncertain future events not wholly within the control of the entity. A provision for a contingent liability should be recorded with a charge to income when the present obligation from a past event exists, the obligation is probable, and the amount can be reasonably estimated. When a range of possible outcomes exists, IFRS requires that the expected value be accrued. The expected value is the midpoint of the range.

## 3.2 Loss Is Reasonably Possible

In the event that both of the conditions above are not met, a financial statement disclosure shall be made when there is at least a reasonable possibility that a loss or an additional loss may have been incurred. The disclosure should include:

- The nature of the contingency.
- An estimate of the possible loss or range of loss, or a statement that an estimate cannot be made.

## 3.3 Loss Is Remote

Generally, no disclosure is necessary for a remote loss contingency; however, disclosure (nature, amount of guarantee, and any expected recovery) should be made for "guarantee-type" remote loss contingencies, such as:

- **Debts** of others guaranteed (officers/related parties);
- **Obligations** of commercial banks under standby letters of credit; and
- **Guarantees** to repurchase receivables (or related property) that have been sold or assigned.

---

### Example 1 — Loss Contingency

**Facts:** Alton Company is the defendant in a wrongful death suit filed as the result of the death of an employee who was working on one of the company's production lines. The plaintiff filed suit in June and has asked for damages of $3,000,000. Alton carries insurance for potential claims of this nature, but the insurance coverage amounts to $1,500,000. Legal counsel for Alton believes that the judge will rule in the plaintiff's favor and that the company will have to pay about $2,200,000, but the settlement could reach $3,000,000.

**Required:** Identify the financial statement treatment for the contingency and prepare the journal entry.

**Solution:**

Alton should record the following entry at year-end:

| | | | |
|---|---|---|---|
| DR | Lawsuit loss | $2,200,000 | |
| CR | Lawsuit liability | | $2,200,000 |

It is probable that the judge will rule against Alton. Because the estimate of the settlement is a range, the $2,200,000 should be recorded as the contingency amount, with disclosures indicating the maximum settlement amount of $3,000,000. The insurance proceeds that may result would be treated as a gain contingency and not recorded until received.

Contingencies and Commitments

| Contingency Treatments | Accrue Amounts | Disclose Amount | Disclose Nature | Ignore |
|---|---|---|---|---|
| Loss contingency that is probable and: Amount or range can be reasonably estimated | ✓ (or minimum) | range | ✓ | |
| Amount cannot be reasonably estimated | | range | ✓ | |
| Loss contingency that is a reasonable possibility | | range | ✓ | |
| Loss contingency that is remote | | | | ✓ |
| Loss contingency that is remote, but is a guarantee for others | | ✓ | ✓ | |
| Gain contingencies that are probable or reasonably possible | | ✓ | ✓ | |
| Gain contingencies that are remote | | | | ✓ |

## 3.4 Potential Loss Contingencies

If it is probable that an unasserted claim will be filed, then it is treated similarly to any other loss contingency.

General or unspecified business risks (such as fire, floods, strikes, and war) do not meet the conditions for accrual, and no loss accrual shall be made (nor is disclosure required).

## 3.5 Appropriation of Retained Earnings

- Any appropriation of retained earnings (such as for general loss contingencies) must be shown within the stockholders' equity section and clearly identified.

- Costs or losses shall not be charged to an appropriation of retained earnings, and no part of the appropriation should be transferred to income.

- Any appropriation should be restored to retained earnings as soon as its purpose is no longer deemed necessary.

# 4 Premiums and Warranties

Premiums and warranties are loss contingencies that are generally accrued by an entity as the expected amounts are probable and can be reasonably estimated.

## 4.1 Premiums

Premiums are offers to customers for the purpose of stimulating sales. They are offered in return for coupons, box tops, labels, etc. The cost of the premium is charged to sales in the period(s) that benefit from the premium offer. Generally, all premiums will not be redeemed in the same period.

Therefore, the number of outstanding premium offers must be estimated accurately to reflect the current liability at the end of each period.

$$\text{Total number of coupons issued} \times \text{Estimated redemption rate} = \text{Total estimated coupon redemptions}$$

### Example 2 — Premiums

**Facts:** AAA Corp. kicked off a sales promotion on August 31, Year 1. AAA included a redeemable coupon on each can of soup sold. Five coupons must be presented to receive a premium that costs AAA $2.00. AAA estimates that 70 percent of the coupons will be redeemed. Information available at December 31, Year 1, is as follows:

| Cans of Soup Sold | Premiums Purchased | Coupons Redeemed |
|---|---|---|
| 1,500,000 | 200,000 | 600,000 |

**Required:** Calculate AAA Corp.'s estimated liability for premium claims.

**Solution:**

The calculation of the estimated liability for premium claims outstanding is as follows:

| | |
|---|---:|
| Total estimated coupon redemptions (1,500,000 × 70%) | 1,050,000 |
| Less: coupons redeemed | (600,000) |
| Coupons to be redeemed | 450,000 |
| Outstanding premium claims (450,000 ÷ 5) | **90,000** |

The estimated liability for premium claims is 90,000 × $2 = $180,000. Note that you were given information about premiums purchased that was not used in the computation in determining estimated liability.

The entry to record the estimated liability for outstanding premium claims is:

| | | | |
|---|---|---|---|
| DR | Premium expense | $180,000 | |
| CR | Premium liability | | $180,000 |

## 4.2 Warranties

Warranties are a seller's promise to "correct" any product defects. Sellers offering warranties must create a liability account if the cost of the warranty can be reasonably estimated.

The entire liability for the warranty should be accrued in the year of sale to "match" the cost with the corresponding revenue. The accrual should take place even if part of the warranty expenditure will be incurred in a later year.

## Example 3  Warranties

**Facts:** ABC Corp. has a three-year warranty against defects in the machinery it sells. When a warranty claim is made, ABC Corp. satisfies the claim by replacing the machinery. Warranty costs are estimated at 2 percent of sales in the year of sale, and 4 and 6 percent in the succeeding years. ABC sales and actual warranty expenses for Year 1–Year 3 were as follows:

|  | Sales | Actual Warranty Costs |
|---|---|---|
| Year 1 | $ 250,000 | $10,000 |
| Year 2 | 500,000 | 20,000 |
| Year 3 | 750,000 | 30,000 |
|  | $1,500,000 | $60,000 |

**Required:** Prepare the journal entries to account for the warranty in Years 1-3 and determine the balance in the warranty liability account at the end of Year 3.

**Solution:** ABC's total liability should be accrued in the year of sale even though it will not be incurred in that year.

*The following journal entries will be recorded in Years 1-3.*

Year 1:

| | | | |
|---|---|---|---|
| DR | Warranty expense ($250,000 × 12%) | $30,000 | |
| CR | Warranty liability | | $30,000 |
| DR | Warranty liability (actual costs) | 10,000 | |
| CR | Inventory | | 10,000 |

Year 2:

| | | | |
|---|---|---|---|
| DR | Warranty expense ($500,000 × 12%) | $60,000 | |
| CR | Warranty liability | | $60,000 |
| DR | Warranty liability | 20,000 | |
| CR | Inventory | | 20,000 |

Year 3:

| | | | |
|---|---|---|---|
| DR | Warranty expense ($750,000 × 12%) | $90,000 | |
| CR | Warranty liability | | $90,000 |
| DR | Warranty liability | 30,000 | |
| CR | Inventory | | 30,000 |

The balance in the account at the end of Year 3 is total liability less actual expenditures and is calculated as follows:

Total liability = Sales × Total estimated expense
 = $1,500,000 × 12% [2% + 4% + 6%]
 = $180,000

Balance, liability account, 12/31/Year 3 = Total liability – Actual expenditures
 = $180,000 – $60,000
 = $120,000

## Question 1    MCQ-00736

During Year 1, Haft Co. became involved in a tax dispute with the IRS. At December 31, Year 1, Haft's tax advisor believed that an unfavorable outcome was probable. A reasonable estimate of additional taxes was $200,000 but could be as much as $300,000. After the Year 1 financial statements were issued, Haft received and accepted an IRS settlement offer of $275,000.

What amount of accrued liability should Haft have reported in its December 31, Year 1 balance sheet?

- a. $200,000
- b. $250,000
- c. $275,000
- d. $300,000

## Question 2    MCQ-00912

On November 10, Year 1, a Garry Corp. truck was in an accident with an auto driven by Dacey. On January 10, Year 2, Garry received notice of a lawsuit seeking $800,000 in damages for personal injuries suffered by Dacey. Garry Corp.'s counsel believes it is reasonably possible that Dacey will be awarded an estimated amount in the range between $250,000 and $500,000, and that $400,000 is a better estimate of potential liability than any other amount. Garry's accounting year ends on December 31, and the Year 1 financial statements were issued on March 6, Year 2. What amount of loss should Garry accrue at December 31, Year 1?

- a. $0
- b. $250,000
- c. $400,000
- d. $500,000

### Question 3 — MCQ-00745

During Year 1, Smith Co. filed suit against West Inc. seeking damages for patent infringement. At December 31, Year 1, Smith's legal counsel believed that it was probable that Smith would be successful against West for an estimated amount in the range of $75,000 to $150,000, with all amounts in the range considered equally likely. In March Year 2, Smith was awarded $100,000 and received full payment thereof. In its Year 1 financial statements, issued in February Year 2, how should this award be reported?

a. As a receivable and revenue of $100,000.
b. As a receivable and deferred revenue of $100,000.
c. As a disclosure of a contingent gain of $100,000.
d. As a disclosure of a contingent gain of an undetermined amount in the range of $75,000 to $150,000.

# MODULE 3: Long-Term Liabilities

FAR 5

## 1 Time Value of Money

Problems involving interest, annuities, and present values, including problems related to long-term liabilities, are all concerned with the use of money over a period of time, which is referred to as the time value of money. The idea of present value is also the basis for the latest foundational concept, SFAC No. 7. The principles used in computing interest, annuities, and present values are applied to many accounting problems. Accounting for leases, pensions, bonds, and long-term debt are some of the more important applications.

### 1.1 Computations

For examination purposes, present value concepts are divisible into six separate types:

- Present value of $1
- Future value of $1
- Present value of an ordinary annuity
- Future value of an ordinary annuity
- Present value of an annuity due
- Future value of an annuity due

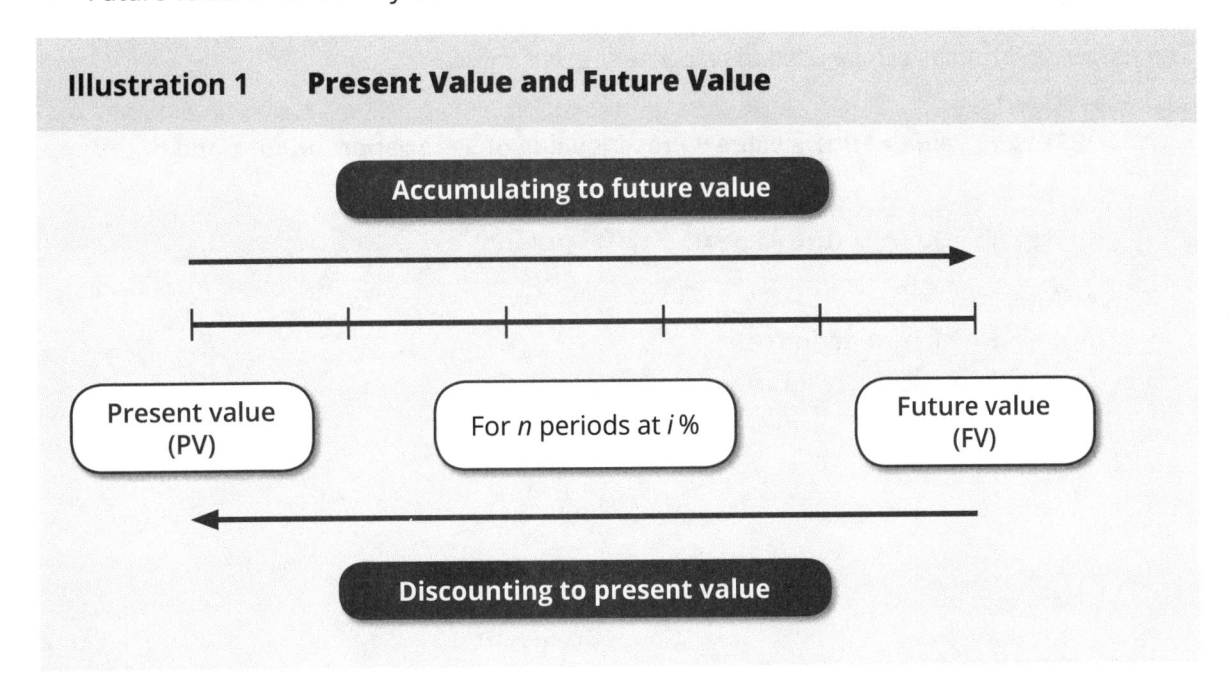

**Illustration 1  Present Value and Future Value**

Accumulating to future value

Present value (PV) — For *n* periods at *i* % — Future value (FV)

Discounting to present value

Long-Term Liabilities                                                                                          FAR 5

## 1.2 Annuities

A large number of business transactions involve multiple payments or receipts. Bond interest payments and lease rental payments are two examples. Annuities are transactions that result in identical periodic payments or receipts at regular intervals. Ordinary annuity (also called "annuity in arrears") payments are made at the end of each period. Annuity due payments occur at the beginning of each period.

The timing of payments is the only difference between an ordinary annuity and an annuity due. This applies to both present value and future value annuities.

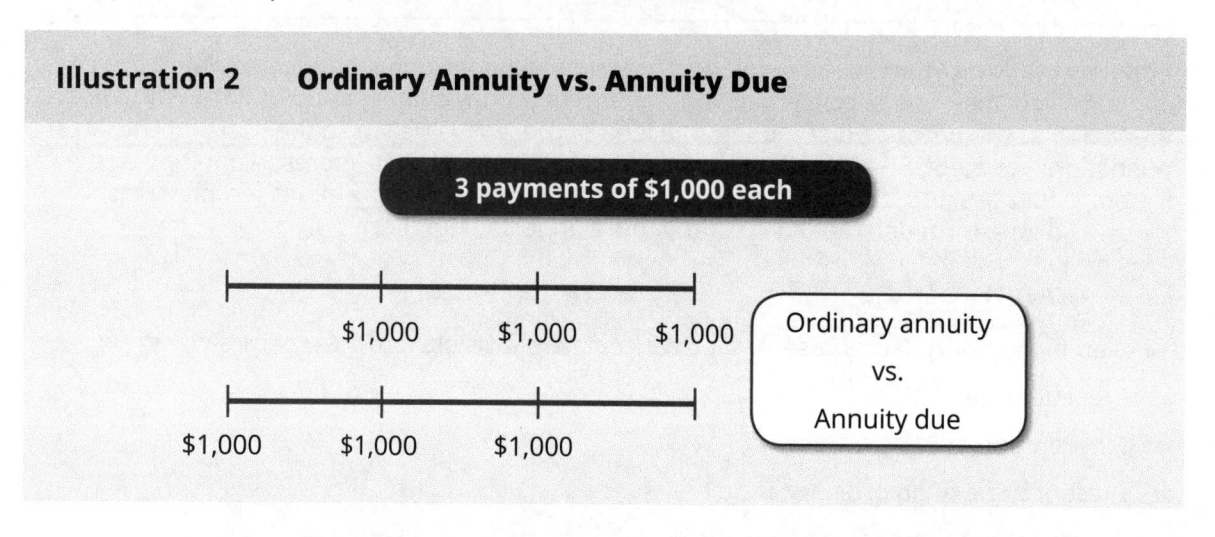

**Illustration 2   Ordinary Annuity vs. Annuity Due**

3 payments of $1,000 each

$1,000   $1,000   $1,000      Ordinary annuity
                              vs.
$1,000   $1,000   $1,000      Annuity due

## 1.3 Present Value of $1

The present value of $1 is the amount that must be invested now at a specific interest rate so that $1 can be paid or received in the future.

The following formulas can be used to calculate present value:

> Present value = Future value × Present value of $1 for appropriate $n$ and $r$
>
> Or:
>
> Present value = Future value / $(1 + r)^n$
>
> Where:
> $n$ = Number of periods
> $r$ = Periodic interest rate

## Example 1 — Present Value of $1

**Facts:** On January 1, Year 1, ABC Corp. received an offer from a competitor to buy ABC's equipment at the end of Year 4. The competitor would pay $500,000 at the end of Year 4. The equipment is worth $300,000 now, and the prevailing interest rate is 10 percent, compounded annually.

**Required:** Using present value calculations, determine whether ABC should accept or reject the offer.

**Solution:** The present value of the $500,000 is calculated as follows:

Present value of $1 for 4 periods at 10% = 0.6830

$500,000 × 0.6830 = $341,500

Alternatively, the present value can be calculated as:

PV = $500,000 / (1 + 0.10)$^4$

= $341,507

Note that the difference between these two calculations is due to the rounding of the present value factor in the first calculation.

ABC should accept the offer of payment at the end of Year 4. The current value of the Year 4 payment is $341,500, which is more than the equipment's current value.

---

### Pass Key

If interest compounds on an other-than-annual basis, the number of periods and the interest rate must be adjusted. For example, if the annual interest rate is 12 percent and interest compounds quarterly over 10 years, then the periodic interest rate is 3 percent and the total number of compounding periods is 40.

---

## 1.4 Future Value of $1

The future value of $1 is more easily understood as compound interest. It is the amount that would accumulate at a future point in time if $1 were invested now. The interest factor causes the future value of $1 to be greater than $1.

The following formula can be used to calculate future value:

> Future value = Present value × Future value of $1 for appropriate *n* and *r*
>
> Or:
>
> Future value = Present value × (1 + *r*)$^n$

# Long-Term Liabilities

## Example 2 — Future Value of $1

**Facts:** Your partner is retiring in five years. It will cost $300,000 to purchase her interest. Assume that you invest $200,000 now, earning 10 percent compounded annually.

**Required:** Using future value calculations, determine whether you will have enough money in five years to purchase your partner's interest.

**Solution:**

Future value of $1 at 10% for 5 periods = 1.6105

$200,000 × 1.6105 = $322,100

Alternatively, the future value can be calculated as:

FV = $200,000 × (1+ 0.10)$^5$
    = $322,102

Note that the difference between these two calculations is due to the rounding of the future value factor in the first calculation.

$322,100 > $300,000, so you will be able to purchase your partner's interest.

### Pass Key

Note that the difference between present value and future value is the amount of interest earned over the period. Also note that the present value factors and future value factors are inverses of each other.

## 1.5 Present Value of an Ordinary Annuity

The present value of an ordinary annuity is the current worth of a series of identical periodic payments to be made in the future. To calculate the present value of an ordinary annuity, the following formula can be used:

$$\text{Present value of ordinary annuity} = \text{Annuity payment} \times \text{Present value of ordinary annuity of \$1 for appropriate } n \text{ and } r$$

> **Example 3** — **Present Value of an Ordinary Annuity**
>
> **Facts:** Parker Inc. enters into a 10-year, noncancelable lease requiring year-end payments of $100,000 each year for 10 years. Parker's borrowing rate is 10 percent compounded annually.
>
> **Required:** Calculate the present value of the lease payments.
>
> **Solution:**
>
> Present value of an ordinary annuity of $1 at 10% for 10 periods = 6.1445
>
> $100,000 × 6.1445 = $614,450
>
> Parker should record the lease at $614,450.

## 1.6 Present Value of an Annuity Due

The only difference in the calculations of an annuity due and an ordinary annuity is the timing of the payments. For an annuity due, the payment occurs at the beginning of the period. When calculating the present value of an annuity due, it is calculated on the day of the first payment. There are several ways to calculate the present value of an annuity due. By adding 1.00 to the present value of an ordinary annuity of 1 for *n* periods, the present value of an annuity due of 1 for *n* + 1 periods may be found.

In addition, if you have the present value of an ordinary annuity of 1 for *n* periods and need the present value of an annuity due of 1 for *n* periods, the following calculation may be used:

> **Present value of annuity due = Present value of ordinary annuity × (1 + *r*)**

In an annuity due, each cash flow is discounted one less period; therefore, the value is higher by (1 + *r*).

> **Illustration 3** — **Ordinary Annuity vs. Annuity Due**
>
> Present value of an ordinary annuity of 1 at 6% for 2 periods = 1.8334
>
> Present value of an annuity due of 1 at 6% for 2 periods = 1.8334 × 1.06 = 1.9434
>
> Present value of an annuity due of 1 at 6% for 3 periods = 1.8334 + 1.00 = 2.8334

Long-Term Liabilities                                                                                                           FAR 5

> ### Example 4 — Present Value of an Annuity Due
>
> **Facts:** Avalanche Inc. enters into a 10-year lease requiring beginning-of-the-year payments of $100,000 each year for 10 years. Avalanche's borrowing rate is 10 percent compounded annually.
>
> **Required:** Calculate the present value of the payments.
>
> **Solution:**
>
> Present value of an annuity due of $1 at 10% for 10 periods  =  6.759
>
> $100,000 × 6.759  =  $675,900

## 1.7 Future Value of an Ordinary Annuity

The future value of an ordinary annuity is the value at a future date of a series of periodic payments. The following formula can be used to calculate the future value of an ordinary annuity:

$$\text{Future value of an ordinary annuity} = \text{Periodic payment} \times \text{Future value of an ordinary annuity of \$1 for appropriate } n \text{ and } r$$

> ### Example 5 — Future Value of an Ordinary Annuity
>
> **Facts:** Jay Planner wants to save for his 12-year-old son's college education. Assume that he sets aside $5,000 at the end of each of the next five years, earning 10 percent compounded annually.
>
> **Required:** Calculate how much money will be in Jay's account at the end of five years.
>
> **Solution:**
>
> Future value of an ordinary annuity of 1 at 10% for 5 periods  =  6.1051
>
> $5,000 × 6.1051  =  $30,525.50

> **Question 1**                                                                                 MCQ-00394
>
> On December 30, Year 1, Chang Co. sold a machine to Door Co. in exchange for a non-interest-bearing note requiring 10 annual payments of $10,000. Door made the first payment on December 30, Year 1. The market interest rate for similar notes at date of issuance was 8 percent. Information on present value factors is as follows:
>
> | Period | Present Value of $1 at 8% | Present Value of Ordinary Annuity of $1 at 8% |
> |---|---|---|
> | 9 | 0.50 | 6.25 |
> | 10 | 0.46 | 6.71 |
>
> In its December 31, Year 1, balance sheet, what amount should Chang report as note receivable?
>
>    **a.**  $45,000
>
>    **b.**  $46,000
>
>    **c.**  $62,500
>
>    **d.**  $67,100

# 2   Long-Term Liabilities

Long-term liabilities are probable sacrifices of economic benefits associated with present obligations that are not payable within the current operating cycle or reporting year, whichever is greater.

## 2.1   Examples

Examples of long-term liabilities include:

- Long-term promissory notes payable
- Bonds payable
- Long-term leases
- Long-term contingent liabilities
- Purchase commitments
- Equipment purchase obligations
- Amounts due under deferred compensation agreements
- Postretirement pension and other benefits payable
- Other financial instruments
- Short-term debt expected to be refinanced (to the extent of post-balance sheet refinancing with support)
- Deferred income taxes payable

Most of these types of liabilities are covered in other sections of this course. This module will focus on notes payable.

## 2.2 Distinguishing Liabilities From Equity

Certain financial instruments have characteristics of both liabilities and equity. The following financial instruments must be classified as liabilities:

- Financial instruments in the form of shares that are mandatorily redeemable (i.e., mandatorily redeemable preferred stock) and represent an unconditional obligation to the issuer to redeem the instrument by transferring assets at a specified date or upon a future event, unless the redemption is required upon the liquidation or termination of the issuer.

- Financial instruments, other than outstanding shares, that represent an obligation to repurchase the issuer's equity shares by transferring assets.

- Financial instruments that represent an obligation to issue a variable number of shares.

# 3 Notes Payable

Notes payable (contractual rights to pay money at a fixed or determinable rate) must be recorded at present value at the date of issuance. If a note is non-interest bearing or the interest rate is unreasonable (usually below market), the value of the note must be determined by imputing the market rate of the note and by using the effective interest method.

Many of these rules apply when notes are exchanged for goods and services and the interest rate varies from the prevailing interest rates. Notes must be recorded at present value so that expense for the period is not distorted.

## 3.1 Stated Interest Factors

A note issued solely for cash equal to its face amount is presumed to earn the interest stated. However, if rights or privileges are attached to the note, they must be evaluated separately. If no rights or privileges are attached and the interest rate on the note reflects prevailing interest rates, record the note payable at face value without any present value considerations.

There is a general presumption that the interest stated on a note resulting from a business transaction entered into at arm's length is fair and adequate.

## 3.2 Imputing Interest

When a note contains either no interest or an unreasonable rate of interest, the substance rather than the form of the transaction must be recorded. This involves determining the present value of the obligation at the appropriate market interest rate, and:

1. recording the payable at its face amount;
2. recording the item received in exchange for the note at the present value of the obligation; and
3. recording any difference between the face amount of the note and its present value as a discount that must be amortized over the life of the note.

## 3.3 Imputing Interest Not Required

The present value calculation at the market rate of interest is not required for certain payables with low or no interest rate when those payables:

- arise in the ordinary course of business, the terms of which do not exceed approximately one year (short-term notes).

- are paid in property or services (not in cash).

- represent security deposits.
- bear an interest rate determined by a government agency.
- arise from transactions between a parent and its subsidiaries.

## 3.4 Amortization of the Discount

Any discount resulting from imputing interest on a note payable must be amortized over the life of the note payable using the effective interest method.

The *effective interest method* is a method under which each payment on a note (or other loan) is allocated to interest and principal as though the note had a constant effective stated rate (or adequate rate) of interest.

## 3.5 Presentation and Disclosure

The *discount* is inseparable from the related note payable and is added to the note payable to determine the carrying value to be reported on the balance sheet.

A full description of the payable, the effective interest rate, and the face amount of the note should be disclosed in the financial statements or notes thereto.

### Example 6 — Effective Interest Method

**Facts:** Company A is making three annual loan payments of $1,000 each to Company B. There is no stated rate of interest. The present value of the aggregate loan payments at the appropriate interest rate of 10 percent is $2,486.

**Required:** Using the effective interest method, allocate the interest and principal for each payment.

**Solution:** Under the effective interest method, each payment would be allocated between interest and principal as follows:

| (a) Cash Payment | (b) Interest Expense (d) × 10% | (c) Principal Paid (a) − (b) | (d) Carrying Value (d) − (c) |
|---|---|---|---|
|  |  |  | $2,486 |
| $1,000 | $249 | $ 751 | 1,735 |
| 1,000 | 174 | 826 | 909 |
| 1,000 | 91 | 909 | -0- |
|  | $514 | $2,486 |  |

This example presents an installment note that has fixed payments over the life of the note. Interest is determined using the remaining balance on the note and the 10 percent effective interest rate. The amount allocated to principal and interest changes as the carrying value of the note decreases.

# Long-Term Liabilities

## Example 7 — Imputed Interest

**Facts:** On January 1, Year 1, a company purchases a machine for $10,000 and issues a $10,000 note payable bearing no interest due in five years. Ten percent is an appropriate interest rate.

The present value of $1 at 10 percent for five years is 0.621. Because the issued note is non-interest bearing, the value of the machine purchased is not $10,000. The present value of the note is also the fair value of the machine.

**Required:** Prepare the journal entries to record the purchase and to amortize the discount on the note payable at the end of Year 1 using the effective interest method. Indicate how the notes payable would appear on the Year 1 balance sheet. Prepare an amortization table showing interest expense and carrying value for the five years of the note.

**Solution:** *Journal entry to record the purchase:*

| | | | |
|---|---|---|---|
| DR | Machine | $6,210 | |
| DR | Discount on note payable | 3,790 | |
| CR | Note payable | | $10,000 |

*Journal entry: Year 1 end of year to amortize the discount on notes payable using the effective interest method:*

| | | | |
|---|---|---|---|
| DR | Interest expense | $621 | |
| CR | Discount on note payable | | $621 |

*Balance sheet presentation at the end of Year 1:*

Notes payable $10,000
Less: discount on notes payable (3,169) [$3,790 − $621]
$ 6,831

In this example, the company records the note at its face amount but records the sale at the present value of the note. The difference between the face amount of the note and its present value is recorded as "discount on notes receivable." This deferred interest is payment for the use of the seller's funds for the five years. Interest expense is recorded each year, using the effective interest method even though no cash interest payments are made during the five-year life of the loan. Interest is built into the face value of the note and will be paid at maturity.

**Amortization Table: No Interest Note Payable**

| Period | Beginning Carrying Value | Interest Expense (10%) | Cash Payment (0%) | Amortization | Ending Carrying Value |
|---|---|---|---|---|---|
| Year 1 | $6,210 | $621 | – | $621 | $ 6,831 |
| Year 2 | 6,831 | 683 | – | 683 | 7,514 |
| Year 3 | 7,514 | 751 | – | 751 | 8,266 |
| Year 4 | 8,266 | 827 | – | 827 | 9,092 |
| Year 5 | 9,092 | 909 | – | 909 | 10,000 |

(rounded)

# 4 Debt Covenants

Creditors use debt covenants in lending agreements to protect their interest by limiting or prohibiting the actions of debtors that might negatively affect the positions of the creditors.

## 4.1 Common Debt Covenants

Debt covenants vary widely. Common debt covenants include the following:

- Limitations on issuing additional debt
- Restrictions on the payment of dividends
- Limitations on the disposal of certain assets
- Minimum working capital requirements
- Collateral requirements
- Limitations on how the borrowed money can be used
- Maintenance of specific financial ratios, including:
  - Debt-to-equity ratio
  - Debt-to-total-capital ratio (debt ratio)
  - Interest coverage ratio (times interest earned)

## 4.2 Violation of Debt Covenants

When debt covenants are violated, the debtor is in technical default and the creditor can demand repayment. Most of the time, concessions are negotiated and real default, as opposed to technical default, is avoided. Concessions can result in the violated covenant(s) being waived temporarily or permanently. Concessions can also result in a change in the interest rate or other terms of the debt.

---

**Example 8 — Debt Covenants**

**Facts:** On December 31, Bike Ride Inc. borrowed $1,000,000 in cash from Creditworthy Bank to purchase a building for the company's production facility. Bike Ride must make annual interest payments at a rate of 6.25 percent. The terms of the borrowing from Creditworthy include the following debt covenants:

- $100,000 of the borrowing must be kept in an account at Creditworthy Bank.
- Bike Ride may not issue any additional debt during the life of the borrowing.
- Bike Ride must maintain a times interest earned ratio of at least 5 during the life of the borrowing.

Bike Ride reported net income of $350,000 and income taxes of $140,000 for the first year.

**Required:** Prepare the journal entry to record the debt at issuance and determine whether Bike Ride's income for the year satisfies the debt covenant requirement.

(continued)

(continued)

**Solution:** *The entry to record the issuance of the debt is:*

| DR | Cash | $900,000 | |
|---|---|---|---|
| DR | Restricted cash | 100,000 | |
| CR | Notes payable | | $1,000,000 |

Every year, Bike Ride must calculate times interest earned.

Times interest earned = Earnings before interest and taxes (EBIT)/Interest expense
= (350,000 + 140,000 + 62,500)/62,500
= 8.84

Bike Ride Inc. meets the terms of the debt covenants for the year.

---

### Question 2    MCQ-06574

On September 30, World Co. borrowed $1,000,000 on a 9 percent note payable. World paid the first of four quarterly payments of $264,200 when due on December 30. In its December 31 balance sheet, what amount should World report as note payable?

   a. $735,800
   b. $750,000
   c. $758,300
   d. $825,800

---

### Question 3    MCQ-03933

In accordance with Sam Company's loan agreement with First Bank, Sam Company must maintain a debt-to-equity ratio of 0.60 or less. At year-end, Sam Company's balance sheet includes total liabilities of $55,000 and total stockholders' equity of $95,500. What is Sam Company's debt-to-equity ratio at year-end, and has Sam Company met the bank's debt covenant requirement?

   a. Sam Company's debt-to-equity ratio at year-end is 0.37 and has satisfied the bank's debt covenant.
   b. Sam Company's debt-to-equity ratio at year-end is 0.58 and has satisfied the bank's debt covenant.
   c. Sam Company's debt-to-equity ratio at year-end is 0.63 and has not satisfied the bank's debt covenant.
   d. Sam Company's debt-to-equity ratio at year-end is 1.74 and has not satisfied the bank's debt covenant.

# MODULE 4 Bonds: Part 1

FAR 5

# 1 Introduction to Bonds Payable

## 1.1 Terminology

Bonds payable are a very common type of long-term liability. The terms below are important to understand when accounting for debt securities such as bonds.

- **Bond Indenture:** The document that describes the contract between the issuer (borrower) and bond holders (lenders).
- **Face (Par) Value:** Face value is the total dollar amount of the bond and the basis on which periodic interest is paid. Bonds are issued at face (par) value when the stated rate of interest equals the market rate of interest.
- **Stated (Nominal or Coupon) Interest Rate:** The stated interest rate, also known as the nominal interest rate or the coupon rate, is the interest to be paid to the investors in cash. This rate is specified in the bond contract.
- **Market (Effective) Interest Rate:** The market interest rate is the rate of interest actually earned by the bondholder and is the rate of return for comparable contracts on the date the bonds are issued.
- **Discount:** If the market rate is higher than the stated rate, the bonds will be issued at a *discount*, in which case the bonds sell for less than the face amount to make up for the lower return being provided.
- **Premium:** If the market rate is lower than the stated rate, the bonds will be issued at a *premium* because the investor will pay more than face value due to the higher return offered.

## 1.2 Types of Bonds

Bonds are an important source of long-term funding for companies needing large amounts of capital. Bonds represent a contractual promise by the issuing corporation to pay investors (bondholders) a specific sum of money at a designated maturity date plus periodic, fixed interest payments (usually made semiannually) based on a percentage of the face amount of the bond. The following are various types of bonds:

- **Debentures:** Debentures are unsecured bonds.
- **Mortgage Bonds:** Mortgage bonds are bonds that are secured by real property.
- **Collateral Trust Bonds:** Collateral trust bonds are secured bonds.
- **Convertible Bonds:** Convertible bonds are convertible into common stock of the debtor (generally) at the option of the bondholder.
    - **Nondetachable Warrants:** The convertible bond itself must be converted into capital stock.
    - **Detachable Warrants:** The bond is not surrendered upon conversion, only the warrants plus cash representing the exercise price of the warrants. The warrants can be bought and sold separately from the bonds.

- **Participating Bonds:** Participating bonds are bonds that not only have a stated rate of interest but participate in income if certain earnings levels are obtained.
- **Term Bonds:** Term bonds are bonds that have a single fixed maturity date. The entire principal is paid at the end of this term/period.
- **Serial Bonds:** Serial bonds are prenumbered bonds that the issuer may call and redeem a portion by serial number (often redeemed pro rata annually/in a series of annual installments).
- **Income Bonds:** Income bonds are bonds that only pay interest if certain income objectives are met.
- **Zero Coupon Bonds:** Zero coupon bonds (also known as "deep discount bonds") are bonds sold with no stated interest but rather at a discount and redeemed at the face value without periodic interest payments.
- **Commodity-Backed Bonds:** Commodity-backed bonds (also known as "asset-linked bonds") are bonds that are redeemable either in cash or a stated volume of a commodity, whichever is greater.

## 2 Bonds Payable vs. Notes Payable

The accounting for long-term notes payable is similar to the accounting for bonds payable. The accounting for long-term, non-interest-bearing notes is similar to the accounting for short-term, non-interest-bearing notes. The following schedule identifies the typical differences between bonds and notes:

| Attribute | Bonds | Notes |
| --- | --- | --- |
| Implementing instrument | Bond | Note |
| Definitive agreement | Indenture | Loan agreement |
| Face amount increments | $1,000 (general) | Negotiated |
| Term | 10 to 30 years | Negotiated |
| Payments prior to maturity | Interest only | Negotiated |
| Payments at maturity | Principal | Negotiated |
| Number of creditors | Many | Few |
| Publicly traded | Yes | No |
| Easily renegotiable | No | Yes |
| Secured | Yes and no | Yes |
| Registered (order) form | Yes | Yes |
| Bearer (coupon) form | Yes | No |
| Right of debtor to call/prepay | Yes | Yes |
| Right of creditor to put w/o default | Yes | No |

# 3 Overview of Bond Terms

Bonds payable should be recorded as a long-term liability at face value and adjusted to the present value of their future cash outflows by either subtracting unamortized discounts or adding unamortized premiums. Bonds payable are recorded at the true present value at the date of issuance based on the market (effective) interest rate at that date.

- Bonds are usually issued in denominations of $1,000.
- Price is always quoted in 100s *(percentage of par value)*.
- Indenture is a contract for purchase of a bond.
- Coupon rate = The stated interest rate on the bond.
- Bond interest (check amount) = Coupon rate × Face. Bonds generally pay interest semiannually in the U.S. and annually in other countries.
- Principal payoff is always the full face amount.
- Premium/discount is the result of the buyer and seller "adjusting" the coupon rate to the prevailing market rate of interest.

# 4 Accounting for the Issuance of Bonds

## 4.1 Bond Selling Price

When a bond is issued, the price is computed as the sum of the present value of the future principal payment *plus* the present value of the future periodic interest payments. Both cash flows are discounted at the prevailing market rate of interest on the date of issuance. This recorded price is the value of the bond at its current cash equivalent.

| Bond |
|---|
| $1,000,000 |
| 10% |
| 5 years |
| Semiannual |
| June 30 and December 31 |

### 4.1.1 Bonds Issued at Par Value

A bond is issued at par value when the stated rate on the bond is equal to the market (effective) interest rate on the date the bonds are issued.

---

**Example 1　　Bonds Issued at Par**

**Facts:** Assume that Kristi Corporation issued a 10 percent, $1,000,000 bond due in five years. The bonds were issued January 1. Interest is due on June 30 and December 31. The yield or market rate is also 10 percent.

| | |
|---|---|
| PV of $1 at 10% for 5 periods | 0.620921 |
| PV of $1 at 5% for 10 periods | 0.613913 |
| PV of an annuity of $1 at 10% for 5 periods | 3.790787 |
| PV of an annuity of $1 at 5% for 10 periods | 7.721735 |

**Required:** Determine the selling price of the bond and prepare the journal entries for borrower and investor to record the bonds at issuance.

(continued)

# Bonds: Part 1

(continued)

**Solution:**

| | 1 | | 2 | | 3 | | 4 | | 5 | | Principal |
|---|---|---|---|---|---|---|---|---|---|---|---|
| | 6/30 | 12/31 | 6/30 | 12/31 | 6/30 | 12/31 | 6/30 | 12/31 | 6/30 | 12/31 | 12/31/X5 |
| | $50,000 | $50,000 | $50,000 | $50,000 | $50,000 | $50,000 | $50,000 | $50,000 | $50,000 | $50,000 | $1,000,000 |

$ 386,087 = $50,000 × 7.721735 (PV of an annuity of $1 at 5% for 10 periods)
$ 613,913 = $1,000,000 × 0.613913 (PV of $1 at 5% for 10 periods)
$1,000,000  Net Present Value

| Borrower | | | | Investor | | | |
|---|---|---|---|---|---|---|---|
| DR | Cash | $1,000,000 | | DR | Investment in bonds | $1,000,000 | |
| CR | Bond payable | | $1,000,000 | CR | Cash | | $1,000,000 |

### 4.1.2 Bonds Issued at a Discount

A bond is issued at a discount when the stated rate on the bond is less than the market (effective) interest rate on the date the bonds are issued.

---

**Example 2 — Bonds Issued at Discount**

**Facts:** Assume that Kristi Corporation issued a 10 percent, $1,000,000 bond due in five years. The bonds were issued January 1. Interest is due on June 30 and December 31. The yield or market rate is 12 percent.

**Required:** Determine the selling price of the bond, noting the amount of discount or premium, and prepare the journal entries for the borrower and investor to record the bonds at issuance.

**Solution:**

| | |
|---|---|
| PV of $1 at 10% for 5 periods | 0.620921 |
| PV of $1 at 12% for 5 periods | 0.567427 |
| PV of $1 at 5% for 10 periods | 0.613913 |
| PV of $1 at 6% for 10 periods | 0.558395 |
| PV of an annuity of $1 at 10% for 5 periods | 3.790787 |
| PV of an annuity of $1 at 12% for 5 periods | 3.604776 |
| PV of an annuity of $1 at 5% for 10 periods | 7.721735 |
| PV of an annuity of $1 at 6% for 10 periods | 7.360087 |

| | 1 | | 2 | | 3 | | 4 | | 5 | | Principal |
|---|---|---|---|---|---|---|---|---|---|---|---|
| | 6/30 | 12/31 | 6/30 | 12/31 | 6/30 | 12/31 | 6/30 | 12/31 | 6/30 | 12/31 | 12/31/X5 |
| | $50,000 | $50,000 | $50,000 | $50,000 | $50,000 | $50,000 | $50,000 | $50,000 | $50,000 | $50,000 | $1,000,000 |

$368,004 = $50,000 × 7.360087 (PV of an annuity of $1 at 6% for 10 periods)
$558,395 = $1,000,000 × 0.558395 (PV of $1 at 6% for 10 periods)
$926,399

(continued)

(continued)

| Borrower | | | Investor | | |
|---|---|---|---|---|---|
| DR Cash | $926,399 | | DR Investment in bonds | $926,399 | |
| DR Discount on bond payable | 73,601 | | CR Cash | | $926,399 |
| CR Bond payable | | $1,000,000 | | | |

### 4.1.3 Bonds Issued at a Premium

A bond is issued at a premium when the stated rate on the bond is greater than the market (effective) interest rate on the date the bonds are issued.

#### Example 3 — Bonds Issued at Premium

**Facts:** Assume that Kristi Corporation issued a 10 percent, $1,000,000 bond due in five years. The bonds were issued January 1. Interest is due on June 30 and December 31. The yield or market rate is 8 percent.

**Required:** Determine the selling price of the bond, noting the amount of discount or premium, and prepare the journal entries for borrower and investor to record the bonds at issuance.

**Solution:**

| | |
|---|---|
| PV of $1 at 10% for 5 periods | 0.620921 |
| PV of $1 at 8% for 5 periods | 0.680583 |
| PV of $1 at 5% for 10 periods | 0.613913 |
| PV of $1 at 4% for 10 periods | 0.675564 |
| PV of an annuity of $1 at 10% for 5 periods | 3.790787 |
| PV of an annuity of $1 at 8% for 5 periods | 3.992710 |
| PV of an annuity of $1 at 5% for 10 periods | 7.721735 |
| PV of an annuity of $1 at 4% for 10 periods | 8.110896 |

| | 1 | | 2 | | 3 | | 4 | | 5 | | Principal |
|---|---|---|---|---|---|---|---|---|---|---|---|
| | 6/30 | 12/31 | 6/30 | 12/31 | 6/30 | 12/31 | 6/30 | 12/31 | 6/30 | 12/31 | 12/31/X5 |
| | $50,000 | $50,000 | $50,000 | $50,000 | $50,000 | $50,000 | $50,000 | $50,000 | $50,000 | $50,000 | $50,000 |

$ 405,545 = $50,000 × 8.110896 (PV of an annuity of $1 at 4% for 10 periods)
$ 675,564 = $1,000,000 × 0.675564 (PV of $1 at 4% for 10 periods)
$1,081,109

| Borrower | | | Investor | | |
|---|---|---|---|---|---|
| DR Cash | $1,081,109 | | DR Investment in bonds | $1,081,109 | |
| CR Premium on bond payable | | $ 81,109 | CR Cash | | $1,081,109 |
| CR Bond payable | | 1,000,000 | | | |

## 4.2 Stated Interest Rate

The stated rate of interest of a bond is typically printed on the bond and included in the bond indenture before the bond is brought to market. The stated rate of a bond does not change, regardless of the market rate at the date of issuance. The amount of cash received by a bondholder at regular interest payment intervals throughout the life of the bonds will always be at the stated rate applied to the face amount of the bond.

Interest is typically paid on bonds twice a year (semiannually), although interest expense will accrue monthly.

## 4.3 Effective Interest Rate

Because the amount of cash to be received in the future is fixed at the time the bond is sold, the market will automatically adjust the issue price of the bond so that the purchaser receives the *market rate of interest* for comparable risk bonds (i.e., the effective interest rate). A discount or premium on the bonds will exist when the bonds are issued with a stated rate that differs from the market rate at the date of issuance.

## 4.4 Discounts

If the market rate of interest is higher than the stated rate of interest on the bond, the bonds will sell at a discount. This means that the bond will sell for *less* than the face value of the bond (at less than 100 percent of par). The difference between the face value of the bond and the sales price of the bond (i.e., the discount) will cause interest expense to be greater than the interest paid in cash to the bondholders.

### 4.4.1 Unamortized Discount

The unamortized discount on bonds payable is a contra-account to bonds payable, which means that it is presented on the balance sheet as a direct reduction from the face (par) value of the bonds to arrive at the bond's carrying value at any particular point in time. The unamortized discount will decrease as the discount is amortized.

| Long-term liabilities: | |
|---|---|
| Bonds payable, 10%, due 12/31/Year X | $1,000,000 |
| Less: unamortized discount | (73,601) |
| | $ 926,399 |

### 4.4.2 Amortization of the Discount

Bond discount represents additional interest to be paid to investors at the bond maturity and is amortized over the life of the bond. The discount is amortized over the life of the bond, with amortized amounts *increasing interest expense* each period. Therefore, the amortization of the discount is added to the amount of cash paid at the stated rate to obtain GAAP interest expense (remember that the amount of cash paid could be zero if the bond is a zero coupon bond).

## 4.5 Premiums

If the market rate of interest is lower than the stated interest rate on the bond, the bonds will sell at a premium. This means that the bonds will sell for more than the face value of the bond (at more than 100 percent of par). The difference between the face value of the bond and the sales price of the bond (i.e., the premium) will cause interest expense to be less than the interest paid in cash.

### 4.5.1 Unamortized Premium

The unamortized premium on bonds payable is presented on the balance sheet as a direct addition to the face (par) value of the bonds to arrive at the bond's carrying value at any particular point in time. The unamortized premium will decrease as the premium is amortized.

| | |
|---|---|
| Long-term liabilities: | |
| Bonds payable, 10%, due 12/31/Year X | $1,000,000 |
| Add: unamortized premium | 81,109 |
| | $1,081,109 |

### 4.5.2 Amortization of the Premium

The bond premium represents interest paid in advance to the issuer by bondholders who then receive a return of this premium in the form of larger periodic interest payments (at the stated rate). The bond premium is amortized over the life of the bond, with amortized amounts *decreasing interest expense* each period. Therefore, the amortization of the premium is subtracted from the amount of cash paid at the stated rate to obtain GAAP interest expense.

## 4.6 Carrying Value

The carrying value of a bond equals face plus the balance of unamortized premium or face minus the balance of unamortized discount. As bonds approach maturity, their carrying values approach face value, so that the carrying value of the bonds equals face value at maturity. The carrying value of a bond with a discount increases to maturity value as the discount is amortized. The carrying value of a bond with a premium decreases to maturity value as the premium is amortized.

| FACE | FACE |
|---|---|
| + Unamortized premium | − Unamortized discount |
| Carrying value | Carrying value |

## 4.7 Bond Issuance Costs

Bond issuance costs are transaction costs incurred when bonds are issued. Examples include legal fees, accounting fees, underwriting commissions, and printing. When bonds are accounted for at amortized cost, bond issuance costs are accounted for as follows:

- Bond issuance costs are presented on the balance sheet as a direct reduction to the carrying amount of the bond, similar to bond discounts.
- When bonds are issued, the bond proceeds are recorded net of the bond issuance costs.
- Bond issuance costs are amortized as interest expense over the life of the bond using the effective interest method.

# Example 4 — Bond With Bond Issuance Costs

**Facts:** On December 31, Year 1, Kristi Corporation issued a 10 percent $1,000,000 bond due in five years. Interest is due on June 30 and December 31. The yield or market rate is 12 percent and the bond sold for $926,399. Bond issuance costs of $20,000 were incurred. The effective interest rate is 12.58 percent.

**Required:** Prepare the journal entry to record the bonds at issuance and indicate how the bonds should be reported on the December 31, Year 1, balance sheet.

**Solution:**

| | | | |
|---|---|---|---|
| DR | Cash | $906,399 | |
| DR | Discount and bond issuance costs | 93,601* | |
| CR | Bonds payable | | $1,000,000 |

*$93,601 = $73,601 discount + $20,000 bond issuance costs

The bonds would be reported as follows on the December 31, Year 1, balance sheet:

Long-term liabilities:
    Principal amount      $1,000,000
    Less: unamortized discount and bond issuance costs      93,601
    Long-term debt less unamortized discount and bond issuance costs      $ 906,399

### 4.7.1 Effective Interest Rate

The inclusion of bond issuance costs and bond discount/premium in the calculation of the carrying amount of the bond results in an effective interest rate for the bond that differs from the market rate. The effective interest rate is used to determine the interest expense for the period as the bond discount/premium and bond issuance costs are amortized. The effective interest rate must be disclosed in the footnotes.

> **Pass Key**
>
> Some CPA Exam questions may make the simplifying assumption that bond issuance costs are recognized as interest expense on a straight-line basis.

### 4.7.2 Deferred Bond Issuance Costs

Bond issuance costs incurred before the issuance of the bonds are deferred on the balance sheet until the bond liability is recorded.

| Example 5 | **Deferred Bond Issuance Costs** |

**Facts:** On November 1, Year 1, Kristi Corporation incurred bond issuance costs of $20,000 related to bonds issued on December 31, Year 1 for $926,399.

**Required:** Prepare the journal entries for Kristi to record these transactions.

**Solution:** *On November 1, Kristi Corporation recorded the following journal entry:*

| DR | Deferred bond issuance costs | $20,000 | |
| CR | Cash | | $20,000 |

*On December 31, Kristi recorded the following journal entry:*

| DR | Cash | $926,399 | |
| DR | Discount and bond issuance costs | 93,601 | |
| CR | Bonds payable | | $1,000,000 |
| CR | Deferred bond issuance costs | | 20,000 |

---

**Question 1** MCQ-00458

The market price of a bond issued at a premium is equal to the present value of its principal amount:

- a. Only, at the stated interest rate.
- b. And the present value of all future interest payments, at the stated interest rate.
- c. Only, at the market (effective) interest rate.
- d. And the present value of all future interest payments, at the market (effective) interest rate.

---

**Question 2** MCQ-00470

On January 2, Year 1, West Co. issued 9 percent bonds in the amount of $500,000, which mature on January 2, Year 11. The bonds were issued for $469,500 to yield 10 percent. Interest is payable annually on December 31. West uses the effective interest method of amortizing bond discount. In its June 30, Year 1 balance sheet, what amount should West report as bonds payable?

- a. $469,500
- b. $470,475
- c. $471,025
- d. $500,000

## NOTES

# MODULE 5: Bonds: Part 2

## 1 Bond Amortization Methods

### 1.1 Amortization Period

Under U.S. GAAP, the period over which to amortize a bond premium or discount and bond issuance costs is the period that the bonds are outstanding (i.e., from the date the bonds are sold). In general, U.S. GAAP amortization is done over the contractual life of the bond.

> **Illustration 1　Bond Amortization Period**
>
> A five-year bond dated January 1 doesn't actually sell until November 1. In this case, the period of amortization is 50 months (not 60 months).

> **U.S. GAAP VS. IFRS**
>
> Under IFRS, amortization is done over the expected life of the bond, not the contractual life of the bond.

### 1.2 Straight-Line Method

To amortize a discount, premium, or bond issuance cost using the straight-line method, simply divide the unamortized discount or premium by the number of periods the bonds are outstanding and amortize the same amount of discount or premium each period. This method of amortization results in a *constant dollar amount of interest expense* each period. The straight-line method is *not GAAP* but is allowed under U.S. GAAP if the results are not materially different from the effective interest method.

Interest expense is calculated as follows:

$$\frac{\text{Premium/discount and bond issuance cost}}{\text{Number of periods bond is outstanding}} = \text{Period amortization}$$

Interest expense = (Face value × Stated interest rate) − Premium amortization
*Or:*
+ Discount and bond issuance cost amortization

## U.S. GAAP VS. IFRS

The straight-line method is not permitted under IFRS.

### Example 1  Bond Discount Amortization: Straight-Line Method

Continuing with the Kristi Corporation example, this is an example of amortization and interest expense calculated under the straight-line method.

**Facts:** Assume that Kristi Corporation issued a 10 percent, $1,000,000 bond due in five years. The bonds were issued January 1. Interest is due on June 30 and December 31. The yield or market rate is 12 percent.

**Required:** Determine the selling price of the bond, noting the amount of discount or premium, and prepare the journal entries for borrower and investor to record the bonds at issuance and for the first interest payment.

**Solution:** $1,000,000 − $926,399 = ($73,601 ÷ 10 periods = $7,360.10)

|  |  |  | Journal Entry Impact ||
|---|---|---|---|---|
|  |  |  | Balance Sheet | Income Statement |
| Date | Net Carrying Value | Straight-Line Amortization | Interest Payment Face × Coupon | Interest Expense Cash Paid + Discount |
| 06/30/Year 1 | $ 926,399.00 | $7,360.10 | $50,000 | $57,360.10 |
| 12/31/Year 1 | 933,759.10 | 7,360.10 | 50,000 | 57,360.10 |
| 06/30/Year 2 | 941,119.20 | 7,360.10 | 50,000 | 57,360.10 |
| 12/31/Year 2 | 948,479.30 | 7,360.10 | 50,000 | 57,360.10 |
| 06/30/Year 3 | 955,839.40 | 7,360.10 | 50,000 | 57,360.10 |
| 12/31/Year 3 | 963,199.50 | 7,360.10 | 50,000 | 57,360.10 |
| 06/30/Year 4 | 970,559.60 | 7,360.10 | 50,000 | 57,360.10 |
| 12/31/Year 4 | 977,919.70 | 7,360.10 | 50,000 | 57,360.10 |
| 06/30/Year 5 | 985,279.80 | 7,360.10 | 50,000 | 57,360.10 |
| 12/31/Year 5 | 992,639.90 | 7,360.10 | 50,000 | 57,360.10 |
| 12/31/Year 5 | $1,000,000.00 |  |  |  |

*(continued)*

(continued)

| Borrower | | | | Investor | | | |
|---|---|---|---|---|---|---|---|
| *January 1, Year 1* | | | | *January 1, Year 1* | | | |
| DR | Cash | $926,399 | | DR | Investment in bonds | $926,399 | |
| DR | Discount on bond payable | 73,601 | | CR | Cash | | $926,399 |
| CR | Bond payable | | $1,000,000 | | | | |
| *June 30, Year 1* | | | | *June 30, Year 1* | | | |
| DR | Bond interest expense | $57,360.10 | | DR | Cash | $50,000.00 | |
| CR | Discount on bond payable | | $ 7,360.10 | DR | Investment in bonds | 7,360.10 | |
| CR | Cash | | 50,000.00 | CR | Bonds interest revenue | | $57,360.10 |

## Example 2 — Bond Premium Amortization: Straight-Line Method

Continuing with the Kristi Corporation example, this is an example of amortization and interest expense calculated under the straight-line method.

**Facts:** Assume that Kristi Corporation issued a 10 percent, $1,000,000 bond due in five years. The bonds were issued January 1. Interest is due on June 30 and December 31. The yield or market rate is 8 percent.

**Required:** Determine the selling price of the bond, noting the amount of discount or premium, and prepare the journal entries for borrower and investor to record the bonds at issuance and the first interest payment.

**Solution:** $1,081,109 − $1,000,000 = ($81,109 ÷ 10 periods = $8,110.90)

|  |  |  | Journal Entry Impact | |
|---|---|---|---|---|
|  |  |  | **Balance Sheet** | **Income Statement** |
| Date | Net Carrying Value | Straight-Line Amortization | Interest Payment Face × Coupon | Interest Expense Cash Paid − Premium |
| 06/30/Year 1 | $1,081,109.00 | $8,110.90 | $50,000 | $41,889.10 |
| 12/31/Year 1 | 1,072,998.10 | 8,110.90 | 50,000 | 41,889.10 |
| 06/30/Year 2 | 1,064,887.20 | 8,110.90 | 50,000 | 41,889.10 |
| 12/31/Year 2 | 1,056,776.30 | 8,110.90 | 50,000 | 41,889.10 |
| 06/30/Year 3 | 1,048,665.40 | 8,110.90 | 50,000 | 41,889.10 |
| 12/31/Year 3 | 1,040,554.50 | 8,110.90 | 50,000 | 41,889.10 |
| 06/30/Year 4 | 1,032,443.60 | 8,110.90 | 50,000 | 41,889.10 |
| 12/31/Year 4 | 1,024,332.70 | 8,110.90 | 50,000 | 41,889.10 |
| 06/30/Year 5 | 1,016,221.80 | 8,110.90 | 50,000 | 41,889.10 |
| 12/31/Year 5 | 1,008,110.90 | 8,110.90 | 50,000 | 41,889.10 |
| 12/31/Year 5 | $1,000,000.00 | | | |

(continued)

# Bonds: Part 2

## (continued)

| Borrower | | | | Investor | | | |
|---|---|---|---|---|---|---|---|
| *January 1, Year 1* | | | | *January 1, Year 1* | | | |
| DR | Cash | $1,081,109 | | DR | Investment in bonds | $1,081,109 | |
| CR | Premium on bond payable | | $ 81,109 | CR | Cash | | $1,081,109 |
| CR | Bond payable | | 1,000,000 | | | | |
| *June 30, Year 1* | | | | *June 30, Year 1* | | | |
| DR | Bond interest expense | $41,889.10 | | DR | Cash | $50,000.00 | |
| DR | Premium on bond payable | 8,110.90 | | CR | Investment in bonds | | $ 8,110.90 |
| CR | Cash | | $50,000.00 | CR | Bonds interest revenue | | 41,889.10 |

## 1.3 Effective Interest Method

Use of the effective interest method of accounting for the amortization of unamortized discounts/premiums is required by both U.S. GAAP and IFRS. Under the effective interest method, interest expense is calculated by multiplying the carrying value of the bond at the *beginning* of the period by the effective interest rate. This method of amortization results in a *constant rate* of interest each period. The difference between interest expense and the cash paid for interest is the amortization for the period of the discount or premium. Interest expense and amortization for the period is calculated as follows:

### 1.3.1 Interest Expense

$$\text{Interest expense} = \text{Carrying value at the beginning of the period} \times \text{Effective (market) interest rate}$$

### 1.3.2 Discount/Premium Amortization

$$\text{Amortization of the discount} = \text{Interest expense} - \text{Interest payment}$$

$$\text{Amortization of the premium} = \text{Interest payment} - \text{Interest expense}$$

## Pass Key

Income statement ⟶ Net carrying value × Effective interest rate = Interest expense
Balance sheet ⟶ Bond face × Coupon rate = <Interest payment>
Difference ⟶ Amortization

| Income Statement | Balance Sheet | Difference |
|---|---|---|
| Net carrying value<br>× Effective interest rate<br>Interest expense | Bond face<br>× Coupon rate<br>− Interest payment | = Amortization |

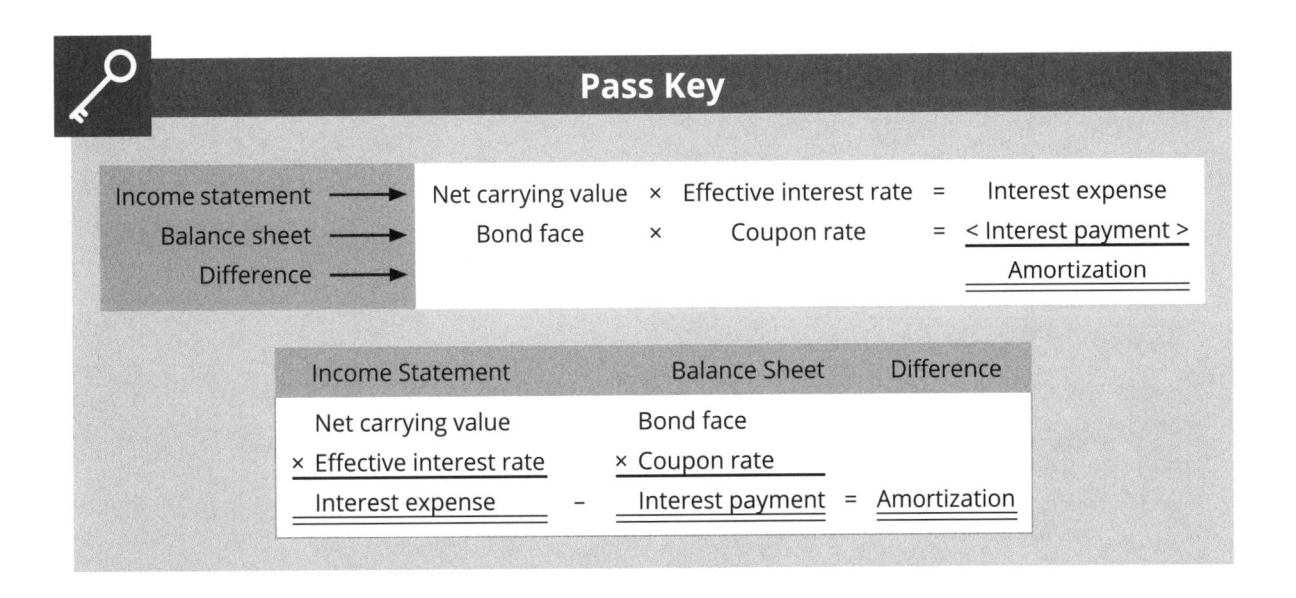

## Example 3  Bond Premium Amortization: Effective Interest Method

**Facts:** Assume that Kristi Corporation issued a 10 percent, $1,000,000 bond due in five years. The bond sold for $1,081,109 on January 1, Year 1, to yield 8 percent. Interest is paid semiannually on June 30 and December 31.

**Required:** Determine the interest expense by the effective interest method and prepare the journal entries for borrower and investor to record the bonds at issuance and for the first two interest payments. Also show the borrower's balance sheet presentation and income statement effect on the Year 1 financial statements.

**Solution:**

*Journal Entry Impact*

| Date | Beginning of Period Net Carrying Value | 4% Semiannual Amortization Interest | Interest Expense (Income Statement) N.C.V. × Effective | Interest Payment (Balance Sheet) Face × Coupon | Amortization (Difference) | End of Period Net Carrying Value |
|---|---|---|---|---|---|---|
| 06/30/Year 1 | $1,081,109 | 4% | $43,244 | $50,000 | $ 6,756 | $1,074,353 |
| 12/31/Year 1 | 1,074,353 | 4% | 42,974 | 50,000 | 7,026 | 1,067,327 |
| 06/30/Year 2 | 1,067,327 | 4% | 42,693 | 50,000 | 7,307 | 1,060,021 |
| 12/31/Year 2 | 1,060,021 | 4% | 42,401 | 50,000 | 7,599 | 1,052,421 |
| 06/30/Year 3 | 1,052,421 | 4% | 42,097 | 50,000 | 7,903 | 1,044,518 |
| 12/31/Year 3 | 1,044,518 | 4% | 41,781 | 50,000 | 8,219 | 1,036,299 |
| 06/30/Year 4 | 1,036,299 | 4% | 41,452 | 50,000 | 8,548 | 1,027,751 |
| 12/31/Year 4 | 1,027,751 | 4% | 41,110 | 50,000 | 8,890 | 1,018,861 |
| 06/30/Year 5 | 1,018,861 | 4% | 40,754 | 50,000 | 9,246 | 1,009,615 |
| 12/31/Year 5 | 1,009,615 | 4% | 40,385 | 50,000 | 9,615 | 1,000,000 |
|  |  |  |  |  | $81,109 |  |

(continued)

(continued)

| Borrower | | | | Investor | | | |
|---|---|---|---|---|---|---|---|
| *January 1, Year 1* | | | | *January 1, Year 1* | | | |
| DR | Cash | $1,081,109 | | DR | Investment in bonds | $1,081,109 | |
| CR | Premium on bonds payable | | $ 81,109 | CR | Cash | | $1,081,109 |
| CR | Bond payable | | 1,000,000 | | | | |
| *June 30, Year 1* | | | | *June 30, Year 1* | | | |
| DR | Bond interest expense | $43,244 | | DR | Cash | $50,000 | |
| DR | Premium on bonds payable | 6,756 | | CR | Investment in bonds | | $ 6,756 |
| CR | Cash | | $50,000 | CR | Bond interest revenue | | 43,244 |
| *December 31, Year 1* | | | | *December 31, Year 1* | | | |
| DR | Bond interest expense | $42,974 | | DR | Cash | $50,000 | |
| DR | Premium on bonds payable | 7,026 | | CR | Investment in bonds | | $ 7,026 |
| CR | Cash | | $50,000 | CR | Bond interest revenue | | 42,974 |

**Balance Sheet Presentation**

Carrying value of the bond at December 31, Year 1:
    Face value                              $1,000,000
  + Unamortized premium        67,327
                                                    $1,067,327

Income statement effect:
    Interest expense for Year 1 = $86,218 [43,244 + 42,974]

## Example 4    Bond Discount Amortization: Effective Interest Method

**Facts:** Assume that Kristi Corporation issued a 10 percent, $1,000,000 bond due in five years. The bond sold for $926,399 on January 1, Year 1, to yield 12 percent. Interest is paid semiannually on June 30 and December 31.

**Required:** Determine the interest expense by the effective interest method and prepare the journal entries for borrower and investor to record the bonds at issuance and for the first two interest payments. Also show the borrower's balance sheet presentation and income statement effect on the Year 1 financial statements.

(continued)

(continued)

**Solution:**

*Journal Entry Impact*

| | | **Income Statement** | **Balance Sheet** | **Difference** | |
|---|---|---|---|---|---|
| Date | Beginning of Period Net Carrying Value | 6% Semiannual Amortization Interest | Interest Expense N.C.V. × Effective | Interest Payment Face × Coupon | Amortization | End of Period Net Carrying Value |
| 06/30/Year 1 | $926,399 | 6% | $55,584 | $50,000 | $ 5,584 | $931,983 |
| 12/31/Year 1 | 931,983 | 6% | 55,919 | 50,000 | 5,919 | 937,902 |
| 06/30/Year 2 | 937,902 | 6% | 56,274 | 50,000 | 6,274 | 944,176 |
| 12/31/Year 2 | 944,176 | 6% | 56,651 | 50,000 | 6,651 | 950,827 |
| 06/30/Year 3 | 950,827 | 6% | 57,050 | 50,000 | 7,050 | 957,876 |
| 12/31/Year 3 | 957,876 | 6% | 57,473 | 50,000 | 7,473 | 965,349 |
| 06/30/Year 4 | 965,349 | 6% | 57,921 | 50,000 | 7,921 | 973,270 |
| 12/31/Year 4 | 973,270 | 6% | 58,396 | 50,000 | 8,396 | 981,666 |
| 06/30/Year 5 | 981,666 | 6% | 58,900 | 50,000 | 8,900 | 990,566 |
| 12/31/Year 5 | 990,566 | 6% | 59,434 | 50,000 | 9,434 | 1,000,000 |
| | | | | | **$73,601** | |

### Borrower

*January 1, Year 1*

| | | | |
|---|---|---|---|
| DR | Cash | $926,399 | |
| DR | Discount on bonds payable | 73,601 | |
| CR | Bond payable | | $1,000,000 |

*June 30, Year 1*

| | | | |
|---|---|---|---|
| DR | Bond interest expense | $55,584 | |
| CR | Discount on bonds payable | | $ 5,584 |
| CR | Cash | | 50,000 |

*December 31, Year 1*

| | | | |
|---|---|---|---|
| DR | Bond interest expense | $55,919 | |
| CR | Discount on bonds payable | | $ 5,919 |
| CR | Cash | | 50,000 |

### Investor

*January 1, Year 1*

| | | | |
|---|---|---|---|
| DR | Investment in bonds | $926,399 | |
| CR | Cash | | $926,399 |

*June 30, Year 1*

| | | | |
|---|---|---|---|
| DR | Cash | $50,000 | |
| DR | Investment in bonds | 5,584 | |
| CR | Bond interest revenue | | $55,584 |

*December 31, Year 1*

| | | | |
|---|---|---|---|
| DR | Cash | $50,000 | |
| DR | Investment in bonds | 5,919 | |
| CR | Bond interest revenue | | $55,919 |

### Balance Sheet Presentation

Carrying value of the bond at December 31, Year 1:

| | |
|---|---|
| Face value | $1,000,000 |
| − Unamortized discount | 62,098 |
| | $ 937,902 |

Income statement effect:
Interest expense for Year 1 = $111,503 [55,584 + 55,919]

Bonds: Part 2

## 1.3.3 Bond Amortization Including Bond Issuance Costs

### Example 5 — Bond Discount Amortization Including Bond Issuance Costs: Effective Interest Method

**Facts:** Assume that Kristi Corporation issued a 10 percent, $1,000,000 bond due in five years. The yield or market rate is 12 percent and the bond sold for $926,399. Bond issuance costs of $20,000 were incurred. The effective interest rate on this bond is 12.58 percent.

**Required:** Determine the interest expense by the effective interest method and prepare the journal entries for borrower and investor to record the bonds at issuance and for the first two interest payments. Also show the borrower's balance presentation and income statement effect on the Year 1 financial statements.

**Solution:**

*Journal Entry Impact*

| Date | Beginning of Period Net Carrying Value | 6.29% Semiannual Amortization Interest | Interest Expense (Income Statement) N.C.V. × Effective | Interest Payment (Balance Sheet) Face × Coupon | Amortization of Discount and Bond Issuance Costs (Difference) | End of Period Net Carrying Value |
|---|---|---|---|---|---|---|
| 06/30/Year 1 | $906,399 | 6.29% | $57,012 | $50,000 | $7,012 | $913,411 |
| 12/31/Year 1 | 913,411 | 6.29% | 57,454 | 50,000 | 7,454 | 920,865 |
| 06/30/Year 2 | 920,865 | 6.29% | 57,922 | 50,000 | 7,922 | 928,787 |
| 12/31/Year 2 | 928,787 | 6.29% | 58,421 | 50,000 | 8,421 | 937,208 |
| 06/30/Year 3 | 937,208 | 6.29% | 58,950 | 50,000 | 8,950 | 946,159 |
| 12/31/Year 3 | 946,159 | 6.29% | 59,513 | 50,000 | 9,513 | 955,672 |
| 06/30/Year 4 | 955,672 | 6.29% | 60,112 | 50,000 | 10,112 | 965,784 |
| 12/31/Year 4 | 965,784 | 6.29% | 60,748 | 50,000 | 10,748 | 976,532 |
| 06/30/Year 5 | 976,532 | 6.29% | 61,424 | 50,000 | 11,424 | 987,955 |
| 12/31/Year 5 | 987,955 | 6.29% | 62,045* | 50,000 | 12,045 | 1,000,000 |

*This amount is adjusted for rounding.

(continued)

(continued)

| Borrower | | | | Investor* | | | |
|---|---|---|---|---|---|---|---|
| *January 1, Year 1* | | | | *January 1, Year 1* | | | |
| DR | Cash | $906,399 | | DR | Investment in bonds | $926,399 | |
| DR | Discount and bond issuance costs | 93,601 | | CR | Cash | | $926,399 |
| CR | Bond payable | | $1,000,000 | | | | |
| *June 30, Year 1* | | | | *June 30, Year 1* | | | |
| DR | Bond interest expense | $57,012 | | DR | Cash | $50,000 | |
| CR | Discount and bond issuance costs | | $ 7,012 | DR | Investment in bonds | 5,584 | |
| CR | Cash | | 50,000 | CR | Bond interest revenue | | $55,584 |
| *December 31, Year 1* | | | | *December 31, Year 1* | | | |
| DR | Bond interest expense | $57,454 | | DR | Cash | $50,000 | |
| CR | Discount and bond issuance costs | | $ 7,454 | DR | Investment in bonds | 5,919 | |
| CR | Cash | | 50,000 | CR | Bond interest revenue | | $55,919 |

*Note that the investor accounting is not affected by the bond issuance costs.

**Balance Sheet Presentation**

Carrying value of the bond at December 31, Year 1:
 Face value $1,000,000
 − Unamortized discount 79,135
 $ 920,865

Income statement effect:
 Interest expense for Year 1 = $114,466 [57,012 + 57,454]

# 2 Bonds Issued Between Interest Dates

Interest payments on bonds are generally made semiannually. However, bonds are usually sold between interest dates, which requires additional entries for accrued interest at the time of sale. The amount of interest that has accrued since the last interest payment is added to the price of the bond. The purchaser pays such interest and is reimbursed at the next payment date on receipt of a full period's interest.

### Example 6 — Bonds Issued Between Interest Dates

**Facts:** On April 1, Year 1, Kristi Corporation issued 10 percent bonds dated January 1, Year 1, in the face amount of $1,000,000. Interest is due on June 30 and December 31. The bonds were issued for $926,399, plus accrued interest for three months (January through March).

**Required:** Determine the cash received and prepare the journal entries to record the sale of the bonds and the first interest payment.

**Solution:**

| | |
|---|---:|
| Selling price ($1,000,000 face) | $926,399 |
| Plus: Accrued interest ($1,000,000 × 10% × 3/12) | 25,000 |
| Total cash received | $951,399 |

*Journal entry to record the sale on April 1:*

| | | | |
|---|---|---:|---:|
| DR | Cash | $951,399 | |
| DR | Discount on bonds payable | 73,601 | |
| CR | Bonds payable | | $1,000,000 |
| CR | Bond interest expense (or payable) | | 25,000 |

*Journal entry to record the first interest payment on June 30 ($1,000,000 × 10% × 6/12):*

| | | | |
|---|---|---:|---:|
| DR | Bond interest expense (or payable) | $50,000 | |
| CR | Cash | | $50,000 |

The interest expense account would then contain a debit balance of $25,000, the proper amount of interest expense for three months at 10% ($1,000,000 × 10% × 3/12 = $25,000).

*Journal entry to record amortization should also be recorded.

# 3 Year-End Bond Interest Accrual

When the date of a scheduled interest payment and the issuer's year-end do not agree, it is necessary to accrue interest by an adjusting entry on the issuer's books at year-end. The accrual must take into account a prorated share of discount or premium amortization.

### Example 7 — Year-End Bond Interest Accrual

**Facts:** Kristi Corporation, whose year-end is December 31, issued $1,000,000 of five-year, 10 percent bonds with interest payable on July 1 and January 1. The bonds sold at a discount for $926,399.

**Required:** Calculate the amount of the year-end accrual for interest and discount amortization and prepare the journal entry to record the accrued interest at year-end.

**Solution:**

Year-end adjustment:

Interest payable
Face value × Coupon rate × Period = $1,000,000 × 10% × 6/12 = $50,000
Amortization (per prior schedule)       5,919

Journal entry on December 31, Year 1:

*To record interest accrual and discount amortization from July 1, Year 1–December 31, Year 1:*

| | | | |
|---|---|---|---|
| DR | Interest expense | $55,919 | |
| CR | Interest payable | | $50,000 |
| CR | Discount on bonds payable | | 5,919 |

# 4 Disclosure Requirements

Companies with many debt issues often report only one balance sheet total, which is supported by comments and schedules in the accompanying notes. Notes often show details regarding the liability maturity dates, interest rates, call and conversion privileges, assets pledged as security, and borrower-imposed restrictions.

## Question 1 — MCQ-00463

On July 1, Year 1, Eagle Corp. issued 600 of its 10 percent, $1,000 bonds at 99 plus accrued interest. The bonds are dated April 1, Year 1 and mature on April 1, Year 11. Interest is payable semiannually on April 1 and October 1. What amount did Eagle receive from the bond issuance?

- a. $579,000
- b. $594,000
- c. $600,000
- d. $609,000

## Question 2 — MCQ-00477

On January 31, Year 2, Beau Corp. issued $300,000 maturity value, 12 percent bonds for $300,000 cash. The bonds are dated December 31, Year 1, and mature on December 31, Year 11. Interest will be paid semiannually on June 30 and December 31. What amount of accrued interest payable should Beau report in its September 30, Year 2, balance sheet?

- a. $27,000
- b. $24,000
- c. $18,000
- d. $9,000

# MODULE 6
# Troubled Debt Restructuring and Extinguishment

**FAR 5**

## 1 Troubled Debt Restructuring

A troubled debt restructuring is one in which the creditor allows the debtor certain concessions to improve the likelihood of collection that would not be considered under normal circumstances. Concessions include items such as reduced interest rates, extension of maturity dates, reduction of the face amount of the debt, and reduction of the amount of accrued interest. The concessions must be made in light of the debtor's financial difficulty, and the objective of the creditor must be to maximize recovery of the investment. Troubled debt restructurings are often the result of legal proceedings or of negotiation between parties.

### 1.1 Accounting and Reporting by Debtors

A debtor accounts for a troubled debt restructuring according to the type, as follows:

#### 1.1.1 Transfer of Assets

The debtor will recognize a gain in the amount of the excess of the carrying amount of the payable (face amount of the payable plus accrued interest, premiums, etc.) over the fair value of the assets given up. The gain or loss on disposition of the asset (i.e., difference between book value and fair value) is reported in income of the period.

- **Recognize Gain/Loss**

    FV asset transferred
    < NBV asset transferred >
    ─────────────────────
    Gain/loss

- **Recognize Gain**

    Carrying amount of the payable
    < FV asset transferred >
    ─────────────────────
    Gain

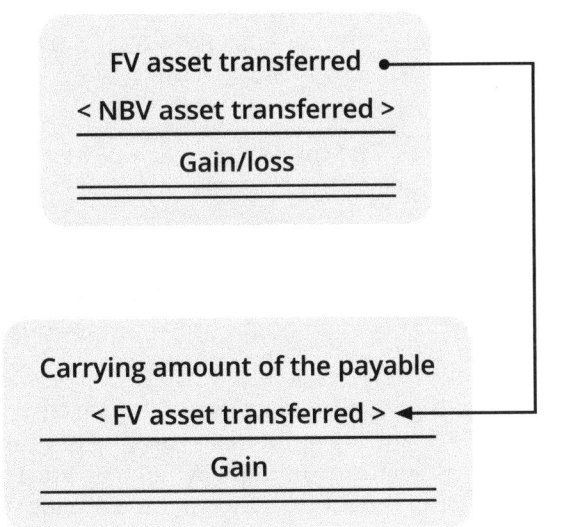

#### 1.1.2 Transfer of Equity Interest

The difference between the carrying amount of the payable and the fair value of the equity interest is recognized as a gain (gain on restructuring of debt) under U.S. GAAP.

- **Recognize Gain**

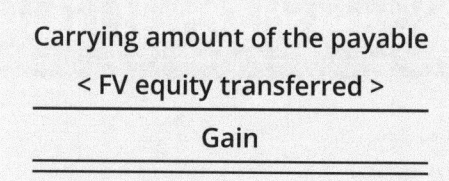

> Carrying amount of the payable
> < FV equity transferred >
> ─────────────────────────
> Gain

### Pass Key

Whether transfer of assets or transfer of equity interest, once the transfer has taken place, the debt has been extinguished.

## 1.1.3 Modification of Terms

A restructuring that does not involve the transfer of assets or equity will often involve the modification of the terms of the debt. In a modification, the debtor usually accounts for the effects of the restructuring prospectively. The debtor does not change the carrying amount unless the carrying amount exceeds the total future cash payments specified by the new terms.

### Pass Key

Under a modification of terms, the debt has not been extinguished; the terms have been adjusted so that the debtor has a greater ability to fulfill its obligation.

- **Total Future Cash Payments:** The total future cash payments are the principal and any accrued interest at the time of the restructuring that continues to be payable by the new terms.

- **Interest Expense:** Interest expense is computed by a method that causes a constant effective rate (e.g., the effective interest method). The new effective rate of interest is the discount rate at which the carrying amount of the debt is equal to the present value of the future cash payments.

- **Future Payments:** When the total (undiscounted) future cash payments are less than the carrying amount, the debtor should reduce the carrying amount accordingly and recognize the difference as a gain restructuring of debt. When there are several related accounts (discount, premium, etc.), the reduction may need to be allocated among them. All cash payments after the restructuring reduce the carrying amount, and no interest expense is recognized after the date of restructure.

    When there are indeterminate future payments, or any time the future payments might exceed the carrying amount, the debtor recognizes no gain and does not adjust the carrying value of the note. When there are indeterminate future payments, the debtor should assume that the future contingent payments will have to be made at least to the extent necessary to obviate any gain.

### 1.1.4 Combination of Type

When a restructuring involves a combination of asset or equity transfers and modification of terms, the fair value of any asset or equity is used first to reduce the carrying amount of the payable. The difference between the fair value and the carrying amount of any assets transferred is recognized as gain or loss. No gain on restructuring can be recognized unless the carrying amount of the payable exceeds the total future cash payments.

All gains on debt restructuring are aggregated and included in net income for the period. They are treated and classified along with other gains of the company, typically in the continuing operations section of the income statement.

## 1.2 Accounting and Reporting by Creditors

### 1.2.1 Recognition of Impairment

A loan is considered impaired if it is probable (likely to occur) that the creditor will be unable to collect all amounts due under the original contract when due. Normal loan procedures should be used to judge whether a loan is impaired. A loan restructured in a troubled debt restructuring is an impaired loan.

### 1.2.2 Measurement of Impairment

- **Receipt of Assets or Equity:** When the creditor receives either assets or equity as full settlement of a receivable, these are accounted for at their fair value at the time of the restructuring. The fair value of the receivable satisfied can be used if it is more clearly determinable than the fair value of the asset or equity acquired. In a partial payment, the creditor must use the fair value of the asset or equity received.

  The excess of the recorded receivable over the fair value of the asset received is recognized as a loss. The creditor accounts for these assets as if they were acquired for cash.

- **Modification of Terms (Use Present Value):** Impairment should be measured based on the loan's present value of expected future cash flows discounted at the loan's historical effective interest rate. The observable market rate can be used if more readily available. Likewise, the fair value of the collateral can be used if the loan is collateral dependent. Any costs to sell should be estimated and should reduce the cash flows.

  The impairment is recorded by creating a valuation allowance with a corresponding charge to bad debt expense:

  | DR | Bad debt expense | $XXX | |
  |----|------------------|------|------|
  | CR | Allowance for credit losses | | $XXX |

## Example 1 — Transfer of Assets

**Facts:** Hull Company is indebted to Apex under a $500,000, 12 percent, three-year note dated December 31, Year 1. Because of Hull's financial difficulties developing in Year 3, Hull owed accrued interest of $60,000 on December 31, Year 3. Under a troubled debt restructuring, on December 31, Year 3, Apex agreed to settle the note and accrued interest for a tract of land having a fair value of $450,000. Hull's acquisition cost of the land is $360,000.

**Required:**

1. Calculate the gain recognized by Hull on the troubled debt restructuring.
2. Prepare the journal entry to record the transaction on Hull's books.
3. Prepare the journal entry to record the transaction on Apex's books.

**Solution:**

1. Hull's total debt is the $500,000 face value of the note plus $60,000 of accrued interest, or $560,000.

The debt was forgiven in exchange for Hull giving Apex (the lender) land worth $450,000, with a cost to Hull of $360,000.

*Hull's total gain is:*

| | |
|---|---:|
| Debt forgiven | $560,000 |
| Carrying value of asset given | (360,000) |
| Total gain | $200,000 ($90,000 + $110,000, per below) |

*Breakout of gain*

Gain on disposal of land (adjustment to fair value)

| | |
|---|---:|
| Fair value of land | $ 450,000 |
| Acquisition cost | (360,000) |
| Holding gain on sale of land | $ 90,000 |

*Gain on restructuring*

| | |
|---|---:|
| Three-year note | $500,000 |
| Accrued interest | 60,000 |
| Amount owed | 560,000 |
| Settlement amount (fair value of land) | (450,000) |
| Gain on restructuring of debt | $ 110,000 |

2. *Journal entry to record the troubled debt restructuring on the books of Hull:*

| | | | |
|---|---|---:|---:|
| DR | Notes payable | $500,000 | |
| DR | Interest payable | 60,000 | |
| CR | Land | | $360,000 |
| CR | Gain on disposal of land | | 90,000 |
| CR | Gain on restructuring | | 110,000 |

(continued)

(continued)

3. *Journal entry to record the troubled debt restructuring on the books of Apex:*

| | | | |
|---|---|---|---|
| DR | Land | $450,000 | |
| DR | Allowance for credit losses | 110,000 | |
| CR | Note receivable | | $500,000 |
| CR | Interest receivable | | 60,000 |

## Example 2 — Transfer of Equity

**Facts:** The same facts as in the previous example, except that on December 31, Year 3, Apex agreed to settle the note and accrued interest for an equity interest in Hull Company having a fair value of $450,000 (100,000 shares of common stock with a market value of $4.50/share and a par value of $2.00/share).

**Required:**

1. Calculate the gain recognized by Hull on the troubled debt restructuring.
2. Prepare the journal entry to record the transaction on Hull's books.
3. Prepare the journal entry to record the transaction on Apex's books.

**Solution:**

1. Hull's total debt is the $500,000 face value of the note plus $60,000 of accrued interest, or $560,000.

The debt was forgiven in exchange for Hull giving Apex (the lender) equity worth $450,000.

*Gain on restructuring:*

| | |
|---|---|
| Carrying amount of payable | $560,000 |
| Settlement amount (fair value of equity) | (450,000) |
| Gain on restructuring of debt | $110,000 |

2. *Journal entry to record the troubled debt restructuring on the books of Hull:*

| | | | |
|---|---|---|---|
| DR | Notes payable | $500,000 | |
| DR | Interest payable | 60,000 | |
| CR | Common stock | | $200,000 |
| CR | Additional paid-in capital | | 250,000 |
| CR | Gain on restructuring | | 110,000 |

3. *Journal entry to record the troubled debt restructuring on the books of Apex:*

| | | | |
|---|---|---|---|
| DR | Equity investments | $450,000 | |
| DR | Allowance for credit losses | 110,000 | |
| CR | Note receivable | | $500,000 |
| CR | Interest receivable | | 60,000 |

# Troubled Debt Restructuring and Extinguishment

## Example 3 — Modification of Terms

**Facts:** The same facts as in the previous example, except that on December 31, Year 3, Apex agreed to modify the terms of the debt. The accrued interest was forgiven, the interest rate was lowered to 3 percent, and the maturity date was extended to December 31, Year 5.

**Required:**

1. Indicate how Hull should report the troubled debt restructuring on its Year 3 income statement.
2. Prepare the journal entry to record the transaction on Hull's books.
3. Prepare the journal entry to record the transaction on Apex's books.

**Solution:**

1. Hull's total debt is the $500,000 face value of the note plus $60,000 of accrued interest, or $560,000.

*Total future cash payments under modified terms:*

| | |
|---|---|
| Face amount of note | $500,000 |
| Year 4 interest | 15,000 = $500,000 × 3% |
| Year 5 interest | 15,000 = $500,000 × 3% |
| Total | $530,000 |

*Gain on restructuring:*

| | |
|---|---|
| Carrying amount of payable | $560,000 |
| Total future cash payments | (530,000) |
| Gain on restructuring of debt | $ 30,000 |

2. *Journal entry to record the troubled debt restructuring on the books of Hull:*

| | | | |
|---|---|---|---|
| DR | Notes payable | $500,000 | |
| DR | Interest payable | 60,000 | |
| CR |    Note payable | | $530,000* |
| CR |    Gain on restructuring | | 30,000 |

*All future payments (principal and interest) will reduce the note payable.

3. *Journal entry to record the troubled debt restructuring on the books of Apex:*

| | | | |
|---|---|---|---|
| DR | Bad debt expense | $136,050 | |
| CR |    Allowance for credit losses | | $136,050* |

*This amount is calculated as the difference between the pre-restructured note balance and the present value of future cash flows ($500,000 and two interest payments of $15,000) discounted at the loan's historical rate of 12 percent.

| | |
|---|---|
| Pre-restructure carrying amount | $ 560,000 |
| Present value of restructured cash flows | $(423,950) |
| Creditor's loss on restructuring | $ 136,050 |

(continued)

(continued)

The present value of restructured cash flows is calculated as follows:

Present value of $500,000 due in two years at 12 percent = 0.7972 × $500,000 = $398,600

Present value of $15,000 interest payable annually for two years at 12 percent = 1.6900 × $15,000 = $25,350

Present value of restructured cash flows = $398,600 + $25,350 = $423,950

# 2 Extinguishment of Debt

Corporations issuing bonds may call or retire them prior to maturity. Callable bonds can be retired after a certain date at a stated price. Refundable bonds allow an existing issue to be retired and replaced with a new issue at a lower interest rate.

## 2.1 Definition of Extinguishment

A liability cannot be derecognized in the financial statements until it has been extinguished. A liability is considered extinguished if the debtor pays or the debtor is legally released.

### 2.1.1 Debtor Pays

A liability is considered extinguished if the debtor pays the creditor and is relieved of its obligation for the liability.

- **Bond Extinguishment at Maturity**

    If a bond is paid at maturity, the carrying value of the bond is equal to the face amount of the bond and no gain or loss is recorded:

    *Journal entry retirement at maturity of a bond issued for $1,081,109 with a face value of $1,000,000. The premium has been fully amortized by maturity.*

    | | | | |
    |---|---|---|---|
    | DR | Bonds payable | $1,000,000 | |
    | CR | Cash | | $1,000,000 |

- **Bond Extinguished Before Maturity**

    If a bond is extinguished before maturity, a gain or loss is generally recorded. The gain or loss is the difference between the carrying value of the bond (Face value less Unamortized discount *or* plus Unamortized premium) and the cash paid to extinguish the bond.

### 2.1.2 Debtor Legally Released

A liability is considered extinguished if the debtor is legally released from being the primary obligor under the liability, either judicially or by the creditor. A troubled debt restructuring would result in the extinguishment of debt only if the debt were forgiven by the creditor as the result of a transfer of assets or the transfer of equity interest. A modification of terms is not extinguishment.

## 2.2 In-Substance Defeasance Not Extinguishment

An in-substance defeasance is an arrangement in which a company places purchased securities into an irrevocable trust and pledges them for the future principal and interest payments on its long-term debt. Because the company remains the primary obligor while there is outstanding debt, the liability is not considered extinguished by an in-substance defeasance.

## 2.3 Gain or Loss on Bond Extinguishment Before Maturity

### 2.3.1 Adjust Items in the Financial Statements

In any bond reacquisition, the following items must be accounted for and adjusted in the financial statements:

- Any related unamortized bond issuance costs;
- Any related unamortized discount or premium; and
- The difference between the bond's face value and the reacquisition proceeds.

### 2.3.2 Calculation of the Gain or Loss

Gain or loss on extinguishment of debt is the difference between the reacquisition price and the net carrying amount of the bond at the date of extinguishment. Any gain or loss on extinguishment of debt is recognized as income from continuing operations (gross of tax) in the income statement.

$$\text{(Gain) or loss} = \text{Reacquisition price} - \text{Net carrying amount}$$

- **Reacquisition Price**

    Reacquisition price is usually shown as a percentage of the bond's face value (e.g., $100,000 at 102 or $100,000 at 95). To calculate the reacquisition price, multiply the percentage by the face value (e.g., $100,000 × 102% = $102,000 or $100,000 × 95% = $95,000).

- **Net Carrying Amount**

    The net carrying amount of the bond is the carrying value (i.e., face value of the bond plus unamortized premium or minus unamortized discount and minus unamortized bond issuance costs).

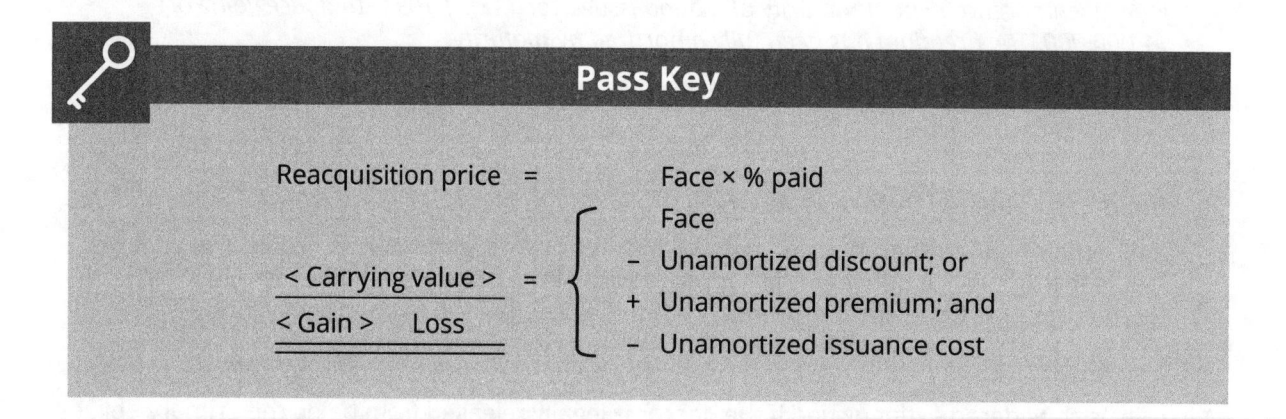

> **Pass Key**
>
> Reacquisition price = Face × % paid
>
> < Carrying value > = Face
> − Unamortized discount; or
> + Unamortized premium; and
> − Unamortized issuance cost
>
> < Gain >   Loss

## Example 4 — Loss on Extinguishment of Bonds

**Facts:** Assume that $1,000,000 bonds due in five years were issued on January 1, Year 1, at a discount for $926,399. Bond issuance costs of $20,000 were incurred. Two years later, on January 1, Year 3, the entire issue is redeemed at 101 and canceled (ignore income tax considerations). On this date, unamortized discount and bond issuance costs totaled $62,792.

**Required:** Calculate the gain or loss recorded when the bonds are extinguished and record the journal entry.

**Solution:**

Reacquisition price:
Face × % paid ($1,000,000 × 101) .................................................... $1,010,000

Bond carrying value:
Face .................................................................... $1,000,000
Less: unamortized discount and bond issuance costs .... (62,792)
Net carrying value .................................................................... (937,208)
Total loss on extinguishment .................................................. $ 72,792

*Components of the loss are:*
Unamortized bond discount and bond issuance costs ..... $ 62,792
Premium paid to retire ($1,000,000 × 1%) ...................... 10,000
Total loss .................................................................... $ 72,792

*Journal entry:*

| | | | |
|---|---|---|---|
| DR | Bonds payable | $1,000,000 | |
| DR | Loss on extinguishment of bonds | 72,792 | |
| CR | Discount on bonds payable and bond issuance costs | | $ 62,792 |
| CR | Cash | | 1,010,000 |

# Example 5: Gain on Extinguishment of Bonds

**Facts:** Assume that $1,000,000 bonds due in five years are issued on January 1, Year 1, at a premium for $1,081,109. The entire issue is redeemed two years later, on January 1, Year 3, for 96 and canceled. (Ignore income tax considerations.) On this date, unamortized premium totaled $52,421.

**Required:** Calculate the gain or loss recorded when the bonds are extinguished and record the journal entry.

**Solution:**

Reacquisition price:
    Face × % paid ($1,000,000 × 96)      $ 960,000

Bond carrying value:
    Face      $1,000,000
    *Plus*: unamortized premium      52,421
    Net carrying value      (1,052,421)
    Total gain on extinguishment      $ (92,421)

*Components of the gain are:*

    Unamortized bond premium      $ 52,421
    Discount to retire ($1,000,000 × 4%)      40,000
    Total gain      $ 92,421

*Journal entry:*

| | | | |
|---|---|---|---|
| DR | Bonds payable | $1,000,000 | |
| DR | Premium on bond payable | 52,421 | |
| CR | Cash | | $ 960,000 |
| CR | Gain on extinguishment of bonds | | 92,421 |

## Question 1 — MCQ-00476

On March 1, Year 1, Somar Co. issued 20-year bonds at a discount. By September 1, Year 6, the bonds were quoted at 106 when Somar exercised its right to retire the bonds at 105. The amount is material and considered to be unusual in nature and infrequently occurring with respect to Somar Co. How should Somar report the bond retirement on its Year 6 income statement under U.S. GAAP?

- a. A gain in continuing operations.
- b. A loss in continuing operations.
- c. A gain in other comprehensive income.
- d. A loss in other comprehensive income.

## Question 2 — MCQ-00471

On July 31, Year 1, Dome Co. issued $1,000,000 of 10 percent, 15-year bonds at par and (as a typical risk-management strategy to Dome Co.) used a portion of the proceeds to call its 600 outstanding 11 percent, $1,000 face value bonds, due on July 31, Year 11, at 102. On that date, unamortized bond premium relating to the 11 percent bonds was $65,000. In its Year 1 income statement, what amount should Dome report as gain or loss from retirement of bonds?

- a. $53,000 gain
- b. $0
- c. $(65,000) loss
- d. $(77,000) loss

# NOTES

# FAR 6

# Leases, Derivatives, Foreign Currency Accounting, and Income Taxes

## Module

| | | |
|---|---|---|
| 1 | Leases: Part 1 | 3 |
| 2 | Leases: Part 2 | 17 |
| 3 | Derivatives and Hedge Accounting | 31 |
| 4 | Foreign Currency Accounting | 43 |
| 5 | Income Taxes: Part 1 | 53 |
| 6 | Income Taxes: Part 2 | 65 |

# NOTES

# MODULE 1

# Leases: Part 1

FAR 6

## 1 Overview

### 1.1 Definitions

Leases are used by public and private entities as a means of gaining access to assets and reducing their exposure to the full risks of asset ownership. A lease is defined as a contractual agreement between a *lessor* who conveys the right to use real or personal property (an asset) and a *lessee* who agrees to pay consideration for this right over a specific period of time. In order for a contract to be a lease or contain a lease, *both* of the criteria below must be met.

- The contract must depend on an identifiable asset in which the lessor does not have a substantive substitution right.

- The contract must convey the right to control the use of the asset over the lease term to the lessee. The lessee will have the right to obtain substantially all of the economic benefits from using the asset and have the right to direct its use.

> **Illustration 1    Definition of a Lease**
>
> Bentley Corp. has a written agreement in place to allow Riggs Inc. to use scientific equipment with a book value of $75,000 for the next five years. Bentley has the right to replace the equipment with a comparable piece of equipment during the term, but Riggs is able to use the asset as it wishes for the next five years while keeping any cash inflows associated with outputs from the equipment.
>
> This is an example of a lease, as there is a contract in place that defines the asset itself, recognizes Bentley's right to substitute the asset, and provides Riggs with the economic benefits of and direction for the use of the asset.

## 2 Lease Contracts

### 2.1 Lease vs. Nonlease Components

The decision as to whether a contract is a lease or contains a lease must be made at contract inception, and only may be reassessed if the terms and conditions of the contract change. As noted earlier, for a contract or a portion of a contract to be considered a lease, the contract must include an identified asset and must convey the right to control this asset.

Once the determination is made that the contract is or contains a lease, the lessee must:

- assess whether multiple contracts should be combined;
- identify the separate lease components within a given contract (or combined contracts); and
- if applicable, determine whether separate lease components within the contract should be combined or separated from any related nonlease components.

### 2.1.1 Combining Contracts

For accounting purposes, contracts should be combined if they meet *all* of the following criteria.

- One or more contracts contains or is a lease.
- The contracts are entered into at approximately the same time.
- The parties to the contract are the same, or are related parties.
- One or more of the following:
  - Performance or price of one contract affects the consideration paid in the other contract(s).
  - The contracts have the same commercial objectives and were negotiated as part of a package.
  - Regarding the use of underlying assets, the rights to use them do not meet the accounting criteria for separate lease components (thereby resulting in a single lease component).

### 2.1.2 Separate Lease Components

Accounting for separate lease components from a lessee perspective is a two-step process.

**Step 1: Identify each right to use an underlying asset within the contract.**

- One right to use an asset = One separate lease component.
- More than one right to use an asset = Lessee must determine whether each right equates to a separate lease component for accounting purposes.
  - Separate if *both* are met:
    - The right benefits the lessee either on a stand-alone basis or together with other resources that are readily available to the lessee.
    - Rights are neither highly dependent on each other nor highly interrelated.

*Note: The right to use land should be accounted for as a separate lease component unless the accounting effect of doing so would be insignificant.*

**Step 2: For a contract that includes both lease and nonlease components, the lessee has two options:**

| Option 1 | Option 2 |
|---|---|
| Lease components are separate units of account from nonlease components. | Each separate lease component is combined with related nonlease components into one unit of account. |

## 2.2 Contract Allocations

Consideration associated with a contract is calculated as:

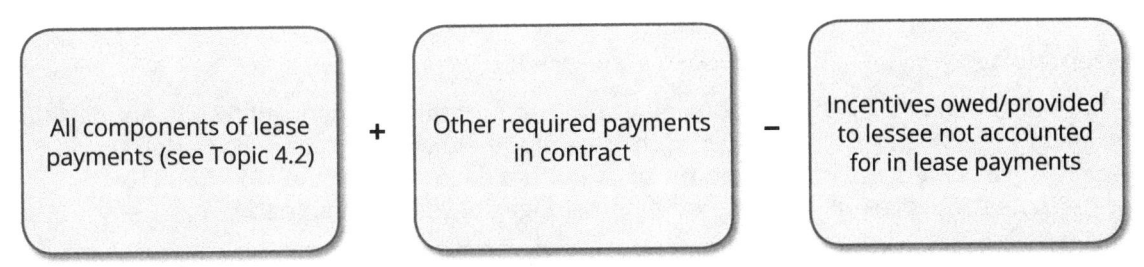

All components of lease payments (see Topic 4.2) **+** Other required payments in contract **−** Incentives owed/provided to lessee not accounted for in lease payments

If Option 1 described above is chosen, contract consideration can be allocated to the separate lease and nonlease components based on relative stand-alone prices. If Option 2 above is chosen, contract consideration will be allocated to each combined unit of account based on relative stand-alone prices. Observable stand-alone prices are the preference, but if those are not available, estimated prices may be used.

### Example 1 Combining Contracts

**Facts:** Fast Science leases two electron microscopes to a university for four years each. Microscope FE is leased for monthly payments of $7,750 and comes with maintenance services. Microscope SQ is leased for monthly payments of $8,600 and also comes with maintenance services. Stand-alone prices for each unit are listed below, with price differentials reflecting the difference in microscope power offered at two distinct university locations.

| Unit | Stand-alone Price |
|---|---|
| Microscope FE | $400,000 |
| Microscope SQ | $450,000 |
| Maintenance, FE | $ 30,000 |
| Maintenance, SQ | $ 35,000 |
|  | **$915,000** |

The university will not pay maintenance fees for the microscopes outside of the agreed upon monthly payments noted above.

**Required:** Calculate the consideration allocation under a scenario in which (1) the lease and nonlease components are treated separately; and (2) the lease and related nonlease components are combined into a single unit of account.

(continued)

(continued)

**Solution:**

**Scenario 1:**

The consideration total of $784,800 equals the two monthly payments of $7,750 and $8,600 (total of $16,350) multiplied by 48 months. The stand-alone prices are used to determine the relative percentage values, and those values are each multiplied by $784,800 to determine the allocation. (Note that the percentages have been rounded.)

| Unit | Stand-alone Price | Relative Value—Stand-alone Price | Consideration Allocation |
|---|---|---|---|
| Microscope FE | $400,000 | 44% | $345,312 |
| Microscope SQ | $450,000 | 49% | $384,552 |
| Maintenance, FE | $ 30,000 | 3% | $ 23,544 |
| Maintenance, SQ | $ 35,000 | 4% | $ 31,392 |
|  | **$915,000** | **100%** | **$784,800** |

**Scenario 2:**

The same logic is applied here that was applied in Scenario 1, except the microscope and the related maintenance are combined for each individual microscope.

| Unit | Stand-alone Price | Relative Value—Stand-alone Price | Consideration Allocation |
|---|---|---|---|
| FE: Microscope and Maintenance | $430,000 | 47% | $368,856 |
| SQ: Microscope and Maintenance | $485,000 | 53% | $415,944 |
|  | **$915,000** | **100%** | **$784,800** |

# 3 Lease Classification as Operating or Finance

Leases transfer substantially all of the benefits and risks inherent in ownership of property to the lessee.

- This is an accounting transaction, which is in substance an installment purchase in the form of a leasing arrangement.

- The lessee accounts for a lease as either an operating or a finance lease, reflective of the acquisition of both an asset and a related liability.

- The lessor accounts for the lease as either an operating lease, sales-type lease, or direct financing lease.

Based on the criteria described in Topic 3.1, a lease will be considered either an operating or a finance lease. Within the finance lease category, two types, sales-type and direct financing, are applicable to lessors.

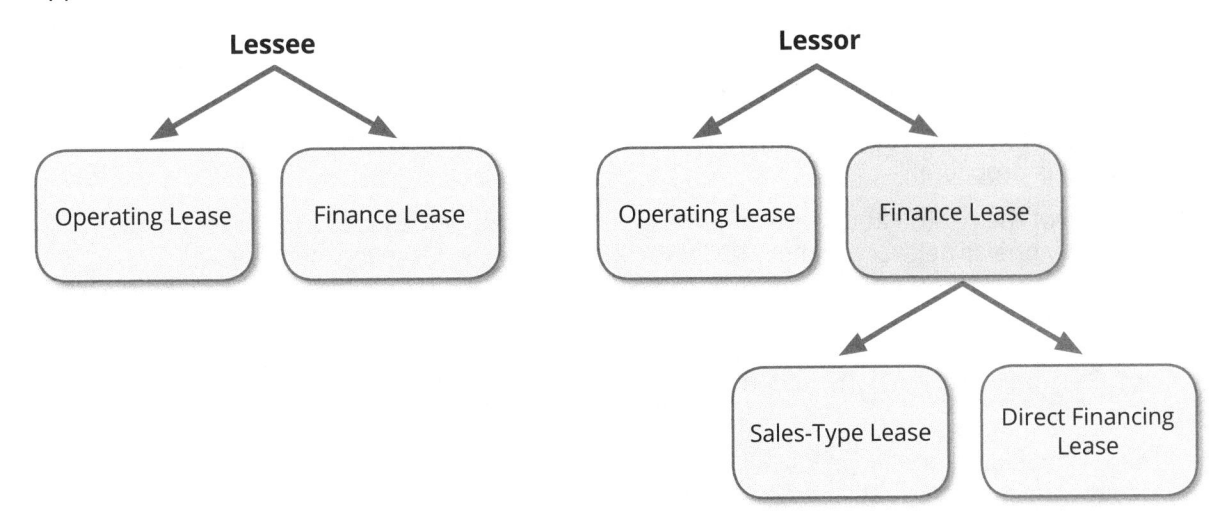

```
                Lessee                                      Lessor
               ↙     ↘                                    ↙        ↘
    Operating Lease   Finance Lease            Operating Lease   Finance Lease
                                                                   ↙       ↘
                                                        Sales-Type Lease   Direct Financing
                                                                                Lease
```

> **Pass Key**
>
> IFRS uses a single model in which lessees only record finance leases; operating leases are not applicable for lessees. Lessors can recognize operating and finance leases.

## 3.1 Criteria

At the onset of a lease, both parties (lessee and lessor) must determine whether the lease will be classified as an operating lease or a finance lease. The assessment, based on a defined set of criteria, shown below, will focus on whether the lessee will in effect assume control of the underlying asset.

The criteria below are applicable to lessors and lessees. If any one of the five criteria is met, the lease will be classified as a sales-type lease by the lessor and a finance lease by the lessee.

- **Ownership** of the underlying asset transfers from the lessor to the lessee by the end of the lease term.
- The lessee has the **written option** to purchase the underlying asset; the option is one that the lessee is "reasonably certain" to exercise.
- The **net present** value of all lease payments and any guaranteed residual value is equal to or substantially exceeds the underlying asset's fair value.
- The term of the lease represents the major part of the **economic life** remaining for the underlying asset.
- The asset is **specialized** such that it will not have an expected, alternative use to the lessor when the lease term ends.

If none of the above criteria are met, or if the lease is considered short term (less than 12 months), it should be treated as an operating lease by the lessee. For the lessor, if none of the criteria above are met, the classification will depend on whether *both* of the following criteria are met.

- **Present** value of the sum of the lease payments, lessee guaranteed residual value not included in the lease payments, and any third-party guaranteed residual value is equal to or substantially exceeds the underlying asset's fair value.
- **Collection** of the lease payments and any amounts necessary to satisfy residual value guarantees is probable.

When both of the criteria above are met, the lessor will classify the lease as a direct financing lease. If only one or neither are met, the lessor will classify the lease as operating.

### Pass Key

There is no explicit guidance in IFRS regarding the collectibility of lease payments and amounts necessary to satisfy a residual value guarantee.

### 3.2 Lessee Decision Tree

In applying the **OWNES** criteria to determine whether a lease should be treated as a finance or an operating lease, the following tree can be used:

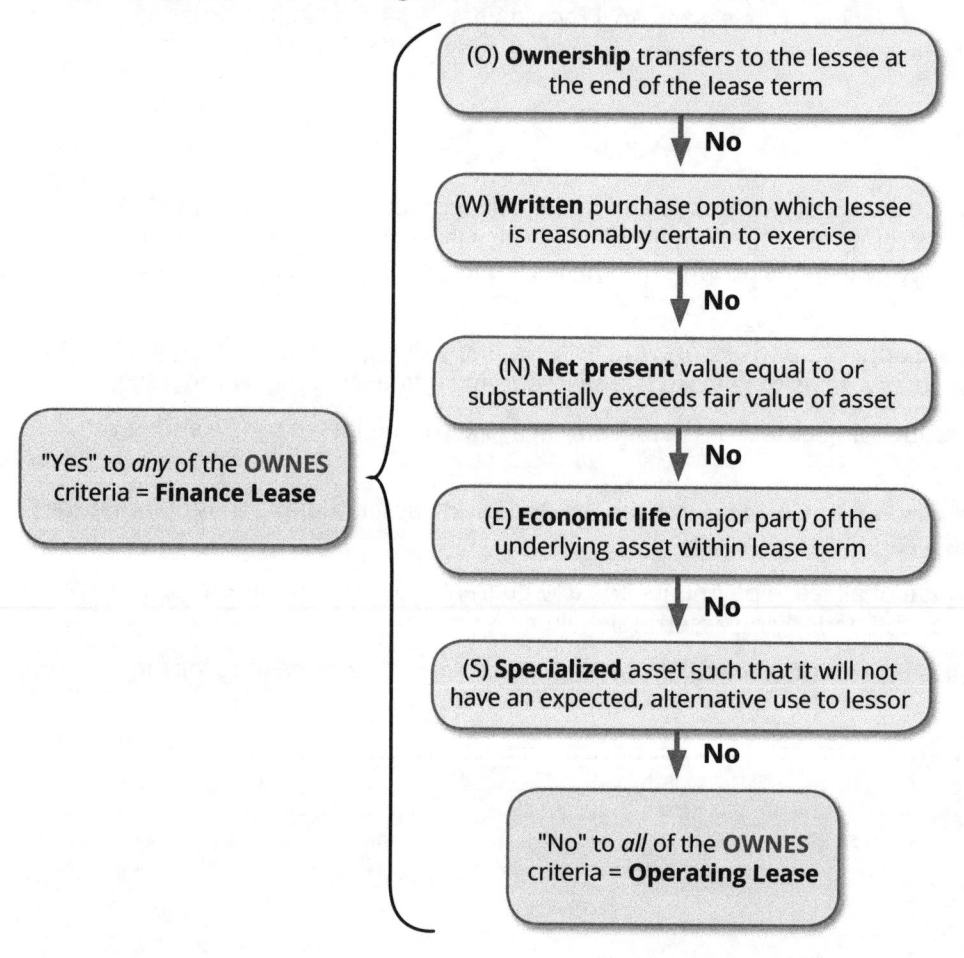

- (O) **Ownership** transfers to the lessee at the end of the lease term
  - ↓ No
- (W) **Written** purchase option which lessee is reasonably certain to exercise
  - ↓ No
- (N) **Net present** value equal to or substantially exceeds fair value of asset
  - ↓ No
- (E) **Economic life** (major part) of the underlying asset within lease term
  - ↓ No
- (S) **Specialized** asset such that it will not have an expected, alternative use to lessor
  - ↓ No
- "No" to *all* of the OWNES criteria = **Operating Lease**

"Yes" to *any* of the OWNES criteria = **Finance Lease**

## 3.3 Quantitative Approach

Although the criteria above do not provide specific, quantitative thresholds for assessing "substantially exceeds" and "major part" determinations, previous FASB guidance can serve as a reasonable approach to determining whether these thresholds are met.

For the **N** criteria, 90 percent or more of the fair value of the underlying asset would reasonably be considered "substantial." For the **E** criteria, a "major part" of the remaining economic life of the asset would reasonably be considered 75 percent or more.

In addition, for the purposes of determining whether a lease commences at or near the end of the underlying asset's economic life, a theoretically reasonable approach would be to use a threshold of 25 percent or less of the underlying asset's total economic life.

### Illustration 2    Finance Lease Criteria

An entity leases equipment with a fair value of $3,500. Lease payments of $1,000 per year are due annually on December 31. The lease term is four years and the asset life is 10 years. The entity's incremental borrowing rate is 10 percent. The lease does not transfer ownership, there is no purchase option, and the asset is not specialized.

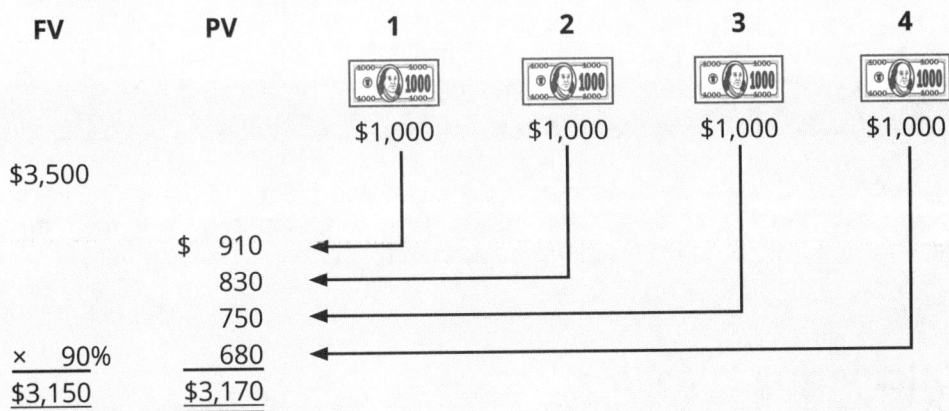

| FV | PV | 1 | 2 | 3 | 4 |
|---|---|---|---|---|---|
|  |  | $1,000 | $1,000 | $1,000 | $1,000 |
| $3,500 | $ 910 ← | | | | |
|  | 830 ← | | | | |
|  | 750 ← | | | | |
| × 90% | 680 ← | | | | |
| $3,150 | $3,170 | | | | |

This lease is accounted for as a finance lease because the present value of the minimum lease payments ($3,170) is greater than 90 percent of the fair value ($3,500 × 90% = $3,150) of the leased equipment.

### Pass Key

Assuming that a lease is greater than 12 months in duration, the determination of how a lessor and lessee account for a lease is based on the **OWNES PC** criteria.

**Lessor**
Sales-Type Lease: At least one of the **OWNES** criteria is met.

Direct Financing Lease: None of the **OWNES** criteria are met, but both of the **PC** criteria are met.

Operating Lease: None of the **OWNES** criteria are met, and either one or no **PC** criteria are met.

**Lessee**
Finance Lease: At least one of the **OWNES** criteria is met.

Operating Lease: None of the **OWNES** criteria are met.

> ### Example 2 — Lease Classification
>
> **Facts:** Landen leases furniture with an economic life of nine years to Haley Inc. for seven years, beginning July 1, Year 1. The present value of the lease payments and residual value are approximately 80 percent of the fair value of the asset. Ownership does not transfer to Haley at the end of the lease and there is no option for Haley to purchase the furniture after the period of seven years ends.
>
> **Required:** Determine whether Haley will likely account for the lease as a finance lease or an operating lease.
>
> **Solution:** A seven-year lease on furniture with a nine-year economic life would equate to 78 percent of the economic life of the asset, which would likely result in Haley classifying the lease as a finance lease. In terms of the other criteria which are not met, the present value, worth 80 percent of the fair value, would likely fall below a threshold at which Haley would consider this a finance lease. Also, there is no ownership transfer, no option to purchase, and furniture is unlikely to be specialized.

> ### Pass Key
>
> IFRS allows a lessee to have a recognition and measurement exemption for leases of assets with a value less than $5,000. U.S. GAAP does not have this exemption, and the criteria described above for recording a lease are applicable regardless of dollar value.

## 4 Calculating Leases

### 4.1 Lease Term

The "commencement date" for a lease is the date for which the lessor makes the underlying asset available to the lessee for use. The lease term begins on this date and extends to the end of the noncancelable period (the period in which the lessee's right is enforceable) for which the lessee has the right to use the underlying asset. A lease that can be terminated by both parties with only minor penalties results in a non-enforceable lease.

An option to terminate exists when one or the other (but not both) has the right to terminate. The lease term will also need to account for any options to extend or terminate the lease as follows:

- Periods covered by an option to extend the lease are included if the lessee is reasonably certain to exercise that option.

- Periods covered by an option to terminate the lease are included if the lessee is reasonably certain not to exercise that option.

- Periods covered by an option to either extend or terminate the lease are included if the exercise is controlled by the lessor.

Lessees must recognize right-of-use (ROU) assets and lease liabilities for all leases that are not considered short term. In order to qualify as short term, the lease will have a term of 12 months or less and there cannot be an option for the lessee to purchase the underlying asset which the lessee is reasonably certain to exercise. These short-term leases will qualify as operating leases and the lessee will recognize payments over the lease term on a straight-line basis.

## 4.2 Lease Payments

In the calculation of the lease payments, the lessee will *include* all of the following.

- **Required contractual fixed payments** (which will include any variable payments that are "in-substance" fixed payments) less any lease incentives paid or payable to the lessee.

- **Exercise option reasonably assured:** the exercise price of an option, which gives the lessee the right to purchase the underlying asset (if it is "reasonably certain" that the lessee will exercise this option).

- **Purchase price at the end of lease:** the stated purchase price of the underlying asset at the end of the lease term (when the lessor has the option to require the lessee to purchase the underlying asset).

- **Only indexed or rate variable payments:** No increase or decrease to future lease payments should be assumed based on increases or decreases in the index or rate. Instead, any difference in the payments due to changes in the index or rate are expensed in the period incurred.

- **Residual guarantees likely to be owed:** The lessee includes the full amount of the residual value guarantee at the end of the lease term in the present value test. The lessee does not consider unguaranteed residual value as part of the present value test.

- **Termination penalties reasonably assured:** Any penalty due from the lessee upon lease termination (the lease term must reflect the lessee exercising an option to terminate the lease).

Lessee lease payments *may or may not* include the following (at the lessee's option):

- **Nonlease** components: amounts allocated to nonlease components of a contract.

Lessee lease payments will specifically *exclude* the following.

- **Guarantees of lessor debt by lessee**
- **Other variable lease payments:** other than those noted above.

---

### Illustration 3     Lease Payments (Included Payments)

Sterling is a lessee for a piece of moveable equipment with a useful life of eight years. Along with the equipment, the lessor is providing scheduled maintenance and upkeep that is accounted for separately from the lease. The terms of the lease include the following: a three-year lease with monthly fixed payments of $3,450 (with the first four months free to the lessee); an option to purchase the asset for $12,500 at the end of the lease, which Sterling is unlikely to exercise; and $8,000 allocated to the maintenance and upkeep component of the agreement.

Lease payments will include the $3,450 in monthly fixed payments for 32 total months (36-month lease with the first four months free). The option to purchase for $12,500 is not included because Sterling is unlikely to exercise the option. The $8,000 allocated to the maintenance and upkeep portion of the contract is also not included in the lease payments.

> **Illustration 4    Lease Payments (Excluded Payments)**
>
> Bowden Corp. is the lessee for two separate lease arrangements. Lease A involves monthly payments that are based on changes in the consumer price index (CPI). Lease B involves monthly lease payments that are based entirely on Bowden's use of the leased asset.
>
> For Bowden, the calculation of the lease payment for Lease A will include the variable monthly payments because they are based on an index/rate. For Lease B, the payments will be recognized as expenses in the period incurred and not included in the lease payments calculation because they are contingent on asset usage, which can fluctuate significantly each period.

> **Pass Key**
>
> IFRS requires a reassessment of variable lease payments that depend on an index or rate when a change in the reference rate or index results in a change in cash flows.

### 4.3 Discount Rate

When calculating the present value of the minimum lease payments, the lessor will use the rate implicit in the lease. The lessee uses either:

- the rate implicit in the lease (if known) or, if this rate is not readily determinable,
- the incremental borrowing rate of the lessee (the rate the lessee would be charged for a collateralized loan with equal payments and a similar lease term to the lease).

### 4.4 Initial Direct Costs

Initial direct costs will be included in the valuation of the ROU asset. These costs are only incurred as a result of the execution of the lease. Any costs incurred prior to signing the lease, which can include lease term negotiations, document preparation, credit checks, etc., are not included in the accounting for direct costs.

# 5  Sale-Leaseback Transactions

A sale-leaseback occurs when one party (the seller) that has control of an asset transfers it to another party (the buyer), with a subsequent lease of the same asset where the seller becomes the lessee and the buyer becomes the lessor. Having control of an asset means being able to direct its use and obtaining substantially all of its remaining benefits.

**ASSET → Transferred from Seller to Buyer**

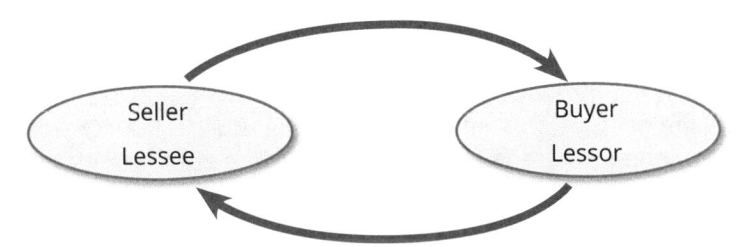

```
    Seller          Buyer
    Lessee          Lessor
```

**ASSET → Leased by the Seller (now the Lessee)
from the Buyer (now the Lessor)**

To qualify as a sale, revenue recognition requirements must be met—in particular, when (1) a contract exists and (2) control has transferred from the seller to the buyer. If the asset transfer does not meet these requirements, this will be treated as a financing transaction.

If an asset transfer involves either of the two key situations below, the transfer may or may not be considered a sale, depending on the circumstances.

1. **Repurchase Option:** To meet the criteria to be a sale, *both* of the following must be met.
   - The option's exercise price already is or will be the same as the underlying asset's fair value at the time of exercise.
   - Alternative assets that are substantially equivalent to the underlying asset are readily available in the marketplace.

   If both of these criteria are not met, the existence of the repurchase option will result in a "failed sale" and this will be treated as a financing transaction.

2. **Residual Value Guarantee:** A sale cannot take place if control of the asset has not transferred to the buyer. It is a qualitative judgment, but the more significant the guarantee, the more unlikely it is that control has transferred.

### 5.1 Sale-Leaseback—Sale Criteria Met

If the criteria are met for a sale, each party must determine whether the transaction is at fair value. (Transactions between related parties do not require this process). To make this determination, two steps are needed.

**Step 1:** Determine which of the two sets of information below are more readily determinable.
- Set 1: Asset sale price and fair value
- Set 2: PV of lease payments and PV of market rental payments

**Step 2:** Of the one that is more determinable, identify any difference between the two data points.

If a difference exists, this will require an adjustment to either the sale price or the purchase price. Any increases in sales or purchase prices will be treated as prepaid rent via an adjustment to the ROU asset in the leaseback, and any decreases in sales or purchase price will be treated as additional financing provided by the buyer-lessor to the seller-lessee.

## Example 3 — Sale-Leaseback (Criteria Met)

**Facts:** Billings Co. held equipment on its books with an original purchase price of $500,000, a remaining useful life of 10 years, and a carrying value of $415,000. On January 1, Year 3, Billings sold the equipment to Crane Inc. for $490,000. The equipment at the time of sale had a fair value of $470,000. Crane agreed to lease back the equipment to Billings for five years at an annual lease cost of $112,396.50 (due on January 1 each year, beginning in Year 4) with an implicit interest rate of 4.75 percent.

**Required:** Assuming that the criteria to qualify the transfer as a sale are met, prepare the journal entry that Billings will record when the transfer takes place.

**Solution:** Given the facts of the question, both the asset sale price ($490,000) and the fair value ($470,000) are readily determinable. As such, the difference of $20,000 will be accounted for as a financing liability on Billings' ledger. The journal entry is as follows:

| | | | |
|---|---|---|---|
| DR | Cash | $490,000 | |
| DR | A/D—Equipment | 85,000 | |
| CR | Equipment | | $500,000 |
| CR | Financing liability | | 20,000 |
| CR | Gain on equipment sale | | 55,000 |

Upon the execution of the sale-leaseback, two transactions will take place:

1. The sale, along with recognition of profit or loss, would be recorded. Note that in order to record a profit or loss, the leaseback will have to be an operating lease. If the lease were to meet the **OWNES** criteria, it would be treated as a finance lease—essentially the equivalent of a repurchase and therefore a "failed sale."

2. The lease would be recorded, based on the same accounting rules as other leases described in this module.

## 5.2 Sale-Leaseback—Sale Criteria Are Not Met

Both the seller (lessee) and the buyer (lessor) will treat a "failed sale" as a financing transaction, which will involve the seller (lessee) recording a financing liability and a buyer (lessor) recording a financing receivable for amounts received from the other party. In regard to the asset, the seller will continue to recognize the asset and the buyer will not recognize it on its books.

## Example 4 — Sale-Leaseback (Criteria Not Met)

**Facts:** Billings Co. held equipment on its books with a remaining useful life of 10 years and a carrying value of $415,000. On January 1, Year 3, Billings sold the equipment to Crane Inc. for $490,000. The equipment at the time of sale had a fair value of $470,000. Crane agreed to lease back the equipment to Billings for five years at an annual lease cost of $112,396.50 per year (due on January 1, beginning in Year 4) with an implicit interest rate of 4.75 percent.

**Required:** Assuming that the criteria to qualify the transfer as a sale are not met, prepare the journal entries that Billings will record on January 1 and on December 31, Year 3.

**Solution:** Because the transfer did not qualify as a sale, the entry on January 1, Year 3, will be as follows:

| | | | |
|---|---|---|---|
| DR | Cash | $490,000 | |
| CR | Financing liability | | $490,000 |

On December 31, Year 3, the entry will be made to record interest as well as depreciation on the equipment that remains on Billings' books. Interest equals the financing liability times the interest rate implicit in the lease ($490,000 × 4.75% = $23,275). Depreciation expense equals the carrying value divided by the useful life ($415,000 / 10 years = $41,500).

| | | | |
|---|---|---|---|
| DR | Interest expense | $23,275 | |
| CR | Financing liability | | $23,275 |
| DR | Depreciation expense | 41,500 | |
| CR | Accumulated depreciation | | 41,500 |

### Pass Key

The only guidance provided by IFRS regarding whether an asset transfer in a sale and leaseback transaction is a sale is if the seller-lessee has a substantive repurchase option, then no sale has taken place.

## Question 1 — MCQ-08768

Watts Inc. enters into an agreement to lease a printer/copier from Jennings Co. The lease is for three years and does not stipulate an ownership transfer or contain a written option to purchase. The printer/copier has a five-year life and the equipment is standard equipment that Jennings can use for many projects and functions. The net present value of the lease payments is approximately half of the overall fair value of the equipment and there is no guaranteed residual value associated with the lease.

Watts and Jennings will account for this lease as:

|    | Watts | Jennings |
|----|-------|----------|
| a. | Finance | Sales-type |
| b. | Finance | Operating |
| c. | Operating | Sales-type |
| d. | Operating | Operating |

## Question 2 — MCQ-08769

Anton owns equipment originally purchased four years ago for $325,000. On January 1, Year 5, Anton sells the equipment to Bridges for $208,000. The equipment has a remaining useful life of six years, a carrying value of $195,000, and a fair value of $202,000. Bridges has agreed to lease the equipment back to Anton for three years with annual payments of $48,375 at an implicit interest rate of 5.25 percent. The lease qualifies as a sale.

When the transfer takes place, Anton will record a financing liability equal to:

a. $0.
b. $6,000.
c. $7,000.
d. $13,000.

# MODULE 2 Leases: Part 2

FAR 6

## 1 Lessee Accounting

As noted previously, when a lease commences, the lessee must evaluate the contract to determine whether a lease should be classified as a finance lease or an operating lease.

### 1.1 Operating Leases

If the lease is an operating lease, the balance sheet will reflect a right-of-use (ROU) asset and lease liability and both will be amortized over the life of the lease using the effective interest method. The ROU asset and lease liability amounts are calculated using the present value of the lease payments, using the appropriate discount rate. On the income statement, lease expense will be recognized each year over the lease term using the straight-line method for expense measurement. Instead of reporting interest expense on the income statement, the lessee will report the interest as part of lease expense.

> **Pass Key**
>
> When calculating the present value of the lease payments for the purpose of calculating the ROU asset and lease liability, keep in mind the following:
>
> Periodic payment
> - Beginning of period = PV of an annuity due
> - End of period = PV of an annuity *(in arrears/ordinary)*
>
> Purchase option
> *Or:*
> Guaranteed residual
> - PV of $1
>
> **Note:** Although leases generally require payment at the beginning of the period (first payment at lease inception), some CPA Exam questions state that the lease payments are made at the end of each period. Read each question carefully to determine whether you are dealing with an annuity due (payment at the beginning of each period) or an ordinary annuity (payment at the end of each period) and be sure to use the correct present value factors.

**Initial Entry:**

| DR | ROU asset | $XXX | |
|---|---|---|---|
| CR | Lease liability | | $XXX |

Leases: Part 2

**Subsequent Entries:**

| DR | Lease expense | $XXX | |
|---|---|---|---|
| CR | Cash/lease liability | | $XXX |

| DR | Lease liability | $XXX | |
|---|---|---|---|
| CR | Accumulated amortization—ROU asset | | $XXX |

### Example 1  Reporting an Operating Lease: Lessee's Books

**Facts:** On January 1, Year 2, a lessee enters into a three-year asset operating (capital) lease with annual payments of $18,000 per year. The first payment will be made December 31 and the interest rate implicit in the lease is 5.75 percent. (The present value of an ordinary annuity for three years at 5.75% = 2.685424.)

**Required:** Prepare the journal entries for the lessee at the commencement date, the end of Year 2, the end of Year 3, and the end of Year 4.

**Solution:**

*Journal Entry—Jan. 1, Year 2*

The present value of $18,000 for three years (first payment made at the end of Year 1) at a rate of 5.75 percent per year is equal to $48,338.

| DR | ROU asset | $48,338 | |
|---|---|---|---|
| CR | Lease liability | | $48,338 |

| Date | Lease Liability | Lease Expense | Interest Expense | Reduction in ROU Asset | Carrying Value of ROU Asset |
|---|---|---|---|---|---|
| | $48,338 | | | | $48,338 |
| 12/31/Year 2 | $33,117 | $18,000 | $2,779 | $15,221 | $33,117 |
| 12/31/Year 3 | $17,021 | $18,000 | $1,904 | $16,096 | $17,021 |
| 12/31/Year 4 | – | $18,000 | $ 979 | $17,021 | – |

*Journal Entry—Dec. 31, Year 2*

The lease payment of $18,000 comprises interest expense and the amortization of the ROU asset, as calculated in the table above.

| DR | Lease expense | $18,000 | |
|---|---|---|---|
| DR | Lease liability | 15,221 | |
| CR | Cash | | $18,000 |
| CR | Accumulated amortization—ROU asset | | 15,221 |

(continued)

(continued)

*Journal Entry—Dec. 31, Year 3*

| | | | |
|---|---|---|---|
| DR | Lease expense | $18,000 | |
| DR | Lease liability | 16,096 | |
| CR | Cash | | $18,000 |
| CR | Accumulated amortization—ROU asset | | 16,096 |

*Journal Entry—Dec. 31, Year 4*

| | | | |
|---|---|---|---|
| DR | Lease expense | $18,000 | |
| DR | Lease liability | 17,021 | |
| CR | Cash | | $18,000 |
| CR | Accumulated amortization—ROU asset | | 17,021 |

Once the final entry has been recorded, the ROU asset is fully amortized.

## 1.2 Finance Leases

If the lease is a finance lease, the lessee will recognize both an ROU asset and a corresponding liability on its balance sheet. The liability will equal the present value of lease payments owed. The ROU asset will include initial direct costs (such as commissions paid, legal and consulting fees, etc.) that were incurred as a result of the lease execution, as well as any lease payments made by the lessee to the lessor at or before lease commencement. Any incentives received by the lessee from the lessor will reduce the value of the asset.

**Initial Entry:**

| | | | |
|---|---|---|---|
| DR | ROU asset | $XXX | |
| CR | Lease liability | | $XXX |

**Subsequent Entries:**

| | | | |
|---|---|---|---|
| DR | Interest expense | $XXX | |
| DR | Lease liability | XXX | |
| CR | Cash/lease payable | | $XXX |

| | | | |
|---|---|---|---|
| DR | Amortization expense | $XXX | |
| CR | Accumulated amortization—ROU asset | | $XXX |

Unlike with operating (capital) leases, the amortization of the ROU asset for a finance lease will be expensed based on how the entity recognizes amortization expense on similar assets.

# Example 2 — Reporting a Finance Lease: Lessee's Books

**Facts:** On January 1, Year 2, a lessee enters into a three-year asset lease with annual payments of $18,000 per year. The first payment will be made December 31 and the interest rate implicit in the lease is 5.75 percent. The lease qualifies as a finance lease.

**Required:** Assuming straight-line amortization, prepare the journal entries for the lessee at the commencement date, the end of Year 2, the end of Year 3, and the end of Year 4.

**Solution:**

*Journal Entry—Jan. 1, Year 2*

The present value of $18,000 for three years (first payment made at the end of Year 1) at a rate of 5.75 percent per year is equal to $48,338.

| DR | ROU asset | $48,338 | |
|---|---|---|---|
| CR | Lease liability | | $48,338 |

| Date | Lease Liability | Total Lease Expense | Interest Expense | Amortization Expense | Carrying Value of ROU Asset |
|---|---|---|---|---|---|
| | $48,338 | | | | $48,338 |
| 12/31/Year 2 | $33,117 | $18,892 | $2,779 | $16,113 | $32,225 |
| 12/31/Year 3 | $17,021 | $18,017 | $1,904 | $16,113 | $16,112 |
| 12/31/Year 4 | – | $17,091 | $ 979 | $16,112 | – |

*Journal Entries—Dec. 31, Year 2*

The lease payment of $18,000 comprises interest expense and the reduction of the lease liability as calculated in the table above. The ROU asset will be amortized at $48,338 over three years, or 16,113 per year.

| DR | Interest expense | $ 2,779 | |
|---|---|---|---|
| DR | Lease liability | 15,221 | |
| CR | Cash | | $18,000 |

| DR | Amortization expense | 16,113 | |
|---|---|---|---|
| CR | Accumulated amortization—ROU asset | | 16,113 |

*Journal Entries—Dec. 31, Year 3*

| DR | Interest expense | $ 1,904 | |
|---|---|---|---|
| DR | Lease liability | 16,096 | |
| CR | Cash | | $18,000 |

| DR | Amortization expense | 16,113 | |
|---|---|---|---|
| CR | Accumulated amortization—ROU asset | | 16,113 |

(continued)

(continued)

*Journal Entries—Dec. 31, Year 4*

| | | | |
|---|---|---|---|
| DR | Interest expense | $ 979 | |
| DR | Lease liability | 17,021 | |
| CR | Cash | | $18,000 |

| | | | |
|---|---|---|---|
| DR | Amortization expense | 16,112 | |
| CR | Accumulated amortization—ROU asset | | 16,112 |

Once the final entry has been recorded, the ROU asset is fully amortized.

## Pass Key

Although GAAP requires measuring the ROU asset using the one methodology described above, IFRS allows for alternative measurement bases based on other standards, such as the Investment Property fair value model (from IAS 40) and the Property, Plant, and Equipment model (from IAS 16).

## Example 3 — Reporting a Lease: Combining Contracts

**Facts:** On January 1, Year 5, a lessee enters into an eight-year asset finance lease with an option to extend for four years, which the lessee is unlikely to exercise. Initial lease payments are $35,000 per year for the first eight years (with payments on January 1 each year, beginning in Year 5) and then $40,000 per year if the lease is extended. Initial direct costs incurred by the lessee are $12,000. The interest rate implicit in the lease is 4.5 percent, and the lessee's incremental borrowing rate is 5.0 percent.

**Required:** Prepare the journal entry for the lessee at the commencement date.

(continued)

(continued)

**Solution:** Cash payouts of $35,000 for the first lease payment and $12,000 for the initial direct costs are recorded, as well as the present value of the seven remaining lease payments. The lease liability is equal to the present value of $35,000 per year for the next seven years at an interest rate of 4.5 percent (the rate implicit in the lease should be chosen as the discount rate, if known). Because the company is unlikely to extend the lease, the four years are not considered in the calculation amount. Seven payments of $35,000 at a rate of 4.5 percent equals a present value of $206,245. The ROU asset will be the combination of these three items.

| DR | ROU asset | $253,245 | |
|---|---|---|---|
| CR | Lease liability | | $206,245 |
| CR | Cash | | 47,000* |

*$35,000 initial payment plus $12,000 initial direct costs.

### Example 4 — Reporting a Finance Lease: Amortization

**Facts:** On January 1, Year 5, a lessee enters into an eight-year asset finance lease with an option to extend for four years, which the lessee is unlikely to exercise. Initial lease payments are $35,000 per year for the first eight years (with payments on January 1 each year, beginning in Year 5) and then $40,000 if the lease is extended. Initial direct costs incurred by the lessee are $12,000. The interest rate implicit in the lease is 4.5 percent, and the lessee's incremental borrowing rate is 5.0 percent.

**Required:** Calculate interest expense, the amortization of the liability, the amortization of the asset (assuming straight-line), and total lease expense for Year 6. (When the first lease payment of $35,000 is made January 1, Year 5, the lease liability is immediately reduced from $241,245 to $206,245.)

**Solution:**

| Date | Lease Payment | Interest (4.5% on Liability) | Reduction of Lease Liability | Lease Liability |
|---|---|---|---|---|
| 1/1/Year 5 | $35,000 | $ 0 | $35,000 | $206,245 |
| 1/1/Year 6 | $35,000 | $9,281 | $25,719 | $180,526 |
| 1/1/Year 7 | $35,000 | $8,124 | $26,876 | $153,650 |
| 1/1/Year 8 | $35,000 | $6,914 | $28,086 | $125,564 |
| 1/1/Year 9 | $35,000 | $5,650 | $29,350 | $ 96,214 |
| 1/1/Year 10 | $35,000 | $4,330 | $30,670 | $ 65,544 |
| 1/1/Year 11 | $35,000 | $2,949 | $32,051 | $ 33,493 |
| 1/1/Year 12 | $35,000 | $1,507 | $33,493 | $ (0) |

The payment made on January 1, Year 7, represents interest expense accrued during Year 6. Year 6 interest expense of $8,124 is equal to the lease liability balance as of 1/1/Year 6 ($180,526) multiplied by the interest rate of 4.5 percent. The reduction of the liability of $26,876 attributable to Year 6 is equal to the difference between the lease payment of $35,000 and the interest expense of $8,124. The asset, worth $253,245 on the lessee's books, will be depreciated over eight years at $31,656 per year. Total lease expense for Year 6 will be equal to $39,780 ($8,124 + $31,656).

In the early years of a finance lease, expense recognition is front-loaded as interest expense, plus asset amortization expense will create a higher total expense than under an operating (capital) lease. In later years, a finance lease will reflect a lower total expense than an operating lease. The overall expense total across the entire lease will be the same under both lease types.

### 1.3 Accounting Policy Election

Lessees can make an accounting policy election and choose to not recognize ROU assets and lease liabilities for leases with terms of 12 months or less. If this election is made, it must be done by the class of the underlying asset and cannot include purchase options for the asset the lessee is reasonably certain to exercise.

## 2 Lessor Accounting

On the commencement date of the lease, lessors will classify a lease as a sales-type, direct financing, or operating lease.

### 2.1 Sales-Type Lease

In a sales-type lease, the lessee gains control of the underlying asset. The lessor will derecognize the asset and recognize a net investment in the lease, as well as a profit or loss, assuming that the collectibility of any residual value guarantee and the lease payments themselves are probable on the date the lease commences. If collectibility is not probable, the lease payments received will be treated as deposit liabilities.

| | | | |
|---|---|---|---|
| DR | Lease receivable | $XXX | |
| CR | Fixed asset | | $XXX |
| CR | Gain (DR if a loss) | | XXX |

For any initial direct costs incurred as part of the lease, if there is a profit or loss, expense the direct costs at commencement date. If there is no profit or loss, defer and recognize the direct costs over the lease term.

---

**Example 5    Reporting a Sales-Type Lease: Lessor's Books**

**Facts:** Jenkins Inc. leases a truck to Briggs Co. for four years at $5,000 per year, with initial direct costs of $450 and an implicit rate of 6 percent. On the date the lease commences (Jan. 1, Year 2), the carrying value and fair value of the truck are $22,000 and $24,216, respectively. Jenkins expects that the truck will be worth $8,700 when the lease ends.

**Required:** If this lease is treated as a sales-type lease and assuming that collection of all amounts owed is probable, determine the lessor's journal entry on Jan. 1, Year 2.

(continued)

(continued)

**Solution:**

| | | | |
|---|---|---|---|
| DR | Lease expense | $ 450 | |
| DR | Residual asset | 6,891 | |
| DR | Lease receivable | 17,325 | |
| CR | Cash | | $ 450 |
| CR | Gain | | 2,216 |
| CR | Truck | | 22,000 |

1. Gross residual asset. This is the present value of $8,700 at 6 percent, or $6,891.
2. Lease receivable. This is the present value of four payments of $5,000 at 6 percent ($17,325).
3. The gain of $2,216 is the difference between the sum of the residual asset and lease receivable, less the carrying value of the truck.

## 2.2 Direct Financing Lease

In a direct financing lease, the lessee does not gain control of the underlying asset. The lessor will derecognize the asset and recognize a net investment in the lease. Any gain will be deferred and amortized over the life of the lease, and any loss will be recognized immediately.

| | | | |
|---|---|---|---|
| DR | Lease receivable | $XXX | |
| DR | Residual asset | XXX | |
| CR | Fixed asset | | $XXX |

For any initial direct costs incurred as part of the lease, they will be deferred and amortized over the lease term. Interest income will be recognized using the interest method over the lease term.

Each period, the lessor will recognize interest income equal to the discount rate applied to both the lease receivable and the residual asset, while the lease payment received will reduce the lease receivable.

| | | | |
|---|---|---|---|
| DR | Cash (lease payment) | $XXX | |
| CR | Interest income | | $XXX |
| CR | Lease receivable | | XXX |

## Example 6　Reporting a Direct Financing Lease: Lessor's Books

**Facts:** Jenkins Inc. leases a truck to Briggs Co. for four years at $5,000 per year, with initial direct costs of $450 and an implicit rate of 6 percent. On the date the lease commences (Jan. 1, Year 2), the carrying value and fair value of the truck are $24,216. Jenkins expects that the truck will be worth $8,700 when the lease ends.

**Required:** If this lease is treated as a direct financing lease, determine the lessor's journal entry at lease inception and when the first payment is received.

**Solution:**

**Lease Inception**

| | | | |
|---|---|---|---|
| DR | Residual asset | $ 6,891 | |
| DR | Lease receivable | 17,775 | |
| CR | Truck | | $24,216 |
| CR | Cash | | 450 |

1. Gross residual asset. This is the present value of $8,700 at 6 percent, or $6,891.
2. Lease receivable. This is the present value of four payments of $5,000 at 6 percent ($17,325) + initial direct costs of $450 = $17,775. The direct costs are included because there is no profit recognized on the commencement date.

**First Payment**

| | | | |
|---|---|---|---|
| DR | Cash | $5,000 | |
| CR | Interest income | | $1,480 |
| CR | Lease receivable | | 3,520 |

Interest income is equal to the implicit rate of 6 percent applied to the PV of both the residual asset and the lease receivable.

### 2.3 Operating Lease

From the perspective of the lessor, any lease that does not qualify as a sales-type or direct financing lease will be an operating lease. The lessor will keep the asset on its balance sheet, which will include depreciating it and recognizing any impairment charges if applicable. Lease income will be recognized on a straight-line basis, and initial direct costs will be deferred and amortized over the lease term.

| | | | |
|---|---|---|---|
| DR | Cash | $XXX | |
| CR | Rental income | | $XXX |

| | | | |
|---|---|---|---|
| DR | Depreciation expense | $XXX | |
| CR | Accumulated depreciation | | $XXX |

Leases: Part 2

# Pass Key

IFRS treats sales-type and direct financing leases similarly. IFRS permits recognition of a selling profit on direct financing leases at the beginning of the lease.

# 3 Financial Statement Presentation

## 3.1 Balance Sheet

ROU assets and associated lease liabilities may either be recognized as separate line items on the balance sheet (in their respective sections) or included with other assets/liabilities and disclosed separately in the notes to the financial statements (indicating which line items in the balance sheet include them). The portion of lease liabilities due within a year or the operating cycle, whichever is longer, should be reported in the current section and the remainder in the long-term section. Finance and operating lease ROU assets and lease liabilities cannot be presented together. The ROU asset will be amortized, and the lease liability will be paid down over the life of the lease.

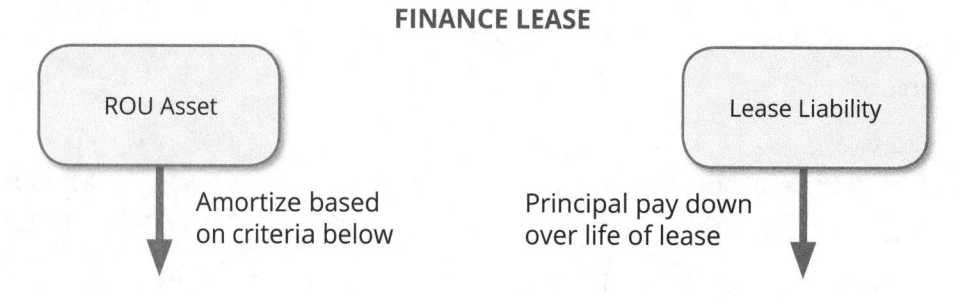

**FINANCE LEASE**

ROU Asset → Amortize based on criteria below

Lease Liability → Principal pay down over life of lease

The ROU asset will be amortized beginning on the commencement date using a straight-line basis (unless another methodology better reflects usage and consumption).

- Criteria for determining amortization:
  - Amortize over the underlying asset's useful life if **ownership** or **written option** criteria are met.
  - Amortize over shorter of the lease term or the useful life of the asset if **net present value**, **economic life**, or **specialized asset** criteria are met.

### Illustration 1    Finance Lease: Amortization

Cooper Industries leases a boat for seven years from Kirkland Inc. There is no ownership transfer at the end of the lease, and Cooper has not been given an option to purchase the boat. The present value of the lease payments is equivalent to the boat's fair value, and the boat has an accounting useful life of five years. On Cooper's books, this will qualify as a finance lease because of the equivalence of the present value of the lease payments to the boat's fair value (the **N** criteria is met). The ROU asset will be amortized over five years because this is the lesser of the useful life of the asset (five years) and the lease term (seven years).

## 3.2 Income Statement

For operating leases, lease expense will be included in income from continuing operations on the lessee's income statement. For finance leases, the income statement will include the amortization of the ROU asset and the portion of the lease expense related to interest on the lease liability.

## 3.3 Cash Flow Statement

For operating leases, lease payments (which include all variable lease payments) are classified as cash flow from operations. Payments for short-term leases are also included in cash flow from operations. Any payments needed to bring the asset to a condition and location in preparation for its intended use are considered investing activities.

For finance leases, the principal portion of the lease payment is a cash flow from financing, the interest portion of the lease payment is a cash flow from operations, and any variable lease payments and short-term lease payments not included in the lease liability are classified as cash flows from operations.

| CFO | CFI | CFF |
|---|---|---|
| **Operating Leases** | | |
| Lease payments | Preparing asset for intended use | |
| Variable lease payments | | |
| Short-term lease payments | | |
| **Finance Leases** | | |
| Interest payments | | Principal payments |
| Variable and short-term lease payments not included in the lease liability | | |

# 4 Disclosures

## 4.1 Lessee Disclosures

A lessee will have to disclose several qualitative pieces of information, including:

- information about the nature of the leases, including any restrictions or covenants;
- options to extend or terminate (existence, terms, conditions);
- residual value guarantees (existence, terms, conditions);
- information on leases that have not commenced but create significant obligations and/or rights for the lessee;
- significant assumptions and judgments made in application (including determination of whether a contract contains a lease, allocation of consideration between lease and nonlease components, discount rate determination, etc.);
- sale-leaseback terms and conditions; and
- the entity's accounting policy related to short-term leases and practical expedients used to combine lease and nonlease components.

Quantitative disclosures will include:

- finance lease costs (separated between the amortization of ROU assets and interest on lease liabilities);
- operating lease costs;
- short-term lease costs;
- the weighted average remaining lease term and discount rate; and
- separate maturity analyses for operating and finance lease liabilities for five years.

### 4.2 Lessor Disclosures

A lessor will have to disclose several qualitative pieces of information, including:

- a description of the lease;
- the existence and terms/conditions of options to extend or terminate the lease;
- options for the lessee to purchase the leased asset;
- significant assumptions and judgments (including whether a contract contains a lease and the allocation of consideration between lease and nonlease components;
- related party leases (if applicable); and
- accounting policies on lessor accounting.

Quantitative disclosures will include:

- profit or loss recognized at commencement date;
- interest income;
- income related to operating lease payments received;
- income from variable lease payments not included in the measurement of the lease receivable;
- components of the net investment in sales-type and direct financing leases (includes lease receivable, unguaranteed residual asset, any deferred selling profit on direct financing leases, minimum lease payments, unguaranteed residual value, initial direct costs, and unearned income);
- information on assets that are subject to operating leases (including associated depreciation and impairment); and
- separate maturity analysis of lease receivables, showing the undiscounted cash flows to be received on an annual basis for a minimum of each of the first five years and a total of the amounts for the remaining years.

## Question 1 — MCQ-08770

At the beginning of Year 2, Kennedy enters into a four-year operating lease with payments due at the end of the year beginning on December 31, Year 2. The rate implicit in the lease is 4.50 percent and Kennedy will owe annual payments of $5,200. The present value factor of an ordinary annuity for four years at 4.50 percent is equal to 3.5875.

The carrying value of the ROU asset at the end of Year 2 will be closest to:

- a. $9,740.
- b. $13,455.
- c. $14,295.
- d. $18,655.

## Question 2 — MCQ-08771

At the beginning of the year, a lessee signs a five-year lease that contains a written purchase option, which the lessee is reasonably certain to exercise. In preparing the annual cash flow statement after year-end, the lessee's cash flow from operations will be:

- a. Positively impacted by the portion of the lease payments that represents interest.
- b. Negatively impacted by variable lease payments not included in the lease liability.
- c. Negatively impacted by the portion of the lease payments that represents principal.
- d. Positively impacted by short-term lease payments not included in the lease liability.

## NOTES

# MODULE 3: Derivatives and Hedge Accounting

FAR 6

## 1 Definitions and Concepts

### 1.1 Derivative Instrument

A *derivative instrument* is a financial instrument that *derives* its value from the value of some other instrument and has all three of the following characteristics:

- One or more underlyings and one or more notional amounts or payment provisions (or both);
- It requires no initial net investment or one that is smaller than would be required for other types of similar contracts; and
- Its terms require or permit a net settlement (i.e., it can be settled for cash in lieu of physical delivery), or it can readily be settled net outside the contract (e.g., on an exchange) or by delivery of an asset that gives substantially the same results (e.g., an asset readily convertible to cash).

### 1.2 Underlying

An *underlying* is a specified price, rate, or other variable (e.g., interest rate, security or commodity price, foreign exchange rate, index of prices or rates, etc.), including a scheduled event (e.g., a payment under contract) that may or may not occur.

### 1.3 Notional Amount

A *notional amount* is a specified unit of measure (e.g., currency units, shares, bushels, pounds, etc.).

### 1.4 Value or Settlement Amount

The *value or settlement amount* of a derivative is the amount determined by the multiplication (or other arithmetical interaction) of the notional amount and the underlying. For example, shares of stock times the price per share.

### 1.5 Payment Provision

A *payment provision* is a specified (fixed) or determinable settlement that is to be made if the underlying behaves in a specified way.

### 1.6 Hedging

*Hedging* is the use of a derivative to offset anticipated losses or to reduce earnings volatility. When a hedge is effective, the change in the value of the derivative offsets the change in value of a hedged item or the cash flows of the hedged item.

# 2 Common Derivatives

## 2.1 Option Contract

A contract between two parties that gives one party the right, but not the obligation, to buy or sell something to the other party at a specified price (the strike price or exercise price) during a specified period of time. The option buyer, or holder, must pay a premium to the option seller, or writer, to enter into the option contract. A call option gives the holder the right to buy from the option writer at a specified price during a specified period of time. A put option gives the holder the right to sell to the option writer at a specified price during a specified period of time.

### Illustration 1    Put Option

On January 1, Year 1, Roberts Company purchased a put option on the stock of Buy Big Inc. The option gave Roberts the right to sell 10,000 shares of Buy Big stock at $75/share during the next 30 days. Roberts paid a premium of $2/share to enter into the option. Roberts exercised the option when Buy Big stock was selling for $69/share.

| | |
|---|---|
| Underlying: | $75/share |
| Notional amount: | 10,000 shares of Buy Big stock |
| Initial net investment: | $2/share × 10,000 shares = $20,000 |
| Settlement amount: | $75/share × 10,000 shares = $750,000 |

Derivatives generally have multiple settlement options. This derivative could be settled in the following ways:

1. Roberts could deliver 10,000 shares of Big Buy stock to the option writer in exchange for $750,000. Note that these shares could either be shares already owned by Roberts, or shares purchased by Roberts for $690,000 ($69/share market price × 10,000 shares) and then delivered to the option writer. Either way, Roberts realizes a gain of $60,000 [($75/share exercise price − $69/share market price) × 10,000 shares]. The option writer realizes a loss of $60,000 because the option writer must pay $75/share for stock with a market value of $69/share.

2. The option writer could pay Roberts $60,000 to settle the contract. This is a net settlement.

Because $20,000 was paid to purchase the put option, Roberts will report a net gain of $40,000 ($60,000 gain − $20,000 premium). If the stock price had remained above $75/share during the 30-day period, Roberts would not have exercised the option.

## 2.2 Futures Contract

An agreement between two parties to exchange a commodity, currency, or other asset at a specified price on a specified future date. One party takes a long position, meaning it agrees to buy a particular item, while the other party takes a short position, meaning it agrees to sell that item. Unlike an option, both parties are obligated to perform according to the terms of the contract. Futures contracts are made through a clearinghouse and have standardized notional amounts and settlement dates.

> **Illustration 2    Futures Contract**
>
> On January 1, Year 1, Jones Company entered into a long position on a futures contract in which it agreed to buy €100,000 for $1.67/€ on April 1, Year 1. On April 1, Year 1, the spot rate was $1.74/€.
>
>     Underlying:                     $1.67/€
>     Notional amount:         €100,000
>     Initial net investment:   $0 (no cost to enter into the futures contract)
>     Settlement amount:     $1.67/€ × €100,000 = $167,000
>
> Derivatives generally have multiple settlement options. This derivative could be settled in the following ways:
>
> 1. Jones could pay $167,000 and receive €100,000. Jones could then realize a $7,000 gain by selling the €100,000 at the spot rate of $1.74/€ ($174,000 – $167,000 = $7,000).
> 2. The other party to the futures contract could pay $7,000 to Jones. This is a net settlement. Jones could then purchase the €100,000 for $174,000 and still show a net outflow of $167,000 ($174,000 purchase price – $7,000 gain).
>
> If the spot rate on April 1 had been $1.59/€, Jones would have realized loss on the contract because Jones would have paid $167,000 for €100,000 that could have been purchased outside the futures contract for only $159,000 (€100,000 × $1.59/€).

## 2.3 Forward Contract

Forward contracts are similar to futures contracts, except that they are privately negotiated between two parties with the assistance of an intermediary, rather than through a clearinghouse. Forward contracts do not have standardized notional amounts or settlement dates. The terms of a forward contract are established by the parties to the contract.

## 2.4 Swap Contract

A private agreement between two parties, generally assisted by an intermediary, to exchange future cash payments. Common swaps include interest rate swaps, currency swaps, equity swaps, and commodity swaps. A swap agreement is equivalent to a series of forward contracts.

> **Illustration 3  Swap Contract**
>
> On January 1, Year 1, East Company and West Company entered into an interest rate swap in which East Company agreed to make to West Company a series of future payments equal to a fixed interest rate of 8% on a principal amount of $1,000,000. In exchange, West Company agreed to make to East Company a series of future payments equal to a floating interest rate of SOFR* + 1% on the principal amount of $1,000,000.
>
> | | |
> |---|---|
> | Underlying: | East Company—8%, and West Company—SOFR + 1% |
> | Notional amount: | $1,000,000 |
> | Initial net investment: | $0 (no cost to enter into the swap contract) |
> | Settlement amount: | East Company—8% × $1,000,000 = $80,000, and West Company—(SOFR + 1%) × $1,000,000 |
>
> On the first settlement date, SOFR was 8.5% and the following amounts were exchanged:
>
> East Company —$80,000→ West Company
> East Company ←$95,000 = $1,000,000 × 9.5%— West Company
>
> Derivatives generally have multiple settlement options. This derivative could be settled in the following ways:
>
> 1. East Company could pay $80,000 to West Company, and West Company could pay $95,000 to East Company.
>
> 2. West Company could pay $15,000 ($95,000 − $80,000) to East Company. This is a net settlement and is the most likely form of settlement in this example.
>
> *SOFR (Secured Overnight Financing Rate) measures the cost of overnight borrowings through repurchase (repo) transactions collateralized with U.S. Treasury securities.

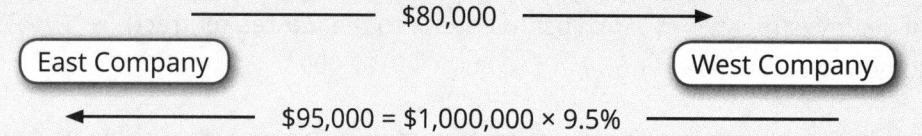

# 3   Derivative Risks

Market risk and credit risk are the inherent risks of all derivative instruments.

## 3.1   Market Risk

Market risk is the risk that the entity will incur a loss on the derivative contract. As demonstrated in the examples above, derivatives are a "zero sum game." Every derivative has a "winner" and a "loser."

## 3.2   Credit Risk

Credit risk is the risk that the other party to the derivative contract will not perform according to the terms of the contract. For example, in the interest rate swap example above, East Company faces the risk that West Company will refuse to pay the net settlement of $15,000.

# 4 Accounting for Derivative Instruments Including Hedges

## 4.1 Balance Sheet

All derivative instruments are recognized in the balance sheet as either assets or liabilities, depending on the rights or obligations under the contracts.

All derivative instruments are measured at fair value.

Accounting for changes in the fair value of a derivative is dependent on whether the derivative has been designated as (and whether it qualifies as) a hedge, combined with the reason for holding the instrument.

## 4.2 Reporting Gains and Losses

### 4.2.1 No Hedging Designation

Gains or losses on a derivative instrument not designated as a hedging instrument are recognized currently in earnings, similar to the accounting for trading securities.

### 4.2.2 Fair Value Hedge

A fair value hedge is an instrument designated as a hedge of the exposure to changes in fair value of a recognized asset or liability, or of an unrecognized firm commitment, that are attributable to a particular risk. Gains/losses on such instruments as well as the offsetting gain/loss on the hedged item are recognized in earnings in the same accounting period. The derivative must be expected to be highly effective in offsetting the fair value change (which could affect income) of the hedged item.

### 4.2.3 Cash Flow Hedge

A cash flow hedge is an instrument designated as hedging the exposure to variability in expected future cash flows attributed to a particular risk. Gains/losses on the *ineffective* portion of a cash flow hedge are reported in current income. Gains/losses on the *effective* portion of a cash flow hedge are deferred and are reported as a component of other comprehensive income until the hedged transaction impacts earnings, as follows:

- If a forecasted sale or expense is hedged, the gain/loss in accumulated other comprehensive income (AOCI) is reclassified to earnings when the sale or expense is recognized in earnings.
- If a forecasted inventory purchase is hedged, the gain/loss in AOCI is reclassified to earnings when the inventory is sold to customers.
- If a forecasted fixed asset purchase is hedged, the gain/loss in AOCI is reclassified to earnings as the fixed asset is depreciated.
- If an existing asset or liability is hedged, the gain/loss in AOCI is reclassified to earnings when the asset or liability impact earnings.

Derivatives and Hedge Accounting

## Private Company Accounting Alternative

Under U.S. GAAP, a private company (an entity that is not a public entity or not-for-profit entity) may elect to apply the following accounting alternative intended to make it easier for certain interest rate swaps to qualify for hedge accounting. Certain conditions must be met, and this alternative is not available to financial institutions.

An eligible company would be able to apply hedge accounting to its receive-variable, pay-fixed interest rate swaps using the following simplified steps:

1. Assume the cash flow hedge has no ineffectiveness as long as certain conditions are met.

2. Recognize the interest rate swap at its settlement value, which excludes nonperformance risk, instead of at its fair value. This provision is optional, and can be elected on a swap-by-swap basis.

3. Complete hedge documentation by the first date on which the financial statements are available to be issued after hedge inception, rather than at hedge inception.

Under this simplified hedge accounting approach, the interest expense reported on the income statement would be similar to the amount that would result if the entity had entered into a fixed-rate borrowing instead of a variable-rate borrowing and a receive-variable, pay-fixed interest rate swap.

### Example 1 — Fair Value Hedge

**Facts:** On September 30, Year 1, Smith Company signed a contract to purchase 100,000 pounds of copper wire on December 31, Year 1, for $1.55/lb.

**Risk:** When it enters into this firm purchase commitment, Smith faces the risk that the price of the copper wire could fall below $1.55/lb. A loss must be recognized on a firm purchase commitment when the contract price exceeds the market price.

**Hedge:** To hedge the risk of loss on the firm purchase commitment, Smith takes a short position in a forward contract in which Smith agrees to sell 100,000 lb. of copper for $0.92/lb. on December 31, Year 1. If the price of copper goes down, Smith will record a gain on the hedge because Smith has "locked in" a higher selling price. This hedge is classified as a fair value hedge because Smith is hedging the change in the value of the firm purchase commitment. Smith expects this hedge to be highly effective because the price of copper wire is directly related to the price of copper.

The prices of copper wire and of the copper forward contract are as follows:

|  | Copper Wire/lb. | Copper Forward/lb. |
| --- | --- | --- |
| September 30, Year 1 | $1.550 | $0.920 |
| December 31, Year 1 | $1.480 | $0.851 |

No journal entries are recorded on September 30, Year 1.

**Required:** Prepare the journal entries that must be recorded on December 31, Year 1.

(continued)

(continued)

**Solution:**

*Journal entry: To record the loss on the firm purchase commitment*
*[($1.480/lb. − $1.550/lb.) × 100,000 lb. = $7,000].*

| DR | Loss on firm purchase commitment | $7,000 | |
|---|---|---|---|
| CR | Firm purchase commitment liability | | $7,000 |

*Journal entry: To record the gain on the forward contract hedge*
*[($0.851/lb. − $0.920/lb.) × 100,000 lb. = $6,900].*

| DR | Fair value hedge | $6,900 | |
|---|---|---|---|
| CR | Gain on fair value hedge | | $6,900 |

Earnings impact of purchase commitment (no hedge) = $7,000 loss

Earnings impact of purchase commitment (with hedge) = $100 loss ($7,000 loss − $6,900 gain)

*Journal entry: To record the net settlement of the forward contract, Smith will receive $6,900 because the forward contract allows Smith to sell copper for $0.92/lb. when the price of copper is $0.851/lb. (The forward price is equal to the spot price of copper on the settlement date).*

| DR | Cash | $6,900 | |
|---|---|---|---|
| CR | Fair value hedge | | $6,900 |

*Journal entry: To record the purchase of 100,000 lb. of copper wire for $1.55/lb. under the firm purchase commitment.*

| DR | Firm purchase commitment liability | $ 7,000 | |
|---|---|---|---|
| DR | Inventory | 148,000 | |
| CR | Cash | | $155,000 |

Note that the inventory is reported at its fair value on December 31, Year 1: 100,000 lb. × $1.480/lb. = $148,000. Because the company entered into the fair value hedge, the cash paid for the inventory totals $148,100 ($155,000 paid under firm purchase commitment − $6,900 net settlement from fair value hedge), which is approximately fair value. This is not a perfect hedge, but it is highly effective.

Derivatives and Hedge Accounting

## Example 2 — Cash Flow Hedge

**Facts:** On September 30, Year 1, Smith Company determined that it will need to purchase 100,000 pounds of copper wire on March 31, Year 2. The current price of copper wire is $1.55/lb.

**Risk:** Smith faces the risk that the price of the copper wire will increase before the purchase is made on March 31, Year 2.

**Hedge:** To hedge the risk that the price of the copper wire will increase, Smith takes a long position in a forward contract in which Smith agrees to buy 100,000 lb. of copper for $0.92/lb. on March 31, Year 2. If the price of copper goes up, Smith will record a gain on the hedge because Smith has "locked in" a lower purchase price. This hedge is classified as a cash flow hedge because Smith is hedging the cash outflow that will be required to purchase the copper wire on March 31, Year 2. Smith expects this hedge to be highly effective because the price of copper wire is directly related to the price of copper. The prices of copper wire and of the copper forward contract are as follows:

|                       | Copper Wire/lb. | Copper Forward/lb. |
|-----------------------|-----------------|--------------------|
| September 30, Year 1  | $1.550          | $0.920             |
| December 31, Year 1   | $1.591          | $0.960             |
| March 31, Year 2      | $1.620          | $0.988             |

**Required:** Prepare the journal entries to account for the cash flow hedge on September 30, Year 1; December 31, Year 1; and March 31, Year 2.

**Solution:**

*September 30, Year 1: No journal entries are recorded.*

*December 31, Year 1: Journal entry to record the gain on the forward contract hedge [($0.960/lb. − $0.920/lb.) × 100,000 lb. = $4,000].*

| DR | Cash flow hedge | $4,000 | |
|----|-----------------|--------|---|
| CR | OCI—Effective portion of hedge* | | $4,000 |

*The entire gain is considered effective because it does not exceed the $4,100 loss on the copper wire during the period [($1.591/lb. − $1.550/lb.) × 100,000 lb. = $4,100].

*March 31, Year 2: Journal entry to record the gain on the forward contract hedge [($0.988/lb. − $0.960/lb.) × 100,000 lb. = $2,800].*

| DR | Cash flow hedge | $2,800 | |
|----|-----------------|--------|---|
| CR | OCI—Effective portion of hedge | | $2,800 |

*Journal entry to record the net settlement of the forward contract.*

| DR | Cash | $6,800 | |
|----|------|--------|---|
| CR | Cash flow hedge | | $6,800 |

Smith will receive $6,800 because under the forward contract Smith purchases copper for $0.92/lb. when the price of copper is $0.988/lb. (the forward price is equal to the spot price of copper on the settlement date).

*(continued)*

*(continued)*

*Journal entry to record the purchase of 100,000 lb. of copper wire for $1.62/lb.:*

| DR | Inventory | $162,000 | |
|---|---|---|---|
| CR | Cash | | $162,000 |

Because the company entered into the cash flow hedge, the net cash paid for the inventory totals $155,200 ($162,000 paid − $6,800 net settlement from the cash flow hedge), only slightly more than the $155,000 that would have been paid if the wire had been purchased on September 30, Year 1. This is not a perfect hedge, but it is highly effective. The $6,800 gain in AOCI will be recognized in earnings when the copper wire is sold to customers.

### 4.2.4 Foreign Currency Hedge

A foreign currency hedge is an instrument designated as hedging the exposure to variability in foreign currency in a variety of foreign currency transactions.

- **Foreign Currency Fair Value Hedge:** Gains and losses from changes in the fair value of foreign currency transaction hedges classified as fair value hedges are accounted for in the same manner as gains/losses on other fair value hedges—in earnings.

- **Foreign Currency Cash Flow Hedge:** Gains and losses from changes in the fair value of foreign currency transaction hedges classified as cash flow hedges are accounted for in the same manner as gains/losses on cash flow hedges—in other comprehensive income for the effective portion and current income for the ineffective portion.

- **Foreign Currency Net Investment Hedge:** Gains and losses from changes in the fair value of foreign currency transaction hedges entered into to hedge a net investment in a foreign operation are reported in other comprehensive income as part of the cumulative translation adjustment for the effective portion and current income for the ineffective portion.

| Type of Hedge Instrument | Accounting for Changes in Fair Value |
|---|---|
| **No hedge designation** | Included in current earnings |
| **Fair value hedge** | Included in current earnings as an offset to the gain/loss from the change in fair value of the hedged item |
| **Cash flow hedge** | |
| Effective portion | Included in other comprehensive income until the hedged transaction impacts earnings |
| Ineffective portion | Included in current earnings |
| **Foreign exchange hedge** | |
| Fair value hedge | Included in current earnings as an offset to the gain/loss from the change in fair value of the hedged item |
| Cash flow hedge | Effective portion—Included in other comprehensive income until the hedged transaction impacts earnings. Ineffective portion—Included in current earnings |
| Net investment hedge | Included in other comprehensive income, as cumulative translation adjustment. |

## 4.3 Reporting Cash Flows

Cash flows from a derivative with no hedging designation should be accounted for in investing activities, unless the derivative is held for trading purposes. If a derivative with no hedging designation is held for trading purposes, the cash flows should be accounted for in operating activities. The cash flows from a derivative held as a hedge may be accounted for in the same category as the item being hedged. If the derivative contains an other-than-insignificant financing element at inception (which is often a matter of judgment), all cash flows associated with that derivative should be reported as cash flows from financing activities, not just those related to the financing element.

# 5 Derivative Disclosures

The following disclosures are required by U.S. GAAP for every period (annual and interim) that a balance sheet and income statement are presented. If derivative information is presented in more than one footnote, then the footnotes should be cross-referenced. IFRS has similar disclosure requirements.

- A description of the entity's objectives for holding or issuing derivatives and its strategies to achieve those objectives. Information should be disclosed about each instrument's primary underlying risk exposure (interest rate, credit, foreign exchange rate, or overall price). Derivatives should be distinguished between those used for risk management (hedging) and those used for other purposes. Derivatives that are used for hedging purposes should be designated as fair value hedging instruments, cash flow hedging instruments, or instruments hedging the foreign currency exposure of a net investment in a foreign operation. If a derivative is not designated as a hedging instrument, then the purpose of the derivative should be described.

- Information on the volume of the company's derivative activity.

- The location and fair values of derivative instruments reported on the balance sheet. Fair value must be presented on a gross basis. Fair value amounts must be presented as separate asset and liability values segregated between derivatives used for hedging purposes and derivatives that are not used for hedging purposes. The disclosure should include the line items in the balance sheet in which the fair value amounts are included.

- The location (line items) and amount of the gains and losses reported on the income statement and in other comprehensive income (OCI). Gains and losses should be presented separately for:

  - Fair value hedges.
  - The effective portion of gains and losses on cash flow hedges and net investment hedges recognized in OCI during the current period.
  - The effective portion of gains and losses on cash flow hedges and net investment hedges reclassified from OCI to the income statement during the current period.
  - The ineffective portion of the gains and losses on cash flow hedges and net investment hedges.
  - Derivative instruments not designated as hedges.

- For derivatives designated as fair value hedges and the related hedged items, the net gain or loss recognized in earnings during the current period, the effective portion of the hedge, and the portion of the gain or loss, if any, excluded from the assessment of effectiveness.
- For derivatives designated as cash flow hedges and the related hedged items, a description of the events that will result in reclassification of gains and losses from OCI to earnings, the estimated reclassification adjustments for the next 12 months, the estimated length of time over which the future cash flows will be hedged, and the amount of gains and losses reclassified to earnings because the forecasted cash flows will not occur and the cash flows hedge has been discontinued.

### Question 1 — MCQ-00943

A derivative designated as a fair value hedge must be:

I. Specifically identified to the hedged asset, liability, or unrecognized firm commitment.
II. Expected to be highly effective in offsetting changes in the fair value of the hedged item.

a. I only.
b. II only.
c. Both I and II.
d. Neither I nor II.

### Question 2 — MCQ-00929

On September 30 of the current year, a U.S. company entered into a futures contract to hedge the value of its inventory. The inventory was reported on the balance sheet at its cost of $250,000 on September 30. On December 31, the market value of the inventory had decreased to $175,000. The entity had a gain of $74,500 on the futures contract at December 31. What is the proper accounting for this hedging transaction on the December 31 year-end financial statements, assuming that the hedge is considered to be highly effective?

a. Other comprehensive income will increase by $74,500.
b. Other comprehensive income will decrease by $500.
c. Net income will increase by $74,500.
d. Net income will decrease by $500.

## NOTES

# MODULE 4: Foreign Currency Accounting

**FAR 6**

## 1 Overview

Foreign currency accounting is concerned with foreign currency transactions and translations.

- **Foreign Currency Transactions:** Transactions with a foreign entity (e.g., buying from and selling to) denominated in (to be settled in) a foreign currency.
- **Foreign Currency Translation:** The conversion of financial statements of a foreign entity into financial statements expressed in the domestic currency (the dollar).

## 2 Terminology

- **Exchange Rate:** Exchange rate is the price of one unit of a currency expressed in units of another currency; the rate at which two currencies will be exchanged at equal value. The exchange rate may be expressed as:
  - **Direct Method:** The direct method is the domestic price of one unit of another currency. For example, one euro costs $1.47.
  - **Indirect Method:** The indirect method is the foreign price of one unit of the domestic currency. For example, 0.68 euro buys $1.00.
- **Current Exchange Rate:** Current exchange rate is the exchange rate at the current date, or for immediate delivery of currency, often referred to as the spot rate.
- **Forward Exchange Rate:** Forward exchange rate is the exchange rate existing now for exchanging two currencies at a specific future date.
- **Historical Exchange Rate:** The historical exchange rate is the rate in effect at the date of issuance of stock or acquisition of assets.
- **Weighted Average Rate:** The weighted average exchange rate is calculated to take into account the exchange rate fluctuations for the period. It would be impractical to account for the actual exchange rate in effect for numerous, recurring transactions (e.g., sales). The average rate, when applied to a transaction normally assumed to have occurred evenly throughout the period, approximates the effect of separate translations of each item.
- **Forward Exchange Contract:** A forward exchange contract is an agreement to exchange at a future specified date and rate a fixed amount of currencies of different countries.
- **Denominated or Fixed in a Currency:** A transaction is denominated or fixed in the currency used to negotiate and settle the transaction, either in U.S. dollars or a foreign currency.
- **Reporting Currency:** The reporting currency is the currency of the entity ultimately reporting financial results of the foreign entity.
- **Functional Currency:** The functional currency is the currency of the primary economic environment in which the entity operates, usually the local currency or the reporting currency.

## Foreign Currency Accounting

- **Foreign Currency Translation:** Foreign currency translation is the restatement of financial statements denominated in the functional currency to the reporting currency using appropriate rates of exchange.

- **Foreign Currency Remeasurement:** Foreign currency remeasurement is the restatement of foreign financial statements from the foreign currency to the entity's functional currency in the following situations:
  - The reporting currency is the functional currency.
  - The financial statements must be restated in the entity's functional currency prior to translating the financial statements from the functional currency to the reporting currency.

- **Monetary Items:** Assets and liabilities that are fixed or denominated in dollars regardless of changes in specific prices or the general price level (e.g., accounts receivable).

- **Nonmonetary Items:** Assets and liabilities that fluctuate in value with inflation and deflation (e.g., a building).

| Monetary and Nonmonetary Items | Monetary | Nonmonetary |
|---|---|---|
| **Assets** | | |
| Cash | ✓ | |
| Marketable common stock | | ✓ |
| Bonds: nonconvertible | ✓ | |
| Accounts/notes receivable (and allowance) | ✓ | |
| Inventory | | ✓ |
| Long-term receivables | ✓ | |
| Investment in subsidiary (equity) | | ✓ |
| Plan, property, and equipment (and accum. depr.) | | ✓ |
| Intangible assets: patents and trademarks | | ✓ |
| **Liabilities** | | |
| Accounts and notes payable | ✓ | |
| Accrued expenses | ✓ | |
| Bonds/notes payable | ✓ | |
| Deferred charges and credits | | ✓ |
| **Equities** | | |
| Preferred stock | | ✓ |
| Common stock | | ✓ |
| Retained earnings is neither. Use as a residual (plug). | | |

# 3 Foreign Financial Statement Translation

Before a parent company can consolidate the financial statements of a foreign subsidiary, the subsidiary's foreign currency financial statements must be restated in the parent company's reporting currency. The method used to restate the foreign subsidiary's financial statements is determined by the functional currency of the foreign subsidiary.

## 3.1 Steps in Restating Foreign Financial Statements

### 3.1.1 Prepare in Accordance With GAAP/IFRS

Before performing any part of the translation process, it is necessary to ensure that the financial statements expressed in the foreign currency were prepared in accordance with U.S. GAAP or IFRS, as appropriate. If necessary, corrections must be made to comply with GAAP or IFRS.

### 3.1.2 Determine the Functional Currency

The functional currency of a foreign entity determines the conversion methodology to use. The functional currency can be the entity's local currency, the currency of the reporting entity, or the currency of another country. Under U.S. GAAP, an entity's local currency qualifies as the functional currency if it is the currency of the primary economic environment in which the company operates, and all of the following conditions exist:

- The foreign operations are relatively self-contained and integrated within the country.
- The day-to-day operations do not depend on the parent's or investor's functional currency.
- The local economy of the foreign entity is *not* highly inflationary, which is defined as cumulative inflation of 100 percent over three years.

### 3.1.3 Determine Appropriate Exchange Rates

The functional currency of the foreign entity determines the exchange rates to be used in converting account balances and the treatment of the gains or losses associated with the translation process.

### 3.1.4 Remeasure and/or Translate the Financial Statements

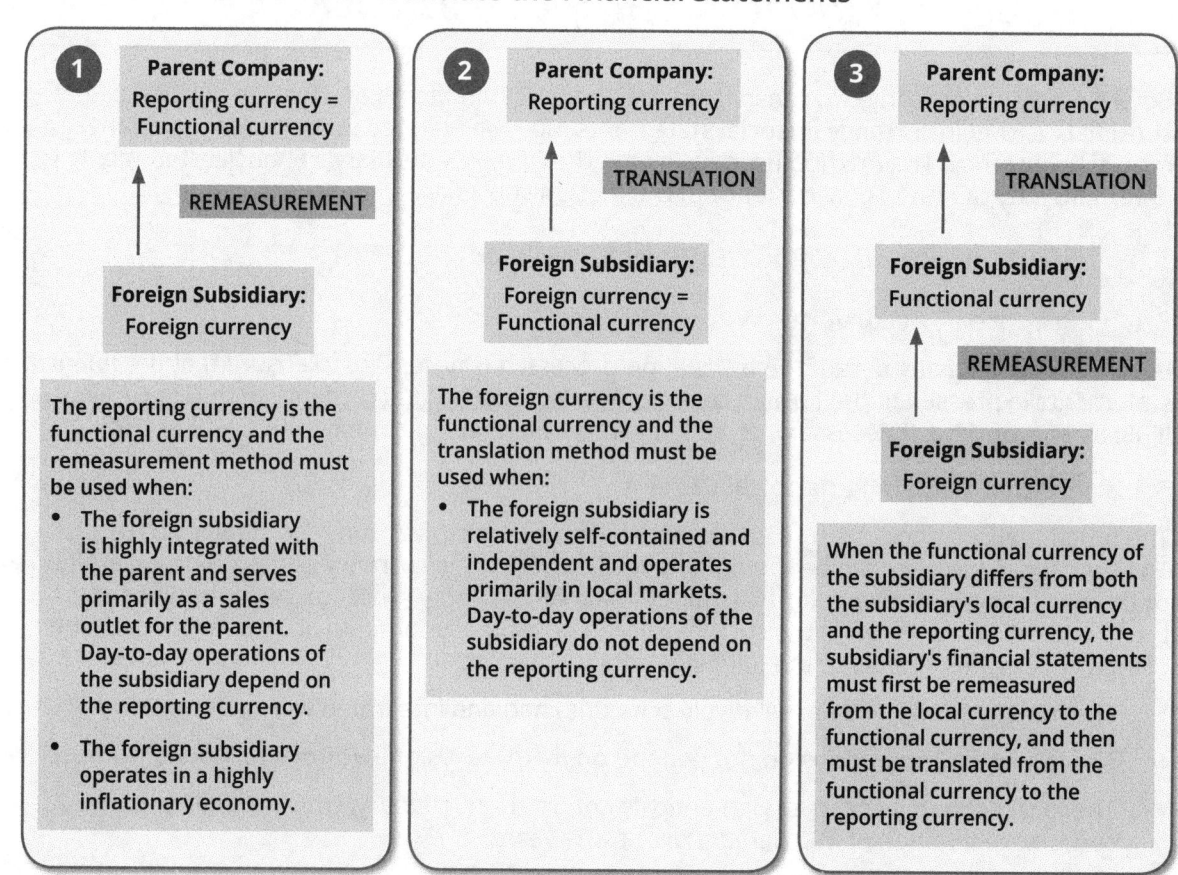

**1** Parent Company: Reporting currency = Functional currency
↑ REMEASUREMENT
Foreign Subsidiary: Foreign currency

The reporting currency is the functional currency and the remeasurement method must be used when:
- The foreign subsidiary is highly integrated with the parent and serves primarily as a sales outlet for the parent. Day-to-day operations of the subsidiary depend on the reporting currency.
- The foreign subsidiary operates in a highly inflationary economy.

**2** Parent Company: Reporting currency
↑ TRANSLATION
Foreign Subsidiary: Foreign currency = Functional currency

The foreign currency is the functional currency and the translation method must be used when:
- The foreign subsidiary is relatively self-contained and independent and operates primarily in local markets. Day-to-day operations of the subsidiary do not depend on the reporting currency.

**3** Parent Company: Reporting currency
↑ TRANSLATION
Foreign Subsidiary: Functional currency
↑ REMEASUREMENT
Foreign Subsidiary: Foreign currency

When the functional currency of the subsidiary differs from both the subsidiary's local currency and the reporting currency, the subsidiary's financial statements must first be remeasured from the local currency to the functional currency, and then must be translated from the functional currency to the reporting currency.

## 3.2 Remeasurement Method (Temporal Method)

If the financial statements of the foreign subsidiary are not in the subsidiary's functional currency, the financial statements are remeasured to the functional currency starting with the balance sheet.

1. **Balance Sheet**
   - Monetary items = Current/year-end rate
   - Nonmonetary items = Historical rate

2. **Income Statement**
   - Non-balance sheet related items = Weighted average rate
   - Balance sheet related items = Historical rate
     — Depreciation/PP&E
     — Cost of goods sold/inventory
     — Amortization/bonds and intangibles

3. **Remeasurement Gain or Loss (Income Statement)**
   Plug "currency gain/loss" to get net income to the required amount needed to adjust retained earnings in order to make the balance sheet balance.

> ### U.S. GAAP VS. IFRS
>
> U.S. GAAP requires the use of the remeasurement method when a foreign subsidiary operates in a highly inflationary economy. Under IFRS, the financial statements of a foreign subsidiary operating in a highly inflationary economy must first be restated for the effects of inflation and then must be converted from the foreign currency to the reporting currency using the current/year-end rate for all elements of both the balance sheet and income statement.

## 3.3 Translation Method (Current Rate Method)

If the financial statements of the foreign subsidiary are in the subsidiary's functional currency, the financial statements are translated to the reporting currency starting with the income statement.

**Foreign currency = Functional currency**

1. **Income Statement**
   - All income statement items = Weighted average rate
   - Transfer net income to retained earnings

2. **Balance Sheet**
   - Assets = Current/year-end rate
   - Liabilities = Current/year-end rate
   - Common stock/APIC = Historical rate
   - Retained earnings = Roll forward
   - Translated retained earnings is equal to the beginning translated retained earnings plus translated net income for the current period less translated dividends declared for the current period.

3. **Translation Gain or Loss (Other Comprehensive Income)**

   Plug "translation adjustment" to other comprehensive income. The translation adjustment is equal to the difference between the debits and credits in the translated trial balance.

Foreign Currency Accounting

> **Pass Key**
>
> To remember the significant differences in order of steps and conversion rates, the summary chart below should help with the basics:
>
> | Method | Step 1 | Step 2 | Plug | Gain/Loss |
> |---|---|---|---|---|
> | Translation | *Income statement*<br>• At weighted average | *Balance sheet*<br>• At year-end rate<br>• Stock and APIC at historical<br>• Roll forward retained earnings | *Equity*<br>• Accumulated other comprehensive income | OCI |
> | Remeasurement | *Balance sheet*<br>• Monetary at year-end rate<br>• Nonmonetary at historical | *Income statement*<br>• At weighted average<br>• Historical for balance sheet related accounts | • Gain/loss so net income is at amount necessary for retained earnings plug | Net income |

## Illustration 1    Translation and Remeasurement

Financial statements of the Kristi Corporation, a foreign subsidiary of the Dollar Corporation (a U.S. company), are shown below at and for the year ended December 31, Year 2. Two examples follow where the statements are first translated using the local currency unit (LCU) as the functional currency (translation method), then the dollar as the functional currency (remeasurement).

**Assumptions:**

1. The parent company organized the subsidiary on December 31, Year 1.

2. Exchange rates for the LCU were as follows:

   | | |
   |---|---|
   | December 31, Year 1, to March 31, Year 2 | $0.18 |
   | April 1, Year 2, to June 30, Year 2 | 0.13 |
   | July 1, Year 2, to September 30, Year 2 | 0.10 |
   | October 1, Year 2, to December 31, Year 2 | 0.10 |
   | Weighted average | 0.1275 |

3. Inventory was acquired evenly throughout the year and sales were made evenly throughout the year.

4. Fixed assets were acquired by the subsidiary on December 31, Year 1.

## Kristi Corporation
### Foreign Currency Financial Statements
Expressed in dollars at and for the year ended December 31, Year 2

|  |  |  | Translation Method |  | Remeasurement Method |  |
|---|---|---|---|---|---|---|
|  |  |  | Exchange Rate | Dollars | Exchange Rate | Dollars |
| **Income Statement** |  |  |  |  |  |  |
| Sales | LCU | $525,000 | $0.1275 | $66,938 | $0.1275 | $66,938 |
| Costs and expenses: |  |  |  |  |  |  |
|   Cost of goods sold | LCU | 400,000 | 0.1275 | $51,000 | 0.1275 | $51,000 |
|   Depreciation expense |  | 22,000 | 0.1275 | 2,805 | 0.18 | 3,960 |
|   Selling expenses |  | 31,000 | 0.1275 | 3,953 | 0.1275 | 3,953 |
|   Other operating expenses |  | 11,000 | 0.1275 | 1,403 | 0.1275 | 1,403 |
|   Income taxes expense |  | 19,000 | 0.1275 | 2,423 | 0.1275 | 2,423 |
| Total costs and expenses | LCU | 483,000 |  | $61,584 |  | $62,739 |
| Currency exchange (gain) |  |  |  |  | PLUG #2 → | (6,854) |
| Net income | LCU | $ 42,000 |  | $ 5,354 |  | $11,053 |
|  |  |  |  |  |  |  |
| **Statement of Retained Earnings** |  |  |  |  |  |  |
| Retained earnings, beginning of year | LCU | -0- |  | -0- |  | -0- |
| Net income |  | 42,000 |  | $ 5,354 |  | $11,053 |
| Retained earnings, end of year | LCU | $ 42,000 |  | $ 5,354 |  | $11,053 |
|  |  |  |  |  |  |  |
| **Balance Sheet—Assets** |  |  |  |  |  |  |
| Cash | LCU | 10,000 | 0.10 | $ 1,000 | 0.10 | $ 1,000 |
| Accounts receivable (net) |  | 50,000 | 0.10 | 5,000 | 0.10 | 5,000 |
| Inventories (at cost) |  | 95,000 | 0.10 | 9,500 | 0.1275 | 12,113 |
| Fixed assets |  | 275,000 | 0.10 | 27,500 | 0.18 | 49,500 |
| Accumulated depreciation |  | (22,000) | 0.10 | (2,200) | 0.18 | (3,960) |
| Total assets | LCU | $408,000 |  | $40,800 |  | $63,653 |
|  |  |  |  |  |  |  |
| **Liabilities and Stockholders' Equity** |  |  |  |  |  |  |
| Accounts payable | LCU | 34,000 | 0.10 | $ 3,400 | 0.10 | $ 3,400 |
| Long-term debt |  | 132,000 | 0.10 | 13,200 | 0.10 | 13,200 |
| Common stock, 10,000 shares |  | 200,000 | 0.18 | 36,000 | 0.18 | 36,000 |
| Retained earnings |  | 42,000 |  | 5,354 | PLUG #1 → | 11,053 |
| Accumulated balance of other comprehensive income |  |  | PLUG → | (17,154) |  |  |
| Total liabilities and stockholders' equity | LCU | $408,000 |  | $40,800 |  | $63,653 |

**Note:** The superimposed numbers are the order of steps in the two examples.

# 4 Individual Foreign Transactions

Foreign currency transaction gains and losses occur when a company buys from or sells to a foreign company with whom it has no ownership interest and agrees to pay or accept payment in a foreign currency. Transactions between subsidiary and parent of a permanent financing nature are not considered foreign currency transactions.

## 4.1 Types of Foreign Currency Transactions

Foreign currency transactions include operating transactions (import, export, borrowing, lending, and investing transactions) and forward exchange contracts (agreements to exchange two different currencies at a specific future date and at a specific rate).

## 4.2 Changes in Exchange Rate

A foreign exchange transaction gain or loss will result if the exchange rate changes between the time a purchase or sale in foreign currency is contracted for and the time actual payment is made.

## 4.3 Transaction Not Settled at Balance Sheet Date

A foreign exchange transaction gain or loss that is recognized in current net income must be computed at each balance sheet date on all recorded transactions denominated in foreign currencies that have not been settled. The difference between the exchange rate used in recording the transaction in dollars and the exchange rate at the balance sheet date (current exchange rate) is an unrealized gain or loss on the foreign currency transaction.

## 4.4 Valuation of Assets and Liabilities

The assets or liabilities resulting from foreign currency transactions should be recorded in the U.S. company's books using the exchange rate in effect at the date of the transaction.

---

### Example 1 — Foreign Currency Transaction

**Facts:** On 12/1/Yr 1, Olinto Company purchased goods on credit for 100,000 pesos. Olinto Company paid for the goods on 2/1/Yr 2. The exchange rates were:

| Date | Rate |
| --- | --- |
| 12/1/Yr 1 | $0.10 |
| 12/31/Yr 1 | $0.08 |
| 2/1/Yr 2 | $0.09 |

**Required:** Prepare the journal entries related to this foreign currency transaction.

**Solution:**

*12/1/Yr 1*

| | | | |
| --- | --- | --- | --- |
| DR | Purchases (100,000 pesos × $0.10 exchange rate) | $10,000 | |
| CR | Accounts payable | | $10,000 |

(continued)

(continued)

*12/31/Yr 1*

| DR | Accounts payable (100,000 pesos × $0.10 − $0.08) | $2,000 | |
|---|---|---|---|
| CR | Foreign exchange transaction gain | | $2,000 |

100,000 pesos can be purchased for $8,000 at 12/31/Yr 1. The difference between the $8,000 and the original recorded liability of $10,000 is a foreign exchange transaction gain that increases net income for Year 1.

*2/1/Yr 2*

| DR | Accounts payable | $8,000 | |
|---|---|---|---|
| DR | Foreign exchange transaction loss [100,000 × ($0.08 − $0.09)] | 1,000 | |
| CR | Cash (100,000 pesos × $0.09) | | $9,000 |

## Question 1 — MCQ-01272

Park Co.'s wholly owned German subsidiary, Schnell Corp., maintains its accounting records in euros. Because all of Schnell's branch offices are in Switzerland, its functional currency is the Swiss franc. Remeasurement of Schnell's Year 4 financial statements resulted in a $7,600 gain, and translation of its financial statements resulted in an $8,100 gain. What amount should Park report as a foreign exchange gain in its income statement for the year ended December 31, Year 4?

a. $0
b. $7,600
c. $8,100
d. $15,700

## Question 2 — MCQ-01274

On September 22, Year 4, Yumi Corp. purchased merchandise from an unaffiliated foreign company for 10,000 units of the foreign company's local currency. On that date, the spot rate was $0.55. Yumi paid the bill in full on March 20, Year 5, when the spot rate was $0.65. The spot rate was $0.70 on December 31, Year 4. What amount should Yumi report as a foreign currency transaction loss in its income statement for the year ended December 31, Year 4?

a. $0
b. $500
c. $1,000
d. $1,500

## NOTES

# MODULE 5: Income Taxes: Part 1

**FAR 6**

## 1 Overview

Accounting for income taxes involves both intraperiod and interperiod tax allocation. Intraperiod allocation matches a portion of the provision for income tax to the applicable components of net income and retained earnings.

Income for federal tax purposes and financial accounting income frequently differ. Obviously, income for federal tax purposes is computed in accordance with the prevailing tax laws, whereas financial accounting income is determined in accordance with GAAP. Therefore, a company's income tax expense and income taxes payable may differ. The incongruity is caused by temporary differences in taxable and/or deductible amounts and requires interperiod tax allocation.

### 1.1 Intraperiod Tax Allocation

Intraperiod tax allocation involves apportioning the total tax provision for financial accounting purposes in a period between the income or loss from:

- **Income** from continuing operations,
- **Discontinued** operations
- **Accounting** principle change (retrospective)
- Other comprehensive income
  - **Pension** funded status change
  - **Unrealized** gain/loss on available-for-sale debt security
  - **Foreign** translation adjustment
  - **Instrument**-specific credit risk
  - **Effective** portion of cash flow hedge
  - **Revaluation** surplus (IFRS only)
- Components of stockholders' equity
  - Retained earnings for prior period adjustments and accounting principle changes (retrospective); and
  - Items of accumulated (other) comprehensive income

Any amount not allocated to continuing operations is allocated to other income statement items, other comprehensive income, or to shareholders' equity in proportion to their individual effects on income tax or benefit for the year. Such items (e.g., discontinued operations) are shown net of their related tax effects.

The amount of income tax expense (or benefit) allocated to continuing operations is the tax effect of pretax income or loss from continuing operations plus or minus the tax effects of changes in:

1. Tax laws or rates.
2. Expected realization of a deferred tax asset.
3. Tax status of the entity.

## 1.2 Comprehensive Interperiod Tax Allocation

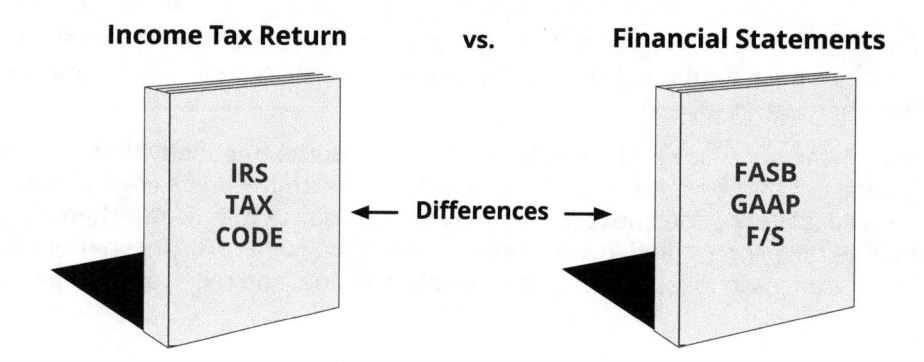

**Income Tax Return** vs. **Financial Statements**

IRS TAX CODE ← Differences → FASB GAAP F/S

### 1.2.1 Objective

The objective of interperiod tax allocation is to recognize through the matching principle the amount of current and future tax related to events that have been recognized in financial accounting income.

- **Current Year Taxes:** Payable (liability) or refundable (asset)

    Or:

- **Future Year Taxes:** Deferred tax asset or deferred tax liability

### 1.2.2 Differences

There are two types of differences between pretax GAAP financial income and taxable income. All differences are either permanent differences or temporary differences.

1. **Permanent Differences**
    - Permanent differences are items of revenue and expense that either:
        — enter into pretax GAAP financial income, but never enter into taxable income (e.g., interest income on state or municipal obligations); or
        — enter into taxable income, but never enter into pretax GAAP financial income (e.g., dividends received deduction).
    - Permanent differences do not affect the deferred tax computation. They only affect the current tax computation. These differences affect only the period in which they occur. They do not affect future financial or taxable income.

2. **Temporary Differences**
    - Temporary differences are items of revenue and expense that may:
        — enter into pretax GAAP financial income in a period *before* they enter into taxable income.
        — enter into pretax GAAP financial income in a period *after* they enter into taxable income.

- Temporary differences affect the deferred tax computation.
- Items that are first recognized for tax purposes will eventually be recognized for GAAP purposes (or vice versa); therefore, the differences are temporary and will eventually "turn around."
- These temporary differences affect future period(s) and require:
  - a liability (for future taxable amounts); or
  - an asset (for future deductible amounts).
- These should be recognized in the financial statement until the difference turns around completely.

### 1.2.3 Comprehensive Allocation

The asset and liability method (sometimes referred to as the balance sheet approach) is required by GAAP for comprehensive allocation. Under comprehensive allocation, interperiod tax allocation is applied to all temporary differences. The asset and liability method requires that either income taxes payable or a deferred tax liability (asset) be recorded for all tax consequences of the current period.

### 1.2.4 Accounting for Interperiod Tax Allocation

- Total income tax expense (GAAP income tax expense) or benefit for the year is the sum of:
  - current income tax expense/benefit, and
  - deferred income tax expense/benefit.
- Current income tax expense/benefit is equal to the income taxes payable or refundable for the current year, as determined on the corporate tax return (Form 1120) for the current year.
- Deferred income tax expense/benefit is equal to the change in deferred tax liability or asset account on the balance sheet from the beginning of the current year to the end of the current year (called the "balance sheet approach").
- Thus, total income tax expense/benefit can be depicted as follows:

$$\text{Current income tax payable or refundable as determined on the corporate tax return} \pm \text{Change in the deferred income tax asset or liability from the beginning to the end of the reporting period} = \text{Total income tax expense or benefit}$$

Tax Return ← Temporary Difference → Financial Statement

× Current tax rate × Future (enacted) tax rate
+ Deferred liability
Current liability − Deferred asset = Total tax expense

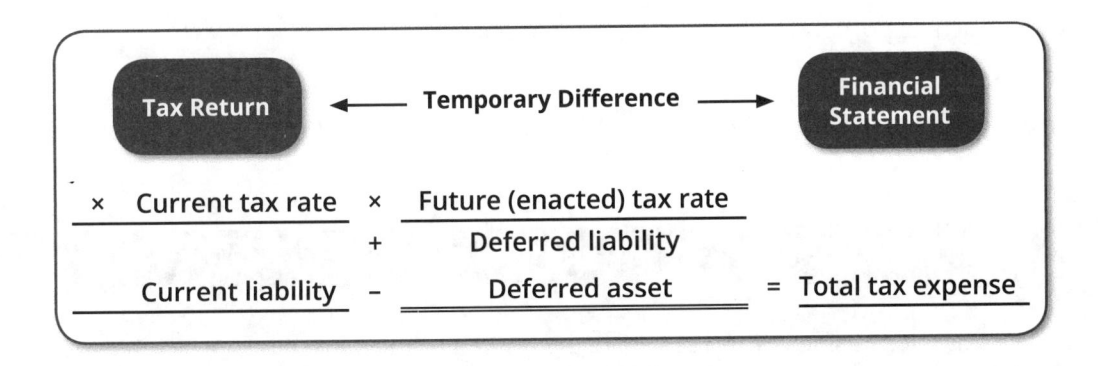

> ## Pass Key
>
> Total tax expense for financial statements is the combination of current tax plus or minus deferred taxes.
>
> The CPA examiners frequently provide an incorrect calculation of financial statement income times the current tax rate. This is an incorrect method to determine the total expense for the following reasons:
>
> - Use of financial statement income (which has permanent differences) is incorrect.
> - Use of the current tax rate ignores future changes to the enacted rate.

## 2 Permanent Differences

A permanent difference is a transaction that affects only income per books or taxable income, but not both. Income tax expense for a period is calculated only on taxable items. For example, tax-exempt interest (municipal and state bonds) is included in financial income, but is excluded in computing income tax expense.

In effect, permanent differences create a discrepancy between taxable income and financial accounting income that will never reverse.

### 2.1 No Deferred Taxes

Because they do not reverse themselves, no interperiod tax allocation is necessary for permanent differences. The income tax provision for financial accounting purposes is computed on the basis of pretax book income adjusted for all permanent differences.

### 2.2 Examples

Permanent differences are either (a) nontaxable, (b) nondeductible, or (c) special tax allowances. Examples are:

- Tax-exempt interest (municipal, state)
- Life insurance proceeds on officer's key man policy
- Life insurance premiums when corporation is beneficiary
- Certain penalties, fines, bribes, kickbacks, etc.
- Nondeductible portion of meal and entertainment expense
- Dividends-received deduction for corporations
- Excess percentage depletion over cost depletion

> ## Pass Key
>
> The deduction for business interest expense is limited to the sum of business interest income plus 30 percent of the adjusted taxable income.

## Example 1 — Permanent Differences

**Facts:** ABC Company reported $200,000 of pretax financial income. Included in this income was $10,000 of life insurance premiums for policies on which the corporation is the beneficiary and interest income on municipal bonds of $50,000.

**Required:** Calculate and record the tax expense for ABC Company, assuming a 21 percent tax rate.

**Solution:**

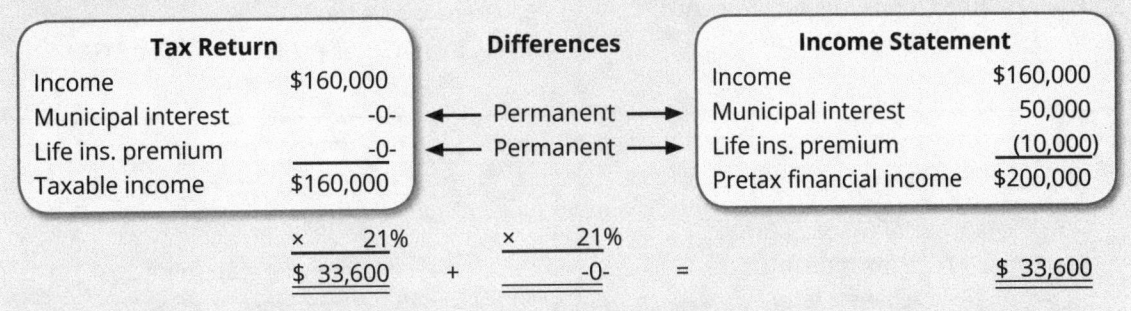

| Tax Return | | Differences | Income Statement | |
|---|---|---|---|---|
| Income | $160,000 | | Income | $160,000 |
| Municipal interest | -0- | ← Permanent → | Municipal interest | 50,000 |
| Life ins. premium | -0- | ← Permanent → | Life ins. premium | (10,000) |
| Taxable income | $160,000 | | Pretax financial income | $200,000 |
| × | 21% | × 21% | | |
| | $33,600 | + -0- = | | $33,600 |

Note that there are no deferred taxes resulting from temporary differences, and that the income tax expense and the income tax liability are the same.

*Journal entry to record income tax expense and income tax liability:*

| DR | Income tax expense | $33,600 | |
|---|---|---|---|
| CR | Income tax payable | | $33,600 |

# 3 Temporary Differences

Temporary differences are the differences between the tax basis of an asset or liability and its reported amount in the financial statements that will result in taxable or deductible amounts in future years when the reported amount of the asset or liability is recovered or settled, respectively.

## 3.1 Transactions That Cause Temporary Differences

There are four basic causes of temporary differences, which reverse in future periods.

1. Revenues or gains that are included in taxable income, after they have been included in financial accounting income, which results in a deferred tax liability.
2. Revenues or gains that are included in taxable income, before they are included in financial accounting income, which results in a deferred tax asset.
3. Expenses or losses deducted from taxable income, after they have been deducted from financial accounting income, which results in a deferred tax asset.
4. Expenses or losses deducted for taxable income, before they are deducted from financial accounting purposes, which results in a deferred tax liability.

Income Taxes: Part 1                                                                                         FAR 6

**① Financial statement income first / Tax return income later**

Tax income later = Future tax liability

1. Installment sales
2. Contractors accounting (% vs. completed)
3. Equity method (undistributed dividends)

**② Tax return income first / Financial statement income later**

Tax income first = Prepaid tax benefit (asset)

1. Prepaid rent*
2. Prepaid interest*
3. Prepaid royalties*
* — The IRC uses the term "prepaid," GAAP uses the term "unearned"

**③ Financial statement expense first / Tax return expense later**

Tax deduct later = Future tax benefit (asset)

1. Bad debt expense (allowance vs. direct w/o)
2. Est. liability/warranty expense
3. Start-up expenses

**④ Tax return expense first / Financial statement expense later**

Tax deduct first = Future tax liability

1. Depreciation expense
2. Amortization of franchise
3. Prepaid expenses (cash basis for tax)

5. Additional causes of temporary differences are:

- Differences between the financial reporting and tax basis of assets and liabilities arising in a business combination accounted for as an acquisition.
- Differences in the tax basis of assets due to indexing, whenever the local currency is the functional currency.

## 3.2 Deferred Tax Liabilities and Assets Recognition

> **Pass Key**
>
> - DTL ⟶ Future tax accounting income > Future financial accounting income
> - DTA ⟶ Future tax accounting income < Future financial accounting income

### 3.2.1 Deferred Tax Liabilities

Deferred tax liabilities are anticipated future tax liabilities derived from situations in which future taxable income will be greater than future financial accounting income due to temporary differences. All deferred tax liabilities are recognized on the balance sheet.

## Example 2 — Deferred Tax Liability

**Facts:** Stone Co. began operations in Year 1 and reported $225,000 in financial income for the year. Stone Co.'s Year 1 tax depreciation exceeded its book depreciation by $25,000. Stone's tax rate for Year 1 and years thereafter was 21 percent. In Year 2, book depreciation exceeded tax depreciation by $25,000. This is a reversal of the temporary difference between GAAP and tax accounting and results in the reversal of the deferred tax liability in Year 2.

**Required:** Prepare the tax journal entries for Year 1 and Year 2.

**Solution:**

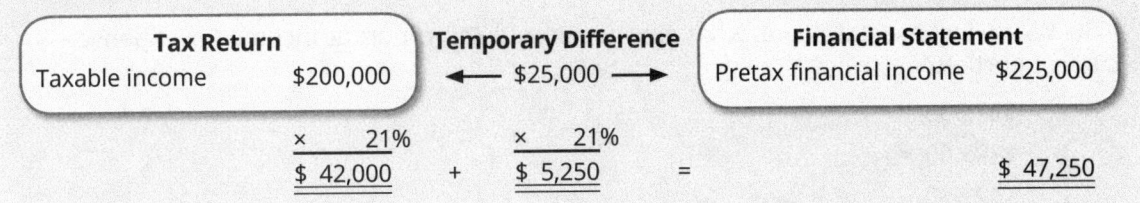

| Tax Return | Temporary Difference | Financial Statement |
|---|---|---|
| Taxable income $200,000 | ← $25,000 → | Pretax financial income $225,000 |
| × 21% | × 21% | |
| $42,000 + | $5,250 = | $47,250 |

The excess depreciation on the tax return results in a future liability, a financial accounting expense in future years that will not be deductible in future years because it was deducted in Year 1. The deferred tax liability reflects the fact that less depreciation will be deducted on the tax return in future years, compared with the financial statements. This yields a future taxable income which will be greater than the future financial accounting income.

*Journal entry to record the taxes in Year 1:*

| | | | |
|---|---|---|---|
| DR | Income tax expense—current | $42,000 | |
| DR | Income tax expense—deferred | 5,250 | |
| CR | Deferred tax liability | | $ 5,250 |
| CR | Income tax payable | | 42,000 |

*Journal entry to record the Year 2 reversal of the deferred tax liability:*

| | | | |
|---|---|---|---|
| DR | Deferred tax liability | $5,250 | |
| CR | Income tax benefit—deferred | | $5,250 |

Income Taxes: Part 1                                                                                                                              FAR 6

### Question 1                                                                                                                                  MCQ-00782

Zeff Co. prepared the following reconciliation of its pretax financial statement income to taxable income for the year ended December 31, Year 1, its first year of operations:

| | |
|---|---:|
| Pretax financial income | $160,000 |
| Nontaxable interest received on municipal securities | (5,000) |
| Long-term loss accrual in excess of deductible amount | 10,000 |
| Depreciation in excess of financial statement amount | (25,000) |
| Taxable income | $140,000 |

Zeff's tax rate for Year 1 is 21 percent.

In its Year 1 income statement, what amount should Zeff report as income tax expense—current portion?

    a.  $27,300
    b.  $29,400
    c.  $32,550
    d.  $33,600

### Question 2                                                                                                                                  MCQ-00783

Zeff Co. prepared the following reconciliation of its pretax financial statement income to taxable income for the year ended December 31, Year 1, its first year of operations:

| | |
|---|---:|
| Pretax financial income | $160,000 |
| Nontaxable interest received on municipal securities | (5,000) |
| Long-term loss accrual in excess of deductible amount | 10,000 |
| Depreciation in excess of financial statement amount | (25,000) |
| Taxable income | $140,000 |

Zeff's tax rate for Year 1 is 21 percent.

In its December 31, Year 1, balance sheet, what should Zeff report as deferred income tax liability?

    a.  $1,050
    b.  $2,100
    c.  $3,150
    d.  $4,200

### 3.2.2 Deferred Tax Assets

Deferred tax assets arise when the amount of taxes paid in the current period exceeds the amount of income tax expense in the current period. They are anticipated future benefits derived from situations in which future taxable income will be less than future financial accounting income due to temporary differences.

### 3.2.3 Valuation Allowance (Contra-Account)

If it is more likely than not (a likelihood of more than 50 percent) that part or all of the deferred tax asset will not be realized, a valuation allowance is recognized. The net deferred tax asset should equal that portion of the deferred tax asset which, based on available evidence, is more likely than not to be realized.

> **U.S. GAAP VS. IFRS**
>
> Valuation allowances are not permitted under IFRS. Instead, a deferred tax asset is recognized when it is probable (more likely than not) that sufficient taxable profit will be available against which the temporary difference can be utilized.

---

**Example 3  Deferred Tax Asset**

**Facts:** Black Co., organized on January 2, Year 1, had pretax accounting income of $500,000 and taxable income of $800,000 for the year ended December 31, Year 1. The enacted tax rate for all years is 21 percent. The only temporary difference is accrued product warranty costs, which are expenses to be paid as follows:

Year 2, $100,000; Year 3, $100,000; Year 4, $100,000

**Required:** Prepare the tax journal entries for Year 1 and Year 2.

**Solution:**

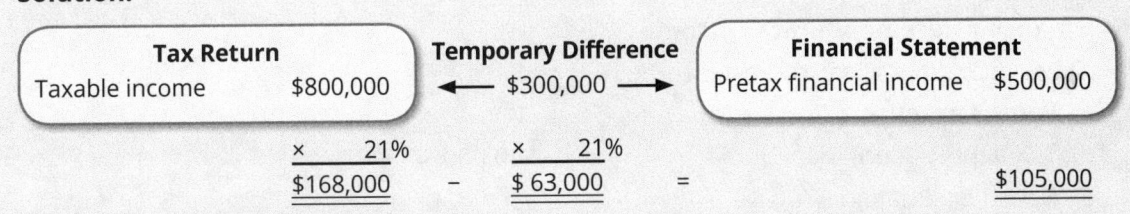

| Tax Return | Temporary Difference | Financial Statement |
|---|---|---|
| Taxable income $800,000 | ← $300,000 → | Pretax financial income $500,000 |
| × 21% | × 21% | |
| $168,000 − | $ 63,000 = | $105,000 |

*Journal entry to record the Year 1 taxes:*

| | | | |
|---|---|---|---|
| DR | Deferred tax asset | $ 63,000 | |
| DR | Income tax expense—current | 168,000 | |
| CR | Income tax payable | | $168,000 |
| CR | Income tax benefit—deferred | | 63,000 |

When the company pays the warranty costs of $100,000 in Year 2, the company will take a $21,000 ($100,000 × 21%) tax deduction related to the warranty costs and will reverse out the related deferred tax asset.

*Journal entry to record reversal of a portion of the deferred tax asset for warranty costs paid and deducted in Year 2.*

| | | | |
|---|---|---|---|
| DR | Income tax expense—deferred | $21,000 | |
| CR | Deferred tax asset | | $21,000 |

# Income Taxes: Part 1

## Example 4 — Valuation Allowance

**Facts:** Black expects to have taxable income of $100,000 in Year 2, but no taxable income after Year 2.

**Required:** Prepare the journal entry to record the deferred tax asset and valuation allowance in Year 1.

**Solution:** The deferred tax asset would be limited to the amount to be realized in Year 2 ($21,000 = $100,000 × 21%). A deferred tax asset of $63,000 would be recognized, but a valuation account of $42,000 would result in a net deferred tax asset of $21,000.

*Journal entry:*

| | | | |
|---|---|---|---|
| DR | Deferred tax asset | $ 63,000 | |
| DR | Income tax expense—current | 168,000 | |
| CR | Deferred tax asset valuation allowance | | $ 42,000 |
| CR | Income tax benefit—deferred | | 21,000 |
| CR | Income tax payable | | 168,000 |

## Example 5 — Permanent and Temporary Differences

**Facts:** Foxy Inc.'s financial statement and taxable income for Year 1 follows (income before the effect of tax-related differences was $140,000):

| | | |
|---|---|---|
| **Financial statement pretax income** | | $115,000 |
| Differences: municipal interest income | | (12,000) |
| Penalty expense | | 7,000 |
| Tax depreciation | $40,000 | |
| Book depreciation | (30,000) | |
| Excess tax depreciation | | (10,000) |
| **Income tax return** | | $100,000 |

The enacted tax rate is 21 percent for this year and future years.

**Required:** Prepare the tax journal entry for Year 1.

*(continued)*

(continued)

**Solution:**

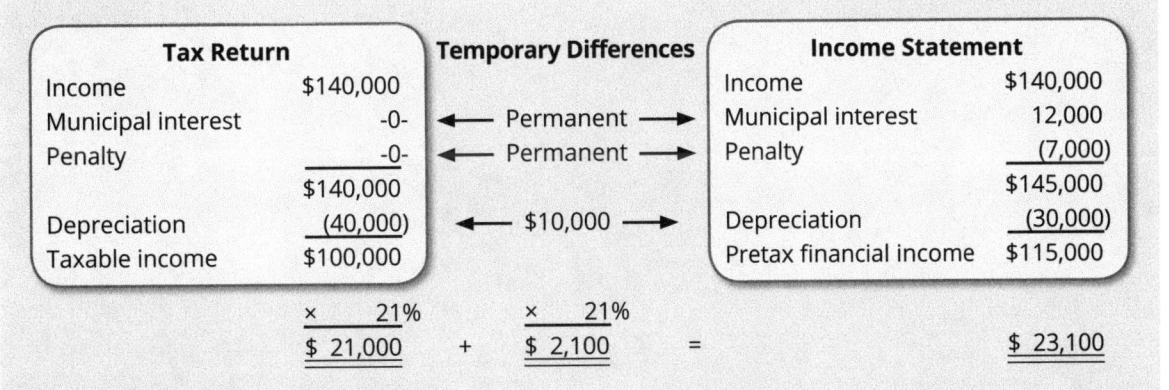

| Tax Return | | Temporary Differences | Income Statement | |
|---|---|---|---|---|
| Income | $140,000 | | Income | $140,000 |
| Municipal interest | -0- | ← Permanent → | Municipal interest | 12,000 |
| Penalty | -0- | ← Permanent → | Penalty | (7,000) |
| | $140,000 | | | $145,000 |
| Depreciation | (40,000) | ← $10,000 → | Depreciation | (30,000) |
| Taxable income | $100,000 | | Pretax financial income | $115,000 |

× 21%    × 21%
$ 21,000  +  $ 2,100  =  $ 23,100

*Journal entry:*

| DR | Income tax expense—current | $ 21,000 | |
|---|---|---|---|
| DR | Income tax expense—deferred | 2,100 | |
| CR | Income taxes currently payable | | $21,000 |
| CR | Deferred tax liability | | 2,100 |

## NOTES

# MODULE 6: Income Taxes: Part 2

FAR 6

## 1 Uncertain Tax Positions

An uncertain tax position is defined as some level of uncertainty of the sustainability of a particular tax position taken by a company. U.S. GAAP requires a more-likely-than-not level of confidence before reflecting a tax benefit in an entity's financial statements.

### 1.1 Scope

A tax position is a filing position that an enterprise has taken or expects to take on its tax return, including:

- A tax deduction (the most common type of tax position).
- A decision to not file a tax return.
- An allocation or shift of income between jurisdictions.
- The characterization of income, or a decision to exclude reporting taxable income, in a tax return.
- A decision to classify a transaction, entity, or other position in a tax return as tax exempt.

### 1.2 Two-Step Approach

#### 1.2.1 Step 1: Recognition of the Tax Benefit

- **Test "More-Likely-Than-Not"**

    The "more-likely-than-not" threshold must be met before a tax benefit can be recognized in the financial statements.

    - The assessment is based on the expected outcome if the dispute with the taxing authority were taken to the court of last resort.

- **Threshold Considerations**

    - The threshold is based on the technical merits of the position.
    - Presume that the relevant taxing authority will examine the tax position and has full knowledge of all relevant information.
    - Each tax position should be evaluated separately.

- **Test Failed**

    - The tax benefit is not recognized in the financial statements if it fails to meet the "more-likely-than-not" test; and
    - Financial statement tax expense is increased.

# Income Taxes: Part 2

## 1.2.2 Step 2: Measurement of the Tax Benefit

- **Recorded Amount**
  - Recognize the largest amount of tax benefit that has a greater than 50 percent likelihood of being realized upon ultimate settlement with the taxing authority.
  - If the tax position is based on clear and unambiguous tax law, recognize the full benefit in the financial statements.

> **Pass Key**
>
> **Step 1:** The evaluation is based on the expected outcome in the court of last resort.
>
> **Step 2:** The evaluation is based on the expected outcome in a settlement with the taxing authority.

### Illustration 1 — Uncertain Tax Position

Foxy Inc. prepared its Year 1 tax return. Foxy Inc. has taken a tax deduction for $2,000 that results in a $420 tax savings (21 percent tax rate). Foxy believes that there is a greater than 50 percent chance that, if audited, the tax deduction would be sustained as filed (the tax deduction meets the "more-likely-than-not" test). However, Foxy concludes that if challenged, it would negotiate a settlement. The following is Foxy's assessment of outcomes:

| Potential Outcomes | Probability | Cumulative Probability |
|---|---|---|
| $420 savings | 26% | 26 |
| $300 savings | 25% | 51 > 50% |
| $200 savings | 21% | 72 |
| $100 savings | 18% | 90 |
| $0 savings | 10% | 100 |

**Result:**

- Based on Foxy Inc.'s assessment of possible outcomes, Foxy should recognize a tax savings/benefit of $300.
- This amount represents the largest benefit that has a greater than 50 percent likelihood of being realized.
- Accordingly, Foxy must record a $120 income tax liability.

# U.S. GAAP VS. IFRS

Uncertain tax positions are not specifically addressed by IFRS. Under IFRS, the tax consequences of events should be accounted for in a manner consistent with the expected resolution of the tax position with tax authorities as of the balance sheet date.

## 2 Enacted Tax Rate

Measurement of deferred taxes is based on the applicable tax rate. This requires using the enacted tax rate expected to apply to taxable items (temporary differences) in the periods the taxable item is expected to be paid (liability) or realized (asset).

### Example 1 — Choice of Tax Rate

**Facts:** Stone Co. began operations in Year 1 and reported $225,000 in income before income taxes for the year. Stone's Year 1 tax depreciation exceeded its book depreciation by $25,000. Stone's tax rate for Year 1 was 30 percent, and the enacted rate for years after is 21 percent.

**Required:** Prepare the tax journal entry for Year 1.

**Solution:**

| Tax Return | Temporary Difference | Financial Statement |
|---|---|---|
| Taxable income  $200,000 | ← $25,000 → | Pretax financial income  $225,000 |
| × 30% | × 21% | |
| $60,000 | + $5,250 | = $65,250 |

| | | | |
|---|---|---|---|
| DR | Income tax expense—current | $60,000 | |
| DR | Income tax expense—deferred | 5,250 | |
| CR | Deferred tax liability | | $5,250 |
| CR | Income tax payable | | 60,000 |

### Pass Key

Use the tax rate in effect when the temporary difference reverses itself. Do not allow the CPA examiners to trick you into using the following tax rates:

- Anticipated
- Proposed
- Unsigned

> **U.S. GAAP VS. IFRS**
>
> IFRS permits the use of enacted or substantively enacted tax rates.

## 3 Treatment of and Adjustment for Changes

### 3.1 Changes in Tax Laws or Rates

The liability method requires that the deferred tax account balance (asset or liability) be adjusted when the tax rates change. Thus if future tax rates have been enacted, not just proposed or estimated, the deferred tax liability and asset accounts will be calculated using the appropriate enacted future effective tax rate.

Changes in tax laws or rates are recognized in the period of change (enactment).

- The amount of the adjustment is measured by the change in applicable laws/rates applied to the remaining cumulative temporary differences.
- The adjustment enters into income tax expense for that period as a component of income from continuing operations.
- An entity must reflect the impact of the enacted change in the annual effective tax rate computation in the interim period that includes the enactment date.

> **U.S. GAAP VS. IFRS**
>
> Under IFRS, adjustments for changes in deferred tax balances due to changes in tax laws or rates are recognized on the income statement, except when the deferred tax balance arises from a transaction or event that is recognized in other comprehensive income. When a deferred tax balance arises from a transaction or event that is recognized in other comprehensive income, adjustments should also be recorded in other comprehensive income.

### 3.2 Change in the Valuation Allowance

A change in circumstances that causes a change in judgment about the ability to realize the related deferred tax asset in future years should be recognized in income from continuing operations in the period of the change.

### 3.3 Change in the Tax Status of an Enterprise

- An entity's tax status may change from taxable to nontaxable (e.g., corporation to partnership) or from nontaxable to taxable (S corporation to C corporation).
- At the date a nontaxable entity becomes a taxable entity, a deferred tax liability or asset should be recognized for any temporary differences.

- At the date a taxable entity becomes a nontaxable entity, any existing deferred tax liability or asset should be eliminated (written off).
- The effect of recognizing or eliminating a deferred tax liability or deferred tax asset should be included in income from continuing operations in the period of the change.

### 3.4 Net Temporary Adjustment (From Beginning Balance)

The deferred tax account is adjusted for the change in deferred taxes (asset or liability), due to the current year's events. The *income tax expense/benefit – deferred* is the difference between the beginning balance in the deferred tax account and the properly computed ending balance in the account.

---

**Example 2    Change in Tax Rate**

**Facts:** Julie Co. had previously recorded temporary differences of $10,000. The enacted rate in the year the temporary differences originated was 20 percent. The deferred tax liability has a beginning balance of $2,000 ($10,000 × 20%). For the current year, taxable income is $100,000 and financial statement income is $120,000. The $20,000 difference is a temporary difference caused by depreciation. The newly enacted rate for the current and future periods is 21 percent. The previously recorded temporary differences have not yet reversed.

**Required:** Prepare the current year tax journal entry.

**Solution:**

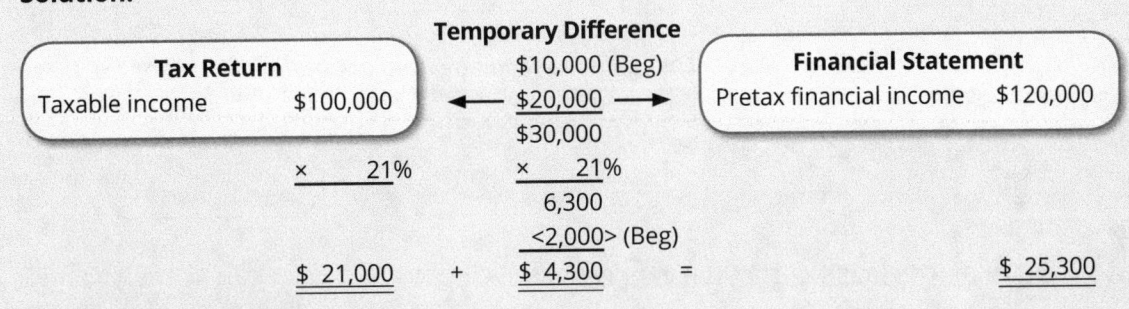

| Tax Return | | Temporary Difference | Financial Statement | |
|---|---|---|---|---|
| Taxable income | $100,000 | $10,000 (Beg) | Pretax financial income | $120,000 |
| | | $20,000 | | |
| | | $30,000 | | |
| × | 21% | × 21% | | |
| | | 6,300 | | |
| | | <2,000> (Beg) | | |
| | $21,000 | + $4,300 = | | $25,300 |

Journal entry to record the taxes:

| DR | Income tax expense—current | $21,000 | |
|---|---|---|---|
| DR | Income tax expense—deferred | 4,300 | |
| CR | Deferred tax liability | | $4,300 |
| CR | Income tax payable | | 21,000 |

---

## 4    Balance Sheet Presentation

Under U.S. GAAP, deferred tax liabilities and assets should be classified and reported as a non-current amount on the balance sheet. This treatment aligns with IFRS. All deferred tax liabilities and assets must be offset (netted) and presented as one amount (a net non-current asset or a net non-current liability), unless the deferred tax liabilities and assets are attributable to different tax-paying components of the entity or to different tax jurisdictions.

# 5 Operating Losses

A net operating loss (NOL) arising in 2018, 2019, or 2020 tax years can be carried back five years (to the oldest year first) and carried forward indefinitely to offset taxable income in other years. NOLs utilized in the five-year carryback period or in 2018, 2019, or 2020 tax years are not subject to a taxable income limitation. NOLs carried forward to taxable years beginning in 2021 or later are limited to 80 percent of taxable income before the NOL deduction. Taxpayers can elect not to carry back and just carry forward. NOLs arising in 2021 and beyond cannot be carried back but can be carried forward indefinitely. Taxable income and financial accounting income will differ for the years in which the loss is incurred and carried back or forward.

## 5.1 Net Operating Loss Carrybacks

If operating losses are carried back to a year before 2018 when the federal corporate tax rate was 35 percent, tax receivables should be measured at the 35 percent rate applicable to the carryback year.

In those cases where a carryback of the NOL is permitted, the tax effects of any realizable loss carryback should be recognized in the determination of the loss period net income. A claim for refund of past taxes is shown on the balance sheet as a separate item from deferred taxes. This income tax refund receivable is usually classified as current.

Tax carrybacks that can be used to reduce taxes due or to receive a refund for a prior period are a tax benefit (asset) and should be recognized (to the extent they can be used) in the period they occur.

*Journal entry to record a current net operating loss that can be used to obtain a refund of $30,000 taxes previously paid:*

| | | | |
|---|---|---|---|
| DR | Tax refund receivable | $30,000 | |
| CR | Tax benefit | | $30,000 |

## 5.2 Operating Loss Carryforwards

If an operating loss is carried forward, the tax effects are recognized to the extent that the tax benefit is more likely than not to be realized. Tax carryforwards should be recognized as deferred tax assets (because they represent future tax savings) in the period in which they occur.

- Net operating loss (NOL) carryforwards should be "valued" using the enacted (future) tax rate for the period(s) they are expected to be used.

- Tax credit carryforwards should be "valued" at the amount of tax payable to be offset in the future. A current net operating loss of $100,000 is carried forward to be used in a period for which the current enacted tax rate is 21 percent.

*Journal entry to record the deferred tax benefit:*

| | | | |
|---|---|---|---|
| DR | Deferred tax asset | $21,000 | |
| CR | Tax benefit * | | $21,000 |

*This is a reduction of the book loss (not a contra-expense).

- The deferred tax asset (DR) will reduce tax payable in a future period.

- The tax benefit (CR) would reduce the net operating loss of the current period.

## Example 3 — Net Operating Losses

**Facts:** The pretax financial accounting income and taxable income of ABC Company were the same for each of the following years. No temporary or permanent differences exist.

|  | Income | Enacted Rates |
|---|---|---|
| 2017 | $10,000 | 35% |
| 2018 | $15,000 | 21% |
| 2019 (current year) | (60,000) | 21% |
| 2020 (expected) | 10,000 | 21% |
| 2021 and forward | -0- | 21% |

**Required:** Assume that it is more likely than not that there will be no taxable earnings after 2020. Assume also that ABC elects to use the five-year carryback. Prepare the journal entry to record the 2019 income taxes and determine how income taxes should be presented in the income statement and the balance sheet.

**Solution:**

**NOL**

| | |
|---|---:|
| 2019 net operating loss (NOL) | $60,000 |
| Carryback to 2017 | (10,000) |
| Carryback to 2018 | (15,000) |
| NOL carryforward to 2020 and future years | $35,000 |

**Carryback**

Income tax receivable:
| | |
|---|---:|
| 2017 ($10,000 × 35%) | $ 3,500 |
| 2018 ($15,000 × 21%) | 3,150 |
| Income tax refund receivable | $ 6,650 |

**Carryforward**

Deferred tax asset (NOL carryforward benefit):
| | |
|---|---:|
| 2020 and future years ($35,000 × 21%) | $ 7,350 |

Deferred tax asset valuation allowance:
| | |
|---|---:|
| NOL carryforward | $35,000 |
| Less: 2020 income | (10,000) |
| Carryforward that will not be used | $25,000 |
| Tax rate (enacted) | × 21% |
| Deferred tax asset valuation allowance | $ 5,250 |
| Net realizable deferred tax asset | $ 2,100 |

*Journal entry to record income taxes for 2019:*

| | | | |
|---|---|---:|---:|
| DR | Income tax refund receivable | $6,650 | |
| DR | Deferred tax asset | 7,350 | |
| CR | Deferred tax asset valuation allowance | | $5,250 |
| CR | Income tax benefit (residual) | | 8,750 |

**Income Statement—2019**

Income tax benefit:
| | |
|---|---:|
| Current | $6,650 |
| Deferred (net) | 2,100 |
| | $8,750 |

**Balance Sheet—2019**

Current assets:
| | |
|---|---:|
| Income tax ref. rec. | $6,650 |

Non-current assets:
| | |
|---|---:|
| Deferred tax asset | $7,350 |
| Less: valuation allow. | (5,250) |
| | $2,100 |

# 6 Investee's Undistributed Earnings

## 6.1 Income Tax Return

Taxable income is the dividend received. Under U.S. tax law, there is a dividend received deduction (exclusion) based on the percentage of ownership in the stock of the other corporation:

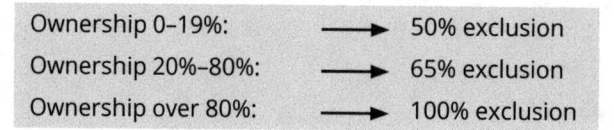

| Ownership | Exclusion |
|---|---|
| Ownership 0–19%: | ⟶ 50% exclusion |
| Ownership 20%–80%: | ⟶ 65% exclusion |
| Ownership over 80%: | ⟶ 100% exclusion |

## 6.2 GAAP Financial Statement

Report percentage of investee's income using the equity method for an investment between 20 and 50 percent.

## 6.3 Temporary Difference

It should be presumed that all undistributed earnings will ultimately be distributed to the investor/parent at some future time. Financial statement income of the investee claimed by the investor/parent as earnings is greater than actual dividends received from the investee that are claimed on the tax return.

---

### Example 4 — Dividends Received Deduction

**Facts:**

- 25 percent owned investee (GAAP requires use of equity method)
- Investee's net income $2,400,000 ($600,000 = GAAP income) ⟵ (Temporary)
- Investee's dividends $2,000,000 ($500,000 = Tax return)
- Tax return: dividend received deduction (exclusion) is 65 percent (permanent)
- Tax rate is 21 percent

**Required:** Calculate the temporary and permanent differences related to the above investment and prepare the tax journal entry.

**Solution:**

| Tax Return | | | Income Statement | |
|---|---|---|---|---|
| Investee div. income | $500,000 | ⟵ Temp & Per ⟶ Equity in earnings | $600,000 |
| 65% exclusion | (325,000) | ⟵ (Permanent) ⟶ | (390,000) |
| Taxable | $175,000 | ⟵ $35,000 ⟶ | $210,000 |
| × | 21% | × 21% | |
| | $ 36,750 | + $ 7,350 = | $ 44,100 |

*Journal entry to record the taxes:*

| | | Debit | Credit |
|---|---|---|---|
| DR | Income tax expense—current | $36,750 | |
| DR | Income tax expense—deferred | 7,350 | |
| CR | Income taxes currently payable | | $36,750 |
| CR | Deferred tax liability | | 7,350 |

# 7 Income Tax Disclosures

## 7.1 Balance Sheet Disclosures

- The components of a net deferred tax liability or asset should be disclosed, including the total of:
  - All deferred tax liabilities
  - All deferred tax assets
  - The valuation allowance for deferred tax assets
- Other balance sheet disclosures include:
  - The net change during the year in the total valuation allowance.
  - The tax effect of each type of temporary difference and carryforward that is significant to the deferred tax liability or asset.

## 7.2 Income Statement Disclosures

The amount of income tax expense (or benefit) allocated to continuing operations and the amount(s) separately allocated to other item(s) must be disclosed.

- The significant components of income tax expense attributable to continuing operations must be disclosed. These include:
  - Current tax expense or benefit
  - Deferred tax expense or benefit
  - Investment tax credits
  - Government grants (that cause a reduction of income tax expense)
  - Benefits of NOL carryforwards
  - Tax expense allocated to shareholders' equity items
  - Adjustments of deferred taxes from changes in tax laws or rates
  - Adjustments of the beginning-of-the-year deferred tax asset valuation due to changes in expectations
- The tax benefit of an operating loss carryforward should be reported in the same manner (income statement location) as the current year source of income or loss that gave rise to the benefit recognition.
- A recognition (in either percentages or dollar amounts) of income tax expense attributable to continuing operations and the amount of income tax expense that would have resulted from applying the statutory rate to pretax income from continuing operations should be presented.

Income Taxes: Part 2 FAR 6

# 8 Corporation Tax Summary

| Corporation Tax Summary | GAAP: Financial Statements | IRC: Tax Return | Temp. | Perm. | None |
|---|---|---|---|---|---|
| **Gross Income** | | | | | |
| Gross sales | Income | Income | | | ✓ |
| Installment sales | Income | Income when received | ✓ | | |
| Rents and royalties in advance | Income when earned | Income when received | ✓ | | |
| State tax refund | Income | Income | | | ✓ |
| *Dividends:* | | | ✓ | | |
|    equity method | Income is subsidiary's earnings | Income is dividends-received | | ✓ | |
|    100/65/50% exclusion | No exclusion | Excluded forever | | | |
| **Items Not Includable in "Taxable Income"** | | | | | |
| State and municipal bond interest | Income | Not taxable income | | ✓ | |
| Life insurance proceeds | Income | Generally not taxable income | | ✓ | |
| Gain/loss on treasury stock | Not reported | Not reported | | | ✓ |
| **Ordinary Expenses** | | | | | |
| Cost of goods sold | Currently expensed | Uniform capitalization rules | | | ✓ |
| Officers' compensation (top) | Expense | $1,000,000 limit | | | ✓ |
| Bad debt | Allowance (estimated) | Direct write-off | ✓ | | |
| Estimated liability for contingency (e.g., warranty) | Expense (accrue estimated) | No deduction until paid | ✓ | | |
| *Interest expense:* business loan | Expense | Deduct (up to limit) | ✓ | | ✓ |
|    Tax-free investment | Expense | Not deductible | | ✓ | |
| Charitable contributions | All expensed | Limited to 10% of adjusted taxable income | ✓ | ✓ | ✓ |
| Loss on abandonment/casualty | Expense | Deduct | | | ✓ |
| Loss on worthless subsidiary | Expense | Deduct | | | ✓ |
| *Depreciation:* MACRS vs. straight-line | Slow depreciation | Fast depreciation | ✓ | | |
| Section 179 depreciation | Not allowed (must depreciate) | $1,040,000 (2020) | ✓ | | |
| Different basis of asset- | Use GAAP basis | Use tax basis | ✓ | | |
| *Amortization:* start-up/ organizational expenses | Expense | $5,000 maximum/amortize excess over 15 years | ✓ | | |
| Franchise | Amortize | Amortize over 15 years | ✓ | | |
| Goodwill | Impairment test | Amortize over 15 years | ✓ | | |
| *Depletion:* percentage vs. straight-line (cost) | Cost over years | Percentage of sales | ✓ | | |
|    Percentage in excess of cost | Not allowed | Percentage of sales | | ✓ | |
| Profit sharing and pension expense | Expense accrued | No deduction until paid | ✓ | | |
| Accrued expense (50% owner/family) | Expense accrued | No deduction until paid | ✓ | | |
| State taxes (paid) | Expense | Deduct | | | ✓ |
| Meals | Expense | Generally 50% deductible | | ✓ | |
| **GAAP Expense Items That Are Not Tax Deductions** | | | | | |
| Life insurance expense (corporation) | Expense | Not deductible | | ✓ | |
| Penalties | Expense | Not deductible | | ✓ | |
| Entertainment | Expense | Not deductible | | ✓ | |
| Lobbying/political expense | Expense | Not deductible | | ✓ | |
| Federal income taxes | Expense | Not deductible | | ✓ | |
| **Special Items** | | | | | |
| Net capital gain (NCG) | Income | Income | | | ✓ |
| Net capital loss (NCL) | Report as loss | Not deductible | ✓ | | |
|    Carryback/carryover (3 years back/5 years forward) | Not applicable | Offset NCGs in other years | ✓ | | |
|    Related shareholder | Report as a loss | Not deductible | | ✓ | |
| Net operating loss | Report as a loss | Carryover indefinitely | ✓ | | |
| Research and development | Expense | Expense/amortize/capitalize | ✓ | ✓ | ✓ |

## Question 1 — MCQ-12688

Mobe Co. reported the following operating income (loss) for its first three years of operations:

| 2019 | $ 300,000 |
| 2020 | (700,000) |
| 2021 | 1,200,000 |

For each year, there were no deferred income taxes (before 2019), and Mobe's effective income tax rate was 21 percent. Mobe elected to forgo the carryback of the 2020 net operating loss. In its 2021 income statement, what amount should Mobe report as total income tax expense?

 a. $84,000
 b. $105,000
 c. $168,000
 d. $252,000

## Question 2 — MCQ-00785

As a result of differences between depreciation for financial reporting purposes and tax purposes, the financial reporting basis of Noor Co.'s sole depreciable asset, acquired in Year 1, exceeded its tax basis by $250,000 at December 31, Year 1. This difference will reverse in future years. The enacted tax rate is 30 percent for Year 1, and 21 percent for future years. Noor has no other temporary differences. In its December 31, Year 1, balance sheet, how should Noor report the deferred tax effect of this difference?

 a. As an asset of $75,000.
 b. As an asset of $52,500.
 c. As a liability of $75,000.
 d. As a liability of $52,500.

## NOTES

# FAR 7

# Pensions and Equity

## Module

| | | |
|---|---|---|
| **1** | Pension Benefits: Part 1 | 3 |
| **2** | Pension Benefits: Part 2 | 15 |
| **3** | Retirement Benefits Other Than Pensions | 27 |
| **4** | Financial Statements of Employee Benefit Plans | 33 |
| **5** | Stockholders' Equity: Part 1 | 39 |
| **6** | Stockholders' Equity: Part 2 | 51 |
| **7** | Stock Compensation | 59 |

# NOTES

# MODULE 1

# Pension Benefits: Part 1

FAR 7

## 1 Overview

A pension plan is an agreement in which the employer provides employees with defined or estimated retirement benefits in exchange for current or past services. Pension benefits are not paid currently; rather, they are a form of deferred compensation and are paid to retired employees, usually on a periodic basis.

In a *defined benefit plan*, the benefits that the employee receives at retirement are determined by formula. It is the sponsor company's responsibility to ensure that contributions to the plan are sufficient to pay benefits as they come due.

In a *defined contribution* plan, the contributions that the sponsor company makes to the plan are determined by formula. The employees' retirement benefits are based on the amount of funds in the plan.

Accounting for defined contribution plans is very simple, whereas accounting for defined benefit plans is complex. For a defined contribution plan, the sponsor company makes just one journal entry and, for defined benefit plans, the sponsor company makes multiple journal entries.

It is very important to note that a pension plan and the sponsoring company are two separate legal entities. The pension plan accounting covered below is not concerned with the pension plan's accounting. Rather, it is concerned with how the sponsor company accounts for the plan.

> ### Pass Key
>
> Accounting for pension plans is concerned primarily with determining the amount of:
> - pension expense that appears on the sponsor company's income statement, and
> - any related pension accounts (asset, liability, and/or other comprehensive income accounts) that appear on the sponsor company's balance sheet.

- For defined benefit and defined contribution plans, pension expenses are not necessarily equal to the amount funded (paid) to the pension trust during the year. Pension accounting is concerned with amounts accrued and expensed by the employer company and the funded status of the plan. It is based on accrual accounting.

- The accounting problems, which arise primarily for defined benefit plans, are caused by necessary use of estimates and assumptions, which affect the timing and measurement of pension costs (expense), gains and losses from investments of plan assets, and liabilities.

## 1.1 Characteristics

A pension plan can be:

- **Written or Implied (Unwritten):** A plan's provisions must be applied to both written plans and those whose existence may be implied from a well-defined, although perhaps unwritten, practice of paying postretirement benefits.
- **Contributory or Noncontributory:** Employees are required to contribute to the plan if it is contributory; only the employer contributes to the plan if it is noncontributory.
- **Funded or Non-funded:** A plan is funded when the employer makes cash contributions to the plan. The amount funded does not have to equal the pension plan expense for the period.
- **Overfunded vs. Underfunded (Funded Status):** Applies only to defined benefit plans.
  - An overfunded plan has assets that exceed its liabilities, whereas an underfunded plan has liabilities that exceed its assets.
  - An overfunded plan results in a net asset on the sponsor's balance sheet; an underfunded plan results in a net liability on the sponsor's balance sheet.

## 1.2 Types of Plans

### 1.2.1 Defined Contribution Plan

This type of plan specifies the periodic amount of contributions to the plan and the way that the contributions should be allocated to employees. A 401(k) plan is an example of a defined contribution plan. When calculating contributions to the plan, the sponsor considers factors such as:

1. Employees' length of service
2. Compensation amounts

### 1.2.2 Defined Benefit Plan

This type of plan defines the benefits to be paid to employees at retirement. Contributions are computed using actuarial assumptions of future benefit payments based on factors such as:

1. Employees' compensation levels at or near retirement.
2. The number of years of employee service.
3. The number of years until the employee retires.
4. The number of years that the plan expects to pay benefits after an employee retires.

## 1.3 Definitions

- **Accumulated Benefit Obligation (ABO):** The actuarial present value of benefits attributed by a formula based on current and past compensation levels. An ABO differs from a PBO only in that the ABO includes no assumption about future compensation levels (uses current salaries).
- **Projected Benefit Obligation (PBO):** The actuarial present value of all benefits attributed by the plan's benefit formula to employee service rendered prior to that date. PBO only uses an assumption as to future compensation levels.

## U.S. GAAP VS. IFRS

Under IFRS, the defined benefit obligation (DBO) is the defined benefit pension plan liability. The DBO (IFRS) and the PBO (U.S. GAAP) are calculated in a similar manner.

- **Vested Benefits:** Benefits are vested when employees have earned their benefits by reason of having reached retirement age and/or having otherwise met unique pension plan requirements (e.g., are fully vested after 10 years of service). The benefits are vested whether or not that person has actually retired, and they are not contingent on remaining in the service of the employer. Generally, pension plan documents require money to be left in the plan until retirement.

- **Service Cost:** The present value of all pension benefits earned by company employees in the current year. It is provided by the actuary. The service cost component increases the projected benefit obligation.

- **Interest Cost:** The increase in the projected benefit obligation (PBO) due to the passage of time. Measuring the PBO as a present value requires accrual of an interest cost on the projected benefit obligation, at rates equal to the assumed discount rates. Interest cost always increases the PBO because the present value of any liability increases as you get closer to the due date.

- **Prior Service Cost:** The cost of benefits based on past service granted for:
  - Service prior to the initiation of a pension plan that employees retroactively receive credit for when the plan is implemented.
  - Subsequent plan amendment, reflecting new or increased benefits, that also is applied to service already provided.

  Prior service cost increases the PBO in the period of the plan initiation or amendment and should be amortized to net periodic pension cost over the future service periods of the affected employees.

- **Actuarial Gains and Losses:** Adjustments to the projected benefit obligation that arise when the actuary changes one or more of the assumptions used to calculate the PBO. Actuarial gains decrease the PBO and actuarial losses increase the PBO.

- **Benefit Payments:** Amounts paid to pension plan participants after retirement. The payment of pension benefits reduces the projected benefit obligation and reduces plan assets.

> ## Pass Key
>
> The following formula can be used to calculate the projected benefit obligation:
>
> ⚪      Beginning projected benefit obligation
>     + Service cost
> ⚪    + Interest cost
>     + Prior service cost from current period plan amendments
>     + Actuarial losses incurred in the current period
>     − Actuarial gains incurred in the current period
> ⚪    − Benefits paid to retirees
> ⚪    Ending projected benefit obligation

- **Plan Assets:** Generally stocks, bonds, and other investments set aside to provide for pension benefits. Plan assets should be reported at fair value. Plan assets increase each period by contributions to the pension plan (funding) and by the return on the plan assets. Plan assets decrease each period by the amount of benefits paid to retired employees.

- **Actual Return on Plan Assets:** Returns on the assets held by the pension plan. Actual return can be calculated based on the fair value of plan assets at the beginning and ending of the period, adjusted for contributions and benefit payments (a squeeze).

> ## Pass Key
>
> The following formula can be used to calculate the ending fair value of plan assets or to solve for the actual return on plan assets:
>
> ⚪      Beginning fair value of plan asset
>     + Contributions
> ⚪    + Actual return on plan assets
> ⚪    − Benefits paid to retirees
> ⚪    Ending fair value of plan assets

## 1.4 Time Line

The following illustrates the various terms and their respective placement within the pension concepts:

### Illustration 1 — Time Line of Pension Plan

Suppose that employee P. Olinto begins work on January 1, Year 1, and that his company does not implement a pension plan until January 1, Year 10. All employees receive credit for all years of service for the company, even those years prior to inception of the plan. In Year 20, the plan is amended to increase the amount of benefits earned each year and this amendment is applied retroactively to the day the employee began to work for the company. Our employee is expected to retire on January 1, Year 30, and die on January 1, Year 40 (these are estimates made by the actuary).

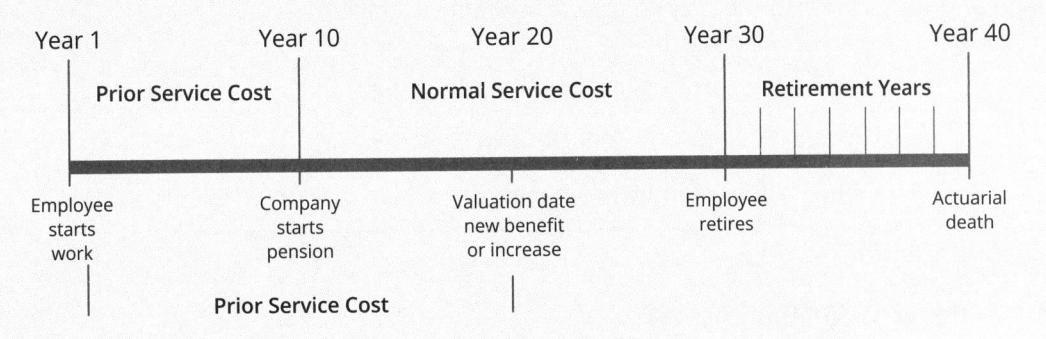

| Year 1 | Year 10 | Year 20 | Year 30 | Year 40 |
|---|---|---|---|---|
| | Prior Service Cost | Normal Service Cost | | Retirement Years |
| Employee starts work | Company starts pension | Valuation date new benefit or increase | Employee retires | Actuarial death |
| | Prior Service Cost | | | |

## 2 Income Statement Accounting

Under U.S. GAAP, pension expense (known as "net periodic pension cost") is the increase in the projected benefit obligation during the period, offset by earnings on plan assets, and adjusted for the effects of certain smoothing mechanisms.

The easy way to remember the elements of U.S. GAAP net periodic pension cost: **SIR AGE**

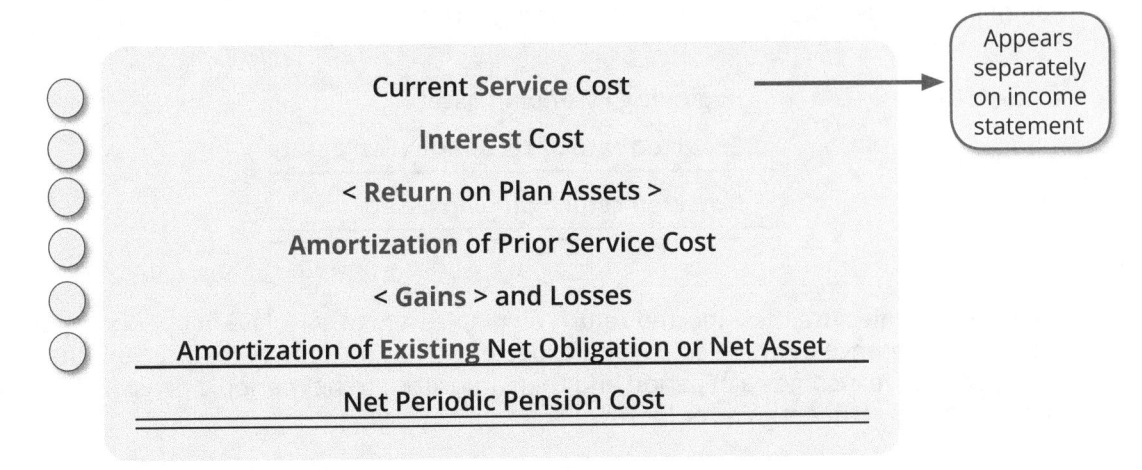

- Current **S**ervice Cost → Appears separately on income statement
- **I**nterest Cost
- < **R**eturn on Plan Assets >
- **A**mortization of Prior Service Cost
- < **G**ains > and Losses
- Amortization of **E**xisting Net Obligation or Net Asset

Net Periodic Pension Cost

Service cost is reported as an operating expense on the income statement in the same line with other compensation costs arising during the period. The other components of net periodic pension cost should be presented on the income statement, separately or in total, below income from operations.

## 2.1 Components of "Net Periodic Pension Cost" Under U.S. GAAP

### 2.1.1 Current **Service** Cost

The present value of all benefits earned in the current period. In other words, the increase in the *projected benefit obligation* (PBO) resulting from employee services in the current period. The pension benefit formula is applied to compute a present value. The actuary provides service cost.

### 2.1.2 **Interest** Cost

The increase in the projected benefit obligation during the current period that is due to the passage of time. (Similar to the recognition of interest expense.)

> Beginning of period PBO
> × Discount rate
> Interest cost

### 2.1.3 < **Return** > on Plan Assets

U.S. GAAP allows companies to offset net periodic pension cost by either the actual return on plan assets or the expected return on plan assets.

- **Actual Return on Plan Assets:** Can be calculated based on the fair value of plan assets at the beginning and ending of the period, adjusted for contributions and benefit payments (a squeeze). Most companies choose not to use the actual return on plan assets in the computation of net periodic pension cost because the actual return can vary drastically from period to period, causing earnings volatility.

- **Expected Return on Plan Assets:** Used in order to "smooth" earnings. The expected return on plan assets is calculated using the following formula:

> Beginning FV of plan assets
> × Expected rate of return on plan assets
> Expected return on plan assets

When companies use the expected return on plan assets to calculate net periodic pension cost, the difference between actual and expected return must be recognized in other comprehensive income each period and then amortized to net periodic pension cost over time with any actuarial gains or losses.

## U.S. GAAP VS. IFRS

Under IFRS, the "service cost" component of defined benefit cost includes both current service cost and past service cost. The "net interest on the defined benefit liability (asset)" component of defined benefit cost is calculated using the following formula:

Net interest on the defined benefit liability (asset) =
Net defined benefit liability (asset) × Discount rate

The net defined benefit liability (asset) is the difference between the defined benefit obligation and the fair value of the plan assets. The net interest on the defined benefit liability (asset) includes interest cost on the defined benefit obligation and interest income on the plan assets.

### 2.1.4 Amortization of Unrecognized Prior Service Cost

Under U.S. GAAP, in the period that a pension plan is initiated or amended, the resulting prior service cost increases the PBO and is recorded as unrecognized prior service cost in other comprehensive income. The unrecognized prior service cost in accumulated other comprehensive income is amortized to net periodic pension cost over the plan participant's remaining years of service. The amortization is calculated using the unrecognized prior service cost balance at the beginning of the period.

```
  Beginning unrecognized prior service cost
÷ Average remaining service life
  ─────────────────────────────────────────
  Amortization of prior service cost
```

### Illustration 2    Prior Service Cost for Plan Amendment

ABC Company has had a defined benefit pension plan for the last 10 years. ABC Company's plan calls for employees who are fully vested to receive 50 percent of their last year's salary with the company upon retirement. ABC Company has now decided to amend the plan and pay a benefit of 55 percent of the last year's salary to retirees. The amendment is to be applied retroactively. The increase in the PBO based on this amendment being applied to services provided in the last 10 years is the prior service cost.

# Pension Benefits: Part 1

## U.S. GAAP VS. IFRS

Under IFRS, prior service cost is referred to as past service cost. When a plan is amended, past service cost increases the DBO and is reported as defined benefit service cost on the income statement. Under IFRS, past service cost is not booked to other comprehensive income.

### 2.1.5 < Gains > and Losses

Gains and losses arise from two sources:

1. The difference between the expected and actual return on plan assets when the expected return on plan assets is used to calculate net periodic pension cost.
2. Changes in actuarial assumptions (actuarial gains and losses).

## Pass Key

It is easy to determine whether something results in a gain or loss by considering whether it is good (i.e., gains) or bad (i.e., losses) for the pension plan. For example:

- If a company actually earns more than expected on its plan assets (actual return > expected return), that is good for the plan (it has more assets than expected); therefore it is a gain.
- If employees are expected to live longer after they retire, that is bad for the pension plan because it increases the amount of benefits it expects to pay; therefore it is a loss (even though it is good for the employee who expects to live longer).

- **Accounting for Gains and Losses:** Under U.S. GAAP, entities have two choices when accounting for gains and losses:
    1. Recognize gains and losses on the income statement in the period incurred; or
    2. Recognize the gains and losses in other comprehensive income in the period incurred and then amortize the unrecognized gains and losses to net periodic pension cost over time using the corridor approach. Most companies choose this option to smooth earnings.

## U.S. GAAP VS. IFRS

Under IFRS, gains and losses are referred to as remeasurements of the net defined benefit liability (asset). Remeasurements of the net defined benefit liability (asset) include actuarial gains and losses and the difference between the actual return on plan assets and the interest income included in the net interest on the defined benefit liability. All remeasurements of the net defined benefit liability (asset) are reported in other comprehensive income and are *not* reclassified (amortized) to the income statement in subsequent periods.

- **The Corridor Approach:** Under the corridor approach, an entity's net unrecognized gain or loss is amortized over the employees' average remaining service period if, as of the beginning of the year, this amount exceeds 10 percent of the *greater* of the beginning of the year balances of:
    - Market related value of plan assets = Assets
    - Projected benefit obligation (PBO) = Liabilities

Beginning of year ⟶ Unrecognized gain or loss
Beginning of year ⟶ < 10% of PBO **OR** Market related value (greater) >
───────────────────
Excess
÷ Average remaining service life
───────────────────
Amortization of unrecognized gain or loss

### 2.1.6 Amortization of **Existing** Net Obligation or Net Asset at Implementation

Under U.S. GAAP, an employer was required to determine the funded status of the pension plan (FV plan assets − PBO) as of the beginning of the first year SFAS 87 (ASC 715) was applied. FAS 87 (ASC 715) was effective for most large companies for fiscal years beginning after December 15, 1986 (December 15, 1988, for nonpublic companies that sponsor plans for 100 or fewer people). This funded status was required to be amortized over the greater of 15 years or the average remaining job life of the company's employees.

Projected benefit obligation
< Fair value plan assets >
───────────────────
Initial unfunded obligation
÷ 15 years OR Average employee job life (greater)
───────────────────
Minimum amortization

Pension Benefits: Part 1

At this time, most companies have fully amortized their SFAS 87 (ASC 715) transition amounts and therefore this amount is no longer a common component of net periodic pension cost.

> ### Pass Key
>
> Pensions are "GREAT"!
>
> - When deciding which balance (assets or liabilities) for the gains/losses component, use the "GREATER" of the two.
>
> - When deciding over which period to amortize the existing obligation (15 years or average service life), use the "GREATER" of the two.

### Example 1 — Annual Pension Cost

**Facts:** The following information pertains to Duffy Corp.'s defined benefit pension plan for Year 1:

| | |
|---|---:|
| Service cost | $300,000 |
| Actual return on plan assets | 80,000 |
| Amortization of unrecognized prior service cost | 70,000 |
| Amortization of actuarial gain | 30,000 |
| Interest on projected benefit obligation | 164,000 |
| Existing net obligation amortization | 20,000 |

**Required:** Calculate the net periodic pension cost to be reported in different locations on the sponsor's Year 1 income statement.

**Solution:** The following items are included in determining net periodic pension cost:

| | |
|---|---:|
| Service cost—reported as compensation cost | **$300,000** |
| Other components of net periodic pension cost: | |
|    Interest on projected benefit obligation | 164,000 |
|    Return on plan assets | (80,000) |
|    **A**mortization of unrecognized prior service cost | 70,000 |
|    **G**ain (actuarial) gain | (30,000) |
|    **E**xisting net obligation amortization | 20,000 |
| **Net periodic pension cost reported separately or in total after income from operations** | **144,000** |
| **Total net periodic pension cost** | **$444,000** |

Service cost ($300,000) is reported as an operating expense on the income statement in the same line with other compensation costs arising during the period. The other components of net periodic pension cost ($144,000) should be presented on the income statement, separately or in total, below income from operations.

## Question 1  MCQ-00690

The following information pertains to Gali Co.'s defined benefit pension plan for the current year.

| | |
|---|---|
| Fair value of plan assets, beginning of year | $350,000 |
| Fair value of plan assets, end of year | 525,000 |
| Employer contributions | 110,000 |
| Benefits paid | 85,000 |

In computing net periodic pension cost, what amount should Gali use as actual return on plan assets?

a. $65,000
b. $150,000
c. $175,000
d. $260,000

## Question 2  MCQ-05054

Carter Components is computing the components of its net periodic pension cost for the current year ended December 31. Carter has calculated that its service cost is $60,000 and has computed interest cost as $42,000. The average remaining service life of its employees is 8 years. The return on $500,000 in plan assets was anticipated to be 8 percent but was actually 8.5 percent. The pension benefit obligation at the beginning of the year was $560,000 and, at the end of the year, $602,000. The company has an unrecognized gain of $60,000. To what extent will the unrecognized gain reduce current-year net periodic pension cost under U.S. GAAP?

a. $25
b. $500
c. $750
d. $1,250

## NOTES

# MODULE 2: Pension Benefits: Part 2

**FAR 7**

## 1 Balance Sheet Accounting

### 1.1 Pension Plan Contributions

A company's contribution to its defined benefit pension plan(s) increases the pension plan asset (overfunded pension plans) or decreases the pension plan liability (underfunded pension plans).

| DR | Pension benefit asset/liability | $XXX | |
|---|---|---|---|
| CR | Cash | | $XXX |

### 1.2 Funded Status

Under U.S. GAAP, companies must report the funded status of their pension plan(s) on the balance sheet as an asset or a liability (or both). The *funded status* of a pension plan is calculated using the following formula:

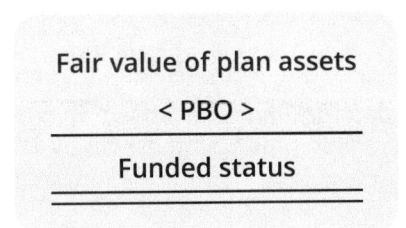

> Fair value of plan assets
> < PBO >
> ―――――――――
> Funded status

If a company has multiple defined benefit pension plans, the funded status of each plan is calculated separately. Note that the fair value of plan assets and PBO must be disclosed separately in the pension footnote disclosures.

#### 1.2.1 Pension Plan Asset (Non-current)

A positive funded status (fair value of plan assets > PBO) indicates that the pension is overfunded. For balance sheet reporting purposes, all overfunded pension plans are aggregated and reported in total as a non-current asset.

#### 1.2.2 Pension Plan Liability (Current, Non-current, or Both)

A negative funded status (fair value of plan assets < PBO) indicates that the pension is underfunded. All underfunded pension plans are aggregated and reported as a current liability, a non-current liability, or both. Underfunded pension plans are reported as a current liability to the extent that the benefit obligation payable within the next 12 months exceeds the fair value of the plans' assets.

Pension Benefits: Part 2

> ### Example 1 — Pension Plan Asset and Liability
>
> **Facts:** ABC Company has three defined benefit pension plans. The company's actuary has provided the company with the following information as of December 31, Year 1.
>
> |  | Plan A | Plan B | Plan C |
> |---|---|---|---|
> | Expected benefit payments—Year 2 | $5,000,000 | $5,000,000 | $5,000,000 |
> | Fair value of plan assets | $7,000,000 | $5,500,000 | $4,500,000 |
> | Projected benefit obligation | $6,000,000 | $6,000,000 | $6,000,000 |
>
> **Required:** Calculate the over (under) funded status of each pension plan and the amounts that should be reported as non-current asset, current liability, and non-current liability on ABC's December 31, Year 1, balance sheet.
>
> **Solution:**
>
> |  | Plan A | Plan B | Plan C | Total |
> |---|---|---|---|---|
> | Fair value of plan assets | $7,000,000 | $5,500,000 | $ 4,500,000 | |
> | Less: PBO | (6,000,000) | (6,000,000) | (6,000,000) | |
> | Over (under) funded status | $1,000,000 | $ (500,000) | $(1,500,000) | $(1,000,000) |
> | Non-current asset | $1,000,000 | -0- | -0- | $ 1,000,000 |
> | Current liability | -0- | -0- | $ 500,000 | $ (500,000) |
> | Non-current liability | -0- | $ 500,000 | $ 1,000,000 | $(1,500,000) |
>
> A current liability will be recorded for Plan C because the expected benefits payable in the next 12 months exceed the fair value of the plan assets by $500,000.

---

### Pass Key

The beginning and ending funded status (FV plan assets − PBO) of a defined benefit pension plan can be reconciled as follows:

  Beginning funded status (pension benefit asset/liability)
  + Contributions
  − Service cost
  − Interest cost
  + Expected return on plan assets
  − Prior service cost incurred in the current period due to plan amendment
  + Net gains incurred during the current period
  − Net losses incurred during the current period
  
  Ending funded status (pension benefit asset/liability)

## U.S. GAAP VS. IFRS

Under IFRS, the funded status (DBO – fair value of plan assets) of the pension plan is reported on the balance sheet as the net defined benefit liability (asset). A liability is reported if the plan is underfunded (DBO > fair value of plan assets) and an asset is reported if the plan is overfunded (DBO < fair value of plan assets). If a net defined benefit asset is reported, the amount of the asset cannot exceed the present value of future economic benefits available to the entity in the form of cash refunds or reductions in future contributions that result from the overfunding. IFRSs do not specify whether an entity should classify the net defined benefit liability (asset) as current or non-current.

### Question 1 — MCQ-05398

Big Books Inc. has the following information related to its defined benefit pension plan:

**December 31, Year 1**

| | |
|---|---|
| Projected benefit obligation | $1,500,000 |
| Fair value of plan assets | 1,400,000 |
| Unrecognized prior service cost | 200,000 |
| Unrecognized net transition asset | 60,000 |

**December 31, Year 2**

| | |
|---|---|
| Projected benefit obligation | $1,740,000 |
| Fair value of plan assets | 1,670,000 |
| Service cost | 220,000 |

**Assumptions**

| | |
|---|---|
| Discount rate | 6% |
| Expected return on plan assets | 8% |

Big Books makes an annual pension plan contribution of $200,000. The company's employees had an average remaining service life of 20 years on December 31, Year 1. The company paid benefits of $70,000 in Year 2 and expects to pay benefits totaling $170,000 to retired employees in Year 3. Big Books has an effective tax rate of 30 percent. The actual return on plan assets was 10 percent. What is the funded status of Big Books' pension plan on December 31, Year 1?

- a. $70,000 underfunded
- b. $70,000 overfunded
- c. $100,000 underfunded
- d. $100,000 overfunded

## 1.3 Accumulated Other Comprehensive Income

U.S. GAAP requires that changes in the funded status of a pension plan due to prior service cost and pension gains and losses be reported in other comprehensive income in the period incurred, unless the company chooses to recognize the pension gains and losses immediately on the income statement. Any remaining unrecognized transition obligation or asset is also reported in accumulated other comprehensive income, net of tax, until amortized to net periodic pension cost.

### 1.3.1 Prior Service Cost and Pension Losses

- **Recognition in Period Incurred:** Prior service cost and pension losses decrease the funded status of the pension plan and are recorded with the following journal entry in the period incurred:

  | DR | Other comprehensive income | $XXX | |
  |---|---|---|---|
  | CR | Pension benefit asset/liability | | $XXX |

- **Amortization to Net Periodic Pension Cost:** When prior service cost, pension losses, and any remaining transition obligation are amortized, they are reclassified out of accumulated other comprehensive income and recognized as a component of net periodic pension cost.

  | DR | Net periodic pension cost | $XXX | |
  |---|---|---|---|
  | CR | Other comprehensive income | | $XXX |

---

### Example 2 — Prior Service Cost in OCI

**Facts:** ABC Company has an underfunded pension plan that is reported on its balance sheet as a non-current pension benefit liability. On October 1, Year 1, ABC Company amended its pension plan and increased the annual benefits to be paid to retired employees from 50 percent to 55 percent of their last year's salary with the company upon retirement. The amendment was applied retroactively and resulted in prior service cost of $1,000,000. This was ABC Company's first plan amendment.

**Required:** Prepare the journal entries to record the prior service cost in Year 1 and the amortization in Year 2.

**Solution:** The following journal entries will be recorded on October 1, Year 1:

*Journal entry to record the prior service cost:*

| DR | Other comprehensive income | $1,000,000 | |
|---|---|---|---|
| CR | Pension benefit liability | | $1,000,000 |

The prior service cost will be amortized over the 20-year average remaining service period of ABC Company's employees starting in Year 2. No amortization will be recorded in Year 1 because amortization is calculated using beginning (January 1) unrecognized prior service cost.

(continued)

(continued)

The following journal entries will be recorded in Year 2:

*Journal entry to record the $50,000 ($1,000,000 ÷ 20 years) reclassification adjustment from OCI to the income statement for the Year 2 amortization of prior service cost:*

| DR | Net periodic pension cost | $50,000 | |
|---|---|---|---|
| CR | Other comprehensive income | | $50,000 |

### 1.3.2 Pension Gains

- **Recognition in Period Incurred:** Pension gains increase the funded status of the pension plan and are recorded with the following journal entry in the period incurred:

| DR | Pension benefit asset/liability | $XXX | |
|---|---|---|---|
| CR | Other comprehensive income | | $XXX |

- **Amortization to Net Periodic Pension Cost:** When pension gains and any remaining net transition assets are recognized in net periodic pension cost through the amortization process, the following reclassification adjustment is recorded.

| DR | Other comprehensive income | $XXX | |
|---|---|---|---|
| CR | Net periodic pension cost | | $XXX |

> **U.S. GAAP VS. IFRS**
>
> Under IFRS, remeasurements of the net defined benefit liability (asset) are included in other comprehensive income and are *not* reclassified (amortized) to the income statement in subsequent periods.

---

**Question 2**  MCQ-08599

At the beginning of Year 1, a company amends its defined benefit pension plan for an additional $500,000 in prior service cost. The amendment covers employees with a 10-year average remaining service life. At the end of Year 1, what is the net entry to accumulated other comprehensive income, ignoring income tax effects?

  a. A $450,000 debit
  b. A $500,000 debit
  c. A $550,000 credit
  d. A $450,000 credit

# Example 3 — Pension Accounting Journal Entries

**Facts:** At December 31, Year 2, Brown House Inc. had the following pension-related information, given an average remaining employee service life of 20 years, an expected and actual return on plan assets of 10 percent, a discount rate of 8 percent, and a net loss incurred during Year 2 of $30,000. The pension loss was incurred when the actuaries changed their assumptions regarding employee compensation levels at retirement.

| | |
|---|---:|
| Service cost | $ 400,000 |
| Interest cost | 116,000 |
| Return on plan assets | (20,000) |
| Amortization of prior service cost | 25,000 |
| Amortization of pension (gain) loss | 19,000 |
| Amortization of existing net transition obligation | 5,000 |
| Year 2 net periodic pension cost | $ 545,000 |

| | Dec. 31, Year 1 | Dec. 31, Year 2 |
|---|---:|---:|
| Fair value of plan assets | $ 200,000 | $ 290,000 |
| Projected benefit obligation | (1,450,000) | (1,646,000) |
| Funded status | $(1,250,000) | $(1,356,000) |
| Items not yet recognized as components of net periodic pension cost: | | |
|   Unrecognized prior service cost | $ 500,000 | $ 475,000 |
|   Unrecognized pension loss | 525,000 | 536,000* |
|   Unrecognized net transition obligation | 100,000 | 95,000 |
| | $ 1,125,000 | $ 1,106,000 |

*The change in the net loss from Year 1 to Year 2 can be calculated as follows:

| | |
|---|---:|
| Beginning unrecognized net loss | $ 525,000 |
| Less: Amortization of net loss | (19,000) |
| Plus: Net loss incurred in Year 2 | 30,000 |
| Ending unrecognized net loss | $ 536,000 |

The company contributed $420,000 to the pension plan during Year 2. The company paid benefits of $350,000 in Year 2 and expects to pay benefits of $250,000 in Year 3.

(continued)

(continued)

**Required:** Prepare the journal entries Brown should record for the pension plan during Year 2.

**Solution:**

*Journal entry to record the contribution to the pension plan during Year 2:*

| | | | |
|---|---|---|---|
| DR | Pension benefit liability—non-current | $420,000 | |
| CR | Cash | | $420,000 |

*Journal entry to record the $30,000 net loss incurred during Year 2:*

| | | | |
|---|---|---|---|
| DR | Other comprehensive income | $30,000 | |
| CR | Pension benefit liability—non-current | | $30,000 |

*Journal entry to record the Year 2 service cost of $400,000, interest cost of $116,000, and return on plan assets of $20,000:*

| | | | |
|---|---|---|---|
| DR | Pension compensation expense | $400,000 | |
| DR | Net periodic pension cost | 96,000 | |
| CR | Pension benefit liability—current | | $496,000 |

*Journal entry to record the $25,000 reclassification adjustment from OCI to the income statement for the Year 2 amortization of prior service cost:*

| | | | |
|---|---|---|---|
| DR | Net periodic pension cost | $25,000 | |
| CR | Other comprehensive income | | $25,000 |

*Journal entry to record the $19,000 reclassification adjustment from OCI to the income statement for the Year 2 amortization of the net loss:*

| | | | |
|---|---|---|---|
| DR | Net periodic pension cost | $19,000 | |
| CR | Other comprehensive income | | $19,000 |

*Journal entry to record the amortization of existing net transition obligations:*

| | | | |
|---|---|---|---|
| DR | Net periodic pension cost | $5,000 | |
| CR | Other comprehensive income | | $5,000 |

(continued)

# Pension Benefits: Part 2

## (continued)

Brown's balance sheet at December 31, Year 2, will reflect the following:

| | |
|---|---:|
| Funded status—December 31, Year 1 | $(1,250,000) |
| + Contributions | 420,000 |
| − Net loss incurred during Year 2 | (30,000) |
| − Service cost / interest cost / return on plan assets | (496,000) |
| Funded status—December 31, Year 2 | $(1,356,000) |
| | |
| AOCI (before tax)—December 31, Year 1 | $(1,125,000) |
| Net loss incurred during Year 2 | (30,000) |
| Amortization of prior service cost | 25,000 |
| Amortization of net loss | 19,000 |
| Amortization of net transition obligation | 5,000 |
| AOCI (before tax)—December 31, Year 2 | $(1,106,000)* |

*Accumulated other comprehensive income is reported on an after-tax basis:
$1,106,000 × (1 − 40%) = $663,600

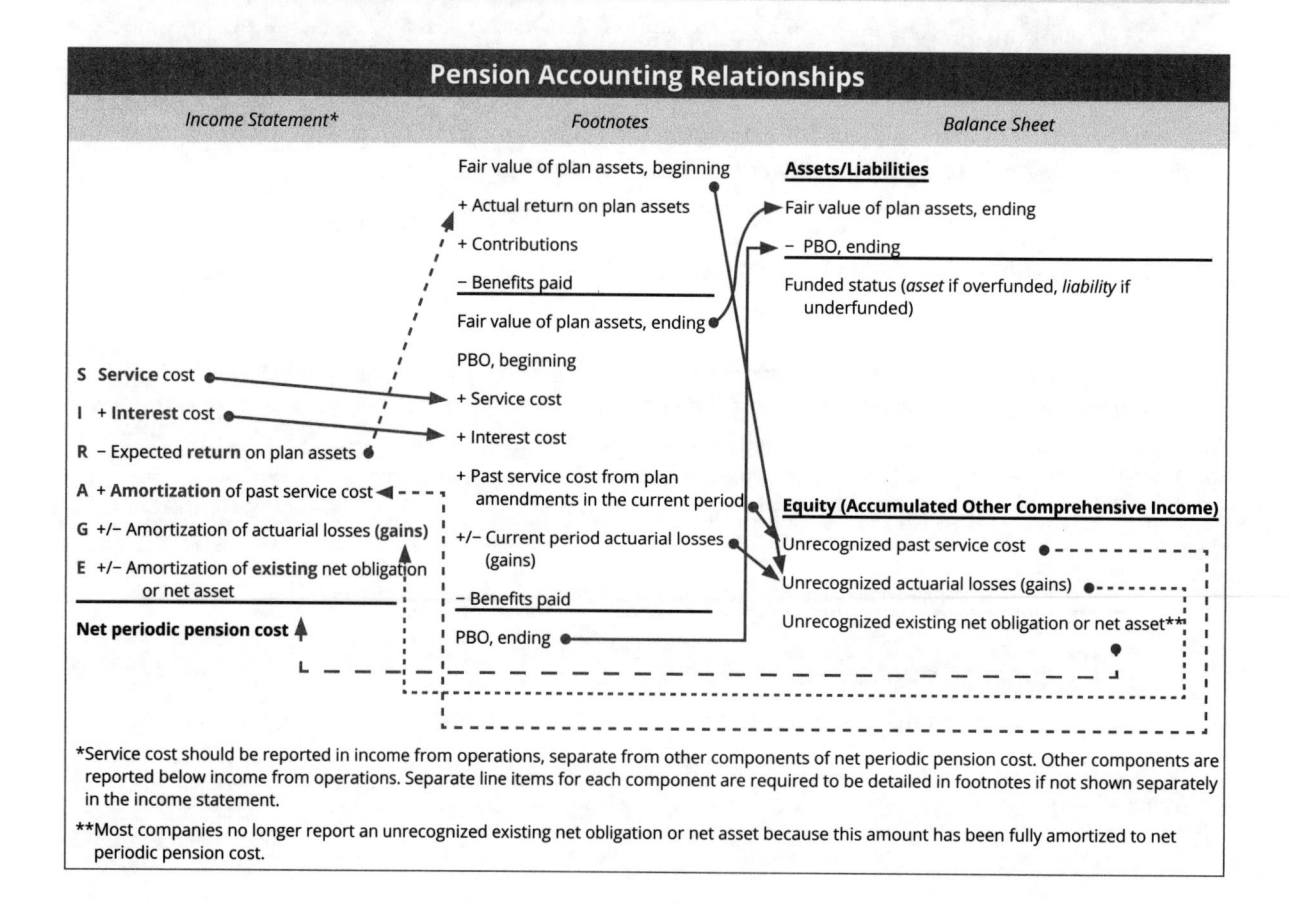

---

## Pension Accounting Relationships

**Income Statement*** 

- **S** Service cost
- **I** + **Interest** cost
- **R** − Expected **return** on plan assets
- **A** + **Amortization** of past service cost
- **G** +/− Amortization of actuarial losses (**gains**)
- **E** +/− Amortization of **existing** net obligation or net asset

**Net periodic pension cost**

**Footnotes**

Fair value of plan assets, beginning
+ Actual return on plan assets
+ Contributions
− Benefits paid
Fair value of plan assets, ending

PBO, beginning
+ Service cost
+ Interest cost
+ Past service cost from plan amendments in the current period
+/− Current period actuarial losses (gains)
− Benefits paid
PBO, ending

**Balance Sheet**

**Assets/Liabilities**
Fair value of plan assets, ending
− PBO, ending

Funded status (*asset* if overfunded, *liability* if underfunded)

**Equity (Accumulated Other Comprehensive Income)**
Unrecognized past service cost
Unrecognized actuarial losses (gains)
Unrecognized existing net obligation or net asset**

*Service cost should be reported in income from operations, separate from other components of net periodic pension cost. Other components are reported below income from operations. Separate line items for each component are required to be detailed in footnotes if not shown separately in the income statement.

**Most companies no longer report an unrecognized existing net obligation or net asset because this amount has been fully amortized to net periodic pension cost.

## 2 Measurement Date

U.S. GAAP requires that the measurement date of the plan assets and benefit obligations of a defined benefit pension plan must be aligned with the date of the employer's balance sheet, with the following exceptions.

- When a plan is sponsored by a subsidiary that has a different fiscal year-end from the parent company, then the subsidiary's plan assets and benefit obligations can be measured as of the subsidiary's balance sheet date.

- When a plan is sponsored by an equity method investee that has a different fiscal year-end from the investor's fiscal year-end, then the investee's plan assets and benefit obligations can be measured as of the date of the investee's financial statements used to apply the equity method.

- When a company's fiscal year-end does not coincide with a month-end, it may elect to measure defined benefit plan assets and obligations using the month-end closest to its fiscal year-end. Contributions made between the measurement date and the fiscal year-end should be disclosed, but will not change the fair value reported at the measurement date.

## 3 Off-Balance Sheet Footnote Disclosures

There are extensive required pension plan footnote disclosures. The disclosure requirements are the same for pension plans and post-retirement benefits.

- **Reconciliations of Beginning and Ending Balances**
    - Reconciliation of the beginning and ending balances of the *benefit obligation*, with separate disclosure of:
        —Service cost.
        —Interest cost.
        —Contributions by plan participants.
        —Actuarial gains and losses.
        —Foreign currency exchange rate changes.
        —Benefits paid.
        —Plan amendments.
        —Business combinations.
        —Divestitures.
        —Curtailments, settlements, and special termination benefits.

- Reconciliation of the beginning and ending balances of the *fair value of plan assets*, including the effects of:
  - Actual return on plan assets.
  - Foreign currency exchange rate changes.
  - Contributions by employer.
  - Contributions by plan participants.
  - Benefits paid.
  - Business combinations.
  - Divestitures.
  - Settlements.
- The measurement date, when it is differs from the fiscal year-end date.

### Funded Status

The funded status of the plan(s) and the amounts recognized on the balance sheet, showing separately the assets and current and non-current liabilities recognized.

### Plan Assets

- A narrative description of investment policies and strategies, including target allocation percentages for the major categories of plan assets.
- The fair value of each major category of plan assets as of the date of each balance sheet presented.
- A narrative description of the basis used to determine the overall expected long-term rate of return on plan assets.
- Information that enables users of financial statements to assess the inputs and valuation techniques used to develop fair value measurements of plan assets at the reporting date.
- The amount and timing of any plan assets expected to be returned to the employer during the 12-month period following the most recent balance sheet date.

### Components of Net Periodic Pension (Benefit) Cost

Amount of net periodic benefit cost recognized, showing separately:

- Service cost component.
- Interest cost component.
- Expected return on plan assets for the period.
- The prior service cost component.
- The gain or loss component.
- The transition asset or obligation component.
- The amount of gain or loss recognized due to a settlement or curtailment.

### Benefit Payments and Contributions

- The accumulated benefit obligation.
- The benefits expected to be paid in each of the next five years and in aggregate for the five fiscal years thereafter.
- The contributions expected to be paid to the plan during the next fiscal year.

- **Impact on Other Comprehensive Income**
  - The net gain or loss and prior service cost recognized in other comprehensive income for the period, and reclassification adjustments of other comprehensive income for the period for the amortization of net gains and losses, prior service cost, and net transition asset or obligation to net periodic pension cost.
  - The amounts in accumulated other comprehensive income that have not been recognized in net periodic pension cost, showing separately the net gain or loss, prior service cost, and net transition asset or obligation.
  - The amounts in accumulated other comprehensive income expected to be recognized in net periodic pension cost during the next fiscal year, showing separately the net gain or loss, prior service cost, and net transition asset or obligation.
- **Rates and Assumptions**

  On a weighted-average basis, the following assumptions are used in accounting for the plan:
  - Assumed discount rate.
  - Rate of compensation increased.
  - Expected long-term rate of return on plan assets.
- **Employer and Related Party Transactions**
  - The amounts and types of securities of the employer and related parties included in plan assets.
  - The amount of future annual benefits of plan participants covered by insurance contracts, including annuity plan contracts issued by the employer or related parties.
  - Any significant transactions between the employer or related parties and the plan during the year.
- **Amortization Methods**

  Any alternative amortization method used to amortize prior service costs or net gains and losses.
- **Assumptions and Commitments**
  - Any substantive commitment (e.g., past practice or a history of regular benefit increases) used as the basis for accounting for the benefit obligation recognized during the period and a description of the nature of the event.
  - An explanation of any significant change in the benefit obligation or plan asset not otherwise apparent in the above disclosures.
  - Disclosure of the estimated future contributions is not required.
- **Termination Benefits**

  The cost of providing special or contractual termination benefits recognized during the period and a description of the nature of the event.
- **Disclosure Requirements for Nonpublic Entities**

  Nonpublic entities are permitted to present less information, essentially eliminating the reconciliations required. The elements included in the net periodic pension cost should be disclosed if they are not presented as separate line items on the income statement.

## NOTES

# MODULE 3: Retirement Benefits Other Than Pensions

FAR 7

## 1 Introduction

### 1.1 Overview

Some companies provide benefits to their employees after the employees have retired. These benefits include:

- Health care insurance
- Life insurance
- Welfare benefits
- Tuition assistance
- Legal services
- Day care

### 1.2 Accrual Requirement

The cost of retiree health and other postretirement benefits must be accrued if:

- the obligation is attributable to employees' services already rendered;
- the employees' rights accumulate or vest;
- payment is probable; and
- the amount of the benefits can be reasonably estimated.

> **U.S. GAAP VS. IFRS**
>
> The accounting for postretirement benefits mirrors pension accounting under both IFRS and U.S. GAAP. The differences between IFRS and U.S. GAAP pension accounting outlined in the previous topic are also differences between IFRS and U.S. GAAP postretirement benefit accounting.

# 2 Definitions

## 2.1 Accumulated Postretirement Benefit Obligation (APBO)

The APBO is the present value of future benefits that have vested as of the measurement date. The APBO is discounted using an assumed discount rate:

- This rate should reflect returns on high-quality, fixed income investments.
- The discount rate is used to determine the APBO, EPBO, and the service and interest cost components of net periodic postretirement benefit cost.

## 2.2 Expected Postretirement Benefit Obligation (EPBO)

The present value of all future benefits expected to be paid as of the measurement date. It includes:

- The amount that has vested (APBO); plus
- The present value of expected future benefits that have not yet vested.

# 3 Income Statement

## 3.1 Income Statement Approach

Costs are allocated in a manner similar to pension costs.

- The benefit-years-of-service approach is used. The expected postretirement benefit obligation is attributed to each year of service in the attribution period.
- The postretirement benefit obligation is accrued during the period the employee works (the attribution period); generally beginning at the employee's date of hire and ending at the full eligibility date.

## 3.2 Income Statement Formula

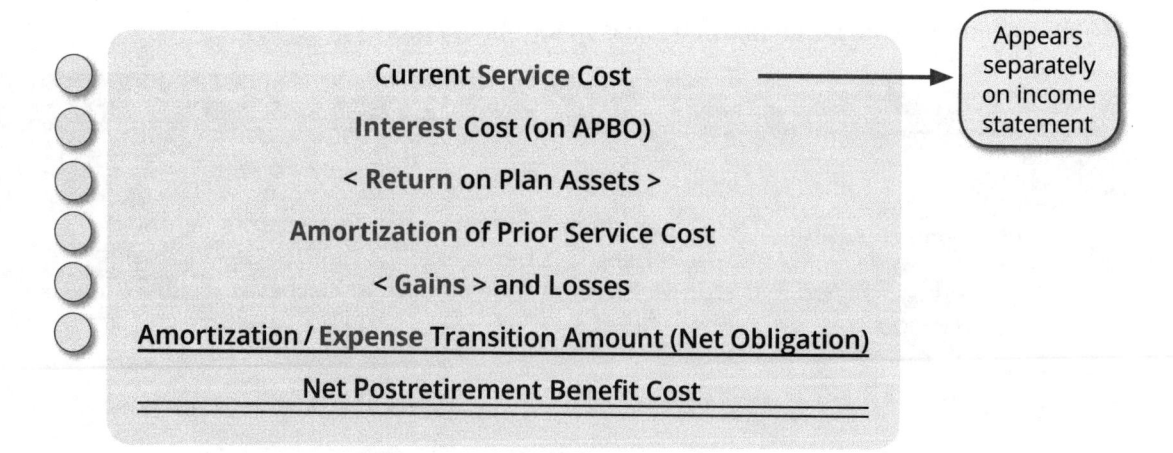

```
    Current Service Cost          ──→  Appears
    Interest Cost (on APBO)             separately
    < Return on Plan Assets >           on income
    Amortization of Prior Service Cost  statement
    < Gains > and Losses
    Amortization / Expense Transition Amount (Net Obligation)
    ─────────────────────────────────────────
    Net Postretirement Benefit Cost
```

An employer should report in the income statement:

- the service cost component in the same line item as other compensation costs which is separated from the rest of the net benefit cost; and
- the other components separately from the service cost component and below income from operations.

## 3.3 Components of "Net Postretirement Benefit Cost"

### 3.3.1 Service Cost
Service cost is the part of the EPBO arising from employee service this period.

### 3.3.2 Interest Cost
Interest cost is the increase in the APBO due to the passage of time. It is calculated as the beginning APBO multiplied by the discount rate.

### 3.3.3 Return on Plan Assets
Net postretirement benefit cost is offset by either the actual return on plan assets or the expected return on plan assets. The expected return on plan assets is calculated as the beginning fair value of plan assets times the expected long-term rate of return. Actual return on plan assets is based on the difference between the fair value of plan assets at the beginning and the end of the period, adjusted for contributions and benefit payments.

### 3.3.4 Amortization of Prior Service Cost
Amortization of prior service cost is the amortization of the cost of retroactive benefits.

### 3.3.5 Gains and Losses
Gains and losses result from two sources:

1. Changes in APBO due to changes in assumptions or experience, and
2. The difference between the expected and actual return on plan assets when expected return on plan assets is used to calculate the net postretirement benefit cost.

   Similar to pension accounting, under U.S. GAAP, gains and losses can be recognized on the income statement in the period incurred or recognized in other comprehensive income and then amortized to net postretirement benefit cost using the corridor approach.

### 3.3.6 Amortization or Expense of the Transition Obligation
Amortization of the transition obligation is the amortization of the effect of adopting SFAS 106 (ASC 740), which was generally effective for fiscal years beginning after December 15, 1992.

Transition to accrual accounting was done in one of two ways:

1. Immediate expense recognition by recording the entire obligation in one year as the effect of a change in accounting principle.
2. Delayed recognition by using straight-line amortization over the average remaining service period of active plan participants. If this period is less than 20 years, a 20-year amortization period may be elected.

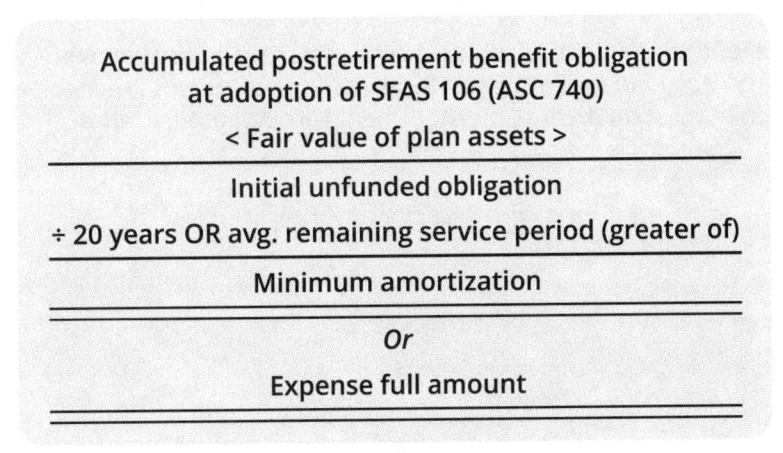

> Accumulated postretirement benefit obligation
> at adoption of SFAS 106 (ASC 740)
> 
> < Fair value of plan assets >
> ─────────────────────────────
> Initial unfunded obligation
> 
> ÷ 20 years OR avg. remaining service period (greater of)
> ─────────────────────────────
> Minimum amortization
> ─────────────────────────────
> Or
> 
> **Expense full amount**

ance Sheet

Postretirement benefit plans are required to have the same balance sheet presentation as pension plans.

## 4.1 Funded Status

Companies must report the funded status of their postretirement benefit plan(s) on the balance sheet as an asset or a liability (or both). The funded status of a postretirement benefit plan is calculated using the following formula:

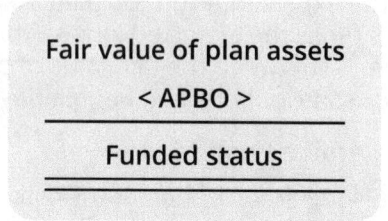

$$\begin{array}{r}\text{Fair value of plan assets} \\ \underline{< \text{APBO} >} \\ \text{Funded status} \end{array}$$

If a company has multiple postretirement benefit plans, the funded status of each plan is calculated separately.

### 4.1.1 Postretirement Benefit Plan Asset (Non-current)

A positive funded status (fair value of plan assets > APBO) indicates that the postretirement benefit plan is overfunded. For balance sheet reporting purposes, all overfunded postretirement benefit plans are aggregated and reported in total as a non-current asset.

### 4.1.2 Postretirement Benefit Plan Liability (Current, Non-current, or Both)

A negative funded status (fair value of plan assets < APBO) indicates that the postretirement benefit plan is underfunded. All underfunded postretirement benefit plans are also aggregated and reported as a current liability, a non-current liability, or both. Underfunded postretirement benefit plans are reported as a current liability to the extent that the benefit obligation payable within the next 12 months exceeds the fair value of the plans' assets.

## 4.2 Accumulated Other Comprehensive Income

Under U.S. GAAP, companies report postretirement benefit gains or losses, prior service costs, and transition net assets or net obligations in other comprehensive income when incurred, unless the amounts are recognized on the income statement in the period incurred. The tax effects of these items are recognized in other comprehensive income.

Postretirement benefit gains or losses, prior service costs and transition net assets or net obligations remain in accumulated other comprehensive income until recognized in net periodic postretirement benefit cost on the income statement through amortization.

# 5 Required Disclosures

Required disclosures are the same as for pension plans and include:

- Reconciliations of beginning and ending balances of the:
    - Accumulated postretirement benefit obligation, and
    - Fair value of plan assets.
- The funded status.
- Plan asset descriptions and fair values.
- The components of the net postretirement benefit cost.
- Benefit payments and contributions.
- The impact on other comprehensive income.
- Rates and assumptions, including:
    - The assumed discount rate.
    - The assumed health care cost trend rate.
    - The effect on the APBO, service cost, and interest cost of a 1 percent increase and a 1 percent decrease in the health care cost trend rate.
- Employer and related party transactions.
- Amortization methods.
- Assumptions and commitments.
- Termination benefits.

---

**Question 1**      MCQ-00701

An employer's obligation for postretirement health benefits that are expected to be provided to or for an employee must be fully accrued by the date the:

    a. Employee is fully eligible for benefits.
    b. Employee retires.
    c. Benefits are utilized.
    d. Benefits are paid.

# NOTES

# MODULE 4
# Financial Statements of Employee Benefit Plans

FAR 7

## 1 Overview

A pension plan and the sponsoring company are two separate legal entities. Pension plan accounting for the sponsoring company focuses on calculating net periodic pension cost using actuarial outputs and reporting the funded status of the plan on the sponsor's balance sheet. In addition to the accounting and reporting done by the sponsor company, U.S. GAAP requires that financial statements be presented by the pension plan itself.

## 2 Required Financial Statements for Defined Benefit Pension Plans

GAAP requires the financial statements of a defined benefit plan to include the following:

1. **Statement of Net Assets Available for Benefits**

   A statement that includes information regarding the net assets available for benefits at the end of the plan year.

2. **Statement of Changes in Net Assets Available for Benefits**

   A statement that includes information regarding the changes during the year in the net assets available for benefits.

3. **Statement of Accumulated Plan Benefits**

   Information regarding the actuarial present value of accumulated plan benefits as of either the beginning or end of the plan year.

4. **Statement of Changes in Accumulated Plan Benefits**

   Information regarding the significant effects of certain factors affecting the year-to-year change in the actuarial present value of accumulated plan benefits.

A *statement of cash flows* is not required, but may be presented if it provides relevant information about the ability of the plan to meet future obligations.

### 2.1 Definitions

- **Accumulated Plan Benefits:** The future benefit payments that are attributable to the employee's services rendered to the benefit information date, including benefits expected to be paid to any of the following:
    - Retired or terminated employees or their beneficiaries
    - Beneficiaries of deceased employees
    - Present employees or their beneficiaries

- **Actuarial Present Value of Accumulated Plan Benefits:** The amount that results from applying actuarial assumptions to the accumulated plan benefits, with the actuarial assumptions being used to adjust the accumulated plan benefits to reflect the time value of money and the probability of payment between the benefit information date and the expected payment date.
- **Net Assets Available for Benefits:** The difference between a plan's assets and liabilities, excluding the participant's accumulated plan benefits.

### Sample Company Pension Plan
### Statement of Net Assets Available for Benefits
### As of December 31

|  | Year 2 | Year 1 |
|---|---|---|
| **Assets** | | |
| Investments, at fair value | | |
|   Common stock | $2,300,000 | $1,910,000 |
|   Corporate bonds | 3,750,000 | 3,320,000 |
|   U.S. government securities | 410,000 | 390,000 |
|   Mortgages | 520,000 | 505,000 |
|   Real estate | 260,000 | 225,000 |
|   Total investments | $7,240,000 | $6,350,000 |
| **Receivables** | | |
|   Employer contributions | 60,000 | 55,000 |
|   Securities sold | 420,000 | 275,000 |
|   Accrued interest and dividends | 105,000 | 97,000 |
|   Total receivables | 585,000 | 427,000 |
| **Cash** | 300,000 | 150,000 |
|   Total assets | $8,125,000 | $6,927,000 |
| **Liabilities** | | |
|   Due to broker for securities purchased | 200,000 | 95,000 |
|   Accounts payable | 65,000 | 40,000 |
|   Accrued expenses | 40,000 | 35,000 |
|   Total liabilities | 305,000 | 170,000 |
| Net assets available for benefits | $7,820,000 | $6,757,000 |

## Sample Company Pension Plan
### Statement of Changes in Net Assets Available for Benefits
### For the Year Ended December 31, Year 2

| | |
|---|---:|
| **Investment income** | |
| Net appreciation in fair value of investments | $ 620,000 |
| Interest | 200,000 |
| Dividends | 150,000 |
| | 970,000 |
| Less investment expenses | 54,000 |
| | 916,000 |
| Employer contributions | 900,000 |
| Total additions | 1,816,000 |
| Benefits paid directly to participants | 678,000 |
| Administrative expenses | 75,000 |
| Total deductions | 753,000 |
| Net increase | 1,063,000 |
| **Net assets available for benefits** | |
| Beginning of year | 6,757,000 |
| End of year | $7,820,000 |

## Sample Company Pension Plan
### Statement of Accumulated Plan Benefits
### As of December 31

| Actuarial present value of accumulated plan benefits | Year 2 | Year 1 |
|---|---:|---:|
| Vested benefits | | |
| Participants currently receiving payments | $ 3,250,000 | $ 3,075,000 |
| Other participants | 7,520,000 | 6,850,000 |
| | 10,770,000 | 9,925,000 |
| Nonvested benefits | 2,450,000 | 2,160,000 |
| Total actuarial present value of accumulated plan benefits | $13,220,000 | $12,085,000 |

Financial Statements of Employee Benefit Plans

|  | Sample Company Pension Plan<br>Statement of Changes in Accumulated Plan Benefits<br>For the Year Ended December 31, Year 2 |  |
|---|---|---|
| Actuarial present value of accumulated plan benefits—beginning of year | | $12,085,000 |
| Increase (decrease) during the year attributable to: | | |
| Plan amendment | | 1,500,000 |
| Change in actuarial assumptions | | (230,000) |
| Benefits accumulated | | 543,000 |
| Benefits paid | | (678,000) |
| Net increase | | 1,135,000 |
| Actuarial present value of accumulated plan benefits—end of year | | $13,220,000 |

# 3 Required Financial Statements for Defined Contribution Pension Plans

GAAP requires the financial statements of a defined contribution plan to include the following:

1. **Statement of Net Assets Available for Benefits**

   A statement that includes information regarding net assets available for benefits at the end of the plan year, with separate amounts for investments carried at fair value and investments carried at contract value.

**Sample Company Defined Contribution Plan**
**Statement of Net Assets Available for Benefits**
For the Year Ended December 31

|  | Year 2 |  | Year 1 |  |
|---|---|---|---|---|
| **Assets** | | | | |
| Investments, at fair value | | $ 8,136,700 | | $7,715,400 |
| Investments at contract value | | 1,650,000 | | 715,000 |
| **Receivables** | | | | |
| Employer contributions | $ 15,400 | | $ 11,000 | |
| Participant contributions | 57,200 | | 55,000 | |
| Notes receivable from participants | 330,000 | | 385,000 | |
| Total receivables | | 402,600 | | 451,000 |
| Total assets | | $10,189,300 | | $8,881,400 |
| **Liabilities** | | | | |
| Accrued expenses | | $ 11,000 | | $ 22,000 |
| Excess contributions payable | | 16,500 | | – |
| Total liabilities | | 27,500 | | 22,000 |
| **Net assets available for benefits** | | **$10,161,800** | | **$8,859,400** |

## 2. Statement of Changes in Net Assets Available for Benefits

A statement that includes information regarding the changes during the year in the net assets available for benefits.

A *statement of cash flows* is not required, but may be presented if it provides relevant information about the ability of the plan to meet future obligations.

---

**Trenton Company Defined Contribution Plan**
**Statement of Changes in Net Assets Available for Benefits**
For the Year Ended December 31, Year 2

**Additions**
Additions to net assets attributed to:
  Investment income:
    Net appreciation in fair value of investments      $308,000
    Interest      405,900
    Dividends      181,500
         $ 895,400

Interest income on notes receivable from participants      22,000

Contributions:
  Employer      $658,900
  Participants      880,000
  Rollovers      220,000
         1,758,900

Total additions      $ 2,676,300

**Deductions**
Deductions from net assets attributed to:
  Benefits paid to participants      $578,600
  Administrative expenses      11,000
Total deductions      589,600
Net increase      $ 2,086,700
Transfer to FGJ plan      (784,300)
Net assets available for benefits:
  Beginning of year      8,859,400
  End of year      $10,161,800

### Question 1 — MCQ-07235

Each of the following is a component of the changes in the net assets available for benefits of a defined benefit pension plan trust, *except*:

    a. The net change in fair value of each significant class of investments.
    b. The net change in the actuarial present value of accumulated plan benefits.
    c. Contributions from the employer and participants.
    d. Benefits paid to participants.

# MODULE 5

# Stockholders' Equity: Part 1

FAR 7

## 1 Overview

Stockholders' equity (also called shareholders' equity or owners' equity) is the owners' claim to the net assets (i.e., assets minus liabilities) of a corporation. It is generally presented on the statement of financial position (balance sheet) as the last major section (following liabilities). The various elements constituting stockholders' equity must be clearly classified according to source.

**Capital Corp.**
**Consolidated Shareholders' Equity—December 31, Year 1**

**Capital Stock (capital equal to par or stated value)**

| | | |
|---|---:|---:|
| Preferred stock, noncumulative, $100 par value, authorized 1,000 shares issued and outstanding 500 shares | | $ 50,000 |
| Common stock, $10 par value, authorized 50,000 shares, issued 30,000 shares of which 5,000 are held in the treasury | | 300,000 |
| | | 350,000 |

**Additional Paid-in Capital (capital in excess of par or stated value)**

| | | |
|---|---:|---:|
| Excess of issue price over par value of common/preferred stock sold | $ 29,000 | |
| Excess of sales price over cost of treasury shares sold | 15,000 | |
| Excess of FMV over par of stock issued as stock dividend | 20,000 | |
| Defaulted stock subscriptions | 10,000 | |
| FMV of common shares contributed by shareholders to corporation | 75,000 | |
| FMV of fixed assets contributed by local government | 60,000 | 209,000 |

**Retained Earnings**

| | | |
|---|---:|---:|
| Appropriated (reserved) for general contingencies | 50,000 | |
| Appropriated (reserved) for possible future inventory decline | 20,000 | |
| Appropriated (reserved) for plant expansion | 40,000 | |
| Appropriated (reserved) for higher replacement cost of fixed assets | 60,000 | |
| Unappropriated (unreserved) | $200,000 | 370,000 |
| | | 929,000 |
| Accumulated other comprehensive income | | 10,000 |
| Less: Cost of shares in treasury | | (85,000) |
| Total Capital Corp. shareholders' equity | | 854,000 |
| Noncontrolling interest | | 25,000 |
| Total equity | | $879,000 |

# 2 Capital Stock (Legal Capital)

*Legal capital* is the amount of capital that must be retained by the corporation for the protection of creditors. The par or stated value of both preferred and common stock is legal capital and is frequently referred to as "capital" stock.

## 2.1 Par Value

Generally, preferred stock is issued with a par value, but common stock may be issued with or without a par value. No-par common stock may be issued as true no-par stock or no-par stock with a stated value. Any excess of the actual amount received over the par or stated value of the stock is accounted for as additional paid-in capital.

## 2.2 Authorized, Issued, and Outstanding

A corporation's charter contains the amounts of each class of stock that it may legally issue, and this is called "authorized" capital stock. When part or all of the authorized capital stock is issued, it is called "issued" capital stock. Because a corporation may own issued capital stock in the form of treasury stock, the amount of issued capital stock in the hands of shareholders is called "outstanding" capital stock. In summary, capital stock may be:

- authorized;
- authorized and issued; or
- authorized, issued, and outstanding.

The number of shares of each class of stock authorized, issued, and outstanding must be disclosed.

## 2.3 Common Stock

*Common stock* is the basic ownership interest in a corporation. Common shareholders bear the ultimate risk of loss and receive the ultimate benefits of success, but they are not guaranteed dividends or assets upon dissolution. Common shareholders generally control management. They have the right to vote, the right to share in earnings of the corporation, and the right to share in assets upon liquidation after the claims of creditors and preferred shareholders are satisfied.

> **Pass Key**
>
> Common shareholders may have preemptive rights to a proportionate share of any additional common stock issued if granted in the articles of incorporation.

### 2.3.1 Book Value per Common Share

Book value per common share measures the amount that common shareholders would receive for each share if all assets were sold at their book (carrying) values and all creditors were paid. Book value per common share can be determined as follows:

$$\text{Book value per common share} = \frac{\text{Common shareholders' equity}}{\text{Common shares outstanding}}$$

### 2.3.2 Common Stockholders' Equity Formula

  Total shareholders' equity
− Preferred stock outstanding (at greater of call price or par value
− Cumulative preferred dividends in arrears
= Common shareholders' equity

## 2.4 Preferred Stock

*Preferred stock* is an equity security with preferences and features not associated with common stock. Preferred stock may include a preference relating to dividends, which may be cumulative or noncumulative and participating or nonparticipating. Preferred stock may also include a preference relating to liquidation. Usually, preferred stock does not have voting rights.

### 2.4.1 Cumulative Preferred Stock

The *cumulative* feature provides that all or part of the preferred dividend not paid in any year *accumulates* and must be paid in the future before dividends can be paid to common shareholders. The accumulated amount is referred to as *dividends in arrears*. The amount of dividends in arrears is not a legal liability, but it must be disclosed in total and on a per-share basis either parenthetically on the balance sheet or in the footnotes.

### 2.4.2 Noncumulative Preferred Stock

With *noncumulative preferred stock,* dividends not paid in any year do not accumulate. The preferred shareholders lose the right to receive dividends that are not declared.

### 2.4.3 Participating Preferred Stock

The *participating* feature provides that preferred shareholders share (participate) with common shareholders in dividends in excess of a specific amount. The participation may be full or partial. *Fully participating* means that preferred shareholders participate in excess dividends without limit. Generally, preferred shareholders receive their preference dividend first, and then additional dividends are shared between common and preferred shareholders. *Partially participating* means preferred shareholders participate in excess dividends, but to a limited extent (e.g., a percentage limit).

# Stockholders' Equity: Part 1

### 2.4.4 Non-participating Preferred Stock

When preferred stock is *nonparticipating,* preferred shareholders are limited to the dividends provided by their preference. They do not share in excess dividends.

### 2.4.5 Preference Upon Liquidation

Preferred stock may include a preference to assets upon liquidation of the entity. If the liquidation preference is significantly greater than the par or stated value, the liquidation preference must be disclosed. The disclosure of the liquidation preference must be in the equity section of the balance sheet, not in the notes to the financial statements.

### 2.4.6 Convertible Preferred Stock

*Convertible* preferred stock may be exchanged for common stock (at the option of the stockholder) at a specified conversion rate.

### 2.4.7 Callable (Redeemable) Preferred Stock

*Callable* preferred stock may be called (repurchased) at a specified price (at the option of the issuing corporation). The aggregate or the per-share amount at which the preferred stock is callable must be disclosed either on the balance sheet or in the footnotes.

### 2.4.8 Mandatorily Redeemable Preferred Stock (Liability)

*Mandatorily redeemable* preferred stock is issued with a maturity date. Similar to debt, mandatorily redeemable preferred stock must be bought back by the company on the maturity date. Mandatorily redeemable preferred stock must be classified as a liability, unless the redemption is required to occur only upon the liquidation or termination of the reporting entity.

---

**Example 1** — **Distribution of Dividends to Participating Preferred Stockholders**

**Facts:** On January 1, Year 1, Samuel Co. issued 100,000 shares of $5 par common stock and 25,000 shares of $10 par fully participating 8 percent cumulative preferred stock. No dividends were paid in Year 1. Cash dividends of $101,000 were declared and paid in Year 2.

**Required:** Determine the dividend to be paid on the preferred and common stock.

**Solution:**

**Schedule 1:** Dividends Remaining for Distribution

| | |
|---|---:|
| Cash dividends | $101,000 |
| Year 1 preferred dividends in arrears [(25,000 × $10) × 0.08] | (20,000) |
| Preferred dividends accumulated in Year 2 | (20,000) |
| | 61,000 |
| Common stock [(100,000 × $5) × 0.08]* | (40,000) |
| Remaining for proration between preferred and common stock | $ 21,000 |

(continued)

(continued)

**Schedule 2:** Proration of Remaining Dividends According to Par Values

*Preferred stock*

$$\frac{250{,}000}{750{,}000} \times \$21{,}000 = \$7{,}000$$

*Common stock*

$$\frac{500{,}000}{750{,}000} \times \$21{,}000 = \$14{,}000$$

**Schedule 3:** Total Dividends Paid on Preferred and Common Stock

| | |
|---|---|
| Preferred stock | $7,000 + $20,000 + $20,000 = $ 47,000 |
| Common stock | $14,000 + $40,000 = 54,000 |
| Total cash dividends distributed | $101,000 |

*The principle applied here is that, with participating cumulative preferred stock, before any proration of dividends may exist, the common shareholders must receive an equal dividend as the preferred shareholders. In this case, preferred shareholders receive an 8 percent dividend first; common shareholders receive an 8 percent dividend second; and the balance ($21,000) is shared pro rata.

# 3 Additional Paid-in Capital

Additional paid-in capital is generally contributed capital in excess of par or stated value. It can also arise from many other different types of transactions. Additional paid-in capital may be aggregated and shown as one amount on the balance sheet.

Examples include:

- Sale of treasury stock at a gain
- Liquidating dividends
- Conversion of bonds
- Small stock dividends

# 4 Retained Earnings

*Retained earnings* (or deficit) is accumulated earnings (or losses) during the life of the corporation that have not been paid out as dividends The amount of accumulated retained earnings is reduced by distributions to stockholders and transfers to additional paid-in capital for stock dividends. Retained earnings does not include treasury stock or accumulated other comprehensive income If the retained earnings account has a negative balance, it is called a deficit.

## 4.1 Formula

> Net income/loss
> − Dividends (cash, property, and stock) declared
> ± Prior period adjustments
> ± Accounting changes reported retrospectively
> ─────────────────────────────────────────
> Retained earnings

## 4.2 Classification of Retained Earnings (Appropriations)

Retained earnings may be classified as either appropriated or unappropriated. The purpose of appropriating retained earnings is to disclose to the shareholders (usually the common shareholders) that some of the retained earnings are not available to pay dividends because they have been restricted for legal or contractual reasons (e.g., a bond indenture) or as a discretionary act of management for specific contingency purposes (e.g., plant expansion). An appropriation of retained earnings may not be used to absorb costs or losses and may not be transferred to Income.

The following entry should be recorded when an appropriation is to be made (and should be reversed when the purpose of the appropriation has occurred):

| | | | |
|---|---|---|---|
| DR | Retained earnings (unappropriated) | $XXX | |
| CR | Retained earnings appropriated for [purpose] | | $XXX |

# 5 Accumulated Other Comprehensive Income

Components of accumulated other comprehensive income include pension adjustments, unrealized gains and losses on available-for-sale securities, foreign currency translation adjustments, deferred gains and losses on the effective portion of cash flow hedges, and revaluation surpluses (IFRS only).

These components of other comprehensive income are not included in determining net income and, therefore, do not enter into retained earnings. Rather, they are recognized in the period in which they occur and are combined with net income to determine comprehensive income. Total accumulated other comprehensive income must be shown in the shareholders' equity section separate from capital stock, additional paid-in capital, and retained earnings.

FAR 7  Stockholders' Equity: Part 1

> **Question 1**  MCQ-01058
>
> At December 31, Year 1, Eagle Corp. reported $1,750,000 of appropriated retained earnings for the construction of a new office building, which was completed in Year 2 at a total cost of $1,500,000. In Year 2, Eagle appropriated $1,200,000 of retained earnings for the construction of a new plant. Also, $2,000,000 of cash was restricted for the retirement of bonds due in Year 3. In its Year 2 balance sheet, Eagle should report what amount of appropriated retained earnings?
>
> a. $1,200,000
> b. $1,450,000
> c. $2,950,000
> d. $3,200,000

# 6 Treasury Stock

Treasury stock is a corporation's own stock that has been issued to shareholders and subsequently reacquired (but not retired). Treasury stockholders are not entitled to any of the rights of ownership given to common shareholders, such as the right to vote or to receive dividends. In addition, a portion of retained earnings equal to the cost of treasury stock may be restricted and may not be used as a basis for the declaration or payment of dividends (depending on applicable state law).

## 6.1 Methods of Accounting for Treasury Stock

Two methods of accounting for treasury stock are permitted:

1. Cost method
2. Legal (or par/state value) method

The primary difference between the two methods is the timing of the recognition of "gain or loss" on treasury stock transactions. Note that under both methods, the "gains and losses" are recorded as a direct adjustment to stockholders' equity and are not included in the determination of net income. Also, under both methods, shares held as treasury stock are not considered to be outstanding shares.

### 6.1.1 Cost Method (Used by Entities Approximately 95 Percent of the Time)

Under the cost method, the treasury shares are recorded and carried at their reacquisition cost. A gain or loss will be determined when treasury stock is reissued or retired, and the original issue price and book value of the stock do not enter into the accounting. The account "additional paid-in capital from treasury stock" is credited for gains and debited for losses when treasury stock is reissued at prices that differ from the reacquisition cost. Losses may also decrease retained earnings if the additional paid-in capital from treasury stock account does not have a balance large enough to absorb the loss. Net income or retained earnings will never be increased through treasury stock transactions.

# Stockholders' Equity: Part 1

## Illustration 1     Cost Method

**Original issue**

10,000 shares $10 par value common stock sold for $15 per share.

| | | | |
|---|---|---|---|
| DR | Cash | $150,000 | |
| CR | Common stock (10,000 × $10 par) | | $100,000 |
| CR | Additional paid-in capital—C/S | | 50,000 |

**Buy back above issue price**

200 shares were repurchased for $20 per share.

| | | | |
|---|---|---|---|
| DR | Treasury stock (200 × $20) | $4,000 | |
| CR | Cash | | $4,000 |

**Reissue above cost**

100 shares repurchased for $20 were resold for $22.

| | | | |
|---|---|---|---|
| DR | Cash (100 × $22) | $2,200 | |
| CR | Treasury stock (100 × $20) | | $2,000 |
| CR | Additional paid-in capital—T/S | | 200 |

*The following journal entry was made after the preceding entry:*

**Reissue below cost**

100 shares repurchased for $20 were resold for $13.

| | | | |
|---|---|---|---|
| DR | Cash (100 × $13) | $1,300 | |
| DR | Additional paid-in capital—T/S | 200 | |
| DR | Retained earnings | 500 | |
| CR | Treasury stock (100 × $20) | | $2,000 |

### 6.1.2 Legal (or Par/Stated Value) Method (Used by Entities Approximately 5 Percent of the Time)

Under the legal method, the treasury shares are recorded by reducing the amounts of par (or stated) value and additional paid-in capital received at the time of the original sale. Treasury stock is debited for its par (or stated) value. APIC—Common Stock is debited (reduced) for the pro rata share of the original issue price attributable to the reacquired shares. Additional paid-in capital from treasury stock is credited for gains and debited for losses when treasury stock is repurchased at prices that differ from the original selling price. Losses may also decrease retained earnings if the "additional paid-in capital from treasury stock" account does not have a balance large enough to absorb the loss. Note that, under this method, the sources of capital associated with the original issue are maintained.

## Illustration 2  Par Value Method

### Original issue

10,000 shares $10 par value common stock sold for $15 per share.

| | | | |
|---|---|---|---|
| DR | Cash | $150,000 | |
| CR | Common stock (10,000 × $10 par) | | $100,000 |
| CR | Additional paid-in capital—C/S | | 50,000 |

### Buy back above issue price

200 shares were repurchased for $20 per share.

| | | | |
|---|---|---|---|
| DR | Treasury stock (200 × $10 par) | $2,000 | |
| DR | Additional paid-in capital—C/S | 1,000 | |
| DR | Retained earnings* | 1,000 | |
| CR | Cash | | $4,000 |

*This entry should be made to retained earnings if there is no balance in the additional paid-in capital–T/S account.

### Buy Back Below Issue Price

200 shares repurchased for $12 per share.

| | | | |
|---|---|---|---|
| DR | Treasury stock (200 × $10 par) | $2,000 | |
| DR | Additional paid-in capital—C/S (200 × $5) | 1,000 | |
| CR | Cash (200 × $12) | | $2,400 |
| CR | Additional paid-in capital—T/S | | 600 |

### Reissue Shares

100 shares repurchased for $20 were resold for $22.

| | | | |
|---|---|---|---|
| DR | Cash (100 × $22) | $2,200 | |
| CR | Treasury stock (100 × $10 par) | | $1,000 |
| CR | Additional paid-in capital—C/S | | 1,200 |

### Reissue Shares

100 shares repurchased for $20 were resold for $13.

| | | | |
|---|---|---|---|
| DR | Cash (100 × $13) | $1,300 | |
| CR | Treasury stock (100 × $10 par) | | $1,000 |
| CR | Additional paid-in capital—C/S | | 300 |

# Stockholders' Equity: Part 1

## Illustration 3 — Effect of Cost and Par Value Methods on Balance Sheet Presentation

The equity sections of the cost balance sheet and par value balance sheet would appear as follows, assuming that the treasury shares were repurchased for $20 per share:

| Cost Method | | Par Value Method | |
|---|---:|---|---:|
| Common stock (par value) | $100,000 | Common stock (par value) | $100,000 |
| Additional paid-in capital | 50,000 | Less: Treasury stock at par | (2,000) |
| Total paid-in capital | 150,000 | Common stock o/s at par | 98,000 |
| Retained earnings | 75,000 | Additional paid-in capital | 49,000 |
| | 225,000 | | 147,000 |
| Less: Treasury stock at cost | (4,000) | Retained earnings | 74,000 |
| Total stockholders' equity | $221,000 | Total stockholders' equity | $221,000 |

## 6.2 Retirement of Treasury Stock

When treasury stock is acquired with the intent of retiring the stock (regardless of whether it is accomplished) and the price paid is in excess of the par or stated value, that excess may be charged against either (1) all paid-in capital arising from past transactions in the same class of stock or (2) retained earnings. When the price paid for the acquired treasury stock is less than par or stated value, the difference must be credited to paid-in capital.

The retirement of treasury stock would be accomplished with the following journal entries under the cost method and the par value method:

## Illustration 4 — Retirement of Treasury Stock

If all 200 treasury shares reacquired for $20 were retired rather than reissued, the following entry would be made:

**Retirement of Shares (Cost Method)**

200 shares of $10 par common stock originally sold for $15 and reacquired for $20 are retired.

| | | | |
|---|---|---:|---:|
| DR | Common stock (200 × $10) | $2,000 | |
| DR | Additional paid-in capital—C/S (200 × $5) | 1,000 | |
| DR | Retained earnings | 1,000 | |
| CR | Treasury stock (200 × $20) | | $4,000 |

To retire treasury stock under the par value method, debit common stock at par and credit treasury stock at par.

**Retirement of Shares (Par Value Method)**

| | | | |
|---|---|---:|---:|
| DR | Common stock (200 × $10 par) | $2,000 | |
| CR | Treasury stock (200 × $10 par) | | $2,000 |

## 6.3 Donated Stock

Donated stock is a company's own stock received as a donation from a shareholder. There is no change in total shareholders' equity as a result of the donation, but the number of shares outstanding decreases, resulting in higher book value per common share. The company should record donated stock at fair market value, as follows:

| | | | |
|---|---|---|---|
| DR | Donated treasury stock (@FMV) | $XXX | |
| CR | Additional paid-in capital (@FMV) | | $XXX |

If the donated stock is sold, the journal entry would be:

| | | | |
|---|---|---|---|
| DR | Cash (@ sales price) | $XXX | |
| DR | Additional paid-in capital (if SP < original FMV) | XXX | |
| CR | Additional paid-in capital (if SP > original FMV) | | $XXX |
| CR | Donated treasury stock (@ book value, or original FMV) | | XXX |

## NOTES

# MODULE 6: Stockholders' Equity: Part 2

**FAR 7**

## 1 Accounting for a Stock Issuance (to Nonemployees)

If par (or stated) value exists, stock may be issued above, at, or below par (or stated) value. Often, stock subscriptions are sold before the stock is actually issued.

### 1.1 Stock Issued Above Par Value

If stock is issued above par value, cash will be debited for the proceeds, common (or preferred) capital stock will be credited for par (or stated) value, and additional paid-in capital will be credited for the excess over par (or stated) value.

### 1.2 Stock Issued at Par Value

If stock is issued at par value, cash will be debited and common (or preferred) capital stock will be credited for the proceeds. There is no entry to additional paid-in capital.

### 1.3 Stock Issued Below Par Value

If stock is issued at less than par (or stated) value, additional paid-in capital would be debited to reflect a discount on the stock. The discount represents a contingent liability to the original owners.

### 1.4 Stock Subscriptions

Frequently, a corporation sells its capital stock by subscription. This means that a contractual agreement to sell a specified number of shares at an agreed-upon price on credit is entered into. Upon full payment of the subscription, a stock certificate evidencing ownership in the corporation is issued.

#### 1.4.1 Sale of Subscriptions

When the subscription method is used to sell capital stock, a subscriptions receivable account is debited and a capital stock subscribed account is credited, as is a regular additional paid-in capital account. Subscriptions not paid for at year-end are treated as a contra-equity item, offsetting the amount of par (or stated) value and additional paid-in capital related to subscriptions not paid for at year-end (if subscriptions are paid after year-end but before the financial statements are issued, the subscriptions receivable may be reported as an asset and will increase paid-in capital at year-end).

*The journal entry to record subscriptions receivable is as follows:*

| | | | |
|---|---|---|---|
| DR | Subscriptions receivable (1,000 shares @ sales price of $100/share) | $100,000 | |
| CR | Common stock subscribed ($10 par × 1,000 shares) | | $10,000 |
| CR | Additional paid-in capital (1,000 shares × $90 share) | | 90,000 |

Stockholders' Equity: Part 2

### 1.4.2 Collection of Subscriptions

Upon payment of the subscription, the subscription receivable account is credited and cash or other assets are debited, as follows. Assume that $85,000 of the $100,000 subscription from above is collected, including $80,000 in full payment of subscriptions and $5,000 in partial subscription payments (common stock cannot be issued until partial payments are paid in full).

| | | | |
|---|---|---|---|
| DR | Cash | $85,000 | |
| CR | Subscriptions receivable | | $85,000 |

### 1.4.3 Issuance of Stock Previously Subscribed

On the actual issuance of the stock certificates, the capital stock subscribed account is debited and the regular capital stock account is credited, as follows (assume that the $80,000 in fully paid subscriptions from above become issued shares):

| | | | |
|---|---|---|---|
| DR | Common stock subscribed (800 shares @ $10) | $8,000 | |
| CR | Common stock (issued) | | $8,000 |

### 1.4.4 Default/Forfeiture of a Subscription

If all or part of a subscription is not collected, the terms of the subscription agreement and corporate policy will determine the appropriate accounting treatment. Generally, the treatment is to reverse the applicable portion of the original entry and either:

- issue stock in proportion to the amount paid;
- refund the partial payment; or
- retain the partial payment (as liquidated damages for breach of contract) by a credit to additional paid-in capital.

## 1.5 Stock Rights

A stock right provides an existing shareholder with the opportunity to buy additional shares. The right usually carries a price below the stock's market price on the date the rights are granted. The issuance of stock rights requires a memorandum entry only. It is possible that the rights may subsequently be redeemed by the company, which will cause a decrease in stockholders' equity in the amount of the redemption price. The exercise of stock rights requires the following journal entry:

| | | | |
|---|---|---|---|
| DR | Cash | [amount received] | |
| CR | Common stock | | [par value] |
| CR | Additional paid-in capital | | [residual] |

## 1.6 Other Stock Valuation Issues

Stock issued for *outside services* should be recorded at the fair value of the stock, and the trading price of the stock is the best evidence of fair value. Stock issued in a *basket sale* with other securities (e.g., bonds) should be allocated a portion of the sales proceeds based on the relative fair market values of the different securities.

# 2 Distributions to Shareholders

A dividend is a pro rata distribution by a corporation based on the shares of a particular class of stock and usually represents a distribution of earnings. Cash dividends are the most common type of dividend distribution, although there are many other types (covered below). Preferred stock usually pays a fixed dividend, expressed in dollars or as a percentage.

## 2.1 Terminology

- **Date of Declaration:** the date the board of directors formally approves a dividend. On the declaration date, a liability is created (dividends payable) and retained earnings is reduced (debited).
- **Date of Record:** the date the board of directors specifies as the date the names of the shareholders to receive the dividend are determined.
- **Date of Payment:** the date on which the dividend is actually disbursed by the corporation or its paying agent.

## 2.2 Cash Dividends

Cash dividends distribute cash to shareholders and may be declared on common or preferred stock. They are paid from retained earnings. Dividends are paid only on authorized, issued, and outstanding shares. They are not paid (or declared) on treasury stock.

## 2.3 Property (In-Kind) Dividends

Property dividends distribute noncash assets (e.g., inventory, investment securities, etc.) to shareholders. They are nonreciprocal transfers of nonmonetary assets from the company to its shareholders. On the date of declaration, the property to be distributed should be restated to fair value and any gain or loss should be recognized in income. The dividend liability and related debit to retained earnings should be recorded at the fair value of the assets transferred.

## 2.4 Scrip Dividends

Scrip dividends are simply a special form of notes payable whereby a corporation commits to paying a dividend at some later date. Scrip dividends may be used when there is a cash shortage. On the date of declaration, retained earnings is debited and notes payable (instead of dividends payable) is credited. Some scrip dividends even bear interest from the declaration date to the date of payment (and, thus, require accrual).

## 2.5 Liquidating Dividends

Liquidating dividends occur when dividends to shareholders exceed retained earnings. Dividends in excess of retained earnings would be charged (debited) first to additional paid-in capital and then to common or preferred stock (as appropriate). Liquidating dividends reduce total paid-in capital.

# U.S. GAAP VS. IFRS

IFRS and the SEC require public entities to present dividends per share and in total for each class of shares in the statement of changes in equity or in the notes to the financial statements.

## 2.6 Stock Dividends

Stock dividends distribute additional shares of a company's own stock to its shareholders. The treatment of stock dividends depends on the size (percentage) of the dividend in proportion to the total shares outstanding before the dividend.

### 2.6.1 Treatment of a Small Stock Dividend (< 20–25 Percent)

When less than 20 to 25 percent of the shares previously outstanding are distributed, the dividend is treated as a small stock dividend because the issuance is not expected to affect the market price of the stock. The fair market value of the stock dividend at the date of declaration is transferred from retained earnings to capital stock and additional paid-in capital. There is no effect on total shareholders' equity, as paid-in capital is substituted for retained earnings (i.e., retained earnings is "capitalized" and made part of paid-in capital).

### Example 1 — Small Stock Dividend

**Facts:** Capital Corporation has 100,000 shares of $10 par value common stock outstanding. The company declares a stock dividend of 5,000 shares when the fair market value is $15 (on the date of declaration). 5,000 shares/100,000 shares = 5%, which is considered a small stock dividend.

**Required:** Prepare the journal entry to record the dividend.

**Solution:**

*Journal entry:*

| | | | |
|---|---|---:|---:|
| DR | Retained earnings (5,000 × $15 FV) | $75,000 | |
| CR | Common stock (5,000 × $10 par value) | | $50,000 |
| CR | Paid-in capital (difference = $75,000 − 50,000) | | 25,000 |

### 2.6.2 Treatment of a Large Stock Dividend (> 20–25 Percent)

When more than 20 to 25 percent of the previously issued shares outstanding are distributed, the dividend is treated as a large stock dividend, as it may be expected to reduce the market price of the stock (similar to a stock split). The par (or stated) value of the stock dividend is normally transferred from retained earnings to capital stock to meet legal requirements. The amount transferred is the number of shares issued multiplied by the par (or stated) value of the stock. However, if state law does not require capitalization of retained earnings for stock dividends (which is rare because it requires amendment to the articles of incorporation), record the stock dividend distribution (like a stock split) by changing the number of shares outstanding and the par (or stated) value per share.

## Example 2 — Stock Dividend Greater Than 20–25 Percent of Previous Outstanding Shares

**Facts:** LMT Corp. declares a 40 percent stock dividend on its 1,000,000 shares of outstanding $10 par common stock (5,000,000 authorized). On the date of declaration, LMT stock is selling for $20 per share.

| | |
|---|---:|
| Total stock dividend (0.40 × 1,000,000) | 400,000 shares |
| Value of 400,000 shares @ $10 per share (par) | $4,000,000 |

**Required:** Prepare the journal entries to record the declaration and distribution of the stock dividend.

**Solution:**

*Journal entry to record the declaration of the stock dividend at par:*

| | | | |
|---|---|---:|---:|
| DR | Retained earnings | $4,000,000 | |
| CR | Common stock distributable | | $4,000,000 |

*Journal entry to record the distribution of the stock dividend at par:*

| | | | |
|---|---|---:|---:|
| DR | Common stock distributable | $4,000,000 | |
| CR | Capital stock, $10 par common | | $4,000,000 |

### 2.6.3 Stock Dividends on Treasury Stock

Stock dividends are generally not distributed on treasury stock because such stock is not considered outstanding. However, an exception is made when:

1. The company is maintaining a ratio of treasury shares to shares outstanding in order to meet stock option or other contractual commitments or
2. State law requires that treasury stock be protected from dilution.

### 2.7 Stock Splits

Stock splits occur when a corporation issues additional shares of its own stock (without charge) to current shareholders and reduces the par (or stated) value per share proportionately. There is no change in the total book value of the shares outstanding. Thus, the memo entry to acknowledge a stock split is merely a formality.

A stock split usually does not affect retained earnings or total shareholders' equity, as is exhibited below:

| | |
|---|---:|
| **Before the Split** | |
| Common stock (10,000 shares outstanding @ $10 par) | $100,000 |
| **After the Split**    (× 2)             (÷ 2) | |
| Common stock (20,000 shares outstanding @ $5 par) | $100,000 |

### 2.7.1 Reverse Stock Splits

A reverse stock split would involve reducing the number of shares outstanding and increasing the par (or stated) value proportionately. One way to reduce the amount of outstanding shares is to recall outstanding stock certificates and issue new certificates.

### 2.7.2 Stock Splits on Treasury Stock

Stock splits are usually not applied to treasury stock because such stock is not considered outstanding. However, an exception is made when:

- the company is maintaining a ratio of treasury shares to shares outstanding in order to meet stock option or other contractual commitments; or
- state law requires that treasury stock be protected from dilution.

## 3 Statement of Changes in Shareholders' Equity

The statement of changes in shareholders' equity provides specific information about changes in an entity's primary equity components, including capital transactions and distributions to shareholders, a reconciliation of retained earnings, and a reconciliation of the carrying amount of each class of equity capital, paid-in capital, and accumulated other comprehensive income.

**Sydney Technologies Inc.**
**Statement of Changes in Stockholders' Equity**
For the Year Ended December 31, Year 1

| | Total | Retained earnings | Accumulated other comprehensive income | Common stock |
|---|---|---|---|---|
| Beginning balance | $30,000,000 | $8,500,000 | $1,500,000 | $20,000,000 |
| Comprehensive income: | | | | |
| Net income | 1,200,000 | 1,200,000 | | |
| Other comprehensive income | 200,000 | | 200,000 | |
| Common stock issued | 1,000,000 | | | 1,000,000 |
| Dividends declared on common stock | (700,000) | (700,000) | | |
| Ending balance | $31,700,000 | $9,000,000 | $1,700,000 | $21,000,000 |

### U.S. GAAP VS. IFRS

U.S. GAAP permits the presentation of the statement of changes in stockholders' equity either as a primary financial statement or within the notes to the financial statements. IFRS and the SEC require the statement of changes in stockholders' equity to be presented as a primary financial statement.

## Question 1 — MCQ-00974

Selected information from the accounts of Row Co. at December 31, Year 5, follows:

| | |
|---|---:|
| Total income since incorporation | $420,000 |
| Total cash dividends paid | 130,000 |
| Total value of property dividends distributed | 30,000 |
| Excess of proceeds over cost of treasury stock sold, accounted for using the cost method | 110,000 |

In its December 31, Year 5, financial statements, what amount should Row report as retained earnings?

a. $260,000
b. $290,000
c. $370,000
d. $400,000

## Question 2 — MCQ-05228

Porter Co. began its business last year and issued 10,000 shares of common stock at $3 per share. The par value of the stock is $1 per share. During January of the current year, Porter bought back 500 shares at $6 per share, which were reported by Porter as treasury stock. The treasury stock shares were reissued later in the current year at $10 per share. Porter used the cost method to account for its equity transactions. What amount should Porter report as paid-in capital related to its treasury stock transactions on its balance sheet for the current year?

a. $1,500
b. $2,000
c. $4,500
d. $20,000

## NOTES

# MODULE 7
# Stock Compensation

**FAR 7**

## 1 Employee Stock Options

A stock option is the right to purchase shares of a corporation's capital stock under fixed conditions of time, place, and amount.

Under traditional stock option and stock purchase plans, an employer corporation grants options to purchase shares of its stock, often at a price lower than the prevailing market, making it possible for the individual exercising the option to have a potential profit at the moment of acquisition. Most option agreements provide that the purchaser must retain the stock for a minimum period, thus eliminating the possibility of speculation. The cost of compensation is measured by the fair value based on an option pricing model. Stock options or purchase plans can be either noncompensatory or compensatory.

### 1.1 Noncompensatory Stock Option/Purchase Plans

#### 1.1.1 Intention

Certain stock options and employee stock purchase plans are used by entities to raise capital or diversify ownership among employees or officers.

#### 1.1.2 Characteristics of Noncompensatory Plans

Under U.S. GAAP, an employee stock purchase plan is noncompensatory if it meets all of the following requirements:

- Substantially all full-time employees meeting limited employee qualifications may participate. Excluded are officers and employees owning a specific amount of the outstanding stock in the corporation.
- Stock is offered to eligible employees equally, but the plan may limit the total amount of shares that can be purchased.
- The time permitted to exercise the rights is limited to a reasonable period.
- Any discount from the market price is no greater than would be a reasonable offer of stock to shareholders or others.

Stock option plans that meet the requirements of a noncompensatory plan do not require the recognition of compensation expense by the sponsoring company. Plans that do not contain these characteristics are usually classified as compensatory plans.

Stock Compensation

> **U.S. GAAP VS. IFRS**
>
> Under IFRS, employee stock purchase plans and stock options are generally considered to be compensatory.

## 1.2 Compensatory Stock Option/Purchase Plans

Compensatory stock options and stock purchase plans are valued at the fair value of the options issued.

### 1.2.1 Definitions

- **Option Price (or Exercise Price):** the price at which the underlying stock can be purchased pursuant to the option contract.

- **Exercise Date:** the date by which the option holder must use the option to purchase the underlying (and typically the date at which the stock options outstanding account is reduced).

- **Fair Value of the Option:** determined by an economic pricing model such as the Black-Scholes method.

- **Grant Date:** the date the option is issued.

- **Vesting Period:** the period over which the employee has to perform services in order to earn the right to exercise the options (i.e., the time from the grant date to the vesting date).

- **Service Period:** the period over which compensation expense is recognized (i.e. the period the employee performs the service). The service period is generally the vesting period.

### 1.2.2 Compensation Expense

Under the fair value method, total compensation expense is measured by applying an acceptable fair value pricing model such as the *Black-Scholes Option Pricing Model*. Any CPA Exam question will supply this number. This compensation expense, calculated on the grant date of the options, is allocated over the service period, in accordance with the matching principle. The service period is the vesting period, which is the time between the grant date and the vesting date.

> ## Example 1  Accounting for Stock Options
>
> **Facts:** On January 1, Year 1, ABC Co. granted options exercisable after December 31, Year 2, to purchase 10,000 shares of $5 par common stock for $25 per share. On the grant date, the market price of the stock was $20 per share. Using an acceptable valuation model, the options had a total fair value of $50,000. The options are to serve as compensation for services during Year 1 and Year 2.
>
> **Required:** Prepare the journal entries to account for the stock.
>
> **Solution:**
>
> **January 1, Year 1**
>
> *No entry required.*
>
> **December 31, Year 1**
>
> *Journal entry to allocate compensation cost to Year 1 operations:*
>
> | | | | |
> |---|---|---|---|
> | DR | Compensation expense | $25,000 | |
> | CR | Additional paid-in capital—stock options | | $25,000 |
>
> **December 31, Year 2**
>
> *Journal entry to allocate compensation cost to Year 2 operations:*
>
> | | | | |
> |---|---|---|---|
> | DR | Compensation expense | $25,000 | |
> | CR | Additional paid-in capital—stock options | | $25,000 |
>
> On January 1, Year 3, all options are exercised. On the exercise date, the market price of the stock was $35 per share.
>
> **January 1, Year 3**
>
> *Journal entry to record the exercise of the options:*
>
> | | | | |
> |---|---|---|---|
> | DR | Cash (10,000 × $25) | $250,000 | |
> | DR | Additional paid-in capital—stock options | 50,000 | |
> | CR | Common stock (10,000 × $5 par) | | $ 50,000 |
> | CR | Additional paid-in capital in excess of par | | 250,000 |

### 1.2.3 Expiration of Options

Expiration of options requires a reclassification of the remaining balance in the "additional paid-in capital—stock options" account. Reclassification is accomplished by means of the following journal entry:

| | | | |
|---|---|---|---|
| DR | Additional paid-in capital—stock options | $XXX | |
| CR | Additional paid-in capital—expired stock options | | $XXX |

**Note:** Compensation expense is not affected by the expiration of options.

# Stock Compensation

### Illustration 1 — Expiration of Options

Assume that in the previous example, only one half of the options are exercised. The journal entry to record the exercise of options follows:

| | | | |
|---|---|---|---|
| DR | Cash (5,000 × $25) | $125,000 | |
| DR | Additional paid-in capital—stock options | 25,000 | |
| CR | Common stock (5,000 × $5) | | $ 25,000 |
| CR | Additional paid-in capital (common stock) | | 125,000 |

If the remaining options expire, the "additional paid-in capital—stock options" account would have to be reclassified as expired. The required journal entry follows:

| | | | |
|---|---|---|---|
| DR | Additional paid-in capital—stock options | $25,000 | |
| CR | Additional paid-in capital—expired stock options | | $25,000 |

## 2 Stock Appreciation Rights (SARs)

A stock appreciation right entitles an employee to receive an amount equal to the excess of the market price of stock at the exercise date over a predetermined amount (usually market price at grant date). This excess multiplied by the number of rights outstanding is recorded as compensation expense and a liability. Compensation expense for stock appreciation rights outstanding must be adjusted annually to account for changes in the market price of the stock. Unlike stock options, stock appreciation rights do not require the employee to make a cash payment.

### Example 2 — Stock Appreciation Rights

**Facts:** On January 1, Year 1, Loud Corp. granted Mort, its president, 10,000 stock appreciation rights expiring on January 3, Year 4. Upon exercise, Mort may receive cash for the excess of market price of the stock on that date over the market price on the grant date, and the service period runs for two years. Market prices were as follows:

| | |
|---|---|
| January 1, Year 1 | $30 |
| December 31, Year 1 | 45 |
| December 31, Year 2 | 40 |

Mort exercised all his stock appreciation rights on January 2, Year 3, when the market value of Loud's stock was still $40.

**Required:** Prepare the journal entries that should be recorded by Loud to account for the stock appreciation rights on December 31, Year 1, December 31, Year 2, and January 2, Year 3.

(continued)

(continued)

**Solution:**

**December 31, Year 1**

| | | |
|---|---|---|
| Market price at December 31, Year 1 | $ | 45 |
| Market price at January 1, Year 1 | | (30) |
| Appreciation in market value | | 15 |
| Number of stock rights outstanding | | × 10,000 |
| Total compensation expense | | $150,000 |

Compensation expense for Year 1 is then ½ × $150,000 because the service period is for two years. Loud's journal entry at 12/31/Yr 1 follows:

| | | | |
|---|---|---|---|
| DR | Compensation expense | $75,000 | |
| CR | Liability for SAR plan | | $75,000 |

A liability account is credited because Mort will receive cash. Otherwise, paid-in capital would be credited if stock is to be issued.

**December 31, Year 2**

| | | |
|---|---|---|
| Market price at December 31, Year 2 | $ | 40 |
| Market price at January 1, Year 1 | | (30) |
| Appreciation in market value | | 10 |
| Number of rights outstanding | | × 10,000 |
| Required balance in liability, Year 2 | | $100,000 |

Compensation expense is $100,000 less the $75,000 previously recognized, or $25,000. The required journal entry for Year 2 follows:

| | | | |
|---|---|---|---|
| DR | Compensation expense | $25,000 | |
| CR | Liability for SAR plan | | $25,000 |

**January 2, Year 3**

When the stock appreciation rights are exercised, Loud would make the following entry:

| | | | |
|---|---|---|---|
| DR | Liability for SAR plan | $100,000 | |
| CR | Cash | | $100,000 |

Stock Compensation

**Question 1**  MCQ-01033

On January 2 of the current year, Kine Co. granted Morgan, its president, compensatory stock options to buy 1,000 shares of Kine's $10 par common stock. The options call for a price of $20 per share and are exercisable for three years following the grant date. Morgan exercised the options on December 31 of the current year. The market price of the stock was $45 on January 2 and $70 on December 31. Using an acceptable options pricing model, Morgan determined that the fair value of the options granted was $30,000. By what net amount should stockholders' equity increase as a result of the grant and exercise of the options?

- a. $20,000
- b. $30,000
- c. $50,000
- d. $70,000

# FAR 8

# EPS, Cash Flows, and NFP Accounting

## Module

| | | |
|---|---|---|
| 1 | Earnings per Share | 3 |
| 2 | Statement of Cash Flows | 15 |
| 3 | Not-for-Profit Financial Reporting: Part 1 | 29 |
| 4 | Not-for-Profit Financial Reporting: Part 2 | 43 |
| 5 | Not-for-Profit Revenue Recognition | 49 |
| 6 | Not-for-Profit Transfers of Assets and Other Accounting Issues | 61 |

# NOTES

# MODULE 1 Earnings per Share

FAR 8

## 1 Overview

Under both U.S. GAAP and IFRS, all public entities (or entities that have made a filing for a public offering) are required to present earnings per share on the face of the income statement. An entity's capital structure determines the manner in which earnings per share are disclosed.

An entity has a simple capital structure if it has only common stock outstanding. The entity presents basic per-share amounts for income from continuing operations and for net income on the face of the income statement.

All other entities must present basic and diluted per-share amounts for income from continuing operations and for net income on the face of the income statement (or statement of income and comprehensive income if the entity is using the one-statement approach).

If the entity reports a discontinued operation, the entity must present the basic and diluted (if applicable) per-share amounts for that item either on the face of the income statement or in the notes to the financial statements.

## 2 Simple Capital Structure (Report Basic EPS Only)

An entity that issues only common stock (or no other securities that can become common stock, such as noncovertible preferred stock) is said to have a simple capital structure. This organization will present EPS for income from continuing operations and for net income on the face of the income statement. The number of common shares outstanding (the denominator) used in the EPS calculation is arrived at by the weighted average method.

### 2.1 Basic EPS Formula

For an organization with a simple capital structure, the formula for earnings per share is as follows:

$$\text{Basic EPS} = \frac{\text{Income available to common shareholders}}{\text{Weighted average number of common shares outstanding}}$$

### 2.2 Income Available to the Common Shareholders

Income available to common shareholders is determined by deducting from the line item income from continuing operations and net income (1) dividends declared in the period on noncumulative preferred stock (regardless of whether they have been paid) and (2) dividends accumulated in the period on cumulative preferred stock (regardless of whether they have been declared).

Earnings per Share

If there is a loss from continuing operations (or a net loss), the amount of the loss should be increased by the preferred shareholders' dividends or claims to determine income available to the common shareholders.

## 2.3 Weighted Average Number of Common Shares Outstanding

The weighted average number of common shares outstanding during the period is the mean (average) of shares outstanding and assumed to be outstanding for EPS calculations. Shares sold or reacquired during the period (including treasury stock) should be weighted for the portion of the period they were outstanding.

> Shares outstanding at the beginning of the period
> + Shares sold during the period (on a time-weighted basis)
> − Shares reacquired during the period (on a time-weighted basis)
> + Stock dividends and stock splits (retroactively adjusted)
> − Reverse stock splits (retroactively adjusted)
> _____
> Weighted average number of common shares outstanding

### 2.3.1 Stock Dividends and Stock Splits

Stock dividends and stock splits (to the same class of shareholders in the same company) must be treated as though they occurred at the *beginning* of the period. The shares outstanding before the stock dividend or stock split must be restated for the portion of the period before the stock dividend/split. If prior periods are presented, the effects of stock dividends and stock splits must be retroactively adjusted for those periods.

- If a stock dividend or stock split occurs after the end of the period but before the financial statements are issued, those shares should enter into the shares outstanding for the EPS calculation for all periods presented.

- Reverse stock splits would retroactively reduce shares outstanding for all periods presented.

### 2.3.2 Rules for Stock Issued in a Business Combination

If the acquisition method is used, the weighted average is measured from the date of the combination.

## Example 1: Weighted Average Number of Shares Outstanding Computation

**Facts:**

| Date | Transaction | Change in Shares | Total Shares |
|---|---|---|---|
| 1/1 | Shares outstanding | | 1,000,000 |
| 3/31 | 2-for-1 stock split | 1,000,000 | 2,000,000 |
| 4/1 | Additional shares sold | 3,000,000 | 5,000,000 |
| 12/1 | Reacquired shares (treasury) | (500,000) | 4,500,000 |

**Required:** Calculate the weighted average number of shares outstanding.

**Solution:**

| Total Shares | × Period Outstanding | × Adjustment for Split | = Weighted Average |
|---|---|---|---|
| 1,000,000 | 3/12 (Jan–Mar) | 2 | 500,000 |
| 5,000,000 | 8/12 (April–Nov) | | 3,333,333 |
| 4,500,000 | 1/12 (Dec) | | 375,000 |
| | | Weighted average shares outstanding | 4,208,333 |

**Alternative Solution:**

| Date | Transaction | Gross Change in Shares | Adjustment to Weighted Average Shares | |
|---|---|---|---|---|
| 1/1 | Shares outstanding | (beginning number) | 1,000,000 | |
| 3/31 | 2-for-1 stock split | 1,000,000 | 1,000,000 | [effective 1/1] |
| 4/1 | Additional shares sold | 3,000,000 | 2,250,000 | [3,000,000 × 9/12] |
| 12/1 | Reacquired shares | (500,000) | (41,667) | [500,000 × 1/12] |
| | Weighted average shares outstanding | | 4,208,333 | |

---

### Question 1 — MCQ-01200

On December 1 of the current year, Clay Co. declared and issued a 6 percent stock dividend on its 100,000 shares of outstanding common stock. There was no other common stock activity during the year. What number of shares should Clay use in determining basic earnings per share for the current year?

a. 100,000
b. 100,500
c. 103,000
d. 106,000

Earnings per Share

FAR 8

> **Question 2** MCQ-01198
>
> Ute Co. had the following capital structure during Year 1 and Year 2:
>
> | | |
> |---|---|
> | Preferred stock, $10 par, 4% cumulative, 25,000 shares issued and outstanding | $ 250,000 |
> | Common stock, $5 par, 200,000 shares issued and outstanding | 1,000,000 |
>
> Ute reported net income of $500,000 for the year ended December 31, Year 2. Ute paid no preferred dividends during Year 1 and paid $16,000 in preferred dividends during Year 2. In its December 31, Year 2, income statement, what amount should Ute report as basic earnings per share?
>
> a. $2.42
> b. $2.45
> c. $2.48
> d. $2.50

# 3  Complex Capital Structure (Report Basic and Diluted EPS)

An entity has a complex capital structure when it has securities that can potentially be converted to common stock and would therefore dilute (reduce) EPS (of common stock). Both basic and diluted EPS must be presented. The basic EPS calculation ignores potentially dilutive securities in the weighted average number of shares outstanding calculation. The objective of diluted EPS is to measure the performance of an entity over the reporting period while giving effect to all potentially dilutive common shares outstanding during the period. Potentially dilutive securities include:

- convertible securities (e.g., convertible preferred stock, convertible bonds, etc.);
- warrants and other options;
- contracts that may be settled in cash or stock; and
- contingent shares.

## 3.1  Diluted EPS Formula

$$\text{Diluted EPS} = \frac{\text{Income available to the common stock shareholder} + \text{Interest on dilutive securities}}{\text{Weighted average number of common shares (assuming all dilutive securities are converted to common stock)}}$$

## 3.2 Dilution From Options, Warrants, and Their Equivalents

The dilutive effect of options and warrants and their equivalents is applied using the treasury stock method. The treasury stock method assumes that the proceeds from the exercise of stock options, warrants, and their equivalents will be used by the company to repurchase treasury shares at the prevailing market price, resulting in an incremental increase in shares outstanding, but not the full amount of shares that are issued on exercise of the common stock equivalents. The equivalents of options and warrants include nonvested stock granted to employees, stock purchase contracts, and partially paid stock subscriptions. Any canceled or issued options or warrants during the period shall be included in the denominator of diluted EPS for the period they were outstanding.

### 3.2.1 Dilutive vs. Antidilutive

Options and similar instruments are only dilutive when the average market price of the underlying common stock exceeds the exercise price of the options or warrants because it is unlikely they would be exercised if the exercise price were higher than the market price. These options or warrants would be "out of the money" and antidilutive. Previously reported EPS should not be adjusted retroactively in the case of options or similar instruments to reflect subsequent changes in market prices of the common stock.

### 3.2.2 Treasury Stock Method

The treasury stock method is applied as follows:

- If the average market price of the stock is greater than the exercise price (called "in the money"), assume that the warrants or other options are exercised at the beginning of the period (or at the time of issue, if later).

- Also assume that the proceeds received (the option or exercise price) are used to purchase common shares at the average market price during the period.

- When the option/warrant is in the money (average market price > exercise price), the proceeds (assumed to be) received will not be sufficient to buy back an (assumed) equal number of shares. This will always result in dilution.

- The difference between the number of shares assumed issued to satisfy the options or warrants and the number of shares assumed to be purchased with the proceeds should be included in the number of shares (denominator) for diluted EPS.

- Previously reported EPS data should not be retroactively adjusted for changes in market price.

The formula to compute additional shares for options and similar instruments is:

$$\text{Additional shares outstanding} = \text{Number of shares} - \left( \frac{\text{Number of shares} \times \text{Exercise price}}{\text{Average market price}} \right)$$

Earnings per Share

> ### Example 2 — Options and Warrants Treasury Stock Method
>
> **Facts:**
>
> 1,000 options to purchase 1,000 common stock shares
> $15.00 exercise price per share
> $20.00 average market price
> $25.00 period-end market price
>
> **Required:** Compute the incremental shares to be added to WACSO when computing diluted EPS using the treasury stock method.
>
> **Solution:**
>
> |  |  | Diluted |
> |---|---:|---:|
> | Options/common stock shares | 1,000 → | 1,000 |
> | Exercise price per share | × $ 15.00 | |
> | Cash corp. received (hypothetically) | $15,000 | |
> | Diluted "repurchase price" | ÷ $ 20.00 | |
> | Repurchase shares (hypothetically) | | <750> |
> | Common shares added to WACSO when computing diluted EPS | | 250 shares |
>
> **Formula Approach**
>
> $$1{,}000 - \frac{1{,}000 \times \$15.00}{\$20.00} = \underline{\underline{250}} \text{ shares}$$

## 3.3 Dilution From Convertible Securities: Bonds or Preferred Stock

The "if-converted" method should be used to determine the dilutive effects of the convertible securities. The if-converted method assumes that the securities were converted to common stock at the *beginning* of the period (or at the time of issue, if later).

### 3.3.1 Convertible Bonds

Use the following steps to apply the if-converted method to convertible bonds:

1. Add to the numerator (i.e., income available to common shareholders) the interest expense, net of tax, due to the assumed conversion of bonds to common stock.

2. Add to the denominator (i.e., weighted average number of shares outstanding) the number of common shares associated with the assumed conversion.

3. If the convertible bonds were issued during the period, assume that the stock was issued at that date for the weighted average calculation.

## Illustration 1   Convertible Bonds: If-Converted Method

| Actual | | Pretend |
|---|---|---|
| $100 | Income | $100 |
| <20> | Bond interest | <0> |
| 80 | Income before taxes | 100 |
| <32> | Taxes (40%) | <40> |
| $ 48 | N.I. available to common stockholders | $ 60 |

### 3.3.2  Antidilution

Use the results of each assumed conversion only if it results in dilution (i.e., reduces EPS). Do not include the results of the *assumed* conversion if it is antidilutive (i.e., increases EPS). In determining whether potential common shares are dilutive or antidilutive, each issue will be considered separately in sequence from most to least dilutive, with options and warrants generally included first. The tests for dilutive or antidilutive effects should be based on income from continuing operations.

### Example 3   Application of the If-Converted Method (Convertible Bonds)

**Facts:** X Company has outstanding 100,000 shares of common stock and $500,000 in 6 percent bonds convertible into 10 shares for each $1,000 bond. Net income for the year is $100,000.

**Required:** Compute the diluted EPS assuming a 34 percent tax rate.

**Solution:**

Diluted shares outstanding:

| | |
|---|---:|
| Common stock | $ 100,000 |
| Convertible bonds (500 × 10) | 5,000 |
| Total common shares outstanding | 105,000 |

Diluted net income:

| | |
|---|---:|
| Net income | $100,000 |
| Add: Interest on bonds, less tax effects [0.06 × $500,000 × (1 − 0.34)] | 19,800 |
| Total net income | $119,800 |
| Diluted EPS ($119,800 ÷ 105,000 shares) | $ 1.14 |

Compare basic EPS computed with the bonds to diluted EPS computed without the bonds to determine whether the inclusion of the convertible bonds in the computation of diluted EPS is antidilutive:

Basic EPS (without conversion) ($100,000 ÷ 100,000 shares)   $ 1.00

Diluted EPS with conversion of the convertible bonds ($1.14) is more than basic EPS without the conversion ($1.00). The convertible bonds are antidilutive and would be excluded.

Earnings per Share

### 3.3.3 Convertible Preferred Stock

Use the following steps to apply the if-converted method to convertible preferred stock:

1. Adjust the numerator (as preferred stock dividends do not affect net income).
2. Add to the denominator the number of shares associated with the assumed conversion.

Antidilution rules apply to convertible preferred stock.

---

**Example 4 — Application of the If-Converted Method (Convertible Preferred Stock)**

**Facts:** Carlin Company has outstanding 100,000 shares of common stock and 10,000 shares of convertible preferred stock, convertible into five shares of common stock for each share of preferred. Net income for the year is $100,000. Dividends declared during the year were $20,000 on the preferred, and $30,000 on the common.

**Required:** Compute the diluted EPS assuming a 34 percent tax rate.

**Solution:**

Diluted shares outstanding:

| | |
|---|---:|
| Common stock | $100,000 |
| Convertible debentures (10,000 × 5) | 50,000 |
| Total common shares outstanding | 150,000 |
| Diluted net income: | $100,000 |
| Diluted EPS ($100,000 ÷ 150,000) | $ 0.67 |

**Note:** The preferred stock dividends are not subtracted from net income. We assume that since the preferred stock was converted into common stock, the preferred stock dividends were not paid.

Antidilution is checked by comparing basic EPS with the calculated diluted EPS:

Basic EPS: $\dfrac{\$100{,}000 - \$20{,}000}{100{,}000} = \$0.80$

Since diluted EPS is less than basic EPS (without conversion), the preferred stock is dilutive, and diluted EPS is $0.67.

---

## 3.4 Dilution From Contracts That May Be Settled in Cash or in Stock

If a contract could be settled in either stock or cash at the election of either the entity or the holder, the facts available each period determine whether it is reflected in the computation of EPS. It is presumed that the contract will be settled in common stock and the resulting shares included in diluted EPS if the effect is more dilutive.

---

**U.S. GAAP VS. IFRS**

Under IFRS, contracts that may be settled in cash or in stock are always presumed to be settled in common shares and included in diluted EPS.

## 3.5 Dilution From Contingent Shares

Contingent issuable shares do not require cash consideration and depend on some future event or on certain conditions being met. Contingent shares (that are dilutive) are also included in the calculation of *basic* EPS if (and as of the date) all conditions for issuance are met.

Issuable shares contingent on the attainment of a certain level of earnings are treated as follows, if dilutive:

- If the necessary conditions have been satisfied by the end of the period, those shares are included in basic EPS as of the beginning of the period in which the conditions were satisfied.

- If the necessary conditions have not been satisfied by the end of the period, the number of contingently issuable shares included in diluted EPS is based on the number of shares that would be issuable, if any, if the end of the reporting period were the end of the contingency period. These shares are included as of the beginning of the period (or as of the date of the contingent stock agreement, if later). If the contingency is due to attainment of future earnings and/or future prices of the shares, both earnings to date and current market price, as they exist at the end of the reporting period, are used.

> **U.S. GAAP VS. IFRS**
>
> Under IFRS, contingently issuable ordinary shares are treated as outstanding and included in the calculation of diluted EPS only if the conditions are satisfied.

# 4 Disclosures

Cash flow per share should not be reported. In addition to reporting basic EPS and diluted EPS for both income from continuing operations and net income and the effects of discontinued operations, the following disclosure requirements must be met:

- A reconciliation of the numerators and the denominators of the basic and diluted per-share computations for income from continuing operations.

- The effect that has been given to preferred dividends in arriving at income available to common stockholders in computing basic EPS.

- Securities that could potentially dilute basic EPS in the future that were not included in the computation of diluted EPS because the effect was antidilutive for the period(s) presented.

- Description of any transaction that occurred after the period end that would have materially affected the number of actual and/or potential common shares outstanding.

Earnings per Share

## Pass Key

|  | Weighted Average | Options and Warrants | Convertible Bond | Convertible P/S | Contingent Issues |
|---|---|---|---|---|---|
| **Basic** | Yes | N/A | N/A | N/A | Conditions have been fully satisfied |
| **Diluted** | Yes | Average market value > Exercise price<br>**Treasury stock method**<br>Repurchase common stock at the *average* price | Any dilutive<br>**If-converted method**<br>Adjust net income for interest expense (not incurred) reduced by taxes | Any dilutive<br>**If-converted method**<br>Do *not* reduce income available to common shareholders by the preferred stock dividend (pretend they were converted) | Based upon conditions having been met to date |

### Question 3                                                                  MCQ-01199

West Co. had earnings per share of $15.00 for the current year before considering the effects of any convertible securities. No conversion or exercise of convertible securities occurred during the year. However, possible conversion of convertible bonds would have reduced earnings per share by $0.75. The effect of possible exercise of common stock options would have increased earnings per share by $0.10. What amount should West report as diluted earnings per share for the current year?

    a. $15.00
    b. $14.35
    c. $14.25
    d. $15.10

## Question 4 — MCQ-05675

Ian Co. is calculating earnings per-share amounts for inclusion in Ian's annual report to shareholders. Ian has obtained the following information from the controller's office as well as shareholder services:

| | |
|---|---|
| Net income from January 1 to December 31 | $125,000 |
| Number of outstanding shares: | |
| January 1 to March 31 | 15,000 |
| April 1 to May 31 | 12,500 |
| June 1 to December 31 | 17,000 |

In addition, Ian has issued 10,000 incentive stock options with an exercise price of $30 to its employees and a year-end market price of $25 per share. What amount is Ian's diluted earnings per share for the year ended December 31?

- a. $4.63
- b. $4.85
- c. $7.35
- d. $7.94

## NOTES

# MODULE 2: Statement of Cash Flows

FAR 8

## 1 Overview

A statement of cash flows is a required part of a full set of financial statements for all business enterprises. The purpose of the statement of cash flows is to provide information about the sources of cash and cash equivalents (i.e., cash receipts) and the uses of cash and cash equivalents (i.e., cash disbursements), including:

- **Operating Cash Flows:** Cash receipts and disbursements from transactions reported on the income statement and current assets and current liabilities (excluding current notes payable and the current portion of long-term debt, which are reported in financing cash flows).
- **Investing Cash Flows:** Cash receipts and disbursements from non-current assets.
- **Financing Cash Flows:** Cash receipts and disbursements from debt (including non-current liabilities) and equity.

The statement also presents information about material noncash events. Cash flow amounts per share are *not* disclosed under U.S. GAAP. IFRS does not prohibit the presentation of cash flow per share.

## 2 Cash and Cash Equivalents

The statement of cash flows reconciles the cash and cash equivalents amount presented on the beginning balance sheet to the cash and cash equivalents amount presented on the ending balance sheet (i.e., the change in cash for the period).

### 2.1 Definitions

- Cash is defined as actual cash (i.e., currency and demand deposits).
- Cash equivalents are defined as short-term, liquid investments that are:
  - quickly convertible into specific amounts of cash *and*
  - so near maturity (i.e., the original maturity date to the investor was within three months of the purchase date) that the risk of changes in the value because of interest rate changes is insignificant.

> **U.S. GAAP VS. IFRS**
>
> Under U.S. GAAP, bank overdrafts are excluded from cash and are classified as financing cash flows. Under IFRS, cash may include bank overdrafts repayable on demand if they are an integral part of an entity's cash management.

## 2.2 Purpose

The cash concept is used because investors, creditors, and other interested parties need information about the entity's available cash and cash needs (i.e., ability to pay obligations, dividends, etc.).

---

**Illustration 1     Summarized Statement Format**

X Company
**Statement of Cash Flows**
For the Year Ended December 31, Year 1

| | |
|---|---:|
| Net cash provided by (used in) operating activities | $XXX |
| Net cash provided by (used in) investing activities | XXX |
| Net cash provided by (used in) financing activities | $XXX |
| Net increase (decrease) in cash | $XXX |
| Cash and cash equivalents at beginning of year | XXX |
| Cash and cash equivalents at end of year | $XXX |

---

# 3   Methods of Presenting the Statement of Cash Flows

There are two ways to prepare the operating section of a statement of cash flows—the *direct method* and the *indirect method*. Both U.S. GAAP and IFRS encourage the use of the direct method. However, most firms use the indirect method. Regardless of the method used, the presentation of investing and financing activities is the same. Only the sections that present operating activities and certain required disclosures are different.

## 3.1   Direct Method

Under the direct method, the operating activities section of the statement of cash flows shows the major classes of *operating* cash receipts and disbursements. Noncash items such as depreciation, amortization, depletion, and income from affiliates under the equity method do not appear in direct method operating cash flow. A reconciliation of net income to net cash flows from operating activities is required to be provided in a separate schedule under U.S. GAAP. This reconciliation is not required under IFRS.

## 3.2   Indirect Method

Companies that choose not to use the direct method are required to report the same amount of net cash flows from operating activities indirectly, by adjusting net income to reconcile it to net cash flows from operating activities, as follows:

$$CFO = \text{Net income} + \text{Noncash expenses/losses} - \text{Noncash income/gains} + \text{Increases (decreases) in operating liabilities/(assets)} - \text{Increases (decreases) in operating assets/(liabilities)}$$

# 4 Sections of the Formal Statement

## 4.1 Operating Activities

Operating activities involve producing goods and delivering services to customers. All transactions not categorized as investing or financing activities (discussed below) are categorized as operating activities. U.S. GAAP requires a reconciliation of net income to net cash provided by operating activities under both the direct method and the indirect method. If the direct method is chosen, the reconciliation will appear in a supplemental schedule. If the indirect method is chosen, this reconciliation is part of the body of the formal statement.

### 4.1.1 Direct Method

If the direct method is used, major classes of cash receipts and disbursements are presented in their gross amounts and totaled to arrive at "net cash flow provided by (used in) operating activities."

The following categories should be reported separately:

1. Cash received from customers (increases cash), calculated as follows:

   >     Revenues
   >   − Increase in receivables
   >   + Decrease in receivables
   >   + Increase in unearned revenue
   >   − Decrease in unearned revenue
   >   ─────────────────────────────
   >     Cash received from customers

2. Interest received (increases cash)
3. Dividends received (increases cash)
4. Other operating cash receipts such as the receipt of insurance proceeds and lawsuit settlements (increases cash)
5. Cash received from the sales of securities classified as trading securities, if classified as current assets (increases cash)

6. Cash paid to suppliers and employees (decreases cash), calculated as follows:

>     Cost of goods sold
>   + Increase in inventory
>   − Decrease in inventory
>   − Increase in accounts payable
>   + Decrease in accounts payable
>   ―――――――――――――――――――
>     Cash paid to suppliers
>
>     Salaries and wages expense
>   − Increase in wages payable
>   + Decrease in wages payable
>   ―――――――――――――――――――
>     Cash paid to employees

7. Interest paid (decreases cash)
8. Income taxes paid (decreases cash)
9. Cash paid to acquire securities classified as trading securities, if classified as current assets (decreases cash)
10. Other operating cash payments (decreases cash), calculated as follows:

>     Other operating expenses
>   − Decrease in prepaid expenses
>   + Increase in prepaid expenses
>   + Decrease in accrued liabilities
>   − Increase in accrued liabilities
>   ―――――――――――――――――――
>     Cash paid for other expenses

### 4.1.2 Indirect Method

Under the indirect method, net income is adjusted to arrive at net cash flows from operating activities. In addition, supplemental disclosure of cash paid for interest and income taxes is required.

- **Adjustment to Net Income:** The adjustment to net income is performed by removing the effects on net income of the following items:
  - All *deferrals* of past operating cash receipts and disbursements (e.g., subtracting increases in inventory and prepaid expenses);

- All *accruals* of expected future operating cash receipts and disbursements (e.g., subtracting increases in accounts receivable and adding increases in accounts payable and accrued expenses);
- All items that are included in net income that *do not affect operating cash receipts and disbursements* (e.g., those that should be omitted altogether or categorized as investing or financing activities, such as adding depreciation and amortization and subtracting gains on sales of productive assets).

■ **Determination of Effect on Cash Flow:** The effect on cash flows for comparative balance sheet changes in asset, liability, and equity accounts can be easily determined (these rules apply to all changes in balance sheet items, including those in the investing and financing activities sections), as follows:

- An increase to an asset or a "debit balance" account (e.g., accounts receivable) will have the effect on the statement of cash flows as a decrease to cash (indirect effect).
- A decrease to an asset of a "debit balance" account (e.g., inventory) will have the effect on the statement of cash flows as an increase to cash (indirect effect).
- An increase in a liability, an equity, or a "credit balance" account (e.g., accounts payable) will have the effect on the statement of cash flows as an increase to cash (direct effect).
- A decrease in a liability, an equity, or a "credit balance" account (e.g., allowance for doubtful accounts) will have the effect on the statement of cash flows as a decrease to cash (direct effect).

■ **Shortcut Cash Flow Effects**
- Changes in debit balance accounts will have the opposite effect on cash flows (because cash is a debit balance account).
- Changes in credit balance accounts will have the same effect on cash flows.

■ **Gains and Losses**
- *Gains* are adjusted out of the operating activities section and (generally) into the investing activities section by *subtracting* their effects from net income.
- *Losses* are adjusted out of the operating activities section and (generally) into the investing activities section by *adding* their effects to net income.

> ### Pass Key
>
> You will be able to easily remember approximately 85 percent of the adjustments made to the operating activities section under the indirect method by remembering the mnemonic **CLAD**.
>
> - Current assets and liabilities
> - Losses and gains
> - Amortization and depreciation
> - Deferred items

## 4.2 Investing Activities

Investing activities include cash flows from the purchase or sale of *non-current assets*:

- Making loans to other entities (cash outflow);
- Purchasing (cash outflow) or disposing of (cash inflow) trading securities (if classified as non-current), available-for-sale securities, and held-to-maturity investment securities of other entities (debt or equity);
- Acquiring (cash outflow) or disposing of (cash inflow) property, plant, and equipment (productive assets); and
- Acquiring another entity under the acquisition method using cash (cash outflow). The payment for the acquisition is shown net of the cash acquired.

## 4.3 Financing Activities

Financing activities include cash flows from *non-current liability* (creditor-oriented) and *equity* (owner-oriented) activities.

### 4.3.1 Equity (Owner-Oriented) Activities

- Obtaining resources from owners, such as issuing stock (cash inflow).
- Providing owners with a return on their investment, such as paying cash dividends or repurchasing stock (cash outflow).

### 4.3.2 Non-current Liability (Creditor-Oriented) Activities

- Obtaining resources from creditors, such as issuing bonds, notes, and other borrowings (cash inflow).
- Payments of principal (not interest, which is part of the operating activities section) on amount borrowed (cash outflow).

## 4.4 Noncash Investing and Financing Activities

Information about material noncash financing and investing activities (those that do not result in cash receipts or payments) should be provided separately in a supplemental disclosure. Of course, any part of the transaction that does involve cash would be included in the statement of cash flows. Examples include:

- A purchase of fixed assets by issuance of stock, which is not a cash transaction, but would likely be a material transaction for the entity.
- The conversion of bonds to equity, which generally does not involve cash.
- Acquiring assets through the incurrence of a capital lease obligation.
- The exchange of one noncash asset for another noncash asset.

## 4.5 Summary of Cash Flow Classifications of Individual Transactions

The following table summarizes the statement of cash flow classifications of individual transactions under U.S. GAAP:

| Transaction | Operating Cash Flow (CFO) | Investing Cash Flow (CFI) | Financing Cash Flow (CFF) | No Net Cash Flow |
|---|---|---|---|---|
| Selling products / collecting receivables | ✓ | | | |
| Purchasing inventory / paying vendors | ✓ | | | |
| Purchasing supplies and services / paying vendors | ✓ | | | |
| Paying taxes | ✓ | | | |
| Purchasing / selling trading securities (general rule) | ✓ | | | |
| Purchasing long-term assets or long-term investments for cash | | ✓ | | |
| Recording depreciation, amortization, or depletion | | | | ✓ |
| Collecting interest on an investment | ✓ | | | |
| Collecting dividends on an investment | ✓ | | | |
| Recording income of equity method affiliates | | | | ✓ |
| Selling long-term assets or investments (noncash equivalents and nontrading securities): cash proceeds | | ✓ | | |
| Borrowing funds (e.g., bank loans, issuing debt) | | | ✓ | |
| Paying interest on debt | ✓ | | | |
| Paying principal on debt | | | ✓ | |
| Issuing common or preferred stock | | | ✓ | |
| Paying dividends on common or preferred stock | | | ✓ | |
| Repurchasing stock (e.g., treasury shares) | | | ✓ | |
| Prepaying debt or paying debt extinguishment costs | | | ✓ | |

**Note:** The statement of cash flows should include amounts generally described as restricted cash or restricted cash equivalents in its reconciliation of beginning-of-period and end-of-period total amounts. U.S. GAAP does not currently provide a definition of restricted cash or restricted cash equivalents. An entity should disclose the nature of any restrictions, if applicable.

# 5 IFRS Differences in Reporting Cash Flows

IFRS allows more flexibility than U.S. GAAP in classifying cash flows related to interest, dividends, and income taxes. The following table summarizes the classification differences between U.S. GAAP and IFRS:

| Transaction | U.S. GAAP | IFRS |
| --- | --- | --- |
| Interest Received | CFO | CFO or CFI |
| Interest Paid | CFO | CFO or CFF |
| Dividends Received | CFO | CFO or CFI |
| Dividends Paid | CFF | CFO or CFF |
| Taxes Paid | CFO | CFO, CFI, CFF |

IFRS classifies taxes paid as CFO, but allows allocation to CFI or CFF for portions specifically identified with investing and financing activities. IFRS also requires disclosure of tax-related cash flows separately within the statement of cash flows. U.S. GAAP requires the disclosure of interest and taxes paid in a footnote if not presented on the statement of cash flows.

# 6 Comparison of Indirect and Direct Methods

**Cox Company**
**Consolidated Statement of Cash Flows**
For the Year Ended December 31, Year 1
Increase (Decrease) in Cash and Cash Equivalents

**CASH FLOWS FROM OPERATING ACTIVITIES**

**Net Income** ............................................................................................................ $ 860

**Adjustments to reconcile net income to net cash provided by operating activities**

| | |
| --- | --- |
| Depreciation and amortization | $445 |
| Provision for losses on accounts receivable | 200 |
| Gain on sale of facility | (80) |
| Undistributed earnings of affiliate | (25) |
| **Change in current assets and liabilities:** | |
| Increase in accounts receivable (gross) | (215) |
| Decrease in inventory | 205 |
| Increase in prepaid expenses | (25) |
| Decrease in accounts payable and accrued expenses | (250) |
| Increase in interest and income taxes payable | 50 |
| Increase in deferred tax liability | 150 |
| Increase in other liabilities | 50 |

**Total adjustments** .................................................................................................. 505

**Net cash provided by operating activities** ......................................................... $1,365

(continued)

(continued)

**CASH FLOWS FROM INVESTING ACTIVITIES**

| | | |
|---|---|---|
| Capital expenditures | $(1,000) | |
| Proceeds from sale of facility | 600 | |
| Payment received on note for sale of plant | 150 | |
| Payment for purchase of Company S, net of cash acquired | (925) | |
| **Net cash used in investing activities** | | **$(1,175)** |

**CASH FLOWS FROM FINANCING ACTIVITIES**

| | | |
|---|---|---|
| Net borrowings under line-of-credit agreement | 300 | |
| Principal payments under capital lease obligation | (125) | |
| Proceeds from issuance of long-term debt | 400 | |
| Proceeds from issuance of common stock | 500 | |
| Dividends paid | (200) | |
| **Net cash provided by financing activities** | | **875** |
| **NET INCREASE IN CASH AND CASH EQUIVALENTS** | | 1,065 |
| Cash and cash equivalents at beginning of year | | 600 |
| **Cash and cash equivalents at end of year** | | **$ 1,665** |

**SUPPLEMENTAL DISCLOSURES OF CASH FLOW INFORMATION**

**Cash paid during the year for:**

| | | |
|---|---|---|
| Interest (net of amount capitalized) | $ 220 | |
| Income taxes | 325 | |

**SUPPLEMENTAL SCHEDULE OF NONCASH INVESTING AND FINANCING ACTIVITIES**

Cox Company purchased all of the capital stock of Company S for $950. In conjunction with the acquisition, liabilities were assumed as follows:

| | | |
|---|---|---|
| Fair value of assets acquired | $ 1,580 | (includes $25 cash) |
| Cash paid for the capital stock | $ (950) | |
| Liabilities assumed | $ 630 | |

A capital lease obligation of $850 was incurred when Cox Company entered into a lease for new equipment.

Additional common stock was issued upon the conversion of $500 of long-term debt. (Each conversion needs to be disclosed separately.)

**DISCLOSURE OF ACCOUNTING POLICY**

For purposes of the statement of cash flows, Cox Company considers all highly liquid debt instruments purchased with an original maturity of three months or less to be cash equivalents.

# Statement of Cash Flows

**COMPARISON TO INDIRECT METHOD**

### Cox Company
### Consolidated Statement of Cash Flows
### For the Year Ended December 31, Year 1
Increase (Decrease) in Cash and Cash Equivalents

**CASH FLOWS FROM OPERATING ACTIVITIES**

| | |
|---|---:|
| Cash received from customers | $13,850 |
| Cash paid to suppliers and employees | (12,000) |
| Dividend received from affiliate | 20 |
| Interest received | 55 |
| Interest paid (net of amount capitalized) | (220) |
| Income taxes paid | (325) |
| Insurance proceeds received | 15 |
| Cash paid to settle lawsuit for patent infringement | (30) |
| **Net cash provided by operating activities** | **$1,365** |

**CASH FLOWS FROM INVESTING ACTIVITIES**

| | |
|---|---:|
| Capital expenditures | (1,000) |
| Proceeds from sale of facility | 600 |
| Payment received on note for sale of plant | 150 |
| Payment for purchase of Company S, net of cash acquired | (925) |
| **Net cash used in investing activities** | **(1,175)** |

**CASH FLOWS FROM FINANCING ACTIVITIES**

| | |
|---|---:|
| Net borrowings under line-of-credit agreement | 300 |
| Principal payments under capital lease obligation | (125) |
| Proceeds from issuance of long-term debt | 400 |
| Proceeds from issuance of common stock | 500 |
| Dividends paid | (200) |
| **Net cash provided by financing activities** | **875** |
| **NET INCREASE IN CASH AND CASH EQUIVALENTS** | **1,065** |
| Cash and cash equivalents at beginning of year | 600 |
| **Cash and cash equivalents at end of year** | **$1,665** |

(continued)

(continued)

**COMPARISON TO INDIRECT METHOD**

**RECONCILIATION OF NET INCOME TO NET CASH PROVIDED BY OPERATING ACTIVITIES**

| | | |
|---|---:|---:|
| Net income | | $ 860 |
| **Adjustments to reconcile net income to net cash provided by operating activities** | | |
| Depreciation and amortization | $ 445 | |
| Provision for losses on accounts receivable | 200 | |
| Gain on sale of facility | (80) | |
| Undistributed earnings of affiliate | (25) | |
| **Change in current assets and liabilities** | | |
| Increase in accounts receivable | (215) | |
| Decrease in inventory | 205 | |
| Increase in prepaid expenses | (25) | |
| Decrease in accounts payable and accrued expenses | (250) | |
| Increase in interest and income taxes payable | 50 | |
| Increase in deferred taxes | 150 | |
| Increase in other liabilities | 50 | |
| Total adjustments | | 505 |
| **Net cash provided by operating activities** | | **$1,365** |

**SUPPLEMENTAL SCHEDULE OF NONCASH INVESTING AND FINANCING ACTIVITIES**

Cox Company purchased all of the capital stock of Company S for $950. In conjunction with the acquisition, liabilities were assumed as follows:

| | |
|---|---:|
| Fair value of assets acquired | $1,580 |
| Cash paid for the capital stock | (950) |
| Liabilities assumed | $ 630 |

A capital lease obligation of $850 was incurred when Cox Company entered into a lease for new equipment.

Additional common stock was issued upon the conversion of $500 of long-term debt.

**DISCLOSURE OF ACCOUNTING POLICY**

For purposes of the statement of cash flows, Cox Company considers all highly liquid debt instruments purchased with a maturity of three months or less to be cash equivalents.

## U.S. GAAP VS. IFRS

IFRS does not require a reconciliation of net income to operating cash flow when using the direct method.

### Summary of Statement of Cash Flows

| Operating Activities: Direct Method | Operating Activities: Indirect Method |
|---|---|
| 1. Cash received from customers.<br>2. Cash paid to suppliers and employees.<br>3. Interest received and paid.<br>4. Dividends received.<br>5. Purchases and sales of trading securities, if appropriate, based on the nature and purpose for which the securities were acquired.<br>6. Income taxes paid.<br>7. All other cash transactions not accounted for elsewhere. | 1. Record net income.<br>2. Adjust net income for noncash items such as depreciation and the impairment of goodwill.<br>3. Reverse the income statement gain or loss shown on the sale of any asset.<br>4. Adjust for changes in current assets and current liabilities except for cash and current interest bearing debt (recorded in financing activities):<br>**Current assets increase:** subtract<br>**Current assets decrease:** add<br>**Current liabilities increase:** add<br>**Current liabilities decrease:** subtract |
| *Financing Activities: Direct and Indirect Methods* | *Investing Activities: Direct and Indirect Methods* |
| 1. All sums borrowed and/or repaid (principal amount only).<br>2. Issuance and/or repurchase of own company stock.<br>3. Dividends paid (not received). | 1. All sums lent and/or repaid (principal only).<br>2. Purchase and/or sale of non-current assets (including fixed assets, intangible assets, and marketable securities). |

### Question 1 — MCQ-05229

New England Co. had net cash provided by operating activities of $351,000; net cash used by investing activities of $420,000; and cash provided by financing activities of $250,000. New England's cash balance was $27,000 on January 1. During the year, there was a sale of land that resulted in a gain of $25,000 and proceeds of $40,000 were received from the sale. What was New England's cash balance at the end of the year?

- a. $27,000
- b. $40,000
- c. $208,000
- d. $248,000

## Question 2 — MCQ-05695

Tam Co. reported the following items in its year-end financial statements:

| | |
|---|---|
| Capital expenditures | $1,000,000 |
| Capital lease payments | 125,000 |
| Income taxes paid | 325,000 |
| Dividends paid | 200,000 |
| Net interest payments | 220,000 |

What amount should Tam report as supplemental disclosures in its statement of cash flows prepared using the indirect method?

a. $545,000
b. $745,000
c. $1,125,000
d. $1,870,000

# NOTES

# MODULE 3
# Not-for-Profit Financial Reporting: Part 1

FAR 8

## 1 Introduction to Not-for-Profit Accounting

### 1.1 Characteristics of Not-for-Profit Organizations

Not-for-profit entities are defined by the FASB as entities that have the following characteristics:

1. Their revenues come from contributions.
2. Their operating purpose does not include profit, although there is nothing to preclude the generation of a profit.
3. Their ownership interests are unlike business enterprises.

### 1.2 Industries That Use Not-for-Profit Accounting

Not-for-profit entities are generally divided into four separate categories related to various industries:

- **Health Care Organizations**
    - Hospitals
    - Nursing homes
    - Hospices
- **Educational Institutions**
    - Colleges and universities
    - Other schools
- **Voluntary Health and Welfare Organizations**
    - United Way
    - American Red Cross
    - March of Dimes
- **Other Private (Not Governmental) Not-for-Profit Organizations**
    - Cemetery organizations
    - Fraternal organizations
    - Labor unions
    - Museums, libraries, and performing arts organizations
    - Professional organizations (e.g., the AICPA)

## 1.3 Users of Not-for-Profit Financial Statements

Users of not-for-profit financial statements include donors, members, creditors, and others who provide resources to the not-for-profit entity (e.g., the government via grants, etc.).

### 1.3.1 Needs of Users

Users of not-for-profit financial statements have common needs. These common needs include the ability to assess:

- The services the organization provides.
- The organization's ability to continue to provide those services.
- The method the organization's managers use to discharge their stewardship responsibility.

### 1.3.2 Financial Statement Information

The following information should be provided in not-for-profit organization financial statements in order to meet these common needs:

- The amount and nature of an organization's assets, liabilities, and net assets (Statement of Financial Position).
- The effects of events and circumstances that change the amount and nature of net assets (Statement of Activities).
- The amount and kinds of inflows and outflows of economic resources occurring within a period (Statement of Activities).
- The relationship between the inflows and outflows (Statement of Activities).
- How an organization obtains and spends cash (Statement of Cash Flows).
- The service efforts of an organization (Statement of Activities or Notes to Financial Statements).

## 1.4 Full Accrual Basis of Accounting

Generally accepted accounting principles require that not-for-profit organizations report using the full accrual basis of accounting.

The primary reporting emphasis is placed on disclosing the sources of the institution's resources and how they were expended, rather than on the periodic determination of net income. The overall emphasis for not-for-profit financial statements is on basic information for the organization as a whole.

> **Pass Key**
>
> The external financial statements of not-for-profit entities do not present funds. The focus of the financial statements is on the basic information of the organization taken as a whole.

# 2 Not-for-Profit Financial Reporting Standards

## 2.1 FASB ASC

The external financial reporting standards for not-for-profit organizations are outlined in the FASB Accounting Standards Codification (ASC). General principles of not-for-profit financial reporting include the following:

- All types of private, not-for-profit organizations are required to have consistent external reporting, making it easier to compare the performance of different not-for-profit organizations.
- Fund accounting is not used for external financial reporting, although separate funds may be maintained for internal purposes.
- External financial statements must focus on the basic information for the organization as a whole.
- Governmental not-for-profits (for example, a state university) are governed by the Government Accounting Standards Board (GASB), not the FASB.

## 2.2 Required Financial Statements

A complete set of general purpose, external financial statements for a not-for-profit entity include the following:

- Statement of Financial Position (equivalent to a commercial Balance Sheet)
- Statement of Activities (equivalent to a commercial Income Statement and Statement of Changes in Retained Earnings)
- Statement of Cash Flows (equivalent to a commercial Statement of Cash Flows using either the direct or indirect method)

## 2.3 Reporting Expenses by Nature and Function

All not-for-profit organizations must report information about the relationships between functional classifications and natural classifications of expenses in one location. Not-for-profits have the latitude to report in one of three ways:

- On the face of the Statement of Activities
- As a schedule in the notes to the financial statements
- In a separate financial statement (no specific title provided by the FASB)

> **Pass Key**
>
> **Functional classifications** of expenses categorize costs by major classes of program and support services. Program services relate to the purpose and mission of the not-for-profit organization; support services relate to such activities as management and general, fundraising, and membership development.
>
> **Natural classifications** of expenses include such descriptions as salaries, rent, utilities, interest expense, supplies, etc., similar to general ledger titles for expense.

# 3 Statement of Financial Position

## 3.1 Components of the Statement of Financial Position

The not-for-profit *statement of financial position* is divided into three major components:

- Assets
- Liabilities
- Net assets (equity)

## 3.2 Sequence of Account Display for Assets and Liabilities

Assets and liabilities should be presented based on the following principles:

- Assets and liabilities should be classified as current or non-current;
- Assets should be sequenced by nearness to cash, and liabilities sequenced by nearness to maturity; and
- Assets restricted or designated for non-current purposes (e.g., debt liquidation, acquisition of long lived assets, etc.) should be displayed as non-current.

## 3.3 Net Assets (With and Without Donor Restrictions)

The components of net assets of not-for-profit organizations may include one or both of the following two classifications: *with* donor restrictions or *without* donor restrictions. Classifications are based on the existence or absence of *donor*-imposed restrictions.

### 3.3.1 Net Assets Without Donor Restrictions

Net assets without donor restrictions are available to finance general operations of a not-for-profit organization and may be expended at the discretion of the governing board.

- Net assets without donor restrictions are not otherwise restricted by external donor-imposed restrictions.
- Internal board-designated funds are classified as net assets without donor restrictions and may include:
  - Board-designated endowment funds
  - Board-designated net assets (for future expenditure)

### 3.3.2 Net Assets With Donor Restrictions

Net assets with donor restrictions are subject to specific, externally imposed limitations made by a donor. Information regarding the nature and amounts of different types of donor-imposed restrictions should be either reported within the financial statement classification of net assets with donor restrictions or in the notes to the financial statements. Examples of various types of donor-imposed restrictions include:

- Support of particular operating activity
- Investment for a specified term
- Use in specified period
- Acquisition of long-lived assets

- Assets that are to be used for a specified purpose and not sold
- Donor-restricted endowments that are perpetual in nature (assets donated with a stipulation that they be invested to provide a permanent source of income)

> **Pass Key**
>
> Internal board-designated funds are classified as net assets without donor restrictions. The examiners sometimes try to trick candidates with incorrect answer options that suggest board-designated endowment funds created by self-imposed limits should be reported as net assets with donor restrictions

## 3.4 Statement of Financial Position Disclosures

Not-for-profit entities must disclose relevant information about the liquidity or maturity of assets and liabilities including restrictions and self-imposed limits on the use of particular items. In addition to information displayed on the face of the statement of financial position, not-for-profit organizations must disclose in the notes of the financial statements:

- Qualitative information useful in assessing liquidity, including how the organization manages its liquid resources to meet cash needs for general expenditures within one year of the statement of financial position date. Additional qualitative disclosures include:
  - A description of the type of asset whose use is limited
  - Nature and amount of limits
  - Contractual limits
  - How and when resources can be used
- Quantitative information that displays or discloses the availability of its liquid resources as affected by:
  - The nature of the resources
  - External limits imposed by donors
  - Internal limits imposed by governing boards

## 3.4.1 Supplemental Disclosures, Net Assets With Donor Restrictions

**Not-for-Profit Organization**
**Notes to Financial Statements**
**Net Assets With Donor Restrictions**
**As of December 31, Year 2**
*(in thousands)*

Net assets with donor restrictions are restricted for the following purposes or periods:

**Subject to expenditure for specified purpose**

| | | |
|---|---:|---:|
| Program Alpha activities | | |
|     Purchase of equipment | $ 3,060 | |
|     Research and seminars | 1,190 | |
| Program Beta activities | | |
|     Disaster relief | 1,025 | |
| Program Gamma activities | | |
|     Building and equipment | 2,150 | |
|     Research | 3,025 | |
| Subtotal | | $ 10,450 |

**Subject to the passage of time**

| | | |
|---|---:|---:|
| For periods after Year 2 | | 3,140 |

**Subject to Not-for-Profit spending policy and appropriations**

| | | |
|---|---:|---:|
| Investment in perpetuity, which once appropriated is expendable to support: | | |
|     Program Alpha activities | $ 33,300 | |
|     Program Beta activities | 15,820 | |
|     Program Gamma activities | 16,480 | |
|     Any activities of the organization | 109,100 | |
| Subtotal | | 174,700 |

**Subject to appropriation and expenditure when a specified event occurs**

| | | |
|---|---:|---:|
| Endowment requiring income to be added to original gift until the fund's value is $2,500 | $ 2,120 | |
| Paid-up life insurance policy that will provide proceeds upon the death of insured for an endowment to support general activities | 80 | |
| Subtotal | | 2,200 |

**Not subject to appropriation or expenditure**

| | | |
|---|---:|---:|
| Land required to be used for a recreational area | | 3,000 |
| **Total net assets with donor restrictions** | | **$193,490** |

## 3.4.2 Supplemental Disclosures, Net Assets Without Donor Restrictions

**Not-for-Profit Organization**
**Notes to Financial Statements**
**Net Assets Without Donor Restrictions**
As of December 31, Year 2
*(in thousands)*

Not-for-Profit Organization's governing board has designated, from net assets without donor restrictions of $92,600, net assets for the following purpose as of December 31, Year 2.

| | |
|---|---:|
| Quasi-endowment | $36,600 |
| Liquidity reserve | 1,300 |
| Total | $37,900 |

**Not-for-Profit Organization**
**Statement of Financial Position**
As of December 31, Year 2 and Year 1
*(in thousands)*

| | Year 2 | Year 1 |
|---|---:|---:|
| **Assets:** | | |
| Cash and cash equivalents | $ 4,575 | $ 4,960 |
| Accounts and interest receivable | 2,130 | 1,670 |
| Inventories and prepaid expenses | 610 | 1,000 |
| Contributions receivable | 3,025 | 2,700 |
| Short-term investments | 1,400 | 1,000 |
| Assets restricted to investment in land, buildings, and equipment | 5,210 | 4,560 |
| Land, buildings, and equipment | 61,700 | 63,590 |
| Long-term investments | 218,160 | 203,500 |
| Total assets | $296,720 | $282,980 |
| **Liabilities and net assets:** | | |
| **Liabilities:** | | |
| Accounts payable | $ 2,570 | $ 1,050 |
| Refundable advance | – | 650 |
| Grants payable | 875 | 1,300 |
| Notes payable | – | 1,140 |
| Annuities obligations | 1,685 | 1,700 |
| Long-term debt | 5,500 | 6,500 |
| Total liabilities | 10,630 | 12,340 |
| **Net assets:** | | |
| Without donor restrictions | 92,600 | 84,570 |
| With donor restrictions | 193,490 | 186,070 |
| Total net assets | 286,090 | 270,640 |
| Total liabilities and net assets | $296,720 | $282,980 |

### Question 1          MCQ-01222

Pharm, a nongovernmental not-for-profit organization, is preparing its year-end financial statements. Which of the following statements is required?

    **a.** Statement of changes in financial position

    **b.** Statement of cash flows

    **c.** Statement of changes in fund balance

    **d.** Statement of revenue, expenses and changes in fund balance

### Question 2          MCQ-01220

Stanton College, a not-for-profit organization, received a building with no donor stipulations as to its use. What type of net assets should be increased when the building was received?

    I.   Net assets without donor restrictions

    II.  Net assets with donor restrictions

    III. Board-designated net assets

        **a.** I only.

        **b.** II only.

        **c.** III only.

        **d.** II or III.

# 4   Statement of Activities

## 4.1   Elements of the Statement of Activities

The not-for-profit statement of activities reports revenues and expenses (shown gross), gains and losses (often shown net), and reclassification between classes of net assets (for example, from net assets with donor restrictions to net assets without donor restrictions, once restrictions have been satisfied).

### 4.1.1   Required Elements

Three required elements are presented in the statement of activities:

**1.** Change in total net assets.

**2.** Change in net assets without donor restrictions.

**3.** Change in net assets with donor restrictions.

### 4.1.2 Format

Preparers have latitude in presentation formats that sequence data in any number of orders, including:

- Revenues, expenses, gains and losses, and reclassification of assets shown last.
- Certain revenues less directly related to expenses, followed by a subtotal, then other revenues and other expenses, gains and losses, and reclassification of net assets.
- Expenses followed by revenues, gains and losses, and the reclassification of net assets.

Other formatting issues to consider include:

- Presentation of intermediate totals such as operating income should be disclosed in the notes to the financial statements.
- Prior period adjustments and changes in accounting principle are reported as adjustments to beginning net assets.
- Items classified as other comprehensive income in commercial accounting are presented in the statement of activities after operating income.

## 4.2 Classification of Revenue, Gains, and Other Support

Revenues are classified into one of two categories, according to the existence or absence of donor-imposed restrictions.

### 4.2.1 Net Assets Without Donor Restrictions

Revenues are classified as net assets without donor restrictions unless the use of the assets received is limited by donor-imposed restrictions. Examples of revenues received without donor restrictions include:

- Fees from rendering services.
- Contributions that have no explicit donor stipulation restricting use.
- Gains and losses recognized on investment that are not accompanied with explicit donor restrictions (investment returns are displayed net of related expenses).

### 4.2.2 Net Assets With Donor Restrictions

Revenues are classified as net assets with donor restrictions (donor-restricted support) if the use of the asset received is limited by donor-imposed restrictions. All restricted revenue is included in the same classification regardless of whether the restriction is perpetual or if the restriction can be satisfied by the recipient. Classification grouping does not, however, preclude the not-for-profit organization from itemizing the character of restrictions on either the face of the financial statements or the notes. Examples of revenues received with donor restrictions include:

- Contributions subject to expenditure for a specified purpose (e.g. programs or capital projects).
- Contributions subject to the passage of time.
- Contributions associated with restrictions that are otherwise temporary in nature.
- Contributions requiring investment in perpetuity with returns eligible for appropriation (e.g., donor-restricted endowment funds).

## 4.3 Reclassification of Restrictions

Contributions with donor-imposed restrictions are recognized as donor-restricted support in the period in which they are received and recognized as an increase to net assets with donor restrictions.

When a donor restriction is satisfied, a reclassification is reported on the statement of activities. Reclassifications are items that simultaneously increase one net asset class and decrease another.

- Donor-imposed restrictions that are met in the same period they are received may be recorded as an increase to net assets without donor restrictions (contribution revenue), provided that the organization discloses and consistently applies this accounting policy.
- Support that results in perpetually restricted net assets ordinarily are not reclassified, because the donor restrictions never expire.
- Revenue, gains, and other support that result in an increase to net assets without donor restrictions ordinarily do not become restricted.

> **Illustration 1  Reclassification**
>
> A not-for-profit clinic receives operating subsidies for indigent care under a state contract. The contract represents a donor-restricted contribution to the clinic; however, the clinic routinely spends adequate amounts on the state-funded services to reclassify the funding from net assets with donor restrictions to net assets without donor restrictions in the year received. Assuming consistent application of its accounting policies, the clinic has the option of immediately reporting the subsidies received under the state contract as an increase to net assets without donor restrictions.

## 4.4 Expense Classification in the Statement of Activities

All expenses (other than investment expenses) are reported as decreases in net assets without donor restrictions. Investment expense is netted against investment returns and classified according to the requirements of the investment revenue. Details of functional classifications and their relationship to natural expense classifications must be presented on the face of the financial statements or the notes. Examples of functional expense classifications are as follows:

### 4.4.1 Program Services

Program services (expenses) are the activities for which the organization is chartered. Examples are:

- **Universities:** Education and research
- **Hospitals:** Patient care and education
- **Union:** Labor negotiations and training
- **Day Care:** Child care

### 4.4.2 Support Services

Supporting services include everything not classified as a program service. Examples are:

- Fundraising
- Management and general (administrative expenses)
- Membership development

### 4.4.3 Combined Costs

Not-for-profit organizations that combine fundraising efforts with educational (or program) services should allocate the combined cost between functions.

**Not-for-Profit Organization**
**Statement of Activities**
For the Year Ended December 31, Year 2
*(in thousands)*

|  | Without Donor Restrictions | With Donor Restrictions | Total |
|---|---|---|---|
| **Revenues, gains, and other support:** | | | |
| Contribution | $ 8,640 | $ 8,390 | $ 17,030 |
| Fees | 5,200 | – | 5,200 |
| Investment return, net | 6,650 | 18,300 | 24,950 |
| Gain on sale of equipment | 200 | – | 200 |
| Other | 150 | – | 150 |
| Net assets released from restrictions | | | |
|   Satisfaction of program restrictions | 8,990 | (8,990) | – |
|   Satisfaction of equipment acquisition restrictions | 1,500 | (1,500) | – |
|   Expiration of time restrictions | 1,250 | (1,250) | – |
|   Appropriation from donor endowment and subsequent satisfaction of any related donor restrictions | 7,500 | (7,500) | – |
| Total net assets released from restrictions | 19,240 | (19,240) | – |
| Total revenues, gains, and other support | 40,080 | 7,450 | 47,530 |
| **Expenses and losses:** | | | |
| Program Alpha | 13,296 | – | 13,296 |
| Program Beta | 8,649 | – | 8,649 |
| Program Gamma | 5,837 | – | 5,837 |
| Management and general | 2,038 | – | 2,038 |
| Fundraising | 2,150 | – | 2,150 |
| Total expenses | 31,970 | – | 31,970 |
| Fire loss | 80 | – | 80 |
| Actuarial loss on annuity obligations | – | 30 | 30 |
| Total expenses and losses | 32,050 | 30 | 32,080 |
| Changes in net assets | 8,030 | 7,420 | 15,450 |
| Net assets at beginning of year | 84,570 | 186,070 | 270,640 |
| Net assets at end of year | $92,600 | $193,490 | $286,090 |

### 4.4.4 Reporting Expenses by Nature and Function

Expense information should include the relationships between functional classifications and natural classifications.

- Functional expenses should be classified as:
  - Major classes of program services; or
  - Supporting activities
- Natural expense components of each functional expense must be presented, including such classifications as:
  - Salaries
  - Rent
  - Electricity
  - Supplies
  - Interest expense
  - Depreciation
  - Awards and grants
  - Professional fees
- Gains and losses and external and direct internal investment expenses that have been netted against the investment return should not be included in the functional expense analysis.

---

**Not-for-Profit Organization**
**Notes to Financial Statements**
**Expenses Classification**
For the Year Ended December 31, Year 2
*(in thousands)*

The table below presents expenses by both their nature and function.

|  | \multicolumn{4}{c}{*Program Activities*} | \multicolumn{3}{c}{*Supporting Activities*} |  |
|---|---|---|---|---|---|---|---|---|
|  | **Alpha** | **Beta** | **Gamma** | **Programs Subtotal** | **Management and General** | **Fund-raising** | **Supporting Subtotal** | **Total Expenses** |
| Salaries and benefits | $ 7,400 | $3,900 | $1,725 | $13,025 | $1,130 | $ 960 | $2,090 | $15,115 |
| Grants to other organizations | 2,075 | 750 | 1,925 | 4,750 | – | – | – | 4,750 |
| Supplies and travel | 890 | 1,013 | 499 | 2,402 | 213 | 540 | 753 | 3,155 |
| Services and professional fees | 160 | 1,490 | 600 | 2,250 | 200 | 390 | 590 | 2,840 |
| Office and occupancy | 1,160 | 600 | 450 | 2,210 | 218 | 100 | 318 | 2,528 |
| Depreciation | 1,440 | 800 | 570 | 2,810 | 250 | 140 | 390 | 3,200 |
| Interest | 171 | 96 | 68 | 335 | 27 | 20 | 47 | 382 |
| Total expenses | $13,296 | $8,649 | $5,837 | $27,782 | $2,038 | $2,150 | $4,188 | $31,970 |

The financial statements report certain categories of expenses that are attributable to more than one program or supporting function. Therefore, these expenses require allocation on a reasonable basis that is consistently applied. The expenses that are allocated include depreciation, interest, and office and occupancy, which are allocated on a square footage basis, as well as salaries and benefits, which are allocated on the basis of estimated time and effort.

## Question 3 — MCQ-01229

At the beginning of the year, the Baker Fund, a nongovernmental not-for-profit corporation, received a $125,000 contribution restricted to youth activity programs. During the year, youth activities generated revenue of $89,000 and had program expenses of $95,000. What amount should Baker report as net assets released from restrictions for the current year?

- a. $0
- b. $6,000
- c. $95,000
- d. $125,000

## Question 4 — MCQ-01257

In its fiscal year ended June 30, Year 1, Barr College, a large, private institution, received $100,000 designated by the donor for scholarships for superior students. On July 26, Year 1, Barr selected the students and awarded the scholarships. How should the July 26 transaction be reported in Barr's statement of activities for the year ended June 30, Year 2?

- a. As both an increase and a decrease of $100,000 in net assets without donor restrictions.
- b. As a decrease only in net assets without donor restrictions.
- c. By footnote disclosure only.
- d. Not reported.

## Question 5 — MCQ-01306

The following expenditures were made by Green Services, a society for the protection of the environment:

| | |
|---|---|
| Printing of the annual report | $12,000 |
| Unsolicited merchandise sent to encourage contributions | 25,000 |
| Cost of an audit performed by a CPA firm | 3,000 |

What amount should be classified as fundraising costs in the society's statement of activities?

- a. $37,000
- b. $28,000
- c. $25,000
- d. $0

## NOTES

# MODULE 4 Not-for-Profit Financial Reporting: Part 2

**FAR 8**

# 1 Statement of Cash Flows

A statement of cash flows is required for all not-for-profit organizations. FASB ASC 230 is applicable to not-for-profit organizations, to the extent that it does not conflict with industry guidance. Identical to commercial standards, the primary purpose of the statement of cash flows is to provide relevant information about the cash receipts and cash payments of the not-for-profit organization during a period. The statement classifies cash receipts and cash payments as operating, investing, and financing activities, and either the direct or the indirect method may be used. The use of the direct method, however, does not require presentation of the reconciliation of net income to cash flows from operations.

## 1.1 Classification of Sources and Uses of Cash

### 1.1.1 Operating Activities

Sources and uses of cash classified by a not-for-profit organization as operating activities include receipts and payments that do not stem from transactions defined as investing or financing, such as:

- Receipts or payments for the settlement of lawsuits.
- Proceeds from insurance settlements (other than those specifically associated with investing activities such as the destruction of a building).
- Refunds from suppliers or refunds to customers.
- Charitable contributions (and disbursements) made by the not-for-profit.

Specifically identified transactions to be classified as cash flows from operations also include:

- Reported activity by major class of gross receipts (when the direct method is used), including contributions, program income, and interest or dividend income.
- Receipts of unrestricted resources designated by the governing body to be used for long-lived assets.
- Proceeds from the sale of financial assets not restricted for long-term purposes.
- Cash payments to suppliers and employees.
- Cash payments for interest.
- Cash activity associated with agency transactions.

> **Pass Key**
>
> Contributions of unrestricted revenue later earmarked (board designated) for construction or purchase of long-lived assets is classified as cash flows from operating activities.

#### 1.1.2 Investing Activities

Sources and uses of cash classified by a not-for-profit organization as investing activities include receipts and payments for such items as:

- Investments in property, plant, and equipment.
- Proceeds from the sale of works of art or disbursements for purchases of works of art.
- Proceeds from the sale of assets that were received in the prior period and whose sale proceeds were restricted to investment in equipment.

#### 1.1.3 Financing Activities

Sources and uses of cash classified by a not-for-profit organization as financing activities include receipts and payments for such items as:

- Proceeds from issuing bonds, mortgages, notes, and other short- or long-term borrowing.
- Repayment of amounts borrowed.
- Receipts from contributions restricted for the purpose of acquiring, constructing, or improving property, plant, and equipment or other long-lived assets.
- Receipts from contributions restricted for the purpose of establishing or increasing a donor-restricted endowment fund.

> **Pass Key**
>
> Cash flows from financing activities not only include the cash transactions related to borrowing that are typically found in a commercial statement of cash flows, but also include cash transactions related to certain restricted contributions. Cash flows from financial activities may be segregated on the face of the financial statements as follows:
>
> - Proceeds from Donor-Restricted Contributions (for long-lived assets)
> - Other Financing Activities

### 1.1.4 Cash and Cash Equivalents

Exclude donor-restricted securities that may otherwise meet the cash equivalent definition in commercial accounting.

> **Pass Key**
>
> Note that in not-for-profit reporting, the statement of cash flows has the three typical commercial classifications: operating activities, financing activities, and investing activities.

### 1.1.5 Noncash Transactions

Noncash transactions that should be disclosed in the statement of cash flows include:

- Contributed securities.
- Construction in progress and other fixed asset purchases included in accounts payable.
- Contributions of beneficial interests (unconditional promises to receive specified cash flows from a charitable trust or other identifiable pool of assets).
- Noncash debt refinancing transactions (e.g., changes in interest rates or other terms, etc.).

### 1.1.6 Direct Method (Supplemental Reconciliation of Cash Flow From Operations Not Required)

Not-for-profits that use the direct method of reporting net cash flows from operations *are not* required to provide a reconciliation of change in net assets to net cash flows from operating activity. This is in contrast to an entity other than a not-for-profit organization (a commercial entity), which is required to provide the reconciliation in a separate schedule.

**Not-for-Profit Organization**
**Statement of Cash Flows**
For the Year Ended December 31, Year 2
*(in thousands)*

**Cash flows from operating activities:**

| | | |
|---|---:|---:|
| Change in net assets | | $15,450 |
| **Adjustments to reconcile change in net assets to net cash used by operating activities:** | | |
|    Depreciation | | 3,200 |
|    Fire loss | | 80 |
|    Actuarial loss on annuity obligations | | 30 |
|    Gain on sale of equipment | | (200) |
|    Increase in accounts and interest receivable | | (460) |
|    Decrease in inventories and prepaid expenses | | 390 |
|    Increase in contributions receivable | | (325) |
|    Increase in accounts payable | | 1,520 |
|    Decrease in refundable advance | | (650) |
|    Decrease in grants payable | | (425) |
|    Contributions restricted for long-term investment | | (2,740) |
|    Interest and dividends restricted for reinvestment | | (300) |
|    Realized and unrealized gains on investments | | (15,800) |
| Net cash used by operating activities | | $(230) |
| **Cash flows from investing activities:** | | |
|    Proceeds on sale of equipment | | 200 |
|    Insurance proceeds from fire loss on building | | 250 |
|    Purchase of equipment | | (1,500) |
|    Proceeds from sale of investments | | 76,100 |
|    Purchase of investments | | (74,900) |
| Net cash used by investing activities | | 150 |
| **Cash flows from financing activities:** | | |
|    Proceeds from contributions restricted for: | | |
|       Investment in perpetual endowment | $ 200 | |
|       Investment in term endowment | 70 | |
|       Investment in land, buildings, and equipment | 1,210 | |
|       Investment subject to annuity agreements | 200 | |
| | 1,680 | |
| **Other financing activities:** | | |
|    Interest and dividends restricted for reinvestment | 300 | |
|    Payments of annuity obligations | (145) | |
|    Payments on notes payable | (1,140) | |
|    Payments on long-term debt | (1,000) | |
| | (1,985) | |
| Net cash used by financing activities | | (305) |
| Net decrease in cash and cash equivalents | | (385) |
| Cash and cash equivalents at beginning of year | | 4,960 |
| Cash and cash equivalents at end of year | | $4,575 |

## Question 1 — MCQ-01255

The Jackson Foundation, a not-for-profit organization, received contributions in Year 1 as follows:

- Cash contributions of $500,000 without donor restrictions.
- Cash contributions of $200,000 with donor restrictions with specific requirements relative to the acquisition of property.

Jackson's statement of cash flows in Year 1 should include which of the following amounts?

|    | Operating Activities | Investing Activities | Financing Activities |
|----|---------------------|----------------------|----------------------|
| a. | $700,000            | $0                   | $0                   |
| b. | $500,000            | $200,000             | $0                   |
| c. | $500,000            | $0                   | $200,000             |
| d. | $0                  | $500,000             | $200,000             |

## NOTES

# MODULE 5
# Not-for-Profit Revenue Recognition

FAR 8

## 1 Revenue From Exchange Transactions

An exchange transaction is one in which the not-for-profit organization earns resources in exchange for a service performed. Revenues from not-for-profit exchange transactions are recognized when realized or realizable and earned.

Revenues from exchange transactions are classified as increases to net assets without donor restrictions.

The following are examples of revenues earned by not-for-profits in exchange transactions:

- Student tuition and fees earned by not-for-profit educational institutions.
- Patient service revenue earned by not-for-profit health care organizations.
- Membership fees earned by not-for-profit membership organizations.

## 2 Contributions Received

### 2.1 Contributions Defined

A *contribution* is defined as an unconditional transfer of cash or assets (collection is certain) to a new owner (title passes) in a manner which is voluntary (the donor is under no obligation to donate) and is nonreciprocal (the donor gets nothing in exchange). Contributions may include cash, services, and other assets.

### 2.2 Recognition

Contributions received are recognized as revenues or gains and reported as either an increase to net assets without donor restrictions or donor-restricted support in the period received and as assets, decreases of liabilities, or expenses, depending on the form of the benefits received. A contribution is classified as revenue if it is part of the ongoing major or central activities of the not-for-profit organization. A contribution is classified as a gain if the transaction is incidental to the purpose of the not-for-profit organization.

### 2.3 Cash Contributions

Cash contributions should be recognized as revenues or gains and reported as contributions that increase net assets without donor restrictions or donor-restricted support in the period in which they are received, and they should be measured at their fair value at the date of the gift.

### 2.4 Promises to Give (Pledges)

#### 2.4.1 Unconditional Promises

An unconditional promise to give (also known as a pledge) is a contribution and is recorded at its fair value when the promise is made. An unconditional promise may be written or verbal. However, verbal pledges should be documented by the organization internally and may be more difficult to collect.

### 2.4.2 Conditional Promises

A conditional promise to give (or pledge) is a transaction that depends on an occurrence of a future and uncertain event. Recognition does not occur until the conditions are substantially met (or when it can be determined that the chances of not meeting the conditions are remote) and the promise becomes unconditional.

Good faith deposits that accompany a conditional promise are accounted for as a refundable advance in the liability section of the statement of financial position.

*To recognize a good faith deposit received before the conditions of a conditional promise are met by the not-for-profit:*

| DR | Cash | $XXX | |
|----|------|------|---|
| CR | Refundable advance | | $XXX |

> **Pass Key**
>
> Conditional promises/pledges are subject to resolution of a contingency. The condition must be resolved before the pledge can be recognized as revenue or gain. Conditions are *not* synonymous with donor restriction. Donor restrictions are satisfied by the not-for-profit organization by use of the donated resources. Conditions are not satisfied by the use of the resources.

### 2.4.3 Multiyear Pledges

Multiyear pledges are recorded at the net present value at the date the pledge is made. Future collections are considered donor-restricted revenues and net assets (time-restricted). The difference between the previously recorded present value and the current amount collected is recognized as contribution revenue, not interest income.

### 2.4.4 Placed-in-Service Approach

In the absence of specific donor restrictions, not-for-profits must use the placed-in-service approach to report the expiration of restrictions on contributions associated with long-lived assets.

> **Illustration 1  Placed-in-Service Approach**
>
> Community Not-for-Profit Inc. receives a building from Gerry Generous at the beginning of the year and immediately begins to use it in a manner consistent with its mission. Gerry places no restrictions on the building. The building has a value of $200,000 and it has a 20-year life. Community Not-for-Profit Inc. would recognize the entire $200,000 donation as a contribution without donor restriction using the placed-in-service approach.
>
> Community Not-for-Profit Inc. also receives a building from the River City. The building is also valued at $200,000 with a 20-year life. The City stipulates that the building must be used for specific community programs and, if it is not used for that purpose, the building's ownership will revert to the City. Community Not-for-Profit Inc. would record the building as an asset and donor-restricted support of $200,000. Each year that Community Not-for-Profit met its restrictions, it would record depreciation expense of $10,000 and would reclassify $10,000 from net assets with restrictions to net assets without restrictions.

### 2.4.5 Allowance for Uncollectible Pledges

An allowance for uncollectible pledges should be recorded in accordance with commercial accounting principles for accounts receivable in order to present the pledge at its net realizable value. However, in contrast to commercial accounting principles, there is no bad debt (or bad contribution) expense recognized at any point. Instead, both the pledge and related contribution revenue are reported net of any allowance.

## 2.5 Split-Interest Agreements

Split-interest agreements represent donor contributions of trusts or other arrangements under which the not-for-profit organization receives benefits that are shared with other beneficiaries.

- Examples include:
  - Charitable lead trust
  - Perpetual trust held by a third party
  - Charitable remainder trust
  - Charitable gift annuity
  - Pooled life income fund
- During the term of the agreement, changes in the value of split-interest agreements should be recognized for:
  - Amortization of discounts
  - Revaluations
- Assets and liabilities recognized under split-interest agreements should be disclosed separately from other assets and liabilities in the statement of financial position.
- Contributions and changes in the value of split-interest agreements should be disclosed as separate line items in the statement of activities (or the related notes).
- Split-interest contributions should be:
  - measured at their fair values at the date of acquisition;
  - estimated based on the present value of the estimated future distributions; and
  - displayed as donor-restricted.

> **Pass Key**
>
> Do not confuse the net asset classification concept of with versus without donor restrictions with the revenue recognition concept of conditional versus unconditional. Unconditional pledges are assured of collection and may be recognized as either with or without donor restrictions. Conditional pledges are still subject to important contingencies and are not recorded.

## 2.6 Donated Services

Donated services received by a not-for-profit organization are generally not recorded because of the difficulty in placing a monetary value on donated services (and the absence of control over them). However, donated services should be recorded as a contribution and expense at fair value if the services meet the following criteria:

1. They create or enhance a nonfinancial asset (e.g., land, building, inventory, etc.); or

2. They require specialized skills that the provider possesses and would otherwise have been purchased by the organization (e.g., attorney, accountant, and doctor services, etc.).

> ### Pass Key
> 
> Contributions of services that do not enhance nonfinancial assets are recognized only **SOME** of the time:
> 
> - **Specialized** skills are required and possessed by the donor
> - **Otherwise** needed by the organization
> - **Measurable**
> - **Easily** (at fair value)

Donated services that qualify for recognition are displayed as nonoperating.

*The following journal entry is used to record contributed services that meet the criteria for recognition:*

| DR | Expense or asset | $XXX | |
|---|---|---|---|
| CR | Contributions—without donor restrictions | | $XXX |

### 2.6.1 Examples

- An attorney provides general counsel services to a not-for-profit organization. Services would be recognized at an appropriate market rate.

- A doctor provides services to a clinic for a vastly reduced fee. The difference between the market rate of the service and the amount paid would be recognized as a contribution.

- An individual volunteers to fill a budgeted position doing general office work. The time will be recognized as a contribution at an appropriate rate. Another individual offers to volunteer to do general office work, but there is no budget for the work performed. The unbudgeted time will not be recognized as a contribution.

> ### Illustration 2 — Donated Services
> 
> A storm damaged the roof of a new building owned by K-9 Shelters, a not-for-profit organization. A supporter of K-9, a professional roofer, repaired the roof at no charge. The value of the repairs was $10,000.
> 
> *In K-9's statement of activities, the repair of the roof should be reported as an increase to expenses and contributions using the following journal entry:*
> 
> | DR | Expense | $10,000 | |
> |---|---|---|---|
> | CR | Contribution without donor restrictions | | $10,000 |

### 2.6.2 Volunteer Recruitment

Costs of soliciting contributed services are considered fundraising expenses regardless of whether services meet recognition criteria.

### 2.7 Donated Collection Items

Donated collection items are contributed works of art or historical treasures. They are not required to be recorded by the recipient not-for-profit organization if all of the following requirements are met:

1. The item is part of a collection, which is held for public viewing, exhibition, education, or research (and not for investment or financial gain);
2. The collection is cared for, preserved, and protected by the organization; and
3. The organization has a policy that requires any proceeds from the sale of donated items to be reinvested in other collection items.

**Note:** If the preceding requirements are not met, the donation must be recognized as an asset and revenue. The policy may not be selectively applied and must be used for all assets.

### 2.8 Donated Materials

*If significant in amount, donated materials should be recorded at their fair value on the date of receipt if the fair value can be objectively determined.*

| DR | Asset | $XXX | |
|---|---|---|---|
| CR | Contribution—support | | $XXX |

Donated materials that merely pass through the organization to an ultimate beneficiary, such as used clothing, should not be recorded, unless the amounts involved are substantial.

*Assuming that donated materials are substantial, they should be recorded as a contribution with an offsetting entry to expenses and appropriately disclosed in the financial statements.*

| DR | Expense | $XXX | |
|---|---|---|---|
| CR | Contributions—supplies | | $XXX |

When donated items are sold at greater than fair value, the amount received in excess of fair value is considered an additional contribution.

### 2.9 Gifts-in-Kind

Noncash contributions, such as donated investments, are called gifts-in-kind. A gift-in-kind is recognized as a contribution at fair value.

Gifts-in-kind that are donated as part of a fundraising appeal are valued at fair value when received and revalued upon their sale as part of the fundraising appeal. The difference between the fair value at the time of donation and the value at the time of sale is accounted for as an additional contribution.

# 3 Accounting for Promises to Contribute and Other Support Transactions

## 3.1 Contributions Without Donor Restrictions

Unconditional promises to contribute in the future are reported as donor-restricted support (implied time restriction), at the present value of the estimated future cash flows using a discount rate commensurate with the risks involved. If the unconditional promises are expected to be collected or paid in less than one year, they may be measured at net realizable value since that amount is a reasonable estimate of fair value.

*Pledges without donor restriction (with implied time restriction and thus initially recognized as donor-restricted):*

| | | | |
|---|---|---|---|
| DR | Pledge receivable—with donor restriction | $XXX | |
| CR | Allowance for doubtful accounts | | $XXX |
| CR | Contributions—with donor restriction | | XXX |

*Later, when collected, assets with donor restrictions are adjusted:*

| | | | |
|---|---|---|---|
| DR | Cash—with donor restriction | $XXX | |
| CR | Pledge receivable—with donor restriction | | $XXX |
| DR | Satisfaction of time restriction—with donor restriction | XXX | |
| CR | Cash—with donor restriction | | XXX |

*Assets without donor restrictions:*

| | | | |
|---|---|---|---|
| DR | Cash—without donor restriction | $XXX | |
| CR | Satisfaction of time restriction—without donor restriction | | $XXX |

Collection of the pledge satisfies the time restriction and results in a reclassification.

---

### Example 1  Accounting for Pledges Receivable

**Facts:** The League, a not-for-profit organization, received the following pledges:

| | |
|---|---|
| Without donor restrictions | $200,000 |
| Donor-restricted for capital additions | 150,000 |

All pledges are legally enforceable; however, the League's experience indicates that 10 percent of all pledges prove to be uncollectible.

**Required:** Determine the amount the League should report as pledges receivable, net of any required allowance account.

**Solution:** Net pledges receivable are gross pledges receivable ($350,000) less allowance for uncollectible (10% × $350,000), or $315,000.

## 3.2 Donor-Restricted Support (Contributions With Donor Restrictions)

A contribution may be restricted by the donor. Donor-imposed restrictions limit the use of contributed assets. They are recognized as revenues, gains, and other support in the period received and as assets, decreases of liabilities, or expenses, depending on the form of the benefits received.

*Increases to net assets with donor restrictions:*

| | | | |
|---|---|---|---|
| DR | Pledge receivable—with donor restrictions | $XXX | |
| CR | Allowance for doubtful accounts | | $XXX |
| CR | Donor-restricted support | | XXX |

*Later, after receivable is collected and when money is spent on restricted purpose, net assets with donor restrictions will be reduced:*

| | | | |
|---|---|---|---|
| DR | Reclassification—satisfaction of donor restriction | $XXX | |
| CR | Cash—with donor restrictions | | $XXX |

*Net assets without donor restrictions are simultaneously increased and decreased:*

| | | | |
|---|---|---|---|
| DR | Cash—without donor restrictions | $XXX | |
| CR | Reclassification—satisfaction of donor restriction | | $XXX |
| DR | Operating expense | XXX | |
| CR | Cash—without donor restrictions | | XXX |

# 4 Fundraising

When a not-for-profit offers premiums (e.g., calendars, coffee mugs, tote bags, etc.) to donors as part of a fundraising campaign, the cost of the premiums is classified as a fundraising expense.

The cost of premiums given to acknowledge donations is also classified as a fundraising expense.

Generally, the difference between the contribution made by the donor and the fair value of any premiums transferred is classified as contribution revenue.

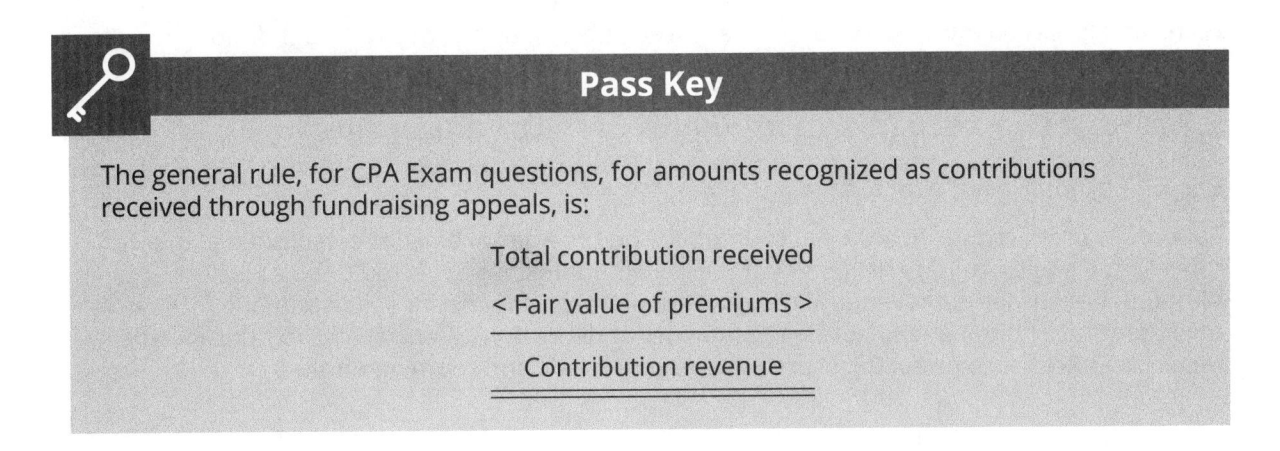

### Pass Key

The general rule, for CPA Exam questions, for amounts recognized as contributions received through fundraising appeals, is:

> Total contribution received
> < Fair value of premiums >
> ───────────────
> Contribution revenue

# 5 Industry-Specific Revenue Recognition

## 5.1 Educational Institutions

### 5.1.1 Revenues

Revenues consist of all increases in net assets without donor restrictions and *all donor-restricted* resources that were actually *expended* during the period, such as:

- Student tuition and fees.
- Government aid, grants, and contracts.
- Gifts and private grants.
- Endowment income.
- Sales and services of educational departments, such as publications and testing services.
- Revenues of auxiliary enterprises, such as food service, residence halls, campus store, and athletics.

> **Pass Key**
>
> Student tuition and fees are reported at the gross amount. Many prior CPA Exam questions have required students to compute gross revenue from tuition and fees:
>
> Assessed student tuition and fees
> < Canceled classes >
> ─────────────────────────────
> Gross revenue from tuition and fees
>
> Scholarships, tuition waivers, and similar reductions are considered either expenditures or a separately displayed allowance reducing revenue.

### 5.1.2 Gains and Losses

Gains and losses on investments and other assets, classified as with or without donor restrictions, are reported in the statement of activities.

## 5.2 Revenue Recognition in Health Care Organizations

### 5.2.1 Patient Service Revenue

Patient service revenue should be accounted for on the accrual basis at established standard rates (usual and customary fees), even if the full amount is not expected to be collected. Although patient service revenue is recorded on a gross basis, deductions are made from gross revenue to recognize patient service revenue net of deductions. Central transactions include medical services such as doctors, surgery, recovery room, and room and board.

- **Charity Care**

    Charity care is defined as health care services that are provided but never expected to result in cash flows to the hospital.

    - Management's policy for providing charity care (as well as the level of charity care provided) should be disclosed in the financial statements.
    - Charity care is not recognized as a receivable or as revenue.
    - Charity care is not recognized as a bad debt expense.

- **Deductions**

    Deductions from patient service revenue to arrive at "net patient service revenue" include the following for uncompensated services:

    - Contractual adjustments for third-party payments.
    - Policy discounts.
    - Administrative adjustments.
    - Bad debts associated with services billed prior to the organization's assessment of the patient's ability to pay (e.g., emergency room services provided and billed at full cost before the likelihood of collection can be determined).

> **Pass Key**
>
> Bad debt may be afforded one of two treatments, depending on the character of the bad debt.
>
> 1. Operating expense: Bad debt resulting from failure to collect revenues that the health care organization anticipated earning (e.g., a self-pay patient screened for ability to pay is billed and does not pay).
> 2. Deduction from revenue: Bad debt resulting from inability to collect large volumes of revenue that the health care organization never assessed for quality or collectibility.

- **Premium Revenue for Capitation Agreements**

    Capitation revenues are the fixed amount per individual that is paid periodically, usually monthly, to a provider as compensation for providing health care services for that period.

> **Pass Key**
>
> Prior CPA Exam questions have required candidates to compute "Patient Service Revenue"; use this formula to answer these questions correctly:
>
> Gross patient service revenue
> < Charitable services >
> ———————————————
> Patient service revenue

### 5.2.2 Other Operating Revenue

Other operating revenue of a health care organization may include:

- Tuition from schools
- Revenue from educational programs
- Donated supplies and equipment
- Specific purpose grants
- Revenue from auxiliary activities
- Cafeteria revenue
- Parking fees
- Gift shop revenue
- Medical transcription fees

### 5.2.3 Nonoperating Revenue and Support Gains and Losses

Nonoperating revenue and gains and losses of a health care organization may include the following transactions that are recognized without donor restrictions:

- Interest and dividend income from investment activities
- Gifts and bequests
- Grants
- Income from endowment funds
- Income from board-designated funds
- Donated services

---

**Pass Key**

Many prior CPA Exam questions have required candidates to identify which of the three categories of revenue a particular item of income is to be reported in:

1. Patient service revenue
2. Other operating revenue (includes donated supplies)
3. Nonoperating revenue (includes donated services)

## Question 1 — MCQ-01225

During Year 7, Jones Foundation received the following support:

- A cash contribution of $875,000 to be used at the board of directors' discretion
- A promise to contribute $500,000 in Year 8 from a supporter who has made similar contributions in prior periods
- Contributed legal services with a value of $100,000, which Jones would have otherwise purchased

At what amounts would Jones classify and record these transactions?

|     | Revenues and Gains Without Donor Restrictions | Revenues and Gains With Donor Restrictions |
| --- | --- | --- |
| a.  | $1,375,000 | $0 |
| b.  | $875,000   | $500,000 |
| c.  | $975,000   | $0 |
| d.  | $975,000   | $500,000 |

## Question 2 — MCQ-01215

Pica, a nongovernmental not-for-profit organization, received unconditional promises of $100,000 expected to be collected within one year. Pica received $10,000 prior to year-end. Pica anticipates collecting 90 percent of the contributions and has a June 30 fiscal year-end. What amount should Pica record as contribution revenue as of June 30?

a. $10,000
b. $80,000
c. $90,000
d. $100,000

## Question 3 — MCQ-01249

A not-for-profit organization receives $150 from a donor. The donor receives two tickets to a theater show and an acknowledgment in the theater program. The tickets have a fair value of $100. What amount is recorded as contribution revenue?

a. $0
b. $50
c. $100
d. $150

## Question 4 — MCQ-04695

Hospital Inc., a not-for-profit organization with no governmental affiliation, reported the following in its accounts for the current year ended December 31:

| | |
|---|---:|
| Gross patient service revenue from all services provided at the established billing rates of the hospital (note that this figure includes charity care of $25,000) | $775,000 |
| Provision for bad debts | 15,000 |
| Difference between established billing rates and fees negotiated with third-party payors (contractual adjustments) | 70,000 |

What amount would the hospital report as net patient service revenue in its statement of activities for the current year ended December 31?

a. $680,000
b. $690,000
c. $705,000
d. $735,000

## Question 5 — MCQ-01287

In April of Year 1, Delta Hospital purchased medicines from Field Pharmaceutical Co. at a cost of $5,000. However, Field notified Delta that the invoice was being canceled and that the medicines were being donated to Delta. Delta should record this donation of medicines as:

a. A memorandum entry only.
b. A $5,000 credit to nonoperating expenses.
c. A $5,000 credit to operating expenses.
d. Other operating revenue.

# MODULE 6

# Not-for-Profit Transfers of Assets and Other Accounting Issues

FAR 8

## 1 Transfers of Assets to a Not-for-Profit Organization or Charitable Trust That Raises or Holds Contributions for Others

An important issue in not-for-profit accounting is the accounting for asset transfers to other not-for-profit organizations, such as foundations, and the circumstances under which those transfers should be accounted for as (1) a contribution, (2) a liability, or (3) a change in interest in net assets.

### 1.1 Financially Interrelated Organizations

Financially interrelated organizations are defined as organizations related by both of the following characteristics:

1. One organization has the ability to influence the operating and financial decisions of the other; and
2. One organization has an ongoing economic interest in the net assets of the other.

### 1.2 Recipient Accounting

A not-for-profit is a recipient entity when it accepts assets from a resource provider and agrees to use the assets on behalf of, or transfer the assets (and/or the return on the assets) to, a specified beneficiary. The accounting by the recipient entity depends on whether the recipient has variance power and whether the recipient and the beneficiary are financially interrelated.

#### 1.2.1 Not Financially Interrelated: Without Variance Power

An organization that accepts assets from a resource provider and agrees to use or manage them on behalf of a specified beneficiary *without variance power* and *without any financial interrelationship* accounts for assets received as follows:

- Assets are valued at fair value.
- The recipient recognizes a *liability* to the beneficiary.

| DR | Asset | $XXX | |
|---|---|---|---|
| CR | Refundable advance liability | | $XXX |

- Assets transferred to recipient organizations are not contributions and are accounted for as liabilities when *any one* of the following conditions are met:
  - The resource provider can change the beneficiary.
  - The resource provider's asset transfer is conditional or otherwise revocable or repayable.
  - The resource provider controls the recipient organization and specifies an unaffiliated beneficiary.
  - The resource provider specifies itself or its affiliate as the beneficiary and does not qualify for equity accounting.

### 1.2.2 Not Financially Interrelated: With Variance Power

When there is no financial interrelationship between the recipient and the beneficiary, an organization that accepts assets from a resource provider and agrees to use or manage them on behalf of a beneficiary follows donee accounting *if it is granted variance power*, the unilateral authority to redirect assets to another beneficiary.

- Assets are valued at fair value.
- Assets are recognized as a contribution when received and expensed when distributed to the beneficiary.

| DR | Asset | $XXX | |
|---|---|---|---|
| CR | Contribution | | $XXX |

### 1.2.3 Financially Interrelated: With or Without Variance Power

An organization *financially interrelated* with a beneficiary that accepts assets from a resource provider and agrees to use or manage them on behalf of a beneficiary follows donee accounting. Regardless of whether variance power is granted:

- Assets are valued at fair value.
- Assets are recognized as a contribution when received and expensed when distributed to the beneficiary.

| DR | Asset | $XXX | |
|---|---|---|---|
| CR | Contribution | | $XXX |

## 1.3 Beneficiary Accounting

Specified beneficiaries recognize their rights to assets held by the recipient unless the recipient is explicitly granted variance power. Rights, when recognized, will be recorded as a receivable and contribution, a beneficial interest, or a change in interest in the net assets of the recipient.

### 1.3.1 Receivable and Contribution

In cases that do not involve financial interrelationship or beneficial interests, the beneficiary recognizes a receivable and a contribution consistent with treatment of all other unconditional promises to give.

| DR | Receivable | $XXX | |
|---|---|---|---|
| CR | Contribution | | $XXX |

### 1.3.2 Not Financially Interrelated: Beneficial Interest

Beneficiaries recognize a beneficial interest in an unconditional right to receive specified cash flows from a pool of assets as contribution revenue, or when donations held by the recipient are nonfinancial.

| DR | Beneficial interest | $XXX | |
|---|---|---|---|
| CR | Contribution | | $XXX |

### 1.3.3 Financially Interrelated: Interest in the Net Assets of the Recipient

Beneficiaries recognize a change in their interest in the net assets of the recipient when the organizations are financially interrelated.

| DR | Interest in recipient net assets | $XXX | |
|---|---|---|---|
| CR | Change in interest in recipient net assets | | $XXX |

---

**Example 1 — Financially Interrelated Recipient and Beneficiary**

**Facts:** Farleigh State University, a private not-for-profit institute of higher learning, established the Farleigh State Foundation Inc. (FSF), a not-for-profit corporation, to raise funds for the university and to account for and manage the investments of the university. The university and the foundation are financially interrelated. During the current year, an alumnus donated investments with a fair value of $25,000,000 to the foundation and specified that the earnings from the investments must be used to fund scholarships at Farleigh State University.

**Required:** Determine how the university and the foundation should account for this donation.

**Solution:**

*Farleigh State Foundation*

The foundation is the recipient of the donation and does not have variance power because the donation must be used to fund university scholarships. *The f*oundation will record the following journal entry because it is financially interrelated with the university:

| DR | Investments | $25,000,000 | |
|---|---|---|---|
| CR | Contribution | | $25,000,000 |

*Farleigh State University*

The university is the beneficiary and will recognize an interest in the change in net assets of the foundation because it is financially interrelated with the foundation:

| DR | Interest in FSF net assets | $25,000,000 | |
|---|---|---|---|
| CR | Change in interest in FSF net assets | | $25,000,000 |

---

**Question 1** — MCQ-05151

The Marble Foundation Inc., a not-for-profit organization, is financially interrelated with its beneficiary organization, Boulder University. Receipts of the Marble Foundation would be displayed/disclosed in the Boulder University financial statements as:

   a. A note disclosure.
   b. An equity transaction within the net asset classification on the balance sheet.
   c. A change in the university's interest in the foundation on the statement of activities.
   d. An increase and decrease in donor-restricted conditional support.

# 2 Other Accounting Issues

## 2.1 Financial Instruments

### 2.1.1 Fair Value

All debt securities and those equity securities that have readily determinable fair values are measured at fair value in the statement of financial position.

### 2.1.2 Gains and Losses

Realized and unrealized gains and losses on investments are reported in the statement of activities as increases or decreases in net assets without donor restrictions unless the use of the investment is donor-restricted, either temporarily or in perpetuity, by explicit donor stipulations or by law. Gains and losses that are limited to specific uses by donor stipulations may be reported as increases in net assets without donor restrictions if the stipulations are met in the same reporting period as the gains and income are recognized.

### 2.1.3 Derivatives

A not-for-profit organization should recognize the change in fair value of all derivatives in the period of the change. Not-for-profits are not permitted to use special hedge accounting rules.

### 2.1.4 Dividends, Interest, and Other Investment Income

Investment income (e.g., dividends and interest) is reported in the period earned as increases in unrestricted net assets unless the use of the investment is restricted by explicit donor stipulations or by law. Investment returns are reported net of any related investment expense.

## 2.2 Endowment Funds

Endowment funds are used to account for assets established to provide income for the maintenance of a not-for-profit entity and may be classified as either net assets without donor restrictions or net assets with donor restrictions. Issues surrounding endowment funds typically relate to their duration, the source of any restriction on them (internal or external), and the accounting issues related to the treatment of changes in value.

### 2.2.1 Duration

Endowment funds may be established in perpetuity or for a specified period of time (sometimes referred to as a term endowment).

### 2.2.2 Source of Restriction

Although endowment funds may be established by a governing board from resources without donor restrictions, they are generally established by a donor-restricted gift. Types of endowment funds include:

- **Board-Designated Endowment Funds**
  - Board-designated endowment funds are created by a not-for profit entity's governing board by designating a portion of its net assets without donor restrictions to provide income for a long but not necessarily specified period of time.
  - Alternative names include funds functioning as endowment or quasi-endowment funds.

- **Donor-Restricted Endowment Funds (Most Common)**
  - An endowment fund created by a donor stipulation requiring investment of the donor's gift in perpetuity or for a specified term.

## 2.2.3 Accounting and Reporting for Endowment Funds

A not-for-profit organization would report an endowment fund in the statement of financial position in one of the following two classes of net assets based on the existence or absence of donor-imposed restrictions:

1. **Net Assets With Donor Restrictions**

    Donor-restricted endowments would be accounted for under net assets with donor restrictions.

> **Illustration 1  Donor-Restricted Endowment Fund**
>
> Ben Benefactor gives $10,000,000 to his alma mater, Private University, a private not-for-profit university, with the stipulation that the principal would not be spent and that earnings from the donation would be used to fund an accounting professor's salary and accounting research. Benefactor's donation would be accounted for as an increase to net assets with donor restrictions and would represent a donor-restricted endowment fund established in perpetuity.

2. **Net Assets Without Donor Restrictions**

    Board-designated endowment funds resulting from an internal designation of net assets without donor restrictions would be classified as net assets without donor restrictions.

> **Illustration 2  Board-Designated Endowment Fund**
>
> The governing board of Private University, a private not-for-profit university, sets aside $8,000,000 from its net assets without donor restrictions to be invested for the next 20 years with related income to be used for a finance professor's salary. The act of the governing board would be accounted for within net assets without donor restrictions and would represent a board-designated endowment established for a specified period of time.

## 2.2.4 Specific Issues Regarding Changes in Value of Donor-Restricted Endowments

- **Inception**
    - The original gifted amount and (generally) related returns shall be initially classified as net assets with donor restrictions.
    - Unless a purpose or other donor restriction exists on the use of the income, investment income is deemed available for spending and is classified as net assets without donor restrictions.

- **Returns on the Endowment Assets Subject to Donor Restriction**
    - Investment returns subject to restriction by donor or by law shall be reported within net assets with donor restriction until appropriated for expenditure.
    - Investment returns are commonly restricted by either time (until appropriated for use) or purpose (until appropriated and expended on the specified purpose described by the donor).
    - Upon approval for expenditure (meeting the requirements of the donor restriction), the funds are deemed to have been appropriated for expenditure.

### Underwater Endowments

- An underwater endowment is a donor-restricted endowment fund for which the fair value of the fund at the reporting date is less than either the original gift amount or the amount required to be maintained by the donor *or* by a law that extends donor restrictions.
- Underwater endowment funds will report accumulated losses together with the endowment fund in net assets with donor restrictions.
- Underwater endowments require the following disclosures in total:
  - The fair value of the underwater endowment;
  - The original endowment gift amount or level required to be maintained by donor stipulations or law; and
  - The amount of the deficiencies of the underwater endowment fund.

---

**Pass Key**

Underwater endowments must disclose how hard it will be for their intended beneficiaries to be **FED**:

- **F**air value of the underwater endowment
- **E**ndowment gift's original amount
- **D**eficiency

---

**Illustration 3    Underwater Endowment**

Ben Benefactor gives a $10,000,000 endowment to Private University, a private not-for-profit entity. The endowment is properly accounted for as an increase in net assets with donor restrictions. At year-end, the endowment had a fair value of $9,750,000. Private University would need to disclose:

| | |
|---|---:|
| Fair value of Ben Benefactor's original gift | $ 9,750,000 |
| Ben Benefactor's original gift | 10,000,000 |
| Deficiency | $ (250,000) |

#### 2.2.5 Required Disclosures for All Endowment Funds

- The governing board's interpretation of the requirements that underlie the net asset classification of the endowment and the ability to spend from underwater endowment funds.
- Policies for the appropriation of endowment assets.
- Investment policies.
- Composition of the not-for-profit endowment by net asset class.
- A reconciliation of the beginning and ending balance of the not-for-profit's endowments by net asset class.

## 2.3 Basis of Assets

Purchased fixed assets are carried at cost, as required by GAAP. Donated fixed assets are recorded at fair value at the date of the gift. Depreciation is recorded in accordance with GAAP for nongovernmental not-for-profit organizations. However, works of art and historical treasures are not depreciated.

**Question 2**  MCQ-07254

Ragg Coalition, a nongovernmental not-for-profit organization, received a gift of Treasury bills. The cost to the donor was $20,000, with an additional $500 for brokerage fees that were paid by the donor prior to the transfer of the Treasury bills. The Treasury bills had a fair value of $15,000 at the time of the transfer. At what amount should Ragg report the Treasury bills in its statement of financial position?

- a. $15,000
- b. $15,500
- c. $20,000
- d. $20,500

**Question 3**  MCQ-05444

RST Charities received equity securities valued at $100,000 as a gift without donor restrictions at the beginning of Year 1. During Year 1, RST received $5,000 in dividends from these securities; at year-end, the securities had a fair market value of $110,000. By what amount did these transactions increase RST's net assets?

- a. $100,000
- b. $105,000
- c. $110,000
- d. $115,000

## NOTES

# FAR 9

# State and Local Governments: Part 1

## Module

| | | |
|---|---|---|
| 1 | Governmental Accounting Overview | 3 |
| 2 | Fund Structure and Fund Accounting | 11 |
| 3 | Transactions and Events: Part 1 | 17 |
| 4 | Transactions and Events: Part 2 | 35 |
| 5 | Governmental Funds Financial Statements: Part 1 | 49 |
| 6 | Governmental Funds Financial Statements: Part 2 | 63 |

# NOTES

# MODULE 1 Governmental Accounting Overview

FAR 9

## 1 Governmental Accounting and Reporting Concepts

### 1.1 Objectives of Governmental Reporting

Governmental financial reporting is designed to demonstrate the accountability of each organization for the stewardship of the resources in their care. Although the accountability for privately owned enterprises may be clearly measured in either the net income of the entity or the increased wealth of its shareholders, governmental organizations are focused on providing efficient and effective delivery of services with public resources in compliance with applicable laws. Identifying and displaying the accountability objectives of governmental organizations is integral to related accounting.

### 1.2 Objectives of Fund Accounting and Reporting

Foundational to governmental accounting is the concept of fund accounting. Fund accounting enables service and mission-driven organizations to easily monitor and report compliance with spending purposes (fund restrictions), spending limits (budget), and other fiscal accountability objectives. Governments use fund accounting to demonstrate fiscal accountability in their external reporting and use funds for internal accounting.

## 2 Industries That Use Governmental Accounting and Reporting Principles

Governmental, not-for-profit, and commercial accounting are applied to entities consistent with their basis of organization and their funding sources, not their industries.

> **Illustration 1    Basis of Organization**
>
> Hospitals could be governmentally funded and accounted for using an enterprise fund (explained later), could be organized as a not-for-profit organization, or could be organized as private businesses that report income and profitability to their shareholders. Although this can be confusing in practice, the CPA Exam is generally very clear as to the manner in which an entity is organized and the applicable accounting principles.

The following industries commonly have the organizational characteristics and funding streams that lend themselves to the accountability objectives met by governmental reporting models.

## 2.1 Governmental Units

Governmental units include federal, state, county, municipal, and a variety of local governmental units (e.g., townships, villages, and special districts) and entities (e.g., hospitals and universities) that are run by governments and use governmental accounting and reporting principles.

## 2.2 Colleges and Universities

Colleges and universities may be governmental entities or nongovernmental entities, depending on whether they are financially accountable to a primary government. In addition, some colleges and universities are organizations operated to earn a profit (i.e., "for-profit" entities); thus, they follow FASB standards for commercial entities rather than the standards developed for governmental entities or not-for-profit entities.

## 2.3 Health Care Organizations

Organizations that provide health care services to individuals include hospitals, nursing care facilities, home health agencies, and clinics. Health care providers can be organized as governmental, not-for-profit, or commercial entities. If the health care entity is financially accountable to a primary government, it could be classified as a component unit (explained in F10) of the government. If a health care entity is organized as a not-for-profit or commercial organization, it follows applicable FASB standards rather than the standards developed for governmental entities.

> **Pass Key**
>
> Not-for-profit organizations not run by governments (e.g., hospitals, universities, voluntary health and welfare organizations, and research organizations) do *not* use governmental accounting and reporting principles.

# 3 Generally Accepted Accounting Principles for Governmental Entities

## 3.1 Governmental Accounting Principles and Standards

The Governmental Accounting Standards Board (GASB), which is the governmental counterpart of the FASB, establishes accounting and reporting standards for governments. The hierarchy of GAAP as it relates to governments was established by GASB 76 as follows:

- GASB Accounting Standards Board Statements (most authoritative—category A)
- GASB Technical Bulletins, GASB Implementation Guides, and literature of the AICPA cleared by the GASB (category B)

Governmental entities should consult guidance in category B documents in the event treatment for a transaction is not specified by a pronouncement in category A.

## 3.2 GASB Conceptual Framework

The GASB has outlined its conceptual framework for governmental financial reporting in GASB Concept Statements Nos. 1–6. These concept statements establish the objectives and concepts that underlie governmental financial reporting but do not establish standards for governmental financial reporting.

According to the conceptual framework, governmental financial reporting communicates financial information to users and fulfills a government's duty to be publicly accountable.

### 3.2.1 Information Used by Financial Report Users

Financial statements are a part of the overall financial reporting done by governments. The information needs of users of governmental financial reports include all of the following:

| All Information Used to Assess Accountability ||||||
|---|---|---|---|---|---|
| All Financial Reporting ||||||
| General Purpose External Financial Reporting |||| Budgets and other special purpose reports (e.g., to grantor agencies) | Other information (e.g., economic indicators) |
| GASB 34 Reporting Requirements ||||||
| Basic financial statements (including notes) | Required supplementary information | Comprehensive annual financial reporting |||

- Financial reporting objectives identified by the framework pertain to *general purpose external financial reporting*, which includes the basic financial statements and required supplementary information, as well as Comprehensive Annual Financial Reporting (CAFR).

- Financial reporting objectives identified by the framework may not fully address budgets, other special purpose reporting or other information (such as stand-alone budget documents or reports to grantor agencies).

### 3.2.2 Governmental-Type and Business-Type Activities

Government entities engage in both governmental-type and business-type activities. Each type of activity requires accounting and reporting standards that address their individual characteristics and user needs. Governmental-type activities are typically supported by taxes and business-type activities are supported by user fees.

### 3.2.3 Users of Governmental Financial Reports

The three groups of primary users of governmental financial reports are:

1. Citizens, including taxpayers, voters, recipients of services, the media, researchers, etc.
2. Legislative and oversight bodies, including state legislators, county and city commissioners, and executives with oversight authority.
3. Investors and creditors, including institutional investors, bond rating agencies, bond insurers, financial institutions, etc.

### 3.2.4 Uses of Financial Reports

Governmental financial reports are used to make economic, social, and political decisions and to assess accountability by:

- Comparing actual financial results to budget
- Assessing financial condition and results of operations
- Assisting in determining compliance with finance-related laws, rules, and regulations
- Assisting in evaluating operating efficiency and effectiveness

### 3.2.5 Accountability and Interperiod Equity

Accountability is the cornerstone of governmental financial reporting. Interperiod equity, or the concept of balancing the budget on an annual basis, is a significant part of accountability.

- **Accountability**
  - Governments provide financial information to the citizenry to justify the raising of resources and demonstrate the purposes for which they are used.
  - Financial reporting plays a major role in fulfilling a government's duty to be publicly accountable.
  - Minimum disclosure includes whether the government operated within the legal constraints imposed by the citizens.

- **Interperiod Equity**
  - Balanced budgets contribute to interperiod equity by enabling a government to meet its commitment to live within its means.
  - Financial reporting should help users assess whether current year revenues are sufficient to pay for the services provided that year and whether future taxpayers will be required to assume burdens for services previously provided.

### 3.2.6 Characteristics of Information in Governmental Financial Reports

Financial information included in governmental financial reports should have the following characteristics:

- **Understandability**

  Information in financial reports should be expressed as simply as possible so the reports can be understood by individuals who may not have detailed knowledge of accounting principles.

- **Reliability**

  Reports should be verifiable and free from bias and should faithfully represent the subject matter. Reliability does not imply precision or certainty.

- **Relevance**

  Information provided should have a close logical relationship to the purpose for which it is needed. Relevance implies reported information will make a difference to users.

- **Timeliness**

  Reported information should be issued in time to have an effect on decisions. Timeliness may supersede absolute precision or detail.

- **Consistency**

    The accounting principles used to prepare financial reports should not change year over year. Accounting principles relate to such issues as transaction valuation, basis of accounting, and the determination of the financial reporting entity.

- **Comparability**

    Financial reports should be comparable. Differences between financial reports should be due to substantive differences in underlying transactions or government structure rather than the selection of methods.

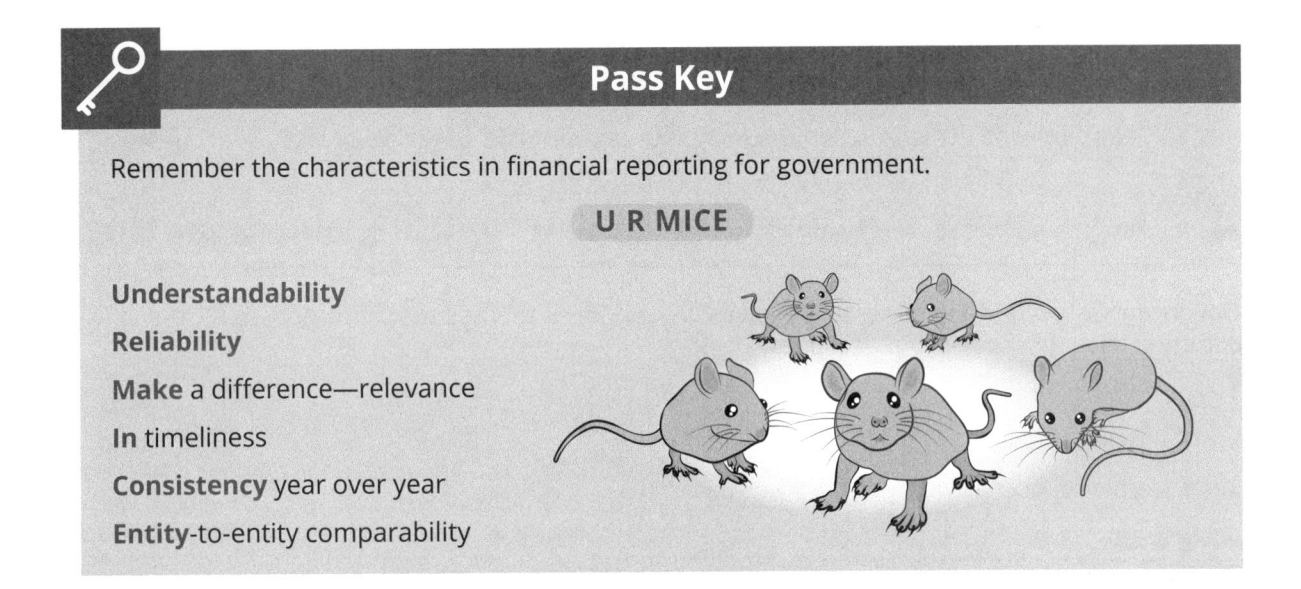

> **Pass Key**
>
> Remember the characteristics in financial reporting for government.
>
> **U R MICE**
>
> **U**nderstandability
> **R**eliability
> **M**ake a difference—relevance
> **I**n timeliness
> **C**onsistency year over year
> **E**ntity-to-entity comparability

### 3.2.7 Limitations on Governmental Financial Reporting

There are some limitations on the information that governmental financial reporting can provide, such as:

- Financial reports use approximate measures that are often based on judgments or estimates.
- Financial reporting is only one source of information for users and might be more useful when used in combination with other pertinent data.
- Financial reports may not meet the diverse needs of all users.
- Cost-benefit relationships must be considered.

### 3.2.8 Financial Reporting Objectives

Accountability is the primary objective of governmental financial reporting and is implicit in the following main objectives of governmental financial reporting:

- Financial reporting should assist in fulfilling a government's duty to be publicly accountable and should enable users to assess that accountability by:
    - Demonstrating whether current year revenues were sufficient to pay for current year services.
    - Demonstrating budgetary and legal or contractual compliance.
    - Providing information that allows users to assess service efforts, costs, and accomplishments of the governmental entity.

- Financial reporting should assist users in evaluating the operating results of the governmental entity for the year by providing information about:
  - Sources and uses of financial resources
  - How the governmental entity financed its activities and met its cash requirements
  - Whether financial position has improved or deteriorated
- Financial reporting should assist users in assessing the level of services that can be provided by the governmental entity and its ability to meet obligations as they come due by providing information about:
  - The financial position and condition of the governmental entity
  - Noncurrent physical assets available to the government and their service potential for future periods
  - Legal or contractual restrictions on resources and risks of potential loss of resources

# 4 Key Concepts in Governmental Accounting and Reporting

Governmental accounting generally revolves around three themes that differentiate it from commercial and not-for-profit accounting:

1. Fund structure
2. Fund accounting
3. External reporting

> **Pass Key**
>
> A fund is a sum of money or other resource segregated for the purpose of carrying on a specific activity or attaining certain objectives in accordance with specific regulations, restrictions, or limitations, constituting an independent fiscal and accounting entity. Each fund is a self-balancing set of accounts.

## 4.1 Fund Structure

GASB 34 defines a fund structure for governments. Eleven fund types (described later) are classified in the following three generic categories:

1. Governmental funds
2. Proprietary funds
3. Fiduciary funds

Fund financial statements should be separately presented for governmental, proprietary, and fiduciary funds to report additional and detailed information about the primary government. A government will establish the minimum number of funds consistent with legal requirements and sound financial administration. A government is not required to have a specific number of funds.

## 4.2 Fund Accounting

Fund classifications within the fund structure defined by the GASB affect the basis of accounting (when revenues and expenditures/expenses are recognized) and the measurement focus (how transactions are recognized; either assuming flow of funds or net income determination) principles associated with each fund category. The application of different accounting principles to the funds in each generic fund grouping described below provides financial data consistent with the reporting accountability objectives of each fund. This feature of governmental accounting is a frequent source of exam questions.

## 4.3 External Reporting

GASB 34 (as amended) establishes minimum reporting requirements to be in compliance with GAAP. Reporting requirements include both fund-based and government-wide financial statement presentations supported by notes to the financial statements and a variety of required supplementary information.

Presentation of a reconciliation of fund financial statements to government-wide financial statements is also required.

---

**Question 1**  MCQ-00888

Which of the following lead(s) to the use of fund accounting by a governmental organization?

|    | Financial Control | Legal Restrictions |
|----|-------------------|--------------------|
| a. | Yes               | Yes                |
| b. | Yes               | No                 |
| c. | No                | No                 |
| d. | No                | Yes                |

# NOTES

# MODULE 2: Fund Structure and Fund Accounting

FAR 9

## 1 Fund Structure

A governmental entity, although a single entity, consists of a number of separate funds. Funds are generally classified into three generic categories:

- Governmental funds
- Proprietary funds
- Fiduciary funds

### 1.1 Governmental Funds

#### 1.1.1 Fund Accounting

Governmental funds are accounted for using the:

- Modified accrual basis of accounting
- Current financial resources measurement focus

The source, use, and balance of the government's current financial resources and the related current liabilities are accounted for through the use of governmental funds. Governmental funds often have a budgetary focus, and seek to measure financial position and the changes therein. The focus of financial reporting is on the *statement of revenues, expenditures, and changes in fund balance*, which is used to demonstrate the use of resources in compliance with laws, rules, and regulations. Accounts are of a "current" nature; thus, the *balance sheet* of governmental funds contains no fixed asset or long-term debt accounts.

#### 1.1.2 Fund Types

Governmental fund types include the following:

- **General Fund:** The *general fund* is set up to account for the ordinary operations of a governmental unit that is financed from taxes and other general revenues. All transactions not accounted for in other funds are accounted for here.
- **Special Revenue Funds:** *Special revenue funds* are set up to account for revenues from specific taxes or other earmarked sources that (by law) are restricted or committed to finance particular activities of government.
- **Debt Service Funds:** *Debt service funds* are set up to account for the accumulation of resources and the payment of interest and principal on all "general obligation debt," other than that serviced by enterprise funds or by special assessments in another fund. Resources of the fund are restricted, committed, or assigned to debt service expenditures.
- **Capital Projects Funds:** *Capital projects funds* are set up to account for resources restricted, committed, or assigned for the acquisition or construction of major capital assets by a governmental unit, except those projects financed by an enterprise fund.
- **Permanent Fund:** *Permanent funds* are used to report resources that are legally restricted to the extent that income, and not principal, may be used for purposes supporting the reporting government's programs (i.e., for the benefit of the public).

| Balance Sheet |
|---|
| Current assets + Deferred outflows |
| Current liabilities + Deferred inflows of resources<br>+ Fund balance |
| Total current liabilities, deferred inflows of resources, and fund balances |

| Statement of Revenues, Expenditures, and Changes in Fund Balance |
|---|
| Revenues |
| < Expenditures ><br>Other financing sources < uses > |
| Net change in fund balance |

## 1.2 Proprietary Funds

### 1.2.1 Fund Accounting

*Proprietary funds* account for business-type activities, and their accounting is similar to commercial accounting. Proprietary funds should be accounted for using the:

- Full accrual basis of accounting
- Economic resources measurement focus

### 1.2.2 Fund Types

Proprietary funds include:

- **Internal Service Funds:** *Internal service funds* are set up to account for goods and services provided by designated departments on a cost-reimbursement fee basis to other departments and agencies within a single governmental unit or to other governmental units. Customers of the internal service fund are primarily internal.

> **Illustration 1  Internal Service Funds**
>
> A central motor pool or building maintenance department may be accounted for with an internal service fund.

- **Enterprise Funds:** *Enterprise funds* are set up to account for the acquisition and operation of governmental facilities and services that are intended to be primarily (more than 50 percent) self-supported by user charges. Customers of the enterprise fund are primarily external.

> **Illustration 2  Enterprise Funds**
>
> Enterprise funds are often used for utilities (water and sewer), airports, and transit systems.

Enterprise funds are required when any one of three criteria is met:

- The activity of the fund is financed by debt secured by a pledge of fee revenue;
- Laws require collection fees adequate to recover costs; or
- Pricing policies are established to produce fees to recover costs.

| Statement of Net Position | Statement of Revenues, Expenses, and Changes in Fund Net Position |
|---|---|
| All assets + Deferred outflows of resources<br>< All liabilities + Deferred inflows of resources ><br>——————————<br>Net position | Operating revenue<br>< Operating expenses ><br>Nonoperating revenue < expenses ><br>——————————<br>Change in net position |

## 1.3 Fiduciary (Trust) Funds

### 1.3.1 Fund Accounting

*Fiduciary funds* account for assets controlled by a government in the capacity of a trust on behalf of beneficiaries with whom a beneficiary relationship exists. Financial statements of fiduciary funds should generally be accounted for using the:

- Full accrual basis of accounting
- Economic resources measurement focus.

### 1.3.2 Fund Types

Fiduciary funds include:

- **Custodial Funds**

  *Custodial funds* usually account for resources in temporary custody of the governmental unit (e.g., taxes collected for another governmental entity) and any fiduciary activities that are not required to be reported in other fiduciary fund classifications.

- **Investment Trust Funds**

  *Investment trust funds* account for external investment pools.

- **Private Purpose Trust Funds**

  *Private purpose trust funds* are used for activities not properly accounted for either as pension or investment trust funds, in which assets are dedicated to providing benefits to recipients in accordance with benefit terms and assets are legally protected from creditors of the government.

- **Pension (and Other Employee Benefit) Trust Funds**

  *Pension trust funds* account for resources of defined benefit plans, defined contribution plans, post-employment benefit plans, and other long-term employee benefit plans.

| Statement of Fiduciary Net Position | Statement of Changes in Fiduciary Net Position |
|---|---|
| All assets + Deferred outflows of resources<br>< All liabilities + Deferred inflows of resources ><br>——————————<br>Net position | Additions<br>< Deductions ><br>——————————<br>Change in net position |

# 2 Fund Accounting

The measurement focus and basis of accounting used in government-wide and fund financial presentations facilitate the reporting of accountability objectives unique to each fund and to the government-wide presentation. The measurement focus of a fund is complemented by the basis of accounting used.

- The modified accrual basis of accounting is used with the current financial resources measurement focus.
- The accrual basis of accounting is used with the economic resources measurement focus.

## 2.1 Measurement Focus

Measurement focus determines the items to be reported on the balance sheet.

### 2.1.1 Current Financial Resources (GRaSPP)

Under the current financial resources measurement focus, fund balance is a measure of available, spendable, or appropriable resources. Only current assets and current liabilities are included on the balance sheet.

- No fixed assets are reported.
- No non-current liabilities are reported.

> **Pass Key**
>
> Adding fixed assets excluded from governmental fund financial statements and subtracting non-current liabilities (also excluded) are two of the most significant reconciling items between governmental funds and government-wide financial statements.

### 2.1.2 Economic Resources (SE-CIPPOE and Government-wide)

Under the economic resources measurement focus, financial reporting centers on the costs of services and the efficiency and effectiveness with which invested capital has been used. All assets and all liabilities (current or non-current) are included on the balance sheet, including certain transactions classified as deferred outflows/inflows of resources. Net position is analyzed and reported in three components: net investment in capital assets, restricted (distinguishing between major categories of external restrictions), and unrestricted.

- Fixed assets are reported.
- Non-current liabilities are reported.

## 2.2 Basis of Accounting

The basis of accounting determines when revenues and expenditures or expenses are recognized and reported in the financial statements.

### 2.2.1 Modified Accrual (GRaSPP)

The modified accrual basis of accounting is used with the current financial resources measurement focus. It is a blend of accrual and cash basis accounting concepts.

- Revenue is recognized when measurable and available to finance the expenditures of the current period. The only difference between the timing of revenue recognition under the modified accrual and full accrual basis of accounting is the manner in which each basis defines the word *available*.
  - Available, under modified accrual, means collectible within the current period or soon enough thereafter to be used to pay liabilities in the current period (generally within 60 days after year-end).
  - Measurable means quantifiable in monetary terms.
- Expenditures are generally recorded when the related fund liability is incurred, with some exceptions. Most notably, debt service expenditures (both principal and interest) are not recognized until either due or paid. Incurred but unpaid debt service expenditures are not accrued.

> **Pass Key**
>
> Addition of accrual basis revenues in excess of modified accrual revenues along with subtraction of accrued interest expenses not recognized in governmental financial statements are frequent reconciling items between the governmental fund financial statements and the government-wide financial statements.

### 2.2.2 Full Accrual (SE-CIPPOE and Government-wide)

The *full accrual* basis of accounting is used with the economic resources measurement focus. It is identical to the accrual basis used in commercial enterprises.

- Revenue is recognized when earned.
- Expenses are recognized when incurred.

## 2.3 Fund Accounting Summary

### 2.3.1 Modified Accrual Basis of Accounting and Current Financial Resources Measurement Focus

Modified accrual basis of accounting and current financial resources measurement focus are used in connection with the governmental funds (**GRaSPP**).

- **General**
- Special **Revenue**

**and**

- Debt **Service**
- Capital **Projects**
- **Permanent**

# Fund Structure and Fund Accounting

## 2.3.2 Economic Resources Measurement Focus and Full Accrual Basis of Accounting

The economic resources measurement focus and full accrual basis of accounting is used for both the government-wide financial statements as well as the fund presentations of the fiduciary and proprietary funds (**SE-CIPPOE**).

- **Service** (internal)
- **Enterprise**
- **Custodial**
- **Investment** trust
- **Private** purpose trust
- **Pension** (and **Other Employee** benefit) trust

> ### Pass Key
>
> To help remember the differences in focus and accounting, use the following:
>
> Governmental funds are **MAC-GRaSPP**
> - **M**odified
> - **A**ccrual accounting
> - **C**urrent financial resources measurement focus
> - **GRaSPP**
>
> Proprietary and fiduciary funds **SCARE**
> - **S**E
> - **C**IPPOE
> - **A**ccrual accounting
> - **R**ecord non-current assets and liabilities
> - **E**conomic resources measurement focus

---

### Question 1     MCQ-00891

The economic resources measurement focus and accrual basis of accounting would be most appropriate for which fund as used in the fund financial statements?

a. General fund
b. Permanent fund
c. Internal service fund
d. Capital projects fund

---

### Question 2     MCQ-00890

Which funds would most appropriately use the current financial resources measurement focus and modified accrual basis of accounting in their fund financial statements?

|    | Governmental | Proprietary | Fiduciary |
|----|--------------|-------------|-----------|
| a. | Yes          | No          | Yes       |
| b. | No           | Yes         | Yes       |
| c. | Yes          | No          | No        |
| d. | Yes          | Yes         | Yes       |

# MODULE 3: Transactions and Events: Part 1

FAR 9

## 1 Accounting for Governmental Funds

> **Pass Key**
>
> Full accrual basis/economic resources measurement focus accounting is used by commercial and not-for-profit entities and is also used to prepare the government-wide, proprietary fund, and fiduciary fund financial statements.
>
> This module focuses on the accounting issues that are unique to the modified accrual basis/current financial resources measurement focus accounting used to prepare governmental fund financial statements.

There are important differences between the modified accrual basis/current financial resources measurement focus accounting used to prepare the financial statements of the governmental funds and the full accrual basis/economic resources measurement focus accounting used to prepare the government-wide financial statements and the financial statements of the proprietary and fiduciary funds.

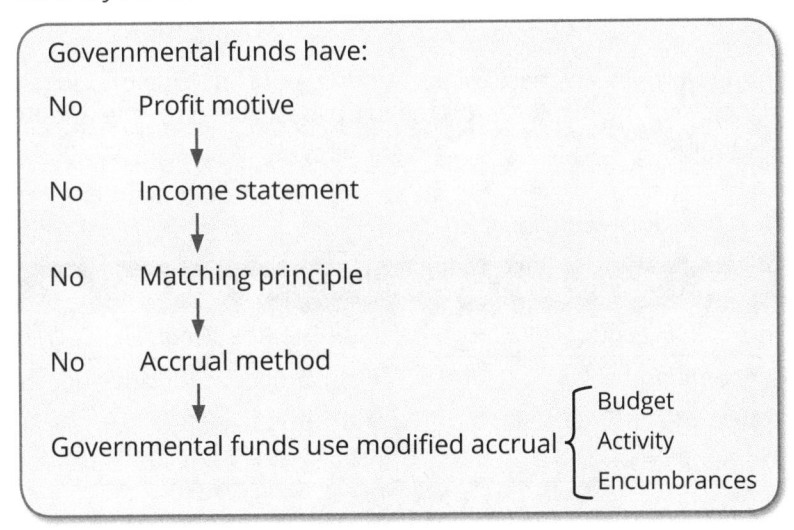

```
Governmental funds have:

No      Profit motive
          ↓
No      Income statement
          ↓
No      Matching principle
          ↓
No      Accrual method
          ↓                              ⎧ Budget
Governmental funds use modified accrual ⎨ Activity
                                         ⎩ Encumbrances
```

These differences demonstrate enhanced accountability and can be summarized in these accounting areas:

- **Budgetary:** Budgetary accounting is used to control spending.
- **Activity:** Activity accounting emphasizes the flow of current financial resources and has an annual budgetary focus.
- **Encumbrance:** Encumbrance accounting is used to record purchase orders and is designed to monitor spending for increased budgetary control.

# Transactions and Events: Part 1

> ## Pass Key
>
> The governmental funds (GRaSPP) use modified accrual accounting, which means separate accounting for each area.
>
> | Book | Close |
> |---|---|
> | Budget | Budget |
> | Activity | Activity |
> | Encumbrances | Encumbrances |

## 2 Budgetary Accounting

| | | | |
|---|---|---|---|
| General fund | | Budget: | Book on opposite side as control |
| Revenue (special) fund | | | Revenue—measurable and available |
| And | Modified accrual | Activity: | Expenditures—all spending |
| Service (debt) fund | | | Assets—expenditured |
| Projects (capital) fund | | | Debts—other financing sources |
| Permanent fund | | Encumbrances: | Commit funds for purchase orders |

Budgetary accounting is used by the "GRaSPP" funds. It is used to control expenditures and to account for the levy of taxes sufficient to cover estimated expenditures.

Budgetary accounting may use any basis of accounting, but reporting of budgetary comparisons to actual performance must be displayed on the same basis used for the adopted budget and reconciled to GAAP if different.

Budgets are based on estimated revenues and appropriations. Governmental resources are typically derived from the following sources:

| Sources of Governmental Resources ||
|---|---|
| *Revenue* | *Other Financing Sources* |
| Taxes—income and sales | Debt proceeds (bonds and notes) |
| Taxes—property and real estate | Interfund transfers |
| Fines and penalties | |

> ## Pass Key
>
> Many governmental accounting questions on the CPA Exam include journal entries. It is important for candidates to understand the basic journal entries in order to properly answer these questions.

## 2.1 Budgetary Accounting Journal Entries

Budgetary accounts are estimated accounts, which are the opposite (in terms of natural debit and credit balances) from real, proprietary, or actual accounts.

Budgetary accounts are posted only twice during the year, unless a supplemental appropriation is made.

### 2.1.1 Beginning of Year

At the beginning of year, the difference between estimated revenues and appropriations goes to an account called *budgetary control* (which is the budgetary "equity account").

*Note:* The credit to appropriations control, below, includes both transfers and estimated expenditures. CPA Exam questions often segregate appropriations and budgeted transfers.

> **Pass Key**
>
> The journal entry that records the budgeted amounts for estimated revenue and approved expenditures (appropriations) is posted on the opposite side of the "T" account compared with actual amounts.

| | | | |
|---|---|---|---|
| DR | Estimated revenue control | $2,000,000 | |
| DR | Budgetary control (negative/deficit) | – | |
| CR | Appropriations control | | $1,950,000 |
| CR | Budgetary control (positive/surplus) | | 50,000 |

### 2.1.2 End of Year

At the end of year, the budget is reversed and closed. The journal entry uses the same amounts that were recorded at the beginning of the period plus or minus any amendments.

> **Pass Key**
>
> The journal entry at period end to reverse the budget is always for the same dollar amounts as the original budgetary journal entry +/– any amendments.

| | | | |
|---|---|---|---|
| DR | Appropriations | $1,950,000 | |
| DR | Budgetary control (positive) | 50,000 | |
| CR | Estimated revenue control | | $2,000,000 |
| CR | Budgetary control (negative) | | – |

> **Pass Key**
>
> Do not be confused by question fact patterns that provide additional information regarding actual activity in amounts different from the budget. The budgetary accounts and actual activity are closed out separately.

# 3 Activity

| | | | |
|---|---|---|---|
| General fund | | Budget: | Book on opposite side as control |
| Revenue (special) fund | | Activity: | Revenue—measurable and available |
| And | Modified accrual | | Expenditures—all spending |
| Service (debt) fund | | | Assets—expenditured |
| Projects (capital) fund | | | Debts—other financing sources |
| Permanent fund | | Encumbrances: | Commit funds for purchase orders |

Governmental fund financial statements emphasize the flow of current financial resources (similar to cash basis reporting) rather than profit and loss. The matching principle is not used. Time and eligibility requirements along with modified accrual concepts (measurable and available) are used to determine the period in which revenue is recognized.

## 3.1 Non-exchange Revenue

Non-exchange transactions are a significant source of revenue for government entities. A non-exchange transaction is a transaction in which an entity gives/receives value without directly receiving/giving equal value in return. Exchange transactions, which are the primary source of revenue for commercial entities and proprietary funds, involve entities giving and receiving equal value in an arm's-length transaction.

### 3.1.1 Types of Non-exchange Revenues

Non-exchange revenues include:

- **Derived Tax Revenues**

    Derived (non-exchange) tax revenues represent taxes imposed on or derived from exchange transactions, such as commercial sales (sales taxes), taxpayer income (income taxes), etc.

- **Imposed Non-exchange Revenues**

    Imposed non-exchange revenues represent taxes imposed on non-exchange transactions (fines) or wealth (property taxes).

    Receivables are recorded when the government has an enforceable legal claim (i.e., when property taxes are levied).

> **Pass Key**
>
> Revenue recognition in governmental funds is always subject to modified accrual standards. Receivables, however, are recognized if the government has an enforceable claim (e.g., a tax levy on property). Recognized revenue will be adjusted to the amount available through the allowance account or deferred inflows of resources account (covered later) even though the receivable is recognized.

### Illustration 1   Property Tax Journal Entries

*Journal entry to record accrual of real property taxes levied and provide for the estimated amount of uncollectible accounts:*

| | | | |
|---|---|---:|---:|
| DR | Real property taxes receivable—current | $1,800,000 | |
| CR | Revenues—property taxes | | $1,620,000 |
| CR | Allowance for uncollectible taxes receivable—current | | 180,000 |

**Note:** When recording receivables, there may be an allowance account but not an uncollectible accounts or "bad debt" expenditure. The recording of the allowance reduces revenue to the measurable and available amount.

*Journal entry to record the collection of property taxes:*

| | | | |
|---|---|---:|---:|
| DR | Cash | $1,458,000 | |
| CR | Real property taxes receivable—current | | $1,458,000 |

*Journal entry to reclassify receivables to delinquent:*

| | | | |
|---|---|---:|---:|
| DR | Property taxes receivable—delinquent | $342,000 | |
| CR | Property taxes receivable—current | | $342,000 |

*Journal entry to reclassify current allowance for uncollectible taxes to delinquent and adjust revenues to accrue available amounts [Revenue adjustment = Revenue previously recognized ($1,620,000) minus measurable and available revenues ($1,458,000)]:*

| | | | |
|---|---|---:|---:|
| DR | Revenues—property taxes | $162,000 | |
| DR | Allowance for uncollectible taxes—current | 180,000 | |
| CR | Allowance for uncollectible taxes—delinquent | | $342,000 |

- **Government-Mandated Non-exchange Transactions**

    Government-mandated non-exchange transactions represent instances in which a higher level of government (e.g., a state) provides funds and mandates certain activities by another level of government (e.g., a county), such as environmental cleanup, etc.

- **Voluntary Non-exchange Transactions**

    Voluntary non-exchange transactions represent instances in which the government receives resources and does not provide equal value (e.g., grant agreements).

### 3.1.2 Revenue Recognition Requirements

The following revenue recognition requirements apply to governmental non-exchange revenues:

- **Time Requirements (Applicable to All Non-exchange Revenues)**

    Revenues are first recognized in the period in which resources must be used or when use may begin.

- **Eligibility Requirements (Applicable to Government-Mandated and Voluntary Non-exchange Transactions)**

    - **Time Requirements:** Revenues are first recognized in the period in which resources must be used or when use may begin, with emphasis on the time limit associated with the revenue (e.g., a grant must be fully expended or returned at the end of a grant period).
    - **Required Characteristics of Recipients:** The resource provider (e.g., the federal government) specifies certain characteristics for the recipient (e.g., the entity receiving the revenue must be a local government).
    - **Reimbursements:** Allowable expenditures must be incurred before revenue may be recognized.
    - **Contingencies (Only Applicable to Voluntary Non-exchange Transactions):** Actions must be taken (e.g., compliance with usage restrictions) before revenue is earned.

> **Pass Key**
>
> - All revenues are subject to time requirements.
> - Derived and imposed tax revenues are only subject to time requirements.
> - Only government-mandated and voluntary non-exchange transactions are subject to eligibility requirements.
> - Only voluntary non-exchange transactions are subject to contingency requirements (a subset of eligibility requirements).
>
> | Application of Revenue Recognition Principles |||
> | Accounts Receivable | Revenue | Deferred Inflow |
> | --- | --- | --- |
> | Measurable amounts for non-exchange levies are recognized as they are assessed. | Both of the following criteria must be met for revenue recognition:<br>▪ Time requirements are met (revenue either must be used or use may begin).<br>▪ Modified accrual requirements are met (revenue is both measurable and available). | Failing revenue recognition criteria, the non-exchange assessment is recorded as a deferred inflow. |

### 3.1.3 Measurable and Available Criteria

Upon satisfaction of recognition standards, governmental fund revenues are subject to basis of accounting rules. Under modified accrual accounting, governmental fund revenues are recorded when measurable and available. This usually means the collection period does not exceed 60 days after fiscal year-end.

> ## Pass Key
>
> The following items are accrued as receivable and revenue when time requirements are met, subject to the measurable and available (collected within 60 days of year-end) criteria:
>
> **Billed/Recorded (= Revenue)**
> - Real estate taxes (due)
> - Fines and penalties
>
> **Received (= Revenue)**
> - Income taxes
> - Sales taxes
>
> **Earned (= Revenue)**
> - Revenue collected in advance, unearned when collected
> - Real estate taxes paid in advance (unearned)
> - Restricted grants (earned when spent)
> - Deferred inflows of resources are recognized in some instances where assets are recorded but related revenues are not eligible for recognition (not available or fails time requirements).
>
> **Imposed non-exchange revenues**
>
> **Derived tax revenue (may not be measurable until received)**

## 3.2 Expenditures

Capital purchases, debt service payments, and operating expenditures are considered spending of funds and are treated as current year expenditures.

### Illustration 2 — Expenditures

Police cars and police officers' salaries are both expenditures treated the same in achieving the primary reporting focus (emphasis) or financial flow of operating data (flow of financial resources), as opposed to capital maintenance (depreciation accounting) or income determination, which are both emphasized in commercial accounting.

> ## Pass Key
>
> The timing of expenditure recognition is consistent with accrual accounting and is governed by when the voucher payable is recorded. The modified accrual basis of accounting does not delay the expenditure until the cash payment is made.

### 3.2.1 Alternatives for Expenditure Recognition

The following methods can be used to account for the purchase and use of the supplies, prepaid assets, and inventory of governmental funds.

- **Purchase Method**
    - Record an expenditure when purchased.
    - Record a current asset and nonspendable fund balance at year-end for any items not used (still on hand).
- **Consumption Method**
    - Record a current asset when purchased.
    - Record an expenditure as consumed during the period.

|  | Purchase | Consumption |
|---|---|---|
| *Buying item* | DR Expenditure<br>CR Vouchers payable | DR Supplies inventory<br>CR Vouchers payable |
| *Use of item* | No entry | DR Expenditure<br>CR Supplies inventory |
| *On-hand at year end* | DR Supplies inventory<br>CR Nonspendable fund balance—inventory | No entry* |

*Regardless of the method used, inventory asset amounts must be balanced with a nonspendable fund balance account to ensure the unassigned fund balance represents available resources. The purchase method assumes adjustment at year-end, and the consumption method, as presented, assumes perpetual inventory maintenance along with related adjustments to fund balance classifications, such that no entry is specifically required at year-end.

### 3.2.2 Classification of Governmental Expenditures

Expenditures of governmental funds are first classified according to the appropriate fund. Within the fund, the expenditures can be further classified using one of several methods.

- **Function or Program**

    Function or program classification provides information on the overall purpose of the expenditures. Function groups expenditures into the major services of the governmental entity. Program groups expenditures into activities, operations, or organizational units that are directed to the attainment of specific purposes or objectives. Both function and program are broad classifications. Examples of function include public safety, highways, education, health and welfare, and general governmental services. Examples of program include programs for the elderly, drug addiction, and education.

- **Organizational Unit**

    Organization unit corresponds to the organizational structure of the governmental entity. An organizational unit may be responsible for carrying out several programs. Examples of organizational units include the police and fire departments. Organizational units roll up into functional presentations. For example, the police and fire departments combine to form the public safety function.

- **Activity**

    By classifying expenditures by specific activity, economy and efficiency of operations can be measured. Measurement standards, such as expenditure per unit of work, can be determined. In addition, this classification serves as a basis for budget preparation. The activity can be an event, a task, or a unit of work with a specific purpose.

- **Character**

    Classification by character refers to determining the basis of the fiscal period the expenditures are presumed to benefit. The major classifications by character are:

    - *Current expenditures*, which benefit the current fiscal period;
    - *Capital outlays*, which are presumed to benefit both the present and future fiscal periods;
    - *Debt service*, which benefits prior fiscal periods as well as current and future periods; and
    - *Intergovernmental*, where one governmental unit transfers resources to another.

- **Object Classes**

    Classification by object classifies the expenditure according to the type of items purchased or services obtained. Examples are personnel services, supplies, and principal and interest payments for debt service expenditures.

## 3.3 Fixed Assets

Fixed assets, whether purchased, constructed or leased, are not expected to contribute to the generation of governmental fund revenue. The acquisition of a fixed asset, therefore, is not capitalized on the fund's books. Instead, it is considered an expenditure of the fund and is not depreciated in the fund financial statements. The fixed assets and related depreciation are reported on the government-wide financial statements.

### Illustration 3 — Capital Outlay Expenditure

A governmental fund purchases a new police car for $25,000. The governmental fund journal entry to record the purchase of the police car follows:

| | | | |
|---|---|---|---|
| DR | Expenditure—capital outlay | $25,000 | |
| CR | Vouchers payable (or cash) | | $25,000 |

### Pass Key

- Governmental funds (GRaSPP) use modified accrual and will "expenditure" fixed asset acquisitions consistent with the current financial resources measurement focus. The fixed assets are reported on the government-wide financial statements.
- Proprietary and fiduciary funds (SE-CIPPOE) use full accrual and will capitalize fixed-asset acquisitions and depreciate them consistent with the economic resources measurement focus.

## 3.4 Debts (Long-Term)

Proceeds from long-term debts are recorded in the governmental funds as "other financing sources." The governmental funds do not record or carry the long-term debt. Rather, it is recorded on the government-wide financial statements. Repayment of long-term debts are recorded as expenditures of both principal and interest.

### Illustration 4 — Proceeds From Bond Issuance

A governmental unit receives the proceeds of a bond issue of $1,000,000. The governmental fund journal entry to record the receipt of the proceeds follows:

| | | | |
|---|---|---|---|
| DR | Cash | $1,000,000 | |
| CR | Other financing sources—bonds issued | | $1,000,000 |

### Illustration 5 — Debt Service Payments

A municipality pays $125,000 in principal and $100,000 in interest on its general long-term debt. The journal entry recorded in the municipality's governmental funds would be:

| | | | |
|---|---|---|---|
| DR | Expenditure—principal | $125,000 | |
| DR | Expenditure—interest | 100,000 | |
| CR | Cash | | $225,000 |

### Pass Key

- Governmental funds (GRaSPP) use modified accrual and will record proceeds from long-term debt as "other financing sources" (*statement of revenues, expenditures, and changes in fund balance*, not the balance sheet) consistent with the current financial resources measurement focus. The debt service fund pays the currently due interest and principal.

- Proprietary and fiduciary funds (SE-CIPPOE) use full accrual, record the long-term debt consistent with the economic resources measurement focus, and directly pay the interest and principal.

## 3.5 Other Financing: Leases

Leases represent the financing of the right to use an underlying asset. The economic substance of this transaction is the same for governments as it is for commercial enterprises. Governmental standards mirror commercial standards while adapting to measurement focus and basis of accounting issues at the fund level. Governmental lease transactions are grouped similarly to commercial accounting but are described using different terminology.

### 3.5.1 Lease Definition

A lease is defined as a contract that conveys control of the right to use another entity's nonfinancial assets as specified in the contract for a period of time. Lease standards typically apply to long-lived tangible assets such as buildings and equipment, and specifically exclude intangible assets, biological assets, inventory, etc.

### 3.5.2 Lease Term

The lease term includes the contract period during which the asset will most likely be used.

The lease term also includes any optional lease extension period which either the lessee or lessor is likely to exercise and periods in which the lessee or lessor will not exercise options to terminate.

Determination of the lease term includes consideration of such matters as the economic incentives or disincentives to exercise options, the history of the parties in exercising options, and the essential qualities of the asset.

### 3.5.3 Lease Classifications

Governmental accounting classifies leases in one of three ways. Leases may be *short-term leases* (similar in character and definition to short-term commercial operating leases) or either *contracts that transfer ownership* (similar in character and definition to commercial sales-type finance leases) or *leases other than short-term leases and contracts that transfer ownership* (similar in character and definition to commercial direct-finance leases and longer-term operating leases).

- **Short-Term Leases**

    Short-term leases have a maximum term of 12 months or less. Short-term leases, by definition, are current and, thus, receive the similar accounting treatment in both governmental and proprietary funds. Accounting is nearly identical to commercial standards.

    - Lessees recognize expenditures or expenses based on payment provisions of the contract. No expenditure or expenses are recognized during rent-free periods.
    - Lessors recognize rent revenue based on the payment provisions of the lease contract. No rent revenues are recognized during rent-free periods.

- **Contracts That Transfer Ownership**

    Contracts that transfer ownership of the underlying asset to the lessee are accounted for as a financed purchase by the lessee and a sale by the lessor.

    - **Lessee Accounting—Governmental Funds:** The lessee accounts for the acquisition of non-current assets with non-current financing as a capital outlay expenditure and other financing source. Payment of the debt is handled in a manner consistent with other debt payments.

Transactions and Events: Part 1

## Illustration 6    Lessee Accounting, Governmental Funds

**Facts:** The city of Lester acquired photocopiers to be used by the city's Finance Department for $25,000 at the beginning of its fiscal year, January 1. Ownership of the copiers will transfer to the city at the end of lease. The lease has a three-year term and carries an interest rate of 10 percent. Payments are to be made annually on December 31 of each year and are computed at $10,053.

**Required:** Prepare the journal entries to:

1. Record the lease at the beginning of the year.
2. Record the first payment on the lease at the end of the year.

**Solution:**

1. The lease is initially recorded as a capital outlay expenditure funded by other financing sources associated with the lease.

   | DR | Expenditure—capital outlay | $25,000 | |
   |---|---|---|---|
   | CR | Other financing sources | | $25,000 |

2. Lease payments on a contract that transfers ownership would be recorded in a manner consistent with other debt service payments.

   | DR | Expenditure—principal | $7,553 | |
   |---|---|---|---|
   | DR | Expenditure—interest | 2,500 | |
   | CR | Cash | | $10,053 |

- **Lessor Accounting—Governmental Funds:** The lessor accounts for the sale of non-current assets with non-current receivables in a manner similar to other measurable but unavailable revenue and recognizes deferred inflows as revenue over time in a systematic and rational manner.

## Illustration 7    Lessor Accounting, Governmental Funds

**Facts:** The city of Lester leased a small parcel of surplus municipal property previously used in the city's general governmental operations to a private company for $25,000 at the beginning of its fiscal year, January 1. Ownership of the parcel will transfer to the private company at the end of lease. The lease has a three-year term and carries an interest rate of 10 percent. Payments are to be made annually on December 31 of each year and are computed at $10,053.

**Required:** Prepare the journal entries to:

1. Record the lease at the beginning of the year.
2. Record the first receipt on the lease at the end of the year.

(continued)

(continued)

**Solution:**

1. The lease is initially recorded as a receivable with recognized revenue to the extent that it is both measurable and available.

| | | | |
|---|---|---|---|
| DR | Lease receivable | $25,000 | |
| CR | Revenue | | $ 7,553 |
| CR | Deferred inflows of resources | | 17,447 |
| | | | |
| DR | Interest receivable | $2,500 | |
| CR | Interest revenue | | $2,500 |

Revenue and deferred inflows are computed using the effective interest method using the assumptions described in the fact pattern. Revenue is equal to the first year of principal with the balance equal to the deferred inflows of resources.

2. Receipts associated with the collection of receivables would be recorded as follows:

| | | | |
|---|---|---|---|
| DR | Cash | $10,053 | |
| CR | Lease receivable | | $7,553 |
| CR | Interest receivable | | 2,500 |

- **Lessee Accounting—Proprietary and Fiduciary Funds and Government-Wide Presentation:** The lessee would account for the acquired asset and associated lease obligation as a financed purchase in a manner consistent with commercial accounting.
- **Lessor Accounting—Proprietary and Fiduciary Funds and Government-Wide Presentation:** The lessor would derecognize the asset sold, record a receivable, and recognize revenue in a manner consistent with commercial accounting.

■ **Leases Other Than Short-Term Leases and Contracts That Transfer Ownership**

Leases not meeting the definition of a short-term lease or that represent contracts that do not transfer ownership are accounted for using principles similar to commercial operating leases as adapted for governmental accounting principles.

- **Lessee Accounting—Governmental Funds:** The lessee accounts for the acquisition of non-current assets with non-current financing as a capital outlay expenditure and other financing source. Payment of the debt is handled in a manner consistent with other debt payments as described above for contracts that transfer ownership.
- **Lessor Accounting—Governmental Funds:** The lessor accounts for the sale of non-current assets with non-current receivables in a manner similar to other measurable but unavailable revenues as described above for contracts that transfer ownership.
- **Lessee Accounting—Proprietary and Fiduciary Funds and Government-Wide Presentation:** At the beginning of the lease, the lessee records an intangible "right-of-use" asset (amortized over the life of the asset or lease term, whichever is less) along with an associated lease liability (amortized using the effective interest method).

  The value of the asset and lease are equal to the discounted lease payments of the contract. The discount rate is the lesser of the interest rate implied in the lease or the lessee's estimated incremental borrowing rate.

  Liabilities may be remeasured if significant changes occur.

# Illustration 8: Lessee Accounting, Proprietary and Fiduciary Funds, and Government-Wide Financial Statements

**Facts:** The city of Lester acquired photocopiers to be used by the city's Water and Sewer Enterprise Fund for $25,000 at the beginning of its fiscal year, January 1. Ownership of the copiers will not transfer to the city at the end of the lease and the city does not have the option to purchase them. The copiers have a useful life of three years, and the lease has a three-year term and carries an interest rate of 10 percent. Payments are to be made annually on December 31 of each year and are computed at $10,053.

**Required:** Prepare the journal entries to:

1. Record the lease at the beginning of the year.
2. Record the entries at the end of the year to recognize lease expense and amortize the associated right-of-use asset.

**Solution:**

1. The lease is neither a short-term lease nor a contract that transfers ownership. It would be recorded as a right-of-use asset and with an associated liability at inception.

| | | | |
|---|---|---|---|
| DR | Right-of-use asset | $25,000 | |
| CR | Lease liability | | $25,000 |

2. Lease payments would be recorded in a manner consistent with other debt service payments. Amortization expense recognizes expiration of the right-of-use asset.

| | | | |
|---|---|---|---|
| DR | Lease liability | $7,553 | |
| DR | Interest expense | 2,500 | |
| CR | Cash | | $10,053 |
| DR | Amortization expense | $8,333 | |
| CR | Accumulated amortization (ROU) | | $8,333 |

Supporting schedule for the right-of-use asset amortization using straight-line amortization over three years and the liability amortization using the effective interest method follows:

| Year | Lease Liability | Principal | Interest | Total Payment | Amortization Expense | Carrying Value of Right-of-Use Asset |
|---|---|---|---|---|---|---|
| Begin | $25,000 | – | – | – | – | $25,000 |
| 1 | $17,447 | $7,553 | $2,500 | $10,053 | $8,333 | $16,667 |
| 2 | $9,139 | $8,308 | $1,745 | $10,053 | $8,333 | $8,334 |
| 3 | $0 | $9,139 | $914 | $10,053 | $8,334 | $0 |

- **Lessor Accounting—Proprietary and Fiduciary Funds and Government-Wide Presentation:** At the beginning of the lease term a lessor should recognize a lease receivable and a deferred inflow of resources. Any initial direct costs should be recorded as an expense.

  The lease receivable is valued at the present value of future lease payments.

  Lease payments include fixed payments, variable payments, residual guaranteed payments, and incentives. Receivables are reduced by periodic payments.

  The deferred inflow is equal to the lease receivable and recognized rationally and systematically as lease revenue over the life of the lease.

  The underlying asset is not derecognized. The asset is reported and depreciated.

### Illustration 9   Lessor Accounting, Proprietary and Fiduciary Funds, and Government-Wide Financial Statements

**Facts:** The city of Lester leased a small parcel of surplus municipal property previously used in the city's Water and Sewer Fund to a private company for $25,000 at the beginning of its fiscal year, January 1. Ownership of the land will not transfer to the private company at the end of the lease and that company does not have the option to purchase it. The lease has a three-year term and carries an interest rate of 10 percent. Payments are to be made annually on December 31 of each year and are computed at $10,053.

**Required:** Prepare the journal entries to:

1. Record the lease at the beginning of the year.
2. Record the first payment on the lease at the end of the year.

**Solution:**

1. The lease is initially recorded as a lease receivable and related benefits as a deferred inflow of resources.

   | | | | |
   |---|---|---|---|
   | DR | Lease receivable | $25,000 | |
   | CR | Deferred inflow of resources | | $25,000 |

2. Lease receipts and revenue recognition on a lease that is not short term and does not transfer ownership would be recorded as follows:

   | | | | |
   |---|---|---|---|
   | DR | Cash | $10,053 | |
   | CR | Interest income | | $2,500 |
   | CR | Lease receivable | | 7,553 |
   | DR | Deferred inflows of resources | $8,333 | |
   | CR | Revenue | | $8,333 |

# Pass Key

Leases are similar to notes receivable and payable but differ in their accounting based on their classification in one of three ways:

### Lessor (Seller)

| Classification | GRSPP Funds DR | GRSPP Funds CR | SE-CIPPOE Funds DR | SE-CIPPOE Funds CR |
|---|---|---|---|---|
| Short-term leases | Receivable | Revenue | Receivable | Revenue |
| Contracts that transfer ownership | Receivable | Current revenue and deferred inflow | Receivable | Revenue |
| Leases other than short-term leases and contracts that transfer ownership | Receivable | Current revenue and deferred inflow | Receivable | Deferred inflow* |

### Lessee (Buyer)

| Classification | GRSPP Funds DR | GRSPP Funds CR | SE-CIPPOE Funds DR | SE-CIPPOE Funds CR |
|---|---|---|---|---|
| Short-term leases | Lease expense | Cash/payable | Lease expense | Cash/payable |
| Contracts that transfer ownership | Capital outlay expenditure | Other financing source | Capital asset acquired | Lease liability |
| Leases other than short-term leases and contracts that transfer ownership | Capital outlay expenditure | Other financing source | Right-of-use asset** | Lease liability |

*Deferred inflows are used in connection with lessor activity recorded in governmental funds because revenues are measurable but not available. Deferred inflows are used by lessors in proprietary and fiduciary funds in response to requirements of the standard.

**Right-of-use assets are only recorded for proprietary and fiduciary fund lessees for leases classified as other than short term and contracts that transfer ownership.

## Question 1 — MCQ-00962

Ridge Township's governing body adopted its general fund budget for the year ended July 31, Year 1, composed of estimated revenues of $100,000 and appropriations of $80,000. Ridge formally integrates its budget into the accounting records.

To record the appropriations of $80,000, Ridge should:

- a. Credit appropriations control.
- b. Debit appropriations control.
- c. Credit estimated expenditures control.
- d. Debit estimated expenditures control.

## Question 2 — MCQ-00964

Ridge Township's governing body adopted its general fund budget for the year ended July 31, Year 1, composed of estimated revenues of $100,000 and appropriations of $80,000. Ridge formally integrates its budget into the accounting records.

To record the $20,000 budgeted excess of estimated revenues over appropriations, Ridge should:

- a. Credit estimated excess revenues control.
- b. Debit estimated excess revenues control.
- c. Credit budgetary control.
- d. Debit budgetary control.

## Question 3 — MCQ-00973

The following information pertains to property taxes levied by Oak City for the calendar year Year 1:

| | |
|---|---|
| Collections during Year 1 | $500,000 |
| Expected collections during the first 60 days of Year 2 | 100,000 |
| Expected collections during the balance of Year 2 | 60,000 |
| Expected collections during January Year 3 | 30,000 |
| Estimated to be uncollectible | 10,000 |
| Total levy | $700,000 |

What amount should Oak report for Year 1 net property tax revenues in its fund financial statements?

- a. $700,000
- b. $690,000
- c. $600,000
- d. $500,000

## Question 4 — MCQ-04673

Dayne County's general fund had the following disbursements during the year:

| | |
|---|---|
| Payment of principal on long-term debt | $100,000 |
| Payments to vendors | 500,000 |
| Purchase of a computer | 300,000 |

What amount should Dayne County report as expenditures in its governmental funds statement of revenues, expenditures, and changes in fund balances?

a. $300,000
b. $500,000
c. $800,000
d. $900,000

## Question 5 — MCQ-00997

It is inappropriate to record depreciation expense in a (an):

a. Enterprise fund.
b. Internal service fund.
c. Private purpose trust fund.
d. Capital projects fund.

# MODULE 4

# Transactions and Events: Part 2

FAR 9

## 1 Encumbrances

| General fund | | Budget: | Book on opposite side as control |
| Revenue (special) fund | | | Revenue—measurable and available |
| And | Modified accrual | Activity: | Expenditures—all spending |
| Service (debt) fund | | | Assets—expenditured |
| Projects (capital) fund | | | Debts—other financing sources |
| Permanent fund | | Encumbrances: | Commit funds for purchase orders |

Open purchase orders represent an encumbrance or commitment of the available appropriations of a government. In order for governmental managers to effectively monitor the degree to which they have used their budgetary appropriations, governmental accounting systems must reflect not only the expenditures but also the obligations to spend (purchase orders). This is done to prevent overspending of appropriations. Subsidiary ledgers are used to record the details of budgetary accounts, encumbrances, and other general ledger accounts that require detail.

### 1.1 Nature of Encumbrances

An encumbrance should not be viewed as a GAAP expenditure. Similarly, the budgetary control account that offsets the encumbrance is not a liability. The budgetary control entry acts as a limitation or constraint that reduces the available fund balance.

---

**Illustration 1    Encumbrances**

Assume that Progressive Township has budgeted or appropriated $100,000 for the purchase of two sanitation trucks at the beginning of the year. Then assume that a purchase order is issued to purchase the two sanitation trucks at an estimated cost of $45,000 each.

*Journal entry to set up the encumbrance and budgetary control in budgetary accounts in the general fund:*

| DR | Encumbrances | $90,000 | |
| CR | Budgetary control | | $90,000 |

The invoice is received for one of the trucks, at an actual cost of $44,000. The entry to the encumbrances account is reversed and the actual expenditure is recorded. Assume that the second truck is back-ordered.

(continued)

*(continued)*

*Journal entry to reverse estimated encumbrances in budgetary accounts:*

| DR | Budgetary control | $45,000 | |
|---|---|---|---|
| CR | Encumbrances | | $45,000 |

*Journal entry to record the actual expenditures of $44,000:*

| DR | Expenditures | $44,000 | |
|---|---|---|---|
| CR | Vouchers payable (or cash) | | $44,000 |

## 1.2 Recording Encumbrances

Encumbrances are recorded for spending/appropriations control purposes, especially in the general and special revenue funds. Encumbrances are not generally used for recurring expenditures, such as salaries. They are more commonly recorded when a purchase order is issued.

### Pass Key

CPA Exam questions may ask about the timing of debits and credits to the encumbrance account and debits and credits to the budgetary control account. Remember that the planned obligations of the government (appropriations) are recorded as credits. All other uses of the appropriation are debits. All you need to remember is to take the sum of the natural balances of the appropriations, expenditure, and encumbrance accounts to arrive at the management objective of this accounting: unexpended appropriations.

The following schedule shows the manner in which the journal entries from the outline would produce management information. Debits are shown without brackets, and credits are shown in brackets. Notice how the activity in the **Budget**, **Activity**, and **Encumbrance** columns are independently maintained by the accounting entries. Also notice how the unexpended appropriation fluctuates first with the encumbrance ($10,000) and then with the recording of the actual transaction ($11,000).

| | Budget | Activity | Encumbrance | |
|---|---|---|---|---|
| Transaction | (Appropriations) | Expenditure | Encumbrance | Unexpended Appropriation |
| 1. Appropriation | $(100,000) | -0- | -0- | $(100,000) |
| 2. Encumbrance | -0- | — | $90,000 | 90,000 |
| Subtotal | (100,000) | — | 90,000 | (10,000) |
| 3. Reverse encumbrance | -0- | -0- | (45,000) | (45,000) |
| 4. Record activity | -0- | $44,000 | -0- | 44,000 |
| Total | $(100,000) | $44,000 | $45,000 | $ (11,000) |

## 1.3 Encumbrances Outstanding at Year-End

If an encumbrance (purchase order) is still outstanding at year-end and appropriations do not lapse (i.e., government will honor outstanding purchase orders), reverse the journal entry and include outstanding encumbrances in an appropriate fund balance classification. Usually encumbrances would be included in "fund balance, committed" or "fund balance, assigned."

Outstanding encumbrances at year-end will be carried forward within the appropriate fund balance classification with a corresponding reduction of unassigned fund balance, if the appropriations do not lapse. Encumbrances will not be specifically detailed on the face of the financial statements but may be disclosed if material. Encumbrances that will be liquidated with restricted, committed, or assigned resources have no effect on the classification of fund balance.

---

**Illustration 2  Closing the Encumbrance at Year-End**

*Journal entry to close outstanding encumbrances at year-end and reserve the fund balance:*

| | | | |
|---|---|---|---|
| DR | Budgetary control | $45,000 | |
| CR | Encumbrances | | $45,000 |

To close budgetary accounts related to outstanding purchase orders.

| | | | |
|---|---|---|---|
| DR | Unassigned fund balance (year-end surplus) | $45,000 | |
| CR | Fund balance, committed | | $45,000 |

To record reclassification of fund balance relative to outstanding prior year purchase orders.

---

### Pass Key

Signs used in this pass key do not attempt to duplicate the consistent Dr (Cr) presentation shown on the previous page. Appropriations are deliberately shown without brackets to represent a positive unspent/unencumbered amount, while encumbrances and expenditures are displayed in brackets to reflect negative amounts that reduce unspent/unencumbered appropriations.

| Transaction | Budget (Appropriations) | Activity Expenditure | Encumbrance Encumbrance | Unexpended Appropriation | Cash | Fund Balance Unassigned | Committed |
|---|---|---|---|---|---|---|---|
| 1. Appropriation | $(100,000) | -0- | -0- | $100,000 | $100,000 | $(100,000) | -0- |
| 2. Encumbrance | -0- | -0- | $ 90,000 | (90,000) | -0- | -0- | -0- |
| 3. Reverse encumbrance | -0- | -0- | (45,000) | 45,000 | -0- | -0- | -0- |
| 4. Record activity | – | $ 44,000 | – | (44,000) | (44,000) | 44,000 | -0- |
| Subtotal | (100,000) | 44,000 | 45,000 | 11,000 | -0- | -0- | -0- |
| 5. Close BAE | 100,000 | (44,000) | (45,000) | (11,000) | -0- | -0- | -0- |
| Subtotal | -0- | -0- | -0- | -0- | 56,000 | (56,000) | -0- |
| 6. Commit encumbered appropriation | -0- | -0- | -0- | -0- | -0- | 45,000 | $(45,000) |
| Total | -0- | -0- | -0- | -0- | $ 56,000 | $ (11,000) | $(45,000) |

## 1.4 Accounting in the Following Year

In the following year, the use (spending/expenditure) of these amounts will be recorded as an expenditure.

### Illustration 3 Subsequent Year Accounting

Journal entry to record the receipt of last year's item and pay for it:

| DR | Expenditure—prior year | $45,000 | |
|---|---|---|---|
| CR | Vouchers payable | | $45,000 |

### Pass Key

The outstanding encumbrance at year-end is treated as a component of an appropriate classification of fund balance (generally committed or assigned). In the following year, when the item is received and paid, it is not reported as an expenditure in the budget and actual comparison schedules because it is not a charge against current period appropriations.

### Example 1 Appropriations and Encumbrances

**Facts:** A county's balances in the general fund included the following:

| | |
|---|---|
| Appropriations | $745,000 |
| Encumbrances | 37,250 |
| Expenditures | 298,000 |
| Vouchers payable | 55,875 |

**Required:** Calculate the remaining appropriations available for use by the county.

**Solution:** Appropriations is a budgetary account. This account represents the governmental unit's approved spending (in this case, $745,000). Expenditures represent the actual incurring of bills, whether paid in cash or recorded as vouchers payable. Encumbrances are the restrictions of the fund balance for purchase orders. Vouchers payable represent expenditures not yet paid.

| | |
|---|---|
| Budget: appropriations | $745,000 |
| Activity: expenditures | (298,000) |
| Encumbrances: | (37,250) |
| Remaining available appropriations | $409,750 |

## Pass Key

Remember to close the budget, activity, and encumbrances (BAE-BAE) separately. Do not try to net them. The rule is:

Budget is booked ⟶ Budget is closed for same amount
Activity is booked ⟶ Activity is closed for actual amount
Encumbrances are booked ⟶ Encumbrance is reversed for same amount

## Pass Key

Encumbrance accounting provides the final dimension to both fiscal accountability and current financial resources measurement focus. Throughout the year, the use of encumbrances helps monitor the degree to which appropriations have been used. At year-end, encumbrances serve to reduce unassigned fund balances to determine the degree of spendable available resources that can be carried forward into the next spending cycle.

### Question 1  MCQ-00940

Which internal account should Spring Township credit when it issues a purchase order for supplies?

- a. Appropriations control
- b. Vouchers payable
- c. Encumbrance control
- d. Budgetary control

### Question 2  MCQ-00969

Elm City issued a purchase order for supplies with an estimated cost of $5,000. When the supplies were received, the accompanying invoice indicated an actual price of $4,950. What amount should Elm debit (credit) to the budgetary control after the supplies and invoice were received?

- a. $(50)
- b. $50
- c. $4,950
- d. $5,000

# 2 Other Transactions and Events

## 2.1 Interfund Activity

Interfund activity represents the flow of resources between funds and between the primary government and its component units. The accounting associated with interfund activity can be classified as follows:

1. Reciprocal interfund activity
2. Nonreciprocal interfund activity

Interfund activity is subject to specific requirements related to financial statement display and disclosure.

### 2.1.1 Reciprocal Interfund Activity

Reciprocal interfund activity includes exchange-type transactions between funds.

- **Interfund Loans:** Interfund loans represent temporary extensions of credit to other funds that are expected to be repaid and are accounted for as interfund receivables and payables (due from/due to). Unrealizable balances are reclassified as transfers.

- **Interfund Services Provided and Used:** Interfund services represent sales and purchases between funds at external pricing. Examples include sales of water and sewer services by an enterprise fund to the city and internal service fund activities. Transactions of this type are accounted for as revenues and expenses/expenditures.

### 2.1.2 Nonreciprocal Interfund Activity

Generally, nonreciprocal interfund activity represents non-exchange transactions between funds.

- **Interfund Transfers:** Flows of assets between funds without the exchange of equivalent value represent interfund transfers. Payments in lieu of taxes made by a proprietary fund to the general fund or the budgeted transfer of pledged revenues from a special revenue fund to a debt service fund to meet bond covenant requirements are examples of interfund transfers. Transfers are normally displayed as other financing sources and uses after nonoperating revenues and expenses.

- **Interfund Reimbursements:** Payments of expenses made by one fund on behalf of another fund are accounted for as reimbursements. The expenditure originally made is reimbursed by the fund actually responsible for the disbursement. Interfund reimbursements serve to reclassify the expenditure or expense associated with the original transaction to the fund ultimately responsible for the obligation satisfied. Interfund reimbursements are not displayed as interfund transactions.

## 2.2 Special Items

### 2.2.1 Characteristics of Special Items

Special items are items under the control of management that are either unusual or infrequent but not both.

- An event or transaction that is unusual in nature possesses a high degree of abnormality and is unrelated to the ordinary and typical activities of government.

- An event or transaction is infrequent in occurrence if it would not reasonably be expected to recur in the foreseeable future.

> **Pass Key**
>
> Special items are distinguished from extraordinary items by their characteristics. Most significantly, *extraordinary* items must be *both* unusual in nature *and* infrequent in occurrence, while *special items* must only be unusual in nature *or* infrequent in occurrence but not both.

### 2.2.2 Examples of Special Items

- Sales of certain governmental capital assets
- Termination benefits resulting from workforce reductions
- Early retirement program offered to all employees
- Significant forgiveness of debt

### 2.2.3 Examples of Extraordinary Items

- Environmental disaster created by a chemical spill from a train wreck
- Significant damage in a community as the result of a terrorist attack

### 2.2.4 Financial Statement Presentation

Special items are reported before extraordinary items.

## 2.3 Deferred Inflows and Outflows

### 2.3.1 Character and Definition

Deferred inflows of resources and deferred outflows of resources result from the acquisition or consumption of net assets (a fund or government's equity) in one period that are applicable to future periods.

Transactions unique to government as well as unusual transactions typically associated with other comprehensive income in commercial settings (e.g., derivative accounting, pension accounting, etc.) are accounted for as deferred inflows/outflows.

- Deferred outflows of resources have a positive effect on net position and are reported following assets but before liabilities.
- Deferred inflows of resources have a negative effect on net position and are reported following liabilities but before equity.

> **Pass Key**
>
> The use of the term *deferred* is limited to items reported as deferred outflows of resources or deferred inflows of resources and should not be used in connection with any other account title.

### 2.3.2 Sources of Deferred Outflows/Inflows of Resources

- **Imposed Non-exchange Revenue Transactions (Time Requirements Not Met)**

    Imposed non-exchange revenue transactions that are reported as receivable prior to their formal levy (such as property taxes recorded in December but not fully levied until January) or transactions recorded as a receivable prior to the period when resources are required to be used (such as occupational licenses billed in November for business license valid in the following year beginning in January) should be reported as deferred inflows.

- **Government-Mandated Non-exchange Transactions and Voluntary Non-exchange Transactions**

    Although multiyear government-mandated non-exchange transactions or voluntary non-exchange transactions may be entirely recognized as revenue, formal time restrictions create the possibility of deferred inflow/outflow treatment. Resources received before time requirements are met, but after all other eligibility requirements are met, should be reported as deferred outflows of resources by the provider and deferred inflows of resources by the recipient.

- **Refunding of Debt**

    The difference between the reacquisition price and the net carrying amount of the old debt should be reported as a deferred outflow (loss) or deferred inflow (gain) and recognized as a component of interest expense over the remaining life of the old or new debt, whichever is shorter.

- **Sales and Intra-entity Transfers of Future Revenues**

    Sales and intra-entity transfers of future revenues should generally be reported as deferred inflows of resources. Governments that factor their receivables initially record the proceeds from the sale as a deferred inflow that is recognized over time.

---

**Illustration 4    Transfer of Future Revenue**

Progressive Township elects to sell its delinquent tax receivables to a state agency specifically established to assist local governments with cash flow issues. The township would receive net proceeds from the state and record deferred inflows of resources.

---

- **Leases**

    Gains or losses arising from sale and leaseback transactions result in a deferred inflow or deferred outflow of resources that are recognized systematically over the life of the lease. In addition, leases classified as other than short-term leases and contracts that transfer ownership are accounted for as a lease receivable and deferred inflow by the lessor.

- **Regulated Operations**

    Deferred inflows of resources may result from rate actions by a regulator that impose limitations on the assets of a government, including:

    - Establishment of current rates at a level adequate to recover costs that are expected to be incurred in the future.

    - Refund of gains or reductions of net allowable costs to be given to customers over future periods.

## Illustration 5   Regulated Operations

The state-regulated Progressive Township Electrical Authority has secured approval from the state to increase electric rates in the coming year. The increase is intended to fund system improvements. The incremental increase associated with the approved rate adjustment would be accounted for as an asset and as a deferred inflow.

- **Assets Associated With Unavailable Revenues (Modified Accrual Criteria Not Met)**

    When an asset is recorded in governmental fund financial statements, but the revenue is not available (e.g., measurable but not collected until more than 60 days after year-end), the government should report a deferred inflow of resources.

- **Asset Retirement Obligations (ARO)**

    A deferred outflow of resources should be recorded in an amount equal to the ARO.

### 2.3.3 Accounting and Financial Reporting for Pensions

Changes in a government's pension liability are accounted for in one of two ways in the sponsoring fund's financial statements and in the government-wide financial statements.

- **Expensed**

    Similar to commercial accounting, changes in a government's pension liability that result from current service costs and interest net of return on plan assets are expensed.

- **Deferred Outflows and Deferred Inflows**

    Changes in a government's pension liability that result from changes in actuarial assumptions, differences between expected and actual return on plan assets, and some (the unearned portion of) prior service costs are accounted for as deferred outflows and deferred inflows. Prior service costs already earned by employees are expensed.

### Pass Key

The use of deferred inflows and deferred outflows in governmental accounting is similar to the use of accumulated other comprehensive income in commercial accounting. For example, changes in the fair value of derivatives that qualify for hedge treatment and certain components of the change in pension liability receive deferred treatment on the statement of financial position through deferred inflow and outflow accounts rather than immediate recognition on the income statement.

### 2.3.4 Derivative Instruments and Hedge Accounting

Derivative instruments are used by state and local governments to manage specific risks or to make investments. Derivatives are reported at fair value. Changes in the fair value of derivatives are reported as follows:

- Changes in value of derivatives used as investments are displayed within the investment revenue classification.

# Transactions and Events: Part 2

- Changes in value of derivatives used for hedging activities are reported as either deferred outflows or deferred inflows of resources.

### Illustration 6 — Forward Contract

Progressive Township plans to purchase fuel for the operation of both its vehicles and its emergency generators for lift station operations in Year 2. The township secures a forward contract to purchase fuel at a specific price in the future. By year-end, however, the price of fuel has fallen below the guaranteed price of the contract, thereby reducing the value of the forward contract by $35,000.

The entry to record the decline in value of the hedge would be as follows:

| | | | |
|---|---|---|---|
| DR | Deferred outflows or resources | $35,000 | |
| CR | Forward contract | | $35,000 |

---

### Question 3     MCQ-08277

The city of Curtain had the following interfund transactions during the month of May:

- Billing by the internal service fund to a department financed by the general fund, for services rendered in the amount of $5,000.
- Transfer of $200,000 from the general fund to establish a new enterprise fund.
- Routine transfer of $50,000 from the general fund to the debt service fund.

What was the total reciprocal interfund activity for Curtain during May?

    a. $5,000
    b. $55,000
    c. $200,000
    d. $255,000

---

### Question 4     MCQ-07265

Assets (such as property taxes receivable) associated with unavailable revenues (such as property taxes collected more than 60 days after year-end) should be recorded by crediting:

    a. An allowance.
    b. A deferred outflow of resources.
    c. A deferred inflow of resources.
    d. An increase to nonspendable fund balance.

# 3 Fund Balances and Components Thereof (GRaSPP)

Fund balance is "equity" in the balance sheets of the governmental funds and is equal to assets (and deferred outflows) minus liabilities (and deferred inflows).

## 3.1 Categories of Fund Balance

Governmental fund balances are reported in a hierarchy that shows up to five degrees of constraint (limitations on use) associated with the current equity of the fund. Constraints, in order, are as follows:

1. **Nonspendable Fund Balance:** Current equity in the fund balance generally comprises available, spendable resources. To the extent that the equity of a governmental fund is represented by current assets that cannot be spent (e.g., prepaid expenditures, inventories, etc.), the fund balance should be displayed as nonspendable.

2. **Restricted Fund Balance:** Fund balance resources associated with assets restricted by external authorities (e.g., legislation, grantors, creditors, etc.) are classified as restricted.

3. **Committed Fund Balance:** Fund balance resources associated with assets obligated by a formal action of the government's highest decision-making authority (e.g., resolutions by a city commission, encumbered appropriations, etc.). Encumbered appropriations are not specifically identified on the face of a government's financial statements but may be disclosed.

4. **Assigned Fund Balance:** Fund balance resources associated with assets that the government intends to obligate (e.g., designations) but has not formally committed. Assignments are not possible if unassigned fund balances are negative.

5. **Unassigned Fund Balance:** Fund balance resources associated with spendable assets that are neither restricted, committed, nor assigned. Unassigned fund balance is a residual equity classification for the general fund. Only the general fund should have a positive unassigned fund balance. Other governmental funds might have negative unassigned fund balances if expenditures incurred for specific purposes exceed the amounts restricted or committed to those purposes.

## 3.2 Summary of Reported Constraints by Fund

The following chart displays the potential (likely) classifications of fund balance in the governmental funds.

| Reported Constraints by Fund: Summary |||||||
| --- | --- | --- | --- | --- | --- |
| Categories | General | Special Revenue | Debt Service | Capital Projects | Permanent |
| Nonspendable | ✓ | ✓ | | | |
| Restricted | ✓ | ✓ | ✓ | ✓ | ✓ |
| Committed | ✓ | ✓ | ✓ | ✓ | |
| Assigned | ✓ | | ✓ | ✓ | |
| Unassigned | Positive X | Negative X | Negative X | Negative X | Negative X |

## 3.3 Summary of Nature/Source of Constraints by Level

| \multicolumn{2}{c}{Nature/Source of Constraints by Level: Summary} ||
|---|---|
| Categories | Nature of Constraint |
| Nonspendable | *Practical*: Monies have been spent, assets are either maturing (e.g., longer-term investments and are not available) or expiring (e.g., prepaids). |
| Restricted | *External*: Legislation, grantor, or creditor requirements must be satisfied. |
| Committed | *Internal*: Highest governing authority establishes limits. |
| Assigned | *Internal*: Intention without formal commitment (designation). |
| Unassigned | No constraint as to use. |

# 4 Net Position and Components Thereof (SE and Government-wide)

Net position is reported in the government-wide and proprietary fund balance sheets and represents net equity (the difference between assets plus deferred outflows and liabilities plus deferred inflows).

## 4.1 Categories of Net Position

Net position must be reported in three categories that focus on the accessibility of the underlying funds.

1. **Net Investment in Capital Assets:** Capital assets reduced by accumulated depreciation and by outstanding debt incurred to acquire, construct, or improve those assets.

    - Net investment includes unamortized original issue discounts or premiums.
    - Associated deferred outflows or inflows related to the capital assets are included in the computation.
    - Debt/obligations must be to parties outside the government (advances from other funds are excluded).
    - A government that has no outstanding capital borrowing will label this portion of net position as "investment in capital assets."
    - Any significant unspent portion of capital-related debt or deferred inflows of resources is excluded from net investment in capital assets and included in restricted net position.

### Pass Key

Capital assets *included* in the calculation of net investment in capital assets include the following:

- Tangible capital assets   (e.g., land, buildings, etc.)
- Intangible capital assets   (e.g., patents, rights, etc.)

Assets *excluded* from the calculation of net investment in capital assets:

- Unspent resources accumulated for capital purposes
- Equity interest in capital assets of joint ventures

2. **Restricted:** Restricted assets and deferred outflows reduced by related liabilities and deferred inflows.
   - Restrictions are externally imposed by creditors, grantors, contributors, or laws and regulations, including those imposed by the government's own constitutional provisions or enabling legislation.
   - No negative restricted amount should be reported. If liabilities exceed related restricted assets, the net negative amount should reduce unrestricted net position.
3. **Unrestricted:** The net amount of the assets plus deferred outflows less liabilities plus deferred inflows that are not included in the determination of net investment in capital assets or restricted net position.
   - Designations of net position representing management's intentions for the use of resources should not be reported on the statement of net position. Designations may be disclosed.

---

**Question 5**                                                                MCQ-06023

General fund resources that are limited as to use by constraints imposed by law through constitutional or enabling legislation would be classified within fund balance as:

   a. Nonspendable.
   b. Restricted.
   c. Committed.
   d. Assigned.

---

**Question 6**                                                                MCQ-06024

The only fund that should show a positive amount in its unassigned fund balance classification would be the:

   a. General fund.
   b. Special revenue fund.
   c. Capital projects fund.
   d. Permanent fund.

## NOTES

# MODULE 5: Governmental Funds Financial Statements: Part 1

FAR 9

## 1 General Fund

| General fund | | Budget: | Book on opposite side as control |
|---|---|---|---|
| Revenue (special) fund | | | Revenue—measurable and available |
| And | Modified accrual | Activity: | Expenditures—all spending |
| Service (debt) fund | | | Assets—expenditured |
| Projects (capital) fund | | | Debts—other financing sources |
| Permanent fund | | Encumbrances: | Commit funds for purchase orders |

The general fund is created at the beginning of the governmental unit, and it exists throughout the life of that unit. The general fund accounts for the general activities of a government that are not accounted for by any other fund.

General fund activities include the administrative and general services of the government.

### 1.1 Revenue Sources

The general fund usually has the largest variety of revenues in a governmental unit. Sources of general fund revenues frequently include all of the earnings types contemplated by governmental reporting models.

- **Taxes**

    General fund revenues in local government often include property taxes as the primary revenue source. Franchise and public service taxes are often recorded in the general fund.

- **Public Safety and Regulation**

    General fund revenues in local government often include fees and fines (police departments, building inspectors, etc., fine individuals for infractions, charge fees for inspections, etc.). General fund revenues also include license and permit revenues (police, fire, or building department licenses for buildings and permits for activities).

- **Intergovernmental**

    Shared or grant revenues from other governments may appear in the general fund.

- **Charges for Services**

    Exchange revenues that support general fund activities may appear in the general fund. The government may elect to use a governmental model instead of proprietary funds for services primarily supported by charges.

- **Other Revenues**

    General fund revenues include investment earnings as well as miscellaneous earnings.

## 1.2 Expenditure Types

The general fund usually has the largest share of expenditures in a governmental unit. Sources of general fund expenditures frequently include most of the current functional expenditure types contemplated by governmental reporting models:

- **General Government**

    General government activities often include the administrative functions of the government, such as the city manager, finance, etc.

- **Public Safety**

    Public safety activities often include the police department, fire department, jail, and building inspections department.

- **Culture and Recreation**

    Culture and recreation activities include parks, libraries, etc.

## 1.3 Unique Accounting Issues

### 1.3.1 Modified Accrual and Budgetary Accounting

The general fund uses the modified accrual basis of accounting, and formally records its budget in its accounting system.

### 1.3.2 Major Fund Status

There is only one general fund per reporting entity and it is always reported as a major fund.

### 1.3.3 Internal Financing

The general fund automatically finances other funds by:

- making a loan (e.g., to a special revenue fund for financing a special assessment).
- making a contribution of equity or revenue (called an "interfund transfer") to a debt service fund or internal service fund.
- making up a deficit in an enterprise fund.

### 1.3.4 Default Classification

The general fund is an operating "catch-all" fund for items not accounted for in other funds, such as:

- major and miscellaneous revenues, and
- major and miscellaneous expenditures.

## 1.4 Financial Statements

The general fund and all other governmental funds produce the following fund financial statements:

- Balance sheet *(Current assets and deferred outflows = Current liabilities and deferred inflows + fund balance)*
- Statement of revenues, expenditures, and changes in fund balance

**Progressive Township**
**Balance Sheet**
**General Fund**
As of December 31, Year 1

| | |
|---|---:|
| **Assets** | |
| Cash | $ 800,000 |
| Receivables | 162,000 |
| Due from other funds | 450,000 |
| Receivables from other governments | 620,000 |
| Inventories | 55,000 |
| **Total assets** | **$ 2,087,000** |
| **Liabilities** | |
| Accounts payable | $ 250,000 |
| Due to other funds | 50,000 |
| Payable to other governments | 65,000 |
| Other liabilities | 95,000 |
| **Total liabilities** | **$ 460,000** |
| **Fund balances** | |
| Nonspendable inventories | $ 55,000 |
| Committed to: | |
|   Sanitation | 45,000 |
| Unassigned: | |
|   General fund | 1,527,000 |
| **Total fund balances** | 1,627,000 |
| **Total liabilities and fund balance** | **$2,087,000** |

**Progressive Township**
**Statement of Revenues, Expenditures, and Changes in Fund Balance**
**General Fund**
For the Year Ended December 31, Year 1

| | |
|---|---:|
| **Revenues** | |
| Property taxes | $1,620,000 |
| Fees and fines | 120,000 |
| Interest earnings | 55,000 |
| Total revenues | $1,795,000 |
| **Expenditures** | |
| Current: | |
| General government | $ 450,000 |
| Public safety | 1,000,000 |
| Culture and recreation | 80,000 |
| Other functional classifications | 200,000 |
| Capital outlay | 25,000 |
| Total expenditures | $1,755,000 |
| Excess (deficiency) of revenues over expenditures | $ 40,000 |
| **Other financing sources (uses)** | |
| Transfers in | $ 85,000 |
| Transfers out | (14,000) |
| Total other financing sources and uses | $ 71,000 |
| **Special item** | |
| Proceeds from sale of land | $ 500,000 |
| Net change in fund balances | 611,000 |
| Fund balances—beginning | 1,016,000 |
| Fund balances—ending | $1,627,000 |

## 2 Special Revenue Fund

| General fund | | Budget: | Book on opposite side as control |
|---|---|---|---|
| **Revenue (special) fund** | | | Revenue—measurable and available |
| And | Modified accrual | Activity: | Expenditures—all spending |
| Service (debt) fund | | | Assets—expenditured |
| Projects (capital) fund | | | Debts—other financing sources |
| Permanent fund | | Encumbrances: | Commit funds for purchase orders |

Special revenue funds account for revenues and expenditures that are legally restricted or committed for specific purposes other than debt service or capital projects. The life of the special revenue fund may be limited or unlimited but resources are expendable.

Examples of special revenue funds include:

- Sales tax fund (e.g., to operate park and tourist facility)
- Gasoline tax fund (e.g., to operate and maintain streets)
- Funds to account for specific fees
    - Special fees (e.g., to operate school programs)
    - Admission fees (e.g., to operate museums)
    - Parking fees (e.g., to operate traffic court)
- Grant funds
    - State grants (state juvenile rehabilitation fund to operate a youth center)
    - Federal grant funds (federal financial assistance programs)

### 2.1 Revenue Sources

Special revenue funds account for revenues legally restricted for specific purposes and are often classified as either intergovernmental revenue or fees. Examples of intergovernmental revenues include specific taxes, shared taxes, and grants.

### 2.2 Expenditure Types

Special revenue fund expenditures include current operating expenditures (e.g., street maintenance) and capital outlays (e.g., highway construction—not special assessments).

### 2.3 Unique Accounting Issues

#### 2.3.1 Expendable Trust Activities

Expendable trust activities (e.g., scholarship and endowment funds) represent funding whose principal and income may be expended in the course of their designated operations so that they are depleted by the end of their designated lives. Expendable trust activity should be accounted for in a special revenue fund.

- **Character of Expenditures:** Expendable trust activities may include capital outlay expenditures, depending on the character of the endowment.

- **Donations:** When a donation is received by an expendable trust, cash or current assets is debited and revenue is credited. Donations may be:
  - Donor/grantor restricted (principal and interest); or
  - Government restricted, such as assets used for illegal activities that are seized and surrendered to the government under various Forfeiture Acts.

### 2.3.2 Grants

When a grant is received, the recipient government monitors and/or determines eligibility. Revenues and expenditures are recognized equally based on payments of the grantor.

> **Pass Key**
>
> The rule of thumb for use of the correct fund is:
> - Monitoring (administrative involvement) = *Special revenue fund*
> - Non-monitoring (no administrative involvement) = *Custodial funds*

## 2.4 Financial Statements

The following financial statement assumes a specific tax (a convention development tax), which is collected and remitted to the government through another government. The sample financial statements assume that revenues recorded in this fund have been pledged to debt payments and are largely transferred out to another fund to support those debt payments.

**Progressive Township**
**Statement of Revenues, Expenditures, and Changes in Fund Balance**
**Convention Development Tax**
For the Year Ended December 31, Year 1

| | |
|---|---:|
| **Revenues** | |
| Intergovernmental | $ 375,000 |
| Interest earnings | 28,000 |
| Total revenues | $ 403,000 |
| **Expenditures** | |
| Current: | |
| Culture and recreation | $ 17,500 |
| Total expenditures | 17,500 |
| Excess (deficiency) of revenues over expenditures | $ 385,500 |
| **Other financing sources (uses)** | |
| Transfers out | $(250,000) |
| Total other financing sources and uses | (250,000) |
| Net change in fund balances | 135,500 |
| Fund balances—beginning | 48,500 |
| Fund balances—ending | $ 184,000 |

# 3 Debt Service Fund

| | | | |
|---|---|---|---|
| General fund | | Budget: | Book on opposite side as control |
| Revenue (special) fund | | Activity: | Revenue—measurable and available |
| And | Modified accrual | | Expenditures—all spending |
| **Service (debt) fund** | | | Assets—expenditured |
| Projects (capital) fund | | | Debts—other financing sources |
| Permanent fund | | Encumbrances: | Not applicable* |

*Fund balance is entirely restricted for debt service.

The debt service fund is created to account for the accumulation of resources (cash and investments) and the payment of currently due interest and principal on long-term general obligation debt (which is generally serial bond debt).

The debt service fund pays off the debt of the GRaSPP funds, but does *not* pay off the debt of the SE-CIPPOE funds.

Examples of debt service funds include:

- Central City Development debt service fund
- Community Redevelopment debt service fund
- Convention Center Development bond debt service fund
- General Revenue bond debt service fund

## 3.1 Revenue and Other Financing Sources

The debt service fund's resources for repayment of new debt are frequently derived from allocated portions of property taxes and transfers from other funds. Proceeds from bond issues to refund (refinance) debt are accounted for in debt service funds as other financing sources.

### Illustration 1 Revenue and Other Financing Source Journal Entries

Assume, independently of all other recorded transactions, that the general fund transferred $10,000 cash to the debt service fund.

*Journal entry to record interfund transfer from the general fund:*

| DR | Cash | $10,000 | |
|---|---|---|---|
| CR | Interfund transfers (from the general fund) | | $10,000 |

(continued)

(continued)

Drawing from the example of the bond issuance for the construction of a new government building described in the next section (the capital projects fund), an $80,000 premium included in the bond proceeds was transferred to the debt service fund as required by the bond indenture.

*Journal entry to record interfund transfer from the capital projects fund:*

| DR | Cash | $80,000 | |
|---|---|---|---|
| CR | Interfund transfers (from the capital projects fund) | | $80,000 |

Interest revenue of $40,000 was transferred from the capital projects fund as required by the bond indenture (see the capital projects example below).

*Journal entry to record interfund transfer from the capital projects fund:*

| DR | Cash | $40,000 | |
|---|---|---|---|
| CR | Interfund transfers (from the capital projects fund) | | $40,000 |

Any income from the investment of resources is recorded as revenue, as follows:

| DR | Cash | $36,000 | |
|---|---|---|---|
| CR | Revenue—investment income | | $36,000 |

### 3.2 Expenditure Types

The debt service fund makes actual expenditures associated with the principal and interest on general obligation long-term debt. When the debt service (debt) payment is legally due, the debt service fund recognizes principal and interest as expenditures. Encumbrance accounts are not used in debt service funds.

---

**Illustration 2   Journalizing Interest Expenditures**

Assume that the semiannual interest payment associated with the bond issue is due ($2,000,000 at 3% × 6/12).

*Journal entry to record payment of interest:*

| DR | Expenditures | $30,000 | |
|---|---|---|---|
| CR | Cash (or matured interest payable if the payment is past due) | | $30,000 |

### Illustration 3 — Journalizing Principal Expenditures

When the face amount of the bonds is due, the debt service fund would make the entry below using the cash that had been transferred from other funds (many times, revenue has been pledged by a special revenue fund for this purpose).

*Journal entry to record the payment of principal on the bonds:*

| DR | Expenditures | $250,000 | |
|---|---|---|---|
| CR | Cash (or matured bonds payable if the payment is past due) | | $250,000 |

Principal and interest expenditures should be recorded when they are legally payable per the bond agreement. There is no profit motive and no need to apply the matching principle, so principal and interest are not accrued during the reporting period.

## 3.3 Unique Accounting Issues

### 3.3.1 Debt Service Fund Requirement

- **Legal Mandate**

  Debt service funds are required only when legally mandated and/or when resources are being accumulated for general long-term debt principal and interest payments maturing in future years.

- **Repayment of Other Governmental Debt**

  The general fund may pay interest and principal directly to the bondholders instead of directly to the debt service fund, unless the use of a debt service fund is mandated. The general fund may incur long-term debt under lease obligations that are either contracts that transfer ownership or leases other than short-term leases and contracts that transfer ownership (e.g., for copiers at city hall) and fully account for the principal and interest payments on that debt.

### 3.3.2 Asset Balances

The operations of this fund are similar to a commercial accounting "sinking fund," which buys investments, earns interest, and eventually pays off the debt with accumulated investments.

### 3.3.3 Debt Balances

The full face value (less current installments) of the general obligation debt is not reported in this fund. Debt service fund expenditures are only used to pay currently payable principal and interest (matured bonds/interest payable).

The balance and interest payable in the debt service fund represent currently due installments only reported in the liabilities sections as matured bonds payable and matured interest payable.

## City of M
### Debt Service Fund: Balance Sheet
As of December 31, Year 3

**Assets**
| | |
|---|---|
| Cash and cash equivalents | $XXX |
| Due from capital projects and other funds | XXX |
| Investments | XXX |
| Interest receivables on investments | XXX |
| Total assets | $XXX |

**Liabilities**
| | |
|---|---|
| Matured bonds payable | $XXX |
| Matured interest payable | XXX |
| Total liabilities | $XXX |

**Fund balance**
| | |
|---|---|
| Restricted debt service retirement | XXX |
| Total liabilities and fund balance | $XXX |

**Note:** There are no unrestricted fund balance accounts in the debt service fund.

### 3.3.4 Closing Entries

The debt service fund closing journal entry illustrated below assumes a budget with estimated revenues of $36,000, appropriations of $30,000, and a fund balance of $6,000 established at the beginning of the year. This entry is similar to that of the general fund shown previously except that there are no encumbrances.

- **Budget Is Closed at Year-End:** *Journal entry to close the budget (reverse for same amount):*

| | | | |
|---|---|---|---|
| DR | Budgetary control | $ 6,000 | |
| DR | Appropriations control | 30,000 | |
| CR | Estimated revenues control | | $36,000 |

- **Activity Is Closed at Year-End:** *Journal entry to close activity for the actual amount:*

| | | | |
|---|---|---|---|
| DR | Interfund transfers from the capital projects fund | $ 80,000 | |
| DR | Interfund transfers from the special revenue fund | 250,000 | |
| DR | Interfund transfers from the capital projects fund | 40,000 | |
| DR | Other revenues | 36,000 | |
| CR | Fund balance, restricted for debt service | | $126,000 |
| CR | Expenditures—interest | | 30,000 |
| CR | Expenditures—principal | | 250,000 |

- **Encumbrances:** Encumbrances are *not applicable* and are therefore not closed at year-end.

### 3.3.5 Composition of Fund Balance

Bond issue proceeds and transfers are temporary or nominal accounts that are closed to fund balance at year-end, consistent with other accounts reported in the funds operating statement. The fund balance consists of:

| | |
|---|---:|
| Beginning restricted fund balance | $ 439,000 |
| Revenue | 36,000 |
| Expenditures—*interest* | (30,000) |
| Expenditures—*principal* | (250,000) |
| Subtotal | 195,000 |
| Interfund transfer from capital projects fund—*bond premium* | 80,000 |
| Interfund transfer from special revenue fund | 250,000 |
| Interfund transfer from capital projects fund—*interest income* | 40,000 |
| Ending restricted fund balance | $ 565,000 |

## 3.4 Financial Statements

### 3.4.1 Balance Sheet

The balance sheet displays the assets accumulated for the repayment of convention center bonds payable from convention development taxes recorded in the special revenue fund illustrated above. No currently payable debt is displayed.

**Progressive Township**
**Balance Sheet**
**Convention Center Bonds**
As of December 31, Year 1

| | |
|---|---:|
| **Assets** | |
| Cash | $505,000 |
| Receivables | 125,000 |
| Due from other funds | 60,000 |
| Total assets | $690,000 |
| **Liabilities** | |
| Accounts payable | – |
| Total liabilities | – |
| **Deferred Inflows Of Resources** | |
| Unavailable revenues—special assessments | 125,000 |
| Total deferred inflows of resources | $125,000 |
| **Fund Balances** | |
| Restricted for: | |
| Debt service | $565,000 |
| Total fund balances | 565,000 |
| Total liabilities, deferred inflows of resources, and fund balances | $690,000 |

# Governmental Funds Financial Statements: Part 1

## 3.4.2 Statement of Revenues, Expenditures, and Changes in Fund Balance

The statement of revenues, expenditures, and changes in fund balance for a debt service fund typically includes investment income, expenditures for debt service and transfers from other funds to support debt service obligations.

**Progressive Township**
**Statement of Revenues, Expenditures, and Changes in Fund Balance**
**Convention Center Bonds**
For the Year Ended December 31, Year 1

| | |
|---|---:|
| **Revenues** | |
| Interest earnings | $ 36,000 |
| Total revenues | 36,000 |
| **Expenditures** | |
| Debt service: | |
| Principal | $ 250,000 |
| Interest and other charges | 30,000 |
| Total expenditures | 280,000 |
| Excess (deficiency) of revenues over expenditures | $(244,000) |
| **Other financing sources (uses)** | |
| Transfers in | $ 370,000 |
| Total other financing sources and uses | 370,000 |
| Net change in fund balances | 126,000 |
| Fund balances—beginning | 439,000 |
| Fund balances—ending | $ 565,000 |

---

### Question 1   MCQ-06615

Brandon County's general fund had the following transactions during the year:

| | |
|---|---|
| Transfer to a debt service fund | $100,000 |
| Payment to a pension trust fund | 500,000 |
| Purchase of equipment | 300,000 |

What amount should Brandon County report for the general fund as other financing uses in its governmental funds statement of revenues, expenditures, and changes in fund balances?

    a. $100,000
    b. $400,000
    c. $800,000
    d. $900,000

## Question 2 — MCQ-01013

Central County received proceeds from various towns and cities for capital projects financed by the county's long-term debt. A special tax was assessed by each local government, and a portion of the tax was properly restricted to repay the long-term debt of the county's capital projects. Central County should account for the restricted portion of the special tax in which of the following funds?

   a. Internal service fund
   b. Enterprise fund
   c. Capital projects fund
   d. Debt service fund

## Question 3 — MCQ-01000

The debt service fund of a governmental unit is used to account for the accumulation of resources for, and the payment of, principal and interest in connection with a:

|    | Fiduciary Fund | Proprietary Fund |
|----|----------------|------------------|
| a. | No             | No               |
| b. | No             | Yes              |
| c. | Yes            | Yes              |
| d. | Yes            | No               |

## Question 4 — MCQ-04665

On January 2, the city of Walton issued $500,000, 10-year, 7 percent general obligation bonds. Interest is payable annually, beginning January 2 of the following year. What amount of bond interest is Walton required to report in the statement of revenues, expenditures, and changes in fund balance of its governmental funds at the close of this fiscal year, September 30?

   a. $0
   b. $17,500
   c. $26,250
   d. $35,000

## NOTES

# MODULE 6: Governmental Funds Financial Statements: Part 2

FAR 9

# 1 Capital Projects Fund

| | | Budget: | Book on opposite side as control |
|---|---|---|---|
| General fund<br>Revenue (special) fund<br>And<br>Service (debt) fund<br>**Projects (capital) fund**<br>Permanent fund | Modified accrual | Activity: | Revenue—measurable and available<br>Expenditures—all spending<br>Assets—expenditured<br>Debts—other financing sources |
| | | Encumbrances: | Commit funds for purchase orders |

Capital projects funds are established for the construction, purchase, or leasing of significant fixed assets [used by governmental funds (GRaSPP) only, not by proprietary or fiduciary fund (SE-CIPPOE)]. The life of the capital projects fund is short and is limited to a construction period of one to three years.

Examples of capital projects funds include:

- Convention center construction fund
- Municipal stadium construction fund
- County courthouse construction fund
- Construction fund accounting for a special assessment project (such as streets and street lights benefiting only those certain property owners who will pay for them)

## 1.1 Revenue and Other Financing Sources

Capital projects funds are generally funded by bond proceeds that are to be used to complete a particular project. The project may also be purely funded by a transfer from another fund, specific tax revenues or capital grants. Investment earnings may also appear in this fund, although the disposition of those earnings may be either to retain them in the fund for the benefit of the project or to immediately transfer them to a debt service fund for the benefit of the bondholders.

### 1.1.1 Investment Earnings

Unexpended capital project resources are typically invested. Earnings recorded in the fund are then handled in a manner prescribed by law.

### 1.1.2 Tax Revenue

Tax revenue specifically identified for construction would be classified as tax revenue of a capital projects fund and recorded in a manner identical to tax revenue in the general fund.

# Governmental Funds Financial Statements: Part 2

### 1.1.3 Capital Grants

Capital grants received in advance are often recorded as a liability and displayed as earned as they are expended (assuming no time restrictions). Government grants may be restricted and are reported as "revenue" when earned (e.g., grant money expended by recipient fund), or may be unrestricted, and recognized immediately.

*Journal entry to record unrestricted government grant:*

| DR | Cash | $XXX | |
|---|---|---|---|
| CR | Revenue | | $XXX |

*Journal entry to record restricted government grants (revenue when spent):*

| DR | Cash | $XXX | |
|---|---|---|---|
| CR | Revenue collected in advance | | $XXX |

*Journal entries to recognize revenue restricted (when spent) by a cost reimbursement contract:*

| DR | Expenditure | $XXX | |
|---|---|---|---|
| CR | Vouchers payable/cash | | $XXX |

*And:*

| DR | Revenue collected in advance | $XXX | |
|---|---|---|---|
| CR | Revenue | | $XXX |

### 1.1.4 General Fund (or Special Revenue Fund) Interfund Transfers

*Journal entry to record a general or a special revenue fund interfund transfer:*

| DR | Cash (or due from "other" fund) | $XXX | |
|---|---|---|---|
| CR | Interfund transfers | | $XXX |

### 1.1.5 Special Assessments

Special assessments are defined as taxes or fees levied against property owners who will directly benefit from the project (e.g., sidewalks and street lights). Accounting for special assessment transactions depends on the degree to which the governmental unit is responsible—or potentially liable for—debt often associated with the assessment.

- **Primarily or Potentially Liable**

    When the governmental unit is primarily or potentially liable for the special assessment debt, the governmental unit should:

    - Account for the capital project and debt-related transactions through the appropriate governmental or proprietary fund.

    - When accounted for in a governmental fund, debt proceeds associated with special assessments for which the governmental unit is either primarily or potentially liable should be classified as "contribution from property owners" on the operating statement to distinguish it from bond proceeds.

    - Assets and liabilities should be reported in the government-wide financial statements under the governmental or business-type activities column as appropriate.

- Special assessment revenues, although technically a tax assessment, are displayed as program revenue on the government-wide financial statements because they specifically defray a particular cost.

■ **Not Primarily or Potentially Liable**

When the governmental unit is *not* primarily or potentially liable and associated revenues do not qualify as revenues of the government (described in more detail in the presentation of fiduciary funds):

- transactions should be reported in a custodial fund; and
- assets and liabilities should be excluded from government-wide presentations.

> **Pass Key**
>
> When the governmental unit is not liable, a custodial fund will account for special assessments.

### 1.1.6 Bond Issue Proceeds

The amount of net bond issue proceeds is presented on the *statement of revenues, expenditures, and changes in fund balances* as "other financing sources."

■ **Bond Premium or Discount**

Premiums and discounts associated with bond proceeds are included in other financing sources and uses and receive no additional accounting after the year in which they are received. There is no amortization of premiums and discounts.

- Bond par value is separately displayed as bond proceeds (sources).
- Bond premiums, if applicable, are separately displayed as a financing source.
- Bond discounts, if applicable, are separately displayed as a financing use.
- Other bond issue costs (bond costs, underwriting fees, etc.) are displayed as debt service expenditures when they are incurred.

■ **Reconciling Items**

The treatment of bond issue proceeds as a resource inflow on fund financial statements (by virtue of using a measurement focus that does not recognize non-current items) creates reconciling items between the governmental fund and the government-wide financial statements.

## Illustration 1  Capital Projects Fund Journal Entries

Assume that a bond issue for $2,000,000 was authorized to build a new convention center (a general government building). The bond was issued for $2,080,000. Assume that the government has been directed to use the premium for the protection of the bondholders.

*Journal entry to record the bond proceeds in the capital projects fund:*

| | | | |
|---|---|---|---|
| DR | Cash | $2,080,000 | |
| CR | Other financing sources—bond issue proceeds | | $2,000,000 |
| CR | Other financing sources—premium on bonds | | 80,000 |

If the sale of the bonds resulted in a premium, as above, the amount of the premium is immediately transferred to the debt service fund, which is used to account for interest and principal payments on the bonds.

*Journal entry to transfer the bond issue premium to the debt service fund:*

| | | | |
|---|---|---|---|
| DR | Interfund transfer (to debt service) | $80,000 | |
| CR | Cash | | $80,000 |

**Note:** If the bonds had been sold at a discount, either the project would have to be reduced by the amount of the discount or the funding shortfall could be transferred in from another source.

If the project is delayed, the proceeds from the bond issue may be invested. Assume that the $2,000,000 is invested in a CD that earned $40,000. The earnings are usually transferred to the debt service fund.

*Journal entry to record investment in the CD:*

| | | | |
|---|---|---|---|
| DR | Investment in CD | $2,000,000 | |
| CR | Cash | | $2,000,000 |

*Journal entry to record interest revenue earned on the investment:*

| | | | |
|---|---|---|---|
| DR | Cash | $40,000 | |
| CR | Revenue—interest income | | $40,000 |

*Journal entry to record the transfer to the debt service fund:*

| | | | |
|---|---|---|---|
| DR | Interfund transfer (to the debt service fund) | $40,000 | |
| CR | Cash | | $40,000 |

The debt service fund would record entries for receipt of this money.

Had the cost of the building been less than the amount provided, the balance would remain in the capital projects fund until proper authorization was enacted for its disposition. On the other hand, if the bond proceeds were completely exhausted before completion of the building, construction would have to cease until new appropriations could be authorized.

## 1.2 Expenditure and Encumbrance Types

Capital projects fund expenditures are usually entirely classified as capital outlay, one of the major character classifications (e.g., current, capital outlay, debt service, etc.). During construction, encumbrances are recorded as commitments are incurred. Vouchers are recorded when a liability is incurred and the expenditure is known. As vouchers are recorded, the encumbrance entry is reversed. Cash is credited and vouchers payable is debited as payments are made.

### Illustration 2    Capital Projects Fund Journal Entries

*Journal entry to record several contracts signed for construction:*

| | | | |
|---|---|---|---|
| DR | Encumbrances | $1,100,000 | |
| CR | Budgetary control | | $1,100,000 |

*Journal entries for one completed contract approved for payment.*

To reverse the encumbrance for the same amount:

| | | | |
|---|---|---|---|
| DR | Budgetary control | $600,000 | |
| CR | Encumbrances | | $600,000 |

To record purchased/constructed assets:

| | | | |
|---|---|---|---|
| DR | Expenditures | $600,000 | |
| CR | Vouchers payable (or cash) | | $600,000 |

### Pass Key

Journal entry amount to report fixed assets in government-wide financial statements:

| Manner Acquired | Amount Recorded |
|---|---|
| Purchase | Cost to buy |
| Construction | Cost to construct |
| Lease obligations structured as contracts that transfer ownership | P.V. lease payments |
| Donated | FV |
| Forfeiture | Lower of cost (to acquire) or market |

## 1.3 Unique Accounting Issues

### 1.3.1 Asset Balances

The cumulative balance of the value of the constructed asset (inception to date construction in progress) is not displayed on the capital projects fund balance sheet.

### 1.3.2 Liability Balances

- **Bond Liability**

    Under the modified accrual basis of accounting, the bond liability is not recorded in the fund financial statements of the capital projects fund. The debt service fund is used to account for the accumulation of resources and the payment of currently due interest and principal on bonds related to capital projects funds.

- **Short-Term Borrowing (Other Financing Sources or Current Liabilities)**

    Short-term borrowing might be necessary to start a project before either bond proceeds or other revenues are received. Often these borrowings are "bond anticipated notes" issued with the expectation that they will be repaid upon issuance of permanent long-term financing (bonds). Bond anticipation notes are generally accounted for as other financing sources, similar to the long-term debt that will replace it.

    *Journal entry to record the short-term borrowing to be refinanced with long-term debt:*

    | | | | |
    |---|---|---|---|
    | DR | Cash | $XXX | |
    | CR | Other financing sources—debt proceeds | | $XXX |

    Short-term financing to be repaid with taxes (tax anticipation notes, or TAN) or other revenues (revenue anticipation notes, or RAN) should be recorded as a current liability:

    *Journal entry to record short-term borrowing to be repaid with revenue:*

    | | | | |
    |---|---|---|---|
    | DR | Cash | $XXX | |
    | CR | Tax or revenue anticipation note payable | | $XXX |

### 1.3.3 Closing Entries

At the end of the period, three closing entries are required in the capital projects fund. Assume that the budget was $2,000,000, expended encumbrances were $500,000, and expenditures were $600,000 to illustrate year-end closings.

- **Budget Is Closed at Year-End**

    *Journal entry to close the budget (reverse for same amount):*

    | | | | |
    |---|---|---|---|
    | DR | Appropriations | $2,000,000 | |
    | CR | Estimated other financing sources | | $2,000,000 |

- **Actual Activity Is Closed at Year-End**

    *Journal entry to close activity (for the actual amount):*

    | | | | |
    |---|---|---|---|
    | DR | Other financing sources—bond issue proceeds | $2,000,000 | |
    | DR | Investment revenue | 40,000 | |
    | DR | Other financing sources—bond premium | 80,000 | |
    | CR | Expenditures | | $ 600,000 |
    | CR | Interfund transfers (to debt service, investment revenue) | | 40,000 |
    | CR | Interfund transfer (to debt service, bond premium) | | 80,000 |
    | CR | Fund balance, restricted | | 1,400,000 |

- **Encumbrances Are Closed at Year-End**

    *Journal entry to close/reverse encumbrances for the same amount:*

    | | | | |
    |---|---|---|---|
    | DR | Budgetary control | $500,000 | |
    | CR | Encumbrances | | $500,000 |

    Outstanding encumbrances at year-end should be carried forward as a component of fund balance. The entire amount of the capital projects fund is presumed to be restricted for capital outlay. Progressive Township would disclose the $500,000 encumbrance as a budgetary obligation of resources restricted for capital projects but would not show the encumbrance on the face of the financial statements or downgrade the constraint associated with the encumbrance from restricted to committed.

### 1.3.4 Composition of Restricted Fund Balance

Note that the restricted fund balance consists of:

| | |
|---|---:|
| Beginning fund balance, restricted | $ 100,000 |
| Proceeds from the bond issue | 2,080,000 |
| Interest income | 40,000 |
| Expenditures | (600,000) |
| Interfund transfer to debt service | (120,000) |
| Ending fund balance, restricted | $1,500,000 |

## 1.4 Financial Statements

The financial statements for the capital projects fund are similar to those already shown for the general fund. Accounts used by individual funds may differ. Some of the common capital projects accounts appear below.

**Progressive Township**
**Balance Sheet**
**Convention Center Construction**
As of December 31, Year 1

| | |
|---|---:|
| **Assets** | |
| Cash | $ 2,100,000 |
| **Total assets** | 2,100,000 |
| **Liabilities** | |
| Accounts payable | $ 600,000 |
| **Total liabilities** | 600,000 |
| **Fund balances** | |
| Restricted for: | |
| Capital projects | 1,500,000 |
| **Total fund balances** | 1,500,000 |
| **Total liabilities and fund balance** | $2,100,000 |

**Progressive Township**
**Statement of Revenues, Expenditures, and Changes in Fund Balance**
**Convention Center Construction**
For the Year Ended December 31, Year 1

| | |
|---|---:|
| **Revenues** | |
| Interest earnings | $ 40,000 |
| Total revenues | 40,000 |
| **Expenditures** | |
| Capital outlay | $ 600,000 |
| Total expenditures | 600,000 |
| Excess (deficiency) of revenues over expenditures | $ (560,000) |
| **Other financing sources (uses)** | |
| Proceeds of long-term capital-related debt | $2,080,000 |
| Transfers out | (120,000) |
| Total other financing sources and uses | 1,960,000 |
| Net change in fund balances | 1,400,000 |
| Fund balances—beginning | 100,000 |
| Fund balances—ending | $1,500,000 |

## Pass Key

The previous discussion described the accounting that Progressive Township would use to pledge tax revenues to the payment of debt service relative to bonds whose proceeds were used for the construction of a convention center. The following condensed financial statements show the relationship between the special revenue, debt service, and capital projects funds.

**Progressive Township**
**Selected Statements of Revenues, Expenditures, and Changes in Fund Balance**
**Convention Center Funding, Debt and Construction**
For the Year Ended December 31, Year 1

|  | Convention Development Tax | Convention Center Bonds | Convention Center Construction | Total Governmental Funds |
|---|---|---|---|---|
| **Revenues** | | | | |
| Property taxes | – | – | – | – |
| Fees and fines | – | – | – | – |
| Intergovernmental | $375,000 | – | – | $ 375,000 |
| Charges for services | – | – | – | – |
| Interest earnings | 28,000 | $ 36,000 | $ 40,000 | 104,000 |
| Total revenues | 403,000 | 36,000 | 40,000 | 479,000 |
| **Expenditures** | | | | |
| Current: | | | | |
| General government | – | – | – | – |
| Public safety | – | – | – | – |
| Culture and recreation | 17,500 | – | – | 17,500 |
| Other functional classifications | – | – | – | – |
| Debt service: | | | | |
| Principal | – | 250,000 | – | 250,000 |
| Interest and other charges | – | 30,000 | – | 30,000 |
| Capital outlay | – | – | 600,000 | 600,000 |
| Total expenditures | 17,500 | 280,000 | 600,000 | 897,500 |
| Excess (deficiency) of revenues over expenditures | 385,500 | (244,000) | (560,000) | (418,500) |
| **Other financing sources (uses)** | | | | |
| Proceeds of long-term capital-related debt | – | – | 2,080,000 | 2,080,000 |
| Transfers in | – | 370,000 | – | 370,000 |
| Transfers out | (250,000) | – | (120,000) | (370,000) |
| Total other financing sources and uses | (250,000) | 370,000 | 1,960,000 | 2,080,000 |
| Net change in fund balances | 135,500 | 126,000 | 1,400,000 | 1,661,500 |
| Fund balances—beginning | 48,500 | 439,000 | 100,000 | 587,500 |
| Fund balances—ending | $ 184,000 | $ 565,000 | $1,500,000 | $2,249,000 |

Examiners have frequently asked candidates not only about the journal entries related to multiple funds involved in a single initiative, but also about the manner in which those same transactions are displayed in the funds involved. Note the *Special Revenue Fund* has operating expenditures, the *Debt Service Fund* has debt service expenditures, and the *Capital Projects Fund* has capital outlay expenditures. Note also that other financing sources and uses include debt proceeds and transfers and that, among these various funds associated with this event, transfers in and out are equal.

# 2 Permanent Funds

| General fund<br>Revenue (special) fund<br>And<br>Service (debt) fund<br>Projects (capital) fund<br>**Permanent fund** | Modified accrual | Budget: | Book on opposite side as control |
|---|---|---|---|
| | | Activity: | Revenue—measurable and available<br>Expenditures—all spending<br>Assets—expenditured<br>Debts—other financing sources |
| | | Encumbrances: | Not applicable |

Permanent funds should be used to report resources that are legally restricted to the extent that only earnings, and not principal, may be used for the purposes that support the reporting government's programs (i.e., that is for the benefit of the public).

A public cemetery perpetual-care fund is an example of a permanent fund. These funds are the equivalent of nonexpendable trusts and may also be used for endowments that are governed by a formal trust agreement with the donor.

## 2.1 Revenue Sources

Revenues may include investment earnings from the trust.

## 2.2 Expenditure Types

Expenditures related to the operating purpose of the fund (e.g., cemetery maintenance).

### Pass Key

Two of the governmental funds (GRaSPP) do not record encumbrances:
- Debt service fund
- Permanent fund

### Pass Key

The easy way to determine where public-restricted funds are recorded is:

| Fund | Available for Public Spending |
|---|---|
| Special revenue fund | Principal and interest |
| Permanent fund | Interest only |

## Question 1　MCQ-05190

A capital projects fund for a new city courthouse recorded a receivable of $300,000 for a state grant and a $450,000 transfer from the general fund. What amount should be reported as revenue by the capital projects fund?

- a. $0
- b. $300,000
- c. $450,000
- d. $750,000

## Question 2　MCQ-00906

Japes City issued $1,000,000 general obligation bonds at 101 to build a new city hall. As part of the bond issue, the city also paid a $500 underwriter fee and $2,000 in debt issue costs. What amount should Japes City report as other financing sources?

- a. $1,010,000
- b. $1,008,000
- c. $1,007,500
- d. $1,000,000

## Question 3　MCQ-05663

Tang City received land from a donor who stipulated that the land must remain intact, but any income generated from the property may be used for general government services. In which fund should Tang City record the donated land?

- a. Special revenue
- b. Permanent
- c. Private-purpose trust
- d. Custodial

## NOTES

# State and Local Governments: Part 2

## Module

| | | |
|---|---|---|
| 1 | Proprietary Funds Financial Statements | 3 |
| 2 | Fiduciary Funds Financial Statements | 15 |
| 3 | Form and Content of the Comprehensive Annual Financial Report | 33 |
| 4 | Government-wide Financial Statements | 41 |
| 5 | Fund Financial Statements | 51 |
| 6 | Deriving Government-wide Financial Statements and Reconciliation Requirements | 65 |
| 7 | Notes and Supplementary Information | 83 |

FAR
10

# NOTES

# MODULE 1: Proprietary Funds Financial Statements

FAR 10

## 1 Internal Service Fund

- **Service (internal) fund** — Full accrual
- Enterprise fund
- Custodial
- Investment trust
- Private purpose trust
- Pension and other employee benefit trust

- Balance sheet—*statement of net position*
- Income statement—*statement of revenues, expenses, and changes in net position*
- Statement of cash flows
- Footnotes

Internal service funds are established to finance and account for services and supplies provided exclusively to other departments within a government unit or to other governmental units, typically on a cost-reimbursement basis.

Examples of internal service funds include:

- Central janitorial departments
- Central garages and motor pools
- Central printing and duplicating services
- Central purchasing and storage departments
- Central repair shops
- Central computer processing department
- Self-insurance

### 1.1 Revenue Sources

#### 1.1.1 Restricted Grant Revenues

*Restricted grant revenues,* if any, would be recognized as revenues in the year monies are spent.

#### 1.1.2 Operating Revenues

*Operating revenues,* or billings for services provided, are recognized when earned.

*Journal entry to record billings for services rendered to other funds:*

| DR | Cash (or due from other fund) | $XXX | |
|---|---|---|---|
| CR | Billings to other departments (operating revenue) | | $XXX |

> **Pass Key**
>
> Even though billing and collection for services is between funds, the transaction is not treated as an interfund transfer. The internal service fund records revenues, and the fund paying for services records an expenditure or expense in an equal amount.

#### 1.1.3 Nonoperating Revenues

*Nonoperating revenues,* such as interest earnings, are segregated from operating revenues for financial statement display.

### 1.2 Expense Types

#### 1.2.1 Operating Expenses

Normal and customary operating expenses related to the delivery of services appear in the internal service funds.

#### 1.2.2 Nonoperating Expenses

*Nonoperating expenses,* such as interest expense, are segregated from operating expenses for financial statement display.

### 1.3 Unique Accounting Issues

#### 1.3.1 Establishing an Internal Service Fund

- Internal service funds may be established by contributions from other funds or interfund transfers from other funds, such as the general fund or an enterprise fund.

  *Journal entry to record interfund transfer (a nonreciprocal transfer):*

  | | | | |
  |---|---|---|---|
  | DR | Cash | $XXX | |
  | CR | Interfund transfer | | $XXX |

  *Journal entry to record contribution of assets to a new internal service fund from the general fund.*

  | | | | |
  |---|---|---|---|
  | DR | Capital assets | $XXX | |
  | CR | Contribution | | $XXX |

- Sale of "general obligation bonds," or (most likely) lease obligations representing contracts that transfer ownership.

  *Journal entry to record the sale of general obligation bonds:*

  | | | | |
  |---|---|---|---|
  | DR | Cash | $XXX | |
  | CR | Long-term bond payable | | $XXX |

- Long-term advances from other funds to be repaid from the earnings to the service (revolving) fund.

*Journal entry to record a long-term payable to another fund:*

| DR | Cash | $XXX | |
|---|---|---|---|
| CR | Due to other fund | | $XXX |

## 1.4 Financial Statements

### 1.4.1 Statement of Net Position

The following is an example of the *statement of net position* provided to emphasize the presentation of non-current items in proprietary fund financial statements. Internal service funds also require presentation of a *statement of revenues, expenses, and changes in net position*, as well as a *statement of cash flows*.

**Progressive Township**
**Statement of Net Position**
**Central Reproduction**
As of December 31, Year 1

**Assets**

| | |
|---|---:|
| Current assets: | |
| Cash | $ 50,000 |
| Receivables | 25,000 |
| Due from other funds | 50,000 |
| Due from other governments | – |
| Inventories | 35,000 |
| Total current assets | 160,000 |
| Non-current assets: | |
| Restricted cash and cash equivalents | – |
| Capital assets: | |
| Land | 50,000 |
| Buildings and equipment | 150,000 |
| Less: accumulated depreciation | (40,000) |
| Total non-current assets | 160,000 |
| **Total assets** | 320,000 |

(continued)

(continued)

**Liabilities**

| | |
|---|---:|
| Current liabilities: | |
|   Accounts payable | 13,000 |
|   Due to other funds | – |
|   Compensated absences | 16,000 |
|   Claims and judgments | – |
|   Bonds, notes, and loans payable | 30,000 |
|     Total current liabilities | 59,000 |
| Non-current liabilities: | |
|   Compensated absences | 28,000 |
|   Claims and judgments | – |
|   Bonds, notes, and loans payable | 70,000 |
|     Total non-current liabilities | 98,000 |
| **Total liabilities** | 157,000 |
| **Net Position** | |
|   Net investment in capital assets | 60,000 |
|   Restricted for debt services | – |
|   Unrestricted | 103,000 |
| **Total net position** | **$163,000** |

### 1.4.2 Reconciling Item

Internal service funds are frequently combined with governmental funds for purposes of displaying governmental activities in the government-wide financial statements, because they are often set up to primarily service the governmental funds of the government. Internal service fund net position and changes in net position are used as reconciling items between the total governmental funds and the government-wide financial statements.

# 2 Enterprise Fund

> Service (internal) fund
> **Enterprise fund**
> Custodial
> Investment trust
> Private purpose trust
> Pension and other employee benefit trust
>
> } Full accrual
>
> Balance sheet—*Statement of net position*
> Income statement—*Statement of revenues, expenses, and changes in net position*
> Statement of cash flows
> Footnotes

*Enterprise funds* are used to account for operations that are financed and operated in a manner similar to private business enterprise. Activities are required to be reported as enterprise funds if any one of the following criteria are met:

- The activity is financed with debt that is secured solely by a pledge of the net revenue from fees and charges.
- Laws and regulations require that the cost of providing services be recovered through fees.
- The pricing policies of the activity establish fees and charges designed to recover its costs.

Examples of enterprise funds include:

- Public utilities (water companies and electric companies)
- Public hospitals (although governmental models may also be used)
- Public universities (although governmental models may also be used)
- Other commercial activities, such as:
  - Public transportation systems
  - Airports
  - Public benefit corporations (e.g., a financing authority that makes publicly funded or regulated loans to promote development of public resources, such as low-cost housing, etc.)
  - Dock and wharf facilities
  - Off-street parking lots and garages
  - Public housing
  - Golf courses and swimming pools
  - Lotteries

## 2.1 Revenue Sources

Revenues for enterprise (and all proprietary funds) must be presented by a major source and distinguished between operating and nonoperating. Classification of transactions as operating or not should be consistent with transaction classification in the *statement of cash flows*.

### 2.1.1 Operating Revenues

*Operating revenues* (and operating expenses) are defined by the main purposes of the fund. Examples of operating revenues include:

- Charges for services, such as the water and sewer billings of a public utility or the greens fees of a golf course
- Miscellaneous operating revenues

### 2.1.2 Nonoperating Revenues

*Nonoperating revenues* are earnings or non-exchange transactions (such as taxes and certain fees and charges) and interest.

- **Shared Revenues**

    Shared revenues are revenues (e.g., from gasoline or sales taxes) collected by one government (e.g., state) and shared on a predetermined basis with another (e.g., local) government. They are nonoperating revenues of the enterprise fund.

## 2.2 Expense Types

### 2.2.1 Operating Expenses

*Operating expenses* are generally classified by object, to include such major categories as *personal services, utilities,* and *depreciation*.

### 2.2.2 Nonoperating Expenses

*Nonoperating expenses* most commonly include interest expense.

## 2.3 Unique Accounting Issues

### 2.3.1 Reporting on the Statement of Revenues, Expenses, and Changes in Net Position

- **Revenue Valuation**

    Revenues are reported either net of discounts and allowance with appropriate disclosure of allowance amounts or reported gross with related discount or allowance amounts reported on the face of the financial statement. Bad debt expense is not recognized.

- **Contributed Capital**

    Resources from capital contributions or additions to endowments are displayed separately after nonoperating revenues and expenses. Contributed capital often arises from contribution of capital assets from governmental funds to proprietary funds. Contributed capital is not shown on the face of the balance sheet.

- **Special and Extraordinary Items**

    Special and extraordinary items are reported separately after nonoperating revenues and expenses (extraordinary items are a recognized reporting category in governmental financial statements).

- **Transfers**

    Interfund transfers are displayed after contributions and special and extraordinary items.

## Pass Key

In case you forget the order of presentation of line items on a proprietary fund *statement of revenues, expenses, and changes in fund net position*, remember **INCASET** and you'll be *encased* in knowledge:

**Income** (operating)

**Nonoperating** income and expense

**Capital** contributions and

**Additions** to endowments

**Special** items (unusual or infrequent)

**Extraordinary** items

**Transfers**

### 2.3.2 Establishing an Enterprise Fund

- **Capital Contributions**

    Capital assets contributed to proprietary funds by governmental funds are recorded as *capital contributions*. Capital contributions will be reported as a separate category reported below the nonoperating revenue and expense section of the operating statement. Capital contributions are not identified as a separate component of net position. Capital contributions are not classified as transfers.

    *Journal entry to record contributions (nonreciprocal interfund activity):*

    | DR | Capital assets | $XXX | |
    |---|---|---|---|
    | CR | Capital contributions | | $XXX |

    Equity transfers from other funds (e.g., transfers of financial assets recognized on the balance sheet of the contributing fund) would be recorded as interfund transfers.

- **Long-Term Debt (or Other Long-Term Financing Agreement, Such as a Lease Contract That Transfers Ownership)**

    The enterprise fund will carry long-term debt, which is backed by the proprietary fund or paid with revenues.

    *Journal entry to issue of "general obligation bond" to be paid from proprietary fund revenues:*

    | DR | Cash | $XXX | |
    |---|---|---|---|
    | CR | Long-term bonds payable | | $XXX |

### 2.3.3 Municipal Landfills (the Dump)

Municipal landfill accounting is governed by *Accounting for Municipal Solid Waste Landfill Closure (MSWLF) and Postclosure Care Costs* (GASB 18).

GASB 18 refers to Environmental Protection Agency (EPA) rules and establishes standards of accounting and reporting for MSWLF closure and postclosure costs required to be incurred by federal, state, or local laws or regulations as a condition for the right to operate in the current period.

- **Reporting and Disclosure:** The estimated total current cost of MSWLF closure and postclosure care should be disclosed as "estimated total current cost of MSWLF closure and postclosure care to be recognized," regardless of their capital or operating nature or the effective date of the regulations requiring the care.
- **Cost Components:** The estimated total current cost of MSWLF closure and postclosure care, based on applicable federal state or local laws or regulations, should include the:
  - Cost of equipment expected to be installed and facilities expected to be constructed near or after the date that the MSWLF stops accepting solid waste and during the postclosure period. This equipment should be limited to items that, once installed or constructed, will be exclusively used for the MSWLF.
  - Cost of a gas monitoring and collection system.
  - Cost of final cover (capping) expected to be applied near or after the date that the MSWLF stops accepting solid waste.
  - This estimate should be adjusted annually. Under proprietary fund reporting, a portion of this estimated cost is recognized as an expense and as a liability, based on usage, each period the MSWLF is operating. All costs are recognized as of the date of closure.
- **Equipment Purchases:** Purchases of equipment anticipated by the liability accrual reduce the liability and do not increase assets.

## 2.4 Financial Statements

### 2.4.1 Statement of Net Position

**Progressive Township**
**Statement of Net Position**
**Water and Sewer Fund**
As of December 31, Year 1

| Assets | |
|---|---:|
| Current assets: | |
| Cash | $ 650,000 |
| Derivative instrument—rate swap | 40,000 |
| Receivables | 500,000 |
| Due from other governments | 100,000 |
| Inventories | 85,000 |
| Total current assets | 1,375,000 |
| Non-current assets: | |
| Restricted cash and cash equivalents | 750,000 |
| Capital assets: | |
| Land | 700,000 |
| Buildings and equipment | 1,800,000 |
| Less: accumulated depreciation | (750,000) |
| Total non-current assets | 2,500,000 |
| **Total assets** | 3,875,000 |

(continued)

(continued)

**Deferred Outflows of Resources**

| | |
|---|---:|
| Accumulated decrease in fair value of hedging derivatives | 35,000 |
| **Total deferred outflows of resources** | 35,000 |

**Liabilities**

Current liabilities:

| | |
|---|---:|
| Accounts payable | 350,000 |
| Due to other funds | 450,000 |
| Forward contract | 35,000 |
| Compensated absences | 75,000 |
| Bonds, notes, and loans payable | 150,000 |
| Total current liabilities | 1,060,000 |

Non-current liabilities:

| | |
|---|---:|
| Compensated absences | 300,000 |
| Bonds, notes, and loans payable | 1,300,000 |
| Total non-current liabilities | 1,600,000 |
| **Total liabilities** | 2,660,000 |

**Deferred Inflows of Resources**

| | |
|---|---:|
| Accumulated increase in fair value of hedging derivatives | 40,000 |
| **Total deferred inflows of resources** | 40,000 |

**Net Position**

| | |
|---|---:|
| Net investment in capital assets | 300,000 |
| Restricted for debt service | 750,000 |
| Unrestricted | 160,000 |
| **Total net position** | $1,210,000 |

### 2.4.2 Statement of Revenues, Expenses, and Changes in Fund Net Position

**Progressive Township**
**Statement of Revenues, Expenses, and Changes in Net Position**
**Water and Sewer Fund**
For the Year Ended December 31, Year 1

**Operating Revenues**

| | |
|---|---:|
| Charges for services | $1,500,000 |
| Miscellaneous | 250,000 |
| **Total operating revenues** | 1,750,000 |

(continued)

(continued)

**Operating Expenses**
| | |
|---|---:|
| Personal services | 975,000 |
| Contracted services | 85,000 |
| Other operating expenses | 300,000 |
| Insurance claims and expenses | – |
| Depreciation expense | 270,000 |
| **Total operating expenses** | 1,630,000 |
| **Operating income (loss)** | 120,000 |

**Nonoperating Revenues (Expenses)**
| | |
|---|---:|
| Interest and investment revenue | 60,000 |
| Interest expense | (100,000) |
| **Total nonoperating revenue (expenses)** | (40,000) |
| **Income (loss) before contributions and transfers** | 80,000 |
| Capital contributions | 300,000 |
| Transfers | – |
| **Change in net position** | 380,000 |
| Total net position—beginning | 830,000 |
| **Total net position—ending** | **$1,210,000** |

### 2.4.3 Statement of Cash Flows

**Progressive Township**
**Statement of Cash Flows**
**Water and Sewer Fund**
For the Year Ended December 31, Year 1

**Cash Flows From Operating Activities**
| | |
|---|---:|
| Receipts from customers | $1,510,000 |
| Payments to suppliers | (334,000) |
| Payments to employees | (903,750) |
| Internal activity—net payments (to) from other funds | 180,000 |
| Net cash provided by operating activities | 452,250 |

**Cash Flows From Noncapital Financing Activities**
| | |
|---|---:|
| Operating subsidies and transfers to other funds | – |

(continued)

(continued)

**Cash Flows From Capital and Related Financing Activities**

| | |
|---|---:|
| Proceeds from capital debt | 800,000 |
| Capital contributions | 300,000 |
| Purchases of capital assets | (800,000) |
| Principal paid on capital debt | (97,500) |
| Interest paid on capital debt | (100,000) |
| Net cash (used) by capital and related financing activities | 102,500 |

**Cash Flows From Investing Activities**

| | |
|---|---:|
| Purchase of investments | (250,000) |
| Interest and dividends | 60,000 |
| Net cash provided by investing activities | (190,000) |
| Net increase in cash and cash equivalents | 364,750 |
| Balances—beginning of the year | 285,250 |
| **Balances—end of the year** | $ 650,000 |

**Reconciliation of Operating Income (Loss) to Net Cash Provided (Used) by Operating Activities**

| | |
|---|---:|
| Operating income (loss) | $ 120,000 |
| Adjustments to reconcile operating income to net cash provided (used) by operating activities: | |
| Depreciation expense | 270,000 |
| Changes in assets and liabilities: | |
| Receivables, net | (240,000) |
| Inventories | (34,000) |
| Accounts and other payables | 302,500 |
| Accrued expenses | 33,750 |
| **Net cash provided by operating activities** | $ 452,250 |

---

### Question 1     MCQ-01029

The billings for transportation services provided to other governmental units are recorded by the internal service fund as:

    a. Transportation appropriations.
    b. Operating revenues.
    c. Interfund exchanges.
    d. Intergovernmental transfers.

## Question 2  MCQ-01032

Cy City's municipal solid waste landfill enterprise fund was established when a new landfill was opened January 3, Year 1. The landfill is expected to close December 31, Year 20. Cy City's Year 1 expenses would include a portion of which of the Year 21 expected disbursements?

I. Cost of a final cover to be applied to the landfill.
II. Cost of equipment to be installed to monitor methane gas buildup.

a. I only
b. II only
c. Both I and II
d. Neither I nor II

## Question 3  MCQ-01040

A state government had the following activities:

I. State-operated lottery          $10,000,000
II. State-operated hospital        $ 3,000,000

Which of the above activities should be most likely accounted for in an enterprise fund?

a. Neither I nor II
b. I only
c. II only
d. Both I and II

# MODULE 2: Fiduciary Funds Financial Statements

FAR 10

## 1 Fiduciary Funds—General

Activities of a governmental entity that qualify for classification as a fiduciary activity must have all of the following characteristics.

- Assets associated with the activity are controlled by the government.
  - Government holds the assets; or
  - Government has the ability to direct the use of the asset for the benefit of specified or intended recipients.

> **Pass Key**
>
> Government control of the assets is not compromised by the presence of retractions (external restraints) that stipulate the asset can be used only for a specific purpose.

- Assets associated with the activity are not derived from revenues that are generated by a government itself (also known as "own source" revenues).
- Assets associated with the activity must have one or more of the following characteristics.
  - The assets are:
    - administered through a trust which the government itself is not a beneficiary.
    - dedicated to providing benefits to recipients in accordance with benefit terms.
    - legally protected from the creditors of the government.
  - The assets are:
    - for the benefit of individuals.
    - not derived from the government's provision of services or goods to the beneficiaries.
    - the government does not have administrative involvement with the assets or direct financial involvement with the assets.

# Fiduciary Funds Financial Statements

## Illustration 1 Fiduciary Funds

Administrative involvement includes such characteristics as:

- Monitoring compliance with the requirements of the activity that are established by the government or by the resource provider that does not receive direct benefits of the activity.
- Determination of eligible expenditures that are established by the government or by a resource provider that does not receive the direct benefits of the activity.
- Has the ability to exercise discretion over how assets are allocated.

Direct financial involvement by a government might include the government providing matching resources for the activity.

### Pass Key

Fiduciary activities have the following general characteristics:
- Assets are controlled by the government
- Assets are not the government's "own-source" revenue
- Assets are not subject to administrative involvement by the government

Fiduciary activities are classified in one of four types of funds:
- Custodial
- Investment trust
- Private purpose
- Pension and other employee benefit

## 2 Custodial Fund

Service (internal) fund
Enterprise fund
**Custodial**
Investment trust
Private purpose trust
Pension and other employee benefit trust
} Full accrual

Balance sheet—*Statement of fiduciary net position*
Income statement—*Statement of changes in fiduciary net position*
Statement of cash flows—*not applicable*
Footnotes

A custodial fund generally collects cash to be held temporarily for an authorized recipient to whom it will be later disbursed. A custodial fund is used when activities are not required to be reported in pension trust funds, investment trust funds, or private purpose trust funds.

Examples of custodial funds include:

- Tax collection funds
- Clearance funds
- Special assessments

## 2.1 Revenue Source Examples

A government may report a single aggregated total for additions in which resources, upon receipt, are normally expected to be held for three months or less. Descriptions should define resource flows:

- Property taxes collected for other governments

## 2.2 Expense-Type Examples

A government may report a single aggregated total for deductions in which resources, upon receipt, are normally expected to be held for three months or less. Descriptions should define resource flows:

- Property taxes distributed to other governments

## 2.3 Unique Accounting Issues

### 2.3.1 Tax Collection Funds

*Tax collection funds* exist when one local government collects a tax for an overlapping governmental unit and remits the amount collected, less administrative charges, to the recipient unit. Examples include sales tax custodial funds, payroll withholding custodial funds, and real estate tax custodial funds.

### 2.3.2 Clearance Funds

*Clearance funds* are used to accumulate a variety of revenues from different sources and apportion them to various operating funds in accordance with a statutory formula or procedure.

Examples of clearance funds, or cash conduit arrangements with no monitoring or administrative involvement, are: pass-through grants; food stamps; traffic citations; and alimony, child support, and other court-ordered payments.

> **Pass Key**
>
> If a governmental unit has monitoring or similar administrative involvement, the special revenue fund is used.

### 2.3.3 Special Assessments

When the governmental unit *is not otherwise obligated* for the debt (i.e., not primarily or potentially liable), the receivables and debt service transaction are appropriately accounted for in the custodial fund.

### 2.3.4 Custodial Fund Title

The custodial fund is the only fiduciary fund type that excludes the word "trust" from the title.

## 2.4 Financial Statements

Custodial funds present a statement of fiduciary net position and a statement of changes in fiduciary net position.

### 2.4.1 Statement of Fiduciary Net Position

Assets and liabilities of custodial funds, often used to account for assets over which the government has temporary custody, are composed of amounts due from taxpayers and due to taxing authorities.

---

**Progressive Township**
**Statement of Fiduciary Net Position**
**Custodial Fund**
As of December 31, Year 1

| | |
|---|---:|
| **Assets** | |
| Cash | $ 50,000 |
| Receivables | |
|   Taxes for other governments | 200,000 |
|     Total receivables | 200,000 |
| **Total assets** | 250,000 |
| **Liabilities** | |
| Due to local governments | 143,000 |
|   **Total liabilities** | 143,000 |
| **Net Position** | |
| Restricted for | |
|   Individuals, organizations, and other governments | $107,000 |

## 2.4.2 Statement of Changes in Fiduciary Net Position

The statement of changes in fiduciary net position are composed predominantly of receipts from taxpayers and payments to benefiting governments.

---

**Progressive Township**
**Statement of Changes in Fiduciary Net Position**
**Custodial Fund**
For the Year Ended December 31, Year 1

| | |
|---|---:|
| **Additions** | |
| Tax collections for other governments | $1,500,000 |
| Miscellaneous | 15,000 |
| **Total additions** | 1,515,000 |
| **Deductions** | |
| Administrative expenses | 3,000 |
| Payments of tax collections to other governments | 1,500,000 |
| **Total deductions** | 1,503,000 |
| **Change in net position** | 12,000 |
| **Net position—beginning of the year** | 95,000 |
| **Net position—end of the year** | $ 107,000 |

# 3 Investment Trust Funds

> Service (internal) fund
> Enterprise fund
> Custodial
> **Investment trust**
> Private purpose trust
> Pension and other employee benefit trust
>
> } Full accrual
>
> Balance sheet—*statement of fiduciary net position*
> Income statement—*statement of changes in fiduciary net position*
> Statement of cash flows—*not required*
> Footnotes

A governmental entity that sponsors one or more external investment pools (sponsoring government) should report the external portion of each pool as a separate investment trust fund.

## 3.1 Revenue (Addition) Sources

Additions include contributions; net appreciation (or depreciation) of the fair value of the plan assets, including realized and unrealized gains and losses; and premiums and discounts on debt securities, which should not be amortized as part of investment income.

## 3.2 Expense (Deduction) Types

Deductions from net position include payments to beneficiaries and administrative expenses.

## 3.3 Unique Accounting Issues

- **Reported Transactions**

    Investment trust financial statements only report the investment assets of those entities using the investment trust's services that are external to the sponsoring government. If the government reporting the investment trust uses the investment trust to serve as trustee for its investments, the asset balances of the government are reported in the funds that own the investments. The government reporting the investment trust treats transactions with the trust as if it were an external party.

- **Asset Valuation**

    For the most part, the plan's net assets (investments) are reported on a fair value basis.

## 3.4 Financial Statements

### 3.4.1 Statement of Fiduciary Net Position

The *statement of fiduciary net position* is prepared on the accrual basis and reports the plan's assets, liabilities, and net position. The statement identifies the major assets of the plan. Reported liabilities should be subtracted from the total assets, and the difference reported as *net position held in investment trust*.

### 3.4.2 Statement of Changes in Fiduciary Net Position

The *statement of changes in fiduciary net position* reports the net increase or decrease in net plan position from the beginning of the year until the end of the year.

# 4 Private Purpose Trust

| | | |
|---|---|---|
| Service (internal) fund | | Balance sheet—*statement of fiduciary net position* |
| Enterprise fund | | Income statement—*statement of changes in fiduciary net position* |
| Custodial | Full accrual | |
| Investment trust | | Statement of cash flows—*not required* |
| **Private purpose trust** | | Footnotes |
| Pension and other employee benefit trust | | |

The *private purpose trust fund* is the designated fund for reporting all other trust arrangements under which principal and income are for the benefit of specific individuals, private organizations, or other governments that are not classified as either pension or investment trusts.

Examples of private purpose trusts include escheat property funds, retainage on construction contracts for the benefit of a contractor, and other trusts. The private purpose trust accounts for fiduciary transactions that relate to specific private, rather than general public, purposes other than:

- public employee retirement systems; or
- investment pools held on behalf of other governments.

## 4.1 Revenue (Addition) Sources

Assume that the principal of a private purpose trust fund is invested and the income received is transferred to a private individual.

- **Private Purpose Trust**

    *Journal entry to record obligation to a private individual:*

    | | | | |
    |---|---|---|---|
    | DR | Deduction | $500 | |
    | CR | Accounts payable | | $500 |

    *Journal entry to record payment:*

    | | | | |
    |---|---|---|---|
    | DR | Accounts payable | $500 | |
    | CR | Cash | | $500 |

## 4.2 Expense (Deductions) Types

- **Expenses (Deductions):** Expenses (deductions) relate to the specific purpose of the trust and may relate to benefits or administrative charges.
- **Capital Gains (Losses):** Capital gains/losses are recorded as adjustments to income/expense.

## 4.3 Unique Accounting Issues

Escheat property is property that reverts to a governmental entity in the absence of legal claimants or heirs at the time the estate is settled. Escheat property generally should be reported as an asset in the governmental or proprietary fund to which the property ultimately escheats. Escheat property held for individuals, private organizations, or other governments should be reported in a private purpose trust fund.

Fiduciary Funds Financial Statements

- Revenue is reduced and a fund liability is reported to the extent that property probably will be reclaimed.

### Pass Key

To determine the correct fund to account for restricted funds, use the following chart:

| Fund | Use | Spending |
|---|---|---|
| Special revenue fund | Public | Interest and principal (expendable) |
| Permanent fund | Public | Interest only (non-expendable) |
| Private purpose fund | Private | Interest and/or principal (expendable) |

## 5 Pension (and Other Employee Benefit) Trust

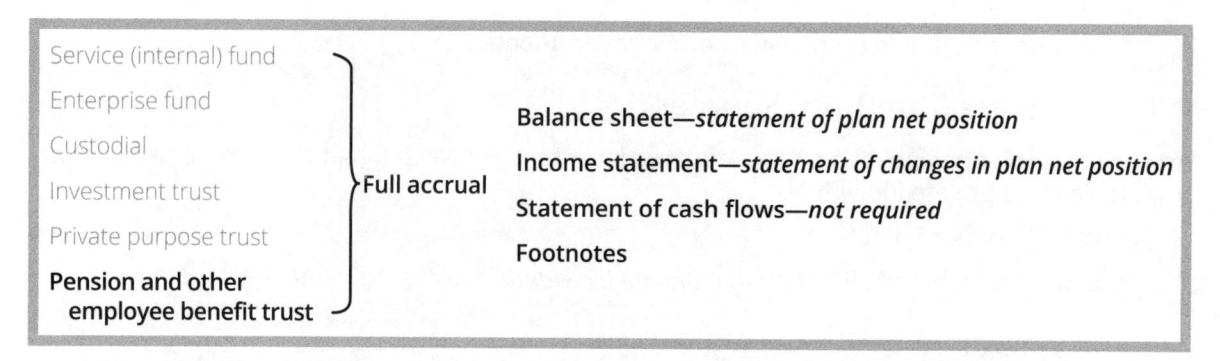

Service (internal) fund
Enterprise fund
Custodial
Investment trust
Private purpose trust
**Pension and other employee benefit trust**
} Full accrual

Balance sheet—*statement of plan net position*
Income statement—*statement of changes in plan net position*
Statement of cash flows—*not required*
Footnotes

Pension (and other employee benefit) trust funds account for government sponsored defined benefit and defined contribution plans and other employee benefits such as postretirement health care benefits.

### 5.1 Revenue (Addition) Sources

#### 5.1.1 Employer and Employee Contributions

Resources received are credited to additions, and further described as either employer or employee contributions. Additions appear on the statement of changes in fiduciary net position.

*Journal entry to record the receipt of money from other funds (additions, not revenue, nor "other financing sources"):*

| DR | Cash | $XXX | |
|---|---|---|---|
| CR | Additions: employer contribution—restricted | | $XXX |

# FAR 10 — Fiduciary Funds Financial Statements

### 5.1.2 Other Fund Contributing Money to the Pension Fund

- **Modified Accrual**

    Journal entry of a GRaSPP fund, which uses modified accrual (expenditures, not "other uses," "transfers"):

    | DR | Expenditures | $XXX | |
    |---|---|---|---|
    | CR | Cash | | $XXX |

- **Full Accrual**

    Journal entry of a SE-CIPPOE fund, which uses full accrual (expenses, not "transfers"):

    | DR | Expenses | $XXX | |
    |---|---|---|---|
    | CR | Cash | | $XXX |

### 5.1.3 Income From Investments

Income from investments is recorded as an addition, in a manner similar to investment earnings in commercial financial statements.

## 5.2 Expense (Deduction) Types

Expenses of pension (NPL) trust funds frequently include benefits payments, refunds, and administrative expense.

## 5.3 Unique Accounting Issues

### 5.3.1 Measurement of Net Pension Liability

The net pension liability is determined in part from data reported in the pension fund financial statements and is reported in the government-wide financial statements, as well as the individual fund financial statements, as appropriate. The net pension liability (NPL) is computed as the total pension liability (TPL) less the amount of the pension plan's fiduciary net position (FNP).

---

**Illustration 2  Measurement of Net Pension Liability**

| | |
|---|---|
| Total pension liability (TPL) | Actuarially determined |
| Less: fiduciary net position (FNP) | Determined from pension fund financial statements |
| Net pension liability (NPL) | |

---

- Actuarial valuations of the total pension liability must be performed every two years, although more frequent valuations are encouraged.

    - Valuations should be performed at year-end based on terms and conditions in effect at year-end or rolled forward to year-end using previous actuarial valuations.

    - Valuations are to be made in conformity with the Actuarial Standards of Practice issued by the Actuarial Standards Board.

    - Actuarial present values are determined using the entry age actuarial cost method attributed to each plan member individually.

Fiduciary Funds Financial Statements

- Discount rates applied to the projected benefit payment used to value the total pension liability should reflect the following:
  - the long-term expected rate of return to the extent that net position is adequate to pay benefits and assets are available for investments; or
  - the tax-exempt bond rate to the extent that conditions for use of the long-term expected rate of return are not met.

> **Illustration 3  Discount Rate for Projected Benefit Payment**
>
> Lower discount rates are used to produce higher liability amounts when net position is not adequate to pay benefits and assets are not available for investment.

### 5.3.2 Reporting Changes in Net Pension Liability

Changes in the net pension liability are reported in one of two ways: They may be reported as a pension expense of the government-wide financial statements and as either an expenditure or expense in the appropriate funds responsible for funding the pension obligation, or they may be reported as deferred outflows or deferred inflows of resources. Components of the change in net pension liability are similar to commercial accounting and include most of the items defined by the mnemonic **SIRAGE**. Reporting treatment is described as follows:

- Changes in the net pension liability that are charged to pension expense in the period of change include:
  - Current period services costs
  - Interest on total pension cost
  - Reductions for projected earnings on pension plan investments
  - Changes in benefit terms not eligible for deferral and therefore required to be included in pension expense immediately (prior service costs)

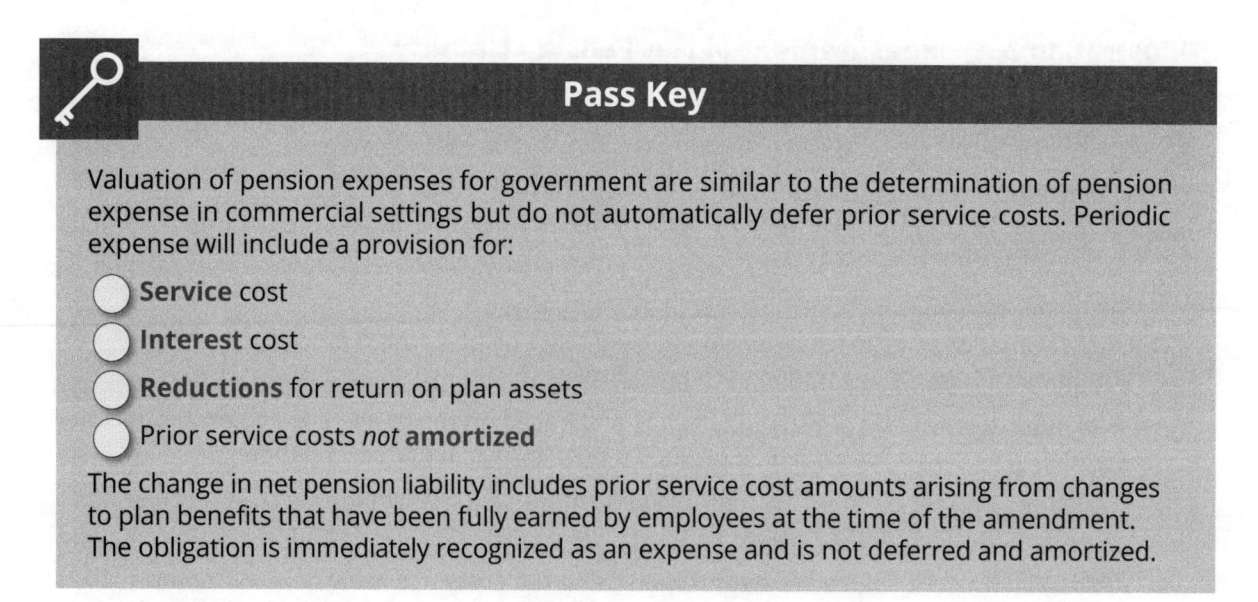

> **Pass Key**
>
> Valuation of pension expenses for government are similar to the determination of pension expense in commercial settings but do not automatically defer prior service costs. Periodic expense will include a provision for:
>
> - **Service** cost
> - **Interest** cost
> - **Reductions** for return on plan assets
> - **Prior** service costs *not* **amortized**
>
> The change in net pension liability includes prior service cost amounts arising from changes to plan benefits that have been fully earned by employees at the time of the amendment. The obligation is immediately recognized as an expense and is not deferred and amortized.

- Other changes in the net pension liability that are accounted for as deferred inflows and outflows of resources (and subsequently amortized to pension expense using a systematic and rational methodology) are:
    - Changes to pension provisions for which benefits have not already been earned by plan participants (unearned benefits of current and former employees) (amortized over the average remaining service life of the employees).
    - Changes of economic and demographic assumptions or other inputs (amortized over the average remaining service life of the employees).
    - Differences between projected earnings and actual experience (amortized over five years).
    - Employer contributions subsequent to the measurement date (recognized in subsequent period).

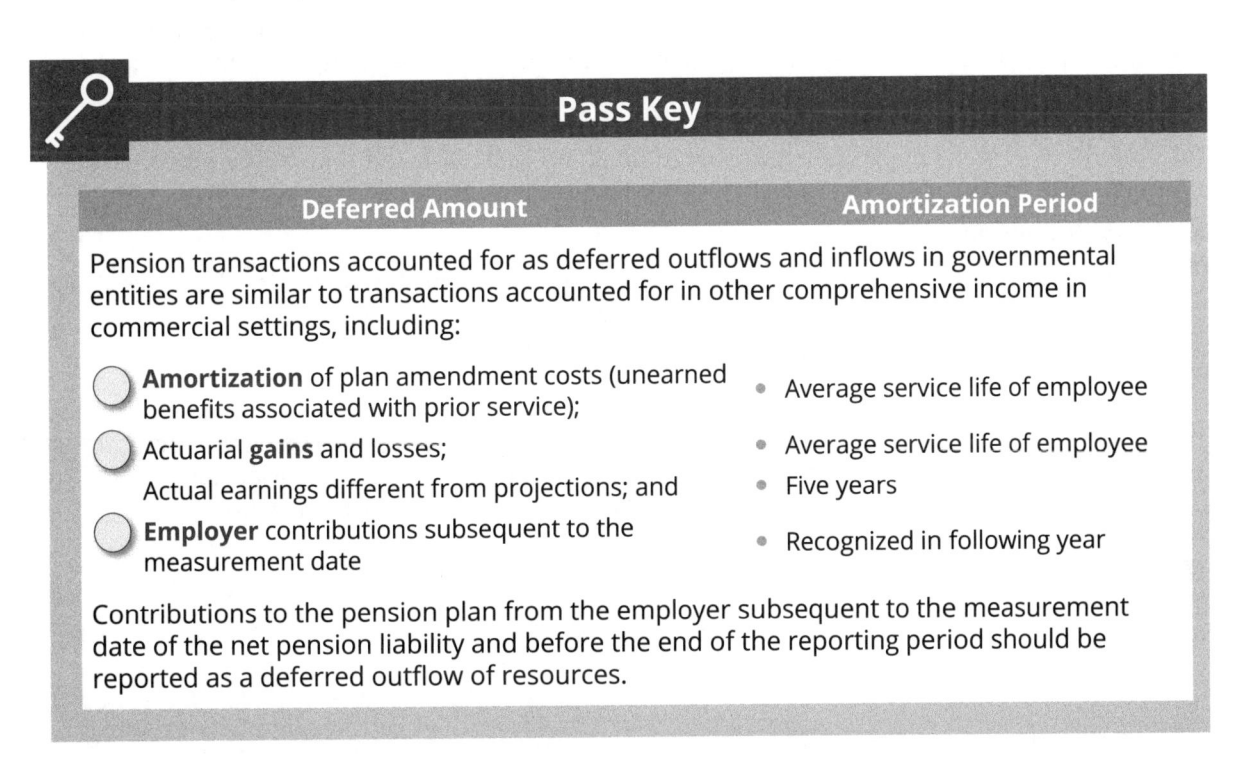

> **Pass Key**
>
> | Deferred Amount | Amortization Period |
> |---|---|
>
> Pension transactions accounted for as deferred outflows and inflows in governmental entities are similar to transactions accounted for in other comprehensive income in commercial settings, including:
>
> - **Amortization** of plan amendment costs (unearned benefits associated with prior service); — Average service life of employee
> - Actuarial **gains** and losses; — Average service life of employee
> - Actual earnings different from projections; and — Five years
> - **Employer** contributions subsequent to the measurement date — Recognized in following year
>
> Contributions to the pension plan from the employer subsequent to the measurement date of the net pension liability and before the end of the reporting period should be reported as a deferred outflow of resources.

- Changes in the pension fund liability are accounted for:
    - as an expense in the government-wide financial statements.
    - as an expense in the proprietary financial statements.
    - as an expenditure and liability in the governmental funds to the extent that the liability is normally expected to be liquidated with expendable available financial resources. Generally, the amount reported is the amount paid plus or minus the change in the current liability displayed.

### 5.3.3 Fiduciary Net Position Accounting

Fiduciary net position is typically reported as net position, restricted. Restrictions are shown as separate line items for pensions and/or post-employment benefits other than pensions.

### 5.3.4 Deferred Compensation Plans for Other Than Enterprise-Fund Employees

Internal Revenue Code (IRC) Section 457 deferred compensation plans are similar to 403(b) and 401(k) defined contribution plans.

IRC Section 457 deferred compensation plans that are reported in the fiduciary funds should be reported as pension (and other employee benefit) trust funds. Furthermore, the investments held by these plans are to be reported (according to GASB 31) at fair value where readily determinable.

## 5.4 Financial Statements

Pension plan assets are generally measured using the accrual basis of accounting applied on a fair value basis, and pension benefit obligations should be recognized when due and payable.

### 5.4.1 Statement of Fiduciary Net Position

The statement of plan net position is prepared on an accrual basis and reports the plan's assets, liabilities, and net position.

- **Asset Valuation**

    For the most part, the plan's net assets (investments) are reported on a fair value basis. This statement identifies the major assets of the plan.

- **Liabilities and Net Position Determination**

    Reported liabilities should be subtracted from the total assets, and the difference should be reported as *net position restricted for pension*. This statement does not report the required actuarial liability. The pension liability is reported in the notes to the financial statements, and further described and analyzed in the required supplementary information.

**Progressive Township**
**Statement of Fiduciary Net Position**
**Pension and Other Employee Benefit Trust Funds**
As of December 31, Year 1

**Assets**

| | |
|---|---:|
| Cash | $1,000,000 |
| Receivables: | |
|    Interest and dividends | 70,000 |
|    Other receivables | 25,000 |
|      Total receivables | 95,000 |
| Investments at fair value: | |
|    U.S. government obligations | 1,000,000 |
|    Corporate bonds | 1,000,000 |
|    Corporate stock | 2,000,000 |
|      Total investments | 4,000,000 |
| **Total assets** | 5,095,000 |
| **Liabilities** | |
| Accounts payable | 30,000 |
| Refunds payable and others | 14,580 |
| **Total liabilities** | 44,580 |
| **Net position—restricted for pension** | $5,050,420 |

### Pass Key

The net pension liability and the change in the net pension liability are not included on the balance sheet of the pension fund financial statements.

### 5.4.2 Statement of Changes in Fiduciary Net Position

The statement of *changes in fiduciary net position* reports the net increase or decrease in net position from the beginning of the year until the end of the year.

- **Additions**

    *Additions* to fiduciary net position include contributions received from employees and employers; net appreciation (or depreciation) of the fair value of the plan assets, including realized and unrealized gains and losses; and premiums and discounts on debt securities, which should not be amortized as part of investment income.

## Deductions

*Deductions* from fiduciary net position include pension benefit payments to retirees and beneficiaries and administrative expenses.

**Progressive Township**
**Statement of Changes in Fiduciary Net Position**
**Pension and Other Employee Benefit Trust Funds**
For the Year Ended December 31, Year 1

| | |
|---|---:|
| **Additions** | |
| Contributions: | |
|   Employer | $ 470,631 |
|   Plan members | 156,900 |
|     Total contributions | 627,531 |
| Investment earnings: | |
|   Net increase (decrease) in fair value of investments | 200,000 |
|   Interest | 130,000 |
|   Dividends | 60,000 |
|     Total investment earnings | 390,000 |
|   Less: investment expense | 40,000 |
|     Net investment earnings | 350,000 |
| **Total additions** | 977,531 |
| **Deductions** | |
| Benefits | 156,895 |
| Refunds of contributions | 62,768 |
| Administrative expenses | 4,896 |
|   Total deductions | 224,559 |
| **Change in net position** | 752,972 |
| **Net position—beginning of the year** | 4,297,448 |
| **Net position—end of the year** | $5,050,420 |

### 5.4.3 Statement of Cash Flows

The *statement of cash flows* is not required.

## Pass Key

The fiduciary and proprietary funds both use full accrual accounting. One significant difference between the fiduciary and proprietary funds involves the cash flow statement:

- Fiduciary funds—*cash flow statement is not required*
- Proprietary funds—*cash flow statement is required*

### 5.4.4 Notes to the Financial Statements

Notes to the financial statements include the following:

- Descriptive information, such as the types of benefits provided, the classes of plan members covered, and the composition of the pension plan board.
- Investment disclosures including:
  - Pension plan investment policies.
  - A description of how fair value is determined.
  - Concentrations of investments with individual organizations exceeding 5 percent of the pension plan fiduciary net position.
  - The annual money-weighted rate of return on pension plan investments.
- Disclosures regarding contributions, reserves, etc.
- The portion of the actuarial present value of the projected benefit payments to be provided through the pension plan to current active and inactive plan members that is attributed to those members' past period of service (the total pension liability).
- The pension plan's fiduciary net position.
- The net pension liability.
- The pension plan's fiduciary net position as a percentage of the total pension liability.
- Significant assumptions and other inputs used to calculate the total pension liability, such as:
  - Inflation
  - Salary changes
  - Post-employment benefit changes and cost-of-living adjustments
  - Inputs to the discount rate
  - Mortality assumptions

### 5.4.5 Required Supplementary Information

The following required supplementary information about employer and nonemployer contributing entity obligations for pensions provided through the pension plan should be presented for each of the 10 most recent fiscal years:

- Sources of changes in the net pension liability.
- Information about the components of the net pension liability and related ratios, including:
  - The pension plan's fiduciary net position as a percentage of the total pension liability.
  - The net pension liability as a percentage of the covered employee payroll.
  - Actuarially determined contributions.
  - The amount of contributions.
- Significant methods and assumptions used in calculating the actuarially determined contributions, presented as notes to the schedules.
- The annual money-weighted rate of return on pension plan investments for each of 10 years presented.
- An explanation of trends in amounts reported in the supplementary schedule, such as changes in benefit terms, population, and assumptions.

Fiduciary Funds Financial Statements  FAR 10

## Matrix of Financial Statements Required for Various Funds

|  |  | Governmental |  |  |  |  | Proprietary |  | Fiduciary |  |  |  |
|---|---|---|---|---|---|---|---|---|---|---|---|---|
|  |  | G<br>General | R<br>Revenue (special) | S<br>Service (debt) | P<br>Projects (capital) | P<br>Permanent | S<br>Service (internal) | E<br>Enterprise | C<br>Custodial | I<br>Investment | P<br>Private purpose | POE<br>Pension and other employee benefit |
| **Balance Sheet** | **Balance sheet**<br>• Current assets<br>• Current liabilities<br>• Fund balance | ✓ | ✓ | ✓ | ✓ | ✓ |  |  |  |  |  |  |
|  | **Statement of net position**<br>• Assets<br>• Liabilities<br>• Net position |  |  |  |  |  | ✓ | ✓ |  |  |  |  |
|  | **Statement of fiduciary net position**<br>• Assets<br>• Liabilities<br>• Net position |  |  |  |  |  |  |  | ✓ | ✓ | ✓ | ✓ |
| **Income Statement** | **Statement of revenues, expenditures, and changes in fund balance**<br>• Revenue<br>• Expenditures<br>• Other financing sources (uses) | ✓ | ✓ | ✓ | ✓ | ✓ |  |  |  |  |  |  |
|  | **Statement of revenues, expenses, and changes in fund net position**<br>• Operating revenue<br>• Operating expenses<br>• Nonoperating revenue and expenses |  |  |  |  |  | ✓ | ✓ |  |  |  |  |
|  | **Statement of changes in fiduciary net position**<br>• Additions<br>• Deductions |  |  |  |  |  |  |  | ✓ | ✓ | ✓ | ✓ |
| **Cash Flows** | **Statement of cash flows**<br>• Operating<br>• Investing<br>• Capital financing<br>• Noncapital financing |  |  |  |  |  | ✓ | ✓ |  |  |  |  |
|  | **Methods of Accounting** |  |  |  |  |  |  |  |  |  |  |  |
|  | Full accrual |  |  |  |  |  | ✓ | ✓ | ✓ | ✓ | ✓ | ✓ |
|  | Modified accrual<br>• Budget<br>• Activity<br>• Encumbrances | ✓<br>•<br>•<br>• | ✓<br>•<br>•<br>• | ✓<br>•<br>•<br>— | ✓<br>•<br>•<br>• | ✓<br>•<br>•<br>— |  |  |  |  |  |  |

## Question 1 — MCQ-01067

Fish Road property owners in Sea County are responsible for special assessment debt that arose from a storm sewer project. If the property owners default, Sea has no obligation regarding debt service, although it does bill property owners for assessments and uses the monies it collects to pay debt holders. What fund type should Sea use to account for these collection and servicing activities?

- a. Custodial
- b. Debt service
- c. Private purpose funds
- d. Capital projects

## Question 2 — MCQ-01082

Arlen City's accounts contained the following cash balances at December 31, Year 1:

| | |
|---|---:|
| Forfeiture Act cash confiscated from illegal activities (disbursements can be used only for law enforcement activities) | $300,000 |
| Sales taxes collected by Arlen to be distributed to other governmental units | 500,000 |

What amount of cash should Arlen report in its private purpose trust funds at December 31, Year 1?

- a. $0
- b. $300,000
- c. $500,000
- d. $800,000

# MODULE 3: Form and Content of the Comprehensive Annual Financial Report

**FAR 10**

## 1 Governmental Financial Reporting Requirements of GASB 34

### 1.1 Overview

#### 1.1.1 Governmental Reporting Standards

The governmental reporting standards established by GASB 34 (as amended) require presentation of basic financial statements and required supplementary information. Basic financial statements are defined as government-wide financial statements, fund financial statements, and notes to the financial statements. Required and other supplementary information covers a wide range of data and presentations, including management's discussion and analysis, which precede the basic financial statements, and other schedules related to budget, pension, and infrastructure.

#### 1.1.2 Accountability

Governmental reporting focuses on two important types of accountability:

- **Operational Accountability**

    The focus of *government-wide financial statements* is to report the extent to which the government has met its operating objectives *efficiently and effectively*, using all resources available for that purpose, and the extent to which it can continue to meet its objectives for the future.

- **Fiscal Accountability**

    The focus of the *fund financial statements* is to demonstrate that the government entity's actions in the current period have *complied* with public decisions concerning the raising and spending of public funds in the short-term (usually one budgetary cycle or one year).

#### 1.1.3 Integrated Approach

The integrated approach requires financial accounting and disclosure to show operational and fiscal accountability individually and to show the relationship between operational and fiscal accountability through a reconciliation. Governmental financial reporting integrates complementary accountability objectives as follows:

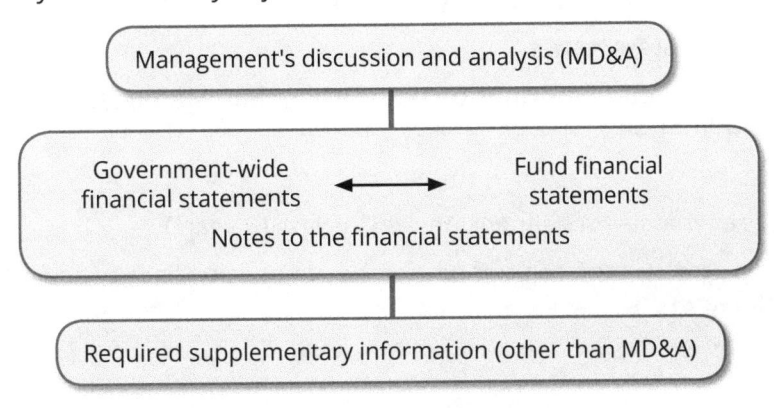

```
        Management's discussion and analysis (MD&A)
                          |
        ┌─────────────────┴─────────────────┐
        │  Government-wide  ⇄  Fund financial │
        │  financial statements    statements │
        │     Notes to the financial statements│
        └─────────────────┬─────────────────┘
                          |
        Required supplementary information (other than MD&A)
```

- The integrated approach requires a reconciliation of the fund financial statements to the government-wide financial statements to link the accountability objectives of the two levels of reporting.
    - This reconciliation may appear on the face of the fund financial statements or in the notes to the government-wide financial statements.
    - Note disclosures are used when summarized aggregated information does not fully disclose the relationship of operational and fiscal accountability.
- Major funds are the focus of the fund statements.
    - Generic fund-type summaries (e.g., all special revenue funds) do not, in and of themselves, provide useful information.
    - Major funds highlight the more significant components of governmental activities (e.g., a single sales tax fund).

## 1.2 Required Reporting for General Purpose Governmental Units

- **Management's Discussion and Analysis (MD&A)**
    - Required supplementary information.
- **Government-wide Financial Statements**
    - Statement of net position
    - Statement of activities
- **Fund Financial Statements**

Major funds shown individually; nonmajor funds shown in total.

- **Governmental Funds**  GRaSPP
    - Balance sheet
    - Statement of revenues, expenditures, and changes in fund balances
- **Proprietary Funds**  SE
    - Statement of net position
    - Statement of revenues, expenses, and changes in fund net position
    - Statement of cash flows
- **Fiduciary Funds**  CIPPOE
    - Statement of fiduciary net position
    - Statement of changes in fiduciary net position

- **Notes to Financial Statements**
- **Required Supplementary Information (RSI) Other Than Management's Discussion and Analysis**
    - **Pension**
        - Sources of changes in net pension liability (last 10 years)
        - Information about the components of the net pension liability and related ratios (last 10 years)

- **Budget**
  - Budgetary comparison schedules
- **Infrastructure**
  - Information about infrastructure (roads, bridges, etc.)
  - Assets for entities using the modified approach

- **Other Supplementary Information (Optional)**
  - Combining statements for nonmajor funds
  - Variance between originally adopted and final amended budget
  - Variance between final amended budget and actual

## 1.3 Comprehensive Annual Financial Report

Governments often present a comprehensive annual financial report (CAFR). A CAFR is not a GAAP requirement; it is a presentation designed by the Government Finance Officers Association that adds an introductory section and a statistical section to the beginning and end of a GASB 34 presentation, as follows:

- **Introductory Section (Unaudited)**
  - Letter of transmittal
  - Organizational chart
  - List of principal officers

- **Basic Financial Statements and Required Supplementary Information (Audited)**
  - Management's discussion and analysis
  - Government-wide financial statements
  - Fund financial statements
  - Notes to the financial statements
  - Required supplementary information

- **Statistical Section (Unaudited)**
  - Ten years of selected financial data
  - Ten years of economic data (e.g., millage rates, appraised values)
  - Other data

## Governmental Reporting Summary

| Fund Structure | Governmental Funds | | | | | Proprietary Funds | | Fiduciary Funds | | | |
|---|---|---|---|---|---|---|---|---|---|---|---|
| | G | R | S | P | P | S | E | C | I | P | POE |
| | General | Revenue (special) | Service (debt) | Projects (capital) | Permanent | Service (internal) | Enterprise | Custodial | Investment | Private purpose | Pension and other employee benefit |

**Fund Accounting**
- Basis of accounting
- Measurement focus
- Specialized accounting

| | Governmental Funds | Proprietary Funds | Fiduciary Funds |
|---|---|---|---|
| Basis / Measurement / Specialized | Modified accrual / Current financial resource / No fixed assets or long-term debt; Budget/activity/encumbrances | Full accrual / Economic resources / None | Full accrual / Economic resources / None |

**External Reporting**
- Accountability objective, government-wide reporting

*Government-wide Financial Statements*
**Operational Accountability**

**Classifications**
- Financial statements
- Basis of accounting
- Measurement focus

| | **Governmental Activities** | **Government Activities** / **Business-type Activities** | **Fiduciary Funds** |
|---|---|---|---|
| | Balance sheet, income statement / Full accrual / Economic resources | Balance sheet, income statement / Full accrual / Economic resources | Not reported |

**External Reporting**
- Accountability objective, fund reporting

*Fund Financial Statements*
**Fiscal Accountability**

**Classifications**
- Accounting
- Budgetary reporting
- Specialized disclosures

| | **Major Funds** | **Major Funds** | **Fund Type** |
|---|---|---|---|
| | Fund accounting | Fund accounting | Fund accounting |
| | Included in RSI *(budget vs. actual + adopted vs. final)* | Not applicable | Not applicable |
| | Reconciliation to government-wide financial statements | Reconciliation to government-wide financial statements | |

---

**Question 1**  MCQ-00975

The statement of activities of the government-wide financial statements is designed primarily to provide information to assess which of the following?

    a. Operational accountability
    b. Financial accountability
    c. Fiscal accountability
    d. Functional accountability

> **Question 2** MCQ-00995
>
> Which of the following statements about the statistical section of the comprehensive annual financial report (CAFR) of a governmental unit is true?
>
> a. Statistical tables may not cover more than two fiscal years.
> b. Statistical tables may not include non-accounting information.
> c. The statistical section is not part of the basic financial statements.
> d. The statistical section is an integral part of the basic financial statements.

# 2 The Financial Reporting Entity

Generally, the financial reporting entity consists of the primary government (i.e., general purpose governmental units and certain special purpose governmental units) and organizations for which the primary government is financially accountable (i.e., component units).

## 2.1 General Purpose Governmental Units

The focus of the government-wide financial statements should be on the primary government.

Consider the following examples of general purpose governmental units:

| States | Counties | Towns | Municipalities | Villages |
| --- | --- | --- | --- | --- |

The primary government consists of all organizations that make up the legal government entity. The primary government is considered the nucleus of the financial reporting entity. Primary government entities include:

- State governments
- General purpose local governments (e.g., a city or a county)
- Special purpose local governments (e.g., a hospital authority or a school district—a governmental unit that has a single or special purpose) that meet all the following criteria:
    - **Separately elected** governing body
    - **Legally** separate
    - **Fiscally** independent of other state and local governments

> **Pass Key**
>
> Primary government reports by "ItSELF."

## 2.2 Special Purpose Governmental Units

Special purpose governmental units that are financially accountable to a primary government are not primary governments. Like any other government, they may be engaged in:

- Governmental activities
- Business-type activities
- Fiduciary activities
- Governmental and business-type activities

## 2.3 Component Unit

A component unit of the primary government is usually an organization for which the elected officials of the primary government are financially accountable. It may also be an organization that by its nature and the significance of its relationship with the primary government cannot be excluded from the primary government's financial statements without making the primary government's financial statements misleading or incomplete.

### 2.3.1 Blended Presentation

Some component units are so intertwined with the primary government that they are, in substance, the same as the primary government.

- The blended method is used when any of the following circumstances is present (only one is required):
  - A board of the component unit is substantively the same as that of the primary government.
  - The component unit serves the primary government exclusively or almost exclusively.
  - The component unit is not a separate legal entity.
- Blended presentation includes the following features:
  - The blended presentation combines financial information with the primary government.
  - Financial information of the component units is not presented in separate columns.

### 2.3.2 Discrete Presentation (or Separate Presentation)

Discrete presentation is used when the criteria for blended presentation are not met.

- Discrete presentation displays component units in separate columns.
- Most component units should use discrete presentation.
- Financial statements of the reporting entity should provide an overview of the entity based on financial accountability.

> **Pass Key**
>
> If a component unit does not meet the requirements for blended presentation, it will be presented discretely. When working CPA Exam questions regarding component units, assume discrete presentation unless the fact pattern specifically provides evidence that the blended presentation criteria have been met.

## The Financial Reporting Entity: Summary

```
Begin
  │
  ▼
Does the entity meet the SELF test?
  ├── YES ──► Primary government
  │
  └── NO ──► Component unit
              │
              ▼
         Is the board of the *primary government* the same as the *component unit*?
         Or:
         Does the *component unit* serve the *primary government* exclusively?
         Or:
         Does the *organization not qualify as a legal entity*?
              ├── YES ──► Blended
              │           *Rare*
              │
              └── NO ──► Discrete
                         *Most often*
```

## 2.4 Reporting Not-for-Profit Entities as a Component Unit

Not-for-profit organizations that provide ongoing support to a primary government or to a component unit of that primary government may also be a component unit of the primary government. Example transactions include:

- Private foundations associated with state universities
- Private foundations associated with public health care facilities

### 2.4.1 Criteria for Discrete Presentation

Legally separate, tax-exempt organizations should be reported as a discrete (separate column) component unit if they meet all of the following criteria:

- Resources held by the tax-exempt organization are for the near-exclusive benefit of the primary government (benefit standard).
- The primary government has access to a majority of the resources held by the tax-exempt organization (access standard).
- Resources held by the tax-exempt organization are significant to the primary government (significance standard).

### 2.4.2 Criteria for Other Component Unit Presentation

Legally separate, tax-exempt organizations meeting the criteria of a financially integrated entity should be classified as a component unit of the primary government if their relationship to that government is so significant as to make the financial statements misleading without component unit treatment.

---

**Example 1 — Not-for-Profit Component Unit**

**Facts:** State University Foundation Inc. was created as a private tax-exempt, not-for-profit organization to support State University, a governmentally organized and supported institute of higher learning.

**Required:** State the criteria for State University Foundation Inc. to be displayed as a discretely reported component unit within the financial statements of State University.

**Solution:** Classification of a private not-for-profit organization as a component unit of a governmental organization with discrete presentation does not require overlapping governance.

Criteria for classification and presentation of a private not-for-profit organization as a discrete component unit of a primary government are all three of the following:

- **Benefit:** The private organization must be for the near exclusive benefit of the primary government.
- **Access:** The primary government must have access to the resources of the private not-for-profit organization.
- **Significance:** Resources of the private not-for-profit organization must be significant to the primary government.

---

**Question 3**      MCQ-01141

South City School District has a separately elected governing body that administers the public school system. The district's budget is subject to the approval of the city council. The district's financial activity should be reported in South City's financial statements by:

    a. Blending only.
    b. Discrete presentation.
    c. Inclusion as a footnote only.
    d. Either blending or inclusion as a footnote.

# MODULE 4: Government-wide Financial Statements

FAR 10

## 1 Overview

- Management's discussion and analysis (MD&A)
- **Government-wide financial statements** → Statement of net position / Statement of activities
- Fund financial statements
- Notes to financial statements
- Required supplementary information
- Other supplementary information

Two statements are included in a set of government-wide financial statements: the statement of net position and the statement of activities. These statements aggregate information for all governmental and all business-type activities. GASB 34 requires the use of the economic resources measurement focus and the full accrual basis of accounting for both statements. Government-wide financial statements include all assets and liabilities over which a government has control or responsibility; therefore, fiduciary funds are excluded and the component units are included.

## 2 Statement of Net Position (a Consolidated Statement)

### 2.1 Net Position Format

Governments are encouraged to report net position as the difference between assets plus deferred outflows of resources and liabilities plus deferred inflows of resources.

```
  Assets and deferred outflows of resources
− Liabilities and deferred inflows of resources
  Net position
```

Net position is divided into each of three components, as applicable.

1. **Net Investment in Capital Assets**

    Net investment in capital assets consists of all capital assets, net of accumulated depreciation, reduced by the outstanding balances of bonds, mortgages, notes, or other borrowings that are attributable to the acquisition, construction, or improvement of those assets. Deferred outflows of resources and deferred inflows of resources that are attributable to these transactions should be included in this component.

2. **Restricted**

    Restricted net position consists of restricted assets reduced by liabilities and deferred inflows of resources related to those assets. Restrictions are imposed by external (not internal) activity.

3. **Unrestricted**

    Unrestricted net position includes the net amount of the assets, deferred outflows of resources, liabilities, and deferred inflows of resources that are not included in the determination of net investment in capital assets or the restricted component of net position.

## 2.2 Treatment of Interfund Receivables and Payables

Elimination of interfund activities within major activity categories (e.g., governmental or business-type activities) displayed for government-wide presentations should be prepared to avoid "grossing up" balances of assets and liabilities.

- Interfund receivables and payables should be eliminated except for the net residual balances of amounts due and payable between governmental activities and business-type activities.

- Receivables and payables to fiduciary funds should be treated like assets and liabilities derived from external sources.

## 2.3 Internal Service Funds

Internal service funds generally should be reported in the governmental activities column.

**Progressive Township**
**Statement of Net Position**
As of December 31, Year 1

|  | Primary Government |  |  |  |
|---|---|---|---|---|
|  | Governmental Activities | Business-type Activities | Total | Component Units |
| **Assets** |  |  |  |  |
| Cash | $4,055,000 | $2,000,000 | $ 6,055,000 | $520,000 |
| Derivative instrument—rate swap | – | 40,000 | 40,000 | – |
| Receivables | 1,065,000 | 670,000 | 1,735,000 | – |
| Internal balances | 450,000 | (450,000) | – | – |
| Inventories | 96,000 | 127,500 | 223,500 | – |
| Capital assets | 2,827,000 | 2,975,000 | 5,802,000 | – |
| **Total assets** | **$8,493,000** | **$5,362,500** | **$13,855,500** | **$520,000** |
| (continued) |  |  |  |  |

(continued)

| | | | | |
|---|---:|---:|---:|---:|
| **Deferred Outflows of Resources** | | | | |
| Accumulated decrease in fair value of hedging derivatives | – | 35,000 | 35,000 | – |
| Total deferred outflows of resources | – | 35,000 | 35,000 | – |
| **Liabilities** | | | | |
| Accounts payable | 1,104,000 | 400,000 | 1,504,000 | 130,000 |
| Forward contract | – | 35,000 | 35,000 | – |
| Other liabilities | 95,000 | – | 95,000 | – |
| Non-current liabilities: | | | | |
|   Due within one year | 46,000 | 337,500 | 383,500 | – |
|   Due in more than one year | 3,518,000 | 2,750,000 | 6,268,000 | – |
| Total liabilities | 4,763,000 | 3,522,500 | 8,285,500 | 130,000 |
| **Deferred Inflows of Resources** | | | | |
| Accumulated increase in fair value of hedging derivatives | – | 40,000 | 40,000 | – |
| Total deferred inflows of resources | – | 40,000 | 40,000 | – |
| **Net Position** | | | | |
| Net investment in capital assets | 1,227,000 | 450,000 | 1,677,000 | – |
| Restricted for: | | | | |
|   Capital projects | 1,574,000 | – | 1,574,000 | – |
|   Debt service | 723,000 | 1,200,000 | 1,923,000 | – |
| Unrestricted | 206,000 | 185,000 | 391,000 | 390,000 |
| **Total net position** | $3,730,000 | $1,835,000 | $5,565,000 | $390,000 |

### Pass Key

The government-wide financial statement includes all assets and liabilities over which a government has control or responsibility. It is important to note that:

- Fiduciary funds (CIPPOE) are not included.
- Component units are included.

# 3 Capital Assets: Capitalization and Depreciation

## 3.1 Capitalization of Assets

The GASB 34 reporting model requires that capital assets, including infrastructure assets, be included in the government-wide financial statements.

### 3.1.1 Valuation

The cost of capital assets should include all ancillary charges necessary to place the asset into its intended location and condition of intended use.

### 3.1.2 Construction Period Interest

Interest cost incurred before the end of a construction period is not included in the historical cost of a capital asset. Interest cost is reported as interest expense on the government-wide financial statements and the financial statements of funds using the economic resources measurement focus (SE-CIPPOE) and displayed as an expenditure on the financial statements using the current financial resources measurement focus (GRSPP).

### 3.1.3 Infrastructure

The term *infrastructure asset* refers to streets, bridges, gutters, and other assets of the government.

Infrastructure assets should be recorded as general capital assets. They are only reported on the government-wide financial statements because of the incompatibility of recording these assets at the fund level with the governmental fund measurement focus and the fact that it would be difficult to allocate general assets to the individual funds.

## 3.2 Required Approach

All assets meeting capitalization requirements should be recorded and depreciated. Depreciation expense that can be specifically identified with a functional category should be included in the direct expenses of that function (e.g., depreciation expense on police cars would be classified as public safety).

## 3.3 Modified Approach

Infrastructure assets that are part of a network or subsystem of a network (hereafter referred to as eligible infrastructure assets) are not required to be depreciated, provided the features of its two requirements (described below) are met.

Under the modified approach, ongoing infrastructure expenditures are typically reported as expenses unless the outlays result in additions or improvements, in which case they would be capitalized.

### 3.3.1 Modified Approach Requirements

Governments may use the modified approach if they meet the following two requirements:

1. **The Asset Management System Meets Certain Conditions**
   - The government maintains an up-to-date inventory of eligible infrastructure assets (e.g., a map of roads, bridges, etc.).
   - A summarized condition assessment (good, poor, etc.) of the eligible infrastructure assets is performed and the results use a measurement scale.
   - Each year, an estimate is made of the amount necessary to maintain and preserve the eligible infrastructure assets at the condition level established and disclosed by the government.

## 2. Documentation Includes Data on Asset Preservation

- A complete condition assessment of eligible infrastructure assets must be performed in a consistent manner at least every three years.

- Reasonable assurance that the results of the three most recently completed condition assessments support assertions that the eligible infrastructure assets are being presented at (or above) the condition level established and disclosed by the government.

### 3.3.2 Modified Approach Reporting Requirements

Two schedules must be presented as required supplementary information as derived from the asset management system and documentation:

1. A schedule reporting the condition of the government's infrastructure; and
2. A comparison schedule of needed and actual expenditures to maintain the government's infrastructure.

### 3.3.3 Modified Approach Accounting Changes (Change in Estimates)

A change from the depreciation (required approach) to the modified approach should be treated as a change in accounting estimate.

A change from the modified approach to the depreciation approach should also be treated as a change in accounting estimate.

## 3.4 Impairment

Governments are required to determine whether impairment of an asset has occurred. Different types of impairment use different measurement techniques. Insurance recoveries are netted against the loss.

- **Physical Damage:** Measured using the *restoration cost approach*. Loss is equal to the estimated cost to restore the asset. The loss value is used to write down historical cost.

- **Enactment of Laws or Obsolescence:** Measured using the *service units approach*. The loss is estimated based on the productive units available before and after the impairment. Unit values are used to quantify the impairment write-off.

- **Asset Life (Duration) or Reduced Utility:** Measured using the *service units approach*.

## 3.5 Artwork and Historical Treasures

As a general rule, governments should capitalize works of art, historical treasures, and similar assets at their historical cost or fair value at date of donation (estimated if necessary), whether they are held as individual items or in a collection.

Under certain circumstances, governments have the option not to capitalize works of art. Regardless of whether collection items are donated or purchased, governments may elect not to capitalize works of art when that collection meets all three of the following conditions:

1. The collection is held for public exhibition, education, or research in furtherance of public service rather than financial gain.
2. The collection is protected, kept unencumbered, cared for, and preserved.
3. The collection is subject to an organizational policy that requires the proceeds from sales of collection items to be used to acquire other items for collections.

# 4 Statement of Activities

> Management's discussion and analysis (MD&A)
> **Government-wide financial statements** { Statement of net position
> Fund financial statements          **Statement of activities**
> Notes to financial statements
> Required supplementary information
> Other supplementary information

Revenue and expenses are reported on the government-wide statement of activities using the full accrual basis. This is a consolidated statement of all governmental and business-type activities.

## 4.1 Program Approach

The government-wide statement of activities uses a net program cost format that is not consistent with commercial accounting. The format provides cost information about the primary functions of the government and indicates each program's dependence on general revenues of the government. Total costs by function are compared to program revenue associated with each function to arrive at the net cost that must be defrayed by tax revenues.

## 4.2 Functions/Programs

The net expense or revenue for each function or program is classified into one of these categories:

- Primary government governmental activities
- Primary government business-type activities
- Component units

## 4.3 Expenses

Expenses are reported by function on the full accrual basis. This category represents expenses directly associated with each of the functions or programs listed.

## 4.4 Program Revenue

Program revenues are revenues directly associated with the function or program on the full accrual basis.

- Exchange revenue is recognized when goods or services are transferred. Revenue recognition is similar to commercial business enterprises (e.g., fees).
- Non-exchange revenue (GASB 33 *Accounting and Financial Reporting for Non-exchange Transactions*) involves transactions in which a government gives (or receives) value without directly receiving (or giving) equal value in exchange (e.g., grants).

## 4.5 Program Revenue Category Types

- **Charges for Services:** Revenues based on exchange or exchange-like transactions, including:
  - Charges for services to customers or applicants who directly benefit from goods or services (e.g., water and sewer fees, licenses, building permits, special assessments, etc.)
  - Charges for services to other governments (e.g., charges to housing prisoners, etc.)
  - Fines and forfeitures
- **Operating Grants and Contributions:** Mandatory and voluntary non-exchange transactions with other governments, organizations, or individuals restricted for use in a particular program.
  - Grant revenues in support of specific programs
- **Capital Grants and Contributions:** Mandatory and voluntary non-exchange transactions with other governments, organizations, or individuals restricted for use in a particular program.
  - Grant revenues in support of specific programs

## 4.6 Net (Expense) Revenue and Changes in Net Position

The net expense or revenue is presented in three categories and a total column:

- Primary government governmental activities column
- Primary government business-type activities column
- Total column (1 and 2)
- Component unit column

## 4.7 General Revenues

General revenues are presented separately in the same three categories and a total column as above. General revenues include taxes, interest earnings, and other revenues that are not specifically associated with a functional expense.

## 4.8 Special Items

Special items are reported separately. Special items are unusual or infrequent (but not both) and are within the control of management.

## 4.9 Change in Net Position

The change in net position is computed by deducting the general revenues from net (expenses) revenues. The net difference is combined with beginning net position to arrive at ending net position.

## 4.10 Eliminations

Generally, internal transactions that artificially "double up" on activity should be eliminated.

- Interfund services, such as water and other utilities, should not be eliminated.
- Internal activity associated with blended component units should be reclassified as interfund activity.
- Internal activity associated with discretely presented component units should be reported as external transactions.

## 4.11 Internal Service Funds

Internal service fund activity generally should be reported in the governmental activities column.

> **Pass Key**
>
> The government-wide statement of activities is the operating statement of the government.
> - The basis of accounting is full accrual—identical to commercial accounting.
> - The net program cost format generally is not used in commercial accounting and reporting.

**Progressive Township**
**Statement of Activities**
For the Year Ended December 31, Year 1

|  |  |  | Program Revenues |  | Net (Expenses) Revenues and Changes in Net Position |  |  |  |
|---|---|---|---|---|---|---|---|---|
|  |  |  |  |  | Primary Government |  |  |  |
| Functions/Programs | Expenses | Indirect Expense Allocation | Charges for Services | Operating Grants and Contrib. | Capital Grants and Contrib. | Governmental Activities | Business-type Activities | Total | Component Units |
| **Primary government:** |  |  |  |  |  |  |  |  |  |
| Governmental activities: |  |  |  |  |  |  |  |  |  |
| General government | $ 555,000 | $(50,000) | $ 215,000 | – | – | $ (290,000) | – | $ (290,000) | – |
| Public safety | 1,025,000 | 35,000 | 78,000 | – | – | (982,000) | – | (982,000) | – |
| Culture and recreation | 107,500 | 10,000 | – | – | – | (117,500) | – | (117,500) | – |
| Other functional classifications | 1,947,000 | 5,000 | – | $1,260,000 | – | (692,000) | – | (692,000) | – |
| Interest on long-term debt | 246,000 | – | 125,000 | – | – | (121,000) | – | (121,000) | – |
| Total governmental activities | 3,880,500 | – | 418,000 | 1,260,000 | – | (2,202,500) | – | (2,202,500) | – |
| Business-type activities: |  |  |  |  |  |  |  |  |  |
| Water | 692,000 | – | 700,000 | – | – | – | $ 8,000 | 8,000 | – |
| Sewer | 1,038,000 | – | 1,050,000 | – | $300,000 | – | 312,000 | 312,000 | – |
| Parking facilities | 465,000 | – | 650,000 | – | – | – | 185,000 | 185,000 | – |
| Total business-type activities | 2,195,000 | – | 2,400,000 | – | 300,000 | – | 505,000 | 505,000 | – |
| Total primary government | $6,075,500 | – | $2,818,000 | $1,260,000 | $300,000 | (2,202,500) | 505,000 | (1,697,500) | – |
| **Component units:** |  |  |  |  |  |  |  |  |  |
| Landfill | 300,000 | – | 500,000 | – | – | – | – | – | $200,000 |
| Public school system | 1,000,000 | – | 100,000 | – | – | – | – | – | (900,000) |
| Total component units | $1,300,000 | – | $ 600,000 | – | – | – | – | – | $(700,000) |
| General revenues |  |  |  |  |  |  |  |  |  |
| Taxes: |  |  |  |  |  |  |  |  |  |
| Property taxes—levied for general purposes |  |  |  |  |  | 1,620,000 | – | 1,620,000 | 1,000,000 |
| Franchise taxes |  |  |  |  |  | 735,000 | – | 735,000 | – |
| Investment earnings |  |  |  |  |  | 205,000 | 60,000 | 265,000 | – |
| Special item—gain on sale of governmental capital property |  |  |  |  |  | 425,000 | – | 425,000 | – |
| Transfers |  |  |  |  |  | 12,000 | (12,000) | – | – |
| Total general revenues, special items, and transfers |  |  |  |  |  | 2,997,000 | 48,000 | 3,045,000 | 1,000,000 |
| Change in net position |  |  |  |  |  | 794,500 | 553,000 | 1,347,500 | 300,000 |
| Net position—beginning |  |  |  |  |  | 2,935,500 | 1,282,000 | 4,217,500 | 90,000 |
| Net position—ending |  |  |  |  |  | $3,730,000 | $1,835,000 | $5,565,000 | $ 390,000 |

## Pass Key

To remember the categories of program revenue, just recall that the government can **SOC** away these revenues:

- **Services** (charges for)
- **Operating** grants and contributions
- **Capital** grants and contributions

---

### Question 1 — MCQ-05949

On March 1, Wag City issued $1,000,000, 10-year, 6 percent general obligation bonds at par with no bond issue costs. The bonds pay interest September 1 and March 1. What amount of interest expense and bond interest payable should Wag report in its government-wide financial statements at the close of the fiscal year on December 31?

- a. Interest expense, $50,000; interest payable, $20,000.
- b. Interest expense, $50,000; interest payable, $0.
- c. Interest expense, $60,000; interest payable, $10,000.
- d. Interest expense, $30,000; interest payable, $0.

---

### Question 2 — MCQ-04670

During the current year, Knoxx County levied property taxes of $2,000,000, of which 1 percent is expected to be uncollectible. The following amounts were collected during the current year:

| | |
|---|---:|
| Prior year taxes collected within the 60 days of the current year | $ 50,000 |
| Prior year taxes collected between 60 days and 90 days into the current year | 120,000 |
| Current year taxes collected in the current year | 1,800,000 |
| Current year taxes collected within the first 60 days of the subsequent year | 80,000 |

What amount of property tax revenue should Knoxx County report in its government-wide statement of activities?

- a. $1,800,000
- b. $1,970,000
- c. $1,980,000
- d. $2,000,000

**Question 3** MCQ-08616

A city government reported a $9,000 increase in net position in the motor pool internal service fund, a $12,000 increase in net position in the water enterprise fund, and a $7,000 increase in the employee pension fund. The motor pool internal service fund provides service primarily to the police department. What amount should the city report as the change in net position for business-type activities in its statement of activities?

- a. $9,000
- b. $12,000
- c. $21,000
- d. $28,000

# MODULE 5: Fund Financial Statements

FAR 10

## 1 Fund Financial Statements

Financial statements are required for the governmental, proprietary, and fiduciary funds. Fund financial statements are presented by major fund rather than by fund type. Reporting by major fund provides more meaningful information.

### 1.1 Major Fund Rules

Major funds are specifically defined as follows: A major fund must meet the 10 percent criteria within its category *and* also meet the 5 percent criteria associated with both categories. Both rules must be met.

#### 1.1.1 10 Percent Test

To meet the 10 percent test, the individual GRSPP funds are individually compared with the total of all governmental funds, and the enterprise funds are individually compared with the total of all enterprise funds.

A fund may be a major fund if it has 10 percent or more of the corresponding total revenues, expenditures/expenses, assets and deferred outflows of resources, or liabilities and deferred inflows of resources of:

- All governmental funds

  *Or:*

- All enterprise funds

#### 1.1.2 5 Percent Test

To meet the 5 percent test, the GRSPP funds are individually compared with the total of all the governmental funds and enterprise funds and each enterprise fund is individually compared with the total of all enterprise funds and governmental funds to meet the 5 percent test.

A fund is a major fund if it meets the 10 percent test and also has 5 percent or more of revenues, expenditures/expenses, assets and deferred outflows of resources, or liabilities and deferred inflows of resources of:

- All governmental funds

  *And:*

- All enterprise funds

## 1.1.3 Other Major Fund Considerations

- Government officials may elect to report a fund as major if they believe that the public interest is served by the reporting, regardless of the quantitative criteria.
- The general fund is always considered a major fund.
- Internal service funds are not considered in the evaluation of major and nonmajor funds. The only proprietary funds used in the determination of major and nonmajor funds are the enterprise funds.
- Extraordinary items and transfers are not considered in major fund determinations.

> **Pass Key**
>
> When determining whether a fund qualifies as a major fund, remember:
> - Aggregate fund balance/equity is not used in either test.
> - The general fund will always be a major fund.
> - Internal service funds will not be considered in the evaluation of major and nonmajor funds.

---

**Question 1**  MCQ-05144

The city of Faberville is evaluating which of its funds it will present as a major fund in its fund financial statements at December 31, Year 1. The city presents the following partial listing of asset data at December 31, Year 1:

| | |
|---|---:|
| Total governmental fund type assets | $3,000,000 |
| Total enterprise fund assets | 2,000,000 |
| General fund assets | 280,000 |
| Community development special revenue fund | 290,000 |
| Sales tax special revenue fund | 350,000 |
| General revenue bonds debt service fund | 120,000 |
| Faberville river bridge capital project fund | 1,500,000 |
| Faberville water and sewer utility fund | 1,800,000 |
| Faberville landfill | 200,000 |

Based purely on assets, how many funds should be displayed as major funds?

- a. Three
- b. Four
- c. Five
- d. Six

# 2 Governmental Funds  GRaSPP

## 2.1 Balance Sheet

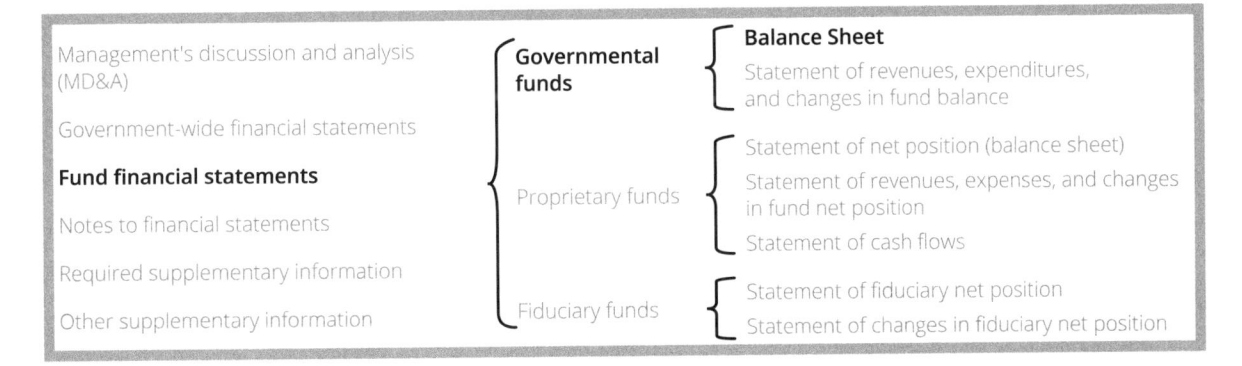

> - Management's discussion and analysis (MD&A)
> - Government-wide financial statements
> - **Fund financial statements**
> - Notes to financial statements
> - Required supplementary information
> - Other supplementary information
>
> Governmental funds
> - Balance Sheet
> - Statement of revenues, expenditures, and changes in fund balance
>
> Proprietary funds
> - Statement of net position (balance sheet)
> - Statement of revenues, expenses, and changes in fund net position
> - Statement of cash flows
>
> Fiduciary funds
> - Statement of fiduciary net position
> - Statement of changes in fiduciary net position

Governmental funds should present financial position in a balance sheet format that displays assets plus deferred outflows of resources equal to liabilities plus deferred inflows of resources plus fund balance.

**Progressive Township**
**Balance Sheet**
**Governmental Funds**
As of December 31, Year 1

|  | General Fund | HUD Programs | Convention Development Tax | Convention Center Bonds | Convention Center Construction | Other Governmental Funds | Total Governmental Funds |
|---|---|---|---|---|---|---|---|
| **Assets** | | | | | | | |
| Cash | $ 800,000 | $80,000 | $250,000 | $505,000 | $2,100,000 | $270,000 | $4,005,000 |
| Receivables | 162,000 | – | – | 125,000 | – | – | 287,000 |
| Due from other funds | 450,000 | – | – | 60,000 | – | – | 510,000 |
| Receivables from other governments | 620,000 | – | 50,000 | – | – | 58,000 | 728,000 |
| Inventories | 55,000 | – | – | – | – | 31,000 | 86,000 |
| **Total assets** | $2,087,000 | $80,000 | $300,000 | $690,000 | $2,100,000 | $359,000 | $5,616,000 |
| **Liabilities** | | | | | | | |
| Accounts payable | $ 250,000 | $20,000 | $ 56,000 | – | $ 600,000 | $100,000 | $1,026,000 |
| Due to other funds | 50,000 | – | 60,000 | – | – | – | 110,000 |
| Payable to other governments | 65,000 | – | – | – | – | – | 65,000 |
| Other liabilities | 95,000 | – | – | – | – | – | 95,000 |
| **Total liabilities** | 460,000 | 20,000 | 116,000 | – | 600,000 | 100,000 | 1,296,000 |
| **Deferred Inflows of Resources** | | | | | | | |
| Unavailable revenues—special assessments | – | – | – | $125,000 | – | – | 125,000 |
| **Total deferred inflows of resources** | – | – | – | 125,000 | – | – | 125,000 |

(continued)

Fund Financial Statements FAR 10

(continued)

**Fund Balances**

| | | | | | | | |
|---|---|---|---|---|---|---|---|
| Nonspendable Inventories | 55,000 | – | – | – | – | 31,000 | 86,000 |
| Restricted for: | | | | | | | |
|    Debt service | – | – | – | 565,000 | – | 158,000 | 723,000 |
|    Capital projects | – | – | – | – | 1,500,000 | 74,000 | 1,574,000 |
| Committed to: | | | | | | | |
|    Urban renewal | – | 60,000 | 184,000 | – | – | – | 244,000 |
|    Sanitation | 45,000 | – | – | – | – | – | 45,000 |
| Assigned: | | | | | | | |
|    Special revenue funds | – | – | – | – | – | 11,000 | 11,000 |
| Unassigned: | | | | | | | |
|    General fund | 1,527,000 | – | – | – | – | – | 1,527,000 |
|    Special revenue funds | – | – | – | – | – | (15,000) | (15,000) |
| **Total fund balances** | 1,627,000 | 60,000 | 184,000 | 565,000 | 1,500,000 | 259,000 | 4,195,000 |
| **Total liabilities, deferred inflows of resources, and fund balances** | $2,087,000 | $80,000 | $300,000 | $690,000 | $2,100,000 | $359,000 | $5,616,000 |

## 2.2 Statement of Revenue, Expenditures, and Changes in Fund Balance

- Management's discussion and analysis (MD&A)
- Government-wide financial statements
- **Fund financial statements**
- Notes to financial statements
- Required supplementary information
- Other supplementary information

Governmental funds
- Balance sheet
- **Statement of revenues, expenditures, and changes in fund balance**

Proprietary funds
- Statement of net position (balance sheet)
- Statement of revenues, expenses, and changes in fund net position
- Statement of cash flows

Fiduciary funds
- Statement of fiduciary net position
- Statement of changes in fiduciary net position

---

**Progressive Township**
**Statement of Revenues, Expenditures, and Changes in Fund Balances**
**Governmental Funds**
For the Year Ended December 31, Year 1

| | General Fund | HUD Programs | Convention Development Tax | Convention Center Bonds | Convention Center Construction | Other Governmental Funds | Total Governmental Funds |
|---|---|---|---|---|---|---|---|
| **Revenues** | | | | | | | |
| Property taxes | $1,620,000 | – | – | – | – | – | $1,620,000 |
| Fees and fines | 120,000 | – | – | – | – | – | 120,000 |
| Intergovernmental | – | $960,000 | $375,000 | – | – | $660,000 | 1,995,000 |
| Charges for services | – | – | – | – | – | 78,000 | 78,000 |
| Interest earnings | 55,000 | – | 28,000 | $36,000 | $40,000 | 40,000 | 199,000 |
| Total revenues | 1,795,000 | 960,000 | 403,000 | 36,000 | 40,000 | 778,000 | 4,012,000 |

(continued)

(continued)

**Expenditures**

| | | | | | | | |
|---|---|---|---|---|---|---|---|
| Current: | | | | | | | |
| General government | 450,000 | – | – | – | – | – | 450,000 |
| Public safety | 1,000,000 | – | – | – | – | – | 1,000,000 |
| Culture and recreation | 80,000 | – | 17,500 | – | – | – | 97,500 |
| Other functional classifications | 200,000 | 940,000 | – | – | – | 757,000 | 1,897,000 |
| Debt service: | | | | | | | |
| Principal | – | – | – | 250,000 | – | 110,000 | 360,000 |
| Interest and other charges | – | – | – | 30,000 | – | 211,000 | 241,000 |
| Capital outlay | 25,000 | – | – | – | 600,000 | 162,000 | 787,000 |
| Total expenditures | 1,755,000 | 940,000 | 17,500 | 280,000 | 600,000 | 1,240,000 | 4,832,500 |
| Excess (deficiency) of revenues over expenditures | 40,000 | 20,000 | 385,500 | (244,000) | (560,000) | (462,000) | (820,500) |

**Other Financing Sources (Uses)**

| | | | | | | | |
|---|---|---|---|---|---|---|---|
| Proceeds of long-term capital-related debt | – | – | – | – | 2,080,000 | – | 2,080,000 |
| Transfers in | 85,000 | – | – | 370,000 | – | 66,000 | 521,000 |
| Transfers out | (14,000) | – | (250,000) | – | (120,000) | (125,000) | (509,000) |
| Total other financing sources and uses | 71,000 | – | (250,000) | 370,000 | 1,960,000 | (59,000) | 2,092,000 |

**Special Item**

| | | | | | | | |
|---|---|---|---|---|---|---|---|
| Proceeds from sale of land | 500,000 | – | – | – | – | – | 500,000 |
| **Net change in fund balances** | 611,000 | 20,000 | 135,500 | 126,000 | 1,400,000 | (521,000) | 1,771,500 |
| Fund balances—beginning | 1,016,000 | 40,000 | 48,500 | 439,000 | 100,000 | 780,000 | 2,423,500 |
| Fund balance—ending | $1,627,000 | $ 60,000 | $ 184,000 | $ 565,000 | $1,500,000 | $ 259,000 | $4,195,000 |

# 3 Proprietary Funds  SE

## 3.1 Statement of Net Position

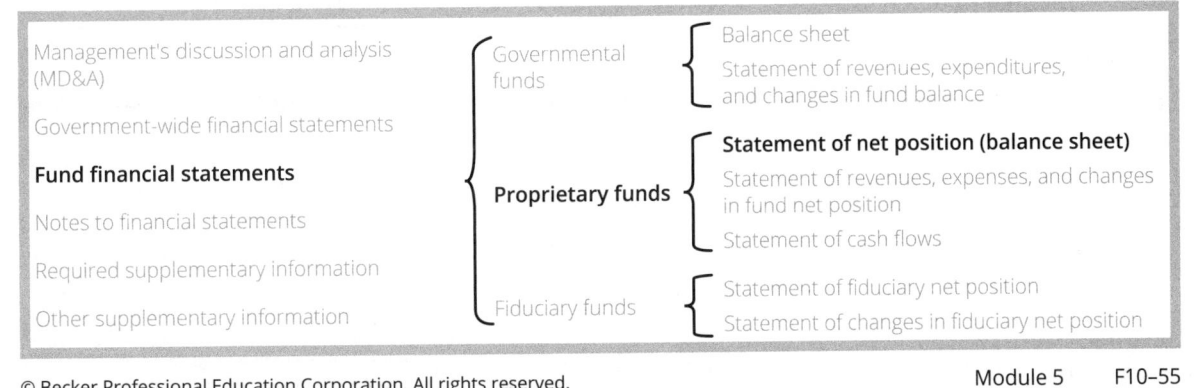

- Management's discussion and analysis (MD&A)
- Government-wide financial statements
- **Fund financial statements**
- Notes to financial statements
- Required supplementary information
- Other supplementary information

Governmental funds:
- Balance sheet
- Statement of revenues, expenditures, and changes in fund balance

Proprietary funds:
- **Statement of net position (balance sheet)**
- Statement of revenues, expenses, and changes in fund net position
- Statement of cash flows

Fiduciary funds:
- Statement of fiduciary net position
- Statement of changes in fiduciary net position

# Fund Financial Statements

Proprietary funds are encouraged to report net position as the difference between assets plus deferred outflows of resources and liabilities plus deferred inflows of resources (similar to the government-wide statement of net position). Proprietary funds can also use a balance sheet format [(Assets + Deferred outflows of resources) = (Liabilities + Deferred inflows of resources) + Net position].

**Progressive Township**
**Statement of Net Position**
**Proprietary Funds**
As of December 31, Year 1

|  | Business-Type Activities Enterprise Funds |  |  | Governmental Activities |
|---|---|---|---|---|
|  | Water and Sewer | Parking Facilities | Totals | Internal Service Funds |
| **Assets** |  |  |  |  |
| Current assets: |  |  |  |  |
| Cash | $ 650,000 | $ 150,000 | $ 800,000 | $ 50,000 |
| Derivative instrument—rate swap | 40,000 | – | 40,000 | – |
| Receivables | 500,000 | 20,000 | 520,000 | 25,000 |
| Due from other governments | 100,000 | 50,000 | 150,000 | 50,000 |
| Inventories | 85,000 | 42,500 | 127,500 | 35,000 |
| Total current assets | 1,375,000 | 262,500 | 1,637,500 | 160,000 |
| Non-current assets: |  |  |  |  |
| Restricted cash and cash equivalents | 750,000 | 450,000 | 1,200,000 | – |
| Capital assets: |  |  |  |  |
| Land | 700,000 | 400,000 | 1,100,000 | $ 50,000 |
| Buildings and equipment | 1,800,000 | 1,200,000 | 3,000,000 | 150,000 |
| Less: accumulated depreciation | (750,000) | (375,000) | (1,125,000) | (40,000) |
| Total non-current assets | 2,500,000 | 1,675,000 | 4,175,000 | 160,000 |
| **Total assets** | 3,875,000 | 1,937,500 | 5,812,500 | 320,000 |
| **Deferred Outflows of Resources** |  |  |  |  |
| Accumulated decrease in fair value of hedging derivatives | 35,000 | – | 35,000 | – |
| **Total deferred outflows of resources** | 35,000 | – | 35,000 | – |

(continued)

(continued)

**Liabilities**

| | | | | |
|---|---:|---:|---:|---:|
| Current liabilities: | | | | |
| Accounts payable | 350,000 | 50,000 | 400,000 | 13,000 |
| Due to other funds | 450,000 | – | 450,000 | – |
| Forward contract | 35,000 | – | 35,000 | – |
| Compensated absences | 75,000 | 37,500 | 112,500 | 16,000 |
| Claims and judgments | – | – | – | – |
| Bonds, notes, and loans payable | 150,000 | 75,000 | 225,000 | 30,000 |
| Total current liabilities | 1,060,000 | 162,500 | 1,222,500 | 59,000 |
| Non-current liabilities: | | | | |
| Compensated absences | 300,000 | 150,000 | 450,000 | 28,000 |
| Claims and judgments | – | – | – | – |
| Bonds, notes, and loans payable | 1,300,000 | 1,000,000 | 2,300,000 | 70,000 |
| Total non-current liabilities | 1,600,000 | 1,150,000 | 2,750,000 | 98,000 |
| **Total liabilities** | 2,660,000 | 1,312,500 | 3,972,500 | 157,000 |

**Deferred Inflows of Resources**

| | | | | |
|---|---:|---:|---:|---:|
| Accumulated increase in fair value of hedging derivatives | 40,000 | – | 40,000 | – |
| **Total deferred inflows of resources** | 40,000 | – | 40,000 | – |

**Net Position**

| | | | | |
|---|---:|---:|---:|---:|
| Net investment in capital assets | 300,000 | 150,000 | 450,000 | 60,000 |
| Restricted for debt service | 750,000 | 450,000 | 1,200,000 | – |
| Unrestricted | 160,000 | 25,000 | 185,000 | 103,000 |
| **Total net position** | $1,210,000 | $625,000 | $1,835,000 | $163,000 |

## 3.2 Statement of Revenues, Expenses, and Changes in Fund Net Position

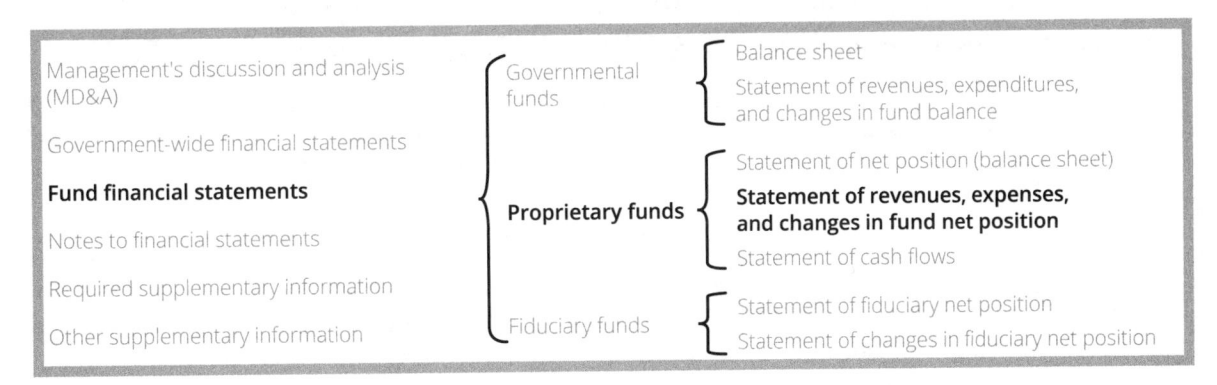

- Management's discussion and analysis (MD&A)
- Government-wide financial statements
- **Fund financial statements**
  - Governmental funds
    - Balance sheet
    - Statement of revenues, expenditures, and changes in fund balance
  - Proprietary funds
    - Statement of net position (balance sheet)
    - **Statement of revenues, expenses, and changes in fund net position**
    - Statement of cash flows
  - Fiduciary funds
    - Statement of fiduciary net position
    - Statement of changes in fiduciary net position
- Notes to financial statements
- Required supplementary information
- Other supplementary information

## Progressive Township
### Statement of Revenues, Expenses, and Changes in Fund Net Position
### Proprietary Funds
For the Year Ended December 31, Year 1

|  | Business-Type Activities Enterprise Funds ||| Governmental Activities |
|---|---|---|---|---|
|  | **Water and Sewer** | **Parking Facilities** | **Totals** | **Internal Service Funds** |
| Operating revenues |  |  |  |  |
| Charges for services | $1,500,000 | $600,000 | $2,100,000 | $ 95,000 |
| Miscellaneous | 250,000 | 50,000 | 300,000 | – |
| **Total operating revenues** | 1,750,000 | 650,000 | 2,400,000 | 95,000 |
| Operating expenses |  |  |  |  |
| Personal services | 975,000 | 150,000 | 1,125,000 | 55,000 |
| Contracted services | 85,000 | 35,000 | 120,000 | 5,000 |
| Other operating expenses | 300,000 | 30,000 | 330,000 | 10,000 |
| Insurance claims and expenses | – | – | – |  |
| Depreciation expense | 270,000 | 200,000 | 470,000 | – |
| **Total operating expenses** | 1,630,000 | 415,000 | 2,045,000 | 70,000 |
| **Operating income (loss)** | 120,000 | 235,000 | 355,000 | 25,000 |
| Nonoperating revenues (expenses) |  |  |  |  |
| Interest and investment revenue | 60,000 | – | 60,000 | 6,000 |
| Interest expense | (100,000) | (50,000) | (150,000) | (5,000) |
| **Total nonoperating revenue (expenses)** | (40,000) | (50,000) | (90,000) | 1,000 |
| **Income (loss) before contributions and transfers** | 80,000 | 185,000 | 265,000 | 26,000 |
| Capital contributions | 300,000 | – | 300,000 | – |
| Transfers | – | (12,000) | (12,000) | – |
| **Change in net position** | 380,000 | 173,000 | 553,000 | 26,000 |
| **Total net position—beginning** | 830,000 | 452,000 | 1,282,000 | 137,000 |
| **Total net position—ending** | $1,210,000 | $625,000 | $1,835,000 | $163,000 |

## 3.3 Statement of Cash Flows

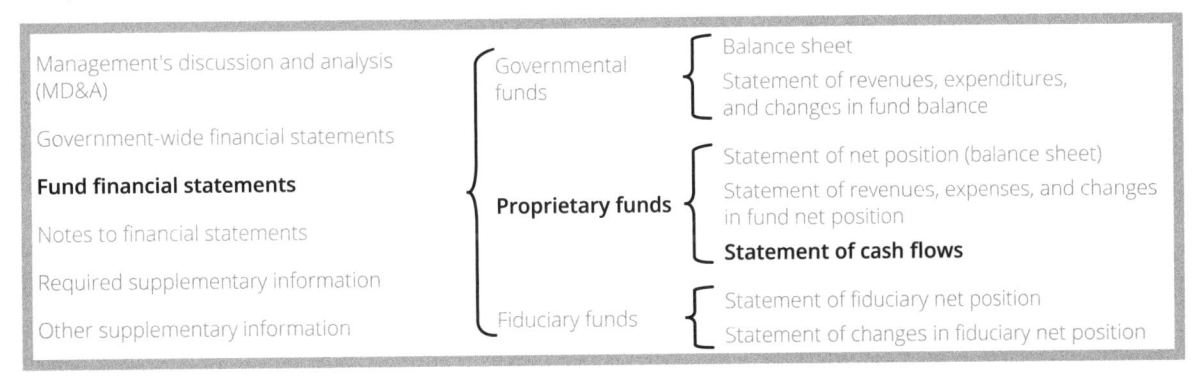

- Management's discussion and analysis (MD&A)
- Government-wide financial statements
- **Fund financial statements**
- Notes to financial statements
- Required supplementary information
- Other supplementary information

Governmental funds
- Balance sheet
- Statement of revenues, expenditures, and changes in fund balance

Proprietary funds
- Statement of net position (balance sheet)
- Statement of revenues, expenses, and changes in fund net position
- **Statement of cash flows**

Fiduciary funds
- Statement of fiduciary net position
- Statement of changes in fiduciary net position

The proprietary funds statement of cash flows is similar to the commercial statement of cash flows, with the following seven differences:

1. The direct method is required (indirect method is not permitted).
2. A reconciliation of operating income (not net income) to net cash provided by operations is required.
3. There are four categories (instead of the three categories in commercial accounting):
   - Operating activities
   - Capital and related financing activities
   - Noncapital financing activities
   - Investing activities
4. The order of financing and investing activities categories are reversed. Governmental entities present the financing categories before investing. Commercial entities present the investing category before financing.
5. Interest income/cash receipts are reported as *investing activities* (not as operating activities).
6. Interest expense/cash payments are either:
   - Capital and related financing; or
   - Noncapital financing.
7. Capital asset purchases are reported as *financing activities* (not as investing activities).

### Pass Key

The reconciliation of operating income to net cash provided by operations includes depreciation and changes in current assets and liabilities, but does not include adjustments for gains and losses because gains and losses and nonoperating items are not included in operating income.

### 3.3.1 Operating Activities

Proprietary fund operating activities include:

- Cash inflows from sales of goods and services
- Cash outflows to suppliers or employees
- Cash inflows from interfund reimbursements and exchanges including payments in lieu of taxes
- Cash transactions not meeting the definition of the other categories

### 3.3.2 Investing Activities

Proprietary fund investing activities include:

- Cash inflows and outflows associated with loans to others (including interest income)
- Cash inflows and outflows associated with equity transactions

### 3.3.3 Capital and Related Financing Activities

- Capital and related financing activities include:
  - Cash flows from issuing debt associated with capital assets (including interest expense)
  - Cash inflows from capital grants
  - Cash inflows from contribution activity associated with capital assets
  - Cash activity related to special assessments associated with capital assets

### 3.3.4 Noncapital Financing Activities

- Noncapital financing activities include:
  - Cash flows from issuing debt for noncapital purposes (including interest expense)
  - Cash receipts from grants or subsidies
  - Cash received from property taxes (not restricted for capital use)
  - Operating transfers

**Progressive Township**
**Statement of Cash Flows**
**Proprietary Funds**
For the Year Ended December 31, Year 1

|  | Business-Type Activities Enterprise Funds ||| Governmental Activities |
|---|---|---|---|---|
|  | Water and Sewer | Parking Facilities | Totals | Internal Service Funds |
| **Cash Flows From Operating Activities** |  |  |  |  |
| Receipts from customers | $1,510,000 | $755,000 | $2,265,000 | $ 65,000 |
| Payments to suppliers | (334,000) | (167,000) | (501,000) | (24,000) |
| Payments to employees | (903,750) | (451,875) | (1,355,625) | (48,250) |
| Internal activity—net payments (to) from other funds | 180,000 | 90,000 | 270,000 | – |
| Net cash provided by operating activities | 452,250 | 226,125 | 678,375 | (7,250) |

(continued)

(continued)

**Cash Flows From Noncapital Financing Activities**

| | | | | |
|---|---|---|---|---|
| Operating subsidies and transfers to other funds | – | (12,000) | (12,000) | – |

**Cash Flows From Capital and Related Financing Activities**

| | | | | |
|---|---|---|---|---|
| Proceeds from capital debt | 800,000 | 400,000 | 1,200,000 | 72,900 |
| Capital contributions | 300,000 | – | 300,000 | – |
| Purchases of capital assets | (800,000) | (400,000) | (1,200,000) | (72,900) |
| Principal paid on capital debt | (97,500) | (48,750) | (146,250) | (37,900) |
| Interest paid on capital debt | (100,000) | (50,000) | (150,000) | (5,000) |
| Net cash provided (used) by capital and related financing activities | 102,500 | (98,750) | 3,750 | (42,900) |

**Cash Flows From Investing Activities**

| | | | | |
|---|---|---|---|---|
| Purchase of investments | (250,000) | (125,000) | (375,000) | – |
| Interest and dividends | 60,000 | 30,000 | 90,000 | 6,000 |
| Net cash provided by investing activities | (190,000) | (95,000) | (285,000) | 6,000 |
| Net increase (decrease) in cash and cash equivalents | 364,750 | 20,375 | 385,125 | (44,150) |
| Balances—beginning of the year | 285,250 | 129,625 | 414,875 | 94,150 |
| Balances—end of the year | $ 650,000 | $150,000 | $ 800,000 | $ 50,000 |

**Reconciliation of Operating Income (Loss) to Net Cash Provided (Used) by Operating Activities**

| | | | | |
|---|---|---|---|---|
| Operating income (loss) | $120,000 | $235,000 | $355,000 | $ 25,000 |
| Adjustments to reconcile operating income to net cash provided (used) by operating activities: | | | | |
| Depreciation expense | 270,000 | 200,000 | 470,000 | – |
| Change in assets and liabilities: | | | | |
| Receivables, net | (240,000) | (180,000) | (420,000) | (30,000) |
| Inventories | (34,000) | (17,000) | (51,000) | (14,000) |
| Accounts and other payables | 302,500 | 75,625 | 378,125 | 11,750 |
| Accrued expenses | 33,750 | (87,500) | (53,750) | – |
| Net cash provided by operating activities | $ 452,250 | $226,125 | $ 678,375 | $ (7,250) |

# 4 Fiduciary Funds  CIPPOE

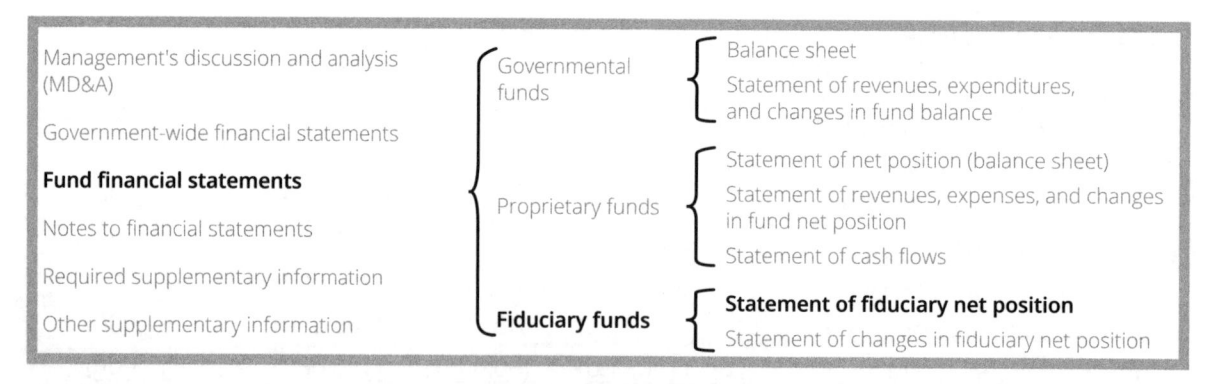

- Management's discussion and analysis (MD&A)
- Government-wide financial statements
- **Fund financial statements**
  - Governmental funds
    - Balance sheet
    - Statement of revenues, expenditures, and changes in fund balance
  - Proprietary funds
    - Statement of net position (balance sheet)
    - Statement of revenues, expenses, and changes in fund net position
    - Statement of cash flows
  - Fiduciary funds
    - Statement of fiduciary net position
    - Statement of changes in fiduciary net position
- Notes to financial statements
- Required supplementary information
- Other supplementary information

Fiduciary funds are required to report net position as the difference between assets plus deferred outflows of resources and liabilities plus deferred inflows of resources (similar to the government-wide statement of net position).

## 4.1 Statement of Fiduciary Net Position

**Progressive Township**
**Statement of Fiduciary Net Position**
**Fiduciary Funds**
As of December 31, Year 1

| | Pension and Other Employee Benefit Trust Funds | Private Purpose Trust Funds | Custodial Funds |
|---|---|---|---|
| **Assets** | | | |
| Cash | $1,000,000 | $ 4,000 | $50,000 |
| Receivables: | | | |
|   Taxes for other governments | – | – | 200,000 |
|   Interest and dividends | 70,000 | – | – |
|   Other receivables | 25,000 | 1,000 | – |
|     Total receivables | 95,000 | 1,000 | 200,000 |
| Investments at fair value: | | | |
|   U.S. government obligations | 1,000,000 | 40,000 | – |
|   Corporate bonds | 1,000,000 | – | – |
|   Corporate stock | 2,000,000 | – | – |
|     Total investments | 4,000,000 | 40,000 | – |
| **Total assets** | $5,095,000 | 45,000 | 250,000 |
| **Liabilities** | | | |
| Accounts payable | 30,000 | 3,000 | – |
| Due to local governments | – | – | 143,000 |
| Refunds payable and others | 14,580 | – | – |
|   **Total liabilities** | $ 44,580 | $ 3,000 | $143,000 |
| **Net Position** | | | |
| Restricted for | | | |
|   Pensions | 5,050,420 | – | – |
|   Individuals, organizations, and other governments | – | 42,000 | 107,000 |
| Total net position | $5,050,420 | $42,000 | $107,000 |

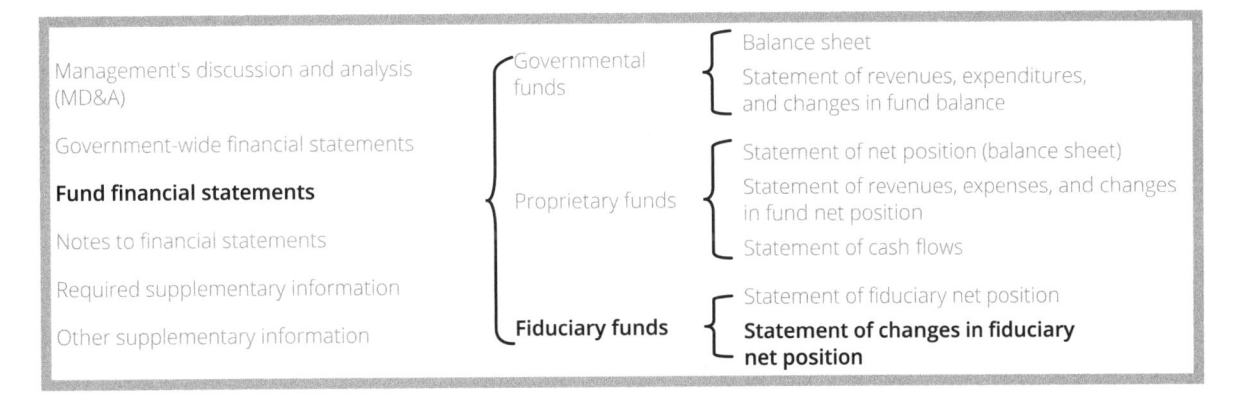

## 4.2 Statement of Changes in Fiduciary Net Position

- Management's discussion and analysis (MD&A)
- Government-wide financial statements
- **Fund financial statements**
  - Governmental funds
    - Balance sheet
    - Statement of revenues, expenditures, and changes in fund balance
  - Proprietary funds
    - Statement of net position (balance sheet)
    - Statement of revenues, expenses, and changes in fund net position
    - Statement of cash flows
  - Fiduciary funds
    - Statement of fiduciary net position
    - Statement of changes in fiduciary net position
- Notes to financial statements
- Required supplementary information
- Other supplementary information

**Progressive Township**
**Statement of Changes In Fiduciary Net Position**
**Fiduciary Funds**
For the Year Ended December 31, Year 1

|  | Pension and Other Employee Benefit Trust Funds | Private Purpose Trust Funds | Custodial Funds |
|---|---|---|---|
| **Additions** | | | |
| Contributions: | | | |
|   Employer | $ 470,631 | – | – |
|   Plan members | 156,900 | – | – |
|     Total contributions | 627,531 | – | – |
| Investment earnings: | | | |
|   Net increase (decrease) in fair value of investments | 200,000 | – | – |
|   Interest | 130,000 | $ 3,200 | – |
|   Dividends | 60,000 | – | – |
|     Total investment earnings | 390,000 | 3,200 | – |
|   Less investment expense | 40,000 | – | – |
|     Net investment earnings | 350,000 | 3,200 | – |
| Tax collections for other governments | – | – | $1,500,000 |
| Miscellaneous | – | – | 15,000 |
| **Total additions** | 977,531 | 3,200 | 1,515,000 |
| **Deductions** | | | |
| Benefits | 156,895 | 5,200 | – |
| Refunds of contributions | 62,768 | – | – |
| Administrative expenses | 4,896 | 1,000 | 3,000 |
| Payments of tax collections to other governments | – | – | 1,500,000 |
|   **Total deductions** | 224,559 | 6,200 | 1,503,000 |
| **Change in net position** | 752,972 | (3,000) | 12,000 |
| **Net position—beginning of the year** | 4,297,448 | 45,000 | 95,000 |
| **Net position—end of the year** | $5,050,420 | $42,000 | $ 107,000 |

## Question 2    MCQ-06820

Abbott Township is preparing its statement of cash flows for its Water and Sewer Enterprise Fund and noted the following transactions:

| | |
|---|---:|
| Cash payments from customers | $ 250,000 |
| Property tax receipts to subsidize operations | 150,000 |
| Special assessment receipts to defray the cost of improved wastewater infrastructure | 50,000 |
| Operating transfers out | (125,000) |

Abbot Township's statement of cash flows should include which of the following amounts?

| | Operating Activities | Noncapital Financing Activities | Capital and Related Financing Activities | Investing Activities |
|---|---|---|---|---|
| a. | $250,000 | $150,000 | $50,000 | $(125,000) |
| b. | $250,000 | $25,000 | $50,000 | $0 |
| c. | $400,000 | $(125,000) | $0 | $50,000 |
| d. | $275,000 | $0 | $50,000 | $0 |

# MODULE 6: Deriving Government-wide Financial Statements and Reconciliation Requirements

FAR 10

## 1 Reconciliation of Governmental Fund Financial Statements to Government-wide Financial Statements

### 1.1 Reconciliation Requirement

Financial statement presentation for governments requires a reconciliation of the equity presented on the balance sheet and the increase/decrease in equity presented in the operating statement from the governmental fund perspective to the government-wide financial statements.

The differences between governmental fund and government-wide financial statements are the result of differences in the measurement focus and basis of accounting used by each presentation.

#### 1.1.1 Measurement Focus Differences

Reconciliation of governmental fund financial statements to the government-wide financial statements involves elimination of the effect of using the current financial resources measurement focus for governmental fund financial statements instead of the economic resources measurement focus used in government-wide financials. Generally, this involves adjustment of capital asset and long-term debt accounts.

#### 1.1.2 Basis of Accounting Differences

Reconciliation of governmental fund financial statements to the government-wide financial statements involves elimination of the effect of using the modified accrual basis of accounting in governmental fund financial statements instead of the full accrual basis of accounting used in government-wide financial statements.

Generally, this involves increasing revenues to show revenues earned rather than only those measurable and available and recognizing expenses when incurred rather than expenditures of current resources.

### 1.2 Reconciliation of the Governmental Funds Balance Sheet to the Government-wide Statement of Net Position

Total fund balance presented in the governmental funds balance sheet must be reconciled to net position from governmental activities presented in the government-wide statement of net position. This reconciliation includes the following:

- Adjustments for the difference in measurement focus:
    - Add **capital** (non-current) assets
    - Subtract related **accumulated** depreciation
    - Subtract **non-current** liabilities

- Adjustments for the difference in basis of accounting:
  - Eliminate deferred inflows associated with recognized revenues (amount of eliminated deferred inflows added)
  - Subtract accrued liability for interest payable
- Consolidation entries:
  - Add internal **service** fund net position

## Pass Key

The balance sheet adjustments can be remembered using the **CANS** mnemonic along with basis of accounting adjustments associated with current year accruals:

|   | |
|---|---|
|   | Total governmental fund balance |
| + | **C**apital assets (existing and current) |
| − | **A**ccumulated depreciation |
| − | **N**on-current liabilities (existing) |
| + | Eliminate/ reverse deferred inflows (add the reduction of deferred inflows associated with revenue recognized and closed to net position as an addition to net position) |
| − | Accrued interest payable |
| + | Internal **s**ervice fund net position |
|   | Net position from governmental activities |

The reconciliation can be presented on the face of the governmental funds balance sheet or in a separate schedule.

**Progressive Township**
**Reconciliation of the Balance Sheet of Governmental Funds to the Statement of Net Position**
As of December 31, Year 1

| | |
|---|---:|
| **Total governmental fund balances** | $4,195,000 |
| **Capital** assets, net of **accumulated** depreciation used in governmental activities that are not reported in fund financial statements | 2,667,000 |
| **Non-current** liabilities, include bonds payable, not recorded in fund financial statements | (3,420,000) |
| Reverse deferred inflows to accrue measurable but unavailable revenue | 125,000 |
| Net position of Internal **service** fund used for governmental activities | 163,000 |
| Net position from governmental activities | $3,730,000 |

## 1.3 Reconciliation of Governmental Funds Statement of Revenues, Expenditures, and Changes in Fund Balance to the Government-wide Statement of Activities

Net change in fund balances presented in the governmental funds statement of revenues, expenditures, and changes in fund balances must be reconciled to the change in net position of governmental activities presented in the government-wide statement of activities. This reconciliation includes the following:

- Adjustments for the difference in measurement focus:
  - Add **capital** outlay expenditures
  - Add **principal** payment on debt
  - Subtract net book values of capital **assets** disposed of during the period
  - Subtract debt proceeds shown as other financing **sources**
- Adjustments for the difference in basis of accounting:
  - Add recognized **revenues** that are measurable but unavailable
  - Accrue **interest** expense
  - Record **depreciation expense**
- Consolidation entries:
  - Add internal **service** fund change in net position

### Pass Key

The operating statement adjustments can be remembered using the **CPAS RIDES** mnemonic:

| | Net change in fund balance—total governmental funds |
|---|---|
| + | **C**apital outlay |
| + | **P**rincipal payments on non-current debt |
| − | **A**sset disposals (net book value) |
| − | **S**ources (other financing sources—debt proceeds) |
| + | **R**evenue (measurable but unavailable) |
| − | **I**nterest expense (accrued) |
| − | **D**epreciation expense |
| + | Internal **s**ervice fund net revenue |
| | Change in net position of governmental activities |

The reconciliation can be presented on the face of the governmental funds statement of revenues, expenditures, and changes in fund balance or in a separate schedule.

### Progressive Township
### Reconciliation of the Statement of Revenues, Expenditures, and Changes in Fund Balances of Governmental Funds to the Statement of Activities
For the Year Ended December 31, Year 1

| | | |
|---|---:|---:|
| Net change in fund balances—total governmental funds | | $1,771,500 |
| **Capital** outlay | | 787,000 |
| **Principal** payments on debt | | 360,000 |
| **Asset** disposal adjustment | | |
|    Proceeds of land sold | $(500,000) | |
|    Gain on sale | 425,000 | |
|    Cost of land sold (excess proceeds over gain on disposal) | | (75,000) |
| **Sources** (other financing)—bond proceeds | | (2,080,000) |
| **Revenues** in the statement of activities that do not provide current financial resources that are not reported as fund revenues | | 125,000 |
| **Interest** accrual (not used in this example) | | – |
| **Depreciation expense** (classified by function) | | |
|    General government | (35,000) | |
|    Public safety | (25,000) | |
|    Culture and recreation | (10,000) | |
|    Other functional classifications | (50,000) | |
|      Total depreciation expense | | (120,000) |
| Net revenue (expense) of Internal **service** funds | | 26,000 |
| Change in net position of governmental activities | | $ 794,500 |

## Example 1     Balance Sheet Reconciliation

**Facts:** Fund balances of Progressive Township's governmental funds totaled $6,555,000 for the year ended December 31, Year 1. Subsidiary accounting records for the township include the following information:

| | |
|---|---:|
| Capital assets | $2,000,000 |
| Accumulated depreciation on capital assets used in governmental activities | 500,000 |
| Long-term debt obligations issued to finance governmental projects | 2,500,000 |
| Internal service fund net position | 200,000 |
| Proprietary fund net position | 7,500,000 |
| Fiduciary fund net position | 650,000 |

**Required:** Calculate net position to be displayed in the governmental activities column of the government-wide financial statement.

(continued)

(continued)

**Solution:** The fund balances of Progressive Township's governmental fund reconcile to the net position displayed in the *governmental activities* column of the government-wide financial statements as follows:

### CANS

| | |
|---|---:|
| Governmental fund balances | $6,555,000 |
| **Capital** assets | 2,000,000 |
| **Accumulated** depreciation | (500,000) |
| **Non-current** liabilities | (2,500,000) |
| Internal **service** fund net position | 200,000 |
| Net position of governmental activities | $5,755,000 |

## Example 2 — Operating Statement Reconciliation

**Facts:** Progressive Township is preparing the reconciliation between the amount reported as "net change in fund balances" for all governmental funds to the amount reported as the "change in net position" for governmental activities on the town's government-wide financial statements for the year ended December 31, Year 1.

Progressive Township reported the following transactions on its governmental fund financial statements.

| | |
|---|---:|
| Net change in fund balance | $ 600,000 |
| Capital outlay expenditures | 250,000 |
| Debt service expenditure—*principal* | 100,000 |
| Debt service expenditure—*interest* | 85,000 |
| Proceeds from issuance of long-term debt | 500,000 |
| Net revenue from enterprise funds | 1,800,000 |
| Net revenue from internal service funds | 53,000 |

The town's subsidiary records also displayed the following information:

| | |
|---|---:|
| Depreciation expense on capital assets used in governmental activities | 45,000 |

**Required:** Calculate the amount that Progressive Township will report as the change in net position for governmental activities on the government-wide financial statements.

**Solution:** The net change in fund balance of Progressive Township's governmental funds reconciles to the change in net position displayed in the governmental activities column of the government-wide financial statements as follows:

### CPAS RIDES

| | |
|---|---:|
| Net change in fund balance | $ 600,000 |
| **Capital** outlay | 250,000 |
| **Principal** payments on debt | 100,000 |
| **Asset** disposal adjustment | – |
| **Sources** (other financing) debt proceeds | (500,000) |
| **Revenue** accrual | – |
| **Interest** accrual | – |
| **Depreciation** expense | (45,000) |
| Internal **service** fund change in net position | 53,000 |
| Change in net position of governmental activities | $ 458,000 |

Deriving Government-wide Financial Statements and Reconciliation Requirements  FAR 10

> **Question 1** MCQ-05142
>
> Bunson Township was incorporated on January 1, Year 1, and is preparing its government-wide financial statements for the year ended December 31, Year 1. The governmental funds displayed a combined change in fund balance of $500,000 for that year and also had the following balances, data, or transactions:
>
> - Capital outlay of $250,000 partially funded by long-term debt proceeds of $225,000
> - Current year depreciation of $60,000 on a capital asset base of $1,200,000
> - Principal payments (on debt) of $40,000
> - Interest payments (on debt) through October 1 of $30,000
> - Principal payments of $10,000 incurred through December 31 but paid on January 2
> - Interest payments of $7,500 incurred through December 31 but paid on January 2
> - Sales tax revenues of $30,000 associated with December 31, Year 1 sales remitted to the State in February and paid to the Township in March
>
> The government-wide change in net position would be displayed as:
>
> a. $455,000
> b. $527,500
> c. $587,500
> d. $597,500

# 2 Deriving Government-wide Financial Statements

## 2.1 Converting the Governmental Fund Financial Statements to Government-wide Financial Statements

The process of preparing the government-wide financial statements from the fund financial statements is similar to the process of preparing consolidated financial statements for commercial entities. However, added complexity comes from the fact that the governmental fund financial statements differ from the government-wide financial statements because of:

1. Measurement focus differences
2. Basis of accounting differences
3. Excluded funds

Workpaper adjustments or eliminations *and* reconciling items result from these three differences.

### 2.1.1 Measurement Focus Differences

The current financial resources measurement focus used to prepare the governmental fund financial statements differs significantly from the economic resources measurement focus used to prepare the government-wide financial statements.

- Significant items reported in the governmental fund financial statements that require workpaper adjustments when preparing the government-wide financial statements include:
  - Capital outlay expenditures in the governmental fund statement of revenues, expenditures, and changes in fund balances that are capitalized on the government-wide statement of net position.
  - Debt service expenditures associated with principal payments on debt in the governmental fund statement of revenues, expenditures, and changes in fund balances that are reductions in the long-term debt reported on the government-wide statement of net position.
  - Debt proceeds included in other financing sources in the governmental fund statement of revenues, expenditures, and changes in fund balances that are reported as long-term liabilities on the government-wide statement of net position.
- Measurement focus differences also may be derived from subsidiary records. The items listed below are common items found in subsidiary records that are recorded on the government-wide statement of net position:
  - Existing capital assets and related accumulated depreciation
  - Existing non-current debts and liabilities

### 2.1.2 Basis of Accounting Differences

Governmental fund financial statements are prepared using the modified accrual basis of accounting, and the government-wide financial statements are prepared using the accrual basis of accounting. Workpaper adjustments and reconciling items result from differences in revenue recognition and also may result from differences in expense vs. expenditure recognition. Primary differences that result in workpaper adjustments and reconciling items when preparing the government-wide financial statements from the governmental fund financial statements include:

- Recognition of measurable but unavailable revenue by elimination of associated deferred inflows of resources reported on the governmental funds balance sheet
- Recognition of unmatured interest payable
- Recognition of depreciation expense

### 2.1.3 Excluded Funds

Governmental activities included on the government-wide financial statements incorporate transactions included in the governmental fund financial statements and the internal service funds. Workpaper entries and reconciliations include:

- Addition of internal service net position to governmental activities reported on the government-wide statement of net position.
- Inclusion of profits earned by internal service funds in governmental activities on the government-wide statement of activities.

## 2.2 Summary of Worksheet Entries and Reconciling Items

The following table summarizes the transactions to be adjusted as part of converting fund financial statements to government-wide financial statements and serve to produce the transactions/differences identified on the reconciliation of the fund financial statements to the government-wide financial statements.

# Deriving Government-wide Financial Statements and Reconciliation Requirements

| Sources | Measurement Focus Differences | | | | Basis of Accounting | | Internal Service | Eliminations |
|---|---|---|---|---|---|---|---|---|
| **Financial statement data** | **Capital** Outlay | **Principal** Payment Expenditure | **Asset** Disposal Adjustment | **Sources** (Other Financing) Debt Proceeds | **Accrued** Revenue | **Interest** and **Depreciation** **Expense** | **Internal** **Service** Fund | Eliminate interfund accounts |
| Balance Sheet: Fund Balance *Reconciled to* Net Position: Governmental Activities | Add increase of asset | Add reduce liability | Subtract net book value of asset disposed of | Subtract increase in liability | Add increase in accrual Subtract decrease in accrual | Subtract interest accrual and depreciation expense | Add positive net position Subtract negative net position | Eliminate interfund receivables and payables |
| Operating Statement: Change in Fund Balance *Reconciled to* Change in Net Position: Governmental Activities | Add expenditure capitalized | Add reduce expenditures | Subtract net book value of asset disposed of | Subtract other financing source classified as debt) | Add increase in revenue Subtract decrease in revenue | Subtract interest accrual and depreciation expense | Add increases in net position Subtract decreases in net position | Eliminate interfund transfers |
| **Mnemonic** | C | P | A | S | R | IDE | S | It (N/A to Recon) |
| **Subsidiary data** | **Capital** Assets | **Accumulated** Depreciation | **Non-current** Debt/ Liability | | | | | |
| Balance Sheet: Fund Balance *Reconciled to* Net Position: Governmental Activities | Add increase capital assets and net position | Subtract reduce capital assets and net position | Subtract increase in non-current liabilities and net position | | | | | |
| **Mnemonic** | C | A | N | | | | | |

## 2.2.1 Workpaper Journal Entries

The following workpaper journal entries are used to convert governmental fund presentations that use the current financial resources measurement focus and the modified accrual basis of accounting to the commercial style of accounting (economic resources measurement focus and accrual basis of accounting) used in government-wide financial statements.

## Measurement Focus Entries

| DR | Capital assets | $XXX | |
|---|---|---|---|
| CR | Net position | | $XXX |

To recognize non-current assets used in governmental activities that were purchased in prior years on the government-wide statement of net position.

| DR | Net position (beginning) | $XXX | |
|---|---|---|---|
| CR | Accumulated depreciation | | $XXX |

To recognize accumulated depreciation related to non-current assets used in governmental activities reported on the government-wide statement of net position.

| DR | Net position (beginning) | $XXX | |
|---|---|---|---|
| CR | Non-current debt (liabilities) | | $XXX |

To recognize non-current liabilities issued in prior years that were used to finance governmental activities on the government-wide statement of net position.

| DR | Capital assets | $XXX | |
|---|---|---|---|
| CR | Capital outlay | | $XXX |

To capitalize assets on the government-wide statement of net position previously shown as expenditures on the governmental fund statement of revenues, expenditures, and changes in fund balance (current year acquisitions).

| DR | Long-term debt | $XXX | |
|---|---|---|---|
| CR | Principal payments (expenditure) | | $XXX |

To reduce long-term debt reported on the government-wide statement of net position for principal payments shown as expenditures on the governmental fund statement of revenues, expenditures, and changes in fund balance.

| DR | Other financing sources: proceeds from asset disposal | $XXX | |
|---|---|---|---|
| DR | Accumulated depreciation | XXX | |
| CR | Cost of asset | | $XXX |
| CR | Gain on disposal | | XXX |

To eliminate the sold asset and related accumulated depreciation from the government-wide statement of net position, recognize the gain on disposal of the asset on the government-wide statement of activities and eliminate the proceeds from the assets disposal reported as other financing sources on the governmental fund statement of revenues, expenditures, and changes in fund balance.

| DR | Other financing sources: debt proceeds | $XXX | |
|---|---|---|---|
| CR | Long-term debt | | $XXX |

To record long-term liabilities as debt on the government-wide statement of net position previously shown as debt proceeds (other financing sources) on the governmental fund statement of revenues, expenditures, and changes in fund balance (current year debt issuance).

## Basis of Accounting Entries

| | | | |
|---|---|---|---|
| DR | Deferred inflows | $XXX | |
| CR | Tax **revenue** | | $XXX |

To recognize measurable but unavailable tax revenue on the government-wide statement of activities previously shown as deferred inflows on the governmental fund balance sheet.

| | | | |
|---|---|---|---|
| DR | **Interest** expense | $XXX | |
| CR | Accrued interest payable | | $XXX |

To accrue interest expense on unmatured debt on the government-wide financial statements previously unrecognized on the governmental fund financial statements.

| | | | |
|---|---|---|---|
| DR | **Depreciation expense** | $XXX | |
| CR | Accumulated depreciation | | $XXX |

To record current period depreciation and accumulated on the government-wide financial statements that was unrecognized on the governmental fund financial statements.

## Internal Service Fund Entries and Eliminations

| | | | |
|---|---|---|---|
| DR | Assets: governmental activities | $XXX | |
| DR | Internal **service** fund revenue | XXX | |
| CR | Liabilities: governmental activities | | $XXX |
| CR | Internal service fund expenses | | XXX |
| CR | Governmental fund expenditures | | XXX |

To integrate internal service fund assets and liabilities into governmental activities on the government-wide statement of net position and eliminate internal service fund profits by reducing governmental expenditures consistent with the cost recovery/breakeven assumption of internal service fund accounting.

**Note:** Consolidation of internal service fund activity with governmental fund activity can be done in numerous ways. The accompanying example uses two entries; however, the example above purely shows the impact of adding balance sheet accounts and eliminating internal services fund revenues and expenses and, where necessary, the fund's profits by reducing governmental fund expenditures.

| | | | |
|---|---|---|---|
| DR | **Interfund** transfers in | $XXX | |
| CR | Interfund **transfers** out | | $XXX |
| DR | Due to other funds | XXX | |
| CR | Due from other funds | | XXX |

To eliminate interfund accounts that would needlessly gross up activity and balances on the government-wide financial statements.

# FAR 10 — Deriving Government-wide Financial Statements and Reconciliation Requirements

## 2.3 Comprehensive Illustration

The following simplified financial statements are presented to illustrate the mechanics of both the reconciliation and the workpaper adjustments.

### 2.3.1 Governmental Fund Financial Statements

**Sample City**
**Governmental Fund Financial Statement Data**
As of and for the Year Ended December 31, Year 1

|  | General Fund | Special Revenue Fund | Debt Service Fund | Capital Projects Fund | All Governmental Funds |
|---|---|---|---|---|---|
| **Assets** | | | | | |
| Cash | $ 10,000 | – | – | – | $ 10,000 |
| Investments | 75,000 | $ 120,000 | $ 25,000 | $ 280,000 | 500,000 |
| Accounts receivable | 60,000 | – | – | – | 60,000 |
| Due from other funds | 35,000 | – | – | – | 35,000 |
| **Total Assets** | $ 180,000 | $ 120,000 | $ 25,000 | $ 280,000 | $ 605,000 |
| **Liabilities** | | | | | |
| Accounts payable | $ 7,000 | $ 15,000 | – | $ 5,000 | $ 27,000 |
| Accrued liabilities | 38,000 | – | – | – | 38,000 |
| Due to other funds | – | 35,000 | – | – | 35,000 |
| **Liabilities** | 45,000 | 50,000 | – | 5,000 | 100,000 |
| **Deferred Inflows of Resources** | 50,000 | – | – | – | 50,000 |
| **Fund Balance** | 85,000 | 70,000 | 25,000 | 275,000 | 455,000 |
| **Total Liabilities, Deferred Inflows and Fund Balance** | $ 180,000 | $ 120,000 | $ 25,000 | $ 280,000 | $ 605,000 |
| | | | | | |
| **Revenues** | | | | | |
| Property taxes | $2,950,000 | – | – | $50,000 | $3,000,000 |
| Intergovernmental revenues | – | 350,000 | – | – | 350,000 |
| Charges for services | 20,000 | 10,000 | – | – | 30,000 |
| **Total Revenues** | 2,970,000 | 360,000 | – | 50,000 | 3,380,000 |
| **Expenditures** | | | | | |
| Current | | | | | |
|   General government | 950,000 | | | | 950,000 |
|   Public safety | 1,650,000 | | | | 1,650,000 |
|   Culture and recreation | 300,000 | 50,000 | | | 350,000 |
| Debt service | | | | | |
|   Principal | – | – | 150,000 | | 150,000 |
|   Interest and other charges | – | – | 110,000 | | 110,000 |
| Capital outlay | – | – | – | 4,800,000 | 4,800,000 |
| **Total expenditures** | $2,900,000 | $ 50,000 | $ 260,000 | $ 4,800,000 | $8,010,000 |
| Excess (deficiency) of revenues over expenditures | 70,000 | 310,000 | (260,000) | (4,750,000) | (4,630,000) |

*(continued)*

(continued)

| | | | | | |
|---|---|---|---|---|---|
| **Other Financing Sources (Uses)** | | | | | |
| Long-term debt issued | – | | | 5,000,000 | 5,000,000 |
| Transfers in | – | | 250,000 | | 250,000 |
| Transfers out | – | (250,000) | – | – | (250,000) |
| Total other financing sources and uses | – | (250,000) | 250,000 | 5,000,000 | 5,000,000 |
| Net change in fund balance | 70,000 | 60,000 | (10,000) | 250,000 | 370,000 |
| **Fund balance: beginning** | 15,000 | 10,000 | 35,000 | 25,000 | 85,000 |
| **Fund balance: ending** | $ 85,000 | $ 70,000 | $ 25,000 | $ 275,000 | $ 455,000 |

### 2.3.2 Internal Service Fund Financial Statements

**Sample City**
**Internal Service Fund Financial Statement Data**
As of and for the Year Ended December 31, Year 1

| | |
|---|---|
| **Assets** | |
| Cash | $ 5,000 |
| Investments | 20,000 |
| Capital assets | 50,000 |
| Accumulated depreciation | (10,000) |
| **Total Assets** | $ 65,000 |
| **Liabilities** | |
| Accounts payable | 2,000 |
| Accrued liabilities | 3,000 |
| Long-term debt | 32,000 |
| **Liabilities** | 37,000 |
| **Deferred Inflows of Resources** | – |
| **Net Position** | 28,000 |
| **Total Liabilities, Deferred Inflows and Net Position** | $ 65,000 |
| **Revenues** | |
| Charges for services | $280,000 |
| Total Revenues | 280,000 |
| **Expenses** | |
| General government | 50,000 |
| Public safety | 205,000 |
| Culture and recreation | 15,000 |
| Total operating expenses | 270,000 |
| Net change in net position | 10,000 |
| **Net position: beginning** | 18,000 |
| **Net position: ending** | $ 28,000 |

## 2.3.3 Additional Facts

**Sample City**
**Additional Facts**
As of and for the Year Ended December 31, Year 1

**Capital Assets**
The city had non-current capital assets of $5,000,000.

**Accumulated Depreciation**
Non-current assets of the city had accumulated depreciation of $1,500,000.

**Non-current Liabilities**
The city had non-current liabilities of $3,000,000.

**Interest on Unmatured Interest**
The city's interest payments on debt fall due on November 30. $10,000 in accrued interest is unpaid at year-end.

**Depreciation Expense**
The city computed $460,000 in deprecation expense and attributed it to the following functional classifications:

| | |
|---|---|
| General government | $140,000 |
| Public safety | 280,000 |
| Culture and recreation | 40,000 |

**Internal Service Funds**
All internal service fund profits of $10,000 resulted from charges to public safety departments.

## 2.3.4 Workpaper Entries

**Sample City**
**Workpaper Entries**
As of and for the Year Ended December 31, Year 1

### Measurement Focus Differences — CAN CPAS

**1**
| | | | |
|---|---|---|---|
| **DR** | Capital assets | $4,800,000 | |
| C  **CR** | Capital outlay | | $4,800,000 |

To capitalize assets on government-wide statement of net position previously shown as expenditures on the governmental fund statement of revenues, expenditures, and changes in fund balance.

**2**
| | | | |
|---|---|---|---|
| **DR** | Long-term debt | $150,000 | |
| P  **CR** | Principal payments (expenditures) | | $150,000 |

To reduce long-term debt for principal payments on government-wide statement of net position previously shown as expenditures on the governmental fund statement of revenues, expenditures, and changes in fund balance.

    **A**  N/A (no asset disposals)

(continued)

(continued)

**3 S**

| DR | Other financing sources—debt proceeds | $5,000,000 | |
|---|---|---|---|
| CR | Long-term debt | | $5,000,0000 |

To record long-term liabilities as debt on the government-wide statement of net position previously shown as debt proceeds (other financing sources) on the governmental fund statement of revenues, expenditures, and changes in fund balance.

**4 C**

| DR | Capital assets | $5,000,000 | |
|---|---|---|---|
| CR | Net position | | $5,000,000 |

To recognize non-current assets used in governmental activities that were purchased in prior years on the government-wide statement of net position.

**5 A**

| DR | Net position | $1,500,000 | |
|---|---|---|---|
| CR | Accumulated depreciation | | $1,500,000 |

To recognize accumulated depreciation related to non-current assets used in governmental activities reported on the government-wide statement of net position.

**6 N**

| DR | Net position (beginning) | $3,000,000 | |
|---|---|---|---|
| CR | Non-current debt (liabilities) | | $3,000,000 |

To recognize non-current liabilities issued in prior years used to finance governmental activities on the government-wide statement of net position.

### Basis of Accounting Differences — RIDE

**1 R**

| DR | Deferred inflows | $50,000 | |
|---|---|---|---|
| CR | Tax revenue | | $50,000 |

To recognize measurable but unavailable tax revenues on the government-wide statement of activities previously shown as deferred inflows on the governmental fund balance sheet.

**2 I**

| DR | Interest expense | $10,000 | |
|---|---|---|---|
| CR | Accrued interest payable (accrued liabilities) | | $10,000 |

To accrue interest expense on unmatured debt on the government-wide financial statements previously unrecognized on the governmental fund financial statements.

**3 DE**

| DR | General government | $140,000 | |
|---|---|---|---|
| DR | Public safety | 280,000 | |
| DR | Culture and recreation | 40,000 | |
| CR | Accumulated depreciation | | $460,000 |

To record current period depreciation and accumulated depreciation on the government-wide financial statements that was unrecognized on the governmental fund financial statements.

(continued)

(continued)

### Consolidation (S)

**1**

| | | | | |
|---|---|---|---|---|
| | DR | Cash | $ 5,000 | |
| | DR | Investments | 20,000 | |
| | DR | Capital assets | 50,000 | |
| | CR | Accumulated depreciation | | $ 10,000 |
| | CR | Accounts payable | | 2,000 |
| | CR | Accrued liabilities | | 3,000 |
| | CR | Long-term debt | | 32,000 |
| S | CR | Internal service fund net position (beginning) | | 18,000 |
| | CR | Charges for services | | 280,000 |
| | DR | Operating expenses: identified with gen. govt. | 50,000 | |
| | DR | Operating expenses: identified with public safety | 205,000 | |
| | DR | Operating expenses: identified with culture & rec. | 15,000 | |

To record internal service fund activity as a governmental activity for government-wide presentation.

**2**

| | | | | |
|---|---|---|---|---|
| | DR | Charges for services | $280,000 | |
| | CR | Operating expenses: identified with gen. govt. | | $ 50,000 |
| | CR | Operating expenses: identified with public safety | | 205,000 |
| | CR | Operating expenses: identified with culture & rec. | | 15,000 |
| S | CR | Internal service fund profits: identified with public safety | | 10,000 |

To eliminate internal service fund revenues and expenses and profits.

### Other Eliminating Entries (Interfund Accounts) (IT)

**3**

| | | | | |
|---|---|---|---|---|
| | DR | Due to other funds | $35,000 | |
| | CR | Due from other funds | | $35,000 |

To eliminate interfund accounts between governmental funds.

**4 IT**

| | | | | |
|---|---|---|---|---|
| | DR | Transfers in | $250,000 | |
| | CR | Transfers out | | $250,000 |

To eliminate interfund accounts between governmental funds.

## 2.3.5 Conversion of Governmental Fund Financial Statements to Government-wide Financial Statements

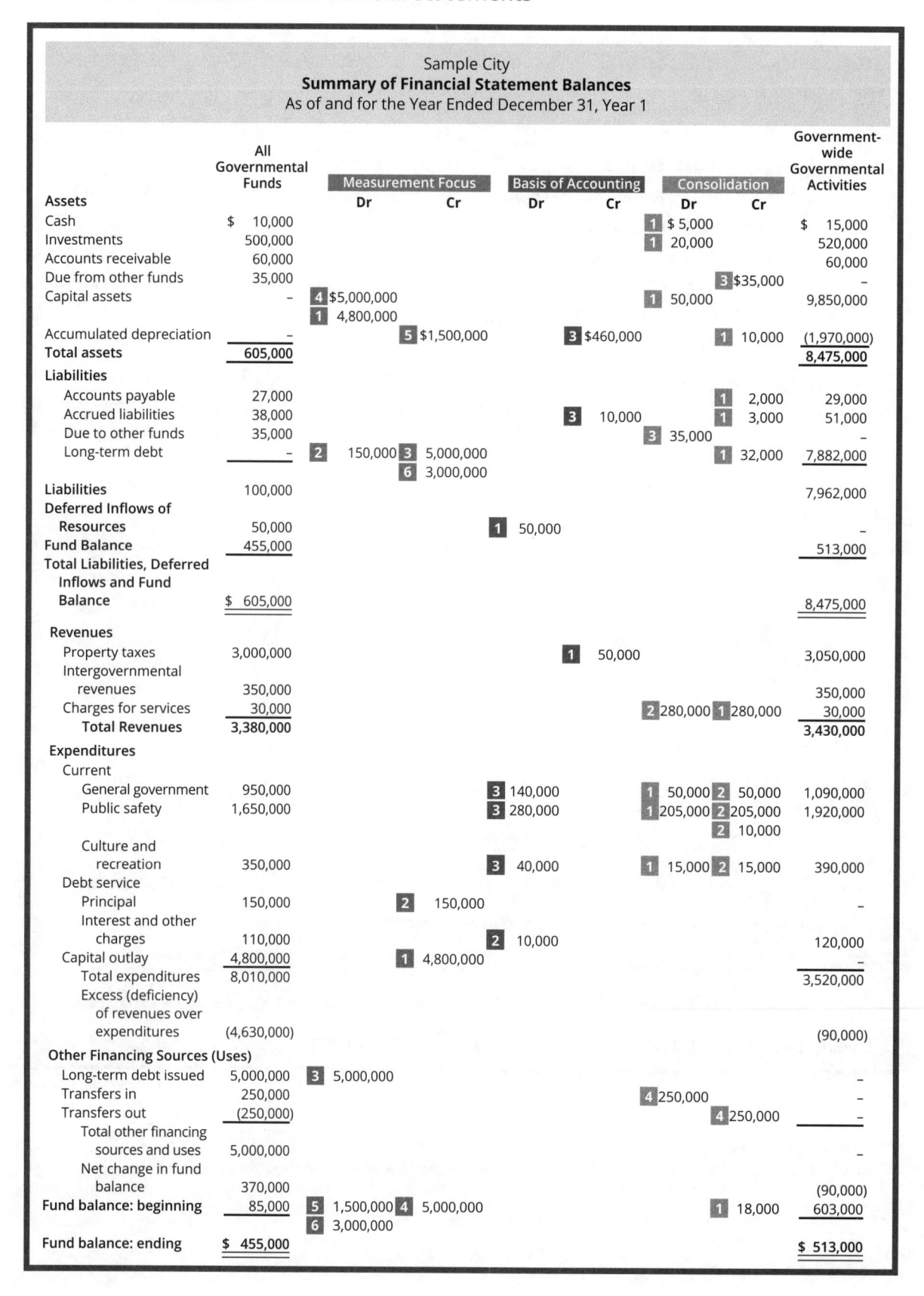

**Sample City**
**Summary of Financial Statement Balances**
As of and for the Year Ended December 31, Year 1

|  | All Governmental Funds | Measurement Focus Dr | Measurement Focus Cr | Basis of Accounting Dr | Basis of Accounting Cr | Consolidation Dr | Consolidation Cr | Government-wide Governmental Activities |
|---|---|---|---|---|---|---|---|---|
| **Assets** |  |  |  |  |  |  |  |  |
| Cash | $ 10,000 |  |  |  |  | **1** $ 5,000 |  | $ 15,000 |
| Investments | 500,000 |  |  |  |  | **1** 20,000 |  | 520,000 |
| Accounts receivable | 60,000 |  |  |  |  |  |  | 60,000 |
| Due from other funds | 35,000 |  |  |  |  |  | **3** $35,000 | – |
| Capital assets | – | **4** $5,000,000 |  |  |  | **1** 50,000 |  | 9,850,000 |
|  |  | **1** 4,800,000 |  |  |  |  |  |  |
| Accumulated depreciation | – |  | **5** $1,500,000 |  | **3** $460,000 |  | **1** 10,000 | (1,970,000) |
| Total assets | 605,000 |  |  |  |  |  |  | 8,475,000 |
| **Liabilities** |  |  |  |  |  |  |  |  |
| Accounts payable | 27,000 |  |  |  |  |  | **1** 2,000 | 29,000 |
| Accrued liabilities | 38,000 |  |  |  | **3** 10,000 |  | **1** 3,000 | 51,000 |
| Due to other funds | 35,000 |  |  |  |  | **3** 35,000 |  | – |
| Long-term debt | – | **2** 150,000 | **3** 5,000,000 |  |  |  | **1** 32,000 | 7,882,000 |
|  |  |  | **6** 3,000,000 |  |  |  |  |  |
| Liabilities | 100,000 |  |  |  |  |  |  | 7,962,000 |
| Deferred Inflows of Resources | 50,000 |  |  | **1** 50,000 |  |  |  | – |
| Fund Balance | 455,000 |  |  |  |  |  |  | 513,000 |
| Total Liabilities, Deferred Inflows and Fund Balance | $ 605,000 |  |  |  |  |  |  | 8,475,000 |
| **Revenues** |  |  |  |  |  |  |  |  |
| Property taxes | 3,000,000 |  |  | **1** 50,000 |  |  |  | 3,050,000 |
| Intergovernmental revenues | 350,000 |  |  |  |  |  |  | 350,000 |
| Charges for services | 30,000 |  |  |  |  | **2** 280,000 | **1** 280,000 | 30,000 |
| Total Revenues | 3,380,000 |  |  |  |  |  |  | 3,430,000 |
| **Expenditures** |  |  |  |  |  |  |  |  |
| Current |  |  |  |  |  |  |  |  |
| General government | 950,000 |  |  | **3** 140,000 |  | **1** 50,000 | **2** 50,000 | 1,090,000 |
| Public safety | 1,650,000 |  |  | **3** 280,000 |  | **1** 205,000 | **2** 205,000 | 1,920,000 |
|  |  |  |  |  |  |  | **2** 10,000 |  |
| Culture and recreation | 350,000 |  |  | **3** 40,000 |  | **1** 15,000 | **2** 15,000 | 390,000 |
| Debt service |  |  |  |  |  |  |  |  |
| Principal | 150,000 | **2** 150,000 |  |  |  |  |  | – |
| Interest and other charges | 110,000 |  |  | **2** 10,000 |  |  |  | 120,000 |
| Capital outlay | 4,800,000 | **1** 4,800,000 |  |  |  |  |  | – |
| Total expenditures | 8,010,000 |  |  |  |  |  |  | 3,520,000 |
| Excess (deficiency) of revenues over expenditures | (4,630,000) |  |  |  |  |  |  | (90,000) |
| **Other Financing Sources (Uses)** |  |  |  |  |  |  |  |  |
| Long-term debt issued | 5,000,000 | **3** 5,000,000 |  |  |  |  |  | – |
| Transfers in | 250,000 |  |  |  |  | **4** 250,000 |  | – |
| Transfers out | (250,000) |  |  |  |  |  | **4** 250,000 | – |
| Total other financing sources and uses | 5,000,000 |  |  |  |  |  |  | – |
| Net change in fund balance | 370,000 |  |  |  |  |  |  | (90,000) |
| Fund balance: beginning | 85,000 |  | **5** 1,500,000 | **4** 5,000,000 |  |  | **1** 18,000 | 603,000 |
|  |  |  | **6** 3,000,000 |  |  |  |  |  |
| Fund balance: ending | $ 455,000 |  |  |  |  |  |  | $ 513,000 |

## 2.3.6 Reconciliation of Fund and Government-wide Presentations

**Sample City**
**Reconciliation of Fund Financial Statements to Government-wide Financial Statements**
As of and for the Year Ended December 31, Year 1

| Fund Financial Statements | | Fund Balance Reconciliation | | Change in Fund Balance Reconciliation |
|---|---|---|---|---|
| Fund balance | | $ 455,000 | | |
| Changes in fund balance | | | | $ 370,000 |

### Measurement Focus Entries

| | | | | | |
|---|---|---|---|---|---|
| Capital assets | [1] | $4,800,000 | | | |
| C Capital outlay | | | [1] | $ 4,800,000 | |
| Principal payment applied to debt | [2] | 150,000 | | | |
| P Principal expenditures | | | [2] | 150,000 | |
| Debt | [3] | (5,000,000) | | | |
| S Other financing sources – Debt proceeds | | | [3] | (5,000,000) | |
| C Capital assets | [4] | 5,000,000 | | – | |
| A Accumulated depreciation | [5] | (1,500,000) | | – | |
| N Non-current debt | [6] | (3,000,000) | | – | |

**Subtotal: Reconciling Items Associated With Measurement Focus Differences** — 450,000 — (50,000)

### Basis of Accounting Differences

| | | | | | |
|---|---|---|---|---|---|
| R Accrue revenue | | | [1] | 50,000 | |
| Reduce deferred inflows | [1] | 50,000 | | | |
| I Interest expense | | | [2] | (10,000) | |
| Accrued interest payable | [2] | (10,000) | | | |
| DE Depreciation expense = Gen. govt. | | | [3] | (140,000) | |
| Depreciation expense – Public safety | | | [3] | (280,000) | |
| Depreciation expense – Culture/rec. | | | [3] | (40,000) | |
| Accumulated depreciation | [3] | (460,000) | | | |

**Subtotal: Reconciling Items Associated With Basis of Accounting Differences** — (420,000) — (420,000)

### Consolidation

| | | | | | |
|---|---|---|---|---|---|
| S Internal service fund net position (beg.) | [1] | 18,000 | | | |
| S Internal service fund net income | [2] | $ 10,000 | [2] | $ 10,000 | |

**Subtotal: Reconciling Items Associated With Integration of Internal Service Funds** — 28,000 — 10,000

**Government-wide Financial Statements**
Net position — $ 513,000
Changes in net position — $ (90,000)

**Note:** Elimination of interfund receivables and payables and interfund transfers has no impact on the reconciliation of either fund balance or changes in fund balance to net position or changes in net position.

# MODULE 7: Notes and Supplementary Information

FAR 10

## 1 Management's Discussion and Analysis

> Management's discussion and analysis (MD&A)
> Government-wide financial statements
> Fund financial statements
> Notes to financial statements
> Required supplementary information
> Other supplementary information

Management's discussion and analysis (MD&A) is part of the supplementary information required in government financial reporting. The MD&A is a narrative that provides a brief, objective, and easily readable analysis of the government's financial activities based on currently known facts, decisions, and conditions. It provides the financial management of the government with the opportunity to present both a short-term and a long-term analysis of activities. The following should be included:

- **Description of the Financial Statements**
    - An easily readable analysis of the government's financial activities based on currently known facts, decisions, and conditions.
    - Condensed financial statement information derived from the government-wide financial statements used to support the government's overall financial position and results of operations. Three years of data are required if the basic financial statements are comparative.
    - Analysis of overall financial position and results of operations, including reasons for changes from the prior year.
    - Analysis of balances and transactions of individual funds, including limitations on future uses of funds.
    - Analysis of significant variations between the original and the final budget.
    - A description of the significant assumptions and implications of use of the modified approach for accounting for infrastructure.
- **Identity of the Primary Government and Discrete Component Units**
- **Economic Conditions and Outlook**

    A description of the effect of the economy on the financial statements.
- **Major Initiatives**

    This section generally describes capital asset and long-term debt activity during the year.

# 2 Notes to the Financial Statements

> Management's discussion and analysis (MD&A)
> Government-wide financial statements
> Fund financial statements
> **Notes to financial statements**
> Required supplementary information
> Other supplementary information

Notes to the financial statements are essential to fair presentation and considered integral to the financial statements. Notes should focus on the primary government, specifically:

- Governmental activities
- Business-type activities
- Major funds
- Nonmajor funds in the aggregate
- Additional information regarding discretely presented component units

## 2.1 Generic Governmental Disclosures

Generic governmental disclosures should include:

- A description of government-wide activities, noting the exclusion of fiduciary funds.
- Policies relating to elimination of internal activity.
- Description of the modified approach for reporting infrastructure, if used.
- Segment information on enterprise funds meeting the following definition of a segment:
  - Enterprise represents an identifiable activity.
  - Enterprise has one or more debt issues outstanding with revenue streams pledged in support of that debt.
  - Enterprise is accounted for separately.

## 2.2 Specific Governmental Disclosures

- Description of activities for:
  - Major funds
  - Internal service funds
  - Fiduciary funds
- The length of time used to define "available" in determining revenue recognition under the modified accrual basis (measurable and available).
- Actions taken to correct material noncompliance with finance-related or legal compliance.
- A schedule of short-term debt and the purpose for which the short-term debt was issued.

- Analysis of interfund account balances by:
  - Maturity (current and non-current)
  - Purpose
  - Individual major fund
  - Nonmajor funds in the aggregate
  - Internal service fund
  - Fiduciary fund types
- Analysis of accounts receivable and accounts payable by:
  - Maturity (current and non-current)
  - Type:
    - Accounts receivable (taxes and special assessments)
    - Accounts payable (vendors, salaries and benefits)
  - Activity and fund:
    - Governmental activities (GRSPP) and internal service
    - Business-type activities (enterprise funds)

# 3 Required Supplementary Information (Other Than MD&A)

> Management's discussion and analysis (MD&A)
> Government-wide financial statements
> Fund financial statements
> Notes to financial statements
> **Required supplementary information**
> Other supplementary information

Required supplementary information includes information that precedes the financial statements (the MD&A) and information included after the basic financial statements. Significant information that follows the basic financial statements includes budgetary comparison reporting, infrastructure information, and pension information.

## 3.1 Budgetary Comparison Reporting

Budgetary comparison schedules must be prepared for the general fund and for each major special revenue fund that has a legally adopted annual budget and may be presented as either required supplementary information or in the basic financial statements.

- Budgetary comparison schedules must show the original budget, the final amended budget, and actual amounts.
  - Computation of variances between budget and actual is optional.
  - Computation of differences between the original and the final amended budget is optional.

Notes and Supplementary Information

- Budgetary comparison may use either GAAP or budgetary formats, or basis of accounting, but must include a reconciliation to GAAP.
- Notes to required supplementary information should disclose excess of expenditure over appropriations in individual funds presented in the budgetary comparison.
- Budgetary comparison schedules should be prepared for the general fund and all special revenue funds that require a budget.

**Progressive Township**
**Budgetary Comparison Schedule**
**General Fund**
For the Year Ended December 31, Year 1

|  | Budgeted Amounts Original | Budgeted Amounts Final | Actual Amounts (Budgetary Basis) | Variance With Final Budget Positive (Negative) |
|---|---|---|---|---|
| Budgetary fund balance, January 1 | $2,975,000 | $1,016,000 | $1,016,000 | – |
| Resources (inflows): |  |  |  |  |
| Property taxes | 1,500,000 | 1,530,000 | 1,620,000 | $ 90,000 |
| Fees and fines | 100,000 | 100,000 | 120,000 | 20,000 |
| Intergovernmental | 260,000 | 260,000 | – | (260,000) |
| Charges for services | 100,000 | 100,000 | – | (100,000) |
| Interest earnings | 40,000 | 40,000 | 55,000 | 15,000 |
| Proceeds from sale of land | – | 500,000 | 500,000 | – |
| Transfers from other funds | 85,000 | 85,000 | 85,000 | – |
| Amounts available for appropriation | 2,085,000 | 2,615,000 | 2,380,000 | (235,000) |
| Charges to appropriations (outflows): |  |  |  |  |
| General government |  |  |  |  |
| Legal | 29,250 | 29,250 | 45,000 | (15,750) |
| Mayor, city council, and city manager | 146,250 | 146,250 | 225,000 | (78,750) |
| Finance and accounting | 102,375 | 102,375 | 157,500 | (55,125) |
| City clerk and elections | 14,625 | 14,625 | 22,500 | (7,875) |
| Public safety |  |  |  |  |
| Police department | 760,500 | 785,500 | 600,000 | 185,500 |
| Fire department | 253,500 | 253,500 | 200,000 | 53,500 |
| Emergency medical services | 190,125 | 190,125 | 150,000 | 40,125 |
| Building inspections | 63,375 | 63,375 | 50,000 | 13,375 |
| Culture and recreation |  |  |  |  |
| Library | 3,900 | 3,900 | 4,000 | (100) |
| Leisure services | 74,100 | 74,100 | 76,000 | (1,900) |

(continued)

(continued)

| | | | | |
|---|---:|---:|---:|---:|
| Other functional classifications | | | | |
|   Public works administration | 23,400 | 23,400 | 40,000 | (16,600) |
|   Street maintenance | 29,250 | 29,250 | 50,000 | (20,750) |
|   Traffic operations | 58,500 | 58,500 | 100,000 | (41,500) |
|   Miscellaneous | 5,850 | 5,850 | 10,000 | (4,150) |
|   Contingency | 165,000 | 165,000 | – | 165,000 |
|   Transfers to other funds | 4,000 | 4,000 | 14,000 | (10,000) |
|   Capital outlay | 30,000 | 30,000 | 25,000 | 5,000 |
| Total charges to appropriations | 1,954,000 | 1,979,000 | 1,769,000 | 210,000 |
| Budgetary fund balance, December 31 | $3,106,000 | $1,652,000 | $1,627,000 | $ (25,000) |

**Note:** Model assumes budget was developed on a GAAP basis; optional variance data included.

### 3.2 Infrastructure Information

The modified approach for reporting infrastructure assumes significant required supplementary disclosures.

- Required supplementary information for all eligible infrastructure assets reported using the modified approach should include schedules that disclose:
  - assessed condition of infrastructure; and
  - estimated annual amount to maintain and preserve infrastructure for each of the past five years.
- Additional disclosures for infrastructure would include:
  - the basis for condition measurement; and
  - the condition level at which the government plans to maintain its infrastructure.

### 3.3 Pension Information

The following required supplementary information should be presented for each of the 10 most recent fiscal years.

- Sources of changes in the net pension liability (NPL).
- Information about the components of the net pension liability and related ratios including:
  - The pension plan's fiduciary net position (FNP) as a percentage of the total pension liability (TPL).
  - The net pension liability as a percentage of the covered-employee payroll.
  - Actuarially determined contributions.
  - The amount of contributions.
- Significant methods and assumptions used to calculate the actuarially determined contributions.

- Annual money-weighted rate of return on pension plan investments for each of the 10 years presented.
- Explanation of trends in amounts reported in the supplementary schedule such as:
  - Changes in benefit terms
  - Changes in the population
  - Changes in assumptions

# 4 Other Supplementary Information (Optional)

> Management's discussion and analysis (MD&A)
> Government-wide financial statements
> Fund financial statements
> Notes to financial statements
> Required supplementary information
> **Other supplementary information**

Optional supplementary information includes:

- Combining statements for nonmajor funds.
- Variance between originally adopted budget and final amended budget.
- Variance between final amended budget and actual.

### Progressive Township
### Balance Sheet
### Nonmajor Governmental Funds
### As of December 31, Year 1

|  | Special Revenue Funds | | Debt Service Funds | | Capital Projects Fund | Permanent Fund | Total Nonmajor Governmental Funds |
|---|---|---|---|---|---|---|---|
|  | Gas Tax | Head Start | East Bridge | Police Dept. Bonds | East Bridge | Inmate Commissary | |
| **Assets** | | | | | | | |
| Cash | $ 10,000 | $ 5,000 | $66,500 | $100,000 | $88,000 | $ 500 | $270,000 |
| Receivables from other governments | 40,000 | 18,000 | – | – | – | – | 58,000 |
| Inventories | 25,000 | – | – | – | – | 6,000 | 31,000 |
| **Total assets** | $ 75,000 | $23,000 | $66,500 | $100,000 | $88,000 | $6,500 | $359,000 |
| **Liabilities** | | | | | | | |
| Accounts payable | $ 65,000 | $12,000 | $ 8,500 | – | $14,000 | $ 500 | $100,000 |
| **Total liabilities** | 65,000 | 12,000 | 8,500 | – | 14,000 | 500 | 100,000 |

(continued)

(continued)

| | Gas Tax | Head Start | East Bridge | Police Dept. Bonds | East Bridge | Inmate Commissary | Total |
|---|---|---|---|---|---|---|---|
| **Fund Balances** | | | | | | | |
| Nonspendable Inventories | 25,000 | – | – | – | – | 6,000 | 31,000 |
| Restricted for: | | | | | | | |
|   Debt Service | – | – | 58,000 | 100,000 | – | – | 158,000 |
|   Capital projects | – | – | – | – | 74,000 | – | 74,000 |
| Assigned: | | | | | | | |
|   Special revenue funds | – | 11,000 | – | – | – | – | 11,000 |
| Unassigned: | | | | | | | |
|   Special revenue funds | (15,000) | – | – | – | – | – | (15,000) |
| **Total fund balances** | 10,000 | 11,000 | 58,000 | 100,000 | 74,000 | 6,000 | 259,000 |
| **Total liabilities and fund balance** | $ 75,000 | $23,000 | $66,500 | $100,000 | $88,000 | $6,500 | $359,000 |

### Progressive Township
### Statement of Revenues, Expenditures, and Changes in Fund Balances
### Nonmajor Governmental Funds
### For the Year Ended December 31, Year 1

| | Special Revenue Funds | | Debt Service Funds | | Capital Projects Fund | Permanent Fund | Total Nonmajor Governmental Funds |
|---|---|---|---|---|---|---|---|
| | Gas Tax | Head Start | East Bridge | Police Dept. Bonds | East Bridge | Inmate Commissary | |
| **Revenues** | | | | | | | |
| Intergovernmental | $ 310,000 | $300,000 | – | – | $ 50,000 | – | $ 660,000 |
| Charges for services | – | – | – | – | – | 78,000 | 78,000 |
| Interest earnings | – | – | $ 20,000 | $ 15,000 | 5,000 | – | 40,000 |
| Total revenues | 310,000 | 300,000 | 20,000 | 15,000 | 55,000 | 78,000 | 778,000 |
| **Expenditures** | | | | | | | |
| Current: | | | | | | | |
| Other functional classifications | 385,000 | 295,000 | – | – | – | 77,000 | 757,000 |
| Debt service: | | | | | | | |
| Principal | – | – | 45,000 | 65,000 | – | – | 110,000 |
| Interest and other charges | – | – | 83,000 | 128,000 | – | – | 211,000 |
| Capital outlay | – | – | – | – | 162,000 | – | 162,000 |
| Total expenditures | 385,000 | 295,000 | 128,000 | 193,000 | 162,000 | 77,000 | 1,240,000 |
| Excess (deficiency) of revenues over expenditures | (75,000) | 5,000 | (108,000) | (178,000) | (107,000) | 1,000 | (462,000) |
| **Other Financing Sources (Uses)** | | | | | | | |
| Transfers in | 12,000 | – | 40,000 | 10,000 | – | 4,000 | 66,000 |
| Transfers out | (40,000) | – | – | – | (85,000) | – | (125,000) |
| Total other financing sources and uses | (28,000) | – | 40,000 | 10,000 | (85,000) | 4,000 | (59,000) |
| Net change in fund balances | (103,000) | 5,000 | (68,000) | (168,000) | (192,000) | 5,000 | (521,000) |
| Fund balances—beginning | 113,000 | 6,000 | 126,000 | 268,000 | 266,000 | 1,000 | 780,000 |
| Fund balances—ending | $ 10,000 | $ 11,000 | $ 58,000 | $ 100,000 | $ 74,000 | $ 6,000 | $ 259,000 |

## Question 1  MCQ-08615

Which of the following is a required part of a local government's management's discussion and analysis (MD&A) as part of its financial statements?

- a. The MD&A should be presented with other required supplementary information.
- b. The MD&A should compare current year results to the prior year with emphasis on the current year.
- c. The MD&A should include an analysis for each fund.
- d. The MD&A should present condensed financial information from the fund financial statements.

## Question 2  MCQ-00980

According to GASB 34, *Basic Financial Statements—and Management's Discussion and Analysis—for State and Local Governments*, certain budgetary schedules are required supplementary information. What is the minimum budgetary information required to be reported in those schedules?

- a. A schedule of unfavorable variances at the functional level.
- b. A schedule showing the final appropriations budget and actual expenditures on a budgetary basis.
- c. A schedule showing the original budget, the final appropriations budget, and actual inflows, outflows, and balances on a budgetary basis.
- d. A schedule showing the proposed budget, the approved budget, the final amended budget, actual inflows and outflows on a budgetary basis, and variances between budget and actual.

# Class Question Explanations

# FAR

**1** Financial 1 .................................................................................3

**2** Financial 2 .................................................................................7

**3** Financial 3 ...............................................................................13

**4** Financial 4 ...............................................................................21

**5** Financial 5 ...............................................................................29

**6** Financial 6 ...............................................................................33

**7** Financial 7 ...............................................................................39

**8** Financial 8 ...............................................................................43

**9** Financial 9 ...............................................................................53

**10** Financial 10 .............................................................................61

**NOTES**

//FINANCIAL 1

Financial 1, Module 1

## 1. MCQ-00010

Choice "b" is correct. Completeness is an ingredient of faithful representation. Other ingredients of faithful representation include neutrality and freedom from error.

Choices "a", "c", and "d" are incorrect. Completeness is an ingredient of faithful representation. Other ingredients of faithful representation include neutrality and freedom from error. The ingredients of relevance are predictive value, confirming value, and materiality.

Financial 1, Module 2

## 1. MCQ-00031

Choice "d" is correct. The transaction resulted in a gain, which should be reported using the net concept (i.e., proceeds less carrying amount). This gain resulted in the recognition of an asset not in the ordinary course of business, but it did not qualify as part of discontinued operations.

Choice "a" is incorrect. Gains (and losses) are reported using the net concept.

Choice "b" is incorrect. Gains and losses from fixed asset sales are reported using the net concept, but are not included in other comprehensive income.

Choice "c" is incorrect. Gains and losses from fixed asset sales are reported using the net concept, but are not included in discontinued operations because a fixed asset is not considered a component of an entity. Discontinued operations are only reported for the disposal of a component of an entity.

## 2. MCQ-00052

Choice "d" is correct. Interest expense is classified as a separate line item on the income statement. Advertising is classified as a selling expense.

Financial 1, Module 3

## 1. MCQ-00549

Choice "d" is correct. For a customer who pays the $540 annual fee in advance, the related revenue should be recognized evenly over the contract year as the services are performed (GAAP-accrual basis of accounting).

Choice "a" is incorrect. Under the cash basis of accounting, revenue is recognized when the cash is collected.

Choice "b" is incorrect. Revenue should not be recognized at the end of the fiscal year; it should be recognized evenly over the contract year.

Choice "c" is incorrect. Revenue should not be recognized at the end of the contract year after all of the services have been performed; it should be recognized evenly over the contract year.

### 2. MCQ-06244

Choice "d" is correct. The journal entries for this transaction for Landon are as follows:

April 15, Year 3: No entry.

July 31, Year 3:

| DR | Cash | $215,000 | |
|---|---|---|---|
| CR | Unearned sales revenue | | $215,000 |

August 31, Year 3:

| DR | Unearned sales revenue | $215,000 | |
|---|---|---|---|
| CR | Sales revenue | | $215,000 |
| DR | Cost of goods sold | 175,000 | |
| CR | Inventory | | 175,000 |

---

**Financial 1, Module 4**

### 1. MCQ-06248

Choice "a" is correct. Although S&B does not take delivery until Year 3, JoJo can recognize the revenue from the sale on September 1, Year 2, because there is a substantive reason for the bill-and-hold arrangement, the roasters were built to S&B's specifications and therefore have been separately identified and cannot be directed to another customer, and the roasters are completed and ready to transfer to S&B on that date.

### 2. MCQ-00654

Choice "d" is correct. The gross profit for the percentage-of-completion method is as follows:

| | |
|---|---|
| Contract price | $3,000,000 |
| Cost to date | 1,800,000 |
| Estimated cost to complete | 600,000 |
| Total cost | $2,400,000 |
| Expected gross profit | 600,000 |
| Percentage complete (18/24) | 75% |
| Profit to date | 450,000 |
| Profit previously recognized | (300,000) |
| Year 2 profit | $ 150,000 |

Choice "a" is incorrect. $450,000 is the total profit earned to date. Only profit earned in Year 2 is to be determined.

Choice "b" is incorrect. $300,000 is the earned profit in Year 1. The profit earned in Year 2 is to be determined.

Choice "c" is incorrect. The total gross profit as of December 31, Year 2 must be computed to determine the profit to be recorded in Year 2.

## 3. MCQ-00659

Choice "d" is correct: Decrease—Decrease. During Year 1, operating income under both the percentage-of-completion method and the completed-contract method will decrease. For "percentage-of-completion" and "completed-contract," the entire estimated loss is recorded for a loss contract in progress (not only the loss incurred to date).

### Financial 1, Module 5

## 1. MCQ-00045

Choice "c" is correct. The Year 3 operating losses would be reported in the Year 3 income statement. The Year 4 operating losses and the gain on disposal would be netted and reported in the Year 4 income statement. Each amount would be reported in the period it occurred.

Choice "a" is incorrect. It reports the total projected gains and losses in Year 4 and nothing in Year 3. Each amount should be reported in the period it occurred.

Choice "b" is incorrect. It reports the total projected gains and losses in Year 3 and nothing in Year 4. Each amount should be reported in the period it occurred.

Choice "d" is incorrect. It reports the total projected losses in Year 3 and the gain in Year 4. Each amount should be reported in the period it occurred.

### Financial 1, Module 6

## 1. MCQ-00071

Choice "d" is correct. Financial statements of all prior periods presented should be restated when there is a "change in entity" such as resulting from:

1. Changing companies in consolidated financial statements.
2. Consolidated financial statements versus previous individual financial statements.

Choice "a" is incorrect. Cumulative-effect adjustments are reported in the retained earnings statement in the year of change.

Choice "b" is incorrect. Restatements are required for changes in entity (of subsidiaries).

Choice "c" is incorrect. Per GAAP, changes involving the cost and equity methods of accounting for investments are not considered to be changes in accounting principle. A change from the cost method to the equity method requires restatement; however, a change from the equity method to the cost method does not require restatement and is accounted for prospectively.

**Note:** IFRS does not discuss the accounting for changes in reporting entity.

## 2. MCQ-00081

Choice "a" is correct. The effect of the new estimate of warranty costs (from $100 to $110) is a change in estimate and will be reported in Year 2 income from continuing operations.

**Rule:** Changes in estimates affect only the current and subsequent periods (not prior periods and not retained earnings).

Choice "b" is incorrect. An accounting change of principle is shown net of tax on the retained earnings statement.

Choice "c" is incorrect. Restating prior years financial statements is only required when comparative financial statements are shown for prior period adjustments of subsequently discovered corrections of errors, changes in entity or changes in accounting principle.

Choice "d" is incorrect. The facts stating a new estimate of warranty costs indicate a change of estimate, not a correction of an error.

Financial 1, Module 7

## 1. MCQ-00102

Choice "c" is correct. Comprehensive income includes all changes in equity during a period except those resulting from owner investments and distributions to owners.

Choice "a" is incorrect. Loss from discontinued operations is included in net income, which is a component of comprehensive income.

Choice "b" is incorrect. Prior period error correction is a change in stockholders' equity not resulting from owner investments and distributions to owners and so is included in comprehensive income.

Choice "d" is incorrect. Unrealized loss on investments in non-current marketable equity securities is a change in stockholders' equity not resulting from owner investments and distributions to owners and so is included in comprehensive income.

Financial 1, Module 8

## 1. MCQ-08238

Choice "b" is correct. When the cash payment was made, the company debited services expense for $90,000. The amount that will be expensed each month over the six-month period is $15,000. Therefore, at the end of Year 1, the total correct expense for November ($15,000) and December ($15,000) would be $30,000. The expense for the next year is $60,000 (4 months × $15,000). The adjusting journal entry to ensure the expense account and prepaid accounts are stated correctly is the following:

| DR | Prepaid services | $60,000 | |
|---|---|---|---|
| CR | Services expense | | $60,000 |

Choice "a" is incorrect. Debiting prepaid services for $30,000 and crediting services expense for $30,000 would result in an overstatement of the services expense and understatement of prepaid services for Year 1.

Choices "c" and "d" are incorrect. The adjusting journal entry must include a debit to prepaid services and credit to services expense to correctly adjust the services expense account and reflect the prepaid services asset for Year 2.

Class Question Explanations     Financial

# FINANCIAL 2

## Financial 2, Module 1

### 1. MCQ-00103

Choice "c" is correct. The method of determining which assets are considered to be cash equivalents is a significant accounting policy.

Choice "a" is incorrect. Debt refinancing would be disclosed in a separate indebtedness note.

Choice "b" is incorrect. Guarantees of other entity's indebtedness would be disclosed in a separate commitments and contingencies note.

Choice "d" is incorrect. Information about pension plan assets and pension plan liabilities is disclosed in a separate pensions note.

## Financial 2, Module 2

### 1. MCQ-03689

Choice "b" is correct. Additional footnote disclosures include management's evaluation of the significance of those conditions and a description of management's plans that alleviated the substantial doubt.

Choice "a" is incorrect. Even though management has plans in place that mitigate the substantial doubt, additional disclosures are required, as explained above.

Choice "c" is incorrect. A supplemental schedule of cash receipts and disbursements is not required.

Choice "d" is incorrect. The balance sheet is still prepared under the going concern basis of accounting. The only time a balance sheet is required under the liquidation basis of accounting is when the entity's liquidation is imminent. In such a case, the entity would no longer be considered a going concern.

## Financial 2, Module 3

### 1. MCQ-00733

Choice "d" is correct. As of February 1, Year 2, Ace Co.'s financial statements have not been issued and the actual amount of the final settlement is known. That amount should be included in Ace Co.'s December 31, Year 1 financial statements and disclosed as a "subsequent event." This is a recognized subsequent event because it relates to litigation that originated in Year 1.

Choice "a" is incorrect. Because the amount of the settlement was known, it must be recorded as well as disclosed.

Choice "b" is incorrect. Whenever an accrual such as this is made, the details must be disclosed.

Choice "c" is incorrect. The general rule governing contingencies only permits no disclosure/no accrual when the outcome is "remote."

## Financial 2, Module 4

### 1. MCQ-06057

Choice "c" is correct. If there is no principal market, then the price in the most advantageous market is the fair value of the stock. The most advantageous market is the market with the best price after considering transaction costs. Although the London quoted market price is higher, after transaction costs the net amount is lower, so New York is the most advantageous market and the fair value is $103.

Choice "a" is incorrect. Transaction costs are considered when determining the most advantageous market, but are not included in the final fair value measurement.

Choice "b" is incorrect. Transaction costs are considered when determining the most advantageous market, but are not included in the final fair value measurement.

Choice "d" is incorrect. Although the London quoted market price is higher, after transaction costs the net amount is lower, so New York is the most advantageous market and the fair value is $103.

## Financial 2, Module 5

### 1. MCQ-00127

Choice "b" is correct. Only Bix and Dil.

| | |
|---|---|
| Total sales to unaffiliated customers | $60,000 |
| Intersegment sales | 23,000 |
| Total combined sales | 83,000 |
| | × 10% |
| Minimum reportable segment | $ 8,300 |

Only Bix and Dil qualify as reportable segments. When using revenues as criteria, a segment must include at least 10 percent of combined revenues, including intersegment sales. Bix and Dil division revenues exceed $8,300, whereas Alo and Cee division revenues do not. Additionally, Bix and Dil together account for more than 75 percent of Timm's total sales to unaffiliated customers (external sales), so no additional reportable segments need to be identified.

## Financial 2, Module 6

### 1. MCQ-06078

Choice "b" is correct. Form 6-K is filed semiannually by foreign private issuers and contains unaudited financial statements. Form 10-Q, which is filed quarterly by U.S. registered companies, also contains unaudited financial statements.

Choice "a" is incorrect. Form 10-K is filed annually by U.S. registered companies and must contain audited financial statements.

Choice "c" is incorrect. Form 40-F is filed annually by specific Canadian companies registered with the SEC and must contain audited financial statements.

Choice "d" is incorrect. Form 20-F is filed annually by non-U.S. registrants registered with the SEC and must contain audited financial statements.

## 2. MCQ-08590

Choice "d" is correct. Form 8-K is a form required to be filed by all companies registered with the Securities and Exchange Commission (SEC). The form reports on major corporate events, including corporate asset acquisitions/disposals, accountant changes, financial statement changes, management changes, changes in securities, etc. Quarterly results of operations will be reported using Form 10-Q.

Choice "a" is incorrect. Assuming they are significant, obligations created under an off-balance sheet arrangement will be reported on Form 8-K.

Choice "b" is incorrect. Changes in securities issued (including sales of equity securities) will be reported on Form 8-K.

Choice "c" is incorrect. A change in the registrant's accountant is significant and will be reported on Form 8-K.

Financial 2, Module 7

## 1. MCQ-00545

Choice "c" is correct. $215,000 service revenue for Year 2.

| | |
|---|---|
| Cash basis revenue | $200,000 |
| + Ending AR | + 60,000 |
| − Beginning AR | − 40,000 |
| − Ending unearned fees | −   5,000 |
| Accrual basis revenue | $215,000 |

## 2. MCQ-08564

Choice "a" is correct. Under accrual accounting, the $10,000 increase in accounts receivable coincides with a $10,000 increase in revenue. If the company had used the cash basis, this revenue would not have affected the income statement until the company was actually paid. So in converting from accrual to cash basis accounting, this $10,000 would be removed.

Under accrual accounting, the $6,000 decrease in accounts payable will coincide with a $6,000 cash payment. If the company had used the cash basis, this cash payment would hit the income statement as an expense in the period in which it was paid (which would be this period). So in converting from accrual to cash basis accounting, this $6,000 would be treated as an expense.

$100,000 [accrual-basis income] − $10,000 [not revenue under the cash basis] − $6,000 [expense under the cash basis] = $84,000 [cash-basis income].

Choice "b" is incorrect. This choice correctly subtracts $10,000 in revenue, but incorrectly adds $6,000 to the accrual-basis income of $100,000.

Choice "c" is incorrect. This choice correctly subtracts $6,000 for cash paid, but incorrectly adds $10,000 in revenue to the accrual-basis income of $100,000.

Choice "d" is incorrect. This choice incorrectly adds both the $10,000 in revenue and the $6,000 cash payment to the accrual-basis income of $100,000.

Financial | Class Question Explanations

Financial 2, Module 8

**1. MCQ-05956**

Choice "a" is correct. To calculate inventory turnover, cost of goods sold must first be calculated:

|   | Beginning inventory | $100,000 |
|---|---|---|
| + | Purchases | + 700,000 |
|   | Goods available for sale | $800,000 |
| − | Ending inventory | − 300,000 |
|   | Cost of goods sold | $ 500,000 |

Inventory turnover is then calculated as follows:

$$\text{Inventory turnover} = \frac{\text{Cost of goods sold}}{\text{Average inventory}} = \frac{\$500}{(\$100 + \$300)/2} = 2.5$$

**2. MCQ-05432**

Choice "b" is correct. To calculate Stent Co.'s debt-to-equity ratio, Stent's total liabilities and total equity must be derived from the facts:

Equity = Capital Stock + Retained earnings
= $150,000 + 215,000
= $365,000

Liabilities = Assets − Equity
= $760,000 − 365,000
= $395,000

Stent's debt-to-equity ratio is then calculated as:

$$\frac{\text{Total liabilities}}{\text{Equity}} = \frac{\$395,000}{\$365,000} = 1.08$$

Choice "a" is incorrect. The denominator of the debt-to-equity ratio is total equity, not just capital stock. See the calculation above.

Choice "c" is incorrect. The debt ratio, not the debt-to-equity ratio, is equal to liabilities divided by total assets.

Choice "d" is incorrect. The debt-to-equity ratio is not equal to equity divided by total assets.

Class Question Explanations                                                                 Financial

## Financial 2, Module 9

### 1. MCQ-04646

Choice "b" is correct, $5,000.

Total equity of new partnership:

| | |
|---|---|
| Eagle | $45,000 |
| Falk | 25,000 |
| Robb | 30,000 |
| Total | $100,000 |

Since Robb is receiving a 25 percent interest in the partnership, his capital account will be credited with 25 percent of the total equity of the new partnership, or $25,000. The difference between his contribution of $30,000, and his capital account balance of $25,000, is credited to the other partners as a bonus.

### 2. MCQ-00721

Choice "d" is correct, $20,000.

Robb's investment:

| | |
|---|---|
| 25% of total capital = | $30,000 |
| Calculate total capital | $30,000 / 0.25 |
| Total capital = | $120,000 |

Less existing capital balances:

| | |
|---|---|
| Eagle | $45,000 |
| Falk | 25,000 |
| Robb | 30,000 |
| Total | $100,000 |

| | |
|---|---|
| Total assets contributed = | $100,000 |
| Goodwill to original partners = | $20,000 |

### 3. MCQ-00722

Choice "a" is correct. Zinc's capital decreased by $1,000 from $100,000 to $99,000.

| Item | Young | Zinc | Profit |
|---|---|---|---|
| Capital | $160,000 | $100,000 | $ 4,000 |
| Interest | 16,000 | 10,000 | (26,000) |
|  | 176,000 | 110,000 | (22,000) |
| Loss allocation | (11,000) | (11,000) | 22,000 |
|  | 165,000 | 99,000 | 0 |
| Net change | $ 5,000 | $ (1,000) | |

Choice "b" is incorrect. If there were no interest allocation, then each capital account would increase by $2,000 [50% × $4,000 profit].

Choice "c" is incorrect. The $11,000 is the loss allocation to Zinc. However, this is offset by the allocation of $10,000 interest.

Choice "d" is incorrect. It is not possible to increase Zinc's capital by both the interest and half the profit because the interest comes "out of" the profit, resulting in a loss.

# FINANCIAL 3

Financial 3, Module 1

### 1. MCQ-00061

Choice "c" is correct: $1,400,000 cash and cash equivalents.

|  | Cash and Cash Equivalents |
|---|---|
| Cash in checking account | $ 350,000 |
| Cash in money market account | 250,000 |
| U.S. Treasury bill, purchased 12/1/Year 2, maturing 2/28/Year 3 (90 days) | 800,000 |
| Total cash and cash equivalents | $1,400,000 |

The U.S. Treasury bond, purchased 3/1/Year 2, maturing 2/28/Year 3, is not a cash equivalent. At the purchase date, it was due in 365 days. Cash equivalents must mature in 90 days or less at the date of purchase.

Financial 3, Module 2

### 1. MCQ-00034

Choice "d" is correct. Factoring receivables without recourse is a sales transaction. Factoring without recourse transfers the risk of uncollectible accounts to the buyer.

Choice "a" is incorrect. Pledging receivables is the process of obtaining a loan using the receivables as collateral.

Choice "b" is incorrect. Assigning receivables is the process of obtaining a loan by transferring to the lender the debtor's right to cash collected on receivables.

Choice "c" is incorrect. Factoring receivables may be treated as a sales transaction. Factoring with recourse leaves the risk of uncollectible accounts with the seller.

### 2. MCQ-00059

Choice "c" is correct: $513,000 cash proceeds received from the bank.

|  | Net Proceeds at discount |
|---|---|
| Face of note | $500,000 |
| Interest rate on note (8% × 1 yr) | × 8% |
|  | 40,000 |
| Maturity value of note | 540,000 |
| Discount by bank (10% × ½ yr) | × 5% |
|  | (27,000) |
| Proceeds from bank | $513,000 |

Financial                                                                                    Class Question Explanations

## Financial 3, Module 3

### 1. MCQ-00114

Choice "c" is correct. The $26,000 understatement of beginning inventory creates an understatement of cost of goods available for sale which leads to a $26,000 understatement of cost of goods sold. The $52,000 overstatement of ending inventory creates a $52,000 understatement of cost of goods sold. Thus, cost of goods sold, in total, is understated by $78,000 ($26,000 plus $52,000).

**Note:** Amounts for beginning and ending balances and purchases are assumed.

|  | As stated | − | Should be | = | Difference |
|---|---|---|---|---|---|
| Beginning balance | $ 0 |  | $ 26,000 |  | $(26,000) |
| Plus purchases | 100,000 |  | 100,000 |  | 0 |
| Less ending inventory | 52,000 |  | 0 |  | 52,000 |
| Cost of goods sold | $48,000 |  | $126,000 |  | $(78,000) |

Choice "a" is incorrect. Cost of goods sold is also understated by $52,000 due to the overstatement of ending inventory.

Choice "b" is incorrect. The $26,000 understatement of beginning inventory creates an understatement, rather than an overstatement, of cost of goods sold. Cost of goods sold is also understated by $52,000 due to the overstatement of ending inventory.

Choice "d" is incorrect. Cost of goods sold is understated, rather than overstated, by $78,000.

### 2. MCQ-00084

Choice "b" is correct.

#### LIFO Perpetual

|  | Units | Unit Cost | Total Cost | Inventory Balance |
|---|---|---|---|---|
| Balance on 1/1 | 2,000 | $1 | $2,000 | $2,000 |
| Purchased on 1/8 | 1,200 | 3 | 3,600 | 5,600 |
| Sold on 1/23 | (1,200) | 3 | (3,600) |  |
|  | (600) | 1 | (600) |  |
| Subtotal | 1,400 | 1 | 1,400 | 1,400 |
| Purchased on 1/28 | 800 | 5 | 4,000 | $5,400 |
|  | 2,200 |  |  |  |

#### LIFO Periodic

Ending inventory in units = 2,200 (from above) × oldest cost = LIFO valuation

|  | Units | Unit Cost | $ |
|---|---|---|---|
| 1/1 Beginning bal. | 2,000 | $1 | $2,000 |
| 1/8 Purchase | 200 | 3 | 600 |
|  |  |  | $2,600 |

CQ–14

Class Question Explanations          Financial

## Financial 3, Module 4

### 1. MCQ-00139

Choice "a" is correct. Land costs include the costs of getting the land ready for intended use which includes razing old buildings less salvage plus title insurance and legal fees.

| | |
|---|---|
| Land | $400,000 |
| Demolition | 50,000 |
| Legal fees | 10,000 |
| Title insurance | 12,000 |
| Salvaged materials | (8,000) |
| Total | $464,000 |

Choice "b" is incorrect. Title insurance and salvaged materials proceeds are included in the cost of the land.

Choice "c" is incorrect. Legal fees and title insurance are included in the cost of the land.

Choice "d" is incorrect. Demolition cost less salvaged materials proceeds are included in the cost of the land.

### 2. MCQ-08592

Choice "b" is correct. The amount of capitalized interest is based on the weighted average amount of accumulated expenditures. The calculation for weighted average expenditures is:

$1,000,000 (12/12) + $1,000,000 (0/12) = $1,000,000

At an interest rate of 8 percent, the amount of interest to be capitalized is equal to $1,000,000 × 8% = $80,000.

Because the company will pay $240,000 in interest on the construction loan, the full $80,000 can be capitalized because it does not exceed $240,000.

Choice "a" is incorrect. Sea may capitalize interest based on the weighted average amount of accumulated expenditures, as long as it does not exceed the total amount of interest costs for the period.

Choice "c" is incorrect. This choice incorrectly uses all expenditures ($2,000,000) for the year in the calculation rather than calculating a weighted average.

Choice "d" is incorrect. Capitalized interest is based on expenditures rather than amounts borrowed.

Financial 3, Module 5

## 1. MCQ-05651

Choice "b" is correct. Under the double (200 percent) declining balance method of depreciation, depreciation expense for Year 2 is calculated as follows:

| Year | Double Percentage* | NBV Remaining | Depreciation Expense |
|------|--------------------|---------------|----------------------|
| 1    | 20%                | $100,000      | $20,000              |
| 2    | 20%                | 80,000        | 16,000               |

*The double-declining balance percentage is calculated as the straight-line rate times 200%: 1/10 × 200% = 20%

Choice "a" is incorrect. This is the Year 2 depreciation incorrectly calculated by subtracting the salvage value from the net book value of the equipment when calculating depreciation. Under declining balance depreciation, the salvage value is not included in the computation of depreciation expense.

Choice "c" is incorrect. This is the Year 1 depreciation incorrectly calculated by subtracting the salvage value from the net book value of the equipment when calculating depreciation. Under declining balance depreciation, the salvage value is not included in the computation of depreciation expense. Additionally, this question asked for depreciation expense in Year 2, not Year 1. Watch the dates!

Choice "d" is incorrect. This is the depreciation expense to be reported in Year 1 under double-declining balance depreciation. The question asked for the depreciation expense in Year 2. Watch the dates!

## 2. MCQ-00143

Choice "b" is correct. The depletion base equals the purchase price ($2,640,000) plus the development costs ($360,000) plus the estimated restoration costs ($180,000) less the expected salvage value ($300,000) or $2,880,000. Depletion is $2.40 per ton ($2,880,000 / 1,200,000 tons). Depletion expense is $144,000 ($2.40 per ton × 60,000 tons sold).

Choice "a" is incorrect. Estimated restoration costs should be included in the calculation of the depletion base.

Choice "c" is incorrect. Estimated restoration costs and estimated salvage value should be included in the calculation of the depletion base.

Choice "d" is incorrect. Estimated salvage value should be included in the calculation of the depletion base.

Class Question Explanations        Financial

## Financial 3, Module 6

### 1. MCQ-00720

Choice "a" is correct: $3,000 (the fair value of the truck surrendered). If a nonmonetary exchange has commercial substance, the transaction is accounted for using the fair value of the asset surrendered or received, whichever is more evident. In this question, it appears that the exchange has commercial substance, as it appears to culminate the earnings process (i.e., a truck is exchanged for stock, which would appear in a business sense to have affected the expected configuration of cash). Therefore, the accounting uses the fair value of the asset surrendered or the fair value of the asset received, whichever is more evident, as the value for the exchange. The question indicates that the fair value of the truck is $3,000 on the date of the exchange, and it does not provide the fair value of the stock (do not use the book value of the stock as an "approximation" of the fair value); therefore, the $3,000 fair value of the truck is used for measuring the transaction.

Choice "b" is incorrect. $2,500 is the book value of the asset surrendered. The book value of the asset surrendered is not used to account for the exchange if the fair value of the asset surrendered is more evident.

Choice "c" is incorrect. $1,500 (25 shares × $60) is Ace's book value of the stock on July 1, Year 1. The book value of the asset received is not used to account for the exchange.

Choice "d" is incorrect. $1,250 (25 shares × $50) is Ace's book value of the stock at December 31, Year 1. The book value of the asset received is not used to account for the exchange.

### 2. MCQ-08514

Choice "c" is correct. When a transaction involving a nonmonetary exchange lacks commercial substance, the reported amount of the nonmonetary asset surrendered is used to record the newly acquired asset. If the transaction has commercial substance, the fair value approach is used.

Choice "a" is incorrect. When the entity's future cash flows are expected to change as a result of the exchange of nonmonetary assets, this exchange is referred to as having commercial substance. In this situation, the fair value method approach is used.

Choice "b" is incorrect. The timing of future cash flows of the asset received differing significantly from the configuration of the future cash flows of the asset transferred is evidence of an exchange with commercial substance in which the fair value approach would be used.

Choice "d" is incorrect. The fair value of the assets surrendered or received is used for reporting when the exchange has commercial substance.

# Financial 3, Module 7

## 1. MCQ-00542

Choice "b" is correct: A $24,000 gain from the sale of the patent in Year 4.

| | |
|---|---:|
| Original patent cost capitalized, Jan. 2, Year 1 | $45,000 |
| Less: 15-year s/l amortization for 3 yrs to Dec. 31, Year 3: 3/15 × $45,000 = | (9,000) |
| Carrying value at Dec. 31, Year 3 | 36,000 |
| Add: successful legal defense costs in Year 4 | 15,000 |
| Carrying value before sale | 51,000 |
| Sales price in Year 4 | 75,000 |
| Gain from sale of patent in Year 4 | $24,000 |

## 2. MCQ-00554

Choice "c" is correct. The $50,000 franchise cost will be amortized on a straight-line basis over 10 years ($5,000 per year). The balance in the franchise account will be $50,000 − $5,000 = $45,000. The 3 percent of franchise operation revenue is an operating expense, unrelated to the intangible asset balance.

## 3. MCQ-05947

Choice "c" is correct. Research and development expense is calculated as follows:

| | |
|---|---:|
| Depreciation of equipment for current and future projects | $ 20,000 |
| Equipment for current projects only | 200,000 |
| R&D salaries | 400,000 |
| Material and labor costs for prototype | 600,000 |
| Total R&D expense | $1,220,000 |

Research and development expense does not include the amount paid for the equipment purchased for current and future projects because the equipment has alternate future uses. This equipment will be capitalized, but the related depreciation expense will be allocated to R&D while the equipment is being used for R&D. The legal fees to obtain the patent are capitalized as an intangible asset.

Class Question Explanations

Financial

## Financial 3, Module 8

### 1. MCQ-06390

Choice "a" is correct. Under U.S. GAAP, impairment analysis begins with a test for recoverability in which the net carrying value of the asset is compared to the undiscounted cash flows expected from the asset. If the net carrying value exceeds the undiscounted cash flows, then an impairment loss is recorded equal to the difference between the carrying value and fair value of the asset. In this situation, the carrying value of $500,000 is less than the undiscounted future cash flows of $515,000, so no impairment loss is recorded.

### 2. MCQ-06570

Choice "a" is correct. There will be no amount recorded because a subsequent reversal of an impairment loss is prohibited under U.S. GAAP (unless the asset is held for disposal). Note that reversal of impairment loss is permitted under IFRS.

Choice "b" is incorrect. This answer is the current value of $130,000 less the original book value of $120,000. No reversal for an impairment loss is allowed.

Choice "c" is incorrect. This represents the reduction in the original carrying amount and does not relate to reversing the loss.

Choice "d" is incorrect. This represents the change in value from the original carrying amount of $100,000 to the new fair value of $130,000. No restoration amount will be booked because reversals of impairment losses are prohibited under U.S. GAAP.

# NOTES

# FINANCIAL 4

## Financial 4, Module 1

### 1. MCQ-00265

Choice "d" is correct. Trading debt securities are reported at fair value, with holding gains and losses included in earnings.

Choice "a" is incorrect. Lower of cost or market valuation is not permitted under IFRS or U.S. GAAP.

Choice "b" is incorrect. Lower of cost or market valuation is not permitted under IFRS or U.S. GAAP.

Choice "c" is incorrect. Trading debt securities are reported at fair value but there is no restriction on the recognition of holding gains.

### 2. MCQ-00273

Choice "b" is correct. Stone must report a net cumulative loss on its statement of stockholders' equity (under "accumulated other comprehensive income") of $22,000 ($148,000 FMV − $170,000 cost). Stone has already reported a $1,500 loss as of 12/31/Y1; therefore, an unrealized loss of $20,500 ($22,000 − $1,500) should be reported in the statement of comprehensive income (as part of other comprehensive income) for Year 2.

### 3. MCQ-00287

Choice "b" is correct. The amount of dividend revenue that should be reported in the investor's income statement for this year would be the portion of the dividends received this year that were not in excess of the investor's share of investee's undistributed earnings since the date of investment.

**Rule:** Dividend revenue, under the fair value method, should be recognized to the extent of cumulative earnings since acquisition and return of capital beyond that point.

Choice "a" is incorrect. This will be characterized as a return of capital or liquidating dividend.

Choices "c" and "d" are incorrect. Part of the dividends will be recognized as income and part will be a return of capital.

Financial                                                                                           Class Question Explanations

Financial 4, Module 2

### 1. MCQ-00320

Choice "b" is correct. Even though Well has only a 10 percent ownership, one can presume that Well has significant influence on Rea because it is the largest single shareholder and has a majority on Rea's board of directors. The equity method is the appropriate accounting method.

| | | | |
|---|---|---|---:|
| B | Beginning investment | | $400,000 |
| A | Add % Rea's income (10% × $500,000) | | 50,000 |
| S | Subtract % Rea's dividends/withdrawals (10% × $150,000) | − | 15,000 |
| E | Ending investment | | $435,000 |

The investment account balance of $400,000 will be increased by the $50,000 equity in earnings (10% × $500,000 net income) and decrease by the $15,000 dividends received (10% × $150,000) for a year-end balance of $435,000.

Choice "a" is incorrect. The investment account must also be decreased for Well's share of the dividends paid by Rea.

Choice "c" is incorrect. The equity method is the correct accounting method for this investment.

Choice "d" is incorrect. The investment account must also be increased for equity in earnings of Rea.

### 2. MCQ-00318

Because Moss owns 40 percent of Dubro's common stock, the equity method is appropriate.

Preferred stock:

$100,000 × 10% = $10,000 dividends

$10,000 dividends × 20% ownership = $2,000 dividends received

Common stock:

| | | |
|---|---:|---|
| Net income | $ 60,000 | |
| Less preferred dividends | (10,000) | |
| Net income available to common shareholders | 50,000 | |
| | × 40% | |
| Moss' percentage owned | $ 20,000 | equity in earnings |

Choice "a" is correct: $20,000 from equity in earnings plus $2,000 from dividend revenue.

### 3. MCQ-00348

Choice "b" is correct. Park would record the additional COGS associated with the undervalued beginning inventory by debiting investment income and crediting the investment in Tun's account. Because the difference between book value and fair market value on land is not amortized, the difference in the land value would have no effect on equity in earnings.

## 4. MCQ-00289

Choice "b" is correct. The allocation of the investment purchase price is calculated as follows:

| Goodwill | Excess = | $200,000 |
|----------|----------|----------|
| FV | × 30% = $180,000 | Purchase Price |
| NBV | × 30% = $150,000 | |

| | |
|---|---|
| Investment | $200,000 |
| Less: NBV ($500,000 × 30%) | (150,000) |
| Total excess | $ 50,000 |

Allocated to identifiable net assets:
| | | |
|---|---|---|
| FV | $ 600,000 | |
| NBV | (500,000) | |
| | $ 100,000 × 30% = | (30,000) |
| Excess to goodwill | | $ 20,000 |

## 5. MCQ-00288

Choice "b" is correct.

Undervalued equipment $100,000 × 40% ownership = $40,000 / 5 years = $8,000

Puff's share of Straw's income:

| | |
|---|---|
| $150,000 × 40% = | $60,000 |
| Less: Excess fair value amortization | (8,000) |
| Equity method investment income | **$52,000** |

---

### Financial 4, Module 3

## 1. MCQ-04697

Choice "b" is correct. Consolidate all majority-owned subsidiaries to have one management and one economic entity, including domestic, foreign, similar, and dissimilar subsidiaries. Consolidated financial statements are prepared when a parent-subsidiary relationship has been formed. An investor is considered to have parent status when control over an investee is established or more than 50 percent of the voting stock of the investee has been acquired.

Choices "a", "c", and "d" are incorrect, per the above.

---

### Financial 4, Module 4

## 1. MCQ-00430

Choice "d" is correct. When the acquisition price exceeds the fair value of net assets acquired, assets and liabilities should be presented at fair value.

Financial                                                                                    Class Question Explanations

### 2. MCQ-00389

Choice "b" is correct. Fees of finders and consultants are expensed in the period incurred. Registration fees for equity securities issued decrease additional paid-in capital (stockholders' equity).

---

Financial 4, Module 5

### 1. MCQ-00391

Choice "b" is correct. The allocation of the investment purchase price is calculated as follows:

| | Sub's Total (100%) | Fair Value = $860,000 | |
|---|---|---|---|
| Goodwill | $160,000 | -0- | NCI |
| Identifiable intangible assets FV | -0- | | |
| Balance sheet FV adjustment | $80,000* | $860,000 | Investment in subsidiary |
| Book value (CAR) | $620,000 | | |

*The balance sheet fair value adjustment is calculated as follows:

$$\begin{aligned}
\text{BS FV adjustment} &= \text{FV net assets} - \text{BV net assets} \\
&= (\$840,000 - \$140,000) - (\$800,000 - \$180,000) \\
&= \$700,000 - \$620,000 \\
&= \$80,000
\end{aligned}$$

### 2. MCQ-06457

Choice "d" is correct. Under U.S. GAAP, goodwill is calculated as follows:

  Goodwill = Fair value of subsidiary − Fair value of subsidiary's net assets

The fair value of the subsidiary is:

  FV of subsidiary × 75% = $300,000
  FV of subsidiary = $400,000

The fair value of the subsidiary's net assets is:

  FV of subsidiary net assets = $40,000 + $380,000 + $60,000 − $200,000 = $280,000

Therefore, the goodwill to be reported under U.S. GAAP is:

  Goodwill = $400,000 − $280,000 = $120,000

## 3. MCQ-06458

Choice "c" is correct. Under the IFRS partial goodwill method, goodwill is calculated as follows:

Goodwill = Acquisition cost − Fair value of subsidiary's net assets acquired

The fair value of the subsidiary's net assets is:

FV of subsidiary's net assets = $40,000 + $380,000 + $60,000 − $200,000 = $280,000

Therefore, the goodwill to be reported under the IFRS partial goodwill method is:

Goodwill = $300,000 − ($280,000 x 75%) = $300,000 − $210,000 = $90,000

### Financial 4, Module 6

## 1. MCQ-00455

Choice "d" is correct. $0 reported as intercompany receivables.

**Rule:** 100 percent of all intercompany balances among members of the consolidated group are eliminated.

**Note:** Here's a quick way to pick up three minutes on the CPA Exam, by carefully reading the question and thus avoiding calculations.

## 2. MCQ-00448

Choice "a" is correct. Sales and cost of goods sold should be reduced by the intercompany sales.

Perez's sales price is Senior's purchase price. When Senior sells to an outside party, this amount becomes Senior's cost of sales. The sales price to the outsider is okay and the original cost of sales on Perez's books is okay, but the sales and cost of sales are overstated, for a like amount, by the intercompany transaction.

**Note:** No inventory adjustment is needed because none of the intercompany goods sold are on hand at year end.

## 3. MCQ-00484

Choice "a" is correct. The effect of the intercompany sale should be eliminated. The machine should be shown on the consolidated statements at Poe's cost of $1,100,000. Depreciation should continue as if the sale had not occurred. Depreciation for the current year is $50,000 [(1,100,000 − 100,000) / 20]. Accumulated depreciation at 12/31/Y10 is $300,000 (250,000 + 50,000).

Financial                                                                                          Class Question Explanations

## Financial 4, Module 7

### 1. MCQ-00427

Choice "c" is correct, $303,000 total consolidated stockholders' equity. Dallas' consolidated stockholders' equity will be the parent company stockholders' equity plus the noncontrolling interest on December 31, Year 1:

| | |
|---|---|
| Common stock | $ 50,000 |
| Additional paid-in capital | 80,250 |
| Noncontrolling interest | 33,000 |
| Retained earnings | 139,750 |
| | **303,000** |

The December 31, Year 1 noncontrolling interest of $33,000 is calculated as follows:

| | | |
|---|---|---|
| Noncontrolling interest, 1/1 | $30,000* | |
| + NCI share of net income | 4,000** | |
| − NCI share of dividends | (1,000) | $ = $5,000 × 20% |
| Noncontrolling interest, 12/31 | **$33,000** | |

*The noncontrolling interest on 1/1 is calculated as follows:

$120,000 acquisition cost = FV of Style × 80%

FV of Style = $150,000

Noncontrolling interest = $150,000 × 20% = $30,000

**The noncontrolling shareholders' share of Style's net income is calculated as follows:

| | |
|---|---|
| Style retained earnings, 1/1 | $36,000 |
| + Net income | 20,000  (plug) |
| - Dividends | (5,000) |
| Style retained earnings, 12/31 | **$51,000** |

Noncontrolling share of Style's net income = $20,000 × 20% = $4,000

### 2. MCQ-00421

Choice "b" is correct. 20 percent of Sago's net income to June 30 and 95 percent of Sago's net income from July 1 to December 31.

**Rule:** In an acquisition, the net income of a newly acquired subsidiary will only be included in consolidated net income from the date of acquisition. Therefore, only 20 percent of Sago net income is included in consolidated earnings until June 30 and 95 percent thereafter.

### 3. MCQ-05920

Choice "b" is correct. When the financial statements of Peace and Surge are consolidated, the equity of Surge, including Surge's retained earnings, will be eliminated. The consolidated statement of retained earnings will include only the $15,000 dividend paid by Peace during the current year.

Class Question Explanations                                                                            Financial

## Financial 4, Module 8

### 1. MCQ-06393

Choice "c" is correct. Under U.S. GAAP, goodwill impairment exists because the $3,310,000 fair value of the reporting unit is less than the $3,450,000 carrying value. The amount of the goodwill impairment loss will be equal to $140,000 ($3,450,000 CV - $3,310,000 FV).

Choice "a" is incorrect. An impairment loss must be recorded because the $3,310,000 fair value of the reporting unit is less than its $3,450,000 carrying value of the reporting unit.

Choice "b" is incorrect. This is the difference between the goodwill line item on the balance sheet and the loss that needs to be booked.

Choice "d" is incorrect. This is simply the amount of the goodwill line item on the balance sheet.

### 2. MCQ-06379

Choice "b" is correct. Under IFRS, the goodwill impairment test is a one-step test in which the carrying value of a cash-generating unit (CGU) is compared to the CGU's recoverable amount, which is the greater of the CGU's fair value less costs to sell and its value in use (PV of future cash flows expected from the CGU). For this CGU, the value in use of $2,400,000 is the recoverable amount because it exceeds the fair value less costs to sell of $2,350,000 ($2,600,000 fair value − $250,000 costs to sell) and the impairment loss is:

Impairment loss = Recoverable amount − Carrying value

Impairment loss = $2,400,000 − $2,425,000 = $(25,000)

Under IFRS, the CGU impairment loss is applied first to the goodwill of the CGU.

Choice "a" is incorrect. An impairment loss must be recorded under IFRS because the carrying value of the cash-generating unit exceeds the cash-generating unit's recoverable amount.

Choice "c" is incorrect. The goodwill impairment loss is not equal to the carrying value of the CGU's goodwill. Under IFRS, the goodwill impairment test is a one-step test in which the carrying value of a cash-generating unit (CGU) is compared to the CGU's recoverable amount, which is the greater of the CGU's fair value less costs to sell and its value in use (PV of future cash flows expected from the CGU). For this CGU, the value in use of $2,400,000 is the recoverable amount because it exceeds the fair value less costs to sell of $2,350,000 ($2,600,000 fair value − $250,000 costs to sell) and the impairment loss is:

Impairment loss = Recoverable amount − Carrying value

Impairment loss = $2,400,000 − $2,425,000 = $25,000

Under IFRS, the CGU impairment loss is applied first to the goodwill of the CGU. The $25,000 impairment loss will reduce the carrying value of the goodwill to $40,000 ($65,000 − $25,000).

Choice "d" is incorrect. The goodwill impairment loss is not equal to the difference between the $2,425,000 carrying value of the CGU and the $2,350,000 fair value less costs to sell of the CGU. Under IFRS, the goodwill impairment test is a one-step test in which the carrying value of a cash-generating unit (CGU) is compared to the CGU's recoverable amount, which is the greater of the CGU's fair value less costs to sell and its value in use (PV of future cash flows expected from the CGU). For this CGU, the value in use of $2,400,000 is the recoverable amount because it exceeds the fair value less costs to sell of $2,350,000 ($2,600,000 fair value − $250,000 costs to sell).

## NOTES

# FINANCIAL 5

## Financial 5, Module 1

### 1. MCQ-03931

Choice "d" is correct. Principal and interest payments were made March 1, Year 2, and March 1, Year 3. From March 1 to December 31, Year 3, the remaining loan balance totals $1,600,000 ($2,000,000 − $200,000 paid 3/1; Year 2 − $200,000 paid 3/1, Year 3). Interest must be accrued on that amount, but only for the months where interest has not been paid in cash (March to December): $1,600,000 × 6% × 10/12 = $80,000.

Choice "a" is incorrect. The interest payable is calculated on the outstanding principal at December 31, Year 3. At that date, the outstanding principal is $1,600,000, not $2,000,000.

Choice "b" is incorrect. $98,000 is the interest revenue for Year 3: Two months of interest on $1,800,000 outstanding loan balance ($18,000) and 10 months of interest on $1,600,000 outstanding loan balance ($80,000). The $18,000 has already been paid in cash.

Choice "c" is incorrect. Interest payable as of December 31, Year 3, is calculated for 10 months (because of the last cash interest and principal payment), not 12 months.

## Financial 5, Module 2

### 1. MCQ-00736

Choice "a" is correct. A contingent liability that is probable and estimable must be recognized. If all amounts within a range of values are equally likely, then the lowest amount in the range is the measurement amount. The final settlement was unknown prior to the issuance of the financial statements, so a contingent liability of $200,000 should have been recorded.

Choice "b" is incorrect. If all amounts within a range of values are equally likely, then the lowest amount in the range should be accrued.

Choice "c" is incorrect. The final settlement was unknown prior to the issuance of the financial statements.

Choice "d" is incorrect. If all amounts within a range of values are equally likely, then the lowest amount in the range should be accrued.

### 2. MCQ-00912

Choice "a" is correct. $0.

**Rule:** Only footnote disclosure is required for a "reasonably possible" (not "probable") loss.

The disclosure should include the range of $250,000 − $500,000 and indicate that the best estimate is $400,000.

Choices "b", "c", and "d" are incorrect. No amount should be accrued for losses that are only "reasonably possible."

### 3. MCQ-00745

Choice "d" is correct. Gain contingencies should be disclosed in the notes unless the likelihood of the gain being realized is remote. The full range of possible settlements should be disclosed. The actual settlement did not occur until after the financial statements were issued.

Choice "a" is incorrect. The actual settlement was not determined until after the financial statements were issued. Gain contingencies are not recognized until realized.

Choice "b" is incorrect. The actual settlement was not determined until after the financial statements were issued. Deferred revenue is an improper account.

Choice "c" is incorrect. The full range of possible settlements must be disclosed. The actual settlement amount of $100,000 was not known until after the financial statements were issued.

## Financial 5, Module 3

### 1. MCQ-00394

Choice "c" is correct. On Dec. 31, Year 1, the first payment will have been received with nine more payments to be received. Present value of this ordinary annuity of nine equal payments with a market interest rate of 8 percent is calculated as $10,000 × 6.25, or $62,500.

Choice "a" is incorrect. The note constitutes an annuity with nine payments since the first payment is made on December 31, Year 1.

Choice "b" is incorrect. The note constitutes an annuity with nine payments since the first payment is made on December 31, Year 1.

Choice "d" is incorrect. The annuity is for nine periods since the first payment is made on December 31, Year 1.

### 2. MCQ-06574

Choice "c" is correct. Each payment of $264,200 will consist of both interest and principal, with only principal reducing the liability owed. The interest portion ($22,500) of the initial payment is equal to $1,000,000 multiplied by the interest rate of 9 percent, and divided by 4 because the payment is quarterly.

Payment of $264,200 − Interest of $22,500 = Principal of $241,700. The principal payment of $241,700 will reduce the liability from $1,000,000 to $758,300.

Choice "a" is incorrect. This choice assumes the entire payment is principal.

Choice "b" is incorrect. This choice assumes there is no interest rate and the payments will be just the $1,000,000 divided by 4.

Choice "d" is incorrect. This choice does not divide the interest amount owed for the year by 4.

### 3. MCQ-03933

Choice "b" is correct. The debt-to-equity ratio is calculated by dividing total liabilities by total stockholders' equity (55,000/95,500 = 0.58). This is less than the debt covenant requirement of 0.60.

Choice "a" is incorrect. 0.37 is total liabilities divided by the sum of liabilities and stockholders' equity [55,000 / (55,000 + 95,500)].

Choice "c" is incorrect. 0.63 is the total stockholders' equity divided by the sum of liabilities and stockholders' equity [95,500 / (55,000 + 95,500)].

Choice "d" is incorrect. 1.74 is the stockholders' equity divided by total liabilities ($95,500/55,000).

Class Question Explanations                                                                                              Financial

Financial 5, Module 4

## 1. MCQ-00458

Choice "d" is correct. To determine the market price of a bond, the present value of the principal is added to the present value of all interest payments, using the market interest rate.

Choice "a" is incorrect. The stated interest rate is used to calculate the amount of interest payment, but not the market price of the bond.

Choice "b" is incorrect. The stated interest rate is used to calculate the amount of interest payment, but not the market price of the bond.

Choice "c" is incorrect. The market interest rate is used in calculating the price of the bond; however, all the interest payments must also be taken into consideration.

## 2. MCQ-00470

Choice "b" is correct.

| Income Statement | Balance Sheet | | $469,500 |
|---|---|---|---|
| $469,500 | $500,000 | | |
| × 10% | × 9% | | |
| $ 46,950 − | $ 45,000 = $1,950 × ½ yr = | | 975 |
| | | | $470,475 |

Choice "a" is incorrect. Amortization of the bond discount should be recorded.

Choice "c" is incorrect. The effective interest method should be used.

Choice "d" is incorrect. The reported valuation of the bond payable is the face value less any unamortized bond discount.

Financial 5, Module 5

## 1. MCQ-00463

Choice "d" is correct. The cash collected equals:

| Face: $600 × $1,000 | | $600,000 | |
|---|---|---|---|
| Issue at: | | × 99% | |
| Bond issue proceeds | | | $594,000 |
| Face | $600,000 | | |
| Coupon | × 10% | | |
| Annual interest | 60,000 | | |
| % Year | × 3/12 | | |
| Accrued interest | | | $ 15,000 |
| Total cash proceeds | | | $609,000 |

Choice "a" is incorrect. Accrued interest should be added rather than subtracted.

Choice "b" is incorrect. Accrued interest collected should be included.

Choice "c" is incorrect. The face value does not equal the issuance price. Accrued interest collected should be included.

## 2. MCQ-00477

Choice "d" is correct. Accrued interest payable on September 30, Year 2 is the interest owed since the June 30, Year 2 payment.

$300,000 × 12% × 3/12 = $9,000

Choice "a" is incorrect. The accrued interest payable on September 30 is only the amount since the June 30 payment. The $27,000 is the interest expense from January 1 through September 30.

Choice "b" is incorrect. The accrued interest payable on September 30 is only the amount since the June 30 payment. The $24,000 is the interest expense from date of issue (January 31) to September 30.

Choice "c" is incorrect. The $18,000 is the interest paid to date in Year 2, but the question is interest payable at September 30.

### Financial 5, Module 6

## 1. MCQ-00476

Choice "b" is correct. The settlement price is greater than the face value of the debt and the face value is greater than the book value. Therefore, the settlement price is greater than the book value and a loss would be recognized on the transaction.

Choice "a" is incorrect. The transaction results in a loss, not a gain.

Choices "c" and "d" are incorrect. The gain or loss on bond retirements is reported in income from continuing operations, not in other comprehensive income.

## 2. MCQ-00471

Choice "a" is correct. A gain of $53,000 is recognized because the $665,000 book value of the debt ($600,000 face value plus $65,000 unamortized premium) is settled for $612,000 ($600,000 at 102). There is no accrued interest because the redemption takes place on an interest date. The proceeds from the new bond issuance are not relevant. Note that the gain is reported as part of continuing operations because the transaction is a typical risk-management strategy of the company.

Choice "b" is incorrect. The retirement price does not equal the book value, so a gain or loss must be recognized.

Choice "c" is incorrect. Gain or loss is not determined solely by the amount of unamortized premium.

Choice "d" is incorrect. The combination of the unamortized premium plus the excess of the retirement price over the bond face value is not relevant.

# FINANCIAL 6

Financial 6, Module 1

## 1. MCQ-08768

Choice "d" is correct. Both Watts (the lessee) and Jennings (the lessor) will account for the lease as an operating lease. None of the "OWNES" criteria are met: there is no ownership transfer; there is no written option to purchase; the net present value is far below the threshold needed to be considered equal to the fair value of the asset; the lease term is only 60 percent of the economic life of the asset; and the equipment is not specialized. As such, Watts must treat the lease as an operating lease. Jennings must also treat the lease as operating because the "sales-type" classification can only be used when at least one of the OWNES criteria are met. Note that although a lessor may also use a "direct financing" classification when the OWNES criteria are not met, in this case that would not be an option because of the relatively low net present value (and absence of guaranteed residual value) compared with the asset's fair value.

## 2. MCQ-08769

Choice "b" is correct. The difference between the sale price ($208,000) and the fair value ($202,000) is recorded as a financing liability on the books of the seller/lessee.

Anton's journal entry will be as follows:

| DR/CR | Account | Debit | Credit |
|---|---|---|---|
| DR | Cash | 208,000 | |
| DR | A/D—Equipment | 130,000 | |
| CR | Equipment | | $325,000 |
| CR | Financing liability | | 6,000 |
| CR | Gain on equipment sale | | 7,000 |

Note that the A/D (accumulated depreciation) on the equipment is derived by comparing the original purchase price of $325,000 with the carrying value of $195,000.

Choice "a" is incorrect. Because there is a difference between the sale price and fair value, a financing liability must be recorded.

Choice "c" is incorrect. $7,000 represents the gain on the equipment sale, which is equal to the fair value of $202,000 versus the carrying value of $195,000.

Choice "d" is incorrect. The difference of $13,000 between the sale price and the carrying value is recorded in two components: the financing liability of $6,000 and the gain on the equipment sale of $7,000.

Financial                                                                                                    Class Question Explanations

Financial 6, Module 2

## 1. MCQ-08770

Choice "c" is correct. As shown in the amortization table below, the carrying value of the ROU asset at the end of Year 2 will be approximately $14,295.

| Date | Lease Expense (Straight-line) | Interest (4.50% on Liability) | Amortization of ROU Asset | Carrying Value of ROU Asset |
|---|---|---|---|---|
|  |  |  |  | $18,655 |
| 12/31/Year 2 | $5,200 | $839 | $4,361 | 14,294 |
| 12/31/Year 3 | 5,200 | 643 | 4,557 | 9,738 |
| 12/31/Year 4 | 5,200 | 438 | 4,762 | 4,976 |
| 12/31/Year 5 | 5,200 | 224 | 4,976 | (0) |

Choice "a" is incorrect. This is the carrying value of the asset at the end of Year 3.

Choice "b" is incorrect. This answer choice incorrectly treats the entire lease payment as amortization without accounting for the interest component of the payment.

Choice "d" is incorrect. At the inception of the lease (beginning of Year 2), the carrying value of the asset is equal to $18,655. ($5,200 x 3.5875 = $18,655)

## 2. MCQ-08771

Choice "b" is correct. Because this lease contains a written purchase option that the lessee is reasonably certain to exercise, it will qualify as a finance lease (it meets the "W" criteria in "OWNES"). Variable lease payments not included in the lease liability are treated as cash outflows from operations and will therefore have a negative impact on bottom-line cash flow from operations.

Choice "a" is incorrect. The interest portion of the lease payment will serve to reduce cash flow from operations, as it is a "CFO" outflow.

Choice "c" is incorrect. The portion of the lease payment that represents principal is a cash flow from financing outflow.

Choice "d" is incorrect. Short-term lease payments not included in the lease liability are treated as cash outflows from operations and will therefore have a negative impact on bottom-line cash flow from operations.

Class Question Explanations                                                                                          Financial

Financial 6, Module 3

## 1. MCQ-00943

Choice "c" is correct. Both I and II. A derivative may be designated and qualify as a fair value hedge if a set of criteria relating to the derivative and the hedged item are met. The most significant criteria are:

1. There is formal documentation of the hedging relationship between the derivative and the hedged item.
2. The hedge must be expected to be highly effective in offsetting changes in the fair value of the hedged item and the effectiveness is assessed at least every three months.
3. The hedged item is specifically identified.
4. The hedged item presents exposure to changes in fair value that could affect income.

## 2. MCQ-00929

Choice "d" is correct. This hedge is classified as a fair value hedge because it is being used to hedge the value of the inventory. Therefore, the gain on the fair value hedge must be recognized in earnings, along with the loss on the inventory, for a net decrease in net income of $500:

   Gain on derivative = $74,500
   Loss on inventory = $175,000 FV − $250,000 BV = $(75,000)
   Net loss on fair value hedge = $(75,000) loss + $74,500 gain = $(500) loss

Choice "a" is incorrect. This hedge is classified as a fair value hedge because it is used to hedge the value of the inventory. The gain on the fair value hedge must be recognized in earnings, along with the loss on the inventory. Other comprehensive income includes gains and losses on the effective portion of hedges classified as cash flow hedges.

Choice "b" is incorrect. The net loss on the hedge will be reported in earnings, not in other comprehensive income, because this hedge is a fair value hedge, not a cash flow hedge.

Choice "c" is incorrect. The gain on the fair value hedge will be reported in earnings, offsetting the loss on the inventory. Therefore, net income will decrease by $500.

Financial 6, Module 4

## 1. MCQ-01272

Choice "b" is correct, $7,600 gain from remeasurement.

**Rule:** "Translation adjustments" are not included in determining net income for the period but are disclosed and accumulated as a component of other comprehensive income in consolidated equity until disposed of.

However, gains or losses from remeasuring the foreign subsidiary's financial statements from the local currency to the functional currency should be included in "income from continuing operations" of the parent company.

**Note:** Assume that the question had asked the following instead:

"What amount should Park report as a foreign exchange gain in its statement of income and comprehensive income (or statement of comprehensive income, by itself)?"

In that case, the answer would have been $15,700.

## 2. MCQ-01274

Choice "d" is correct. On September 22, the liability denominated in dollars equals $5,500 (10,000 units × $0.55 spot rate). On December 31, the liability denominated in dollars equals $7,000 (10,000 units × $0.70 spot rate). At year-end, the foreign currency transaction loss equals $1,500 ($7,000−$5,500).

Choice "a" is incorrect. Because the spot rate at year-end is different from the spot rate at September 22, a foreign currency transaction gain or loss must be recognized.

Choice "b" is incorrect. Only the loss as of December 31 should be recognized.

Choice "c" is incorrect. Only the loss as of December 31 should be recognized.

### Financial 6, Module 5

## 1. MCQ-00782

Choice "b" is correct. The current portion of the income tax expense equals $29,400, income tax payable on taxable income [$140,000 × 21%].

Choice "a" is incorrect. The tax rate is applied to taxable income, not to pretax financial income less the permanent difference and tax depreciation in excess of accounting depreciation.

Choice "c" is incorrect. The tax rate is applied to taxable income, not to pretax financial income less the permanent difference.

Choice "d" is incorrect. The tax rate is applied to taxable income, not to pretax financial income.

|  | Tax |  |  |  | F/S |
|---|---|---|---|---|---|
| Income | $160,000 |  | Income |  | $160,000 |
| Muni | (5,000) | ← Permanent → |  |  | – |
| Est. Loss | 10,000 | ← (10,000) → |  |  | – |
| Excess Depr. | (25,000) | ← $25,000 → |  |  | – |
| Taxable income | $140,000 | $15,000 |  |  | $160,000 |
|  | × 21% | × 21% |  |  |  |
|  | $ 29,400 | + $ 3,150 | = |  | $ 32,550 |

## 2. MCQ-00783

Choice "c" is correct. The deferred income tax liability equals the 21 percent tax rate times $15,000 future taxable amount computed as the net of the future taxable amounts [$25,000 depreciation] and the future deductible amounts [$10,000].

|  | Tax |  |  |  | F/S |
|---|---|---|---|---|---|
| Income | $160,000 |  | Income |  | $160,000 |
| Muni | (5,000) | ← Permanent → |  |  | – |
| Est. Loss | 10,000 | ← (10,000) → |  |  | – |
| Excess Depr. | (25,000) | ← $25,000 → |  |  | – |
|  | $140,000 | $15,000 |  |  | $160,000 |
|  | × 21% | × 21% |  |  |  |
|  | $ 29,400 | + $ 3,150 | = |  | $ 32,550 |

Financial 6, Module 6

### 1. MCQ-12688

Choice "d" is correct, $252,000 total income tax expense for 2019.

*2020*

| DR | Deferred tax asset ($700,000 × 21%) | 147,000 | |
|---|---|---|---|
| CR | Income tax benefit | | $147,000 |

*2021*

```
                    Beg:    700,000
         Tax                                    I/S
       $1,200,000                            $1,200,000
NOL      700,000  ←  (700,000)  →                —
       $ 500,000           -0-               $1,200,000
    ×       21%       ×       21%
                    End       -0-
                    Beg   $147,000
       $ 105,000    +    $147,000    =    $ 252,000
```

| DR | Income tax expense | $252,000 | |
|---|---|---|---|
| CR | Income tax payable | | $105,000 |
| CR | Deferred tax asset | | 147,000 |

**Note:** NOLs utilized in the five-year carryback period or in 2018, 2019, or 2020 tax years are not subject to a taxable income limitation. NOLs carried forward to taxable years beginning in 2021 or later are limited to 80 percent of taxable income before the NOL deduction. In this example, 80 percent of $1,200,000 equals $960,000. The $700,000 NOL does not exceed the 80 percent limitation for 2021.

### 2. MCQ-00785

Choice "d" is correct, as a deferred tax liability of $52,500, because tax depreciation exceeds book depreciation. The 21 percent tax rate for the period(s) the difference is expected to reverse should be used.

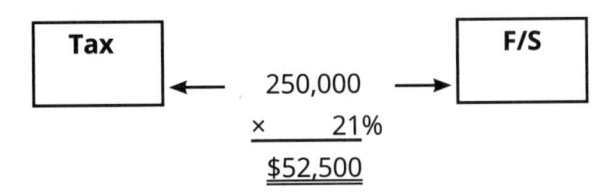

```
  Tax                    F/S
         ←  250,000  →
            ×    21%
            $52,500
```

# FINANCIAL 7

## Financial 7, Module 1

### 1. MCQ-00690

Choice "b" is correct.

| | | |
|---|---|---|
| B | Beginning plan assets | $ 350,000 |
| A | + Contributions | 110,000 |
|   | + Actual return | 150,000 Squeeze |
| S | − Benefits paid | (85,000) |
| E | Ending plan assets | $ 525,000 |

The actual return must equal $150,000.

Choice "a" is incorrect. Year-end plan assets equal beginning plan assets plus contributions less distributions plus actual return on plan assets.

Choice "c" is incorrect. Year-end plan assets equal beginning plan assets plus contributions less distributions plus actual return on plan assets.

Choice "d" is incorrect. Year-end plan assets equal beginning plan assets plus contributions less distributions plus actual return on plan assets.

### 2. MCQ-05054

Choice "b" is correct. Under U.S. GAAP, unrecognized gains and losses are recognized in net periodic pension cost using the following formula:

$$\frac{\text{Unrecognized gain or loss}}{\text{(10\% of the greater of the PBO or FMV of plan assets at the beginning of the year)}}$$

$$\frac{\text{Excess}}{\div \text{Average remaining service life}}$$

Minimum recognized amount to be reported

| | | |
|---|---|---|
| Unrecognized gain | | $60,000 |
| Greater of PBO or FMV of plan assets | | |
| As of the beginning of the year | $560,000 | |
| 10 percent | × 10% | |
| 10 percent of PBO | | 56,000 |
| Excess | | 4,000 |
| Average remaining service life | | ÷ 8 years |
| Minimum recognized amount | | $ $500 |

Note that the gain due to the difference between the expected and actual return on plan assets will be amortized starting in the next year.

Choices "a", "c", and "d" are incorrect. These wrong answers are derived by using either the incorrect threshold amount (FMV of assets instead of PBO) or using the amount at the end of the year, rather than the beginning.

## Financial 7, Module 2

**1. MCQ-05398**

Choice "c" is correct. The funded status of the pension plan at December 31, Year 1, is computed as follows:

Fair value of plan assets − PBO = $1,400,000 − 1,500,000 = $(100,000)

Because the PBO exceeds the fair value of the pension plan assets, this is an underfunded pension plan.

Choice "a" is incorrect. This answer incorrectly uses the Year 2 PBO and fair value of plan assets to compute the Year 1 funded status.

Choice "b" is incorrect. On December 31, Year 2, the plan is $70,000 underfunded.

Choice "d" is incorrect. Big Book's pension plan is underfunded, not overfunded, by $100,000 at December 31, Year 1.

**2. MCQ-08599**

Choice "a" is correct. The initial journal entry for a prior service cost will include a debit to other comprehensive income of $500,000 and a corresponding credit to the pension plan asset/liability. The amortization of the prior service costs will be $50,000 for Year 1, which is the beginning balance of $500,000 divided by the average remaining service life of 10 years. The amortization entry will debit net periodic pension cost and credit other comprehensive income for $50,000. The net effect to other comprehensive income will be a debit of $450,000.

Choice "b" is incorrect. This choice incorrectly ignores the amortization of $50,000.

Choice "c" is incorrect. This choice incorrectly counts the initial $500,000 as a credit (rather than debit) to other comprehensive income.

Choice "d" is incorrect. This choice incorrectly credits the initial $500,000 and debits the amortization of $50,000.

## Financial 7, Module 3

**1. MCQ-00701**

Choice "a" is correct. Postretirement health benefits are accrued in a manner similar to pension benefits. The expected postretirement health benefits must be fully accrued by the date the employee is fully eligible for the benefits. The accrual will begin when the employee is hired through the eligibility (vesting) date.

## Financial 7, Module 4

### 1. MCQ-07235

Choice "b" is correct. The statement of changes in net assets available for benefits shows the appreciation in the fair value of investments, any other investment income, investment expenses, contributions, benefits paid, and administrative expenses to arrive at the net increase or decrease in net assets available for benefits during the period. The change in actuarial present value of accumulated plan benefits is shown on the statement of changes in accumulated plan benefits.

Choice "a" is incorrect. The net change in fair value is reported on the statement of changes in net assets available for benefits.

Choice "c" is incorrect. Contributions to the plan, whether from the employer or participants, are reported on the statement of changes in net assets available for benefits.

Choice "d" is incorrect. Benefits paid are reported on the statement of changes in net assets available for benefits.

## Financial 7, Module 5

### 1. MCQ-01058

Choice "a" is correct. $1,200,000 appropriated retained earnings at Dec. 31, Year 2 (for the construction of a new plant only). When the purpose of the appropriation has been achieved, it should be restored to unappropriated retained earnings.

Choices "b" and "c" are incorrect. When the new ($1,500,000) office building was completed in Year 2, $1,750,000 was restored to unappropriated retained earnings.

Choice "d" is incorrect. "Cash restricted for the retirement of bonds" (an asset account called "sinking fund cash") typically reduces regular cash and does not affect retained earnings. (There may also be an appropriation, but this would have to be specifically mentioned in the question.)

## Financial 7, Module 6

### 1. MCQ-00974

Choice "a" is correct. Look at each item given and decide how it affects retained earnings: income since incorporation equals unadjusted ending retained earnings (RE), that is, current year income is included; cash dividends is a direct deduction from RE on the date of declaration; property dividends are deducted from RE at market value on the date of declaration; the excess proceeds from the sale of treasury stock is considered additional paid-in capital. Thus: Ending retained earnings = Unadjusted retained earnings − Cash dividends − Property dividends = $420,000 − $130,000 − $30,000 = $260,000.

Choice "b" is incorrect. This amount does not include the effect of the property dividends. Property dividends are deducted from RE at market value on the date of declaration.

Choice "c" is incorrect. This amount incorrectly includes the proceeds from the sale of the treasury stock. The cost method of accounting for treasury stock affects retained earnings only if the shares are sold below cost and the difference exceeds any additional paid-in capital from treasury stock.

Choice "d" is incorrect. This amount omits property dividends and incorrectly includes the proceeds from the sale of the treasury stock. Property dividends are deducted from RE at market value on the date of declaration. Treasury stock sold in excess of cost does not affect retained earnings.

## 2. MCQ-05228

Choice "b" is correct. Using the cost method, the treasury stock transactions include the reissuance of the treasury shares at $10 per share ($4 per share to APIC × 500 shares = $2,000). The additional paid-in capital from the original issuance of the stock is not paid-in capital related to the treasury stock and is not included.

Choice "a" is incorrect. This is equal to 500 shares at $3 per share, which is the amount of additional paid-in capital generated on the original issuance of the stock. Additional paid-in capital from the original issuance of the stock is not included.

Choice "c" is incorrect. This is equal to 500 shares at $9 per share, which is the difference between the price at which the treasury shares were reissued ($10 reissuance price − $1 par value = $9 × 500 = $4,500).

Choice "d" is incorrect. This is equal to 10,000 shares originally issued at the additional paid-in capital amount that was generated in the original issuance ($3 issuance price − $1 per share = $2 x 10,000 = $20,000).

### Financial 7, Module 7

## 1. MCQ-01033

Choice "a" is correct. $20,000 increase in stockholders' equity.

Compensation cost should be charged to expense over the service period. In this problem, because the options are exercised in the same period as the grant date, the total compensation cost must be charged to expense in Year 1.

|  | DR | CR | Effect on Stockholders' Equity |
|---|---|---|---|
| **Jan. 2, Year 1 (when options granted)** |  |  |  |
| Compensation expense* | $30,000 |  | $(30,000) |
|    Paid-in capital-stock-options-outstanding |  | $30,000 | 30,000 |
| **Dec. 31, Year 1 (when options exercised)** |  |  |  |
| Cash ($20 × 1,000) | 20,000 |  |  |
| Paid-in capital-stock-options-outstanding | 30,000 |  | (30,000) |
|    Common stock at par ($10 × 1,000) |  | 10,000 | 10,000 |
|    Paid in capital in excess of par (squeeze) |  | 40,000 | 40,000 |
| Net effect on stockholders' equity |  |  | $20,000 |

*Note: A charge to expense lowers retained earnings.

Class Question Explanations                                                         Financial

# FINANCIAL 8

Financial 8, Module 1

## 1. MCQ-01200

Choice "d" is correct. A 6 percent stock dividend equals 6,000 shares with a total of 106,000 shares outstanding after the distribution of the dividend. Stock dividends and stock splits require restatement of the shares outstanding before the stock dividend or stock split. Thus, the stock dividend would be treated as if it had occurred at the beginning of the fiscal year.

Choice "a" is incorrect. This calculation ignores the fact that 6,000 shares were issued due to the stock dividend.

Choice "b" is incorrect. In this calculation, the stock dividend shares are weighted for the one month in which they were outstanding. However, stock dividends are treated as if they had occurred at the beginning of the fiscal year.

Choice "c" is incorrect. Stock dividends are treated as if they had occurred at the beginning of the fiscal year.

## 2. MCQ-01198

Choice "b" is correct. $2.45 earnings per share.

|  | Year 1 | Year 2 |
|---|---|---|
| Net income | ? | $ 500,000 |
| Less: cumulative preferred stock dividend "requirement" ($10 par × 25,000 shares × 4%) | (10,000) | (10,000) |
| Income available to common shares |  | 490,000 |
| Divide by average common shares O/S |  | ÷ 200,000 |
| Basic earnings per common share |  | $ 2.45 |

**Note:** Because the preferred stock dividends are cumulative, when they are declared or paid is not relevant.

Choice "a" is incorrect. This answer is calculated by incorrectly subtracting the $16,000 preferred dividend paid in Year 2. When preferred stock is cumulative, the dividend accumulated during the period must be subtracted to calculate basic earnings per share.

Choice "c" is incorrect. This amount is calculated by incorrectly subtracting preferred dividends of $4,000. This amount is not supported by the question facts.

Choice "d" is incorrect. This amount is equal to net income divided by the average common shares outstanding. When calculating basic earnings per share, preferred dividends accumulated during the period on cumulative preferred stock or preferred dividends declared during the period on noncumulative preferred stock must be subtracted from net income to calculate the income available to common shareholders, which is then divided by the average common shares outstanding.

Financial                                                                                               Class Question Explanations

### 3. MCQ-01199

Choice "c" is correct. $14.25 diluted earnings per share.

|  | Basic EPS | Diluted EPS |
|---|---|---|
| EPS before the effect of any convertibles | $15.00 | $15.00 |
| Possible conversion of bonds | – | (0.75) |
| Diluted earnings per share | $15.00 | $14.25 |

**Note:** The possible exercise of common stock options would increase EPS by $0.10, so they are not used because of the antidilution rule. Each potentially dilutive security is considered separately for its dilutive effect.

### 4. MCQ-05675

Choice "d" is correct. Ian's diluted earnings per share will be equal to its basic earnings per share because the stock options are out of the money. Out of the money stock options are antidilutive because the exercise price exceeds the market price of the stock. Ian's basic and diluted earnings per share are calculated as follows:

$$\text{Basic (and diluted) EPS} = \frac{\text{Income available to common shareholders}}{\text{Weighted average number of common shares}}$$

$$\text{Basic (and diluted) EPS} = \frac{\$125,000}{15,750^*} = \$7.94$$

*The weighted average number of common shares outstanding is:

| Total Shares | Period Outstanding | Weighted Average |
|---|---|---|
| 15,000 | 3/12 | 3,750 |
| 12,500 | 2/12 | 2,083 |
| 17,000 | 7/12 | 9,917 |
|  |  | Total 15,750 |

Choices "a", "b", and "c" are incorrect, per the above.

## Financial 8, Module 2

### 1. MCQ-05229

Choice "c" is correct. New England's cash balance at the end of the year includes the cash balance at the beginning of the year, the net cash provided by operating activities, the net cash used by investing activities, and the net cash provided by financing activities ($27,000 + $351,000 − $420,000 + $250,000 = $208,000). The sale of the land was included in the cash from the investing activities and does not have to be considered separately. When working this type of question, be sure to distinguish between the net cash used and the net cash provided.

Choice "a" is incorrect. The cash balance at the end of the year certainly includes more than just the cash balance at the beginning of the year.

Choice "b" is incorrect. The cash balance at the end of the year certainly includes more than just the proceeds from the land.

Choice "d" is incorrect. The proceeds from the sale of the land are already included in the net cash from investing activities. It does not have to be considered separately and does not have to be added.

### 2. MCQ-05695

Choice "a" is correct. When the indirect method is used, a supplemental disclosure of cash paid for interest and income taxes is required. Tam will report total cash paid for interest and income taxes of $545,000 ($325,000 income taxes paid + $220,000 net interest payments).

Choice "b" is incorrect. Under the indirect method, supplemental disclosures will include the cash paid for interest and income taxes, but will not include the dividends paid. Supplemental disclosure is not required for dividend payments because dividends paid is a line-item disclosure in the financing section.

Choice "c" is incorrect. Under the indirect method, a supplemental disclosure of cash paid for interest and income taxes is required. However, a supplemental disclosure of capital expenditures and capital lease payments is not required because capital expenditures is a line-item disclosure in the investing section and the principal portion of capital lease payments is a line-item disclosure in the financing section.

Choice "d" is incorrect. When the indirect method is used, a supplemental disclosure of cash paid for interest and income taxes is required. Tam will report total cash paid for interest and income taxes of $545,000 ($325,000 income taxes paid + $220,000 net interest payments). However, supplemental disclosure of dividends paid, capital expenditures, and capital lease payments is not required.

## Financial 8, Module 3

### 1. MCQ-01222

Choice "b" is correct. Not-for-profit corporations are required to produce the following financial statements:

- Statement of financial position
- Statement of activities
- Statement of cash flows

Not-for-profit corporations are also required to disclose, display, or separately report the relationship between functional classifications and natural classifications of expenses.

Choice "a" is incorrect. The statement of changes in financial position is no longer used by not-for-profit corporations.

Choice "c" is incorrect. Not-for-profits do not account for fund balances in financial statements issued for external use and therefore do not produce a statement of changes in fund balance.

Choice "d" is incorrect. Not-for-profits do not account for fund balances in financial statements issued for external use and therefore do not produce a statement of revenues, expenses and changes in fund balance.

### 2. MCQ-01220

Choice "a" is correct. Assets received by a not-for-profit organization that do not have donor-imposed restrictions increase net assets without donor restrictions. Long-lived assets would be recognized as an increase to net assets without donor restrictions using the placed-in-service approach.

Choice "b" is incorrect. Classification of assets as donor-restricted support that increases net assets with donor restrictions would be used if assets were restricted in perpetuity or if there are restrictions that can be satisfied as to purpose, timing, or asset acquisition requirements. Absent these requirements or an accounting policy implying a time restriction, the contribution of assets is classified as an increase to net assets without donor restrictions.

Choice "c" is incorrect. Classification of net assets as board-designated would come in response to a specific action by the governing board. The fact pattern is silent as to any specific actions by Stanton College.

Choice "d" is incorrect. Classification of a contribution as an increase to board-designated net assets *or* net assets with donor restrictions is usually impossible and, regardless, is inappropriate in this case.

## 3. MCQ-01229

Choice "c" is correct. Restricted donations are released from restriction when conditions or eligibility requirements have been satisfied. The Baker Fund has satisfied the restriction on $95,000 by spending the money on program expenses.

Choice "a" is incorrect. The Baker Fund met donor stipulations during the year. The fund's actions released the restrictions.

Choice "b" is incorrect. The donor did not stipulate in the bequest restrictions that the program income be used to reduce the eligible expenses.

Choice "d" is incorrect. The entire amount of the donation was not released from restriction, only the amount used to satisfy the donor's stipulations.

## 4. MCQ-01257

Choice "a" is correct. Net assets without donor restrictions would increase by the amount of the reclassification of net assets with donor restrictions whose restrictions have been satisfied and then reduced by scholarship expense. The net effect of the July 26 transaction is a simultaneous increase and decrease in net assets without donor restrictions.

The tuition fees from students should be recognized as gross revenue regardless of whether they are funded by scholarships (an increase in net assets without donor restrictions), whereas scholarships to the students are considered expenses (a reduction in net assets without donor restrictions). The exchange transaction of providing credit hours for tuition is usually recognized as gross revenue, with scholarships being recognized as expenses.

The journal entries to record the satisfaction of donor restrictions and issuance of scholarships would include:

| | | | |
|---|---|---|---|
| DR | Satisfaction of program restrictions, donor-restricted | $100,000 | |
| CR | Satisfaction of program restrictions, without donor restrictions | | $100,000 |

*To record satisfaction of donor-restricted contributions used for scholarships.*

| | | | |
|---|---|---|---|
| DR | Scholarship expense | $100,000 | |
| CR | Tuition revenues | | $100,000 |

*To record award of scholarships.*

Choice "b" is incorrect. Although net assets without donor restrictions decrease in response to the recognition of scholarship expense, they are also increased by the satisfaction of restrictions.

Choice "c" is incorrect. The satisfaction of donor restrictions is displayed on the financial statements in addition to being disclosed.

Choice "d" is incorrect. Satisfaction of donor restrictions is fully reported.

## 5. MCQ-01306

Choice "c" is correct. Fundraising expenses are incurred to induce contributions. Of the expenses listed, only the unsolicited merchandise sent to encourage contributions qualifies as fundraising. The printing of the annual report and the cost of an audit would be reported under supporting services—management and general expenses.

### Financial 8, Module 4

## 1. MCQ-01255

Choice "c" is correct. The cash contributions without donor restrictions totaling $500,000 are reported as increases in operating activities in the statement of cash flows. The $200,000 cash contributions with donor restrictions are reported as increases in financing activities because the restriction is the acquisition of property, not general operations.

Choices "a", "b", and "d" are incorrect, per above.

### Financial 8, Module 5

## 1. MCQ-01225

Choice "d" is correct. Contributions available for use at the board's discretion are classified as revenues and gains without donor restrictions. No specific requirement is associated with that revenue. Contributed services are similarly considered to be revenues and gains without restrictions. Services are rendered and consumed simultaneously as expenses. Expenses are classified as reductions of net assets without donor restrictions. To be restricted, the donation must be restricted by the donors, creditors, grantors, or laws or regulations. A promise to contribute carries an implied time restriction until conditions (collection) or eligibility requirements (date, etc.) have been satisfied. Classification of revenues is computed as follows:

|  | *Revenues and Gains Without Donor Restrictions* | *Revenues and Gains With Donor Restrictions* |
|---|---|---|
| Cash contribution | $875,000 | $ – |
| Promise to contribute | – | 500,000 |
| Donated services | 100,000 | – |
|  | **$975,000** | **$500,000** |

## 2. MCQ-01215

Choice "c" is correct. Pica would recognize contribution revenue based on the net realizable value of its pledges receivable.

| | |
|---|---|
| Total pledge receivable | $100,000 |
| Net realizable value | × 90% |
| Contribution revenue | $ 90,000 |
| Allowance for doubtful accounts | $ 10,000 |

**Rule:** Recording promises to give are journalized as follows:

| | | | |
|---|---|---|---|
| DR | Pledge receivable | $100,000 | |
| CR | Allowance for doubtful accounts | | $10,000 |
| CR | Contribution revenue | | 90,000 |

Note that the examiners have asked for total revenue without respect to classification. The collection of a portion of the pledge prior to year-end is irrelevant.

Choice "a" is incorrect. Pica would recognize contributions in the amount of unconditional pledges whose collection is deemed to be probable along with actual receipts. Pica would not limit its recognition of contribution revenue to only those amounts received.

Choice "b" is incorrect. Pica would recognize contributions in the amount of unconditional pledges whose collection is deemed to be probable and in addition to amounts actually received. Pica would not limit its recognition of contribution revenue to only the uncollected amounts whose receipt is deemed to be probable.

Choice "d" is incorrect. Pica would not recognize the full amount of pledges as contribution revenue if some amounts are deemed to be uncollectible.

## 3. MCQ-01249

Choice "b" is correct. Contributions to a not-for-profit include transactions which are unconditional (not requiring a future event to occur), nonreciprocal, voluntary, and not of an ownership investment. The FMV of the theater tickets (the exchange part of the transaction) would not be considered in determining the amount of the contribution revenue. The $50 above the FMV of the tickets is contribution revenue.

Choice "a" is incorrect. Contributions to a not-for-profit include transactions which are unconditional (not requiring a future event to occur), nonreciprocal, voluntary, and not of an ownership investment. Part of the $150 from the donor can be considered contribution revenue meeting these criteria.

Choice "c" is incorrect. Contributions to a not-for-profit include transactions that are unconditional (not requiring a future event to occur), nonreciprocal, voluntary, and not of an ownership investment. The $100 from the donor is an exchange transaction, as the donor received theater tickets with an FMV of $100.

Choice "d" is incorrect. Contributions to a not-for-profit include transactions which are unconditional (not requiring a future event to occur), nonreciprocal, voluntary, and not of an ownership investment. The $150 from the donor includes both an exchange transaction and contribution revenue.

Financial                                                                                           Class Question Explanations

## 4. MCQ-04695

Choice "a" is correct. Hospital Inc. would report net patient revenue in an amount equal to its gross patient service revenue net of both charity care and the difference between established billing rates and fees negotiated with third-party payors (sometimes called contractual adjustments). Net patient revenue for Hospital Inc. for the current year ended December 31 is computed as follows:

| | |
|---|---:|
| Gross patient revenues including charity care of $25,000 | $775,000 |
| Less: charity care | (25,000) |
| Less: contractual adjustments | (70,000) |
| Net patient service revenue | $680,000 |

Choice "b" is incorrect. The amount represented by this selection ($690,000) is the amount properly recognized as net patient service revenue ($680,000) plus charity care of $25,000 and net of bad debt expense of $15,000 given in the fact pattern. Charity care is improperly included and should not be recognized and bad debt expense is recognized as an expense, not a contra-revenue.

Choice "c" is incorrect. The amount represented by this selection ($705,000) is the amount properly recognized as net patient service revenue ($680,000) plus charity care of $25,000. Charity care is improperly included and should not be recognized.

Choice "d" is incorrect. The amount represented by this selection ($735,000) is the amount properly recognized as net patient service revenue ($680,000) plus contractual adjustments of $70,000 and net of bad debt expense of $15,000 given in the fact pattern. Contractual adjustments are improperly included and should not be recognized and bad debt expense is recognized as an expense, not a contra-revenue.

## 5. MCQ-01287

Choice "d" is correct. Donations of medicines are included as other operating revenue at the fair value of the medicine, because the medicine constitutes part of the ongoing major operation of the hospital.

Choice "a" is incorrect. Donated goods are recorded on the books and records of a not-for-profit organization. A memorandum entry is not adequate.

Choice "b" is incorrect. Pharmaceuticals represent part of the ongoing and central operations of the hospital. Donated items would represent other operating revenue and, ultimately, operating expenses.

Choice "c" is incorrect. Donated pharmaceuticals represent operating revenue, not a reduction in expenses. Amounts would be presented as gross income, not net.

Financial 8, Module 6

## 1. MCQ-05151

Choice "c" is correct. Beneficiaries (e.g., Boulder University) with a financial interest in recipient organizations (e.g., Marble Foundation) recognize the change in their interest of the recipient organization on their statement of activities. The interest in the net assets of the recipient is adjusted for the beneficiary's share of the change with the following entry:

| DR | Interest in net assets | $XXX | |
|---|---|---|---|
| CR | Interest in Marble Foundation net assets (statement of activities) | | $XXX |

Choice "a" is incorrect. Beneficiaries with a financial interest in recipient organizations do not limit their reporting of recipient equity to disclosures only.

Choice "b" is incorrect. Beneficiaries with a financial interest in recipient organizations report changes in recipient interest through their statements of activities, not directly within the net asset classification on the balance sheet.

Choice "d" is incorrect. "Conditional support" is a contradiction in terms and represents a distracter.

## 2. MCQ-07254

Choice "a" is correct. Ragg would report the Treasury bills at their fair value of $15,000 on the statement of financial position. All debt securities that have readily determinable fair values are measured at fair value in the statement of financial position.

Donated items are valued at fair value upon receipt. Securities are marked to market and valued at fair value at the balance sheet date. The question is silent as to the receipt date and the value at year-end, so we are left to assume that the value on the statement of financial position is the last fair value provided, $15,000.

Choice "b" is incorrect. The fair value plus brokerage costs is not the valuation used by the recipient. The recipient would purely use the fair value.

Choice "c" is incorrect. The donor's basis is not the valuation used by the recipient. The recipient would use the fair value.

Choice "d" is incorrect. The donor's basis plus brokerage costs is not the valuation used by the recipient. The recipient would use the fair value.

## 3. MCQ-05444

Choice "d" is correct. RST's net assets increased $115,000 as a result of the contribution of equity securities; the increase in market value and the dividends received is computed as follows:

| | |
|---|---:|
| Equity security received | $100,000 |
| Change in market value | 10,000 |
| Fair market value at year-end | 110,000 |
| Dividends received | 5,000 |
| Total | $115,000 |

All debt securities and those equity securities that have readily determinable fair values are measured at fair value in the statement of financial position. Gains and losses on investments are reported in the statement of activities. Investment income (e.g., dividends and interest) is reported in the period earned as an increase in net assets.

Choice "a" is incorrect. The proposed solution excludes changes in market value and dividends from increases in net assets in error. Both the change in market value and the dividend would be considered as an increase in net assets.

Choice "b" is incorrect. The proposed solution excludes changes in market value from increases in net assets in error. Both the change in market value and the dividend would be considered as an increase in net assets.

Choice "c" is incorrect. The proposed solution excludes dividends from increases in net assets in error. Both the change in market value and the dividend would be considered as an increase in net assets.

# FINANCIAL 9

### Financial 9, Module 1

## 1. MCQ-00888

Choice "a" is correct. Fund accounting enables service and mission-driven organizations to easily monitor compliance with spending purpose (legal restrictions), spending limits (budget and financial control), and other fiscal accountability objectives.

### Financial 9, Module 2

## 1. MCQ-00891

Choice "c" is correct. The internal service fund's fund financial statement would be prepared using an economic resources measurement focus and the accrual basis of accounting. The governmental funds, which include the general fund, permanent fund, and capital projects fund, would be prepared using the current financial resources measurement focus and the modified accrual basis of accounting.

Choices "a", "b", and "d" are incorrect, per the explanation above.

## 2. MCQ-00890

Choice "c" is correct. Governmental funds use the current financial resources measurement focus and modified accrual basis of accounting in their fund financial statements. Proprietary and fiduciary funds use the economic resources measurement focus and accrual basis of accounting.

Choices "a", "b", and "d" are incorrect, per the explanation above.

### Financial 9, Module 3

## 1. MCQ-00962

Choice "a" is correct. To record the budget, the journal entry would be:

| | | | |
|---|---|---|---|
| DR | Estimated revenues | $100,000 | |
| CR | Appropriations | | $80,000 |
| CR | Budgetary control | | 20,000 |

Choice "b" is incorrect. Appropriations is credited, not debited.

Choice "c" is incorrect. Estimated expenditures control is not an appropriate account title.

Choice "d" is incorrect. Estimated expenditures control is not an appropriate account title. In addition, the $80,000 would be credited, not debited.

Financial                                                                                                   Class Question Explanations

## 2. MCQ-00964

Choice "c" is correct. To record the budget, the journal entry would be:

| DR | Estimated revenues | $100,000 |          |
|----|--------------------|----------|----------|
| CR | Appropriations     |          | $80,000  |
| CR | Budgetary control  |          | 20,000   |

Choice "a" is incorrect. Estimated excess revenues control is not an appropriate account title.

Choice "b" is incorrect. Estimated excess revenues control is not an appropriate account title. In addition, the $20,000 is credited, not debited.

Choice "d" is incorrect. Budgetary control would be credited, not debited.

## 3. MCQ-00973

Choice "c" is correct. The net property tax revenues would include the $500,000 collections during the year plus the $100,000 expected collections within 60 days of year-end, for a total of $600,000. The remaining expected collections of $90,000 ($60,000 + $30,000) would be recorded as deferred inflows of resources and not revenues. The $10,000 estimated to be uncollectible would not be considered because revenues are accounted for net of the estimated uncollectible amount.

|                          |                     | Revenue Recognition Criteria: Imposed Non-exchange Transactions |                                  |                       |
|--------------------------|---------------------|--------------------------|------------------------|-----------------------|
| Collection Date          | Amount Collected    | Time Requirements*       | Modified Accrual Requirements** | Revenue Recognized    |
|                          |                     | _Year 1_                 | _Year 1_               | _Year 1_              |
| Throughout Year 1        | $500,000            | Yes                      | Yes                    | $500,000              |
| First 60 days of Year 2  | 100,000             | Yes                      | Yes                    | 100,000               |
| Remaining days of Year 2 | 60,000              | Yes                      | No                     | –                     |
| January Year 3           | 30,000              | Yes                      | No                     | –                     |
| Uncollectible            | (10,000)            | N/A                      | N/A                    | –                     |
| **Total recognized**     |                     |                          |                        | **$600,000**          |

*Yes, the requirements are met in the indicated year.
**No, the requirements are not met in the indicated year.

Choice "a" is incorrect. The revenues account would include neither the $90,000 expected collections beyond 60 days after year-end nor the $10,000 uncollectible amount.

Choice "b" is incorrect. The revenues account would not include the $90,000 expected collections beyond 60 days after year-end.

Choice "d" is incorrect. The revenues account would include the $100,000 expected collections shortly after year-end (within 60 days).

## 4. MCQ-04673

Choice "d" is correct. Governmental funds use the current financial resources measurement focus. As a result, the governmental fund statement of revenues, expenditures and changes in fund balance will emphasize the financial flow of resources and recognize all of the disbursements described for Dayne County as an expenditure:

| | |
|---|---:|
| Current: expenditures (payments to vendors) | $500,000 |
| Capital outlay: computer purchase expenditure | 300,000 |
| Debt service: principal payment on long term debt | 100,000 |
| Total reported expenditures | $900,000 |

Choice "a" is incorrect. The total expenditures reported by Dayne County would not be limited to the capital outlay expenditure for computer equipment of $300,000.

Choice "b" is incorrect. The total expenditures reported by Dayne County would not be limited to the vendor payments of $500,000.

Choice "c" is incorrect. The total expenditures reported by Dayne County would not be limited to the total of $800,000 represented by the vendor payments of $500,000 and the capital outlay expenditure for computer equipment of $300,000.

## 5. MCQ-00997

Choice "d" is correct. The capital projects fund is a governmental fund. The measurement focus of governmental funds is the flow of financial resources. Because depreciation expense does not reflect the use of financial resources, it is not recorded in the capital projects fund.

Choice "a" is incorrect. An enterprise fund is a proprietary fund that uses full accrual accounting and has capital maintenance as its measurement focus. Such funds record depreciation expense.

Choice "b" is incorrect. An internal service fund is a proprietary fund that uses full accrual accounting and has capital maintenance as its measurement focus. Such funds record depreciation expense.

Choice "c" is incorrect. A private purpose trust fund is a fiduciary fund that uses full accrual accounting and has capital maintenance as its measurement focus. Such funds record depreciation expense.

### Financial 9, Module 4

## 1. MCQ-00940

Choice "d" is correct. A purchase order is a binding document and thus is recorded when issued. The journal entry made for internal accounting when a purchase order is issued is:

| | | | |
|---|---|---:|---:|
| DR | Encumbrances | $XXX | |
| CR | Budgetary control | | $XXX |

Choice "a" is incorrect. Appropriations control is credited when the budget is set up, not when a purchase order is issued.

Choice "b" is incorrect. Vouchers payable is credited when goods are received.

Choice "c" is incorrect. Encumbrance control is credited when goods are received and budgetary control is debited.

Financial                                                                 Class Question Explanations

## 2. MCQ-00969

Choice "d" is correct. After the supplies and invoice are received, Elm should debit the internal account for budgetary control for the same $5,000 estimated amount that the account was credited when the purchase order was issued. The journal entries would be:

*When the purchase order was issued:*

| DR | Encumbrances (estimated) | $5,000 | |
|---|---|---|---|
| CR | Budgetary control | | $5,000 |

*When the supplies and invoice are received:*

| DR | Budgetary control | $5,000 | |
|---|---|---|---|
| CR | Encumbrances | | $5,000 |
| DR | Expenditures (actual) | 4,950 | |
| CR | Vouchers payable | | 4,950 |

Choices "a" and "b" are incorrect. Budgetary control is debited for the same estimated amount that it was originally credited for when the purchase order was issued. Do not take the difference between the estimated amount and the actual amount.

Choice "c" is incorrect. The $4,950 is the actual invoice amount. Budgetary control is debited for the estimated amount.

## 3. MCQ-08277

Choice "a" is correct. Reciprocal interfund activity for the city of Curtain is $5,000. Reciprocal interfund activity includes interfund loans and interfund services provided and used. Billing by the internal service fund to a department financed by the general fund for services rendered is the only transaction meeting this definition. Nonreciprocal transfers include interfund transfers (which are displayed as either other financing sources or uses on the governmental fund financial statements or purely as transfers in proprietary fund financial statements) and interfund reimbursements (which are not shown on the face of the financial statements).

Choice "b" is incorrect. This response incorrectly combines a routine transfer (nonreciprocal activity) of $50,000 with a $5,000 reciprocal transfer (an internal service fund billing).

Choice "c" is incorrect. This response incorrectly classifies a transfer (nonreciprocal activity) of $200,000 as a reciprocal transfer. Reciprocal transfers are defined above as payments for services provided and used, and loans. Internal capitalization of a new fund is not considered reciprocal.

Choice "d" is incorrect. This response incorrectly combines a both a routine transfer (nonreciprocal activity) of $50,000 and a nonroutine transfer (also nonreciprocal) of $200,000 with a $5,000 reciprocal transfer (an internal service fund billing).

## 4. MCQ-07265

Choice "c" is correct. Assets associated with unavailable revenues should be recorded by crediting deferred inflows of resources as follows:

| DR | Accounts receivable | $XXX | |
|---|---|---|---|
| CR | Deferred inflows of resources | | $XXX |

Choice "a" incorrect. An allowance account is used for earnings that are not expected to be collectible, not that they are simply collected subsequent to the common deadline for recognition under modified accrual (60 days).

Choice "b" incorrect. Assets associated with unavailable revenues would be recorded along with deferred inflows of resources, not deferred outflows of resources.

Choice "d" incorrect. Unavailable revenues are not recognized as a component of fund balance. They are recognized as a deferred inflow of resources.

## 5. MCQ-06023

Choice "b" is correct. Restricted fund balances represent resources whose use has been limited by external sources such as creditors (e.g., debt covenants), contributors, other governments, laws, constitutional provisions, or enabling legislation.

Choice "a" is incorrect. Nonspendable fund balances represent resources in a form that cannot be spent (e.g., inventories or prepaid expenditures) or are legally or contractually required to remain whole (e.g., permanent fund principal).

Choice "c" is incorrect. Committed fund balances represent resources that can only be used for specific purposes pursuant to constraints imposed by formal action of the government's highest level of decision-making authority.

Choice "d" is incorrect. Assigned fund balances are constrained by the government's intent to be used for specific purposes, but are neither restricted nor committed.

## 6. MCQ-06024

Choice "a" is correct. Unassigned fund balance is the residual classification for the general fund. This classification represents fund balance that has not been assigned to other funds and has not been restricted, committed or assigned to specific purposes within the general fund.

Choice "b" is incorrect. The general fund should be the only fund that shows a positive unassigned fund balance amount. Over-expenditure of resources in special revenue funds may result in a reported negative unassigned fund balance.

Choice "c" is incorrect. The general fund should be the only fund that shows a positive unassigned fund balance amount. Over-expenditure of resources in capital project funds may result in a reported negative unassigned fund balance.

Choice "d" is incorrect. The general fund should be the only fund that shows a positive unassigned fund balance amount. Permanent funds would display a restricted balance.

Financial 9, Module 5

## 1. MCQ-06615

Choice "a" is correct. The transfer to a debt service fund is a transfer out, which will fall under "other financing uses" on the statement of revenues, expenditures, and changes in fund balances.

Choice "b" is incorrect. The purchase of equipment ($300,000) is an expenditure and would not be considered an "other financing use" in combination with transfers.

Choice "c" is incorrect. This choice includes both the payment to a pension trust fund and the purchase of equipment (both expenditures) but fails to include the transfer to a debt service fund (an "other financing use").

Choice "d" is incorrect. The payment to a pension trust fund and the purchase of equipment are both classified as expenditures.

## 2. MCQ-01013

Choice "d" is correct. The debt service fund accounts for the accumulation of resources for, and the payment of, general long-term liability principal and interest. The restricted portion of the special tax is for the repayment of the long-term debt of the county's capital projects, which would be serviced from the debt service fund. The capital projects fund is a governmental fund for the acquisition or construction of capital assets.

Choice "a" is incorrect. The internal service funds provide goods or services to other departments on a cost-reimbursement basis. General long-term debt would not be serviced from this fund.

Choice "b" is incorrect. Enterprise funds provide goods or services to the general public, similar to a for-profit enterprise. General long-term debt would not be serviced from this fund.

Choice "c" is incorrect. Capital project funds account for the resources to be used for the acquisition or construction of major capital facilities. Long-term liabilities are not recorded in or serviced from this fund.

## 3. MCQ-01000

Choice "a" is correct. The debt service fund services general debt. Both fiduciary funds and proprietary funds record their own long-term liabilities and service their own debt.

Choices "b", "c", and "d" are incorrect, per the explanation above.

## 4. MCQ-04665

Choice "a" is correct. The city of Walton would not record any interest expenditures in its current year financial statements. Interest expenditures should be recorded when legally payable per the bond agreement. Interest expenditures should not be accrued between payment dates. Bonds were issued January 2, the balance sheet date is September 30 and the payment date is the following January 2. No interest expenditure would be recognized.

Choice "b" is incorrect. The city of Walton pays interest annually according to the fact pattern. Although it is not unusual for bonds to required payment of interest twice a year, six months of interest expenditures, $17,500 ($500,000 × 7% × 6/12), would not be recorded unless actually paid.

Choice "c" is incorrect. The city of Walton would not accrue interest expenditures. Nine months of interest expenditures suggested by this answer, $26,250 ($500,000 × 7% × 9/12), would not be recorded.

Choice "d" is incorrect. The city of Walton would record interest expenditures as they are paid or as they mature. Recognition of a full year of interest, $35,000 ($500,000 × 7%), would not be appropriate nine months after issuance of the bonds and three months before the first payment (September 30).

### Financial 9, Module 6

## 1. MCQ-05190

Choice "b" is correct. The state grant of $300,000 would be reported as revenue in the capital projects fund, and the transfer from the general fund of $450,000 would be recorded as "other financing sources." The accrual of a receivable associated with a state grant indicates that revenues have been earned by the city by either incurring eligible capital outlay expenditures to be paid by grant revenues or by satisfaction of other pertinent grant requirements prior to accruing the receivable.

Choice "a" is incorrect. Per the above explanation, the $300,000 state grant is revenue, so this answer cannot be correct.

Choice "c" is incorrect. The $450,000 transfer from the general fund is not revenue. It is classified as an "other financing source."

Choice "d" is incorrect. The $450,000 transfer from the general fund is not revenue, so this answer, which combines the $300,000 in revenue with the $400,000 transfer, is incorrect.

Financial                                                          Class Question Explanations

## 2. MCQ-00906

Choice "a" is correct. Japes City would account for proceeds from the issuance of general obligation bonds (both face amount and premium) as other financing sources. Debt related transaction costs would not be netted against debt proceeds. Other financing sources are computed as follows:

| | |
|---|---:|
| Bond face amount | $1,000,000 |
| Bond premium | 101 |
| Total proceeds | $1,010,000 |

Underwriter's fees of $500 and other debt issues costs of $2,000 would be accounted for as debt service expenditures.

Choice "b" is incorrect. Japes City would not report total proceeds net of other debt issue costs as other financing sources. No debt related transactions are shown on net basis.

Choice "c" is incorrect. Japes City would not report total proceeds net of bond issues costs and other debt issues costs as other financing sources. No debt related transactions are shown on a net basis.

Choice "d" is incorrect. Japes City would not report only the face amount of the issued bonds as other financing sources and exclude bond premium.

## 3. MCQ-05663

Choice "b" is correct. The fact pattern describes the circumstances required for a permanent fund. Permanent funds should be used to report resources that are restricted to the extent that only earnings, and not principal, may be used for the purposes that support the government (that benefit the public). The land received by Tang City is to be kept intact with income used for general government services.

Choice "a" is incorrect. Selection of a special revenue fund would not be appropriate. Although the special revenue fund has many features that would be compatible with the fact pattern, special revenue funds are expendable. The donor specified that the land must be kept in perpetuity.

Choice "c" is incorrect. A private-purpose trust is inappropriate. Although the private-purpose fund is designed for the safekeeping of assets for the use of a beneficiary, it contemplates a specific beneficiary, not the general public.

Choice "d" is incorrect. A custodial fund is appropriate for the safeguarding of assets to be purely given to another group, not used on their behalf. Tang City is charged with using the land or its proceeds for the public good, not simply to pass it along. A custodial fund is not appropriate for the Tang City for this transaction.

# FINANCIAL 10

Financial 10, Module 1

## 1. MCQ-01029

Choice "b" is correct. Billings for transportation services provided to other governmental units are considered quasi-external transactions and are treated as revenues by the internal service fund. The journal entry is as follows:

| DR | Due from other funds | $XXX | |
|---|---|---|---|
| CR | Operating revenues | | $XXX |

Choices "a", "c", and "d" are incorrect, per the journal entry explanation above.

## 2. MCQ-01032

Choice "c" is correct. Municipal solid waste landfills (MSWLF) owners and operators are required to incur a variety of costs to provide for protection of the environment both during the period of landfill operations and during the postclosure period. The estimated total current cost of MSWLF closure and postclosure care, based on applicable federal state or local laws or regulations, should include:

a. Cost of equipment expected to be installed and facilities expected to be constructed near or after the date that the MSWLF stops accepting solid waste and during the postclosure period. This equipment should be limited to items that, once installed or constructed, will be exclusively used for the MSWLF. This may include gas monitoring and collection systems.

b. Cost of final cover (capping) expected to be applied near or after the date that the MSWLF stops accepting solid waste.

## 3. MCQ-01040

Choice "d" is correct. An enterprise fund may be used to account for the provision of goods and services that are financed mainly by user charges. Both a state-operated lottery and a state-operated hospital are financed mainly by user charges.

Choice "a" is incorrect. Both a state-operated lottery and a state-operated hospital are financed mainly by user charges and would most likely be accounted for as enterprise funds.

Choice "b" is incorrect. Although the proposed answer properly identifies the lottery as an enterprise fund, it incorrectly excludes the hospital from classification as an enterprise fund. Hospitals are typically supported by patient service revenues (a fee paid by external users) and would, therefore, be most likely classified as an enterprise fund.

Choice "c" is incorrect. Although the proposed answer properly identifies the hospital as an enterprise fund, it incorrectly excludes the lottery from classification as an enterprise fund. Lotteries are typically supported by fees from ticket/lottery sales to external users. The fund would, therefore, be most likely classified as an enterprise fund.

## Financial 10, Module 2

### 1. MCQ-01067

Choice "a" is correct. The debt service transactions of a special assessment issue for which the government is not obligated in any manner should be reported in a custodial fund, rather than a debt service fund, to reflect the fact that the government's duties are limited to collecting and remitting funds without administrative involvement for the assessed property owners and bondholders.

Choice "b" is incorrect. The debt service fund would service the debt for special assessments where the government is obligated in some manner, which is not the case here.

Choice "c" is incorrect. Private purpose funds would not be used for special assessment projects.

Choice "d" is incorrect. The capital project fund would account for the project inflows and outflows where the government is obligated in some manner, which is not the case here.

### 2. MCQ-01082

Choice "a" is correct. The $300,000 should be reported in a special revenue fund because the government is agreeing to accept cash and spend it in a specified way and the $500,000 belongs in a custodial fund. Escheat property held for individuals, private organizations, or another government should be reported in a private purpose trust fund, or in the governmental or proprietary fund in which otherwise reported.

Choice "b" is incorrect. The $300,000 results from the government's agreement to accept resources and to spend them in a specified way (i.e., law enforcement activities). This is an example of a special revenue fund.

Choices "c" and "d" are incorrect. The $500,000 belongs in a custodial fund because Arlen is collecting sales taxes to be remitted to other governmental units.

## Financial 10, Module 3

### 1. MCQ-00975

Choice "a" is correct. Government-wide financial statements focus on operational accountability.

Rule: The focus of government-wide financial statements is the government's responsibility to report the extent to which it has met its operating objectives efficiently and effectively, using all resources available for that purpose, and the extent to which it can continue to meet its objectives for the future.

Choice "b" is incorrect. Although all financial statements serve to demonstrate financial accountability is some way, the government-wide financial statements most specifically focus on operational accountability.

Choice "c" is incorrect. Fund financial statements focus on fiscal accountability. Fund financial statement accountability objectives complement government-wide financial statement accountability objectives.

Choice "d" is incorrect. Functional accountability is a distracter.

## 2. MCQ-00995

Choice "c" is correct. A comprehensive annual financial report is divided into three sections: an introductory section, the basic financial statements along with other required supplementary information mandated by GASB 34, and the statistical section. The statistical section, by definition, is not part of the basic financial statements.

Choice "a" is incorrect. Statistical tables generally provide ten years of historical financial information. There is no limitation with regard to presenting two years or less of data.

Choice "b" is incorrect. Statistical tables include a variety of accounting and non-accounting data including property values, tax rates on overlapping governments, demographic statistics, etc.

Choice "d" is incorrect. The statistical tables are not viewed as an integral part of the basic financial statements.

## 3. MCQ-01141

Choice "b" is correct. South City School District meets the test of component unit of the city; it is financially accountable to South City. Thus, its financial data needs to be reported with South City's financial data. However, because the school district is not substantively the same as the city, because it is a legally separate entity, and because the school district does not exclusively service or benefit South City itself, the financial data should be reported using the discrete presentation method.

Choice "a" is incorrect. Because South City School District meets the test of component unit, its financial data needs to be reported with South City's financial data. The financial data would not be blended because the school district does not meet the tests for blending; the school district is not substantively the same as South City and the school district does not exclusively service or benefit the city itself.

Choice "c" is incorrect. South City School District meets the test of component unit of the city; it is financially accountable to South City. Thus, its financial data needs to be reported with the city's financial data. However, because the school district is not substantively the same as the city and because the school district does not exclusively service or benefit the city itself, the financial data should be reported using the discrete presentation method. The discrete presentation is either in condensed financial statements with the notes to the reporting entity's financial statements, or in combining statements in its general purpose financial statement. The inclusion of the word "only" makes this answer choice incorrect.

Choice "d" is incorrect. Because South City School District meets the test of component unit, its financial data needs to be reported with the city's financial data. The financial data would not be blended because the school district does not meet the tests for blending; the school district is not substantively the same as the city and the school district does not exclusively service or benefit the city itself.

### Financial 10, Module 4

## 1. MCQ-05949

Choice "a" is correct. The government-wide financial statements are prepared using the economic resources measurement focus and the full accrual basis of accounting. Therefore, interest expense should include all interest accrued from March 1 through December 31 (10 months) and interest payable should include the amount accrued after the interest payment on September 1 (4 months).

Interest expense = $1,000,000 × 6% × 10/12 = $50,000

Interest payable = $1,000,000 × 6% × 4/12 = $20,000

## 2. MCQ-04670

Choice "c" is correct. Knoxx County would report revenue from its governmental funds on the full accrual basis in its government-wide statement of activities. As such, Knoxx County would recognize revenues from property taxes, net of estimated refunds and estimated uncollectible amounts in the period in which they are levied. The examiners provide additional irrelevant data necessary to compute earnings on the modified accrual basis. Earnings on the accrual basis are computed as follows:

| | |
|---|---|
| Property tax levy | $2,000,000 |
| Estimated uncollectible (1 percent) | (20,000) |
| Revenue recognized | $1,980,000 |

Collection data shown in the fact pattern would be useful in computing revenue on the modified accrual basis for display in fund financial statements, but is not relevant to the computation of accrual basis revenue displayed in the government-wide financial statements.

Choice "a" is incorrect. The amount collected from the current year levy ($1,800,000) would not be the amount recognized as property tax revenue on the accrual basis.

Choice "b" is incorrect. The total of all amounts collected in the current year from both prior year and current year levies ($1,970,000 = $50,000 + $120,000 + $1,800,000) would not be the amount recognized as property tax revenue on the accrual basis.

Choice "d" is incorrect. The total amount of the levy ($2,000,000) or the revenue computed on the modified accrual basis (also $2,000,000 representing the sum of the $120,000 collected after the 60-day availability criteria from the prior year, the $1,800,000 in current year collections and the $80,000 collected within 60 days of the current year) would not be the amount recognized as property tax revenue on the accrual basis.

## 3. MCQ-08616

Choice "b" is correct. The statement of activities is the government-wide financial statement used to report revenues and expenses for governmental and business-type activities. The only fund type that will fall in the "business-type" classification is the enterprise fund, which in this example is the water enterprise fund. Because the net position of the water enterprise fund increased by $12,000, this amount will be reported under business-type activities in the statement of activities. The $9,000 for the motor pool internal service fund will be reported under "governmental activities" and the $7,000 change in fiduciary net position for the pension fund will be excluded from government-wide presentations. Fiduciary fund activity is only displayed in the fund financial statements.

Choice "a" is incorrect. This choice incorrectly includes the $9,000 for the motor pool internal service fund as a business-type activity and excludes the $12,000 for the water enterprise fund.

Choice "c" is incorrect. This choice incorrectly includes the $9,000 for the motor pool internal service fund as a business-type activity.

Choice "d" is incorrect. This choice incorrectly includes the $9,000 for the motor pool internal service fund and the $7,000 for the pension fund as business-type activities.

## Financial 10, Module 5

### 1. MCQ-05144

Choice "b" is correct. Four funds would be treated as major funds.

Major fund treatment for purposes of fund financial statement presentation requires that a fund be both 10 percent of its fund category's assets, revenues, or expenditures/expenses and 5 percent of the combined governmental and enterprise assets, revenues, and expenditures/expenses.

Three of the funds meet the specific criteria for major fund treatment. The general fund, even though it does not meet the criteria, is always treated as a major fund. This question's focus is based purely on assets. The computation of major funds treatment based on asset criteria is as follows:

| Fund Description | Amount | 10% | 5% | Quantitative Criteria | Judgmental Criteria |
|---|---|---|---|---|---|
| Governmental funds | $3,000,000 | $300,000 | | | |
| Enterprise funds | 2,000,000 | 200,000 | | | |
| Combined governmental and enterprise | $5,000,000 | | $250,000 | | |
| *Governmental* | | | | | |
| General fund | 280,000 | No | Yes | No | Yes |
| Community development special revenue fund | 290,000 | No | Yes | No | |
| Sales tax special revenue fund | 350,000 | Yes | Yes | Yes | Yes |
| General revenue bond debt service fund | 120,000 | No | No | No | |
| Faberville river bridge capital projects fund | 1,500,000 | Yes | Yes | Yes | Yes |
| *Enterprise* | | | | | |
| Faberville water and sewer utility fund | 1,800,000 | Yes | Yes | Yes | Yes |
| Faberville landfill fund | 200,000 | Yes | No | No | |

### 2. MCQ-06820

Choice "b" is correct. The transactions listed in the fact pattern would be distributed as follows:

- Cash payments from customers of $250,000 are classified as cash flows from operating activities.

- Property tax receipts (sources of $150,000) and operating transfers out (uses of $125,000) would produce net noncapital financing activities of $25,000 (source).

- Special assessments for capital improvements (such as enhanced wastewater infrastructure) would be displayed as capital and related financing activities.

- There are no investing activities.

Choice "a" is incorrect. Operating transfers out are classified as noncapital financing activities, not investing activities.

Choice "c" is incorrect. Property tax receipts are classified as noncapital financing activities, not operating activities. In addition, special assessments that fund capital improvements are classified as capital and related financing activities.

Choice "d" is incorrect. Property taxes and operating transfers are classified as noncapital financing activities, not operating activities.

## Financial 10, Module 6

### 1. MCQ-05142

Choice "b" is correct. The reconciliation of change in governmental fund balances to change in net position for governmental activities in the government-wide financial statements would be computed using the **CPAS RIDES** mnemonic as follows:

| | |
|---|---:|
| Change in governmental fund balances | $ 500,000 |
| Capital outlay | 250,000 |
| Principal payments | 40,000 |
| Asset disposals | 0 |
| Sources (other financing) | (225,000) |
| Revenue—sales tax | 30,000 |
| Interest expense | (7,500) |
| Depreciation expense | (60,000) |
| Internal service fund | 0 |
| Change in net position | $ 527,500 |

Choices "a", "c", and "d" are incorrect per the above calculation.

## Financial 10, Module 7

### 1. MCQ-08615

Choice "b" is correct. One of the major components of the MD&A is the description of the financial statements, which includes an analysis of the government's overall financial position and the results of operations, including reasons for changes from the prior year.

Choice "a" is incorrect. The MD&A should be presented independently, with other supplementary information presented separately.

Choice "c" is incorrect. The MD&A is a narrative covering all of the government's financial activities; the analysis of the individual funds will be included in the notes to the financial statements.

Choice "d" is incorrect. The MD&A should present condensed financial information from the government-wide financial statements.

### 2. MCQ-00980

Choice "c" is correct. Budgetary comparison schedules should be prepared for the general fund and each major special revenue fund, which requires a budget. Budgetary comparison schedules should display the original budget, final appropriations budget, and actual inflows, outflows, and balances on a budgetary basis.

Choice "a" is incorrect. Presentations of variances are optional.

Choice "b" is incorrect. Budgetary presentation must display original as well as final amended budgets in comparison to each other as well as actual results displayed on a budgetary basis.

Choice "d" is incorrect. Budgetary presentations need not include originally proposed budgets, only the originally approved budgets along with other items as described in the rule. In addition, variance presentations are optional.

Material from *Uniform CPA Examination Blueprints*,
© 2018, American Institute for CPAs. All rights reserved.
Used by permission.

# Blueprint
# FAR

## Financial Accounting and Reporting (FAR)

### Summary blueprint

**Content area allocation** — **Weight**

| Content area | Weight |
|---|---|
| I. Conceptual Framework, Standard-Setting and Financial Reporting | 25–35% |
| II. Select Financial Statement Accounts | 30–40% |
| III. Select Transactions | 20–30% |
| IV. State and Local Governments | 5–15% |

**Skill allocation** — **Weight**

| Skill | Weight |
|---|---|
| Evaluation | — |
| Analysis | 25–35% |
| Application | 50–60% |
| Remembering and Understanding | 10–20% |

© Becker Professional Education Corporation. All rights reserved.

Financial Accounting and Reporting (FAR)

## Area I – Conceptual Framework, Standard-Setting and Financial Reporting (25–35%)

### A. Conceptual framework and standard-setting for business and nonbusiness entities

| Content group/topic | Skill: Remembering and Understanding | Skill: Application | Skill: Analysis | Skill: Evaluation | Representative task |
|---|---|---|---|---|---|
| 1. Conceptual framework | ✓ | | | | Recall the purpose and characteristics in the conceptual framework for business and nonbusiness entities. |
| 2. Standard-setting process | ✓ | | | | Recall the due process steps followed by the FASB to establish financial accounting and reporting standards. |

### B. General-purpose financial statements: for-profit business entities

| Content group/topic | Skill: Remembering and Understanding | Skill: Application | Skill: Analysis | Skill: Evaluation | Representative task |
|---|---|---|---|---|---|
| 1. Balance sheet/ statement of financial position | | ✓ | | | Prepare a classified balance sheet from a trial balance and supporting documentation. |
| | | ✓ | | | Adjust the balance sheet to correct identified errors. |
| | | | ✓ | | Detect, investigate and correct discrepancies while agreeing the balance sheet amounts to supporting documentation. |
| | | | ✓ | | Calculate fluctuations and ratios and interpret the results while reviewing comparative balance sheets. |
| 2. Income statement/ statement of profit or loss | | ✓ | | | Prepare a multiple-step income statement from a trial balance and supporting documentation. |
| | | ✓ | | | Prepare a single-step income statement from a trial balance and supporting documentation. |
| | | ✓ | | | Adjust the income statement to correct identified errors. |
| | | | ✓ | | Detect, investigate and correct discrepancies while agreeing the income statement amounts to supporting documentation. |
| | | | ✓ | | Calculate fluctuations and ratios and interpret the results while reviewing comparative income statements. |

Uniform CPA Examination Blueprints: Financial Accounting and Reporting (FAR)

# Financial Accounting and Reporting (FAR)

## Area I – Conceptual Framework, Standard-Setting and Financial Reporting (25–35%) (continued)

### B. General-purpose financial statements: for-profit business entities (continued)

| Content group/topic | Remembering and Understanding | Application | Analysis | Evaluation | Representative task |
|---|---|---|---|---|---|
| 3. Statement of comprehensive income | | > | | | Prepare a statement of comprehensive income from a trial balance and supporting documentation. |
| | | > | | | Calculate reclassification adjustments for items of other comprehensive income. |
| | | > | | | Adjust the statement of comprehensive income to correct identified errors. |
| | | | > | | Detect, investigate and correct discrepancies while agreeing the statement of comprehensive income amounts to supporting documentation. |
| 4. Statement of changes in equity | | > | | | Prepare a statement of changes in equity from a trial balance and supporting documentation. |
| | | > | | | Adjust the statement of changes in equity to correct identified errors. |
| | | | > | | Detect, investigate and correct discrepancies while agreeing the statement of changes in equity amounts to supporting documentation. |
| 5. Statement of cash flows | | > | | | Prepare a statement of cash flows using the direct method and required disclosures from supporting documentation. |
| | | > | | | Prepare a statement of cash flows using the indirect method and required disclosures from supporting documentation. |
| | | > | | | Adjust a statement of cash flows to correct identified errors. |
| | | | > | | Detect, investigate and correct discrepancies while agreeing the statement of cash flows amounts to supporting documentation. |
| | | | > | | Derive the impact of transactions on the statement of cash flows. |

# Area I – Conceptual Framework, Standard-Setting and Financial Reporting (25–35%) (continued)

## B. General-purpose financial statements: for-profit business entities (continued)

| Content group/topic | Skill: Remembering and Understanding | Application | Analysis | Evaluation | Representative task |
|---|:---:|:---:|:---:|:---:|---|
| 6. Notes to financial statements | | ✓ | | | Adjust the notes to the financial statements to correct identified errors and omissions. |
| | | | ✓ | | Compare the notes to the financial statements to the financial statements and supporting documentation to identify inconsistencies and investigate those inconsistencies. |
| 7. Consolidated financial statements (including wholly owned subsidiaries and noncontrolling interests) | ✓ | | | | Recall basic consolidation concepts and terms (e.g. controlling interest, noncontrolling interest, primary beneficiary, variable interest entity). |
| | | ✓ | | | Prepare consolidated financial statements (includes adjustments, eliminations and/or noncontrolling interests) from supporting documentation. |
| | | ✓ | | | Adjust consolidated financial statements to correct identified errors. |
| | | | ✓ | | Detect, investigate and correct discrepancies identified while agreeing the consolidated financial statement amounts to supporting documentation. |
| 8. Discontinued operations | | ✓ | | | Prepare the discontinued operations portion of the financial statements from a trial balance and supporting documentation. |
| 9. Going concern | ✓ | | | | Recall the requirements for disclosing uncertainties about an entity's ability to continue as a going concern. |

Financial Accounting and Reporting (FAR)

## Area I – Conceptual Framework, Standard-Setting and Financial Reporting (25–35%) (continued)

### C. General-purpose financial statements: nongovernmental, not-for-profit entities

| Content group/topic | Remembering and Understanding | Application | Analysis | Evaluation | Representative task |
|---|---|---|---|---|---|
| 1. Statement of financial position | ✓ | | | | Recall the purpose and objectives of the statement of financial position for a nongovernmental, not-for-profit entity. |
| | | ✓ | | | Prepare a statement of financial position for a nongovernmental, not-for-profit entity from a trial balance and supporting documentation. |
| | | ✓ | | | Adjust the statement of financial position for a nongovernmental, not-for-profit entity to correct identified errors. |
| 2. Statement of activities | ✓ | | | | Recall the purpose and objectives of the statement of activities for a nongovernmental, not-for-profit entity. |
| | | ✓ | | | Prepare a statement of activities for a nongovernmental, not-for-profit entity from a trial balance and supporting documentation. |
| | | ✓ | | | Adjust the statement of activities for a nongovernmental, not-for-profit entity to correct identified errors. |
| 3. Statement of cash flows | ✓ | | | | Recall the purpose and objectives of the statement of cash flows for a nongovernmental, not-for-profit entity. |
| | | ✓ | | | Prepare a statement of cash flows and required disclosures using the direct method for a nongovernmental, not-for-profit entity. |
| | | ✓ | | | Prepare a statement of cash flows and required disclosures using the indirect method for a nongovernmental, not-for-profit entity. |
| | | ✓ | | | Adjust the statement of cash flows for a nongovernmental, not-for-profit entity to correct identified errors. |
| 4. Notes to financial statements | | ✓ | | | Adjust the notes to the financial statements to correct identified errors and omissions. |

Uniform CPA Examination Blueprints: Financial Accounting and Reporting (FAR)                 FAR10

Financial Accounting and Reporting (FAR)

## Area I – Conceptual Framework, Standard-Setting and Financial Reporting (25–35%) (continued)

| Content group/topic | Skill: Remembering and Understanding | Skill: Application | Skill: Analysis | Skill: Evaluation | Representative task |
|---|---|---|---|---|---|
| D. Public company reporting topics (U.S. SEC reporting requirements, earnings per share and segment reporting) | | | | | |
| | > | | | | Recall the purpose of forms 10-Q, 10-K and 8-K that a U.S. registrant is required to file with the U.S. Securities and Exchange Commission under the Securities Exchange Act of 1934. |
| | > | | | | Identify the significant components of Form 10-Q and Form 10-K filed with the U.S. Securities and Exchange Commission. |
| | | > | | | Prepare financial statement note disclosures for reportable segments. |
| | | > | | | Calculate basic earnings per share. |
| | | > | | | Calculate diluted earnings per share. |
| E. Financial statements of employee benefit plans | | | | | |
| | > | | | | Identify the required financial statements for a defined benefit pension plan and a defined contribution pension plan. |
| | | > | | | Prepare a statement of changes in net assets available for benefits for a defined benefit pension plan and a defined contribution pension plan. |
| | | > | | | Prepare a statement of net assets available for benefits for a defined benefit pension plan and a defined contribution pension plan. |

Uniform CPA Examination Blueprints: Financial Accounting and Reporting (FAR)

# Financial Accounting and Reporting (FAR)

## Area I – Conceptual Framework, Standard-Setting and Financial Reporting (25–35%) (continued)

| Content group/topic | Skill | | | | Representative task |
|---|---|---|---|---|---|
| | Remembering and Understanding | Application | Analysis | Evaluation | |
| **F. Special purpose frameworks** | | | | | |
| | > | | | | Recall appropriate financial statement titles to be used for the financial statements prepared under a special purpose framework. |
| | | > | | | Perform calculations to convert cash basis or modified cash basis financial statements to accrual basis financial statements. |
| | | > | | | Prepare financial statements using the cash basis of accounting. |
| | | > | | | Prepare financial statements using a modified cash basis of accounting. |
| | | > | | | Prepare financial statements using the income tax basis of accounting. |

Financial                                                                                                                         Blueprint

Financial Accounting and Reporting (FAR)

## Area II – Select Financial Statement Accounts (30–40%)

| Content group/topic | Skill | | | | Representative task |
|---|---|---|---|---|---|
| | Remembering and Understanding | Application | Analysis | Evaluation | |
| A. Cash and cash equivalents | | > | | | Calculate cash and cash equivalents balances to be reported in the financial statements. |
| | | > | | | Reconcile the cash balance per the bank statement to the general ledger. |
| | | | > | | Investigate unreconciled cash balances to determine whether an adjustment to the general ledger is necessary. |
| B. Trade receivables | | > | | | Calculate trade receivables and allowances and prepare journal entries. |
| | | > | | | Prepare any required journal entries to record the transfer of trade receivables (secured borrowings, factoring, assignment, pledging). |
| | | > | | | Prepare a rollforward of the trade receivables account balance using various sources of information. |
| | | | > | | Reconcile and investigate differences between the subledger and general ledger for trade receivables to determine whether an adjustment is necessary. |
| C. Inventory | | > | | | Calculate the carrying amount of inventory and prepare journal entries using various costing methods. |
| | | > | | | Measure impairment losses on inventory. |
| | | > | | | Prepare a rollforward of the inventory account balance using various sources of information. |
| | | | > | | Reconcile and investigate differences between the subledger and general ledger for inventory to determine whether an adjustment is necessary. |

Uniform CPA Examination Blueprints: Financial Accounting and Reporting (FAR)                                       FAR13

BL-8                                                             © Becker Professional Education Corporation. All rights reserved.

Financial Accounting and Reporting (FAR)

## Area II – Select Financial Statement Accounts (30–40%) (continued)

| Content group/topic | Remembering and Understanding | Application | Analysis | Evaluation | Representative task |
|---|---|---|---|---|---|
| **D. Property, plant and equipment** | | | | | |
| | | > | | | Calculate the gross and net property, plant and equipment balances and prepare journal entries. |
| | | > | | | Calculate gains or losses on the disposal of long-lived assets to be recognized in the financial statements. |
| | | > | | | Measure impairment losses on long-lived assets to be recognized in the financial statements. |
| | | > | | | Calculate the amounts necessary to prepare journal entries to record a nonmonetary exchange. |
| | | > | | | Determine whether an asset qualifies to be reported as held for sale in the financial statements. |
| | | > | | | Adjust the carrying amount of assets held for sale and calculate the loss to be recognized in the financial statements. |
| | | | > | | Prepare a rollforward of the property, plant and equipment account balance using various sources of information. |
| | | | > | | Reconcile and investigate differences between the subledger and general ledger for property, plant and equipment to determine whether an adjustment is necessary. |
| **E. Investments** | | | | | |
| 1. Financial assets at fair value | > | | | | Identify investments that are eligible or required to be reported at fair value in the financial statements. |
| | | > | | | Calculate the carrying amount of investments measured at fair value and prepare journal entries (excluding impairment). |

## Area II – Select Financial Statement Accounts (30–40%) (continued)

### E. Investments (continued)

| Content group/topic | Remembering and Understanding | Application | Analysis | Evaluation | Representative task |
|---|---|---|---|---|---|
| 1. Financial assets at fair value, (continued) | | ✓ | | | Calculate gains and losses to be recognized in net income or other comprehensive income for investments measured at fair value and prepare journal entries. |
| | | ✓ | | | Calculate investment income to be recognized in net income for investments measured at fair value and prepare journal entries. |
| | | ✓ | | | Measure impairment losses to be recognized on applicable investments reported at fair value in the financial statements. |
| 2. Financial assets at amortized cost | ✓ | | | | Identify investments that are eligible to be reported at amortized cost in the financial statements. |
| | | ✓ | | | Calculate the carrying amount of investments measured at amortized cost and prepare journal entries (excluding impairment). |
| | | ✓ | | | Measure impairment losses to be recognized on investments reported at amortized cost in the financial statements. |
| 3. Equity method investments | ✓ | | | | Identify when the equity method of accounting can be applied to an investment. |
| | | ✓ | | | Calculate the carrying amount of equity method investments and prepare journal entries (excluding impairment). |
| | | ✓ | | | Measure impairment losses to be recognized in the financial statements on equity method investments. |

Financial Accounting and Reporting (FAR)

## Area II – Select Financial Statement Accounts (30–40%) (continued)

| Content group/topic | Skill | | | | Representative task |
|---|---|---|---|---|---|
| | Remembering and Understanding | Application | Analysis | Evaluation | |
| F. Intangible assets – goodwill and other | ✓ | | | | Identify the criteria for recognizing intangible assets in the statement of financial position and classify intangible assets as either finite-lived or indefinite-lived. |
| | ✓ | | | | Identify impairment indicators for goodwill and other indefinite-lived intangible assets. |
| | | ✓ | | | Calculate the carrying amount of finite-lived intangible assets reported in the financial statements (initial measurement, amortization and impairment) and prepare journal entries. |
| | | ✓ | | | Calculate the carrying amount of goodwill and other indefinite-lived intangible assets reported in the financial statements (includes initial measurement and impairment) and prepare journal entries. |
| G. Payables and accrued liabilities | | ✓ | | | Calculate the carrying amount of payables and accrued liabilities and prepare journal entries. |
| | | ✓ | | | Identify and calculate liabilities arising from exit or disposal activities and determine the timing of recognition in the financial statements. |
| | | ✓ | | | Calculate the liabilities and assets resulting from asset retirement obligations and prepare journal entries. |
| | | | ✓ | | Reconcile and investigate differences between the subledger and general ledger for accounts payable and accrued liabilities to determine whether an adjustment is necessary. |
| H. Long-term debt (financial liabilities) | | | | | |
| 1. Notes and bonds payable | ✓ | | | | Classify a change to a debt instrument as either a modification of terms or an extinguishment of debt. |
| | ✓ | | | | Understand when a change to the terms of a debt instrument qualifies as a troubled debt restructuring. |
| | ✓ | | | | Classify a financial instrument as either debt or equity, based on its characteristics. |

Uniform CPA Examination Blueprints: Financial Accounting and Reporting (FAR)

FAR16

Financial Accounting and Reporting (FAR)

## Area II – Select Financial Statement Accounts (30–40%) (continued)

| Content group/topic | Skill | | | | Representative task |
|---|---|---|---|---|---|
| | Remembering and Understanding | Application | Analysis | Evaluation | |
| **H. Long-term debt (financial liabilities)** (continued) | | | | | |
| 1. Notes and bonds payable, (continued) | | ✓ | | | Calculate the interest expense attributable to notes and bonds payable reported in the financial statements (including discounts, premiums or debt issuance costs). |
| | | ✓ | | | Calculate the carrying amount of notes and bonds payable and prepare journal entries. |
| 2. Debt covenant compliance | | ✓ | | | Perform debt covenant calculations as stipulated in a debt agreement to ascertain compliance. |
| **I. Equity** | | ✓ | | | Prepare journal entries to recognize equity transactions in the financial statements. |
| | | ✓ | | | Calculate net asset balances for a nongovernmental, not-for-profit entity and prepare journal entries. |
| **J. Revenue recognition** | ✓ | | | | Recall concepts of accounting for revenue. |
| | | ✓ | | | Determine the amount and timing of revenue to be recognized under a contract and prepare journal entries. |
| | | ✓ | | | Determine revenue to be recognized by a nongovernmental, not-for-profit entity for contributed services received and prepare journal entries. |
| | | | ✓ | | Interpret agreements, contracts and/or other supporting documentation to determine the amount and timing of revenue to be recognized in the financial statements. |
| | | | ✓ | | Reconcile and investigate differences between the sales subledger and the general ledger to determine whether an adjustment is necessary. |

Uniform CPA Examination Blueprints: Financial Accounting and Reporting (FAR)

FAR17

Financial Accounting and Reporting (FAR)

## Area II – Select Financial Statement Accounts (30–40%) (continued)

| Content group/topic | Skill: Remembering and Understanding | Skill: Application | Skill: Analysis | Skill: Evaluation | Representative task |
|---|---|---|---|---|---|
| **K. Compensation and benefits** | | | | | |
| 1. Compensated absences | | > | | | Calculate the carrying amount of the liability for compensated absences and prepare journal entries. |
| 2. Retirement benefits | | > | | | Use actuarial outputs to calculate the costs and the funded status for a defined benefit pension plan or a defined benefit postretirement plan and prepare journal entries. |
| 3. Stock compensation (share-based payments) | > | | | | Recall concepts associated with share-based payment arrangements (grant date, vesting conditions, inputs to valuation techniques, valuation models). |
| | | > | | | Calculate compensation costs to be recognized for a share-based payment arrangement classified as equity and prepare journal entries. |
| | | > | | | Calculate compensation costs to be recognized for a share-based payment arrangement classified as a liability and prepare journal entries. |
| **L. Income taxes** | > | | | | Recall the accounting treatment for uncertainty in income taxes. |
| | > | | | | Recall the criteria for recognizing or adjusting a valuation allowance for a deferred tax asset in the financial statements. |
| | | > | | | Calculate the income tax expense, current taxes payable/receivable and deferred tax liabilities/assets to be reported in the financial statements. |
| | | > | | | Prepare journal entries to record the tax provision in the financial statements. |

Uniform CPA Examination Blueprints: Financial Accounting and Reporting (FAR)

FAR18

# Financial Accounting and Reporting (FAR)

## Area III – Select Transactions (20–30%)

| Content group/topic | Skill: Remembering and Understanding | Skill: Application | Skill: Analysis | Skill: Evaluation | Representative task |
|---|---|---|---|---|---|
| **A. Accounting changes and error corrections** | | | | | |
| | | > | | | Calculate a required adjustment to the financial statements due to an accounting change or error correction and determine whether it requires prospective or retrospective application. |
| | | | > | | Derive the impact to the financial statements and related note disclosures of an accounting change or an error correction. |
| **B. Business combinations** | | | | | |
| | | > | | | Prepare journal entries to record the identifiable net assets acquired in a business combination that results in the recognition of goodwill. |
| | | > | | | Prepare journal entries to record the identifiable net assets acquired in a business combination that includes a noncontrolling interest. |
| | | > | | | Prepare journal entries to record the identifiable net assets acquired in a business combination that results in the recognition of a bargain purchase gain. |
| | | > | | | Adjust the financial statements to properly reflect changes in contingent consideration related to a business combination. |
| | | > | | | Calculate the consideration transferred in a business combination. |
| | | > | | | Adjust the financial statements to properly reflect measurement period adjustments related to a business combination. |

Uniform CPA Examination Blueprints: Financial Accounting and Reporting (FAR)     FAR19

# Blueprint

Financial Accounting and Reporting (FAR)

## Area III – Select Transactions (20–30%)
(continued)

| Content group/topic | Skill | | | | Representative task |
|---|---|---|---|---|---|
| | Remembering and Understanding | Application | Analysis | Evaluation | |
| **C. Contingencies and commitments** | | | | | |
| | > | | | | Recall the recognition and disclosure criteria used to identify commitments and contingencies. |
| | | > | | | Calculate amounts of contingencies and prepare journal entries. |
| | | | > | | Review supporting documentation to determine whether a commitment or contingency requires recognition or disclosure in the financial statements. |
| **D. Derivatives and hedge accounting (e.g., swaps, options, forwards)** | | | | | |
| | > | | | | Identify the characteristics of a freestanding and/or embedded derivative financial instrument to be recognized in the financial statements. |
| | > | | | | Identify the criteria necessary to qualify for hedge accounting. |
| | | > | | | Prepare journal entries for hedging transactions. |
| | | > | | | Prepare journal entries for derivative financial instruments (swaps, options and forwards). |
| **E. Foreign currency transactions and translation** | | | | | |
| | > | | | | Recall the basic functional currency concepts including the indicators to be considered when determining an entity's functional currency. |
| | | > | | | Calculate transaction gains or losses recognized from monetary transactions denominated in a foreign currency. |
| | | > | | | Adjust an entity's financial statements (local currency to reporting currency or functional currency to reporting currency) and recognize the effect on equity through net income or other comprehensive income. |

Uniform CPA Examination Blueprints: Financial Accounting and Reporting (FAR)

FAR20

Financial                                                                                                          Blueprint

Financial Accounting and Reporting (FAR)

## Area III – Select Transactions (20–30%)
(continued)

| Content group/topic | Skill | | | | Representative task |
|---|---|---|---|---|---|
| | Remembering and Understanding | Application | Analysis | Evaluation | |
| **F. Leases** | | | | | |
| | ✓ | | | | Recall the appropriate accounting treatment for residual value guarantees, purchase options and variable lease payments included in leasing arrangements. |
| | ✓ | | | | Identify the criteria for classifying a lease arrangement. |
| | | ✓ | | | Calculate the carrying amount of lease-related assets and liabilities and prepare journal entries that a lessee should record. |
| | | ✓ | | | Calculate the carrying amount of lease-related assets and prepare journal entries that a lessor should record. |
| | | ✓ | | | Calculate the lease costs that a lessee should recognize in the income statement. |
| | | ✓ | | | Prepare journal entries that the seller/lessee should record for a sale-leaseback transaction. |
| | | ✓ | | | Calculate the amount of lease income that a lessor should recognize in the income statement. |
| | | | ✓ | | Interpret agreements, contracts and/or other supporting documentation to determine the appropriate accounting treatment of a leasing arrangement and prepare the journal entries that the lessee should record. |
| **G. Nonreciprocal transfers** | | | | | |
| | ✓ | | | | Recall the recognition requirements associated with conditional and unconditional promises to give (pledges) for a nongovernmental, not-for-profit entity. |
| | ✓ | | | | Identify transfers to a nongovernmental, not-for-profit entity acting as an agent or intermediary that are not recognized as contributions in the statement of activities. |

Uniform CPA Examination Blueprints: Financial Accounting and Reporting (FAR)                                        FAR21

## Financial Accounting and Reporting (FAR)

## Area III — Select Transactions (20–30%)
(continued)

| Content group/topic | Skill: Remembering and Understanding | Skill: Application | Skill: Analysis | Skill: Evaluation | Representative task |
|---|---|---|---|---|---|
| **G. Nonreciprocal transfers** (continued) | | | | | |
| | | > | | | Calculate the carrying amount of donated assets (financial assets or long-lived assets) to be reported in the statement of financial position. |
| | | > | | | Calculate increases in net assets attributable to contributions for a nongovernmental, not-for-profit entity. |
| **H. Research and development costs** | | | | | |
| | > | | | | Identify research and development costs and classify the costs as an expense in the financial statements. |
| | | > | | | Calculate the research and development costs to be reported as an expense in the financial statements. |
| **I. Software costs** | | | | | |
| | > | | | | Identify the criteria necessary to capitalize software costs (software for internal use or sale) in the financial statements. |
| | | > | | | Calculate capitalized software costs (software for internal use or sale) to be reported in the financial statements and the related amortization expense. |
| **J. Subsequent events** | | | | | |
| | > | | | | Identify a subsequent event and recall its appropriate accounting treatment. |
| | | > | | | Calculate required adjustments to financial statements and/or note disclosures based on identified subsequent events. |
| | | | > | | Derive the impact to the financial statements and required note disclosures due to identified subsequent events. |

Uniform CPA Examination Blueprints: Financial Accounting and Reporting (FAR)  FAR22

# Financial Accounting and Reporting (FAR)

## Area III – Select Transactions (20–30%)
(continued)

| Content group/topic | Skill | | | | Representative task |
|---|---|---|---|---|---|
| | Remembering and Understanding | Application | Analysis | Evaluation | |
| **K. Fair value measurements** | | | | | |
| | > | | | | Identify the valuation techniques used to measure fair value. |
| | | > | | | Use the fair value hierarchy to determine the classification of a fair value measurement. |
| | | > | | | Use the fair value concepts (e.g. highest and best use, market participant assumptions, unit of account) to measure the fair value of assets and liabilities. |
| **L. Differences between IFRS and U.S. GAAP** | | | | | |
| | > | | | | Identify accounting and reporting differences between IFRS and U.S. GAAP. |
| | | > | | | Determine the impact of the differences between IFRS and U.S. GAAP on the financial statements. |

Financial Accounting and Reporting (FAR)

# Area IV – State and Local Governments (5–15%)

| Content group/topic | Skill | | | | Representative task |
|---|---|---|---|---|---|
| | Remembering and Understanding | Application | Analysis | Evaluation | |
| **A. State and local government concepts** | | | | | |
| 1. Conceptual framework | ✓ | | | | Recall the purpose and characteristics of the conceptual framework for state and local governments. |
| 2. Measurement focus and basis of accounting | ✓ | | | | Recall the measurement focus and basis of accounting used by state and local governments for fund and government-wide financial reporting. |
| 3. Purpose of funds | | ✓ | | | Determine the appropriate fund(s) that a state or local government should use to record its activities. |
| **B. Format and content of the financial section of the comprehensive annual financial report (CAFR)** | | | | | |
| 1. Government-wide financial statements | ✓ | | | | Identify and recall basic concepts and principles associated with government-wide financial statements (e.g., required activities, financial statements and financial statement components). |
| | | ✓ | | | Prepare the government-wide statement of net position for a state or local government from trial balances and supporting documentation. |
| | | ✓ | | | Prepare the government-wide statement of activities for a state or local government from trial balances and supporting documentation. |
| 2. Governmental funds financial statements | ✓ | | | | Identify and recall basic concepts and principles associated with governmental fund financial statements (e.g., required funds, financial statements and financial statement components). |
| | | ✓ | | | Prepare the statement of revenues, expenditures and changes in fund balances for the governmental funds of a state or local government from trial balances and supporting documentation. |
| | | ✓ | | | Prepare the balance sheet for the governmental funds of a state or local government from trial balances and supporting documentation. |

Uniform CPA Examination Blueprints: Financial Accounting and Reporting (FAR)   FAR24

Financial Accounting and Reporting (FAR)

## Area IV – State and Local Governments (5-15%)
(continued)

| Content group/topic | Skill | | | | Representative task |
|---|---|---|---|---|---|
| | Remembering and Understanding | Application | Analysis | Evaluation | |
| **B. Format and content of the financial section of the comprehensive annual financial report (CAFR)** (continued) | | | | | |
| 3. Proprietary funds financial statements | > | | | | Identify and recall basic concepts and principles associated with proprietary fund financial statements (e.g., required funds, financial statements and financial statement components). |
| | | > | | | Prepare the statement of revenues, expenses and changes in fund net position for the proprietary funds of a state or local government from trial balances and supporting documentation. |
| | | > | | | Prepare the statement of net position for the proprietary funds of a state or local government from trial balances and supporting documentation. |
| | | > | | | Prepare the statement of cash flows for the proprietary funds of a state or local government. |
| 4. Fiduciary funds financial statements | > | | | | Identify and recall basic concepts and principles associated with fiduciary fund financial statements (e.g., required funds, financial statements and financial statement components). |
| | | > | | | Prepare the statement of changes in fiduciary net position for the fiduciary funds of a state or local government from trial balances and supporting documentation. |
| | | > | | | Prepare the statement of net position for the fiduciary funds of a state or local government from trial balances and supporting documentation. |
| 5. Notes to financial statements | > | | | | Recall the disclosure requirements for the notes to the basic financial statements of state and local governments. |
| 6. Management's discussion and analysis | > | | | | Recall the objectives and components of management's discussion and analysis in the comprehensive annual financial report for state and local governments. |

Uniform CPA Examination Blueprints: Financial Accounting and Reporting (FAR)

Financial Accounting and Reporting (FAR)

## Area IV – State and Local Governments (5–15%) (continued)

| Content group/topic | Skill | | | | Representative task |
|---|---|---|---|---|---|
| | Remembering and Understanding | Application | Analysis | Evaluation | |
| **B. Format and content of the financial section of the comprehensive annual financial report (CAFR)** *(continued)* | | | | | |
| 7. Budgetary comparison reporting | > | | | | Recall the objectives and components of budgetary comparison reporting in the comprehensive annual financial report for state and local governments. |
| 8. Required supplementary information (RSI) other than management's discussion and analysis | > | | | | Recall the objectives and components of required supplementary information other than management's discussion and analysis in the comprehensive annual financial report for state and local governments. |
| 9. Financial reporting entity, including blended and discrete component units | > | | | | Recall the criteria for classifying an entity as a component unit of a state or local government and the financial statement presentation requirements (discrete or blended). |
| **C. Deriving government-wide financial statements and reconciliation requirements** | | | | | |
| | | > | | | Prepare worksheets to convert the governmental fund financial statements to the governmental activities reported in the government-wide financial statements. |
| | | > | | | Prepare the schedule to reconcile the total fund balances and the net change in fund balances reported in the governmental fund financial statements to the net position and change in net position reported in the government-wide financial statements. |

Uniform CPA Examination Blueprints: Financial Accounting and Reporting (FAR)

Financial Accounting and Reporting (FAR)

## Area IV – State and Local Governments (5-15%)
(continued)

D. Typical items and specific types of transactions and events: measurement, valuation, calculation and presentation in governmental entity financial statements

| Content group/topic | Remembering and Understanding | Application | Analysis | Evaluation | Representative task |
|---|:---:|:---:|:---:|:---:|---|
| 1. Net position and components thereof | | ✓ | | | Calculate the net position balances (unrestricted, restricted and net investment in capital assets) for state and local governments and prepare journal entries. |
| 2. Fund balances and components thereof | | ✓ | | | Calculate the fund balances (assigned, unassigned, nonspendable, committed and restricted) for state and local governments and prepare journal entries. |
| 3. Capital assets and infrastructure assets | ✓ | | | | Identify capital assets reported in the government-wide financial statements of state and local governments. |
| | | ✓ | | | Calculate the net general capital assets balance for state and local governments and prepare journal entries (initial measurement and subsequent depreciation and amortization). |
| 4. General and proprietary long-term liabilities | ✓ | | | | Identify general and proprietary long-term liabilities reported in the government-wide financial statements of state and local governments. |
| | | ✓ | | | Calculate the total indebtedness to be reported in the government-wide financial statements of a state or local government. |
| | | ✓ | | | Calculate the net general long-term debt balance for state and local governments and prepare journal entries (debt issuance, interest payments, issue premiums or issue discounts). |
| 5. Interfund activity, including transfers | | ✓ | | | Prepare eliminations of interfund activity in the government-wide financial statements of state and local governments. |
| | | ✓ | | | Prepare journal entries to recognize interfund activity within state and local governments. |

Uniform CPA Examination Blueprints: Financial Accounting and Reporting (FAR)

FAR27

BL–22

© Becker Professional Education Corporation. All rights reserved.

# Area IV – State and Local Governments (5–15%) (continued)

D. Typical items and specific types of transactions and events: measurement, valuation, calculation and presentation in governmental entity financial statements (continued)

| Content group/topic | Remembering and Understanding | Application | Analysis | Evaluation | Representative task |
|---|---|---|---|---|---|
| 6. Nonexchange revenue transactions | | ✓ | | | Calculate the amount of nonexchange revenue to be recognized by state and local governments using the modified accrual basis of accounting and prepare journal entries. |
| | | ✓ | | | Calculate the amount of nonexchange revenue to be recognized by state and local governments using the accrual basis of accounting and prepare journal entries. |
| 7. Expenditures and expenses | | ✓ | | | Calculate expenditures to be recognized under the modified accrual basis of accounting (paid from available fund financial resources) for state and local governments and prepare journal entries. |
| | | ✓ | | | Calculate expenses to be recognized under the accrual basis of accounting for state and local governments and prepare journal entries. |
| 8. Special items | ✓ | | | | Identify transactions that require presentation as special items in government-wide financial statements for state and local governments. |
| 9. Budgetary accounting and encumbrances | ✓ | | | | Recall and explain the types of budgets used by state and local governments. |
| | | ✓ | | | Prepare journal entries to record budgets (original and final) of state and local governments. |
| | | ✓ | | | Prepare journal entries to record encumbrances of state and local governments. |
| 10. Other financing sources and uses | | ✓ | | | Calculate the amount to be reported as other financing sources and other financing uses in the governmental funds financial statements. |

## NOTES

# Glossary
# FAR

**Account Analysis Format:** An account analysis format is an analysis format for any balance sheet account. It has the general format of beginning balance, add something, subtract something, and ending balance. An account analysis format can readily be used to solve for any of these four amounts when the others are known or can be calculated. The amounts to be added or the amounts to be subtracted or both may be single or multiple amounts.

**Accounting Alternative:** In 2014, the Financial Accounting Standards Board (FASB) started issuing Accounting Standards Updates (ASUs) that provide simplified accounting alternatives for some or all private companies. These accounting alternatives reflect decisions reached by the Private Company Council (PCC) and endorsed by the FASB. An example is the accounting alternative for goodwill, issued in early 2014.

**Accounting Principles Board (APB) Opinions:** APB Opinions were published by the Accounting Principles Board from 1959 to 1973. APB Opinions that were not superseded are included in the FASB Accounting Standards Codification.

**Accounting Research Bulletins (ARB):** Accounting Research Bulletins were published by the AICPA's Committee on Accounting Procedure from 1939 to 1959. Accounting Research Bulletins that were not superseded are incorporated in the FASB Accounting Standards Codification.

**Accounts Receivable:** Accounts receivable are oral promises to pay debts. They are generally classified as current assets and also either as trade receivables (accounts receivable from purchasers of goods and services) or nontrade receivables (accounts receivable from persons other than customers, such as advances to employees, tax refunds, etc.). *See also* current assets *and* notes receivable.

**Accounts Receivable Turnover:** The accounts receivable turnover ratio is sales (net) divided by average accounts receivable (net).

**Accretion Expense:** Accretion expense is the increase in the ARO liability due to the passage of time calculated using the appropriate accretion rate. The accretion expense is added to the ARO liability each period. *See also* asset retirement obligation (ARO).

**Accrual Accounting:** Accrual accounting is required by U.S. GAAP and IFRS. Revenues are recognized when the performance obligation is satisfied and expenses are recognized in the same period as the related revenue, not necessarily in the period in which the cash is received or expended by the company. *See also* deferral *and* matching principle.

**Accrued Expenses:** Accrued expenses (accrued liabilities) are expenses recognized or incurred through the passage of time (or other criteria) but not yet paid by the entity (accrued interest payable, accrued wages, etc.). *See also* deferred charges *and* prepaid expenses *and* estimated liabilities *and* accrued liability.

**Accrued Liability:** An accrued liability (accrued expense) is an expense recognized or incurred (through the passage of time or other criteria) but not yet paid. *See also* estimated liabilities *and* accrued expenses.

© Becker Professional Education Corporation. All rights reserved.

**Accumulated Benefit Obligation (ABO):** The accumulated benefit obligation is the actuarial present value of pension benefits attributed by a formula based on current and past compensation levels. ABO differs from PBO only in that ABO includes no assumptions about future compensation levels and uses current salaries.

**Accumulated Depreciation:** Accumulated depreciation is the depreciation accumulated to date for fixed assets. It is a contra-asset to fixed assets. *See also* fixed assets.

**Accumulated Other Comprehensive Income:** Accumulated other comprehensive income is a component of equity that includes the total of other comprehensive income for the current period and previous periods. Comprehensive income for the current period is "closed" to this account. Accumulated other comprehensive income is the parallel to retained earnings for items of other comprehensive income. *See also* comprehensive income *and* other comprehensive income *and* retained earnings.

**Accumulated Postretirement Benefit Obligation (APBO):** The APBO is the present value of future postretirement benefits that have vested as of the measurement date.

**Acquisition Method:** The method used under U.S. GAAP and IFRS to account for the acquisition of a subsidiary. Under the acquisition method, the acquirer recognizes all acquired assets and liabilities and any noncontrolling interest at fair value.

**Activity Classification:** Activity classification is the classification of governmental expenditures by specific activity. The activity can be an event, a task, or a unit of work with a specific purpose. *See also* function (program) classification *and* character classification.

**Actual Return on Plan Assets:** The actual return on (pension) plan assets is the return on the assets held by a pension plan. Actual return can be calculated based on the fair value of plan assets at the beginning and the end of the period, adjusted for employer contributions and benefit payments. *See also* expected return on plan assets.

**Additional Paid-in Capital:** Additional paid-in capital is generally contributed capital in excess of par or stated value. It can also arise from many other different types of transactions. Examples include the sale of treasury stock at a "gain," the issuance of liquidating dividends, the conversion of bonds, and the declaration of a small stock dividend. Additional paid-in capital from these sources may be aggregated and shown as one amount on the balance sheet. *See also* common stock *and* retained earnings.

**Additions:** In fixed asset accounting, additions increase the quantity or improve the quality of fixed assets and are capitalized. *See also* improvements *and* replacements *and* repairs.

**Agency Transaction:** Agency transactions consist of resources received by a not-for-profit organization over which the organization has little or no discretion or variance power. *See also* variance power.

**Allowance Method:** Under the allowance method of accounting for bad debts, an estimate is made of the accounts receivable that will be written off and that amount is charged to bad debts expense for the period. The allowance method is GAAP because it matches the bad debts expense to the sales revenue that generated it. *See also* direct write-off method *and* bad debt expense.

**Amortization:** Amortization is the allocation of the cost of an asset over its useful life. Amortization of fixed assets is called depreciation, and amortization of wasting assets is called depletion. *See also* intangible assets.

**Annuity Due:** An annuity due (annuity in advance) is an annuity with payments at the beginning of the period. *See also* ordinary annuity.

**Antidilution:** For EPS calculations, the results of an assumed conversion should be used only if it results in dilution (reduces EPS). The results of an assumed conversion should not be used if it is antidilutive (increases EPS). *See also* diluted earnings per share.

**Appropriated Retained Earnings:** Appropriated retained earnings is that portion of retained earnings that has been appropriated/designated for some purpose. Appropriations of retained earnings are a means of disclosure, but they do restrict the dividends that can be declared. *See also* retained earnings *and* unappropriated retained earnings.

**Appropriations:** Appropriations (which can be thought of as estimated expenditures) is the budgetary account that is credited at the beginning of the year. *See also* estimated revenues *and* budgetary fund balance *and* expenditures.

**Assets:** Assets are probable future economic benefits to be received as a result of past transactions or events. Valuation accounts may be used to show reductions to or increases in an asset that reflect adjustments beyond the historical cost or carrying amount of the asset. *See also* liabilities *and* equity.

**Asset Group:** For discontinued operations reporting, an asset group is a collection of assets to be disposed of together as a group in a single (disposal) transaction and the liabilities directly associated with those assets that will be transferred in that same transaction. *See also* component of an entity *and* held for sale.

**Asset Retirement Obligation (ARO):** A legal obligation associated with the retirement of a tangible long-lived asset that results from the acquisition, construction, or development and/or normal operation of a long-lived asset, except for certain lease obligations (minimum lease payment and contingent rentals).

**Asset Turnover:** The asset turnover ratio is net sales divided by average total assets.

**Assigned Fund Balance:** Fund balance resources associated with assets the government intends to obligate but has not formally committed.

**Authorized Shares:** Authorized shares is the number of shares of common stock that are authorized for a corporation to issue. The number of authorized shares is disclosed. *See also* issued shares *and* outstanding shares.

**Available-for-Sale Debt Securities:** Available-for-sale debt securities are those not meeting the definitions of the other classifications (trading or held-to-maturity). Debt securities classified as available-for-sale are reported as either current assets or non-current assets, depending on intent. *See also* trading debt securities *and* held-to-maturity debt securities.

**Bad Debt Expense:** Bad debt expense is the amount charged to income for the period for bad debts. It is also called doubtful accounts expense. *See also* allowance method *and* percentage of accounts receivable at year-end method.

**Basic Earnings per Share:** For an organization with a simple capital structure, the formula for basic earnings per share is the income available to common shareholders divided by the weighted average number of common shares outstanding. *See also* diluted earnings per share.

**Basic Financial Statements:** For governmental organizations, the basic financial statements are the government-wide financial statements, the fund financial statements, and the notes to the financial statements. *See also* government-wide financial statements *and* fund financial statements.

**Basket Purchase:** A basket purchase is a purchase of two or more assets for a single price. The single price must be allocated to the individual assets purchased.

**Blended Presentation:** Some component units are so intertwined with the primary government that they are, in substance, the same as the primary government. In these cases, blended presentation is preferred. The blended presentation combines financial information with the primary government. Financial information of the component units is not presented in separate columns. *See also* financial reporting entity *and* component unit *and* discrete presentation.

**Board-Designated Endowment Fund:** An endowment fund created by a not-for-profit entity's governing board by designating a portion of its net assets without donor restrictions to be invested to provide income for a long but not necessarily specified period. Board-designated endowments are also referred to as funds functioning as an endowment or quasi-endowment funds. *See also* endowment fund.

**Bond Indenture:** A bond indenture describes the contract between the issuer (the borrower) and bondholders (the lenders). *See also* stated interest rate.

**Bond Issuance Costs:** Bond issuance costs are the transaction costs of a bond issue. Examples are legal fees, accounting fees, underwriting commissions, and printing. Under U.S. GAAP and IFRS, bond issue costs decrease the carrying value of the bond and are amortized using the effective interest method.

**Bond Selling Price:** The bond selling price is the sum of the present value of the future principal amount plus the total present value of the future interest amounts, all discounted at the prevailing effective interest rate. The same procedure is used to value a bond at any other date (not necessarily the date of sale of the bond). Depending on the relationship of the bond's stated rate to the effective interest rate (at the time, for bonds of similar risk), the bond may sell at a premium or a discount. *See also* effective interest rate *and* premium *and* discount.

**Book Value per Common Share:** Book value per common share measures the amount that common shareholders would receive for each share of common stock if all assets were sold at their book (carrying) values and all creditors were paid.

**Budgetary Accounting:** Budgetary accounting is used to control expenditures and to account for the levy of taxes sufficient to cover estimated expenditures. The major features of budgetary accounting are the use of budgetary accounts and the use of encumbrances. *See also* encumbrances.

**Budgetary Accounts:** Budgetary accounts are estimated accounts that are the opposite (in terms of natural debits and credits) from real or actual accounts. Budgetary accounts are normally posted only twice a year—once at the beginning of the year and again at the end of the year. *See also* encumbrances.

**Budgetary Fund Balance:** Budgetary fund balance is the account that is credited when estimated revenues and transfers-in for the year are greater than appropriations and transfers-out for the year. It is debited when estimated revenues and transfers-in for the year are less than appropriations and transfers-out for the year. *See also* appropriations *and* transfers-in *and* transfers-out.

**Business (as used in discontinued operations):** An integrated set of activities and assets that is conducted and managed for the purpose of providing a return to investors or other owners, members, or participants.

**Business-Type Activities:** Business-type activities in governmental accounting are normally financed by fees. *See also* governmental activities.

**Call Option:** Gives the holder the right to buy from the option writer at a specified price during a specified period of time.

**Capital and Related Financing Activities:** For governmental organizations, a statement of cash flows has four types of activities, instead of the three categories in commercial organizations. The normal financing activities are divided into capital and related financing activities and noncapital financing activities. Capital asset purchases are reported as financing activities rather than investing activities. *See also* financing activities and investing activities.

**Capital Grants:** Capital grants are grants for capital expenditures.

**Capital Grants and Contributions:** Capital grants and contributions are mandatory and voluntary non-exchange transactions with other governments, organizations, or individuals that are restricted for use in a particular program for capital expenditures. *See also* operating grants and contributions.

**Capital Projects Fund:** Capital projects funds are set up to account for resources used for the acquisition or construction of major capital assets by a governmental unit, except those projects financed by an enterprise fund. *See also* general fund *and* special revenue fund *and* debt service fund *and* permanent fund *and* custodial trust fund.

**Capital Stock:** Legal capital is the amount of capital that must be retained by a corporation for the protection of creditors. The par or stated value of both preferred and common stock is legal capital and is frequently referred to as capital stock. *See also* par value (of stock) *and* common stock *and* preferred stock.

**Capitalization of Interest Period:** The capitalization of interest period is the period during which construction period interest is capitalized. The period begins when expenditures for the asset have been made, when activities necessary to get the asset ready for its intended use are in progress, and when interest costs are being incurred. The period ends when the asset is substantially complete and ready for its intended use. *See also* construction period interest *and* weighted average of accumulated expenditures.

**Cash:** Cash includes both currency and demand or similar deposits with banks and/or other financial institutions. Cash may be either restricted for some special purpose or unrestricted. *See also* cash equivalents *and* restricted cash.

**Cash Conversion Cycle:** The cash conversion cycle is days in inventory plus days sales in accounts receivable minus days of payables outstanding.

**Cash Discount:** A cash discount is a discount for early payment, generally based on a percentage of the sales price. For example, a discount of 2/10, n/30 offers the purchaser a discount of 2 percent of the sales price if payment is made within 10 days. If the discount is not taken, the entire (gross) amount is due in 30 days. Sales may be recorded either on a gross basis or a net basis with respect to cash discounts. *See also* gross method (of recording sales) *and* net method (of recording sales) *and* trade discounts.

**Cash Dividend:** A dividend is a pro rata distribution by a corporation based on the shares of a particular class of stock and usually represents a distribution of earnings. Cash dividends are the most common type of dividend distribution, although there are many other types. Dividends are paid only on authorized, issued, and outstanding shares; they are not paid on treasury stock. *See also* property dividend *and* retained earnings *and* stock dividend.

**Cash Equivalents:** Cash equivalents include cash and short-term, highly liquid investments that are both readily convertible to cash and so near their maturity when acquired (90 days or less from the date of purchase) that they present insignificant risk of changes in value. *See also* cash.

**Cash Flow Hedge:** A cash flow hedge is a financial instrument designated as hedging exposure to variability in expected future cash flows attributed to a particular risk. Gains/losses on the effective portion of a cash flow hedge are deferred and reported as a component of other comprehensive income until the cash flows associated with the hedged item are realized. Gains/losses on the ineffective portion of a cash flow hedge are reported in current income. *See also* derivative *and* fair value hedge *and* foreign currency hedge.

**Cash-Generating Unit:** The smallest identifiable group of assets that generates cash inflows that are largely independent of the cash inflows from other assets or groups of assets. Under IFRS, goodwill impairment is analyzed at the cash-generating unit level.

**Change in Accounting Entity:** A change in accounting entity occurs when the entity being reported on has changed composition. Examples include consolidated or combined financial statements that are presented in place of statements of the individual companies and changes in the companies included in the consolidated or combined financial statements from year to year.

**Change in Accounting Estimate:** A change in accounting estimate occurs when it is determined that an estimate previously used was incorrect. Changes in accounting estimate are reported prospectively in the current period and future periods if the change affects both. Note that a change in depreciation method is reported as a change in accounting estimate.

**Change in Accounting Principle:** An accounting principle may be changed only if the alternative principle is preferable and more fairly presents the information. Changes in accounting principle are normally reported using the cumulative effect approach and are reported retrospectively as a change to the opening balance of retained earnings if the cumulative effect can be determined. Changes in accounting principle are reported net of tax.

**Character Classification:** Character classification refers to determining the basis of the fiscal period the expenditures are presumed to benefit. The major character classifications are current expenditures, capital outlays, debt service, and inter-governmental. *See also* function (program) classification *and* activity classification.

**Collateral Trust Bond:** A collateral trust bond is a bond that is secured by financial assets like stocks or bonds. *See also* debenture *and* mortgage bond *and* convertible bond.

**Committed Fund Balance:** Fund balance resources associated with assets obligated by a formal action of the government's highest decision-making authority. Encumbered appropriations are not displayed as committed fund balance.

**Commodity-Backed Bond:** A commodity-backed bond (also known as an asset-linked bond) is a bond that is redeemable either in cash or a stated volume of a commodity, whichever is greater.

**Common Stock:** Common stock is the basic ownership interest in a corporation. Common shareholders bear the ultimate risk of loss and receive the ultimate benefits of success, but they are not guaranteed dividends or assets upon dissolution. Common shareholders generally control management. They have the right to vote, the right to share in earnings of the corporation, a preemptive right to a proportionate share of any additional common stock issued, and the right to share in assets upon liquidation after satisfaction of creditors' claims and those of preferred shareholders. *See also* preferred stock *and* additional paid-in capital *and* retained earnings.

**Comparability:** Comparability is the quality of information that enables financial statement users to identify similarities in and differences between two sets of economic phenomena. Comparability allows users to compare the information with similar information for other business enterprises. *See also* consistency.

**Compensated Absences:** Compensated absences are accrued if all of the criteria for accrual are satisfied. The criteria include (1) the employee has performed the services to which the vacation or sick pay is attributable; (2) the liability is vested or accumulated; (3) payment is probable; and (4) the amount can be reasonably estimated. The accrual of nonvesting but accumulating sick pay is not required.

**Compensatory Stock Option Plan:** A compensatory stock option plan is one that is intended to compensate employees. *See also* stock option *and* noncompensatory stock purchase plan.

**Completed Contract Accounting:** Under U.S. GAAP, the completed contract method is used to account for long-term construction contracts when contract costs cannot be reasonably estimated. Under the completed contract method, income is recognized only upon completion of the contract.

**Complex Capital Structure:** A complex capital structure is one that is not a simple capital structure. An entity has a complex capital structure when it has securities that can potentially be converted to common stock and would therefore dilute (reduce) EPS (of common stock). *See also* simple capital structure.

**Component Depreciation:** Component depreciation is depreciation of individual identifiable pieces of a fixed asset (or group of fixed assets). Component depreciation is required under IFRS. *See also* composite depreciation.

**Component of an Entity:** For discontinued operations reporting, a component of an entity is a part of an entity (the lowest level) for which operations and cash flows can be clearly distinguished, both operationally and for financial reporting purposes, from the rest of the entity. A component of an entity may be an operating segment, a reportable segment (as those terms are defined in segment reporting), a reporting unit (as that term is defined in goodwill impairment testing), a subsidiary, or an asset group. *See also* asset group *and* held for sale *and* discontinued operations.

**Component Unit:** A component unit of a primary government is a legally separate organization for which the elected officials of the primary government are financially accountable. It may also be a separate organization, but its nature and the significance of its relationship with the primary government are such that exclusion of the unit's financial information would cause the primary government's financial statements to be misleading or incomplete. *See also* financial reporting entity *and* primary government *and* special-purpose governmental unit.

**Composite Depreciation:** Composite depreciation is the process of averaging the economic lives of a number of dissimilar property units and depreciating the entire class of assets over a single life, thus simplifying record keeping of assets and depreciation calculations. It is a specialized depreciation accounting method in which no gain or loss is recognized when one asset of the group is sold or retired. *See also* group depreciation.

**Comprehensive Allocation:** Under comprehensive (income tax) allocation, interperiod tax allocation is applied to all temporary differences. The liability method requires that either income taxes payable or a deferred tax liability (asset) be recorded for all tax consequences of the current period. *See also* interperiod tax allocation *and* temporary difference *and* permanent difference.

**Comprehensive Annual Financial Report (CAFR):** The CAFR includes the basic financial statements and required supplementary information, an introductory section, and a statistical section. *See also* basic financial statements.

**Comprehensive Income:** Comprehensive income is the change in equity (net assets) of a business enterprise during a period from transactions and other events and circumstances from nonowner sources. It includes all changes in equity during a period except those resulting from investments by owners and distributions to owners. *See also* other comprehensive income *and* accumulated other comprehensive income.

**Computer Software Developed for Internal Use:** Under U.S. GAAP, the cost of computer software developed for internal use only is divided into categories, and the accounting for each category is different. Cost incurred during the preliminary project state and cost incurred for training and maintenance are expensed. Cost incurred after the preliminary project state and for upgrades and enhancements, including the direct cost of materials and services, the cost of employees directly associated with the project, and interest cost incurred for the project are capitalized.

**Computer Software Development Costs:** Under U.S. GAAP, the costs of computer software to be sold, leased, or licensed are separated into categories, and the accounting for each category is different. Costs (coding, testing, and producing product masters) incurred after technological feasibility has been established are capitalized and amortized. Costs incurred to actually produce the software are inventoried. *See also* technological feasibility.

**Concentration of Credit Risk:** Credit risk is the risk that the other party to a transaction (counterparty) will partially or completely fail to perform. A concentration of credit risk exists if a number of counterparties are engaged in similar activities and have similar economic characteristics that would cause their ability to meet contractual obligations to be similarly affected by changes in economic or other conditions. Concentrations of credit risk are disclosed. *See also* market risk.

**Conditional Promise:** A conditional promise to give is a transaction that depends on an occurrence of a future and uncertain event. Recognition does not occur until the conditions are substantially met (or when it can be determined that the chances of not meeting the conditions are remote) and the promise becomes unconditional. Good faith deposits that accompany a conditional promise are accounted for as a refundable advance in the liability section of the statement of financial position. *See also* contribution *and* unconditional promise.

**Conservatism Principle:** When selecting alternative accounting methods, the method that is least likely to overstate assets (and revenues/gains) and understate liabilities (and expenses/losses) in the current period is selected.

**Consigned Goods:** In a consignment arrangement, the seller (the consignor) delivers goods to an agent (the consignee) to hold and sell on the consignor's behalf. The consignor includes the consigned goods in its inventory because title and risk of loss is retained by the consignor even though the consignee possesses the goods.

**Consistency:** In order for financial statement users to be able to compare the performance of an organization in one period with the performance of the same organization in another period, consistent accounting policies and procedures must be applied by the organization from period to period. This does not mean that the organization cannot change accounting policies if the new method more fairly presents the information; however, the effect of the change is accounted for and disclosed in the financial statements. *See also* comparability.

**Consolidated Financial Statements:** Consolidated financial statements represent the results of operations, cash flows, and financial position of a single entity, even if multiple legal entities are involved. The presumption is that consolidated financial statements are more meaningful than parent company financial statements and/or parent company financial statements together with separate subsidiary financial statements.

**Consolidation:** Consolidation is the combination of the financial statements of two or more entities into a single set of financial statements representing a single economic unit. The cost method, the equity method, and consolidation are the three methods of accounting for intercompany investments, depending on the amount of control. *See also* consolidated financial statements *and* intercompany transactions *and* cost method *and* equity method.

**Construction Period Interest:** Construction period interest is interest incurred during the construction period for a fixed asset or special order goods. Construction period interest during the capitalization of interest period is capitalized. *See also* weighted average of accumulated expenditures *and* capitalization of interest period.

**Consumption Method:** For certain governmental fund expenditures, the consumption method may be used. With the consumption method, supplies and prepaid amounts, such as prepaid insurance, and inventory are booked into a current asset account when the purchase is made. Any amount on hand at the end of the period is removed from the current asset account and treated as an expenditure. There must be a reservation of fund balance for the amount in the current asset account. *See also* purchase method.

**Contingency:** A contingency is an existing condition, situation, or set of circumstances involving varying degrees of uncertainty that may result in the increase or decrease in an asset or the incurrence or avoidance of a liability. *See also* gain contingency *and* loss contingency.

**Contingent Shares:** Contingent shares (contingently issuable shares) do not require cash consideration and depend on some future event or on certain conditions being met. Contingent shares (that are dilutive) are also included in the calculation of basic earnings per share if (and as of the date) all conditions for issuance are met. *See also* basic earnings per share.

**Contribution:** A contribution is an unconditional transfer of cash or assets (collection is certain) to a new owner (title passes) in a manner that is voluntary (the donor is under no obligation to donate) and is nonreciprocal (the donor gets nothing in exchange). *See also* unconditional promise *and* conditional promise.

**Contributions With Donor Restrictions:** A contribution may be restricted by the donor. Donor-imposed restrictions limit the use of contributed assets. They are recognized as revenues, gains, and other support in the period received and as assets, decreases of liabilities, or expenses depending on the form of the benefits received. May also be referred to as donor-restricted support. *See also* contributions without donor restrictions.

**Contributions Without Donor Restrictions:** Unconditional promises to contribute in the future are reported as restricted support (implied time restriction) at the present value of the estimated future cash flows using a discount rate commensurate with the risks involved. If the unconditional promises are expected to be collected or paid in less than one year, they may be measured at net realizable value since that amount is a reasonable estimate of fair value. *See also* contributions with donor restrictions.

**Contributory Plan:** A contributory plan is a plan to which employees are required to contribute. *See also* noncontributory plan.

**Control:** For consolidation purposes, an investor is considered to have parent status when control over an investee is established or more than 50 percent of the voting stock of the investee has been acquired. *See also* significant influence.

**Conventional Retail Inventory Method:** The conventional retail inventory method approximates the results that would be obtained by taking a physical inventory count and pricing the goods at the lower of cost or market. Subtracting the markdowns from the total available for sale results in a lower cost complement percentage, which results in a lower ending inventory. This, in turn, results in an automatic lower of cost or market valuation.

**Convertible Bond:** A convertible bond is convertible into common stock of the debtor (generally) at the option of the bondholder. With a convertible bond, the bond must be surrendered to obtain the common stock. *See also* debenture *and* mortgage bond *and* collateral trust bond.

**Cost:** Cost is an amount (measured in money) expended for items such as capital assets, services (e.g., payroll), and merchandise received. Cost is the amount actually paid for something. *See also* unexpired cost *and* expenses.

**Cost Method:** An investor accounts for an investment in securities using the cost method if the investor does not have the ability to exercise significant influence over the investee (ownership of less than 20 percent is presumed to be a lack of significant influence). The rules of marketable equity securities are followed and the investment is generally carried at fair value through net income (FVTNI). *See also* equity method *and* investment in subsidiary *and* liquidating dividends.

**Cost Method (of Treasury Stock Accounting):** Under the cost method of treasury stock accounting, treasury shares are recorded and carried at their reacquisition cost. A gain or loss is determined when treasury stock is reissued or retired, and the original issue price and book value of the stock do not enter into the accounting. Additional paid-in capital from treasury stock is credited for gains and debited for losses when treasury stock is reissued at prices that differ from the original selling price. Losses may also decrease retained earnings if additional paid-in capital from treasury stock does not have a balance large enough to absorb the loss. Net income or retained earnings is never increased through treasury stock transactions. The cost method is required under IFRS. *See also* treasury stock *and* par value method (of treasury stock accounting).

**Cost Recovery Method:** The cost recovery method is a method of revenue recognition in which no profit is recognized on a sale until all costs have been recovered.

**Cumulative Effect of Change in Accounting Principle:** Most changes in accounting principle are reported using the cumulative effect approach. The cumulative effect is equal to the difference between the amount of beginning retained earnings in the period of change and what the retained earnings would have been if the accounting change had been retroactively applied to all prior affected periods. It includes direct effects and only those indirect effects that are entered in the accounting records. Changes in accounting principle are normally reported using the cumulative effect approach and are reported retrospectively as a change to the opening balance of retained earnings of the earliest year presented if the cumulative effect can be determined. *See also* change in accounting principle.

**Cumulative Preferred Stock:** The cumulative feature provides that all or part of the preferred dividend not paid in any year accumulates and must be paid in the future before dividends can be paid to common shareholders. The accumulated amount is referred to as dividends in arrears. The amount of dividends in arrears is not a legal liability, but it is disclosed in total and on a per share basis either parenthetically on the balance sheet or in the footnotes. *See also* preferred stock *and* noncumulative preferred stock.

**Current Assets:** Current assets are those resources that are reasonably expected to be realized in cash, sold, or consumed during the normal operating cycle of a business or one year, whichever is longer. *See also* current liabilities.

**Current Cost:** Current cost is the cost that would be incurred at the present time to replace an asset, the replacement cost or the lower recoverable amount. *See also* historical cost.

**Current Exchange Rate:** The current exchange rate is the exchange rate at the current date, or for immediate delivery of a currency. It is often referred to as the spot rate. *See also* exchange rate *and* forward exchange rate.

**Current Financial Resources Measurement Focus:** The current financial resources measurement focus seeks to value and report fund balances as a measure of available, spendable, or appropriable resources. Only current assets and current liabilities are included on the balance sheet. No fixed assets are reported. No non-current liabilities are reported. *See also* measurement focus *and* economic resources measurement focus *and* modified accrual basis of accounting.

**Current Income Tax Expense:** Current income tax expense/benefit is equal to the income taxes payable or refundable for the current year, as determined on the corporate tax return. *See also* deferred income tax expense *and* total income tax expense.

**Current Liabilities:** Current liabilities are obligations whose liquidation is reasonably expected to require the use of current assets or the creation of other current liabilities. Obligations for items that have entered the operating cycle are classified as current liabilities. The concept of current liabilities includes estimates or accrued amounts that are expected to be required to cover expenditures within the year for known obligations when the amount can be determined only approximately or where the specific person(s) to whom payment will be made is unascertainable. *See also* current assets.

**Current Method:** In foreign currency reporting, once all of the financial statements to be reported on are measured in their functional currencies, it is necessary to translate them to their reporting currency (provided that the functional currency is not the reporting currency). *See also* temporal method *and* functional currency *and* reporting currency.

**Current Ratio:** The current ratio is current assets divided by current liabilities. *See also* working capital *and* quick ratio *and* current assets *and* current liabilities.

**Curtailment:** In pension plan accounting, curtailments are events that reduce the expected remaining years of service for present employees or eliminate the accrual of defined benefits for future services of a significant number of employees. *See also* settlement.

**Custodial Trust Fund:** Custodial trust funds (or custodial funds) account for resources in the temporary custody of a governmental unit (taxes collected for another governmental entity). *See also* fiduciary funds *and* pension trust fund *and* private purpose trust fund *and* investment trust fund.

**Debenture:** A debenture is an unsecured bond. *See also* mortgage bond *and* collateral trust bond *and* convertible bond.

**Debt Security:** A debt security is any security that represents a creditor relationship with an entity. *See also* equity security.

**Debt Service Fund:** Debt service funds are set up to account for the accumulation of resources and the payment of interest and principal on all general obligation debt other than that serviced by enterprise funds or by special assessments in another fund. *See also* general fund *and* special revenue fund *and* capital projects fund *and* permanent fund.

**Debt/Equity Ratio:** The debt/equity ratio is total liabilities divided by total common stockholders' equity.

**Declaration Date:** The declaration date is the date the board of directors formally approves a dividend. On the declaration date, a liability is created (dividends payable) and retained earnings are reduced. *See also* record date.

**Declining Balance Depreciation:** Declining balance depreciation is an accelerated method of depreciation that provides higher depreciation in the early years of an asset's life and lower depreciation in the later years. The rate used is normally 150 percent or 200 percent of the straight-line rate; salvage value is not included in the calculation other than as a lower limit to the amount that can be depreciated. *See also* straight-line depreciation *and* sum-of-the-years'-digits depreciation *and* units-of-production depreciation.

**Deferral:** Deferral of revenues or expenses occurs when cash is received or expended but is not recognizable for financial statement purposes. Deferral typically results in the recognition of a liability or a prepaid expense. *See also* accrual accounting.

**Deferred Charges:** Deferred charges result from expenditures or accruals that cannot be charged to a tangible asset but that do pertain to future operations. Deferred charges are often referred to as long-term prepaid assets. *See also* prepaid expenses.

**Deferred Credits:** Deferred credits refers to when cash is received in advance of the recognition of the revenue. Examples are prepaid interest income (the cash is received in advance before the interest income is recognized) and prepaid rental income (the cash is received in advance before the rental income is recognized).

**Deferred Income Tax Expense:** Deferred income tax expense/benefit is equal to the change in the deferred tax liability or asset on the balance sheet from the beginning of the current year to the end of the current year. *See also* current income tax expense *and* total income tax expense.

**Deferred Inflow of Resources:** An acquisition of net assets by a government that is applicable to a future reporting period. Deferred inflows of resources have a negative effect on net position, but are not liabilities, and are reported as a separate subheading following liabilities but before equity.

**Deferred Outflow of Resources:** Consumption of net assets by a government that is applicable to a future reporting period. Deferred outflows of resources have a positive effect on net position that is similar to assets, but are not assets, and are reported as a separate subheading following assets but before liabilities.

**Deferred Tax Asset:** A deferred tax asset is the estimated future tax effect of temporary differences and carryforwards when future taxable income (and thus taxes payable) will be less than future financial accounting income (and thus income tax expense). All deferred tax assets may not be reported on the balance sheet because there may be a valuation allowance. *See also* valuation allowance.

**Deferred Tax Liability:** A deferred tax liability is the estimated future tax effect of temporary differences and carryforwards when future taxable income (and thus taxes payable) will be greater than future financial accounting income (and thus income tax expense). All deferred tax liabilities are reported on the balance sheet.

**Defined Benefit Plan:** In a defined benefit plan, the benefits that employees will receive at retirement are determined by a formula based on such factors as employee length of service and compensation. Contributions are computed using actuarial estimates of future benefit payments based on factors such as the employee's compensation levels at or near retirement, the number of years of employee service, the number of years until the employee retires, the number of years the plan expects to pay benefits after an employee retires, etc. It is the sponsoring organization's responsibility to ensure that contributions to the plan are sufficient to pay benefits as they come due.

**Defined Contribution Plan:** In a defined contribution plan, the contributions that the sponsoring organization makes to the plan are determined by a formula. Employees' retirement benefits are based solely on the amount of funds in the plan. A good example of a defined contribution plan is a 401(k) plan.

**Depletion:** Depletion is the allocation of the cost of wasting natural resources such as oil, gas, timber, and minerals to the production process. Cost depletion is GAAP; percentage depletion is not GAAP. *See also* depreciation *and* amortization.

**Depreciation:** Depreciation is the allocation of the cost of a fixed asset over its useful life. *See also* depletion *and* amortization.

**Derecognition:** In a transfer of financial assets or extinguishment of liabilities, derecognition is the removal of previously recognized items from the balance sheet. Derecognition of assets occurs when control over the assets has been surrendered, and derecognition of liabilities occurs when the liabilities have been extinguished. *See also* pledging of accounts receivable *and* factoring of accounts receivable.

**Derivative:** A derivative is a financial instrument for which the value or settlement amount is derived from the value of something else. A derivative has all three of these characteristics: It has one or more underlying and one or more notional amounts or payment provisions; it requires no initial net investment or one that is smaller than would be required for other types of similar contracts; and its terms require or permit a net settlement. Forwards, futures, option contracts, and swap contracts are examples of derivatives. *See also* financial instrument *and* underlying *and* notional amount *and* settlement amount *and* payment provision.

**Derived Tax Revenues:** Derived (non-exchange) tax revenues are taxes imposed on or derived from exchange transactions such as commercial sales (sales taxes), taxpayer income (income taxes), etc. *See also* imposed non-exchange revenues *and* government mandated non-exchange transactions *and* voluntary non-exchange transactions.

**Diluted Earnings per Share:** Diluted earnings per share is the (income available to the common stock shareholder + interest on dilutive securities) divided by the weighted average number of common shares outstanding assuming all dilutive securities are converted to common stock. The objective of diluted earnings per share is to measure the performance of an entity over the reporting period while giving effect to all potentially dilutive common stock shares outstanding during the period. *See also* basic earnings per share.

**Direct Financing Lease:** Under U.S. GAAP, from the standpoint of the lessor, finance leases are divided into direct financing leases and sales-type leases. A direct financing lease is a lease that meets one of the five finance lease criteria and two other criteria and where there is no manufacturers' or dealers' profit. *See also* sales-type lease *and* finance lease (U.S. GAAP) *and* finance lease criteria *and* operating lease.

**Direct Method:** GAAP encourages enterprises to report cash flows from operating activities using the direct method by showing major classes of operating cash receipts and disbursements. A reconciliation of net income and net cash flows from operating activities is required in a separate schedule. *See also* indirect method *and* operating activities.

**Direct Write-off Method:** Under the direct write-off method of accounting for bad debts, an account receivable is written off and a bad debt is recognized when the account becomes uncollectible. The direct write-off method is not GAAP because it does not properly match the bad debt expense with the sales revenue that generated it. *See also* allowance method.

**Discontinued Operations:** Discontinued operations is a separate component of the income statement that is reported after income from continuing operations (I). Discontinued operations are reported net of tax. *See also* income from continuing operations *and* operating segment *and* reportable segment.

**Discount:** In bond accounting, bonds are sold at a discount if the market interest rate is higher than the stated interest rate. The bond has to sell at a discount because investors can obtain a higher interest rate on other investments. *See also* premium *and* stated interest rate *and* effective interest rate *and* par value (of a bond) *and* bond selling price.

**Discounted Notes Receivable:** Discounted notes receivable arise when the holder of the note endorses the note (with or without recourse) to a third party and receives cash. The difference between the cash received by the holder and the maturity value of the note is called the discount. *See also* notes receivable.

**Discrete Presentation:** Discrete presentation (separate presentation) is used when the criteria for blended presentation are not met. Most component units should use discrete presentation. Discrete presentation displays component units in separate columns. *See also* component unit *and* blended presentation.

**Dollar Value LIFO:** Under the regular LIFO method, inventory is measured in units and is priced at unit prices. Under the dollar value LIFO method, inventory is measured in dollars and is adjusted for changing price levels. When converting from LIFO inventory to dollar value LIFO, a price index is used to adjust the inventory value. *See also* LIFO method.

**Donated Collection Item:** Donated collection items are contributed works of art or historical treasures. They are not required to be recorded by the recipient not-for-profit organization if all of the following requirements are met: the item is part of a collection which is held for public viewing, exhibition, education, or research (and not for investment or financial gain); the collection is cared for, preserved, and protected by the organization; and the organization has a policy that requires any proceeds from the sale of donated items to be reinvested in other collection items.

**Donated Services:** Donated services received by a not-for-profit organization are generally not recorded because of the difficulty in placing a monetary value on donated services (and the absence of control over them). However, donated services are recorded as contribution revenue and expense at fair value if the services meet the following criteria: They create or enhance a nonfinancial asset (land, buildings, inventory, etc.) or they require specialized skills that the provider possesses and would otherwise have been purchased by the organization (attorney, accountant, doctor services, etc.).

**Donated Stock:** Donated stock is a corporation's own stock received as a donation from a shareholder. There is no change in total shareholders' equity as a result of the donation. The corporation should record donated stock at fair value.

**Donor-Imposed Restrictions:** Donor-imposed restrictions represent donor stipulations that specify a use for a contribution more specific than the broad limits associated with the nature of the not-for-profit organization, the environment in which it operates, or the purposes defined by the articles of incorporation. Donor-imposed restrictions may be temporary or perpetual in nature.

**Economic Resources Measurement Focus:** The economic resources measurement focus seeks to determine the costs of services and the efficiency and effectiveness with which invested capital has been used. All assets and all liabilities (current or non-current) are included on the balance sheet. Net position is analyzed and normally reported separately as restricted, unrestricted, and net investment in capital assets. Fixed assets are reported. Non-current liabilities are reported. *See also* measurement focus *and* current financial resources measurement focus.

**Effective Interest Method:** The effective interest method of bond amortization is a method of amortization that results in a constant rate of interest each period. Interest expense is calculated by multiplying the carrying amount of the bond at the beginning of the period by the effective interest rate. The difference between the interest expense and the cash paid for interest is the amortization for the period of the discount or premium. *See also* effective interest rate *and* discount *and* premium.

**Effective Interest Rate:** The effective or market interest rate is the rate of interest actually earned by the bondholders and is the rate of return for comparable bonds at the date of issuance. *See also* stated interest rate *and* par value (of a bond) *and* discount *and* premium *and* bond selling price.

**Enacted Tax Rate:** Measurement of deferred taxes is based on an applicable tax rate. This measurement requires using the enacted tax rate expected to apply to temporary differences in the periods the temporary differences are expected to be paid (liability) or realized (asset). *See also* temporary difference.

**Encumbrances:** Open purchase orders represent an encumbrance or reduction of the appropriations of a government. In order for governmental managers to effectively monitor the degree to which they have used their budgetary appropriations, governmental accounting systems reflect not only the expenditures but also the obligations to spend (purchase orders). This is done to prevent overspending of appropriations. *See also* expenditures *and* budgetary accounts.

**Endowment Fund:** An endowment fund is an established fund of assets to provide income for the maintenance of a not-for-profit entity. The use of the fund may be with or without donor-imposed restrictions. Endowment funds are generally established by donor-restricted gifts to provide a source of income either in perpetuity or for a specified period. *See also* board-designated endowment fund *and* underwater endowment fund.

**Enterprise Fund:** Enterprise funds are set up to account for the acquisition and operation of governmental facilities and services that are intended to be primarily (over 50 percent) self-supported by user charges. Examples of enterprise funds are those used for utilities (often water and sewer), airports, and transit systems. Enterprise funds are required when any one of three criteria is met: the activity of the fund is financed by debt secured by a pledge of fee revenue; laws require collection fees adequate to recover cover costs; or pricing policies are established to produce fees that recover costs. *See also* proprietary funds *and* internal service fund.

**Entity Assumption:** Under U.S. GAAP, it is assumed that economic activity can be accounted for only when considering an identifiable set of activities (a separate corporation, division, etc.). *See also* going concern assumption *and* monetary unit assumption *and* periodicity assumption *and* historical cost principle.

**Equity:** Equity is the residual interest in the assets of an entity that remains after deducting its liabilities. *See also* assets *and* liabilities.

**Equity Method:** The equity method is used to account for an investment in securities if significant influence is exercised by the investor over the investee. The critical criterion for using the equity method is that the investor exerts significant influence over the operating and financial policies of the investee. If no direct evidence of significant influence exists, ownership of 20 percent to 50 percent of the investee's voting stock is deemed to represent significant influence. *See also* cost method.

**Equity Method Goodwill:** Equity method goodwill is goodwill generated in an equity method investment. It is not separately identified as goodwill and is merely included as a part of the equity method investment. Equity method goodwill is not amortized or separately tested for impairment; instead it is tested for impairment as part of the equity method investment. *See also* goodwill (and goodwill impairment) *and* equity method.

**Equity Security:** An equity security is any security representing an ownership interest in an entity (common stock, preferred stock, and other forms of capital stock); the right to acquire ownership shares (stock warrants, rights, and call options); and the right to dispose of ownership shares (put options). Equity securities do not include preferred stock, treasury stock, convertible bonds, options contracts, futures contracts, forward contracts, leases, and normal trade accounts and notes receivable. *See also* debt security.

**Escheat Property:** Escheat property is property that has been forfeited as a result of the passage of time or process of law. *See also* private purpose trust fund.

**Estimated Liabilities:** Estimated liabilities represent the recognition of probable future charges that result from a prior act (the estimated liability for warranties, trading stamps, or coupons). They are not the same as accrued liabilities. *See also* accrued liability.

**Estimated Revenues:** Estimated revenues is the budgetary account that is debited at the beginning of the year. *See also* appropriations *and* budgetary fund balance.

**Exchange Rate:** The exchange rate is the price of one unit of a currency expressed in units of another currency – the rate at which two currencies would be exchanged at equal value. The exchange rate may be expressed either by a direct method (the domestic price for one unit of a foreign currency) or the indirect method (the foreign price of one unit of the domestic currency). *See also* current exchange rate *and* forward exchange rate.

**Exchange Revenue:** Exchange revenue is revenue recognized when goods and services are transferred. *See also* non-exchange revenue.

**Executory Costs:** Executory costs are amounts such as insurance, maintenance, and taxes paid in connection with leased property. Executory costs are not included in minimum lease payments.

**Exercise Price:** The exercise price (often called the strike price) of a stock option is the amount of money that must be exchanged for the stock to exercise a stock option. *See also* stock option *and* grant date.

**Expected Postretirement Benefit Obligation:** The present value of all future postretirement benefits expected to be paid as of the measurement date, including the amount that has vested (APBO) plus the present value of expected future benefits that have not yet vested.

**Expected Return on Plan Assets:** Expected return on (pension) plan assets is the return that is expected on pension plan assets at the beginning of the year. The expected return on plan assets is a component of net periodic pension cost. *See also* actual return on plan assets.

**Expendable Trust Fund:** Expendable trust funds (scholarship and endowment funds) are those for which principal and income may be expended in the course of their designated operations so that they are depleted by the end of their designated lives. Expendable trust funds are accounted for in special revenue funds. *See also* special revenue fund.

**Expenditures:** Expenditures are amounts expended for either current (operating) items or non-current (capital) items. In governmental accounting, there are no expenses. *See also* encumbrances.

**Expenses:** Expenses are outflows, uses of assets, or the incurring of liabilities from delivering goods or services as part of normal operations over a period of time. A loss is a cost expiration either not in the ordinary course of business (a loss on the sale of investment assets) or without the generation of revenue (an abandonment). *See also* revenues *and* gains *and* losses *and* cost.

**Expired Cost:** An expired cost is a cost that expires during the period because it has no future benefit. *See also* unexpired cost.

**External Investment Pool:** An external investment pool is an arrangement that commingles the money of more than one legally separate entity and invests that money in an investment portfolio. *See also* investment trust fund.

**Extinguishment of Debt:** An extinguishment of debt is a transaction in which the debtor pays the creditor and is relieved of its obligation for the liability or the debtor is legally released from being the primary obligor under the liability. *See also* in-substance defeasance.

**Face Value:** The face value of a bond is the par value of the bond. *See also* par value (of a bond).

**Factoring of Accounts Receivable:** Factoring of accounts receivable is the process by which accounts receivable are converted into cash by assigning/selling them to a factor either with or without recourse. If accounts receivable are assigned without recourse, the assignment is normally at a considerable discount. *See also* pledging of accounts receivable.

**Fair Value:** The price to sell an asset or transfer a liability in an orderly transaction between market participants at the measurement date.

**Fair Value Hedge:** A fair value hedge is a financial instrument designated as hedging exposure to changes in the fair value of an asset or liability or an identified portion thereof that is attributed to a particular risk. Gains/losses on such instruments as well as the offsetting losses/gains on the hedged item are recognized in earnings in the same accounting period. A fair value hedge must also be expected to be highly effective in offsetting fair value of the hedged item. *See also* derivative *and* cash flow hedge *and* foreign currency hedge.

**Fair Value Method:** When accounting for compensatory stock options, the compensation cost for a stock option is the fair value of the option at the grant date.

**Fair Value of Plan Assets:** The fair value of (pension) plan assets is the fair value of assets in the pension plan.

**Fair Value Option:** On specified election dates, entities may choose to measure eligible financial instruments at fair value. Under the fair value option, unrealized gains and losses are reported in earnings. The fair value option is irrevocable and is applied to individual financial instruments.

**FASB Accounting Standards Codification:** The single source of authoritative nongovernmental U.S. GAAP.

**Feedback Value:** Feedback value enables decision makers to confirm prior expectations or to adjust or correct the assessment made. *See also* relevance *and* predictive value *and* timeliness.

**Fiduciary Funds:** Fiduciary funds account for assets received when the government acts in the capacity of a trust or custodial fund. All fiduciary funds, except for certain pension liabilities and post-employment health care plans, utilize the full accrual basis of accounting and the economic resources measurement focus. *See also* pension trust fund *and* custodial trust fund *and* private purpose trust fund *and* investment trust fund.

**FIFO Method:** Under FIFO, the first costs inventoried are the first costs transferred to cost of goods sold. Ending inventory includes the most recently incurred costs; thus, the ending inventory balance approximates replacement cost. In periods of rising prices, income may be overstated because the FIFO method results in the highest ending inventory, the lowest costs of goods sold, and the highest net income (current costs are not matched with current revenues). *See also* specific identification method *and* weighted average method *and* moving average method *and* LIFO method.

**Finance Lease Criteria:** Under U.S. GAAP, one of five criteria must be satisfied for a lease to be a finance lease:

- Ownership transfers at the end of the lease.
- There is a written purchase option.
- The net present value of the minimum lease payments is greater than or equal to 90 percent of the fair value of the leased asset.
- Economic life (major part) of the underlying asset within lease term.
- Specialized asset such that it will not have an alternative use to lessor.

*See also* finance lease (U.S. GAAP) *and* operating lease.

**Finance Lease (U.S. GAAP):** From the standpoint of the lessee, a finance lease is a lease that transfers substantially all of the benefits and risks inherent in ownership of property to the lessee. A finance lease is in substance an installment purchase in the form of a lease. Both a right-of-use (ROU) asset and a liability are recorded. Under IFRS, a lease is classified as a finance lease by both the lessee and lessor when the lease transfers substantially all the risks and rewards of ownership to the lessee. *See also* operating lease *and* direct financing lease *and* sales-type lease *and* finance lease criteria.

**Financial Accounting Standards Board (FASB):** The FASB is the organization that currently establishes accounting standards. *See also* Statement of Financial Accounting Standard (SFAS) *and* Governmental Accounting Standards Board (GASB).

**Financial Instrument:** A financial instrument is cash, foreign currency, demand deposits, evidence of an ownership interest in an entity (stock certificates, partnership interests, and limited liability company interests), and contracts that result in an exchange of cash or ownership interests in an entity. Contracts either (1) impose on one entity a contractual obligation to deliver cash or another financial instrument to a second entity or to exchange other financial instruments on potentially unfavorable terms with the second entity or (2) convey to that second entity a contractual right to receive cash or another financial instrument from the first entity or to exchange other financial instruments on potentially favorable terms with the first entity. Financial instruments include derivatives. *See also* derivative.

**Financially Interrelated Organization:** Financially interrelated organizations are organizations related by both of the following characteristics: one organization has the ability to influence the operating and financial decisions of the other and one organization has an ongoing economic interest in the net assets of the other.

**Financial Reporting Entity:** The financial reporting entity consists of the primary government (general-purpose governmental units), organizations for which the primary government is financially accountable (special-purpose governmental units), and certain other specially defined organizations (component units). *See also* primary government *and* special-purpose governmental unit *and* component unit.

**Financing Activities:** Financing activities include obtaining resources from owners by issuing stock; providing owners with a return on their investment by paying dividends or repurchasing stock; obtaining resources from creditors by issuing bonds, notes, and other borrowings; and paying principal (not interest, which is part of the operating activities section) on amounts borrowed. *See also* operating activities *and* investing activities.

**Firm Purchase Commitment:** A firm purchase commitment is a legally enforceable agreement to purchase a specified amount of goods at some time in the future. All material firm purchase commitments are disclosed in either the financial statements or the notes thereto.

**Fiscal Accountability:** The focus of fund financial statements is to demonstrate that the government entity's actions in the current period have complied with public decisions concerning the raising and spending of public funds in the short-term (usually one budgetary cycle or one year). *See also* operational accountability *and* fund financial statements.

**Fixed Assets:** Fixed assets are assets that possess physical substance, that are acquired for use in operations and not for resale, and that are long term in nature and subject to depreciation. Fixed assets are categorized as land (used in operations and not an investment) and buildings and equipment. *See also* accumulated depreciation.

**FOB Destination:** Free on Board (FOB) destination means that the seller of the goods is required to deliver the goods to the destination point at the seller's expense. Goods shipped FOB destinations are included in the buyer's inventory upon receipt. *See also* inventory.

**FOB Shipping Point:** FOB shipping point means that the seller of the goods is required to deliver the goods to the shipping point at the seller's expense. Goods shipped FOB shipping point are included in the buyer's inventory upon shipment. *See also* inventory.

**Foreign Currency Hedge:** A foreign currency hedge is a financial instrument designated as hedging exposure to variability in foreign currency in a variety of foreign currency transactions. Gains and losses on changes in fair value of foreign currency transaction hedges entered into as fair value hedges are accounted for in the same manner as gains/losses on other fair value hedges—in earnings. Gains and losses on changes in fair value of foreign currency transactions entered into as cash flow hedges are accounted for in the same manner as gains/losses on cash flow hedges–in other comprehensive income for the effective portion. *See also* fair value hedge *and* cash flow hedge.

**Foreign Currency Transaction:** A foreign currency transaction is a transaction with a foreign entity (buying from and selling to) denominated in (to be settled in) a foreign currency. *See also* remeasurement.

**Foreign Currency Translation:** Foreign currency translation is the conversion of financial statements of a foreign entity into financial statements expressed in the domestic currency (the dollar).

**Form 6-K:** This SEC form is filed semiannually by foreign private issuers. This form is similar to the Form 10-Q and contains unaudited financial statements, interim period MD&A, and certain disclosures.

**Form 8-K:** This SEC form is filed to report major corporate events such as corporate asset acquisitions or disposals, changes in securities and trading markets, changes to accountants or financial statements, and changes in corporate governance or management.

**Form 10-K:** An SEC form that must be filed annually by U.S. registered companies (issuers). This form contains financial disclosures, including a summary of financial data, management's discussion and analysis (MD&A), and audited financial statements prepared using U.S. GAAP.

**Form 10-Q:** An SEC form that must be filed quarterly by U.S. registered companies (issuers). This form contains unaudited financial statements prepared using U.S. GAAP, interim period MD&A, and certain disclosures.

**Form 11-K:** The annual report of a company's employee benefit plan(s) that must be filed with the SEC.

**Forms 3, 4, and 5:** SEC forms that are required to be filed by directors, officers, or beneficial owners of more than 10 percent of a class of equity securities of a registered company.

**Forms 20-F and 40-F:** These forms must be filed with the SEC annually by foreign private issuers. Form 40-F is filed by specific Canadian companies registered with the SEC and Form 20-F is filed by other non-U.S. registrants. These forms are similar to Form 10-K and contain financial disclosures, including a summary of financial data, management's discussion and analysis (MD&A), and audited financial statements.

**Forward Contract:** Forward contracts are similar to futures contracts, except that they are privately negotiated between two parties with the assistance of an intermediary, rather than through a clearinghouse. Forward contracts do not have standardized notional amounts or settlement dates. The terms of a forward contract are established by the parties to the contract.

**Forward Exchange Contract:** A forward exchange contract is an agreement to exchange a fixed amount of currencies of different countries at a specified future date and rate.

**Forward Exchange Rate:** A forward exchange rate is the exchange rate existing now for exchanging two currencies at a specific future date, often referred to as the forward rate. *See also* exchange rate *and* current exchange rate.

**Foundations:** Foundations are private trusts and foundations that are organized for specific benefit to society (educational purposes, religious purposes, or for some other charitable purpose). *See also* health care organizations *and* voluntary health and welfare organizations.

**Franchise:** A franchise is the right to operate a particular business under a franchise agreement (license) for a fee. Franchise fees might be initial franchise fees or continuing franchise fees. Both franchisor and franchisee have specialized accounting rules.

**Full Accrual Basis of Accounting:** For governmental accounting, the full accrual basis of accounting is used with the economic resources measurement focus and is identical to the accounting methods used in commercial enterprises. Revenue is recognized when earned. Expenses are recognized when incurred. The full accrual basis of accounting is used by SE and PAPI funds. *See also* modified accrual basis of accounting.

**Full Disclosure Principle:** It is important that the user be given information that would make a difference in the decision process but not too much information so that the user is impeded in analyzing what is important.

**Functional Currency:** The functional currency is the currency of the primary economic environment in which an entity operates, usually the local currency or the reporting currency. *See also* reporting currency *and* translation *and* remeasurement.

**Functional Depreciation:** Functional depreciation arises from the obsolescence of an asset or the inadequacy of an asset to perform efficiently. *See also* physical depreciation.

**Function (Program) Classification:** Function (program) classification provides information on the overall purpose of expenditures. Function classification groups expenditures into the major services of the governmental entity. Program classification groups expenditures into activities, operations, or organizational units that are directed to the attainment of specific purposes or objectives. Both function and program are broad classifications. Examples of functions include public safety, highways, education, health and welfare, and general governmental services. Examples of programs are programs for the elderly, drug addiction, and education. *See also* activity classification *and* character classification.

**Fund:** A fund is a sum of money or other resource segregated for the purpose of carrying on a specific activity or attaining certain objectives in accordance with specific regulations, restrictions, or limitations, and constituting an independent fiscal and accounting entity. Each fund is a self-balancing set of accounts.

**Funded Plan:** A funded plan is one in which the sponsoring organization makes cash contributions to the plan. An overfunded plan is one in which plan assets exceed the plan liabilities, and an underfunded plan is one in which plan assets are less than plan liabilities. *See also* fair value of plan assets.

**Funded Status:** The difference between the fair value of a defined benefit pension plan's assets and the pension plan's projected benefit obligation (PBO). Under U.S. GAAP, the funded status is reported on the balance sheet as a non-current asset if the pension plan is overfunded, and as a current liability, non-current liability, or both if the pension plan is underfunded. Under IFRS, the funded status is disclosed in the notes to the financial statements.

**Fund Financial Statements:** In fund financial statements, major funds are shown individually, and nonmajor funds are shown in total. For governmental funds, the fund financial statements are the balance sheet and the statement of revenues, expenditures, and changes in fund balance. For proprietary funds, the fund financial statements are the statement of net position, the statement of revenues, expenses, and changes in fund net position, and the statement of cash flows. For fiduciary funds, the fund financial statements are the statement of fiduciary net position and the statement of changes in fiduciary net position. *See also* governmental funds (GRASPP) *and* proprietary funds *and* fiduciary funds *and* major funds *and* nonmajor funds.

**Fundraising Expenses:** Fundraising expenses should also be classified functionally and be separately disclosed in the financial statements. They include the costs of transmitting appeals to the public and the salaries of personnel connected with fundraising campaigns. *See also* program support expenses *and* management and general expenses.

**Future Value of $1:** The future value of $1 is the amount that will accumulate if $1 were invested now. *See also* present value of $1.

**Future Value of an Annuity of $1:** The future value of an annuity of $1 is the amount that will accumulate from a series of identical periodic payments to be made in the future. *See also* present value of an annuity of $1.

**Futures Contract:** An agreement between two parties to exchange a commodity or currency at a specified price on a specified future date. One party takes a long position and agrees to buy a particular item, while the other party takes a short position and agrees to sell that item. Unlike an option, both parties are obligated to perform according to the terms of the contract. Futures contracts are made through a clearinghouse and have standardized notional amounts and settlement dates.

**Gain Contingency:** A contingency is an existing condition, situation, or set of circumstances involving varying degrees of uncertainty that may result in the increase in an asset or the avoidance of a liability. *See also* contingency *and* loss contingency.

**Gains:** Gains are increases in equity from peripheral transactions and other events except revenue and investments from owners. A gain is the recognition of an asset either not in the ordinary course of business (a gain on the sale of a fixed asset) or without the incurrence of an expense. *See also* revenues *and* expenses *and* losses.

**General Fund:** The general fund is set up to account for the ordinary operations of a governmental unit that are financed from taxes and other general revenues. All transactions not accounted for in some other fund are accounted for in the general fund. All accounts of the general fund are of a current nature; thus the fund contains no fixed-asset accounts or long-term debt accounts. *See also* governmental funds (GRASPP) *and* special revenue fund *and* debt service fund *and* capital projects fund *and* permanent fund.

**Gifts-in-Kind:** Gifts-in-kind are noncash contributions.

**Going Concern Assumption:** It is assumed that the entity will continue to operate in the foreseeable future. *See also* entity assumption *and* monetary unit assumption *and* periodicity assumption *and* historical cost principle.

**Goodwill (and Goodwill Impairment):** The intangible resources and elements connected with an entity (management or marketing expertise or technical skill and knowledge that cannot be identified or valued separately). Goodwill is capitalized excess earnings power. Goodwill results from acquisition method business combinations and is recognized only in consolidated financial statements. Goodwill is not amortized, but is tested at least annually for impairment.

**Government Accountability Office (GAO):** The GAO became the Government Accountability Office as of July 7, 2004. It formerly was called the General Accounting Office. The GAO gathers information to help Congress determine how well executive branch agencies are doing their jobs. The GAO's work routinely answers such basic questions as whether government programs are meeting their objectives or providing good service to the public.

**Government-Mandated Non-exchange Transactions:** Government-mandated non-exchange transactions are instances in which a higher level of government (a state) provides funds and mandates certain activities by another level of government (a county) such as environmental cleanup, etc. *See also* derived tax revenues *and* imposed non-exchange revenues *and* voluntary non-exchange transactions.

**Governmental Accounting Standards Board (GASB):** The GASB is the governmental counterpart of the FASB. *See also* Financial Accounting Standards Board (FASB) *and* Governmental Finance Officers Association (GFOA).

**Governmental Acquisition:** The acquisition of one legally separate entity by another legally separate entity in exchange for significant consideration, resulting in the continuation of the acquiring government.

**Governmental Activities:** Governmental activities are normally financed through taxes, intra-governmental revenues, and other non-exchange revenues. *See also* business-type activities.

**Governmental Finance Officers Association (GFOA):** The GFOA is the governmental counterpart of the AICPA. *See also* Governmental Accounting Standards Board (GASB).

**Governmental Funds (GRASPP):** Governmental funds include the general fund, the special revenue fund, the debt service fund, the capital projects fund, and the permanent fund. All governmental funds utilize the modified accrual basis of accounting and the current financial resources measurement focus.

**Governmental Merger:** The combination of legally separate entities without the exchange of significant consideration, resulting in the elimination of an entity or entities and either the continuation of a single merged entity or the creation of a new government.

**Governmental Units:** Governmental units include federal, state, county, municipal, and a variety of local governmental units (townships, villages, and special districts) and entities (hospitals and universities) that are run by governments. *See also* not-for-profit organizations.

**Government-wide Financial Statements:** Government-wide financial statements convert disaggregated fund-based financial statements using multiple measurement focuses and bases of accounting to a single consolidated set of financial statements that use the full accrual basis of accounting and the economic resources measurement focus. Financial activity of the primary government is classified into governmental activities and business-type activities. Government-wide financial statements are the statement of net position and the statement of activities. *See also* fund financial statements.

**Grant Date:** For stock option accounting, the grant date is the date at which an employee receives the option. Compensation cost is measured at the grant data of the option. *See also* stock option.

**Gross Concept:** Revenues are reported at their gross amounts (less an allowance for returns and discounts given). *See also* net concept.

**Gross Method (of Recording Sales):** The gross method of recording sales records sales without regard to an available cash discount. If payment is received within the discount period, a sales discount (contra-revenue) account is debited to reflect the cash discount. *See also* cash discount *and* net method (of recording sales).

**Gross Profit Method:** The gross profit method is used for interim financial statements as part of a periodic inventory system. Inventory is valued at retail, and the average gross profit percentage is used to determine the inventory cost for the interim financial statements. The gross profit percentage is known and is used to calculate the cost of goods sold. *See also* interim financial reporting.

**Group Depreciation:** Group depreciation is the process of averaging the economic lives of a number of similar property units and depreciating the entire class of assets over a single life, thus simplifying record keeping of assets and depreciation calculations. It is a specialized depreciation accounting method in which no gain or loss is recognized when one asset of the group is sold or retired. *See also* composite depreciation.

**Guaranteed Residual Value (by the Lessee):** The guaranteed residual value of a lease is the amount guaranteed by the lessee to the lessor for the estimated residual value of the asset at the end of the lease term. *See also* unguaranteed residual value.

**Health Care Organizations:** Health care organizations are organizations that provide health care services to individuals, including hospitals, nursing care facilities, home health agencies, and clinics. Health care organizations can be organized as governmental, not-for-profit, or commercial entities. If the health care entity is financially accountable to a primary government, it could be classified as a component unit of the government.

**Hedge:** A hedge is a trading strategy in which derivatives are used to reduce or completely offset a counterparty's risk exposure to an underlying asset. *See also* fair value hedge *and* cash flow hedge *and* foreign currency hedge.

**Held for Sale:** Under U.S. GAAP, for discontinued operations reporting, a component of an entity is classified as held for sale in the period in which all of the following criteria are met:
1. Management commits to a plan to sell the component.
2. The component is available for immediate sale in its present condition.
3. An active program to locate a buyer has been initiated.
4. The sale of the component is probable and the sale is expected to be complete within one year.
5. The sale of the component is being actively marketed.
6. Actions required to complete the sale make it unlikely that significant changes to the plan will be made or that the plan will be withdrawn.

*See also* component of an entity *and* discontinued operations.

**Held-to-Maturity Debt Securities:** Investments in debt securities are classified as held-to-maturity debt securities if the corporation has the positive intent and ability to hold these securities to maturity. If the intent is to hold the security for an indefinite period of time, but not necessarily to maturity, the security would be classified as available-for-sale. *See also* trading debt securities *and* available-for-sale debt securities.

**Highest and Best Use:** The use that maximizes the value of an asset or group of assets.

**Historical Cost:** Historical cost is the actual exchange value in dollars at the time of the transaction. *See also* current cost.

**Historical Cost Principle:** As a general rule, it is assumed that financial information is accounted for and based on cost, not fair value. Measurement is shifting toward fair value, however. More and more items on the balance sheet are being measured at fair value. *See also* entity assumption *and* going concern assumption *and* monetary unit assumption *and* periodicity assumption.

**IASB Framework:** Developed by the IASB to assist in developing future IFRSs and evaluating existing IFRSs. The Framework provides a basis for reducing the number of alternative accounting treatments permitted by IFRS.

**If-Converted Method:** For earnings per share calculations, the if-converted method is used to determine the dilutive effects of convertible securities. The if-converted method assumes that the securities were converted to common stock at the beginning of the period (or at the time of issue, if later). *See also* treasury stock method *and* diluted earnings per share.

**Impairment (of Assets to Be Held and Used or to Be Disposed of):** An impairment of assets to be held and used or to be disposed of occurs if the book value of those assets is determined not to be recoverable. Under U.S. GAAP, the impairment test is divided into two steps. Under IFRS, the impairment test is a one-step test.

**Impairment of Debt Securities:** Based on the current expected credit losses (CECL) model, available-for-sale and held-to-maturity debt securities should be reported on the balance sheet at the net amount expected to be collected. Credit losses on held-to-maturity securities will equal the amount by which amortized cost exceeds present value. The credit loss for an available-for-sale security is capped at the amount by which amortized cost exceeds fair value, with any additional loss reported in other comprehensive income. The income statement each period may reflect increases and decreases in expected credit losses for these securities. *See also* held-to-maturity debt securities *and* available-for-sale debt securities *and* impairment (of assets to be held and used or to be disposed of).

**Impairment of Equity Securities:** Equity securities that do not have readily determinable fair values are measured at cost minus impairment (the practicality exception). When a qualitative assessment indicates that impairment exists, the cost basis of the security is written down to fair value and the amount of the write-down is accounted for as a realized loss and included in earnings.

**Impairment of Loans:** A loan is considered impaired if it is probable (likely to occur) that the creditor will be unable to collect all amounts due under the original contract when due. *See also* troubled debt restructuring.

**Imposed Non-exchange Revenues:** Imposed non-exchange revenues are taxes imposed on non-exchange transactions (fines) or wealth (property taxes). *See also* derived tax revenues *and* government-mandated non-exchange transactions *and* voluntary non-exchange transactions.

**Improvements:** In fixed asset accounting, improvements (betterments) improve the quality of fixed assets and are capitalized. *See also* additions *and* replacements *and* repairs.

**Imputing Interest:** Certain receivables and payables (contractual rights to receive or pay money at a fixed or determinable rate) must be recorded at true present value at the date of issuance. If a note is non-interest bearing or the interest rate is unreasonable (usually below market), the value of the note is determined by imputing the market rate of the note by using the effective interest method. *See also* effective interest method.

**Inception of the Lease:** The inception of the lease is the date of the lease agreement or the date of a written commitment signed by the parties involved that sets forth the principal provisions of the lease transaction.

**Income Available to Common Shareholders:** For earnings per share calculations, income available to common shareholders is determined by deducting from the income from continuing operations and net income the dividends declared in the period on noncumulative preferred stock (regardless of whether they have been paid) and the dividends accumulated on cumulative preferred stock (regardless of whether they have been declared). *See also* basic earnings per share *and* weighted average number of common shares outstanding.

**Income Bond:** An income bond is a bond that only pays interest if certain income objectives are met.

**Income From Continuing Operations:** Income from continuing operations includes operating activities (revenues, cost of goods sold, selling expenses, and administrative expenses); nonoperating activities (other revenues and gains and other expenses and losses); and income taxes. Amounts in income from continuing operations are reported gross of tax, and the income tax related to these amounts are reported separately as income taxes. *See also* discontinued operations.

**Incremental Borrowing Rate:** The lessee's incremental borrowing rate is the rate of interest that a lessee would have to pay at the inception of the lease to borrow the funds, on similar terms, to purchase the leased property. *See also* interest rate implicit in the lease.

**Indirect Method:** The indirect method of reporting cash flows from operating activities adjusts net income to reconcile it to net cash flows from operating activities. The same amount of cash flows from operating activities is reported under the direct or indirect methods. *See also* direct method *and* operating activities.

**Infrastructure Assets:** Infrastructure assets are streets, bridges, gutters, and other assets of a government. *See also* required approach *and* modified approach.

**Initial Franchise Fees:** Initial franchise fees are amounts paid by the franchisee for receiving initial services from the franchisor. Such services might include site selection, supervision of construction, bookkeeping services, and quality control.

**In-substance Defeasance:** An in-substance defeasance is an arrangement in which securities are placed into an irrevocable trust and are pledged for future principal and interest payments on long-term debt. The liability is not considered extinguished. *See also* extinguishment of debt.

**Intangible Assets:** Intangible assets are certain long-lived legal rights and competitive advantages developed or acquired by a business enterprise. Intangible assets are typically acquired to be used in operations of a business and provide benefits over several accounting periods. Intangible assets with finite (determinable) lives are amortized and tested for impairment. Intangible assets with indefinite lives cannot be amortized and are just tested for impairment.

**Integrated Approach:** The integrated approach to governmental entity financial reporting integrates operational accountability and fiscal accountability. The integrated approach requires a reconciliation of the fund financial statements to the government-wide financial statements. The purpose of the reconciliation is to link the two levels of financial reporting. *See also* operational accountability *and* fiscal accountability *and* fund financial statements *and* government-wide financial statements.

**Intercompany Bond Transactions:** If one member of the consolidated group acquires an affiliate's debt from an outsider, the debt is considered to be retired and a gain/loss is recognized. The gain/loss is reported as a gain/loss on the extinguishment of debt and is calculated as the difference between the price paid to acquire the debt and the book value of the debt. The gains/loss is recorded through an elimination entry.

**Intercompany Profit in Inventories:** When affiliated companies sell inventory/merchandise to one another, this inventory/merchandise is normally sold at a profit. The total amount of the intercompany sale and cost of goods sold is eliminated in preparing consolidated financial statements. In addition, any intercompany profit remaining in the ending inventory (not sold) is eliminated from the ending inventory and the cost of goods sold of the purchasing affiliate. 100 percent of the profit is eliminated even if the parent's ownership interest is less than 100 percent. The intercompany profit in beginning inventory that was recognized by the selling affiliate in the previous year is eliminated by an adjustment (debit) to retained earnings.

**Intercompany Profit on Fixed Assets:** The gain or loss on the intercompany sale of a depreciable asset is unrealized from a consolidated financial statement perspective until the asset is sold to an outsider. Both the gain/loss on the intercompany sale and the extra or decreased accumulated depreciation of the acquired asset are eliminated in preparing consolidated financial statements.

**Intercompany Transactions:** Intercompany transactions are transactions between affiliated companies. The effects of intercompany transactions are eliminated in consolidation. *See also* consolidation.

**Interest Cost:** Interest cost is the increase in the projected benefit obligation due to the passage of time. Measuring the projected benefit obligation as a present value requires the accrual of an interest cost, at rates equal to the assumed discount rates. Interest cost always increases the projected benefit obligation because the present value of any liability increases closer to the due date. Interest cost is a component of net periodic pension cost. *See also* projected benefit obligation *and* net periodic pension cost.

**Interest Rate Implicit in the Lease:** The interest rate implicit in the lease is the rate that results in an aggregate present value equal to the fair value of the leased property at the beginning of the lease term. *See also* incremental borrowing rate.

**Interfund Activity:** Interfund activity represents the flow of resources between funds and between the primary government and its component units. *See also* primary government *and* component unit.

**Interfund Reimbursement:** Interfund reimbursements are payments of expenses made by one fund on behalf of another fund.

**Interfund Transfer:** Interfund transfers are flows of assets between funds without the exchange of equivalent value.

**Interim Financial Reporting:** Interim financial reporting is generally concerned with the quarterly reports filed by public companies.

**Internal Service Fund:** Internal service funds are set up to account for goods and services provided by designated departments on a (cost reimbursement) fee basis to other departments and agencies within a single governmental unit or to other governmental units. *See also* proprietary funds *and* enterprise fund.

**International Accounting Standards Board (IASB):** The organization that establishes International Financial Reporting Standards (IFRS). The IASB was established in 2001 as part of the International Accounting Standards Committee Foundation. The purpose of the IASB is to develop a single set of high-quality, global accounting standards.

**International Financial Reporting Interpretations Committee (IFRIC):** The committee appointed to assist the IASB in establishing and improving standards of financial accounting and reporting. The IFRIC provides guidance on newly identified financial reporting issues not addressed in the IFRSs and assists the IASB in achieving international convergence of accounting standards.

**International Financial Reporting Standards (IFRS):** The accounting standards issued by the IASB.

**Interperiod Tax Allocation:** Interperiod tax allocation is the recognition of the income tax effects of all revenues, expenses, gains, losses, and other events that create differences between the tax bases of assets and liabilities and their amounts for financial reporting. *See also* temporary difference *and* permanent difference.

**Intraperiod Tax Allocation:** Intraperiod tax allocation involves apportioning the total income tax provision for financial accounting purposes in a period between the income or loss from continuing operations, discontinued operations, the cumulative effect of accounting changes (recorded on the statement of retained earnings), and comprehensive income. All of these amounts are reported net of tax.

**Inventory:** Inventories are asset items held for sale in the ordinary course of business or goods that will be used or consumed in the production of goods to be sold. Inventories are often classified as retail inventories (held for sale), raw materials inventory, work in process (WIP) inventory, and finished goods inventory.

**Inventory Turnover:** The inventory turnover ratio is cost of goods sold divided by average inventory.

**Investing Activities:** Investing activities include making loans to other entities, purchasing or disposing of available-for-sale and held-to maturity debt securities and equity securities, and acquiring or disposing of property, plant, and equipment (productive assets). *See also* operating activities *and* financing activities.

**Investment in Subsidiary:** The investment in subsidiary account is the cost or carrying amount of the investment in a subsidiary under the cost method or the equity method. The investment in subsidiary is eliminated when preparing consolidated financial statements. *See also* cost method *and* equity method *and* consolidation.

**Investment Trust Fund:** Investment trust funds account for external investment pools. *See also* fiduciary funds *and* pension trust fund *and* custodial trust fund *and* private purpose trust fund.

**Involuntary Conversion:** An involuntary conversion is the conversion of property due to fire, theft, etc., of a nonmonetary asset. An involuntary conversion results in a gain or loss for financial accounting purposes.

**Issued Shares:** Issued shares are the number of shares that have been issued by the corporation. *See also* authorized shares *and* outstanding shares.

**Large Stock Dividend:** When more than 20 percent to 25 percent of the shares previously issued and outstanding are distributed, a stock dividend is treated as a large stock dividend because the issuance is expected to reduce the market price of the stock (similar to a stock split). *See also* stock dividend *and* small stock dividend.

**Lease Bonus:** A lease bonus is an amount paid in addition to normal rent or as a prepayment in an operating lease. *See also* operating lease.

**Lease Term:** The lease term includes, among other factors, any fixed noncancelable term, any period covered by a bargain renewal option, any period covered by ordinary renewal options preceding the date on which a bargain purchase option is exercisable, and any period representing renewals or extensions of the lease at the lessor's option.

**Leasehold Improvement:** A leasehold improvement is an improvement that is permanently affixed to leased property and reverts to the lessor at the termination of the lease. In general, if the property is not moveable from the premises by the tenant, the improvement is a leasehold improvement. Leasehold improvements are amortized over the lesser of the term of the lease or the useful life of the asset.

**Level 1 Inputs:** In fair value measurement, quoted prices in active markets for identical assets or liabilities that the reporting entity has access to on the measurement date.

**Level 2 Inputs:** In fair value measurement, inputs other than quoted market prices (Level 1) that are directly or indirectly observable for the asset or liability.

**Level 3 Inputs:** In fair value measurement, unobservable inputs for an asset or liability.

**Liabilities:** Liabilities are probable future sacrifices of economic benefits arising from a present obligation to transfer assets or provide services to other entities in the future as a result of past transactions or events. *See also* assets *and* equity.

**LIFO Layers:** The U.S. GAAP LIFO method of inventory accounting requires that records be maintained for base year inventory amounts plus any additional layers that may be added in years in which ending inventory is greater than beginning inventory. An additional LIFO layer is priced at the earliest costs of the year in which it was created.

**LIFO Method:** Under U.S. GAAP LIFO, the last costs inventoried are the first costs transferred to cost of goods sold. Ending inventory, thus, includes the oldest costs. The ending balance of inventory will typically not approximate replacement cost. LIFO does not generally relate to actual flow of goods because most organizations sell or use their oldest goods first to prevent holding old or obsolete items. *See also* specific identification method *and* FIFO method *and* weighted average method *and* moving average method *and* LIFO layers *and* dollar value LIFO.

**Liquidating Dividends:** Liquidating dividends occur when dividends to shareholders exceed retained earnings. Dividends in excess of retained earnings are charged first to additional paid-in capital and then to common or preferred stock. Liquidating dividends reduce total paid-in capital. *See also* retained earnings.

**Liquidation Basis of Accounting:** A basis of accounting required under U.S. GAAP for public and private companies and not-for-profit organizations that are facing imminent liquidation. This basis of accounting helps financial statement users understand how much the organization will have available to distribute to investors after disposing of its assets and settling its obligations.

**Liquidation Preference on Preferred Stock:** If an entity issues preferred stock or other senior stock that has a preference in involuntary liquidation considerably in excess of the par or stated value of the shares, it is required to disclose this information in the equity section of the statement of financial position. *See also* preferred stock.

**Loan Funds:** In not-for-profit accounting, funds used to account for loans made to students, employees, and other constituents and the resources available for these purposes. Fund balances represent amounts available to lend and can be any classification of net assets.

**Long-Term Liabilities:** Long-term liabilities are probable future expenditures associated with current obligations that are not payable within the current operating cycle or reporting year, whichever is greater.

**Loss Contingency:** A loss contingency is an existing condition, situation, or set of circumstances involving varying degrees of uncertainty that may result in the decrease in an asset or the incurrence of a liability. *See also* contingency *and* gain contingency.

**Losses:** Losses are decreases in equity from peripheral transactions and other events except expenses and distributions to owners. *See also* expenses *and* revenues *and* gains.

**Lower of Cost of Market:** The lower of cost or market method is an inventory valuation method to write down inventory to its lower utility value, if the market value of the inventory is lower than its cost. The purpose of the lower of cost or market method is to recognize a decline in value of inventory in the period it occurs. Cost in the lower of cost or market formula is the original cost. Market starts at current replacement cost. Market cannot be greater than the selling price less the cost to complete (the ceiling) or less than the selling price less the cost to complete and less a normal profit margin (the floor).

**Major Funds:** Major funds are funds whose revenues, expenditures/expenses, assets, or liabilities are at least 10 percent of the corresponding totals for all governmental or enterprise funds and at least 5 percent of the aggregate amount for all governmental and enterprise funds. *See also* nonmajor funds.

**Management and General Expenses:** Management and general costs include expenses for the overall direction of the organization, general record keeping, business management, budgeting, general board activities, and related purposes. *See also* program support expenses *and* fundraising expenses.

**Management Discussion & Analysis (MD&A):** MD&A is part of required supplementary information but is presented before the regular financial information. *See also* required supplementary information.

**Mandatorily Redeemable Preferred Stock:** Mandatorily redeemable preferred stock is issued with a maturity date. Similar to debt, mandatorily redeemable preferred stock must be bought back by the company on the maturity date. Mandatorily redeemable preferred stock must be classified as a liability, unless the redemption is required to occur only upon the liquidation or termination of the reporting entity.

**Market Participants:** Buyers and sellers who are independent (not related parties), knowledgeable about the asset or liability, able to transact for the asset or liability, and willing to transact for the asset or liability.

**Market Risk:** Market risk is the possibility of loss from changes in market value, not necessarily due to the failure of another party, but due to changes in economic circumstances. Market risk should be, but is not required to be, disclosed under U.S. GAAP. Market risk is required to be disclosed under IFRS. *See also* concentration of credit risk.

**Matching Principle:** The matching principle indicates that expenses are recognized in the same period in which the related revenue is recognized when it is practicable to do so. Matching of revenues and costs is the simultaneous or combined recognition of the revenues and expenses that results directly and jointly from the same transactions or events. For those expenses that do not have a cause and effect relationship to revenue, a systematic and rational approach to expense recognition is used (amortization and depreciation of long-lived assets). If there is no systematic and rational approach, immediate expensing is used. *See also* accrual accounting.

**Measurable and Available:** Measurable and available is the basis of the current financial resources measurement focus. Revenue is recognized when measurable and available to finance the expenditures of the current period (generally within 60 days). *See also* current financial resources measurement focus *and* modified accrual basis of accounting.

**Measurement Focus:** Measurement focus refers to the economic values emphasized and reported in the financial presentation. *See also* current financial resources measurement focus *and* economic resources measurement focus.

**Modified Accrual Basis of Accounting:** The modified accrual basis of accounting is used with the current financial resources measurement focus and is a blend of accrual and cash basis accounting concepts into an entirely different basis of accounting. Revenue is recognized when measurable and available to finance the expenditures of the current period. Expenditures are generally recorded when the related fund liability is incurred. The modified accrual basis of accounting is used by GRASPP funds. *See also* full accrual basis of accounting *and* current financial resources measurement focus.

**Modified Approach:** Infrastructure assets that are part of a network or subsystem of a network are not required to be depreciated provided two requirements are met. Under the modified approach, infrastructure expenditures are typically reported as expenses, unless the outlays result in additions or improvements, in which case they would be capitalized. *See also* required approach.

**Monetary Item:** A monetary asset or liability is an asset or liability that is fixed in dollars regardless of changes in specific prices or changes in the general price level (cash, accounts and notes receivable, etc.). *See also* nonmonetary item.

**Monetary Unit Assumption:** It is assumed that money is an appropriate basis by which to measure economic activity. The assumption is that the monetary unit does not change over time; thus, the effects of inflation are not reflected in the financial statements. *See also* entity assumption *and* going concern assumption *and* periodicity assumption *and* historical cost principle.

**Mortgage Bond:** A mortgage bond is a bond that is secured by real property. *See also* debenture *and* collateral trust bond *and* convertible bond.

**Most Advantageous Market:** The market with the best price for the asset or liability, after considering transaction costs. The price in the most advantageous market will be the fair value measurement only if there is no principal market.

**Moving Average Method:** The moving average method of inventory accounting computes the weighted average cost after each purchase. A perpetual inventory system is necessary to use the moving average method. *See also* specific identification method *and* FIFO method *and* weighted average method *and* LIFO method.

**MSWLF:** An MSWLF is a municipal solid waste landfill (a dump).

**Multiple Element Arrangement:** Sales that include multiple products or services. The fair value of multiple element arrangements must be allocated to the separate contract elements. Revenue is recognized separately for each element.

**Multiple-Step Income Statement:** A multiple-step income statement reports operating revenues and expenses separately from nonoperating revenues and expenses and other gains and losses. *See also* single-step income statement.

**Net Assets:** Net assets are assets less liabilities. *See also* net assets with donor restrictions *and* net assets without donor restrictions.

**Net Assets With Donor Restrictions:** For not-for-profit organizations, the portion of net assets of a not-for-profit entity that is subject to donor-imposed restrictions. Donor-imposed restrictions represent donor stipulations that specify a use for a contribution more specific than the broad limits associated with the nature of the not-for-profit organization, the environment in which it operates, or the purposes defined by the articles of incorporation. Donor-imposed restrictions may be temporary or perpetual in nature. *See also* net assets *and* net assets without donor restrictions.

**Net Assets Without Donor Restrictions:** For not-for-profit organizations, the portion of net assets of a not-for-profit entity that is not subject to donor-imposed restrictions. These net assets are available to finance general operations of the particular organization, and may be expended at the discretion of the governing board. Internal board-designated funds are classified as net assets without donor restrictions. *See also* net assets *and* net assets with donor restrictions.

**Net Concept:** Gains are reported at their net amounts (proceeds less net book value or carrying amount). Losses are reported at their net amounts (proceeds less net book value or carrying amount). *See also* gross concept *and* gains *and* losses.

**Net Investment Hedge:** A net investment hedge is a hedge of a net investment in a foreign operation. Gains and losses on changes in fair value of foreign currency transactions entered into to hedge a net investment in a foreign operation are reported in other comprehensive income as part of the cumulative foreign currency translation adjustment. *See also* cash flow hedge *and* fair value hedge *and* foreign currency hedge.

**Net Investment in Capital Assets:** For governmental organizations, net investment in capital assets is capital assets reduced by the accumulated depreciation on those assets and any debt that is attributable to the acquisition, construction, or improvement of those assets. *See also* net position *and* restricted net position *and* unrestricted net position (governmental).

**Net Method (of Recording Sales):** The net method of recording sales records sales and accounts receivable net of the cash discount. An adjustment is not needed if payment is received within the discount period. However, if payment is received after the discount period, a discount not taken account (revenue) must be credited. *See also* cash discount *and* gross method.

**Net Operating Loss (NOL):** A net operating loss occurs when a taxpayer's deductions exceed income for the year. NOL rules on carrybacks and carryforwards as well as taxable income limitations are year-specific. Taxable income and financial accounting income will differ for the years in which the loss is incurred and carried back or forward.

**Net Periodic Pension Cost:** Net periodic pension cost is equal to the total of service cost, interest cost, the expected return on plan assets, amortization of prior service cost, (amortization of) gains and losses, and amortization of existing net obligation or net asset.

**Net Position:** In governmental accounting, the difference between assets plus deferred outflows and liabilities plus deferred inflows of resources.

**Net Postretirement Benefit Cost:** The net postretirement benefit cost is the parallel for postretirement benefits to the net periodic pension cost for pensions. *See also* net periodic pension cost.

**Net Realizable Value (of Accounts Receivable):** The net realizable value of accounts receivable is the balance of the accounts receivable account less the allowance for uncollectible accounts.

**Neutrality:** Neutrality means that the information is free from bias and free from outside influences. *See also* reliability *and* representational faithfulness *and* verifiability.

**Noncash Operating and Financing Activities:** Noncash financing and investing activities are those that do not result in cash receipts or payments. Information about these activities should be provided separately in a supplemental disclosure. Any part of the transaction that does involve cash would be included in the statement of cash flows. Examples include a purchase of fixed assets by issuance of stock, the conversion of bonds to equity, and the exchange of one noncash asset for another noncash asset. *See also* operating activities *and* investing activities *and* financing activities *and* direct method *and* indirect method.

**Noncompensatory Stock Purchase Plan:** Under U.S. GAAP, certain stock options and stock purchase plans may not be intended primarily to compensate employees. For example, a corporation may wish to raise capital or diversify ownership of its stock among its employees or officers. Where the difference is no larger per share than that in an offer to all shareholders for the purpose of raising the same amount of capital, there is no compensation involved. *See also* stock option *and* compensatory stock option plan.

**Noncontributory Plan:** A noncontributory plan is one in which employees are not required to contribute to the plan. *See also* contributory plan.

**Noncontrolling Interest:** Business combinations that do not establish a 100 percent ownership of an investee by an investor result in a portion of the investee's equity being attributed to minority shareholders. That interest is called a noncontrolling interest.

**Noncumulative Preferred Stock:** With noncumulative preferred stock, dividends that are not paid in any year do not accumulate. The preferred shareholders lose the right to receive dividends that are not declared. *See also* preferred stock *and* cumulative preferred stock.

**Non-exchange Revenue:** Non-exchange revenue is revenue recognized when a government gives (or receives) value without directly receiving (or giving) equal value in exchange. *See also* exchange revenue.

**Nonexpendable Trust Fund:** Nonexpendable trust funds are those whose principal may not be expended in the course of their designated operations but whose income may be expended. *See also* expendable trust fund *and* permanent fund.

**Nonmajor Funds:** Nonmajor funds are funds that are not classified as major funds. *See also* major funds.

**Nonmonetary Exchange:** Under U.S. GAAP, nonmonetary exchanges are divided into two categories: exchanges of assets that have commercial substance and exchanges of assets that lack commercial substance. An exchange has commercial substance if future cash flows of the entity involved in the exchange change as a result of the transaction. Gains and losses are always recognized in exchanges having commercial substances and are not normally recognized in exchanges lacking commercial substance (in exchanges lacking commercial substances, there might be an impairment loss which is recognized before or as part of the transaction).

**Nonmonetary Item:** A nonmonetary asset or liability is an asset or liability that is not fixed in dollars and instead fluctuates with changes in the price level. *See also* monetary item.

**Nonprofit Activity (as used in discontinued operations):** An integrated set of activities and assets that is conducted and managed for the purpose of providing benefits, other than goods or services at a profit, to fulfill an entity's purpose or mission.

**Nonreciprocal Interfund Activity:** Nonreciprocal interfund activity refers to non-exchange transactions between funds. *See also* reciprocal interfund activity.

**Nonrecognized Subsequent Events:** Subsequent events that provide information about conditions that occurred after the balance sheet date and did not exist at the balance sheet date. Entities should not recognize nonrecognized subsequent events in the financial statements (balance sheet and income statement).

**Nonspendable Fund Balance:** Current equity in the fund balance generally comprises available, spendable resources. To the extent that the equity of a governmental fund is represented by current assets that cannot be spent (e.g., prepaid expenses, inventories, etc.), the fund balance should be displayed as nonspendable.

**Notes Receivable:** Notes receivable are written promises to pay a debt, and the writing is called a promissory note. Notes receivable are sometimes discounted, where the holder endorses the note to a third party and receives an amount of cash. *See also* accounts receivable.

**Not-for-Profit Organizations:** Not-for-profit organizations are organizations that are not run by governments (hospitals, universities, voluntary health and welfare organizations, and research organizations). Not-for-profit entities are entities whose revenues come from contributions and whose operating purpose does not include profit. *See also* foundations and health care organizations *and* voluntary health and welfare organizations.

**Notional Amount:** A notional amount is a specified unit of measure (currency units, shares, bushels, pounds, etc.). *See also* derivative *and* underlying *and* settlement amount *and* payment provision.

**Object Class:** Object class classification categorizes governmental expenditures according to the type of items purchased or services obtained. Examples are personnel services, supplies, and principal and interest payments for debt service expenditures. *See also* function (program) classification *and* activity classification *and* character classification.

**Operating Activities:** Operating activities involve producing goods and delivering services to customers. Operating activities also is a residual category in that all transactions not categorized as investing or financing activities are categorized as operating activities. There are differences in the direct and indirect methods of the statement of cash flows in the operating activities section, but not in the other sections. Receiving and paying interest and receiving dividends are operating activities under U.S. GAAP. *See also* investing activities *and* financing activities *and* direct method *and* indirect method.

**Operating Grants and Contributions:** Operating grants and contributions are mandatory and voluntary non-exchange transactions with other governments or individuals that are restricted for use in a particular program for operating expenditures. *See also* capital grants and contributions.

**Operating Lease:** An operating lease is a lease that does not qualify as a finance lease. Both lessees and lessors may classify leases as operating leases. *See also* finance lease (U.S. GAAP) *and* direct financing lease *and* sales-type lease.

**Operating Loss Carryback:** Under present U.S. tax law, no operating loss carryback is allowed.

**Operating Loss Carryforward:** If an operating loss is carried forward, the tax effects are recognized to the extent that the tax benefit is more likely than not to be realized.

**Operating Segment:** For segment reporting, an operating segment is a segment of an enterprise that engages in business activities from which revenues may be earned and in which expenses are incurred, whose operating results are regularly reviewed by the enterprise's chief operating decision maker, and for which discrete financial information is available. *See also* segment reporting *and* reportable segment.

**Operational Accountability:** The focus of government-wide financial statements is to report the extent to which the government entity has met its operating objectives efficiently and effectively, using all resources available for that purpose, and the extent to which it can continue to meet its objectives for the future. *See also* fiscal accountability *and* government-wide financial statements.

**Option Contract:** A contract between two parties that gives one party the right, but not the obligation, to buy or sell something to the other party at a specified price (the strike price or exercise price) during a specified period of time. The option buyer, or holder, must pay a premium to the option seller, or writer, to enter into the option contract.

**Orderly Transaction:** A transaction in which the asset or liability is exposed to the market for a period before the measurement date long enough to allow for marketing activities that are usual and customary for transactions involving such assets or liabilities. An orderly transaction cannot be a forced transaction.

**Ordinary Annuity:** An ordinary annuity is an annuity with payments at the end of the period. *See also* annuity due.

**Other Comprehensive Bases of Accounting (OCBOA):** Non-GAAP financial statement presentations that have wide-spread understanding and support, also known as special purpose financial statements.

**Other Comprehensive Income:** Other comprehensive income includes those items (gains and losses) in comprehensive income that are excluded from net income. Items of other comprehensive income are pension adjustments, unrealized gains and losses on available-for-sale debt securities, foreign currency translation adjustments, and the effective portion of cash flow hedges. Revaluation surplus is also recognized in other comprehensive income under IFRS. *See also* comprehensive income *and* accumulated other comprehensive income.

**Other Financing Sources:** For governmental funds, other financing sources are amounts such as operating transfers from other funds (transfers-in) and bond issue proceeds. *See also* transfers-in.

**Other Financing Uses:** For governmental funds, other financing uses are amounts such as operating transfers to other funds (transfers-out). See also transfers-out.

**Outstanding Shares:** Outstanding shares is the number of shares that have been issued and have not been reacquired as treasury stock. See also authorized shares and issued shares.

**Overfunded:** A defined benefit pension plan is overfunded when the fair value of the pension plan assets exceeds the projected benefit obligation (PBO).

**Participating Bond:** A participating bond is a bond that not only has a stated rate of interest but also participates in income if certain earnings levels are obtained. See also stated interest rate.

**Participating Preferred Stock:** Participating preferred stock is preferred stock that includes a participating feature which provides that preferred shareholders share (participate) with common shareholders in dividends in excess of a specific amount. The participation may be full or partial. Generally, preferred shareholders receive their preference dividend first, and then additional dividends are shared between common and preferred shareholders. See also preferred stock.

**Par Value (of a Bond):** The par value of a bond is the total dollar amount of the bond that will be repaid at the expiration of the bond term. Bonds are valued at par value when the stated interest rate is equal to the effective interest rate. See also face value.

**Par Value (of Stock):** Generally, preferred stock is issued with a par value, but common stock may be issued with or without a par value. No-par common stock may be issued as true no-par stock or no-par stock with a stated value. See also capital stock.

**Par Value Method (of Treasury Stock Accounting):** Under the par value method of treasury stock accounting, treasury shares are recorded by reducing the amounts of par (or stated) value and additional paid-in capital received at the time of the original sale. Treasury stock is debited for its par (or stated) value. Additional paid-in capital is debited for the pro rata share of the original issue price attributable to the reacquired shares. Retained earnings is debited for any excess of treasury stock cost over the original issue price. Additional paid-in capital is credited for any excess of the original issue price over the treasury stock cost. Under the par value method, the sources of capital associated with the original issue are maintained. The par value method of accounting for treasury stock is not permitted under IFRS. See also treasury stock and cost method (of treasury stock accounting).

**Patient Service Revenue:** Patient service revenue for a health care organization should be accounted for on the accrual basis at established standard rates (usual and customary fees), even if the full amount is not expected to be collected. Although patient service revenue is accounted for on a gross basis, deductions are made from gross revenue for reporting purposes.

**Payment Provision:** A payment provision is a specified (fixed) or determinable settlement that is to be made if the underlying behaves in a specified way. See also derivative and underlying and notional amount and settlement amount.

**Pension Trust Fund:** Pension trust funds account for resources of defined benefit plans, defined contribution plans, post retirement benefit plans, and other long-term employee benefit plans. See also fiduciary funds and custodial trust fund and private purpose trust fund and investment trust fund.

**Percentage of Accounts Receivable at Year-End Method:** The percentage of accounts receivable at year-end method is a method of calculating bad debt expense as a percentage of accounts receivable at year-end (possibly by an aging of the accounts receivable). The amount is the ending balance in accounts receivable and the bad debt expense is plugged (possibly by using an account analysis format). See also allowance method.

**Percentage-of-Completion Accounting:** Under percentage-of-completion accounting, revenue is recognized as production takes place. Percentage-of-completion accounting can be used for long-term construction contracts having costs that can be reasonably estimated. If costs cannot be reasonably estimated, the completed contract method must be used under U.S. GAAP and the cost recovery method must be used under IFRS. See also completed contract accounting.

**Period Costs:** Period costs are costs that are not charged to a product (inventory). Instead, they are charged to the period.

**Periodic Inventory System:** With a periodic inventory system, the quantity of inventory is determined only by physical count, usually annually. Units of inventory are counted and valued at the end of the accounting period. The actual cost of goods sold is calculated using the cost of goods sold account analysis format: beginning inventory plus purchases less ending inventory equals cost of goods sold. See also perpetual inventory system.

**Periodicity Assumption:** It is assumed that economic activity can be divided into meaningful time periods. See also entity assumption and going concern assumption and monetary unit assumption and historical cost principle.

**Permanent Difference:** Permanent differences do not affect the deferred tax computation. They only affect the current tax computation, only the period in which they occur and not future financial or taxable income. Permanent differences are items of revenue and expense that either enter into pretax financial income but never into taxable income or enter into taxable income, but never into pretax financial income. In effect, a permanent difference is a difference between taxable income and financial income that will never reverse. *See also* temporary difference.

**Permanent Fund:** Permanent funds are used to report resources that are legally restricted to the extent that income, and not principal, may be used for purposes that support the reporting government's programs (for the benefit of the public). *See also* general fund *and* special revenue fund *and* debt service fund *and* capital projects fund *and* nonexpendable trust fund.

**Perpetual Inventory System:** With a perpetual inventory system, the inventory record for each item of inventory is updated for each purchase and each sale as it occurs. The actual cost of goods sold is determined and recorded with each sale. Therefore, the perpetual inventory system keeps a running total of inventory balances. *See also* periodic inventory system.

**Pervasive Constraints:** The pervasive constraints for accounting information per the FASB conceptual framework is cost vs. benefits (the benefits of accounting information must be greater than the cost of obtaining and presenting that information) and materiality (the use of the information or the lack of the information could make a difference in decisions made by the users).

**Physical Depreciation:** Physical depreciation is the wear and tear on an asset over a period of time. *See also* functional depreciation.

**Pledging of Accounts Receivable:** Pledging is the process whereby existing accounts receivable are used as collateral for a loan. Title to the accounts receivable is retained but the proceeds are used to pay the loan. *See also* factoring of accounts receivable.

**Post-employment Benefits:** Post-employment benefits are benefits that are paid to former employees after they have been terminated.

**Postretirement Benefits:** Postretirement benefits are benefits that are paid to former employees after their employment.

**Predictive Value:** When information has predictive value, it has the ability to assist financial statement users in evaluating past, present, or future events. *See also* relevance *and* feedback value *and* timeliness.

**Preferred Stock:** Preferred stock is an equity security with preferences and features not associated with common stock. Preferred stock may include a preference relating to dividends, which may be cumulative or noncumulative and participating or nonparticipating. Preferred stock also may include a preference relating to liquidation. Usually, preferred stock does not have voting rights. *See also* common stock *and* cumulative preferred stock.

**Premium:** In bond accounting, bonds are sold at a premium if the market interest rate is less than the stated interest rate. The bond has to sell at a premium because investors cannot obtain a higher interest rate in other investments. *See also* discount *and* stated interest rate *and* effective interest rate *and* par value (of a bond) *and* bond selling price.

**Prepaid Expenses:** Prepaid expenses relate to expenditures with a residual value (prepaid insurance with a cancellation value). *See also* accrued expenses *and* deferred charges.

**Present Value Calculations:** SFAC 7 allows the use of two approaches to determine present value depending on the circumstances. These two approaches are the traditional approach (one discount rate is used to determine the present value of a cash flow stream) and the expected cash flow approach (the risk-free rate of return is used as the discount rate and the expected future cash flows are adjusted to take risk into account).

**Present Value of $1:** The present value of $1 is the amount that must be invested now at a specific interest rate so that $1 is received in the future. *See also* future value of $1.

**Present Value of an Annuity of $1:** The present value of an annuity of $1 is the value now of a series of identical periodic payments to be made in the future. *See also* future value of an annuity of $1.

**Primary Beneficiary:** The entity that is required to consolidate a VIE. The primary beneficiary is the entity that has the power to direct the activities of a variable interest entity that most significantly impact the entity's economic performance and 1) absorbs the expected VIE losses, or 2) receives the expected VIE residual returns.

**Primary Government:** A primary government consists of all organizations that make up the legal government entity. The primary government is considered the nucleus of the financial reporting entity. *See also* financial reporting entity.

**Principal Market:** The market with the greatest volume or level of activity for the asset or liability. If there is a principal market for an asset or liability, the price in that market will be the fair value measurement, even if there is a more advantageous price in a different market.

**Prior Period Adjustment:** Prior period adjustments consist of corrections of errors in the financial statements of prior periods.

**Prior Service Cost:** Prior service cost is the cost of benefits granted to employees for 1) services provided before the initiation of a pension plan that grants retroactive benefits and 2) plan amendments that provide new or increased benefits for services already provided. Amortization of prior service cost is a component of net periodic pension cost. *See also* unrecognized prior service cost *and* net periodic pension cost.

**Private Company Council:** The Private Company Council (PCC) serves as the primary advisory body to the FASB on the appropriate treatment for private companies for items under active consideration on the FASB's technical agenda. The PCC and the FASB work jointly to decide whether and when alternatives within U.S. generally accepted accounting principles (GAAP) are warranted for private companies.

**Private Purpose Trust Fund:** Private purpose trust funds are the designated funds for all other trust fund arrangements under which principal and income are for the benefit of specific individuals, private organizations, and other governments. Often, the government will need to record escheat property in a private purpose trust fund. *See also* fiduciary funds *and* pension trust fund *and* custodial trust fund *and* escheat property.

**Probable:** In accounting for contingencies, probable is likely to occur. *See also* reasonably possible *and* remote *and* contingency.

**Product Costs:** Product costs are costs that are charged to a product. *See also* period costs.

**Program Approach:** The program approach provides cost information about the primary functions of the government and indicates each program's dependence on the general revenues of the government.

**Program Revenue:** Program revenue is revenue directly associated with a function or program on the full accrual basis.

**Program Services:** Program services are the activities for which an organization was chartered. *See also* support services.

**Program Support Expenses:** Program support expenses are expenses that are directly related to the organization's program. For example, if an organization's program was cancer research then only those expenses directly related to the actual research on cancer should be classified as program support expenses. *See also* fundraising expenses *and* management and general expenses.

**Progress Billings:** In construction accounting, construction in progress is the amount that has been spent for the construction (effectively an inventory account). Progress billings are the amount that has been billed for the construction. The difference between construction in progress and progress billings is reported as a current asset if construction in progress is greater than progress billings and as a current liability if construction in progress is less than progress billings.

**Projected Benefit Obligation (PBO):** The projected benefit obligation is the actuarial present value of all benefits attributed by the plan's benefit formula to employee service rendered prior to that date. PBO uses an assumption as to future compensation levels. *See also* accumulated benefit obligation (ABO).

**Property Dividend:** Property dividends distribute noncash assets (inventory, investment securities, etc.) to shareholders. They are nonreciprocal transfers of nonmonetary assets from a corporation to its shareholders. On the declaration date, the property to be distributed is restated to fair value and any gain or loss is recognized in income. The dividend liability and related debit to retained earnings is recorded at the fair value of the assets transferred. *See also* cash dividend *and* stock dividend.

**Proprietary Funds:** Proprietary funds include internal service funds and enterprise funds. Proprietary funds account for business-type activities and their accounting is similar to commercial accounting. All proprietary funds utilize the full accrual basis of accounting and the economic resources measurement focus. *See also* internal service fund *and* enterprise fund *and* economic resources measurement focus *and* the full accrual basis of accounting.

**Purchase Method:** For certain governmental fund expenditures, the purchase method may be used. With the purchase method, supplies and prepaid amounts such as prepaid insurance and inventory are treated as expenditures in total when the purchase is made. Any amount on hand at the end of the period is reversed into a current asset account. The amount in the current asset account must be a reservation of fund balance. This purchase method has nothing to do with the purchase method used to account for business combinations. *See also* consumption method.

**Purchasing Power Gain:** A purchasing power gain is recognized on holding monetary assets during a period of deflation and on holding monetary liabilities during a period of inflation.

**Purchasing Power Loss:** A purchasing power loss is recognized on holding monetary assets during a period of inflation and on holding monetary liabilities during a period of deflation.

**Put Option:** Gives the holder the right to sell to the option writer at a specified price during a specified period of time.

**Quick Ratio:** The quick ratio is (cash and cash equivalents plus short-term marketable securities plus receivables [net]) divided by current liabilities. It is the current ratio without inventories and prepaid assets in the numerator. *See also* current ratio *and* current liabilities.

**Realization:** Realization occurs when the entity obtains cash or the right to receive cash (i.e., from the sale of assets) or has converted a noncash resource into cash. *See also* recognition.

**Reasonably Possible:** In accounting for contingencies, reasonably possible is somewhere between probable and remote. *See also* probable *and* remote *and* contingency.

**Reciprocal Interfund Activity:** Reciprocal interfund activity is exchange-type transactions between funds. *See also* nonreciprocal interfund activity.

**Reclassification:** In marketable securities accounting, a reclassification is any transfer of a particular security from one group (trading, available-for-sale, or held-to-maturity) to another group (trading, available-for-sale, or held-to-maturity).

**Recognition:** Recognition is the actual recording of transactions and events in the financial statements. *See also* realization.

**Recognized Subsequent Events:** Subsequent events that provide additional information about conditions that existed at the balance sheet date. Entities must recognize the effects of all recognized subsequent events in the financial statements.

**Record Date:** The record date is the date the board of directors specifies as the date the names of the shareholders to receive a dividend are determined. *See also* declaration date.

**Regulation S-X (17 CFR part 210):** SEC regulation in which the SEC sets forth the form and content of and requirements for interim and annual financial statements to be filed with the SEC.

**Relative Sales Value Method:** The relative sales value method of costing is used when costs cannot be determined individually. Joint products, lump-sum purchases of assets (basket purchases), and large assets that are subdivided (real estate tracts) are examples of items that are cost by the relative sales value method.

**Relevance:** In order for information to be useful, it has to be relevant (it has to make a difference) to the decision-making process. Under the FASB Conceptual Framework, the quality of relevance has three subcategories: predictive value, feedback value, and timeliness (PFT mnemonic). Under the IASB Framework, the subcategories of relevance are predictive value, feedback value, and materiality. *See also* reliability *and* predictive value *and* feedback value *and* timeliness.

**Reliability:** In order for information to be reliable, financial statement users must be able to reasonably depend on it to be free from error and bias and to be faithfully representative of what it claims to represent. Under the FASB Conceptual Framework, the quality of reliability has three subcategories: neutrality, representational faithfulness, and verifiability (VRFN mnemonic). Under the IASB Framework, the subcategories of reliability are neutrality, representational faithfulness, substance over form, prudence, and completeness. *See also* relevance *and* neutrality *and* representational faithfulness *and* verifiability.

**Remeasurement:** Foreign currency remeasurement is the restatement of financial statements denominated in a foreign currency to the entity's functional currency. Remeasurement is required when an entity's books are not maintained in its functional currency. *See also* translation *and* functional currency.

**Remote:** In accounting for contingencies, remote is a slight chance of occurring. *See also* probable *and* reasonably possible *and* contingency.

**Repairs:** In fixed asset accounting, ordinary repairs are expensed as repair and maintenance. Extraordinary repairs are capitalized. *See also* additions *and* improvements.

**Replacements:** In fixed asset accounting, replacements involve a determination of the unit of depreciation. If the entire unit is the unit of depreciation, the replacement is expensed as a repair. If units of the fixed asset are separated (component method), the original cost and the related accumulated depreciation of the component are removed from the account and a gain/loss is recognized and the cost of the replacement is capitalized. *See also* additions *and* improvements.

**Reportable Segment:** For segment reporting, segments are operating segments of an enterprise that meet the criteria for separate reporting. *See also* segment reporting *and* operating segment.

**Reporting Currency:** The reporting currency is the currency of the entity ultimately reporting financial results of the foreign entity. *See also* functional currency.

**Reporting Unit (goodwill impairment):** An operating segment, or one level below an operating segment. Under U.S. GAAP, goodwill impairment is analyzed at the reporting unit level.

**Reporting Unit (governmental accounting):** For governmental reporting, the reporting unit is the primary governmental unit and its component units. *See also* primary government *and* component unit.

**Representational Faithfulness:** Representational faithfulness is agreement between financial reporting and the resources or events represented. It means that the information is valid (economic substance over legal form). *See also* reliability *and* neutrality *and* verifiability.

**Required Approach:** Depreciation expense that can be specifically identified with a functional category should be included in the direct expenses of that function. *See also* modified approach.

**Required Supplementary Information:** In governmental accounting, required supplementary information includes a schedule of funding progress, a schedule of employer contributions, budgetary comparison schedules, and information about infrastructure analysis. In addition, there is certain other supplementary information, which is optional. *See also* management discussion & analysis (MD&A).

**Research and Development Expenses:** Research is planned efforts to discover new information that will help either create a new product, service, process, or technique, or significantly improve the one in current use. Development takes the findings generated by research and formulates a plan to create the desired item or to significantly improve the existing one. Under U.S. GAAP, research and development costs are normally expensed (if an R&D cost has alternative future uses, it is capitalized and expensed and depreciated over its useful life). Under IFRS, research costs are expensed and development costs may be capitalized if certain criteria are met.

**Restricted Cash:** Restricted cash is cash that has been set aside for a specific use or purpose. *See also* cash *and* unrestricted cash.

**Restricted Fund Balance:** Fund balance resources associated with assets restricted by external authorities (e.g., laws, grantors, creditors, etc.) are classified as restricted.

**Restricted Net Position:** For governmental organizations, the restricted component of net position consists of restricted assets reduced by liabilities and deferred inflows of resources related to those assets. *See also* net position *and* unrestricted net position (governmental) *and* net investment in capital assets.

**Retained Earnings:** Retained earnings (or deficit) is accumulated earnings (or losses) during the life of the corporation that have not been paid out as dividends. The amount of accumulated retained earnings is reduced by distributions to stockholders and transfers to additional paid-in capital for stock dividends. Retained earnings do not include treasury stock or accumulated other comprehensive income. If the retained earnings account has a negative balance, it is called a deficit. *See also* common stock *and* additional paid-in capital *and* accumulated other comprehensive income.

**Return on Assets:** Return on assets is net income divided by average total assets.

**Return on Equity:** Return on equity is (net income less preferred dividends) divided by the average equity.

**Revaluation Model:** Under IFRS, long-lived assets, including fixed assets and intangible assets, are initially recognized at cost and then revalued to fair value at a subsequent revaluation date. Revalued assets are reported at the fair value on the revaluation date adjusted for subsequent amortization/depreciation and impairment. Revaluations must be performed regularly so that at the end of each reporting period the carrying value of the long-lived asset does not differ materially from fair value.

**Revaluation Surplus:** Gains recognized in other comprehensive income when intangible assets and fixed assets are revalued under IFRS.

**Revenue Recognition:** Revenue is recognized when an entity satisfies a performance obligation by transferring either a good or a service to a customer. *See also* realization *and* recognition.

**Revenues:** Revenue recognition occurs when an entity satisfies a performance obligation by transferring either a good or a service to a customer. Revenue should be recognized at an amount that reflects the expected consideration the entity is entitled to receive in exchange for the good or service provided. *See also* expenses *and* gains *and* losses.

**Revenues (for GASB 34 Purposes):** Revenues are based on exchange or exchange-like transactions including charges for services to customers, charges for services to other governments, and fines and forfeitures. *See also* operating grants and contributions.

**Reverse Stock Split:** A reverse stock split is a stock split that reduces the number of shares outstanding and increases the par (or stated) value proportionately. One way to reduce the amount of outstanding shares is to recall outstanding stock certificates and issue new certificates. *See also* stock split.

**Sale-Leaseback:** In a sale-leaseback transaction, the owner of property (seller-lessee) sells the property and simultaneously leases it back from the purchaser-lessor. Usually there is no visible interruption in the use of the property.

**Sales-Type Lease:** From the standpoint of the lessor, finance leases are divided into direct financing leases and sales-type leases under U.S. GAAP. A sales-type lease is a lease that meets one of the five finance lease criteria and two other criteria and in which there is a manufacturers' or dealers' profit. *See also* operating lease *and* direct financing lease *and* finance lease (U.S. GAAP) *and* finance lease criteria.

**Salvage Value:** Salvage value (residual value) is an estimate of the amount that will be realized at the end of the useful life of a depreciable asset. Frequently, depreciable assets have little or no scrap value at the end of their estimated useful life and, if immaterial, the amount(s) may be ignored in calculating depreciation. *See also* useful life.

**Scrip Dividends:** Scrip dividends are simply a special form of note payable whereby a corporation commits to paying a dividend at some later date. Scrip dividends may be used when there is a cash shortage. On the declaration date, retained earnings are debited and notes payable (instead of dividends payable) is credited. Some scrip dividends even bear interest from the declaration date to the date of payment. *See also* cash dividend *and* property dividend.

**Securities and Exchange Commission (SEC):** A U.S. government regulatory body established by the Securities Exchange Act of 1934. All companies that issue securities in the United States are subject to SEC rules and regulations.

**Securities Offering Registration Statement:** A registration statement that must be filed with the SEC when a company issues new securities.

**Segment Reporting:** Segment reporting is the presentation of information about certain parts of an enterprise. The objective of requiring segment disclosures is to provide information on the business activities and the economic environment of an enterprise to help the users of financial statements. *See also* operating segment *and* reportable segment.

**Service Cost:** Service cost (also called current service cost) is the present value of all pension benefits earned by employees in the current year. It is provided by an actuary. Service cost increases the projected benefit obligation and is unaffected by the funded status of the plan. Service cost is a component of net periodic pension cost. *See also* projected benefit obligation *and* net periodic pension cost.

**Settlement:** In pension plan accounting, settlements occur when the pension plan assets increase in value to the point that sale of the pension plan assets allows an organization to purchase annuity contracts to satisfy pension obligations. The remaining funds from the sale of the assets may, with restrictions, be used by the organization. *See also* curtailment.

**Settlement Amount:** The settlement amount (or value) of a derivative is the amount determined by the multiplication (or other arithmetical interaction) of the notional amount and the underlying. *See also* derivative *and* underlying *and* notional amount *and* payment provision.

**Severe Impact:** A significant financially disruptive effect of the normal functioning of an entity.

**Short-Term Obligations Expected to Be Refinanced:** A short-term obligation expected to be refinanced is a short-term obligation that may be excluded from current liabilities and included in noncurrent debt if the intent is to refinance it on a long-term basis and the intent is supported by the ability to do so. The ability to refinance is evidenced either by the actual refinancing prior to the issuance of the financial statements or the existence of a noncancelable financing agreement from a lender having the financial resources to accomplish the refinancing. *See also* current liabilities.

**Significant Influence:** Significant influence is presumed when an investor owns 20 percent to 50 percent of an investee's voting stock. Significant influence can occur even if an investor owns less than 20 percent, but it is not presumed. *See also* cost method *and* equity method *and* control.

**Simple Capital Structure:** A simple capital structure is one with common stock only (or no other securities that can become common stock, such as nonconvertible preferred stock). *See also* basic earnings per share *and* complex capital structure.

**Single-Step Income Statement:** In a single-step income statement, presentation of income from continuing operations and total expenses (including income tax expense) are subtracted from total revenues; thus, the income statement has a single step. *See also* multiple-step income statement.

**Small Stock Dividend:** When less than 20 percent to 25 percent of the shares previously issued and outstanding are distributed, a dividend is treated as a small stock dividend, because the issuance is not expected to affect the market price of the stock. *See also* stock dividend *and* large stock dividend.

**Special Assessments:** Special assessments are defined as taxes or fees levied against property owners who will directly benefit from the project (such as sidewalks and street lights). Accounting for special assessment transactions depends on the degree to which the governmental unit is responsible or potentially liable for debt often associated with the assessment. *See also* capital projects fund *and* custodial trust fund.

**Special-Purpose Governmental Unit:** Special-purpose governmental units that are not primary governments are organizations that are financially accountable to a primary government. They are typically entities engaged in governmental activities, business-type activities, fiduciary activities, and governmental and business-type activities. *See also* financial reporting entity *and* primary government *and* component unit.

**Special Revenue Fund:** Special revenue funds are set up to account for revenues from specific taxes or other earmarked sources that by law are designated to finance particular activities of a government. Note that transactions accounted for in expendable trust funds previous to GASB 34 are accounted for in special revenue funds under GASB 34. The expendable trust fund no longer exists as a fund type. *See also* governmental funds (GRASPP) *and* general fund *and* debt service fund *and* capital projects fund *and* permanent fund *and* expendable trust fund.

**Specific Identification Method:** Under the specific identification method, the cost of each item in inventory is uniquely identified to that item. The cost follows the physical flow of the item in and out of inventory to cost of goods sold. Specific identification is usually used for physically large or high-value items and allows for a greater opportunity for manipulation of income. *See also* FIFO method *and* weighted average method *and* moving average method *and* LIFO method.

**Split-Interest Agreement:** Split-interest agreements are donor contributions of trusts or other arrangements under which a not-for-profit organization receives benefits that are shared with other beneficiaries.

**Start-up Costs:** Start-up costs are expenses incurred in the formation of a corporation (legal fees) and are considered organizational costs. Start-up costs are expensed when incurred.

**Stated Interest Rate:** The stated (or nominal) interest rate is the interest to be paid to the bondholders. This rate is specified in the bond contract. *See also* bond indenture *and* effective interest rate.

**Statement of Financial Accounting Concept (SFAC):** Statements of Financial Accounting Concepts are published by the Financial Accounting Standards Board. They establish the concepts and objectives to be used by the FASB in developing accounting standards. They do not establish GAAP. *See also* Statement of Financial Accounting Standard (SFAS) *and* Accounting Principles Board (APB) opinions *and* Accounting Research Bulletins (ARB).

**Statement of Financial Accounting Standard (SFAS):** Statements of Financial Accounting Standards were published by the Financial Accounting Standards Board. All active (non-superseded) SFAS were included in the FASB Accounting Standards Codification.

**Step-by-Step Acquisition:** An investor may acquire an investment in an investee in more than one transaction. In this case, goodwill is computed at the time of each transaction.

**Stock Appreciation Right:** A stock appreciation right entitles an employee to receive an amount equal to the excess of the market price of the stock at the exercise date over a predetermined amount (usually market price at grant date). This excess times the number of rights outstanding is the compensation cost of the corporation. Compensation cost for stock appreciation rights outstanding is adjusted annually to account for changes in the market price of the stock. Unlike stock options, stock appreciation rights do not require the employee to make a cash payment. *See also* stock option.

**Stock Dividend:** Stock dividends distribute additional shares of a corporation's own stock to its shareholders. The treatment of stock dividends depends on the size (percentage) of the dividend in proportion to the total shares outstanding before the dividend. *See also* large stock dividend *and* small stock dividend *and* cash dividend *and* property dividend *and* stock split.

**Stock Option:** A stock option is the right to purchase shares of a corporation's capital stock under fixed conditions of time, place, and amount. Stock options are normally compensatory and require a payment at the exercise date. *See also* fair value method.

**Stock Right:** A stock right provides an existing shareholder with the opportunity to buy additional shares. The right usually carries a price below the stock's market price on the date the rights are granted. The issuance of stock rights requires a memorandum entry only.

**Stock Split:** Stock splits occur when a corporation issues additional shares of its own stock (without charge) to current shareholders and reduces the par (or stated) value per share proportionately. There is no change in the total book value of the shares outstanding. Thus, the memo entry to acknowledge a stock split is merely a formality. *See also* reverse stock split *and* stock dividend.

**Stock Subscription:** Sometimes, a corporation sells its capital stock by subscription. This means that a contractual agreement to sell a specified number of shares at an agreed-upon price on credit is entered into. Upon full payment of the subscription, a stock certificate evidencing ownership in the corporation is issued.

**Stockholders' Equity:** Stockholders' equity (also called shareholders' equity or owners' equity) is the owners' claim to the net assets (assets minus liabilities) of a corporation. It is generally presented on the statement of financial position (balance sheet) as the last major section following liabilities.

**Straight-Line Depreciation:** Straight-line depreciation is a method of depreciation where depreciation is recognized evenly over the life of the asset. Salvage value is included in the calculation. *See also* sum-of-the-years'-digits depreciation *and* declining balance depreciation *and* units-of-production depreciation.

**Summary of Significant Accounting Policies:** U.S. GAAP and IFRS require that a description of all significant accounting policies be included as an integral part of the financial statements. The preferred presentation is to include the "Summary of Significant Accounting Policies" as the first or second note to the financial statements.

**Sum-of-the-Years'-Digits Depreciation:** Sum-of-the-years'-depreciation is an accelerated method of depreciation that provides higher depreciation in the early years of the asset's life and lower depreciation in the later years. A specific formula is used to calculate the depreciation for each year; salvage value is included in the calculation. *See also* straight-line depreciation *and* declining balance depreciation *and* units-of-production depreciation.

**Support Services:** Support services are all services that are not program services. *See also* program services.

**Swap Contract:** A private agreement between two parties, generally assisted by an intermediary, to exchange future cash payments. Common swaps include interest rate swaps, currency swaps, equity swaps, and commodity swaps. A swap agreement is equivalent to a series of forward contracts.

**Technological Feasibility:** For computer software development accounting under U.S. GAAP, technological feasibility is established upon completion of a detailed program design or completion of a working model. *See also* computer software developed for internal use *and* computer software development costs.

**Temporal Method:** Foreign currency remeasurement, also known as the temporal method, is the restatement of financial statements denominated in a foreign currency to the entity's functional currency. Remeasurement is required when an entity's books are not maintained in its functional currency. *See also* translation *and* current method *and* functional currency.

**Temporary Difference:** Temporary differences affect the deferred tax computation. Temporary differences are items of revenue and expense that enter into pretax financial income in a period before they enter into taxable income or enter into pretax financial income in a period after they enter into taxable income. Temporary differences reverse in future periods. *See also* permanent difference *and* comprehensive allocation.

**Term Bond:** A term bond is a bond that has a single fixed maturity date.

**Termination Benefits:** Termination benefits arise when employees are paid to terminate their rights to future pension payments. *See also* settlement *and* curtailment.

**Timeliness:** Timeliness is having the information available while it is able to influence decisions. *See also* relevance *and* predictive value *and* feedback value.

**Times Interest Earned:** Times interest earned is income before interest and taxes divided by interest. Times interest earned is also known as the interest coverage ratio.

**Total Income Tax Expense:** Total income tax expense or benefit for a period is the sum of current income tax expense/benefit and deferred income tax expense/benefit. *See also* current income tax expense *and* deferred income tax expense.

**Trade Discounts:** Trade discounts are quantity discounts. Sales and accounts receivable are recorded net of trade discounts. *See also* cash discount.

**Trading Debt Securities:** Trading debt securities are those securities that are bought and held principally for the purpose of selling them in the near term. Trading debt securities generally reflect active and frequent buying and selling with the objective of generating profits on short-term differences in price. Securities classified as trading debt securities are normally reported as current assets. *See also* available-for-sale debt securities *and* held-to-maturity debt securities.

**Transfers-In:** Transfers-in are transfers into one fund from another. They represent the source of financial resources. Transfers-in are other financing sources. *See also* other financing sources *and* transfers-out.

**Transfers of Operations:** A combination of a government's activities (less than a legal entity) with either an existing government or with a new government.

**Transfers-Out:** Transfers-out are transfers out of one fund to another. They represent the use of financial resources. Transfers-out are other financing uses. *See also* other financing uses *and* transfers-in.

**Translation:** Foreign currency translation is the restatement of financial statements denominated in the functional currency to the reporting currency using an appropriate rate of exchange. *See also* remeasurement *and* functional currency.

**Treasury Bond:** A treasury bond is a bond that has been reacquired, but not retired, by the issuer (like treasury stock). Its par value is shown on the balance sheet as a deduction from bonds payable.

**Treasury Stock:** Treasury stock is a corporation's own stock that has been issued to shareholders and subsequently reacquired but not retired. Treasury stock is not generally considered an asset because it is widely held that a corporation cannot own part of itself. Treasury stock is not entitled to any of the rights of ownership given to common stock, such as the right to vote or to receive dividends. In addition, a portion of retained earnings equal to the cost of treasury stock may be restricted and may not be used as a basis for the declaration or payment of dividends (depending on applicable state law). *See also* cost method (of treasury stock accounting) *and* par value method (of treasury stock accounting).

**Treasury Stock Method:** For earnings per share calculations, the dilutive effect of options and warrants and their equivalents is applied using the treasury stock method. The treasury stock method assumes that the proceeds from the exercise of stock options, warrants, and their equivalents will be used by the corporation to repurchase treasury shares at the prevailing (or average) market price, resulting in an incremental increase in shares outstanding, but not the full amount of shares that are issued on exercise of the common stock equivalents. *See also* diluted earnings per share *and* if-converted method.

**Troubled Debt Restructuring:** A troubled debt restructuring (impaired loan) is a debt restructuring in which the creditor allows the debtor certain concessions to improve the likelihood of collection that would not be considered under normal circumstances. Concessions include items such as reduced interest rates, extension of maturity dates, reduction of the face amount of the debt, and reduction of the amount of accrued interest. The concessions must be made in light of the debtor's financial difficulty, and the objective of the creditor must be to maximize recovery of the investment. Troubled debt restructurings are often the result of legal proceedings or of negotiation between the parties. *See also* impairment of loans.

**Unamortized Discount (Premium):** Unamortized discount (premium) is the amount of the original discount or premium on the bond that has not yet been amortized. *See also* discount *and* premium.

**Unappropriated Retained Earnings:** Unappropriated retained earnings is that portion of retained earnings that has not been appropriated. *See also* retained earnings *and* appropriated retained earnings.

**Unassigned Fund Balance:** Fund balance resources associated with spendable assets neither restricted, committed, nor assigned. Unassigned fund balance is a residual equity classification for the general fund. Only the general fund should have a positive unassigned fund balance. Other governmental funds might have negative unassigned fund balances if all their other fund balance classifications have no balance.

**Unconditional Promise:** An unconditional promise to give (the promise is also known as a pledge) is a contribution, and is recorded as revenue at its fair market value when the promise is made. An unconditional promise may be written or verbal. However, verbal pledges should be documented by the organization internally and may be more difficult to collect. *See also* contribution *and* conditional promise.

**Underfunded:** A defined benefit pension plan is underfunded when the fair value of the pension plan assets is less than the projected benefit obligation (PBO).

**Underlying:** An underlying is a specified price, rate, or other variable (interest rate, security or commodity price, foreign exchange rate, index of prices or rates, etc.), including a scheduled event that may or may not occur. *See also* derivative *and* notional amount *and* settlement amount *and* payment provision.

**Underwater Endowment Fund:** A donor-restricted endowment fund for which the fair value of the fund at the reporting date is less than either the original gift amount or the amount required to be maintained either by the donor or by law that extends donor restrictions. *See also* endowment fund.

**Unearned Revenue:** Unearned revenue (revenue received in advance) is recorded as a liability because it is an obligation to perform a service in the future and is reported as revenue in the period in which it is earned, that is, when no further future service is required. Examples include rent received in advance, interest received in advance on notes receivable, and subscriptions received in advance.

**Unexpired Cost:** An unexpired cost is a cost that will expire in future periods and be charged (matched or allocated in a systematic and rational manner) against revenues from future periods. *See also* cost *and* expenses *and* matching principle *and* expired cost.

**Unguaranteed Residual Value:** The unguaranteed residual value of the lease is the estimated fair value of the leased property at the end of the lease term that is not guaranteed by either the lessor or by a third party unrelated by the lessor. *See also* guaranteed residual value (by the lessee).

**Units-of-Production Depreciation:** The units-of-production method relates depreciation to the estimated production capability of an asset and is expressed in a rate per unit or hour. *See also* straight-line depreciation *and* sum-of-the-years'-digits depreciation *and* declining balance depreciation.

**Unrealized Gains and Losses:** In marketable securities accounting, unrealized gains and losses are those that are determined in the marking-to-market of the securities. If the unrealized gains and losses are for trading debt securities, the unrealized gains and losses are treated as realized gains and losses and included in income. If the unrealized gains and losses are for available-for-sale debt securities, the unrealized gains and losses are included in other comprehensive income. Equity securities are generally reported at fair value through net income (FVTNI). Unrealized holding gains and losses on equity securities are included in earnings as they occur. *See also* trading debt securities *and* available-for-sale debt securities.

**Unrecognized Prior Service Cost:** Unrecognized prior service cost is the portion of prior service cost that has not yet been recognized (amortized) by the employer in net periodic pension cost. *See also* net periodic pension cost *and* prior service cost.

**Unrestricted Cash:** Unrestricted cash is used for all current operations. *See also* cash *and* restricted cash.

**Unrestricted Current Funds (unrestricted operating or general):** Funds used to record a not-for-profit's activities that are supported by resources over which the governing boards have discretionary control. Fund balances generally consist of unrestricted net assets.

**Unrestricted Net Position (governmental):** For governmental organizations, the unrestricted component of net position includes the net amount of the assets, deferred outflows of resources, liabilities, and deferred inflows of resources that are not included in the determination of net investment in capital assets or the restricted component of net position. *See also* net position *and* restricted net position *and* net investment in capital assets.

**Useful Life:** Useful life is the period of time over which an asset's cost will be depreciated. *See also* salvage value.

**Valuation Allowance:** In deferred tax accounting, a valuation allowance is recognized under U.S. GAAP when it is more likely than not that part or all of a deferred tax asset will not be realized. *See also* deferred tax asset.

**Variable Interest Entity:** A corporation, partnership, trust, LLC, or other legal structure used for business purposes that either does not have equity investors with voting rights or lacks the sufficient financial resources to support its activities.

**Variance Power:** Variance power is the ability to use assets in any way a not-for-profit organization deems appropriate. *See also* agency transaction.

**Verifiability:** If information is verifiable (objective), it means that the same results could be duplicated with the same measurement techniques (which is the primary concern for auditors of financial statements). *See also* reliability *and* neutrality *and* representational faithfulness.

**Vested Benefits:** Vested benefits are pension plan benefits that already belong (vest) to employees who have earned their benefits by reason of having reached retirement age and/or who otherwise meet unique pension plan requirements (fully vested after only five years of service). The benefits are vested whether that person has actually retired, and they are not contingent on remaining in the service of the employer. Generally, pension plans require money to be left in the plan until retirement.

**Voluntary Health and Welfare Organizations:** Voluntary health and welfare organizations include organizations for the blind, mental health associations, the Salvation Army, and a variety of other not-for-profit organizations. Organizations that are funded primarily by contributions and that provide services which are not funded to any great degree by any other source and which benefit community health or welfare are voluntary health and welfare organizations. *See also* foundations *and* health care organizations *and* not-for-profit organizations.

**Voluntary Non-exchange Transactions:** Voluntary non-exchange transactions are instances in which the government receives resources and does not provide equal value (grants). *See also* derived tax revenues *and* imposed non-exchange revenues *and* government-mandated non-exchange transactions.

**Weighted Average Method:** Under the weighted average method of inventory accounting, the average cost of each item in inventory is the weighted average of the cost of all of the items in inventory at the end of the period. The weighted average is determined by dividing the total cost of inventory available by the total number of units of inventory available, remembering that the beginning inventory is included in both totals. This method is particularly suitable for homogenous products and a periodic inventory system. *See also* specific identification method *and* FIFO method *and* moving average method *and* LIFO method.

**Weighted Average Number of Common Shares Outstanding:** For earnings per share calculations, the weighted average number of common shares outstanding during a period is the mean (average) of shares outstanding and assumed to be outstanding for earnings per share calculations. Shares sold or reacquired during the period (including treasury stock) should be weighted for the portion of the period they were outstanding. *See also* basic earnings per share *and* income available to common shareholders.

**Weighted Average of Accumulated Expenditures:** Interest to be capitalized for a particular period is determined by applying an interest rate to the average amount of accumulated expenditures for the qualifying asset during the period (known as avoidable interest). *See also* construction period interest *and* capitalization of interest period.

**With Recourse:** If an assignment of accounts receivable is with recourse, the factor has an option to resell any uncollectible receivables to the original assignor. If an assignment of accounts receivable is with recourse, two treatments are possible. The transfer may be considered either a sale or a borrowing (with the accounts receivable as collateral). *See also* factoring of accounts receivable *and* pledging of accounts receivable.

**Without Recourse:** If an assignment of accounts receivable is without recourse, the assignee (the factor) assumes the risk of any losses on collections. If the assignee is unable to collect all of the accounts receivable, it has no recourse against the assignor. *See also* factoring of accounts receivable *and* pledging of accounts receivable.

**Working Capital:** Working capital is current assets minus current liabilities. *See also* current ratio *and* current assets *and* current liabilities.

**Written Purchase Option:** A written purchase option is a lessee's option to purchase the leased property at a sufficiently low price that the exercise of the option is relatively certain.

**Zero Coupon Bond:** A zero coupon bond (also known as a deep discount bond) is a bond sold with no stated interest but rather at a discount and redeemed at face value. *See also* stated interest rate *and* face value.

# Index FAR

## A

| | |
|---|---|
| Account analysis format | F3-9 |
| Accounting alternatives | F1-4, F6-36 |
| Accounting Principles Board | F1-3 |
| Accounts receivable | F3-9 |
|     turnover | F2-44 |
| Accretion expense | F5-12 |
| Accrual accounting | F1-9 |
| Accrued liabilities | F5-3 |
| Accumulated benefit obligation (ABO) | F7-4 |
| Accumulated other comprehensive income | F1-60, F7-18, F7-30, F7-44 |
| Accumulated plan benefits | F7-33 |
| Accumulated postretirement benefit obligation (APBO) | F7-28 |
| Activity accounting, governmental | F9-20, F9-25 |
| Actual return on plan assets | F7-6, F7-8 |
| Actuarial gains and losses | F7-5 |
| Additional paid-in capital | F7-43 |
| Adjusting journal entries | F1-67 |
| Admission of a partner | F2-53 |
| Allocating the transaction price | F1-23 |
| Allowance method | F3-12, F3-14 |
| Amortization | F3-70 |
| Annuity due | F5-26, F5-29 |
| Antidilutive | F8-7, F8-9 |
| Appropriations control | F9-19 |
| Artwork and historical treasures | F10-45 |
| Asset retirement | |
|     cost | F5-12 |
|         obligations | F5-11 |
| Asset turnover | F2-46 |
| Assigned fund balance | F9-45 |
| Authorized capital stock | F7-40 |
| Available-for-sale securities | F4-4 |

© Becker Professional Education Corporation. All rights reserved.

## B

Bad debt expense ............................................. F3-12, F3-14
Balance sheet ................................................................ F1-17
    approach ................................................................ F6-55
Bank reconciliations ................................................... F3-4
Basic EPS .................................................................... F8-3
Basis of accounting .................................................. F9-14
Basket purchase ....................................................... F3-42
Beneficial interest .................................................... F8-62
Beneficiary accounting ........................................... F8-62
Benefit payments ....................................................... F7-5
Bill-and-hold arrangements .................................. F1-35
Blended presentation ............................................ F10-38
Bond amortization methods ................................. F5-47
Bonds payable
    indenture ............................................................... F5-37
    issuance costs ..................................................... F5-43
    issued at a discount .......................................... F5-40
    issued at a premium ........................................ F5-41
    issued at par value ............................................ F5-39
    selling price ......................................................... F5-39
Bond terms ................................................................. F5-39
Bonuses ......................................................................... F5-7
Bonus method—partnerships .............................. F2-55
Book value per common share ............................ F7-41
Budgetary
    accounting .......................................................... F9-18
    control .................................................................... F9-19
    information ....................................................... F10-85
Buildings .................................................................... F3-42

## C

Callable preferred stock ......................................... F7-42
Capital assets (capitalization and depreciation) .... F10-44
Capital grants and contributions ...................... F10-47
Capitalization of interest costs ............................. F3-44
Capital projects funds ............................... F9-11, F9-63
Capital stock .............................................................. F7-40
Carrying value ........................................................... F5-43
Cash ................................................................. F3-3, F8-15

Cash basis .................................................................. F2-33
Cash dividends ......................................................... F7-53
Cash equivalents ...................................................... F8-15
Cash flow hedge ....................................................... F6-35
Categories of funds ................................................. F9-11
Change in accounting entity ................................ F1-55
Change in accounting estimate ........................... F1-51
Change in accounting principle .......................... F1-52
Character .................................................................... F9-25
Charges for services ............................................. F10-47
Classification of governmental expenditures ....... F9-24
Classification of governmental fund balances
    (GRaSPP) ............................................................. F9-45
Classified balance sheet ......................................... F1-17
Clearance funds ..................................................... F10-17
Collateral trust bonds ............................................. F5-37
Combined costs ........................................................ F8-39
Commercial substance ........................................... F3-61
Committed fund balance ...................................... F9-45
Committee on Accounting Procedure ................. F1-3
Common stock ......................................................... F7-40
Common stockholders' equity ............................. F7-41
Compensation for future absences ....................... F5-8
Compensatory stock option ................................. F7-60
Completed contract method ................................ F1-42
Complex capital structure ...................................... F8-6
Component depreciation ...................................... F3-50
Component of an entity ........................................ F1-45
Component unit ..................................................... F10-38
Comprehensive allocation .................................... F6-55
Comprehensive annual financial report
    (CAFR) ................................................................. F10-35
Comprehensive income ......................................... F1-59
Computer software development costs ............ F3-76
Concentration of credit risk ................................. F4-14
Concentrations ........................................................... F2-5
Conceptual frameworks ........................................... F1-4
Conditional promises ............................................. F8-50
Consigned goods ..................................................... F3-22
Consignment sales .................................................. F1-36

Consolidated balance sheet .................................... F4-73
Consolidated statement of cash flows .................. F4-75
Consolidated statement of changes in equity ....... F4-75
Consolidated statement of income ...................... F4-74
Construction period interest ................................... F3-44
Consumption method ............................................. F9-24
Contingencies .......................................................... F5-17
Contingent shares ................................................... F8-11
Contributions and recognition ............................... F8-49
Control ..................................................................... F4-31
Convertible bonds .................................................. F5-37
Convertible preferred stock ................................... F8-10
Corridor approach .................................................. F7-11
Cost
    approach ........................................................... F2-18
    depletion ........................................................... F3-57
    flow assumptions ............................................. F3-29
    method .............................................................. F7-45
    model ................................................... F3-40, F3-71
Costs ........................................................................ F1-13
Costs to fullfill a contract ........................................ F1-31
Credit risk ................................................................ F6-34
Cumulative effect .................................................... F1-53
Cumulative preferred stock ................................... F7-41
Current expected credit losses
    (CECL) model ........................................ F3-12, F4-7
Current financial resources (GRaSPP) ................... F9-14
Current rate method .............................................. F6-47
Current ratio ........................................................... F2-43
Current service cost ................................................ F7-8
Custodial funds ...................................................... F9-13

# D

Days in inventory ................................................... F2-45
Days sales in accounts receivable ......................... F2-44
Debentures ............................................................. F5-37
Debt covenants ...................................................... F5-35
Debt instruments ................................................... F4-16
Debt service funds ..................................... F9-11, F9-55
Debt-to-equity ....................................................... F2-49

Deferred tax
    assets ................................................................ F6-60
    liabilities ............................................................ F6-58
Defined benefit pension plan
    financial statements ........................................ F7-33
Defined benefit plan ................................... F7-3, F7-4
Defined contribution plan .......................... F7-3, F7-4
Depletion ................................................................ F3-56
Deposits in transit .................................................. F3-5
Depreciation ........................................................... F3-49
Derivative instruments ............................. F6-31, F6-35
Derivative risks ....................................................... F6-34
Derived tax revenues ............................................. F9-20
Determining the transaction price ....................... F1-22
Diluted EPS ............................................................. F8-6
Dilutive ................................................................... F8-7
Direct financing lease ............................................ F6-7
Direct method ............................................ F8-16, F8-17
Direct write-off method ............................ F3-12, F3-14
Discontinued operations ....................................... F1-45
Discount ..................................... F5-33, F5-37, F5-42
Discount and premium amortization ................... F5-47
Discounting notes receivable ............................... F3-17
Discrete presentation ............................................ F10-38
Disposals ................................................................. F3-56
Dividend payout .................................................... F2-51
Dividends ............................................................... F7-53
Dollar-value LIFO ................................................... F3-34
Donated collection items ...................................... F8-53
Donated materials ................................................. F8-53
Donated services ................................................... F8-51
Donated stock ........................................................ F7-49
Double-declining-balance method ....................... F3-54
DuPont return on assets ........................................ F2-47

# E

Earnings per share ................................................. F2-50
Economic resources (SE-CIPPOE) ......................... F9-14
Effective interest method .......................... F5-33, F5-50
Effective interest rate ............................................ F5-42

Elements of financial statements............................ F1-9
Enacted tax rate .................................................. F6-67
Encumbrances...................................................... F9-35
Enhancing qualitative characteristics.................... F1-6
Enterprise funds............................................ F9-12, F10-7
Equipment .......................................................... F3-43
Equity
    instruments.................................................. F4-16
    investment at risk ...................................... F4-35
    method ........................................................ F4-19
    securities..................................................... F4-10
Equity multiplier.................................................. F2-50
Error correction................................................... F1-55
Escheat property................................................. F10-21
Estimated revenue control ................................. F9-19
Estimated useful life ........................................... F3-49
Estimates in the preparation
    of financial statements............................... F2-5
Exact method ..................................................... F2-54
Exchange rate..................................................... F6-43
Exercise price...................................................... F7-60
Existing net obligation ........................................ F7-11
Exit or disposal activities.................................... F5-10
Expected postretirement benefit obligation
    (EPBO)......................................................... F7-28
Expected return on plan assets ........................ F7-8
Expendable trusts .............................................. F9-53
Expenditures ...................................................... F9-23
Expense classification in the statement
    of activities ................................................. F8-38
External reporting............................................... F9-9
Extinguishment of debt...................................... F5-65

# F

Face value ........................................................... F5-37
Factoring ............................................................. F3-16
Fair value ............................................................. F2-15
    hedge .......................................................... F6-35
    option ......................................................... F4-3
Fiduciary (trust) funds ........................................ F9-13

Finance lease...................................................... F6-7
Financial Accounting Standards Board (FASB) ........ F1-3
Financial instruments ........................................ F8-64
Financially interrelated...................................... F8-61
Financial reporting entity .................................. F10-37
Financing activities............................................. F8-20
Financing cash flows.......................................... F8-15
First in, first out (FIFO) method ........................ F3-29
Fiscal accountability........................................... F10-33
Fixed assets ........................................................ F3-39
    impairment................................................. F3-83
    under IFRS .................................................. F3-40
    under U.S. GAAP ........................................ F3-39
FOB destination.................................................. F3-21
FOB shipping point ............................................ F3-21
Foreign currency
    hedge .......................................................... F6-39
    items............................................................ F1-60
    transactions..................................... F6-43, F6-50
    translation .................................................. F6-43
Foreign financial statement translation................. F6-45
Form 8-K.............................................................. F2-28
Form 10-K............................................................ F2-27
Form 10-Q........................................................... F2-27
Forward contract................................................ F6-33
Franchise accounting......................................... F3-72
Free or reduced rent ......................................... F6-4
Full accrual......................................................... F9-15
Full set of financial statements ........................ F1-8
Function ............................................................. F9-24
Functional currency ........................................... F6-43
Functional depreciation .................................... F3-49
Fund accounting................................................ F9-9
Fundamental assumptions................................ F1-8
Fundamental qualitative characteristics.................. F1-5
Funded status............................................. F7-15, F7-30
Fund financial statements ................................ F10-34
Fundraising......................................................... F8-55

Fund structure ............................................. F9-8
Futures contract ......................................... F6-33
Future value of $1 .................................... F5-27
Future value of an ordinary annuity ...... F5-30

## G

Gain contingency ....................................... F5-17
Gains and losses ....................................... F7-10
General fund .............................. F9-11, F9-49
Generally accepted accounting principles
  (GAAP) ................................................. F1-3
Going concern ............................................ F2-7
Goodwill ...................................... F4-22, F4-85
Goodwill impairment ................................ F4-85
Goodwill method—partnerships ............. F2-56
Governmental Accounting Standards Board
  (GASB) ................................................. F9-4
Governmental funds ................................ F9-11
Governmental units ................................... F9-4
Government mandated non-exchange
  transactions ....................................... F9-21
Government-wide financial
  statements ............................. F10-34, F10-41
Grants ....................................................... F9-54
Gross profit method ................................. F3-36
Guarantees ............................................... F5-19

## H

Hedging ..................................................... F6-31
Held for sale ............................................. F1-46
Held-to-maturity securities ........................ F4-5
Highest and best use ................................ F2-17
Historical cost .......................................... F3-39
Historical exchange rate .......................... F6-43

## I

Identifying the contract ............................. F1-19
Identifying the performance obligations
  in the contract .................................... F1-21
If-converted method .................................. F8-8
Impairment ....................... F3-40, F3-79, F5-61
Impairment of securities ........................... F4-7

Imposed non-exchange revenues ........... F9-20
Improvements .......................................... F3-43
Income approach ..................................... F2-18
Income statement ..................................... F1-13
Income tax
  basis ................................................... F2-35
  disclosures ........................................ F6-73
Income taxes ........................................... F6-53
Incremental costs of obtaining a contract ............. F1-31
Indirect method ........................... F8-16, F8-18
Infrastructure ................. F10-35, F10-44, F10-87
Intangible assets ..................................... F3-69
Integrated approach ............................... F10-33
Intercompany
  bond transactions ............................. F4-68
  inventory/merchandise transactions ............... F4-66
  profit on sale of depreciable fixed assets ........ F4-69
  sale of land ........................................ F4-69
  transactions ...................................... F4-65
Interest cost ............................. F7-5, F7-8, F7-29
Interfund activity .................................... F9-40
Internal service funds ........... F9-12, F10-3, F10-42, F10-48
International Financial Reporting Standards
  (IFRS) .................................................. F1-4
Interperiod tax allocation ............. F6-54, F6-55
Intraperiod tax allocation ....................... F6-53
Inventory turnover .................................. F2-45
Investee's undistributed earnings .......... F6-72
Investing activities ................................... F8-20
Investing cash flows ............................... F8-15
Investment trust funds .............. F9-13, F10-20
Involuntary conversions ......................... F3-67
Issued capital stock ................................. F7-40

## L

Lacking commercial substance .............. F3-63
Land .......................................................... F3-41
  improvements .................................... F3-42
Last in, first out (LIFO) method ............... F3-32
Lease classification ................................... F6-6

Lease contract ............................................................. F6-3
Lease definition ........................................................... F6-3
Lease disclosures ...................................................... F6-27
Lease discount rate .................................................. F6-12
Lease (governmental) ................................................ F9-27
Lease payments ........................................................ F6-11
Lessee accounting .................................................... F6-17
Lessor accounting ..................................................... F6-23
Legal method ............................................................. F7-46
Level 1 inputs ............................................................ F2-18
Level 2 inputs ............................................................ F2-18
Level 3 inputs ............................................................ F2-18
Liquidating dividends ................................................. F7-53
Liquidation of a partnership ....................................... F2-61
Long-term construction contracts .............................. F1-39
Long-term liabilities ................................................... F5-31
Loss contingency ........................................... F5-17, F5-18
Lower of cost and net realizable value ...................... F3-24
Lower of cost or market ............................................. F3-23

## M

Major fund reporting criteria ................................... F10-51
Management's discussion and analysis
 (MD&A) .................................................. F10-34, F10-83
Mandatorily redeemable preferred stock .................. F7-42
Marketable securities reclassification ........................ F4-6
Market approach ....................................................... F2-17
Market risk .................................................... F4-14, F6-34
Matrix of financial statements required
 for various funds ................................................ F10-30
Measurable and available .......................................... F9-15
Measurement focus ................................................... F9-14
Modification of terms ................................................. F5-60
Modified accrual accounting ...................................... F9-15
Modified approach ................................................... F10-44
Modified cash basis ................................................... F2-33
Most advantageous market ....................................... F2-16
Moving average method ............................................ F3-31
Multiple-step income statement ................................ F1-14
Multiyear pledges ...................................................... F8-50
Municipal landfills (the dump) .................................. F10-9

## N

Net assets available for benefits .............................. F7-34
Net investment
 hedge ................................................................. F6-39
Net operating loss (NOL) ............................................ F6-70
Net periodic pension cost ............................................ F7-8
Net realizable value ....................................... F3-23, F3-24
Noncash investing and financing activities ............... F8-20
Noncompensatory stock option ................................. F7-59
Nonconforming goods ................................................ F3-21
Nonmonetary exchanges ........................................... F3-61
Nonreciprocal interfund activity ................................. F9-40
Nonrecognized subsequent events ........................... F2-11
Nonspendable fund balance ...................................... F9-45
Non-sufficient funds (NSF) ........................................... F3-5
Notes payable .............................................. F5-32, F5-38
Notes receivable ........................................................ F3-17
Notes to financial statements ..................... F2-3, F10-84
Notional amount ........................................................ F6-31

## O

Object classes ........................................................... F9-25
Operating
 activities ............................................................. F8-17
 cash flows .......................................................... F8-15
 grants and contributions .................................. F10-47
 loss carryforwards .............................................. F6-70
 segment ............................................................. F2-22
Operating lease ............................................................ F6-7
Operational accountability ...................................... F10-33
Option contract .......................................................... F6-32
Orderly transaction .................................................... F2-16
Ordinary annuity ........................................................ F5-26
Organizational costs .................................................. F3-73
Organizational unit .................................................... F9-24
Other comprehensive bases of accounting ............... F2-33
Other comprehensive income .................................... F1-59
Outstanding capital stock ......................................... F7-40
Outstanding checks ..................................................... F3-5

## P

Participating preferred stock .................................. F7-41
Par value ........................................................................ F7-40
Partnerships ................................................................. F2-53
Payables ........................................................................... F5-3
Payment provision ........................................................ F6-31
Pension adjustments .................................................... F1-59
Pension expense ............................................................. F7-7
Pension plan .................................................................... F7-4
    asset ........................................................................ F7-15
    contributions ......................................................... F7-15
    contributory ............................................................. F7-4
    liability .................................................................... F7-15
    noncontributory ...................................................... F7-4
Pension trust funds ..................................... F9-13, F10-22
Percentage depletion .................................................... F3-57
Percentage-of-completion method ............................. F1-39
Periodic inventory system ............................................ F3-27
Permanent differences ..................................... F6-54, F6-56
Permanent funds ............................................... F9-11, F9-72
Perpetual inventory system ......................................... F3-27
Physical depreciation .................................................... F3-49
Plan assets ....................................................................... F7-6
Pledging ........................................................................... F3-16
Postretirement benefits ............................................... F7-27
    cost ........................................................................ F7-29
    plan asset .............................................................. F7-30
    plan liability .......................................................... F7-30
    plan gains and losses ......................................... F7-29
Preferred stock ............................................................. F7-41
Premium ............................................................ F5-37, F5-42
Present value measurement ........................................ F1-10
Present value of $1 ...................................................... F5-26
Present value of an ordinary annuity ........................ F5-28
Price earnings ratio ...................................................... F2-50
Primarily or potentially liable .................................... F9-64
Primary beneficiary ...................................................... F4-33
Primary government ................................................. F10-37
Principal market ........................................................... F2-16

Principal vs. agent ........................................................ F1-32
Prior service cost ................................... F7-5, F7-9, F7-29
Private Company Council .............................................. F1-4
Private purpose trust funds ....................... F9-13, F10-21
Profit margin ................................................................ F2-47
Program ........................................................................ F9-24
    approach ............................................................ F10-46
    revenue category types .................................. F10-47
    services ................................................................ F8-38
Projected benefit obligation (PBO) ............................. F7-4
Property (in-kind) dividends ...................................... F7-53
Proprietary funds ........................................................ F9-12
Prospective ................................................................... F1-51
Purchase commitments ............................................... F3-36
Purchase method ........................................................ F9-24

## Q

Quick ratio ................................................................... F2-43

## R

Ratio analysis .............................................................. F2-41
Realized gains and losses ............................................. F4-5
Recipient accounting .................................................. F8-61
Reciprocal interfund activity ..................................... F9-40
Reclassification adjustments ..................................... F1-60
Reclassification of restrictions .................................. F8-38
Recognized subsequent events ................................. F2-11
Reconciliation of governmental fund
    financial statements to government-wide
    financial statements .......................................... F10-65
Refund liabilities ......................................................... F1-38
Regulation S-X ............................................................. F2-28
Remeasurement method ........................................... F6-46
Repairs .......................................................................... F3-43
Replacements .............................................................. F3-43
Reportable segment ................................................... F2-22
Reporting currency ..................................................... F6-43
Repurchase agreements ............................................. F1-33
Required supplementary information .... F10-34, F10-85
Research and development costs ............................. F3-74
Restricted cash .............................................................. F3-3

Restricted fund balance ............................. F9-45
Retained earnings ...................................... F7-44
Retrospective ............................................. F1-52
Return on assets ........................................ F2-47
Return on equity ........................................ F2-48
Return on plan assets ........................ F7-8, F7-29
Revaluation gains and losses ................... F3-40
Revaluation model ............................ F3-40, F3-71
Revaluation surplus ................................... F1-60
Revenue recognition (U.S. GAAP) ............ F1-19
Reverse stock splits ................................... F7-56
Revised financial statements ................... F2-12
Right to return ............................................ F1-38
Risks and uncertainties ............................. F2-5

## S

Sale-leaseback transactions .................... F6-12
Sales discount ............................................ F3-10
Sales-type lease ......................................... F6-7
Salvage value .................................. F3-49, F3-54
Scrip dividends ........................................... F7-53
Securities and Exchange Commission (SEC) ............ F1-3
    interactive data rule ............................ F2-31
Securities offering registration statements ........... F2-27
Segment reporting ..................................... F2-21
Serial bonds ................................................ F5-38
Service cost ......................................... F7-5, F7-29
Settlement amount ................................... F6-31
Significant influence .................................. F4-19
Simple capital structure ............................ F8-3
Single-step income statement ................. F1-16
Special assessments .................................. F9-64
Special items .............................................. F10-47
Special purpose entities ............................ F4-36
Special purpose frameworks ..................... F2-33
Special purpose governmental units ....... F10-38
Special revenue funds ..................... F9-11, F9-53
Specific governmental disclosures .......... F10-84
Specific identification method .................. F3-29
Split interest agreements ......................... F8-51

Start-up costs ............................................ F3-73
Stated interest rate .......................... F5-37, F5-42
Statement of activities ..................... F8-36, F10-46
Statement of cash flows ............................ F8-15
    not-for-profit ......................................... F8-43
    proprietary funds ................................. F10-59
Statement of changes in shareholders' equity ..... F7-56
Statement of comprehensive income .......... F1-59, F1-61
Statement of consolidated
    comprehensive income ....................... F4-74
Statement of financial position ................ F8-32
Statement of net position ......................... F10-41
Statement of retained earnings ............... F1-56
Stock
    dividends ............................................... F7-54
    options .................................................. F7-59
    rights ..................................................... F7-52
    splits ...................................................... F7-55
    subscriptions ........................................ F7-51
Straight-line depreciation ......................... F3-52
Subsequent events ................................... F2-11
Summary of significant accounting policies ........... F2-3
Sum-of-the-years'-digits method ............. F3-52
Support services ........................................ F8-38
Swap contract ............................................ F6-33

## T

Temporal method ...................................... F6-46
Temporarily restricted ............................... F8-37
Temporary differences .................... F6-54, F6-57
Times interest earned ............................... F2-50
Time value of money ................................. F5-25
Total debt ratio .......................................... F2-49
Trade discounts ......................................... F3-11
Trading securities ...................................... F4-4
Transition obligation ................................. F7-29
Translation method ................................... F6-47
Treasury stock ............................................ F7-45
Treasury stock method ............................. F8-7
Troubled debt restructuring ..................... F5-59

## U

Unassigned fund balance ........................... F9-45
Uncertain tax positions ............................... F6-65
Uncollectible accounts receivable ............ F3-12
Unconditional promises ............................. F8-49
Underlying ..................................................... F6-31
Units-of-production method ..................... F3-54
Unrealized gains and losses ...................... F1-60

## V

Valuation ........................................................ F4-5
Valuation allowance .................................... F6-61
Valuation of inventory ................................ F3-23
Variable interest entities ............................ F4-33
Variance power ............................................ F8-61
Vested benefits ............................................. F7-5
Voluntary non-exchange transactions ... F9-21

## W

Warranties ............................................ F1-37, F5-21
Weighted average amount of accumulated expenditures ............................................ F3-44
Weighted average exchange rate ............ F6-43
Weighted average method ........................ F3-30
Weighted average number of common shares outstanding .................................. F8-4
Withdrawal of a partner ............................. F2-60
Without recourse ................................. F3-16, F3-17
With recourse ....................................... F3-16, F3-17
Write-off ......................................................... F3-14

## X

XBRL (eXtensible Business Reporting Language) ................................................... F2-30

## Z

Zero coupon bonds ..................................... F5-38

## NOTES